Art & Architecture Thesaurus

THE GETTY
ART HISTORY
INFORMATION
PROGRAM

The Art and Architecture Thesaurus
is a program of
The Getty Art History Information Program

Art & Architecture Thesaurus

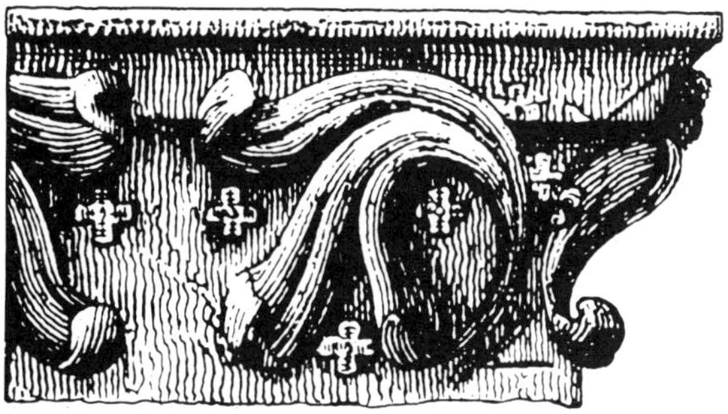

Toni Petersen
DIRECTOR

Volume 1

Part I: Introduction
Part II: Hierarchical Displays

Published on behalf of
The Getty Art History Information Program

OXFORD UNIVERSITY PRESS

New York · 1990 · *Oxford*

Oxford University Press

Oxford New York Toronto
Delhi Bombay Calcutta Madras Karachi
Petaling Jaya Singapore Hong Kong Tokyo
Nairobi Dar es Salaam Cape Town
Melbourne Auckland

and associated companies in
Berlin Ibadan

Published by Oxford University Press, Inc.,
200 Madison Avenue, New York, New York 10016

Library of Congress Cataloging-in-Publication Data
Art & architecture thesaurus / Toni Petersen, director.
p.
21½x28 cm.
Half t.p.: The Getty Art History Information Program.
Includes bibliographical references.
Contents: v. 1, pt. 1. Introduction. pt. 2. Hierarchical displays — v. 2. Alphabetical display, A and–Knotted — v. 3. Alphabetical display, Knotting–Zutujil.
ISBN 0-19-506403-8 (set)
1. Subject headings—Art. 2. Art—Abstracting and indexing. 3. Subject headings—Architecture. 4. Architecture—Abstracting and indexing. I. Petersen, Toni. II. Getty Art History Information Program. III. J. Paul Getty Trust. IV. Title: Art and architecture thesaurus.
Z695.1.A7A76 1990 89-26479
025.4'97—dc20 CIP

9 8 7 6 5 4 3 2 1

Printed in the United States of America
on acid-free paper

Designed by Jonathon Nix, The Studley Press, Dalton, Massachusetts
Illustrations on pp. 1 and 133 copyright reserved to Her Majesty Queen Elizabeth II

Contents

Foreword

ONE OFTEN HEARS THAT new technology will make the use of databases more effective and natural than ever before. However, such optimistic assertions also send another message: the long-term institutional investment in automation projects in the visual arts is unlikely to reside in continually evolving computer systems. For data in the Humanities to remain useful to their intended audiences, and for opportunities to integrate and share information to be fully realized, the future will have to be built into the information itself.

Especially true of databases in the arts, cataloging objects, their reproductions, and the literature of art history represent extraordinary expenditures of time, money, and expertise. Descriptive language, in the form of controlled vocabularies, plays a vital role in the consistency and reliability of documentation. Institutions have successfully constructed their own internal vocabulary standards for cataloging in manual as well as automated systems. However, multiple standards have the drawback of balkanizing information by institution or medium, divisions which fragment intellectual content and research interests. Moreover, the re-invention of controlled vocabularies for each project constitutes an enormous redundancy of effort. Developing collective, controlled vocabularies that can be used and broadly shared among institutions offers an alternative approach by concentrating greater effort and review than could be brought to bear by any single project. Such an enterprise carries with it enormous ambition and the responsibility to build consensus.

The publication of the *Art and Architecture Thesaurus* marks the first general availability of a remarkable resource for those faced with documenting materials in the visual arts. From the perspective of the Getty Art History Information Program, we are especially gratified to contribute in the area of vocabulary standards. Our participation allows us to help institutions that collect art-historical information; to see our effort reused by many projects; and to support the primary means by which information can be made compatible across multiple data sources.

The sheer scale of the material surely embodies the most evident accomplishment of the *AAT*, and is ample testimony to the dedication Toni Petersen and her staff have brought to the project. Perhaps less obvious, in the ten years since its inception, the developers of the *AAT* have demonstrated steadfast willingness to adapt to new and more flexible ideas of how vocabularies could be constructed.

FOREWORD

Originally envisioned as a compendium of subject heading lists used in art libraries, the *AAT* has evolved into a faceted hierarchical structure that can accommodate diverse levels of cataloging detail, and that explicitly supports the variability in terminology that inevitably arises from institutional preferences or multilingual applications.

Still less apparent, but fundamental to the significance of the *AAT*, is the process of its development. The thesaurus has been created as a collaboration with art historians, architects, librarians, visual resource curators, archivists, museum personnel, and specialists in thesaurus construction. Practically, this commitment to absorbing diverse interests and points of view has meant long and difficult discussions and negotiations, with repeated revisions of the terms and their structure.

This publication represents the first phase of the *AAT*'s distribution: twenty-three hierarchies of a projected forty hierarchies are being published simultaneously in print and on floppy disk by the the Oxford University Press. While considerable work remains for the *AAT* staff to complete outstanding hierarchies, the future of the thesaurus will depend increasingly on another constituency, the *AAT* user community. The willingness of that constituency to act as critics, to share their experience in applying the *AAT*, and to submit new terminology as their material warrants will be essential to keep the *AAT* a vital and relevant tool for the field.

Michael Ester, Director
The Getty Art History Information Program

The Art and Architecture Thesaurus Project, 1980–1990

PROJECT DIRECTOR: Toni Petersen (1980–)
CO-DIRECTOR: Dora P. Crouch (1980–1983), Pat Molholt (1980–1985)

EDITORIAL STAFF

Built Environment: J.A. Chewning (1981–1986), Daniel C. Williamson (1986–1988), Donald H. Sanders (1987–)

Furnishings and Equipment: Marguerite d'Aprile-Smith (1983–), Mary Hodge (1984–1987)

Visual and Verbal Communication: Isabel Wellisz (1983–1986), Elma B. Sanders (1987–)

Production: Cheryl V. Reeves (1983–1985), Cathleen K. Whitehead (1985–1988), Dagmar Jaunzems (1988–)

User Services: Marguerite d'Aprile-Smith (1984–1986), Cathleen K. Whitehead (1988–)

Authority Work: Susan Carpenter (1983–1984), Cathleen K. Whitehead (1984–1986), Martha Cordova (1985–1986), Alison A.L. Chipman (1986–)

Lexicography: Eugene M. Hoffman (1981–1982)

Editorial Assistance: Hugh D. Arbor, Amelia P. Blomquist, Greta Earnest, Barclay A. Gessner, Rebecca S. Krysiak, Elisa Lanzi, Katherine B. Meyers, Peggie Partello

ADMINISTRATIVE STAFF

Sandra L. Brookner, Katherine L. Engle, Teresa A. Ferrelli, Penelope E. Hawkins, Victoria N. Peacock, Eileen Satrape, Charlotte L. Welch, Peter C. Wirth

ART HISTORY INFORMATION PROGRAM

SPECIAL CREDIT must be given to the Art History Information Program, directed by Michael Ester, and to the members of the Scholarly Information Development Group. As a group they were responsible for the technical development of the *AAT's* computer system from design of the database through production of the computer tape for this publication. Headed by Program Manager John Logan, whose advice was always well taken, the group included Project Manager Joseph Busch and Programmer/Analyst Songqiao Liu, who patiently translated our constant requests for new features and enhancements into reality, and Sofia Dondoe, Richard Dolen, Aaron Gross, Raul Guerrero, Mike Hariri, and Scott Smith.

THE *AAT* PROJECT, 1980-1990

BENEFACTORS

THE FOLLOWING FUNDING AGENCIES are thanked for the generous support that has made the *Art and Architecture Thesaurus* a reality:

J. Paul Getty Trust
National Endowment for the Humanities
Andrew W. Mellon Foundation
Council on Library Resources
National Endowment for the Arts

Bennington College and Rensselaer Polytechnic Institute, the founders' institutions, gave generously of space and time in the first five years of the project's development and enthusiastically supported the idea of a new art thesaurus.

COLLABORATORS

A PROJECT OF THIS LENGTH and size could be accomplished only through the aid of a great many contributing scholars and information scientists, numerous libraries and librarians, and a few key thesaurus construction experts. Since it is impractical to give a detailed account of our indebtedness to so many collaborators, we here record their names with very real gratitude, adding a note of apology to those whose names may have slipped through the cracks of our record-keeping system over the last decade.

Research for *AAT* terminology requires the use of many excellent research libraries. The staffs of the following institutions have our thanks for their generous assistance:

Columbia University Libraries, especially Avery Architectural and Fine Arts Library
Frances Loeb Library, Graduate School of Design, Harvard University
Dumbarton Oaks Libraries
Edward C. Crossett Library, Bennington College
Museum of Modern Art Library
Green Architectural Library, Rensselaer Polytechnic Institute
Sterling and Francine Clark Art Institute Library
Williams College Library
Winterthur Museum Library
Boston Museum of Fine Arts Library
Thomas J. Watson Library of the Metropolitan Museum of Art
J. Paul Getty Center Library
New York State Historical Association
State University of New York at Albany, Dewey Library at the School of Information Science and Policy
British Architectural Library, Royal Institute of British Architects

Scholarly review of the *AAT* is an important avenue to validate the work in progress. The final stage in the construction of a hierarchy includes the calling together of a scholarly review team. Twenty-eight of these reviews, lasting from one day to two and a half days, have occurred in the last decade. The most cohesive and longest lasting of these teams is the Architecture Advisory Group chaired by Henry Millon. Meeting seven times between 1983 and 1989 to review the five Built Environment hierarchies at various stages of their development, this team played a major role in the way sets of terms are structured and in the choice of terms. The *AAT* project staff will remain in the debt of this careful and energetic group of scholars who always were willing to put aside time in impossibly busy schedules to come together to make the architecture hierarchies the best they could be.

Henry Millon, Center for Advanced Study in the Visual Arts, National Gallery of Art
Stanford Anderson, Massachusetts Institute of Technology
Margaret DePopolo, Rotch Library, Massachusetts Institute of Technology
Kevin Lynch (deceased)
Donlyn Lyndon, Department of Architecture, University of California at Berkeley
Laurie Olin, Hanna/Olin Associates
Daniel Schodek, Graduate School of Design, Harvard University

Our thanks go as well to those scholars who participated in reviews of the other hierarchies included in this edition of the *AAT*, and to Marilyn Schmitt, Susan Siegfried, and Deborah Wilde, art historians from the staff of the Getty Art History Information Program, who joined all of the review teams.

Associated Concepts Hierarchy

May 11, 1987

David Bearman, Archives and Museum Informatics
Leendert Couprie, University of Leiden
Henry Millon, CASVA, National Gallery of Art
Matthew Rohn, Williams College
Elaine Svenonius, University of California at Los Angeles
Michael Tomlan, Cornell University

Styles and Periods Hierarchy

July 11-12, 1983

Jonathan Fairbanks, Boston Museum of Fine Arts
Elizabeth McLachlan, Rutgers, The State University of New Jersey
Henry Millon, CASVA, National Gallery of Art
Adolf K. Placzek, Avery Librarian Emeritus, Columbia University
Gillian Wilson, J. Paul Getty Museum

February 13, 1985

Priscilla Farah, Metropolitan Museum of Art
Eileen Fry, Indiana University
Eleanor Manikka, University of Michigan
Sara Jane Pearman, Cleveland Museum of Art
Helene Roberts, Harvard University

Janice Sorkow, Boston Museum of Fine Arts
Ingeborg Wald, Cornell University

April 19, 1985

Pat Barnett, Metropolitan Museum of Art
Priscilla Farah, Metropolitan Museum of Art
Eileen Fry, Indiana University
Eleanor Manikka, University of Michigan
Sara Jane Pearman, Cleveland Museum of Art
Helene Roberts, Harvard University
Janice Sorkow, Boston Museum of Fine Arts
Ingeborg Wald, Cornell University

July 11-12, 1985

Pat Barnett, Metropolitan Museum of Art
Jonathan Fairbanks, Boston Museum of Fine Arts
Virginia Kerr, Avery Library of Columbia University
Elizabeth McLachlan, Rutgers, The State University of New Jersey
Henry Millon, CASVA, National Gallery of Art
Adolf K. Placzek, Avery Librarian Emeritus, Columbia University
William Tronzo, Dumbarton Oaks, Center for Byzantine Studies
Gillian Wilson, J. Paul Getty Museum

March 17, 1988

Nancy Allen, Boston Museum of Fine Arts
Vishakha Desai, Boston Museum of Fine Arts
Denise Leidy, Boston Museum of Fine Arts
Janice Sorkow, Boston Museum of Fine Arts

Design Elements and Processes and Techniques Hierarchies

July 31-August 1, 1986

James Blackaby, Mercer Museum
Kathryn Boardman, Farmers Museum
Albert Dietz, Massachusetts Institute of Technology, Emeritus
Samuel Y. Edgerton, Jr., Williams College
Thomas Krens, Williams College, Museum of Art
Dennis McFadden, New York State Capitol Project
Daniel Schodek, Graduate School of Design, Harvard University
Joyce Zucker, New York State Bureau of Historic Sites

Colors Hierarchy

November 14, 1986

Samuel Y. Edgerton, Jr., Williams College
Marcia B. Hall, Temple University
Charles Parkhurst, Williams College
Joyce Zucker, New York State Bureau of Historic Sites

People and Occupations, Disciplines, and Processes and Techniques Hierarchies

March 9-10, 1987

David Bearman, Archives and Museum Informatics
Thomas Krens, Williams College, Museum of Art
Charles Parkhurst, Williams College
Kathleen Roe, New York State Archives

Materials Hierarchy

June 21, 1985

Pat Barnett, Metropolitan Museum of Art
Elaine Dee, Cooper-Hewitt Museum
Albert Dietz, Massachusetts Institute of Technology, Emeritus
Henry Millon, CASVA, National Gallery of Art
Daniel Schodek, Graduate School of Design, Harvard University
Michael Tomlan, Cornell University

Decorative Arts Planning Session

April 1-2, 1984

Kenneth Ames, Winterthur Museum
Melissa Banta, Peabody Museum of Archaeology and Ethnology
Anne Golovin, National Museum of American History
Henry Hawley, Cleveland Museum of Art
Ivor Noel Hume, Colonial Williamsburg
David McFadden, Cooper-Hewitt Museum
Dianne Pilgrim, Brooklyn Museum
William Rieder, Getty Photo Archives
Lynn S. Roberts, Art Institute of Chicago
Gilbert Vincent, Cooperstown Graduate Program
Sir Francis Watson, formerly Keeper of the Queen's Works of Art, Windsor
John Watson, New York State Museum

Tools and Equipment Hierarchy

October 24-25, 1985

James Blackaby, Mercer Museum
Kathryn Boardman, Farmers Museum
Elaine Dee, Cooper-Hewitt Museum
Albert Dietz, Massachusetts Institute of Technology, Emeritus
Thomas Krens, Williams College, Museum of Art
Daniel Schodek, Graduate School of Design, Harvard University

May 29-30, 1986

James Blackaby, Mercer Museum
Kathryn Boardman, Farmers Museum
Elaine Dee, Cooper-Hewitt Museum
Albert Dietz, Massachusetts Institute of Technology, Emeritus
Thomas Krens, Williams College, Museum of Art
Daniel Schodek, Graduate School of Design, Harvard University
Joyce Zucker, New York State Bureau of Historic Sites

Furniture Hierarchy

October 28-29, 1984

Kenneth Ames, Winterthur Museum
John Kirk, Boston University
David McFadden, Cooper-Hewitt Museum
William Rieder, Getty Photo Archives
Rodris Roth, National Museum of American History
Gilbert Vincent, Cooperstown Graduate Program
Sir Francis Watson, formerly Keeper of the Queen's Works of Art, Windsor
Gillian Wilson, J. Paul Getty Museum

June 19-20, 1989

Kenneth Ames, Winterthur Museum
Christopher Gilbert, Temple Newsam House
Anne Golovin, National Museum of American History
Morrison Heckscher, Metropolitan Museum of Art
Simon Jervis, Victoria and Albert Museum
David McFadden, Cooper-Hewitt Museum
Milo Naeve, Art Institute of Chicago
Patricia Tice, Strong Museum

Fine Arts Advisory Group

May 10-11, 1988

Elaine Gazda, Kelsey Museum of Ancient and Medieval Archaeology, University of Michigan
Victor Margolin, University of Illinois at Chicago
James Marrow, University of California at Berkeley
Lee Parry, University of Arizona
Clive Phillpot, Museum of Modern Art Library
Robert Rainwater, New York Public Library
Gerald Silk, Tyler School of Art, Temple University
William Stapp, National Portrait Gallery

Drawings Hierarchy

November 18, 1987

Howard Burns, Harvard University
Mimi Cazort, Canadian Centre for Architecture
Elaine Dee, Cooper-Hewitt Museum
Diane DeGrazia, National Gallery of Art
Jill Lever, Royal Institute of British Architects

Photographs Hierarchy

April 30-May 1, 1984

James Anderson, University of Louisville
Miles Barth, International Center of Photography
Elizabeth Betz, Library of Congress, Prints and Photos Department
Andrew Birrell, Public Archives of Canada

Andrew Eskind, George Eastman House
Diane Hopkins, Public Archives of Canada
Terrence Pitts, Center for Creative Photography
Mary Kay Porter, Getty Conservation Institute
James T. Reilly, Rochester Institute of Technology
Diane Vogt-O'Connor, Smithsonian Institution Archives

June 27, 1988

M. Susan Barger, Johns Hopkins University
Roy Flukinger, Harry Ransom Humanities Research Center, University of Texas at Austin
Lori Gross, Canadian Centre for Architecture
Marnie Sandweiss, Amon Carter Museum
William Stapp, National Portrait Gallery
Diane Vogt-O'Connor, Smithsonian Institution Archives

May 2-3, 1989

M. Susan Barger, Johns Hopkins University
Andrew Eskind, George Eastman House
Roy Flukinger, Harry Ransom Humanities Research Center, University of Texas at Austin
Ellen Handy, Metropolitan Museum of Art
Ann McCauley, University of Massachusetts at Boston
Jeff Rosen, Columbia College, Chicago

Document Types Hierarchy

October 4, 1983

J. Thomas Converse, State Historical Society of Kentucky
Max J. Evans, State Historical Society of Wisconsin
H. Thomas Hickerson, Cornell University Libraries
Tom Mills, New York State Archives
Brent Thompson, Latter-day Saints Historical Department
Victoria Walch, archival consultant, Iowa City
Lisa Weber, Society of American Archivists

January 6, 1989

Lawrence Dowler, Harvard University Library
John Fleckner, Smithsonian Institution Archives
H. Thomas Hickerson, Cornell University Libraries
Avra Michelson, National Archives and Records Administration
Alden Monroe, Alabama Department of Archives and History
Kathleen Roe, New York State Archives

African Art Planning Session

May 31-June 1, 1984

Monni Adams, Peabody Museum of Archaeology and Ethnology, Harvard University
Daniel Biebuyck, University of Delaware

Henry Drewel, Cleveland State University
Werner Gillon, furniture specialist, London
Labelle Prussin, University of Washington
Philip Ravenhill, West African Museums Project
Roy Sieber, National Museum of African Art
Janet Stanley, National Museum of African Art
John Vlach, George Washington University
Frank Willett, Hunterian Art Gallery, University of Glasgow

A MAJOR ROLE in the development of the *AAT* was played by a number of thesaurus experts and information scientists who gave of their expertise to the novices who set out to construct this thesaurus. The content of the vocabulary is the province of art and architectural historians; the conceptualization of its structure and display was immeasurably aided by the collective experience and wisdom of the following:

Jean Aitchison, thesaurus consultant, Letchworth, England
James Anderson, Graduate School of Communications, Rutgers, The State University of New Jersey
C. David Batty, thesaurus consultant, Silver Spring, Maryland
David A. Bearman, Archives and Museum Informatics
Everett Brenner, American Petroleum Institute
Mary Dykstra, School of Library and Information Studies, Dalhousie University
Charles R. Hildreth, consultant, Read, Ltd.
F.W. Lancaster, Graduate Library School, University of Pennsylvania
Carol Mandel, Columbia University Libraries
Karen L. Markey, School of Information and Library Studies, University of Michigan
Elaine Svenonius, Graduate School of Library and Information Science, University of California at Los Angeles
Geraldene Walker, School of Information Science and Policy, State University of New York at Albany
Bella Hass Weinberg, Division of Library and Information Science, St. John's University

WITH FULL KNOWLEDGE that there must be omissions, for which we apologize, the following group of persons whom we called upon for help at various stages of the work deserves acknowledgment: Jean Shaw Adelman, Nancy Allen, Donald Anderle, Charles S. Ash, Kathleen Bales, Patricia Barnett, Lynn Lady Bellardo, James Birch, Sir John Boardman, Eric J. Bransby, Carole Cable, Helen Chillman, D. Sherman Clarke, James Coleman, Christiane C. Collins, Paul Connor, David Craven, Barbara L. Daniels-Swannack, Theodore Dell, David deLorenzo, John Dojka, Lamia Doumato, Marcy C. Dunnigan, Robert Engass, Nancy Goyne Evans, Robin Evans, Dolores Fairbanks, Lane Faison, Rafael Fernandez, Quentin W. Fitzgerald, Walter F. Geisinger, Angela Giral, Wendy Greenhouse, Peter W. Guenther, David Haberstich, Katherine Haskins, Susan Hoover, Jeffrey L. Horrell, Richard B. Hubbard, Jr., Christina Huemer,

Thomas Jacoby, Ruth Kamen, Robert Kaufmann, Sydney Keaveney, Virginia Kerr, Ann Ketterer, Phyllis Lambert, Alan Lathrop, Diedre Lawrence, Roger Lawson, Douglas Lewis, Elizabeth M. Lewis, Maryellen LoPresti, Eileen Markson, Karen Meizner, Bethany Mendenhall, Eileen Michaels, Christine Minter-Dowd, Peter Murray, Denys Peter Myers, Nyal E. Nelson, Arlene Noble, Christian Otto, Robert T. Packard, David Parke, James A. Parker, Richard Pearce-Moses, Ford Peatross, Katherine Poole, Catha Rambusch, John W. Reps, Zelda Richardson, Daphne Roloff, William D. Rust, Jr., T. Witthus Rutherford, Lenore Sarasan, Karol Schmiegel, Nancy Schuller, Adeline Schuster, Wendy Shay, Anna Smislova, Merrill Smith, Maryly Snow, Janet Stanley, Norman D. Stevens, Marsha Stevenson, Damie Stillman, Fred Stitt, Patricia Sullivan, Jane Sunderland, Christine L. Sundt, Richard Szary, Eleanor (Neville) McD. Thompson, Robert Trent, Alan Tucker, Ruta Butkus Vanderheide, Robert Vogel, Faith H. Vosburgh, Murray Waddington, Lisa B. Weber, Margaret N. Webster, Dustin Wees, Janice Woo, Susan Wyngaard, Karel Yasko, John Zukowsky.

Since this project began, it has been our good fortune to have received the support of a number of associations and potential users. In some cases, such as with the Art Libraries Society of North America's *AAT* Advisory Committee and the Art and Architecture Program Committee of the Research Libraries Group's Subcommittee on *AAT* Implementation, it has meant five or six years of work on specific tasks. In others, such as the Society of American Archivists and the American Institute of Architects, it has meant collaboration in developing certain areas of terminology in the *AAT*. The Library of Congress Network Development and MARC Standards Office has been helpful in promoting changes to the MARC format suggested by the *AAT*. Efforts to prepare proposals for such changes have been aided by welcome advice from RLG staff.

From the earliest days of the *AAT* project, we have sought to test the developing terminology in actual indexing and cataloging environments. From a small group of ten or twelve organizations in 1983, a network of over 150 groups using advance drafts of the *AAT* has grown. These users provide us with valuable information on how the *AAT* taxonomy is being applied and suggest new candidate terms for inclusion as well as pointing out instances where terms need to be changed or modified. We wish especially to cite the *Avery Index to Architectural Periodicals* and the AVIADOR project of the Avery Library of Columbia University, the Foundation for the Documents of Architecture project, and *RILA (International Repertory of the Literature of Art)* for their contribution to the *AAT's* growth.

Finally, we must note those organizations who generously supplied us with copies of their subject term lists in 1980. The lists were incorporated into the *AAT* database and form the very foundation of the thesaurus.

Avery Index to Architectural Periodicals
Library of Congress Subject Headings (LCSH)
RIBA Architectural Periodicals Index
RILA (International Repertory of the Literature of Art)

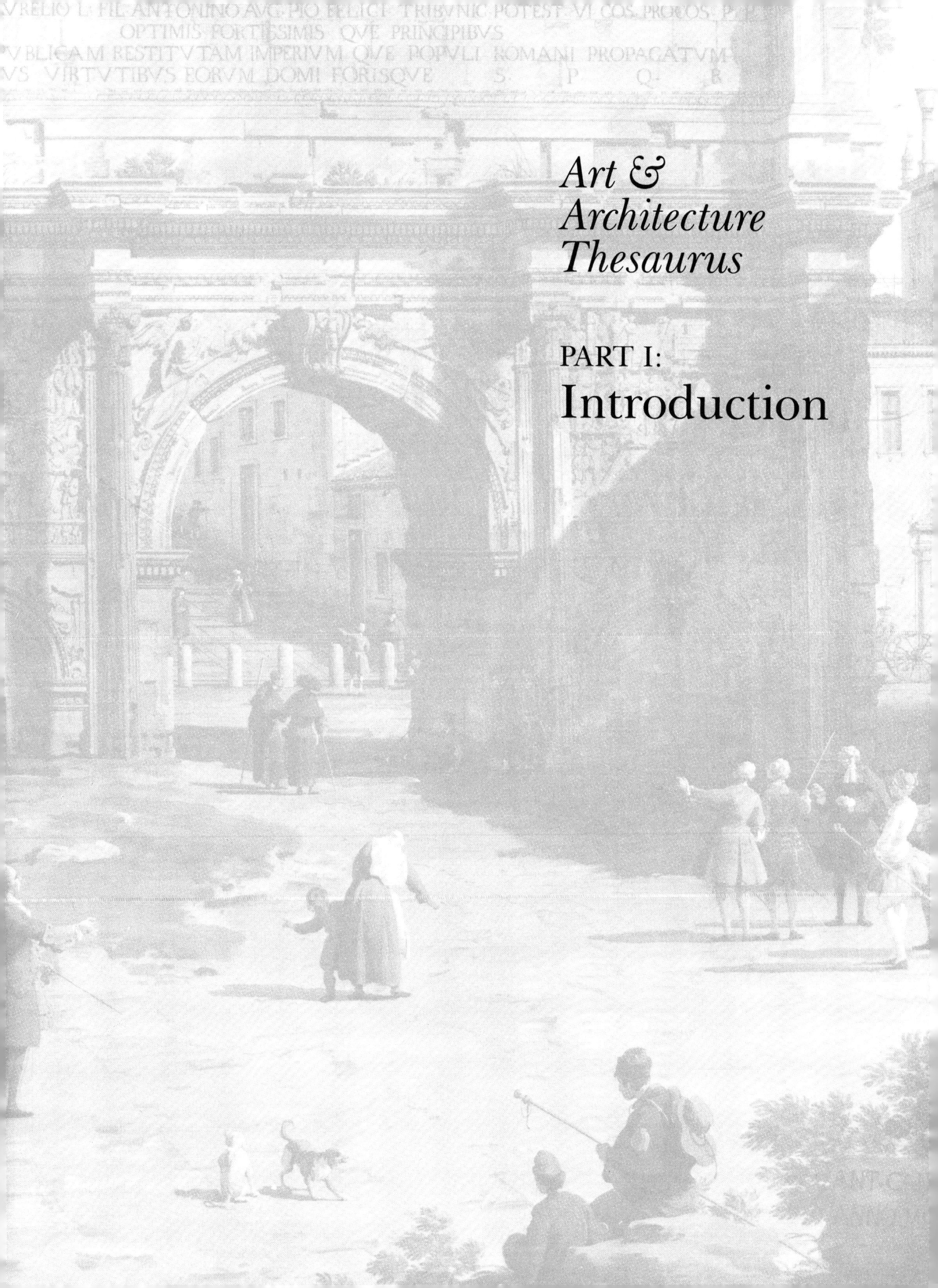

Art & Architecture Thesaurus

PART I: Introduction

History of the Project

The *Art and Architecture Thesaurus*, more often known by its initials, *AAT*, celebrated its tenth anniversary in 1989. The decade since its inception witnessed many developments in the field of information science in general and in art information handling in particular. The advent of the microcomputer encouraged the proliferation of online databases and a tighter control of collections of materials, whether books, journals, or objects. It also allowed vast quantities of data to be stored and retrieved easily and cheaply. At the same time, the development of relational databases for the microcomputer enabled scholars to link a variety of information within one system. All of this new-found functionality had a significant influence on the move toward the automation of collections of materials in the field of art and architecture. In contrast, the field of thesaurus construction and its applications in information retrieval was already well established during this period, having had its major development in the post-World War II era.

The *AAT*'s role in this environment has been an important one. Despite warnings that the information being stored in the many new art related databases might be inaccessible without a standard vocabulary to guide access to them, it has not always been clear to the database producers that the use of a controlled vocabulary is, in fact, indispensable to this task.

Marilyn Schmitt of the J. Paul Getty Trust's Art History Information Program, writing on the need for improved information handling in the humanities, noted that the development of databases in the humanities has proceeded with "a certain relentless inevitability."[1] On the other hand, she states that scholars working in the humanities have the most complicated information needs. All past data, no matter how ancient, is important; verbal expression is rich and uncontrolled, that is to say, inconsistent; and vocabulary control is considered alien to the scholarly task—hampering thought processes and even likely to impoverish the variety of humanistic activity.

Researchers and scholars, in describing their work, have clearly articulated the problems:

- the agony of tracking down information when indexes are inadequate
- the difficulty of organizing visual and written information
- the threat of the loss of information due to lack of certainty of what that information is called in different indexing systems

· the impossibility of finding what you need in unindexed archives[2]

The Beginnings of the Project

It is often frustration that serves as the catalyst for change. In 1979, Dora Crouch, an architectural historian and professor at Rensselaer Polytechnic Institute in Troy, New York, found herself increasingly frustrated with the constant difficulties she encountered in trying to assemble slides for her lectures. To solve this problem, Crouch—who was also editor of *The Society of Architectural Historians Newsletter*—called a meeting in February 1979 of about a half-dozen archivists, librarians, prints and drawings curators, and indexers in order to initiate the Universal Access System for Slides (UAS).

At this first meeting the group set out a program to gain diversified support for the UAS project. It also acknowledged the need for a thesaurus of art and architectural terms. Crouch emphasized the need for a controlled vocabulary that would provide for the consistent representation of information by determining the preferred ways of referring to concepts, bringing together synonyms, and noting other relationships, such as broader and narrower terms. Such a vocabulary would lighten the burden of indexers and catalogers and bring about the most comprehensive retrieval of information possible on a particular topic by linking terms whose meanings are related.

In May 1979 a larger group was assembled at the headquarters of the Committee for the Preservation of Architectural Records in New York City for the second meeting of the UAS Planning Group. Among the new participants were Pat Molholt, associate director of libraries at Rensselaer and Toni Petersen and Michael Rinehart from *RILA (International Repertory of the Literature of Art)*.

Discussion focused on the need for a means to use the latest technology in computerized cataloging and indexing projects. Each of the participants noted the handicap of the lack of a controlled vocabulary in their projects, and the need for an art and architecture thesaurus was again raised. Henry Millon, dean of the Center for Advanced Study in the Visual Arts (CASVA) at the National Gallery of Art, who was unable to attend, sent his recommendation for the ideal thesaurus. His concerns summarized the issues addressed by the committee. He wrote:

> A thesaurus for computer needs to be arranged hierarchically, so that it collapses within itself, to make a nest of terms. This is a key problem in making subject categories. Designing such a thesaurus will take real collaboration among architectural historians.

In this statement Millon identified key elements that became guiding principles in the development of the *Art and Architecture Thesaurus*. The idea that the thesaurus should be hierarchically structured and that it should be based on the collaboration of scholars in the field became two of the earliest operating principles of the *AAT*. Millon's understanding and forethought regarding the pivotal role of his colleagues later gave him a critical role, as chair of the *AAT*'s Architecture Advisory Group, which was established in 1983 to review and guide *AAT* research and production.

Foundation of the *AAT*

As it happened, the UAS never materialized. The group disbanded after the second meeting, but its momentum and energy were captured by the formation of the *Art and Architecture Thesaurus* project. A trio from the UAS group consisting of Pat Molholt, Toni Petersen, and Dora Crouch set to work to prepare grant proposals and to plan the thesaurus. Petersen was executive editor of *RILA*. Since 1973, *RILA* had been publishing an index to art historical literature using a manually-produced card catalog of subject terms. Although it followed standard library techniques of authority control (i.e., "see" and "see also" references), it was futile to expect consistent links between terms when one could not clearly see the conceptual relationships in the alphabetically arranged file. At an indexing seminar held by the National Federation of Abstracting and Indexing Services (NFAIS), Petersen had recently been converted from the library techniques of constructing alphabetically arranged authority files to the information science techniques of constructing hierarchical thesauri. Molholt, associate director of the Rensselaer Polytechnic Institute libraries, was impressed with the advantages of the hierarchically arranged *Medical Subject Headings (MeSH)* thesaurus, and suggested using it as a model. Molholt also brought to the group experience with automated systems.

Their first grant, received from the Council on Library Resources in early 1980, enabled the group to investigate and establish the need for an art and architecture thesaurus. The investigators wrote to, spoke with, and visited numerous authorities regarding art subject indexing and thesaurus construction. Copies of approximately a dozen major subject lists and thesauri in art and architecture in use at the time as well as several small lists used in projects in individual institutions were acquired and analyzed. The resulting report, *Indexing and Abstracting in the Arts: A Survey and Analysis*, was finished later that year and was made available through the ERIC document service.[3] It concluded that while each was tailored to meet the needs of its own project, none was adequate in itself to provide the comprehensive thesaurus needed for the whole field.

In September 1980 a one-year planning grant from the National Endowment for the Humanities (NEH) was received. At this point Crouch, Molholt, and Petersen officially became the co-directors of the *Art and Architecture Thesaurus* project. They were granted partial release time from their respective institutions (Petersen had by this time accepted the directorship of the Bennington College Library). Rensselaer became the administering institution for the one-year grant and agreed to give the infant project a home in its Folsom Library.

Thus the *AAT* project set out to build a consistent, comprehensive, and controlled vocabulary that could be used by database developers but that at the same time would not conflict with the working language of the scholars and researchers who would be the users of those databases, The thesaurus was envisioned as a set of terms that would include the history and the making of the visual arts; that is, it would form a hinge between objects and their replicas or representations and the bibliography about them. Its coverage would be geographically and historically comprehensive but would not include terminology for iconographical themes. The terminology would be hierarchically organized and optimized for computerized use. Scholars in the field would review the work at all stages. These few tenets were the first principles in the developing methodology of the *AAT*.

Relationship to the *Library of Congress Subject Headings*

The initial task of gathering terminology from existing glossaries, subject lists, and thesauri underscored yet another basic principle of the *AAT*, that it would build upon vocabulary already in use in the field. In this way, the developers hoped to increase its relevance and enable indexing and cataloging organizations to absorb the new thesaurus easily. With this in mind, priority was to be given to the eighty year-old *Library of Congress Subject Headings (LCSH). LCSH*, which is used in the majority of libraries in the United States, already formed the basis for many of the subject lists developed by bibliographic indexing services in the field of art and architecture. The work plan focused on drawing from *LCSH* all relevant terms and inputting them into a computer file. The intention was to merge all the collected lists, with the resulting body of terminology forming the basis of the new thesaurus.

As the work has progressed over the past decade, however, more and more differences have emerged between *LCSH* and the developing *AAT*. Basic differences in the way terms are chosen and structured were analyzed by Petersen in a 1983 article, in which issues such as inverted word order versus natural word order (e.g., *houses, Victorian* versus *Victorian houses*), as well as other more serious problems that violated thesaurus standards for term construction, were raised.[4]

By the time the *AAT* was ready for publication, there were major differences in form and philosophy between the *AAT* and *LCSH*. The attempt to incorporate *LCSH* was confounded for several reasons:

- The *AAT* is hierarchically arranged according to a rigorously constructed, internally consistent structure. This allows a cataloger to see terms graphically organized by concept, with terms that are broader and others that are narrower or more specific in meaning. *LCSH* terms are available only in an alphabetical array.
- *AAT* terms are chosen from available sources to form a conceptual whole within their hierarchical arrays. There are both general terms in the *AAT*, such as *houses*, and narrower terms related to it, such as *country houses* and *bungalows*. *LCSH* terms are more often general, because they are used to describe the subject of whole books rather than a specific object in an image or the subject of a periodical article. They are also generated only when a need for a term arises. Thus, many terms available in the *AAT* will not be found in *LCSH*.
- Rather than expressing single concepts, *LCSH* terms are often "precoordinated"; that is, they are complex concepts put together at the time the heading is generated, and they remain in the authority list in that specific combination. For example, *Wooden doors* is an *LCSH* heading, as is *Renaissance painting*. In the *AAT*, because of its faceted structure, *wood* is found in

the Materials hierarchy, *doors* in the Built Works Components hierarchy, *Renaissance* in the Styles and Periods hierarchy and *painting* in the Disciplines hierarchy. Indexers are free to use terms separately, or to combine them into headings that they precoordinate at the time of indexing to match the item they are describing.[5]

Despite these divergencies, the compilers of the *AAT* sought to give priority to *LCSH* terms because of *LCSH*'s long-term preeminence as an indexing vocabulary. *LCSH* terms were thus always preferred, provided that their forms met the strict requirements for thesaurus construction set out in national and international standards. However, when necessary, *LCSH* terms were modified. Each concept in *LCSH*, whether adopted intact or modified, was noted in the *AAT*'s records. It was hoped that this would enable libraries using the *AAT* to track their older bibliographic records containing *LCSH* headings and to connect bibliographic records for similar subjects. Another important step was to prepare the *AAT* databases for use in the MARC format, the communications format in use by most *LCSH*-based library and bibliographic systems.

Construction of the Early *AAT*

The project's first setback occurred in 1981, when the NEH was asked to support a major grant to construct the whole of the *AAT* over a three-year period. Unfortunately, this request coincided with new restrictions on the NEH budget, and a grant for only one year was given, with the proviso that the *AAT* limit its work to the field of architecture, where there were already several existing subject lists available upon which to build.

In the fall of 1981 a lexicographer with experience in the construction of hierarchical thesauri, a part-time computer programmer, a secretary, and some student assistants began work. The work plan involved defining all the categories or possible hierarchies that would be necessary to cover the field of architecture and associated areas and writing a computer program that would generate single termsheets for each term in the computerized lists that had been generously supplied to the *AAT* project by the *Journal of the Society of Architectural Historians*, the *Avery Index to Architectural Periodicals*, the Picture Division of the Public Archives of Canada, *RILA*, and the *Architectural Periodicals Index* of the Royal Institute of British Architects. Since there was no computerized *LCSH* file available at the time, relevant terms had to be painstakingly identified in the printed *LCSH* volumes and a computerized file created.

This first gathering of potential candidate terms for the *AAT* resulted in a stack of approximately thirty thousand separate termsheets. The terms were to be studied for overlaps and omissions as well as style of headings and addition of cross-references.

In order to process the termsheets most efficiently, three consultants were brought to Troy for a week in January 1982 to work with the staff and the three overextended part-time co-directors. The visitors included Angela Giral, then the director of the Graduate School of Design Library at Harvard University but soon to become the Avery Librarian at Columbia University; J. Chewning, a doctoral candidate in architectural history at the Massachusetts Institute of Technology, and Susan Blandy, a librarian from the Troy area.

To the participants, this week was both daunting and exhilarating. Petersen wrote of the experience:

> The seven of us began in a huge room in the School of Architecture at Rensselaer, equipped with banks of large, empty, rough study tables. Before us were the waist-high stacks of term sheets; on each table were sign posts for each of the then-identified eighteen or nineteen separate categories or hierarchies, such as Architectural Components, Settlements and Towns, Landscape and Gardening, Design and Practice, Construction, Education, People, and Industries. We each took armloads of termsheets and wove our way around the tables, dropping off the termsheets that corresponded to each category with much chatting and exchanging of advice among ourselves.
>
> As I recall, this took about two and a half days. The remainder of the week was spent alphabetizing the resulting sorted stacks of terms, and stapling together sets of termsheets for terms that were identical or similar in concept but had been generated from different indexing lists.

The next job was to arrange each stack of termsheets into hierarchies, a process called shingling. Again, help was needed and J. Chewning returned as a part-time consultant, along with Bethany Mendenhall, head of technical services at the J. Paul Getty Museum Library, who was given leave to spend six months at the *AAT*, from February to June of 1982.

By May of that year a great deal of progress had been made. The first set of hierarchies had been completed and an advisory board had been named and had met three times in the course of the year. Its function was to comment on the plan of work, to review the structure of the hierarchies, and to help define the scope of the project. Members included Christina Huemer of the Avery Library of Columbia University; Helen Chillman of the Photo and Slide Library of Yale University; Christian Otto, architectural historian at Cornell University; Ford Peatross of the Department of Prints and Photographs, Library of Congress; and Michael Rinehart of *RILA*.

The January working group had thought that the matching and merging task would generate every known term for the cataloging and indexing of architectural materials. However, the first attempt to create hierarchies revealed the unexpected presence of large gaps throughout the vocabulary. The tens of thousands of termsheets that had been generated did not, in fact, provide a complete set of terms. The explanation was twofold. First, when terms that have been developed for an alphabetically arranged list are rearranged by concepts, missing terms quickly become apparent. As Molholt has said, "When the parts of a bicycle are laid out by size, it's hard to see what may be missing. When those parts are laid out in the form of a bicycle, missing parts are easy to detect." The second reason for gaps was that most subject lists derived from indexing and cataloging systems contain only those terms needed to index or catalog existing documents or objects heretofore encountered. The terms can be no more comprehensive than the documents and objects so far described.

A small experiment was conducted in which terms believed to be absolutely necessary to the scholarly community were added to one subsection of one hierarchy. That section nearly doubled in size as a result. This was a major watershed for the *AAT*, for it was now clear that the original set of lists could not be depended upon to provide a consistent set of terms in a hierarchical array. The scholarly mandate of the *AAT* required a decision to search out missing terms in reference works and scholarly monographs, a costly and labor-intensive task.

The year of intense labor from 1981 to 1982 established most of the basic principles for construction of the *AAT*, principles that have subsequently been clarified and codified:

- The *AAT* would be constructed using standard thesaurus conventions, such as those outlined in the American National Standards Institute's *Guidelines for the Construction of Monolingual Thesauri*.
- It would be structure hierarchically, drawing on the model of the *Medical Subject Headings Thesaurus (MeSH)* for its tree structures and alphabetical displays.
- It would be based on terminology that is current, that is warranted for use in standard literary sources, and that is validated by the scholarly community. If possible, it would incorporate existing lists that may be enhanced or modified.
- It would be responsible to its constituency and take cognizance of the needs of that constituency in the depth and scope of its terminology.
- The data comprising the thesaurus would be made available in machine-readable forms lending themselves to a variety of automated systems.
- The necessary financial commitment would be sought, not only to build the original vocabulary but to maintain it over the long term.
- A commitment would be made to the user groups that the vocabulary would not be changed arbitrarily. Although change is inevitable, it should be planned for and promulgated with the agreement of the user community.

In addition to setting these principles, by November 1982—when the project's final report to the NEH came due—the *AAT* staff reported completion of a number of major tasks, including the following:

- Nineteen hierarchies had been developed in draft form, and more than half had been already heavily edited and polished.
- Both hierarchical and alphabetical lists of the hierarchies had been computer-based.
- Materials to guide the external review process had been written.
- Methodological problems of form and topical subdivisions, including rules for use, had been resolved.
- Publicity was continuing through presentations before professional societies.
- Endorsements for the proposed thesaurus had multiplied.

- Consultants had routinely added their expertise to the staff's deliberations.
- A major paper about the project was slated for imminent publication.

The *AAT* Under the Sponsorship of the J. Paul Getty Trust

With the end of the one-year (plus a three-month extension) NEH grant in January 1983, there was a dramatic change in the structure and operating mode of the *AAT* project. The directors accepted the offer of the J. Paul Getty Trust to become an operating unit of the trust. Soon after, Dora Crouch, who had major responsibility for overseeing the architecture hierarchies, resigned to return to her own research and teaching. The fledgling project, with a staff of two editors and a secretary, was moved from Rensselaer to a site on the Bennington College campus. Toni Petersen now divided her time equally between the Bennington College Library and the *AAT* project, where her major responsibility was administration of the staff and construction of the thesaurus. Pat Molholt continued on 20 percent release time from Rensselaer and was mainly responsible for management of the budget and the computer system. Both directors took an active role in in-house review of work in progress and the setting of policy.

With the change from federal funding to the assumption of responsibilities as an operating unit of the J. Paul Getty Trust, the beginning of 1983 became a time for taking stock. A meeting was held during the first week of January to discuss the status of the project. Attending from outside the *AAT* staff were Pat Barnett of the Thomas J. Watson Library at the Metropolitan Museum of Art, Angela Giral, Carol Mandel, then of the Association of Research Libraries, Bethany Mendenhall, Michael Rinehart, and Elaine Svenonius of the Graduate School of Library and Information Science at the University of California at Los Angeles. The hierarchies that had been constructed thus far were examined, along with current operating procedures. The following conclusions emerged, most of which had been raised before in other settings:

- The model for the architecture section would need to be augmented with additional rules and procedures for decorative and fine arts terminology.
- The *AAT* was to define those areas considered "core" to its scope, areas where it should attempt comprehensiveness, and those that are "peripheral," which would not be treated so exhaustively.
- Even with respect to core areas, limits were to be imposed on attempts at completeness or comprehensiveness. A mechanism for long-term maintenance and for the addition of new terms was to be developed.
- A need was expressed for adding scope notes (essentially abridged definitions) to distinguish near synonyms and to explain the scope of terms.
- The *AAT* compilers were to establish an authority record for each term to include all information about the term, including sources used in term choice.
- The importance of what were then seen as subdivision lists was affirmed, especially in the area of styles and periods, place names, dates, document types, and topical subdivisions.

Issues and Problems of Thesaurus Construction

By 1983 the conceptual framework of the *AAT*'s hierarchies—or "tree structures," structures that display genus-species relationships—had been well articulated. Work on the term level, however, had not been so successful. Not only was it evident that the major assembled lists were gapingly incomplete, but it was also apparent that they presented concepts in different and inconsistent ways. One list would give a compound term in natural language order (e.g., *wooden floors*); another would provide a similar term for the same concept in inverted order (floors, wood), still another would use cryptic faceting codes (*floors: wood: firehouses*).

In addition to the inconsistencies that resulted from such "inherited" terms, it became apparent that many of the combinations of terms could not be maintained in the *AAT*. To enumerate all possible combinations of style or period and object name, or material and object name (such as *Victorian cottages* or *marble floors*) would cause the size of the thesaurus to burgeon uncontrollably. Elaine Svenonius later made this clear at the Second International Conference on Automatic Processing of Art History Data and Documents in Pisa in 1984.[6]

The decision to develop separate hierarchies for styles and periods, materials, and objects instead of precoordinating terms would not end the pre- and post-coordination problem, however. As the staff struggled to write rules that would clearly articulate the instances where multiword terms might be considered "bound" and where they might be "decoordinated," it became necessary to consult the large body of literature on the subject, much of which seemed to confuse rather than elucidate the issues. Finally, in the spring of 1985, a number of thesaurus experts were assembled for a two-day meeting to try to crack the problem. The discussions included James Anderson of Rutgers University, Everett Brenner of the American Petroleum Institute, F. W. Lancaster of the University of Pennsylvania, Elaine Svenonius, and John Logan of the Getty Art History Information Program. Despite progress on several well-articulated rules for *AAT* editorial procedures, case-by-case judgment calls often continue to be used to determine how and when a multiword term signifies a single, bound concept and when it should be "decoordinated" and its component parts placed in separate hierarchies.

Another issue that has raised problems relates to terms for abstract concepts, such as *harmony, Renaissance,* and *circular*, terms not necessarily in noun form, the prescribed form for thesaurus entries. Abstract terms are much more difficult to classify. Not only are genus-species relationships difficult to construct, but in many cases the hierarchy tends to be more shallow than in the object hierarchies, where one routinely finds ten or more levels of specificity.

There is also the problem that there is often no "real" indexing term to use as a broader or collocating term under which to array a group of similar terms, or "siblings." The *AAT* followed the lead of some other thesauri in establishing "node labels," or "guide terms"—terms within brackets that express the broader concept but are not suitable as indexing terms, e.g., <*chairs by form*>.

Organizing terms into hierarchies limits their classification as well. Building a network of related terms—the next step in the process and a feature that will be added in the next few years once the *Art and Architecture Thesaurus* is completed—is a necessary step for the representation of knowledge in a field. In a sense, one builds alternate hierarchies from the paths made by related terms. For example, in the architecture hierarchies, all single architectural structures are classified within their genus-species relationships: *chapels* is a division of *churches*, as is *cathedrals*. Through related term references, one is able to relate the parts to the whole. *Pews* and *pulpits* will point to *chapels, churches*, and other terms for religious structures.

Scholarly Review of the *AAT*

As early as 1982, in accord with the stated goal of the *AAT* to seek validation of its work from scholars in the field, a number of hierarchies in the architecture set had been sent for review to about thirty persons, mainly architectural historians, architecture librarians, and slide curators. The results of this review were insubstantial. It was clear that it was difficult for reviewers to assimilate, in isolation, such a large body of material with little or no orientation by the *AAT* staff. Equally problematic was the fact that those reviewers who did comment on the content and/or arrangement of terms frequently contradicted one another. The review process was rethought and the decision was made to bring together small groups of scholars for concentrated periods of work with the *AAT* staff from then on. These working groups would review well-defined portions of the thesaaurus rather than judge several hierarchies at one time, and they would resolve differences of opinion in the course of the meeting.

The summer of 1983 was the occasion for the first scholarly review meeting on an *AAT* hierarchy, following the new procedure. At this point the *AAT* contained about thirteen thousand terms; one-fifth of them resided in the Styles and Periods hierarchy, the subject of the first review. The points raised then have been raised by all subsequent review groups, regardless of the nature of the hierarchy under discussion. They include the question of who the *AAT*'s users are and how their needs affect term choice and hierarchical arrangement, and what sources are consulted in the gathering of terms. Reviewers also want to know how the *AAT* accommodates changes in the forms of terms through history, and whether or not non-English terms are included. Time and again reviewers have become engrossed in analyzing the structure of a hierarchy, and they have often played a significant role in modifying—or completely changing—its arrangement.

Scholarly review groups are assembled during the final stage in the construction of hierarchies. Twenty-eight of these reviews, lasting from one half to two and a half days, have occurred since 1983. The most cohesive and enduring of the review teams is the Architecture Advisory Group, chaired by Henry Millon and including five other scholars and architects representing a broad spectrum of the field. This group, which met seven times between 1984 and 1989 to review the architecture hierarchies as they developed, has played a major role in the way these sets of terms are structured and in the choice of terms.

Following the example of this group, advisory groups in the areas of the decorative and fine arts were planned. A Fine Arts Advisory Group met for the first time in May 1988. Two days of spirited discussion resulted in an analysis of the relationship between the various traditional fields of painting and sculpture and the contemporary fields of design and nontraditional media, and in a renaming of the section, which had been called Fine Arts, than Art Forms, and is now Verbal and Visual Communication. The influence of this group of scholars could dramatically change the way in which the language of the field is perceived and could provide new modes of description for cataloging and indexing.

Work with the scholarly community and with a growing group of *AAT* test users has underscored the conviction that while comprehensiveness and standardization of vocabulary is an important goal, successful thesauri can be neither immutable nor authoritarian. They must be able to respond to the living, evolving language from which they are drawn—to assimilate both the language of scholars in the field and the more popular language found in basic literary sources. The *AAT* seeks to maintain a delicate balance between providing standardization of a body of terms that is as full a representation of an area or field as possible and responding to patterns of usage and the subtleties of language. It must be understood that total comprehensiveness is not truly possible, given the restraints of time and resources and the changeable nature of language itself. A thesaurus must be seen as a living tool, a body of language that can be added to and changed as it responds to the needs of its users.

Further Developments

It was only with the advent of the Getty Trust support in 1983 that resources became available to carry out some of the more important suggestions raised by the *AAT*'s many expert consultants. From this point on, the rule of literary warrant was emphasized for each term. Rather than accept terms, even with modifications, as they were received from various indexing sources, each term was also researched in several reference sources, including scholarly monographs, glossaries, and catalogs. A record was kept of all sources consulted, and definitions of the term as found in the sources were noted. Attention was directed to choosing a form of the term that not only captures the way a concept is currently expressed by the scholarly community but that also reflects the principles of thesaurus term construction. Variant forms were included as lead-in terms. Even so, because of staff and time limitations, it was to be three more years before scope notes appeared as part of the alphabetic displays distributed to the *AAT*'s users.

In mid-1983 the *AAT* staff was expanded by the addition of two editors and work was begun on the decorative and fine arts, as they were then labled. The co-directors, along with Marguerite d'Aprile-Smith, decorative arts editor, began a program to introduce the *AAT* to museum curators and registrars. In a two-year period, presentations were given at the Winterthur Museum, the

Metropolitan Museum of Art, the Boston Museum of Fine Arts, the Strong Museum, the Cleveland Museum of Art, the Victoria and Albert Museum, the Art Institute of Chicago, the Cooper-Hewitt Museum, the Smithsonian Institution, and at various museum conferences.

One final grant was received by the *AAT* just before the project moved to Bennington. It was a grant from the National Endowment for the Arts, matched by a similar grant from the J. Paul Getty Trust, for testing the *AAT* in a controlled environment. Unused for some time, this grant ultimately became the basis for a project at the Architecture Slide Library at Rensselaer, which resulted in the recataloging of fifty thousand slides, integrating their records in the online public access catalog at Rensselaer, and using the *AAT* as the subject access vocabulary.

In 1985 the *AAT* entered a new phase under the direction of Michael Ester at the Getty Art History Information Program (AHIP). Half a decade of work had yet to yield a product that could be officially distributed. With AHIP's help, a series of more realistic goals was set. First of all, the scope of the thesaurus was narrowed to focus on Western art and architecture. Work on the decorative and fine arts sections was suspended until architecture, and all its supporting sections, could be completed. The organizational structure of the *AAT* staff was revamped to reflect the workflow more accurately. A new position of production manager, with supervisory functions over the editorial process, was added. The development of a new computer program brought out certain inadequacies of the *AAT*'s input termsheet. A new termsheet was designed that took into account how the terms are researched and included space for sources consulted and definitions found in those sources.

Building on the *AAT*'s principle of mapping terms from major sources to their placement in the *AAT*'s structure, the *AAT* took on a more coordinative role. The mapping of terms brought with it the possibility that the *AAT* might become a switching language, enabling users to choose from a number of variant terms expressing a particular concept.

In January 1986, Petersen left her position at Bennington College to assume the full-time directorship of the *AAT* project. Pat Molholt returned to her full-time position at Rensselaer, although her association with the *AAT* remained close. The *AAT* staff, now numbering twelve, moved to comfortable offices in Williamstown, Massachusetts, close by its sister AHIP organization, *RILA*, in the summer of 1986, where it will remain until its last anticipated move in the mid-1990s to the permanent Getty facility under construction in Brentwood, California.

Building a Constituency

From the earliest days of the project, financial support was only one kind of sponsorship sought by the co-directors. Preparing for the NEH grant proposals had brought the endorsements of the Society of Architectural Historians, the College Art Association, and the Art Libraries Society of North America (ARLIS). At the 1982 annual conference of ARLIS, an *AAT* Advisory Committee was formed with the aim of serving as a liaison between the *AAT* and the ARLIS membership. The previous year the Subject Heading Task Force of the Art and Architecture Program Committee (AAPC) of the Research Libraries Group (RLG) had officially endorsed the *AAT*. In 1982, responding to the suggestion that the *AAT* serve as an alternative subject heading authority file in RLIN (RLG's Research Libraries Information Network), the AAPC formed a Subcommittee on AAT Implementation, which has been working with RLG staff toward this goal since 1984. In 1982 the *AAT* was also endorsed by the American Institute of Architects (AIA), the Council on Library Resources (CLR), and the Association of Architecture School Librarians (AASL).

International interest in the *AAT* was sparked by Pat Molholt at the International Federation of Library Associations (IFLA) in the summer of 1981. Here it was suggested that the Art Library Group within IFLA adopt as a project the problem of converting the *AAT* into a multilingual thesaurus, one of the stated long-term goals of the co-directors. That same year, the Royal Institute of British Architects' British Architectural Library, about to computerize and integrate its collection catalogs, offered to supply British terminology to the *AAT*. The Victoria and Albert Museum expressed an interest in assisting in this task. Clearly, the same need for a well-conceived and comprehensive controlled vocabulary that originally fueled the formation of the *AAT* in America was being felt in the international community.

International interest in the *AAT* sparked the quest for a miltilingual thesaurus. Scholars conducting research by means of automated databases want to find material in at least the major European languages via terms in their own languages. Such a desire on the part of scholars has led to investigations into the possbility of a multilingual art and architecture thesaurus by a committee of international art historians called Thesaurus Artis Universalis (TAU). Since 1984 this committee—charged by its parent organization, the International Committee for the History of Art (CIHA)—has studied the issue, and in 1989 it recommended a collaborative plan to translate the *AAT* into French, German, Italian, Spanish, and British English. Translation teams in several countries are envisioned, with the American English of the *AAT* serving as the base language and the *AAT* offices as the maintenance center for a central database.

In the winter of 1988-89, an experiment was carried out to translate a small section of one of the architecture hierarchies into the four other official CIHA languages. Translation teams in Montreal, Rome, Madrid, and Marburg, working on special bilingual termsheets produced by the *AAT* staff, successfully provided data to the *AAT* that produced bilingual hierarchies. The participants' reports set out the difficulties encountered: sometimes there was no equivalent for an English term; sometimes there were many different terms in the European language for a single English term. In addition, there was the problem of arranging the terms in a hierarchy, since researchers occasionally found that the conceptualization of the hierarchical structure in another language was different from that in English. All of the translation teams agreed that the inclusion of illustrations of the terms to be translated would have aided the process immeasurably. Despite these inherent difficulties, the experiment was seen as a positive step toward enhancing communication among international art historical communities.

It was not only endorsements and working groups that influenced the direction of the *AAT*. The first critique of the project was delivered by Trevor Fawcett in his keynote speech at the International Seminar on Information Problems in Art History at Oxford in 1982. Among his recommendations were that the *AAT* should be highly prescriptive, with detailed instructions for the application of terms; that there be copious scope notes; and that there be a high degree of specificity qualified by clearly stated constraints. He stressed the importance of having the *AAT* accepted by the major producers of bibliographic records. Prophetically, each of these recommendations has proved to be a necessity.

Seeking the acceptance of the major producers of bibliographic records especially necessitated several years of preparatory work. Although producers of indexing services such as the *Avery Index to Architectural Periodicals* and *RILA* have had little problem in adopting the *AAT* (and indeed have been using the terminology in draft form since late 1984), the art library community, which expressed the most dissatisfaction with its existing subject heading list, *LCSH*, and which had expressed the most need for an art and architecture thesaurus, was the least prepared to adopt it. Multitudes of its records already existed in national bibliographic networks with *LCSH* headings on them. Not only would it be difficult to switch to a new subject authority list, but the costs involved in training catalogers and in having to generate more specific headings to describe the contents of books would be considerable.

To aid library catalogers solve part of this problem, the *AAT* maps all relevant *LCSH* concepts where they appear in the *AAT*. Catalogers who wish to link old records containing *LCSH* terms with new records containing *AAT* terms have the opportunity to do so. By the spring of 1989, the *AAT* compilers had also produced MARC tapes of the *AAT* for use by national bibliographic networks or in local online library catalogs. Several sample tapes of the *AAT* in the MARC format have been test-mounted by individual libraries and by RLIN.

In the course of the mapping into MARC, it became clear that the USMARC Authorities Format would need modifications and that new fields should be added to hold and display hierarchically organized thesauri. The director of the *AAT*, with the support of RLG's Art and Architecture Program Committee, proposed and successfully shepherded a set of modifications and new fields through the Library of Congress Network Development and Standards Office, and then through the national committee that permits changes to the MARC format, the MARBI (Machine Readable Bibliographic Information) Committee. In addition to needed changes in the MARC Authorities Format, the MARC subject field (650) was inadequate for coding terms drawn from separate hierarchies. The implementation of a new subject field (654) now allows catalogers using faceted thesauri like the *AAT* to code and identify uniquely each term that has been combined into a more complex heading, noting the facets from which the terms came, and also to code a "focus" term—the term that is the main concept of the indexing string.

The *AAT*'s Faceted Structure

The *AAT* arrived at its current faceted structure slowly, and only with some prodding from classification experts such as Jean Aitchison, a British thesaurus expert, and then British librarians and classification experts gathered in 1984 by the British Architectural Library at the Royal Institute of British Architects (RIBA). British classification theorists have led the way, following S. R. Ranganathan in the 1930s, in the movement toward the classification of knowledge into faceted categories. Facets are seen as homogeneous, mutually exclusive units of information that share characteristics that demonstrate their differences from each other. For example, materials are different from objects made from them; each may thus be considered a facet of categorization. At the 1984 RIBA meeting, however, faceted classification was not raised to the level of complexity it has since taken in the *AAT*. At a much simpler level, and with the help of attendees familiar with the Bliss Classification System, the hierarchies were rearranged to start with the most abstract concepts and proceed to terms for styles and periods of art, agents, activities, materials, and finally object types.

One year later, John Logan, program manager, AHIP, recognized that this classification scheme actually paved the way for the *AAT* hierarchies to reside in different facets according to the syntactic meaning of the terms they held. This breakthrough has allowed for the subsequent refinement of *AAT* terminology and for the placing of terms in rational hierarchical arrangements. The development of the *AAT*'s faceted classification scheme has continued to be refined. Since 1989 a unique code for each term, called a classification notation, has identified its facet and hierarchical location, both to allow for the automatic configuring of the hierarchy, and for the scanning from broader to narrower terms in order to change the scope of a search. The classification notation was worked out in meetings with Bella Hass Weinberg of St. John's University and thesaurus expert David Batty and has resulted in a classification scheme and notation which is truly expressive of the *AAT*'s faceted structure. This development was consistent with a suggestion from a technical report by David Bearman on the issues that emerged as the *AAT* began to be used as an indexing language in local systems.

Contributions of Thesaurus Experts and Information Scientists

Throughout its development, the *AAT* has benefited from the advice the staff has received, not only from scholars in the fields that the *AAT* covers but also from thesaurus experts and information scientists who have helped to define its procedures and develop its system. The first sustained relationship of this nature began in the summer of 1983, when Elaine Svenonius worked with the *AAT* staff on theories of thesaurus construction and on practical problems of *AAT* development; helped to put together a "Prototype" document that set out conventions used in the *AAT* and provided sample displays for an audience that, until then, had heard much but seen little of the AAT; and worked on the first draft of the project's editorial manual. Subsequently, she has reviewed all completed hierarchies for consistency of thesaurus standards.

Songqiao Liu, a Ph.D. candidate under Svenonius at UCLA, was hired by AHIP in 1985, and developed the *AAT*'s thesaurus construction system. Liu's work produced a complex yet easy-to-use program that allows for hierarchies to be built automatically from term records. The new production system both builds the hierarchies and edits and revises vocabulary supplied from outside users. An enhancement includes a multilingual component—used to produce the bilingual hierarchies in the 1988 TAU experiment—and a dial-in access component that has been extended to some of the *AAT*'s most active users.

The issue of the *AAT*'s outreach to its user community was first raised in 1981 by Bethany Mendenhall. She stressed the necessity of demonstrating how to apply the *AAT*'s vocabulary in different environments if the *AAT* were to be successful in attracting a body of users. The next year Trevor Fawcett, as was noted earlier, stressed the importance of gaining support for the *AAT* among potential users. Most controlled vocabularies are developed internally and in a limited context by individual institutions or organizations; they reflect the content of the local collection being indexed or cataloged. The *AAT*, on the other hand, is an external standard independent of any individual application. It is intended to be flexible enough to meet diverse needs, whether they be to index text about a work of art or architecture, visual or archival documentation of the work, or the original work itself. The *AAT* sets out to establish a common vocabulary that can forster communication between, and enhance access to, a variety of art and archival information resources. In order to accomplish these ambitious goals, it was necessary to attract users from an early stage in the development of the project.

In September 1983, Mendenhall and staff from the Getty Center for the History of Art and the Humanities Library, along with David Patten and Michael Rinehart of *RILA*, met with the *AAT* co-directors, Nancy Englander and Marilyn Schmitt of the Getty Trust, and two indexing specialists, James Anderson of Rutgers University and Elaine Svenonius, to discuss application issues. The group concluded that an indexing system with syntactic rules could indeed be devised but that not all databases and cataloging organizations would be content to adopt it. Some would want to construct their own systems based on their internal needs. All would need guidance from the *AAT*.

In November 1983 and May 1984, groups of potential users met to assist in developing guidelines for use of the *AAT*, to develop mechanisms for communication with user projects, and to establish procedures for the *AAT* to assist individual projects to apply the thesaurus.

The year 1984 also saw a number of meetings of the RLG/AAPC's Subcommittee on *AAT* Implementation, which set itself the task of producing an application protocol that would instruct users in the building of complex combinations of terms. The subcommittee's work culminated in 1988 in the successful proposal for the new 654 subject field in the MARC format. In addition, the subcommittee worked hard on a general set of application rules that would be helpful to all users. It developed the idea of an *AAT* "expression": a strictly defined construction of *AAT* terms that together form a limited concept consisting of any main term modified by the appropriate style, material, or other descriptive terms (e.g., *round stone towers*). Further elaboration resulted in the concept of a "string," which was seen as a construction of two or more expressions separated by some kind of punctuation. (e.g., *Baroque churches—Switzerland—restoration*). This simple set of rules has become the basis for subsequent work on an application protocol. A formal version written by Mary Dykstra, dean of the Library School at Dalhousie University in Halifax, accompanies the thesaurus as an aid for those users wishing to develop indexing systems for their applications (see Appendix D to the Guide to Use).

Use of the *AAT*

By the end of 1984 it was decided that a small test group of *AAT* users should begin to apply the terminology in their databases. The first *AAT* user services coordinator had joined the staff, and a Candidate Term form and a Comment form had been developed. These forms were introduced to test users at the Avery Library, the Smithsonian, and the Architectural Drawings Advisory Group (ADAG), which has since been incorporated into the Foundation for Documents of Architecture. The first seven hierarchies, which were then considered completed in first draft (Styles and Periods, Drawings, Document Types, and the four architecture hierarchies), were distributed to about twelve organizations that had requested them. By 1989, the test-user group had grown to over 200 organizations. It continues to grow at the rate of about five new users per month. This process has had a two-way benefit. Indexing and cataloging organizations in the field of art and architecture that were just beginning to build online databases needed a controlled vocabulary, and the *AAT* staff needed to know if the vocabulary it was building was adequate and useful.

In the spring of 1988, members of the *AAT* staff visited over fifty users to gather information on what kinds of organization they were, what computer systems they used, and how they were making use of the thesaurus. These formal interviews—conducted by Toni Petersen, director of the project; Cathy Whitehead, user services coordinator; and Joseph Busch, project manager for the *AAT* at AHIP—resulted in the following findings:

- Most *AAT* users are responsible for handling architectural and archival information. (Since these sections of the *AAT* were the first constructed, this finding was hardly a surprising discovery.)
- Many *AAT* users manage archival and visual material collections.
- Manual systems of indexing provide limited access by subject to archival, slide and photograph collections; managers are therefore open to new thesauri as they begin to automate their indexes. (The *AAT* staff has worked with both the Society of American Archivists and the Visual Resources Association to provide for the special needs of these fields in the areas of subject terminology, giving workshops and demonstrations and meeting with groups within these societies to develop particular areas of the thesaurus.)

- *AAT* users employ a wide variety of computer systems, but most use microcomputers. (This finding has helped the project staff to plan for the types of machine-readable distribution of the *AAT* that will be most widely useful.)
- *AAT* users will need software and training in mounting the thesaurus in their systems.

During the interviews, participation in the *AAT*'s candidate-term process was also evaluated. When the hierarchies first began to be distributed in draft form, a formal procedure had been instituted with test users to encourage them to participate in the development of the *AAT* by suggesting new terms and commenting on existing ones. The submission and processing of candidate terms has become a valuable part of the editorial process. Each term so proposed is assigned to an editor and is researched as rigorously as all other terms being considered for the thesaurus. Regular meetings to discuss the disposition of the suggested terms sharpen the editorial process, raising issues to be resolved. When difficulties with new concepts arise, *AAT* editors consult with the submitting organizations to discuss the necessity for a particular term and how it might be applied. The *AAT* user services coordinator acts as liaison with submitting organizations, receiving and returning candidate terms and suggestions and communicating general editorial policies that might help users in their indexing and cataloging tasks.

AAT users currently include slide, drawing, and photograph collections, archives, museums, libraries, indexing services, architecture and design firms, and art and architecture dictionary and encyclopedia projects. The majority of these users have automated or are planning to automate their collections. Through the 1988 survey—and through personal communication with a number of actual and potential *AAT* users—a clear sense of the need to provide guidance and training in the use of controlled subject vocabulary has developed. Guidelines ranging from general rules on term selection to the use of *AAT* terms in complex indexing systems are needed. A series of training workshops that began in 1987 will be expanded to reach all constituents who need guidance in the use of the thesaurus. The primary stance of the project staff toward *AAT* users has tended to be one of openness and flexibility: openness to a variety of information systems, and their particular needs, and flexibility to change the *AAT*, as required, by both the user community and by new developments in the field of information science. The *AAT*-user liaison will continue to be an indispensable element of the long-term maintenance and growth of the thesaurus.

This publication is in further service of *AAT* users. With more than 200 organizations using the thesaurus in draft form, it became imperative to issue a formal, even though incomplete, version. The twenty-three hierarchies included here, covering as they do the field of architecture and all modifying terminology, along with several hierarchies from the decorative and fine arts sections that have been the most requested over the years, form a set that should fill the needs of many users. Those who have been using the draft hierarchies may now be assured that the terminology covered here is stable and will not be changed unless there is an error in a particular term. All users have the opportunity to participate in maintaining the *AAT* by reporting their requests on the Candidate Term Forms and Comment Forms (see Appendixes A and B to the Guide to Use).

Supplementary volumes including new terms and any changes to existing terms will be published by Oxford University Press on a regular basis. Completion of all projected hierarchies is anticipated within the next few years, and a new edition will then be released that includes the entire set. The *AAT* looks forward to fruitful interaction with its users, not only for enrichment and maintenance of the present terminology but also for information on needed areas of expansion in the future.

References

1. Marilyn Schmitt, "A Database of Databases," *The J. Paul Getty Trust Bulletin* (Winter 1989): 6-7.

2. "Researching Research," *The J. Paul Getty Trust Bulletin* (Fall 1987): 4-5.

3. Dora Crouch, Pat Molholt, and Toni Petersen. *Indexing in Art and Architecture: An Investigation and Analysis*. Report to the Council on Library Resources. Washington D.C., Council on Library Resources, 1981.

4. Toni Petersen, "The AAT: A Model for the Restructuring of LCSH," *Journal of Academic Librarianship* (September 1983) 9:207-210.

5. Toni Petersen, "Subject Control in Visual Collections," *Art Documentation* (Winter 1988) 132-33.

6. Elaine Svenonius, "Information Retrieval Thesauri in the Field of Art" (paper delivered at the Second International Conference on *Automatic Processing of Art History Data and Documents*, Pisa, Italy, 24-27 September 1984).

Guide to Use

1. Purpose

A thesaurus is the controlled vocabulary of an indexing system, arranged in a known order and structured so that synonymous, hierarchical, and associative relationships among terms are clearly displayed and identified by standardized relationship indicators. Its purposes are to ensure consistency in indexing, especially in information management and retrieval systems, and to facilitate the retrieval of information. Regardless of the material being cataloged or indexed, whether works of art, journal articles, architectural drawings, photographs, the contents of books, or sets of family papers, successful information management and retrieval depends upon the ability of the cataloger or indexer to anticipate the needs and viewpoints of their users and to determine the essence of meaning within a document or the name and physical characteristics of an object. Users' needs and the analysis of the items being indexed must then be translated into consistent, appropriate language.

Languages develop both by evolution and by revolution. Word forms and spellings change slowly, but new words and new meanings for "old" words appear virtually overnight. The multiple labels we assign objects and concepts complicate matters further. Some labels are based on cultural differences, some on a user's point of view as an artist, art historian, curator, or archivist. It is the role of a thesaurus to draw together terms scattered by accident of the alphabet or by cultural and function-based biases. A good thesaurus, by definition, is never finished. If the work is to reflect its environment, it must change over time as the disciplines it helps to define change.

A thesaurus not only draws together synonyms and differentiates homographs, it structures information according to the hierarchical principle of genus and species to aid in the browsing and selection of appropriate terminology. Terminology for a thesaurus springs from many sources: subject lists of indexing and cataloging organizations, scholarly monographs, catalogs, glossaries, specialized dictionaries, and the like.

It is anticipated that users of the *AAT* will include staff members at libraries, archives, museums, indexing and abstracting services, historical collections, drawings collections, and photographic collections, as well as scholars and students engaged in independent research. Further, it is expected that this user population will be diverse, not only from the standpoint of its understanding of the subject content of the thesaurus but also in its expertise in navigating the various displays in these volumes. Users who are unfamiliar with hierarchical displays and the general syndetic structure of a thesaurus are cautioned to pay careful attention to the explanations and assistance offered in this guide to use.

2. Scope

The *Art and Architecture Thesaurus* (*AAT*) covers terminology for art and architecture of the Western world from antiquity to the present. Fields within art and architecture are defined as follows:

Built Environment Built works and the human elaboration of the natural environment

Furnishings and Equipment Artifacts with a primarily utilitarian purpose, often embellished

Visual and Verbal Communication Communicative artifacts created according to aesthetic, conceptual, or symbolic principles

The largest proportion of terms in this publication are names of objects of the built environment. Although terms for some objects of visual and verbal communication and of furnishings and equipment are included, sections covering these fields are still under development and will be completed for the next edition. The thesaurus is expected to be issued in its entirety within the next few years. Expansion into areas beyond the Western world will be considered as a possible later development of the *AAT*.

Besides supplying a vocabulary for objects, the *AAT* also provides terminology necessary for the description of these objects, which includes the materials and techniques of their construction, their physical attributes, such as shape and color, and terminology associated with their production and study, such as the roles of persons and concepts relating to their history, theory, criticism, and purpose. This "supporting terminology" will be expanded as work on terminology relating to visual and verbal communication and to furnishings and equipment continues.

Terminology that describes the depiction or representation of iconographical themes, such as religious and mythological subjects of paintings or carvings, is generally excluded. Some terms that designate genres of work, such as *portraits*, *landscapes*, and *caricatures*, and some terms that specify design motifs and patterns are provided.

3. Conceptual Framework

The *AAT* vocabulary is organized into seven facets and forty hierarchies, or subdivisions of the facets. A complete listing of the planned coverage of the *AAT* is given in Appendix A. This first edition of the thesaurus contains twenty-three of the projected forty hierarchies:

ASSOCIATED CONCEPTS FACET
- Associated Concepts

PHYSICAL ATTRIBUTES FACET
- Design Attributes
- Design Elements
- Colors

STYLES AND PERIODS FACET
- Styles and Periods

AGENTS FACET
- People and Organizations

ACTIVITIES FACET
- Disciplines
- Functions
- Events
- Processes and Techniques

MATERIALS FACET
- Materials

OBJECTS FACET

Built Environment
- Settlements, Systems and Landscapes
- Built Complexes and Districts
- Single Built Works and Open Spaces
- Building Divisions and Site Elements
- Built Works Components

Furnishings and Equipment
- Tools and Equipment
- Hardware and Joints
- Furniture

Visual and Verbal Communication
- Image and Object Genres
- Drawings
- Photographs
- Document Types

The conceptual framework of facets and hierarchies was developed in conjunction with classification specialists and has been validated by review within the scholarly communities served by the *AAT*.

3.1 Facets Facets constitute the major subdivisions of terminology. A facet is a homogeneous class of terms whose members share characteristics that distinguish them from the members of other classes. When a term is first nominated for inclusion in the *AAT*, the fundamental category, or facet, to which it belongs must be determined. For example, *marble*, meaning a type of substance used in the creation of objects, is found as a descriptor in the Materials facet, while *Impressionist*, denoting visually distinctive works of art, is listed as a descriptor in the Styles and Periods facet. The faceted approach to subject analysis and indexing was first introduced by Shiyali Ramamrita Ranganathan in 1933. Dividing knowledge into five fundamental classes—Personality, Matter, Energy, Space, and Time—he categorized subjects of documents according to these facets. Since then, indexers influenced by Ranganathan have developed discipline-specific systems by using his primary categories or by inventing others pertinent to their scope.

In constructing the *AAT* it was quickly discovered that much of the terminology within its scope related to object names. It was also soon apparent that noun phrases denoting objects of art and architecture often contain adjectives (designating material, style, technique, and function, among others) and that these adjectives recur in infinite combinations throughout the built environment (*Victorian houses*), material culture (*painted furniture*), and the fine arts (*charcoal drawings*). Rather than enumerate the nearly infinite number of object and subject descriptions needed by thesaurus users, the *AAT* decided to provide the building blocks of these descriptors in the form of a faceted vocabulary. To date, the *AAT* staff has identified seven facets from which these subject and object descriptions can be created:

Associated Concepts
Physical Attributes
Styles and Periods
Agents
Activities
Materials
Objects

The facets are conceptually organized in a scheme that proceeds from abstract concepts to concrete, physical artifacts. To these *AAT* facets, indexers may add other facets for time and place in order to construct more complex indexing strings.

The **Associated Concepts** facet contains terms for abstract concepts, qualities, and phenomena that relate directly to the study and execution of art and architecture (*adaptive reuse, beauty, balance, connoisseurship*), as well as those aligned with other disciplines not directly included in the scope of the thesaurus but useful in relation to art or architecture (*metaphor, electricity*). Also included are terms for general theories, critical concepts, ideologies, attitudes, and social or cultural movements (*privacy, freedom, socialism, romanticism*).

The **PHYSICAL ATTRIBUTES** facet contains terms descriptive of the appearance or quality of artifacts, especially relating to their design or decoration, such as shape attributes (*round*), color attributes (*light green*), and other aspects of design (*exterior*). Also included are terms for individual and repeating design elements (*strapwork, lotus*), and areas of decoration (*borders, panels*).

The **STYLES AND PERIODS** facet contains terms for concepts denoting visually distinctive traits assigned by scholars in the description and classification of man-made works of architecture, fine arts, or decorative arts. These terms include those derived from the names of peoples or cultures (*Inuit*), geographic areas and sites (*French, Angkor Vat*), names of rulers (*Louis XIV*), historical periods (*Xia*), as well as terms that are descriptive or interpretive (*Black-figure, Abstract Expressionism*).

The **AGENTS** facet contains terms for persons or groups of persons associated by some role or occupation (*printmakers*) and generic names of groups and organizations (*corporations*).

The **ACTIVITIES** facet contains terms for actions, endeavors, and tasks as well as for methods or techniques used to accomplish some end. Included are terms for branches of learning and professional endeavor (*archaeology, engineering*), conceptually executed processes (*analyzing*), discrete occurrences and events (*contests, death*), and processes performed on or with materials and objects (*conservation, drawing, weaving*).

The **MATERIALS** facet contains terms for naturally or synthetically derived substances. These terms range from names of raw materials (*iron, clay*) and functional classes of materials (*adhesives, emulsifiers*) to manufactured materials and products (*artificial ivory, millwork*) used in the construction of various objects and components.

The **OBJECTS** facet contains terms for inanimate entities that are perceptible, especially by touch or sight, and that are usually the product of human activity. Included are terms for built works and elements of the natural environment important to design (*arches, rivers*), man-made artifacts, including those with a utilitarian purpose (*tools*), and those that are usually associated with aesthetic or symbolic principles (*still lifes, capricci*).

As a result of the faceted approach, many common phrases, such as "painted Victorian furniture" are not explicitly listed as thesaurus descriptors since they contain words that are listed separately in different facets:

painted	in Activities facet
Victorian	in Styles and Periods facet
furniture	in Objects facet

Such combined statements that are not listed in the thesaurus as single terms must be created by the indexer at the time of indexing or the researcher at the time of searching. Rules for recombining terms to form subject statements or object descriptions are found in Appendix D.

3.2 Hierarchies Hierarchies may be thought of as subfacets of the general facets in that they are also homogeneous groupings of terminology within the basic facets. The Objects facet contains the hierarchies Built Works Components, Furniture, and Drawings, among others, while the Activities facet contains the hierarchies Functions, Processes and Techniques, Events, and Disciplines. Hierarchies graphically display genus-species or class-subclass relationships for a specific family of terms.

Each hierarchy included in this volume is preceded by an explanatory statement of its scope, arrangement, and usage, followed by an outline or summary of its organization, called a synopsis. The synopsis gives an overview of the hierarchy's content by showing the first three or four levels of terms contained in the hierarchy. Section 4.2 below explains the conventions used in the hierarchies.

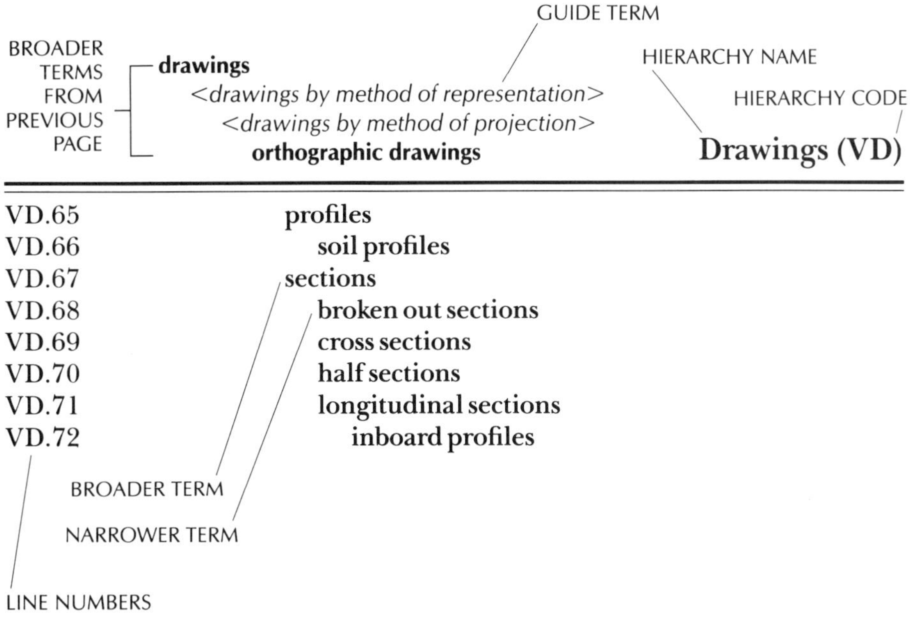

FIGURE 1. *Sample from Hierarchical Display*

4. Editorial Principles and Conventions

The *AAT* has been constructed according to the principles and conventions outlined in the following standards:

American National Standards Institute. *Guidelines for Thesaurus Structure, Construction, and Use.* New York: American National Standards Institute, 1980. (ANSI Z39.19)

British Standards Institution. *Guidelines for the Establishment and Development of Monolingual Thesauri.* 2d ed. London: British Standards Institution, 1987. (BS 5273)

The International Organization for Standardization. *Guidelines for the Establishment and Development of Monolingual Thesauri.* 2d ed. Geneva: International

Organization for Standardization, 1986. (ISO 2788)

UNISIST Guidelines for the Establishment and Development of Monolingual Thesauri. 2nd ed. Paris: United Nations Educational, Scientific, and Cultural Organization, 1986. (PGI-81/ws/15)

A list of other sources used to augment these standards can be found in the bibliography, section 10.

This edition of the *AAT* consists of two types of display: a hierarchical display and an alphabetical display. Sample displays are shown in Figures 1 and 2. The two displays each contain all the descriptors in this edition of the *AAT* and are designed to be used as complementary tools.

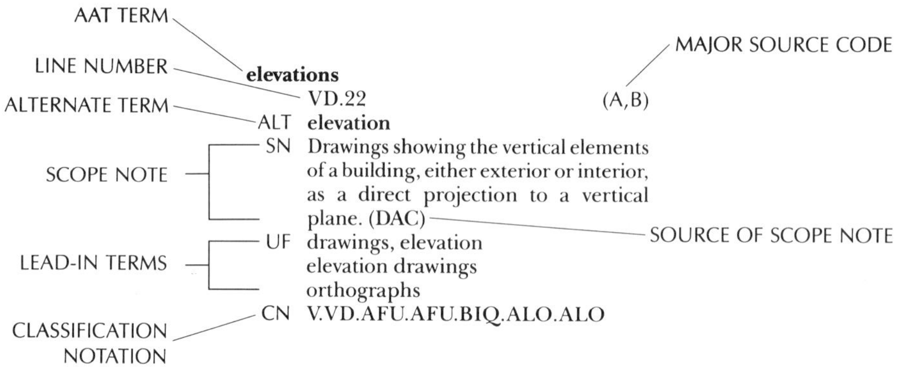

FIGURE 2. *Sample from Alphabetical Display*

4.1 Alphabetical Display The alphabetical display serves as an index to the hierarchical displays and provides detailed information about each entry, such as a scope note, synonym(s), and its classification number. Alphabetization is word by word; hyphens and commas file after spaces.

4.1.1 Descriptors Based on its editorial procedures, the *AAT* gathers all forms of a term and selects one, called the descriptor, that is recommended for use. Synonyms and certain spelling variants of this descriptor are included as lead-in vocabulary. Descriptors are also called main terms, preferred terms, authorized terms, postable terms, or established terms in various vocabulary systems.

4.1.1.1 Form of Descriptors The form of a descriptor represents the conventional usage of the term in the field and the most widely accepted spelling. Most descriptors are nouns (*buildings*) or noun phrases (*historic buildings*). Free-standing adjectives are included as descriptors in some hierarchies so they can be used as modifiers of other descriptors. Their inclusion serves to avoid undue enumeration of phrases composed of adjectives plus nouns (*circular rooms, circular stairs, circular barns*, etc.). Certain descriptors, in particular those in the Styles and Periods hierarchy and the Materials hierarchy, may be used both as nouns and as adjectives. For example, the term *stone* may be used alone or in combination with a noun to make a phrase such as *stone columns*. Gerund forms are also included in the hierarchies in the Activities facet (*repairing*). Active verbs are never used as descriptors but in some instances are provided as lead-in vocabulary (*repair*, for example, is a lead-in term to *repairing*). Prepositional phrases and phrases containing conjunctives are generally excluded from the thesaurus, except when they express single concepts (*wattle and daub*). Terms containing connective punctuation, such as commas or colons, are not allowed as descriptors.

All terms are spelled with an initial lowercase letter with the exception of proper nouns (*Inuit, Louis XVI*) and some proper adjectives (*German, Ionic*). Another exception is for trademarks used as descriptors. These appear with an initial uppercase letter followed by the code TM in parentheses (*Kodachrome (TM)*). Compound terms used as descriptors appear in natural word order (*public buildings*); inverted forms are included as lead-in vocabulary (*buildings, public* is a lead-in term to *public buildings*).

Use of the singular or plural form has been decided on the basis of literary warrant, common usage, and the recommendations found in the thesaurus standards cited earlier. Generally, count nouns—terms that answer the question "how many?"—are in the plural (*chairs*), and mass nouns—terms that answer the question "how much?"—are in the singular (*concrete*). Singular forms are available for use as alternate terms (see section 4.1.4 below).

Possessives used in a compound phrase are generally pluralized (*artists' marks*), except when the phrase indicates an actual object name (*potter's wheels*).

4.1.1.2 Establishing *AAT* Descriptors *AAT* descriptors reflect, as far as possible, the vocabulary used by scholars and other researchers. An effort has been made to include vocabulary used by archivists and other information professionals who organize and describe information in the areas covered by the thesaurus. Terms were initially gathered from the following controlled vocabularies already used in the field:

Avery Index to Architectural Periodicals
Library of Congress Subject Headings (LCSH)
RIBA Architectural Periodicals Index
RILA (*International Repertory of the Literature of Art*)

Relevant headings and other information from these lists, such as the preferred or nonpreferred status of headings, have been systematically mapped to the *AAT*. Mapping is a process whereby information about the original status and form of a term in a source is preserved within the *AAT*'s term record. Source codes indicating where terms from these major sources appear in the *AAT* are given in entries in the alphabetic displays.

The *AAT* includes terms as they are found in the sources cited above unless they fail to meet *AAT* term form and selection criteria (i.e., if the term is in inverted form, or contains punctuation marks). Terms from the above sources that do not conform to *AAT* editorial policy are usually included as lead-in terms.

Some terms from these sources that are relevant to the scope of the *AAT* but that are unacceptable either as descriptors or as lead-in vocabulary because of their form are mapped to the appropriate term(s) in the online *AAT* term record. For example, the Library of Congress heading "Architecture—Designs and plans" is mapped to the *AAT* descriptor *architectural drawings*. It is hoped that such mapping will facilitate the transition from one vocabulary to another as well as the coexistence of two or more vocabularies in the same system. The form in which a descriptor appears in sources consulted by the *AAT* is available only in the *AAT* thesaurus construction database and in authority records distributed in the USMARC authorities format.

Each *AAT* descriptor, no matter what its source, must be validated against the literature of the field. Each descriptor is checked in several sources in order to establish its form and meaning and to ensure that all word forms (i.e., synonyms and alternate spellings) are included. The actual form of a descriptor must have literary warrant. It is not enough that the concept a descriptor denotes is discussed within the body of a text; the term itself must be used in the text.

Relatively new terms, such as *intelligent buildings*, are accepted into the thesaurus on a provisional basis. The usage of such terms is monitored to ensure that the form of the descriptor is actually the form being used in the literature.

4.1.1.3 Terms in Other Languages *AAT* terms are based on American English usage. Therefore, terms from other languages, including British English, must appear in common usage in authoritative American English sources before they are considered for inclusion in the *AAT*. The inclusion and treatment of foreign-language terms are determined by editorial staff on a case-by-case basis. Generally, if terms in another language meet *AAT* term-selection criteria, they are placed in the following manner:

1. If a term from another language is commonly used in authoritative American English sources and has no American English equivalent, then it is included as a descriptor.

   EXAMPLES: *mihrabs*, *pagodas*

2. If a term from another language is commonly used in authoritative American English sources and does have an American English equivalent, then it is also included as a descriptor but is placed as a narrower term to its American English counterpart.

   EXAMPLES: *domus* is a narrower term to *houses*.
   bonheurs-du-jour is a narrower term to *lady's writing tables*.

3. If a term does appear in authoritative American English sources but is used interchangeably for the American English equivalent, it is considered a true synonym and is included as a lead-in term.

   EXAMPLES: *souks* USE *bazaars*
   allés couvertes USE *gallery graves*

4.1.1.4 Compound Terms Following standard thesaurus guidelines, *AAT* descriptors represent single concepts with precise meanings. Single concepts may be expressed by one word (*broadsides*) or by more than one word (*curtain walls*). As a general rule, users will not find multiword phrases that contain descriptors from two different facets as in the following instances:

MATERIAL + OBJECT (*charcoal drawings*): The descriptor *charcoal* is in the Materials facet. The descriptor *drawings* is in the Drawings hierarchy of the Objects facet.

STYLE + OBJECT (*Ionic columns*): The descriptor *Ionic* is in the Styles and Periods facet. The descriptor *columns* is in the Built Works Components hierarchy of the Objects facet.

ACTIVITY + OBJECT (*painted chairs*): The descriptor *painted* is in the Processes and Techniques hierarchy of the Activities facet. The descriptor *chairs* is in the Furniture hierarchy of the Objects facet.

PHYSICAL ATTRIBUTE + OBJECT (*round photographs*): The descriptor *round* is in the Design Attributes hierarchy of the Physical Attributes facet. The descriptor *photographs* is in the Photographs hierarchy of the Objects facet.

Other multiword phrases are excluded as descriptors when they express the following relationship:

SUBJECT + FORM/GENRE (*furniture pattern books, war photographs*): The descriptor *furniture* is in the Furniture hierarchy and the descriptor *pattern books* is in the Document Types hierarchy. The descriptor *war* is in the Associated Concepts facet. The descriptor *photographs* is in the Photographs hierarchy of the Objects facet.

Compound terms, that is, multiword terms that express a single concept, are included as descriptors and referred to as "bound terms" when they meet one or more of the following conditions:

1. When the meaning of the term would be lost if its components were broken apart and would lead to false drops in retrieval (*cabinet pictures* conveys a different concept than the combination of the separate terms *cabinets* and *pictures*)
2. If the compound phrase is encountered so frequently in the literature of the field that it is considered for practical purposes to be a single concept (*marriage certificates*)
3. If it contains a term that is not a valid term in its own right (*three-point perspective*, where *three-point* is not a valid term in the *AAT*)
4. If the precombined term is the name of an object and is therefore a single concept (*carpenter's squares*)

4.1.2 Line Number The line number is a computer-generated, alphanumeric code used in the printed version of the thesaurus to provide a link from a descriptor in the alphabetical display to its location in the hierarchical display. Line numbers consist of a two-letter code followed by the number of the line at which the term appears in that hierarchy (VD.36 = line 36 in the Drawings hierarchy). Because line numbers are purely sequential and will change as new terminology is added in subsequent editions, they should never be used in place of a descriptor. The classification notation, described in the following section, should be used for this purpose.

4.1.3 Classification Notation Each descriptor is assigned a unique identifier called a classification notation (CN), which may be used to substitute for a descriptor in an automated database. They are not devices to find a term in a hierarchy; line numbers should be used for this purpose. This identifying code begins with a one-letter facet notation (V = Objects facet) followed by a period, a two-letter hierarchy code (VD = Drawings hierarchy), and three-letter elements, separated by periods that specify level of indentation (V.VD.AFU.-AFU.ALO).

Classification notations are expressive in that they convey the sequence of descriptors in a hierarchy and indicate the relative position of a descriptor within that hierarchy. Furthermore, they are permanent. The insertion of new terms will not affect the notation of already established descriptors. Should a descriptor become obsolete in a future edition of the thesaurus, the classification notation will not be reassigned.

Because they are expressive, classification notations may also be used to generate the hierarchy in systems that wish to maintain the thesaurus online. Line numbers used in the printed thesaurus should not be used for this purpose.

4.1.4 Alternate Term An alternate term (ALT) is sometimes given for other grammatical forms of a descriptor when they are needed for indexing and cataloging purposes. For example, because there are strong historic differences between bibliographic indexing practice and visual resources and museum cataloging practice, both the singular and the plural forms of nouns are given. The user must decide which form is appropriate to the application at hand and apply the terminology consistently. These terms have the same hierarchical relationships as the descriptor, but they appear only in the alphabetical display. Alternate terms may be of the following types:

1. The noun form of an adjective:
   (**Impressionist**
   ALT **Impressionism**)
2. The adjectival form of a noun:
   (**Buddhism**
   ALT **Buddhist**)
3. The adjectival form of a gerund:
   (**painting**
   ALT **painted**)
4. The singular form of a plural noun:
   (**museums**
   ALT **museum**)

4.1.5 Major Source Codes One or more single-letter codes appearing in parentheses to the right of the line number indicate that the concept denoted by the term was found in one of the following controlled vocabularies:

A = Avery Index Authority Reference File
B = RIBA Architectural Periodicals Index, *Architectural Keywords*
L = *Library of Congress Subject Headings* (LCSH)
N = *Revised Nomenclature for Museum Cataloging*
R = *International Repertory of the Literature of Art (RILA) Subject Heading List*

These codes indicate only that the concept was found in the source. No indication of the form of the concept or its preferred/nonpreferred status is given. For example, following the line number for *special libraries* will be found the parenthetical notation (L,B), indicating that the *AAT* concept is used in LCSH and RIBA. However, no indication is given that the forms of the term used are, respectively, "Libraries, Special" and "Libraries: special." Only a code for each source is given in this printed edition of the *AAT*.

4.1.6 Scope Notes A scope note (SN) is a statement that clarifies the meaning and usage of a term within the thesaurus. The functions of scope notes are the following:

1. To indicate the meaning, scope, or usage of a term within the *AAT*
2. To guide users in selecting the most appropriate term
3. To distinguish a given term from others
4. To direct users to related or overlapping concepts

Scope notes should be viewed in conjunction with the term's placement in a hierarchy, since the hierarchical context also serves to clarify meaning.

Scope notes that define terms in the *AAT* are called definitional scope notes. Scope notes that provide guidance on usage in the thesaurus are called instructional scope notes. Scope notes may be definitional, instructional, or both.

4.1.6.1 Instructional Scope Notes Instructional scope notes are used to restrict the use of a term, to distinguish between terms that have overlapping meanings, or to provide other advice on term usage. Instructional scope notes usually contain one of the following phrases:

Use when . . .
Where possible use . . .
Includes . . . excludes . . .
Use only when . . .
Distinguished from . . . by . . .
Distinct from . . . in that . . .

When reference is made to other *AAT* terms in a scope note, a reciprocal scope note is found for each term mentioned.

EXAMPLES:

dogtrots

SN Use for passages, sharing a roof common with the rest of the building, connecting two parts of a log house of the American folk architecture tradition. Distinguished from "breezeways" by its folk architecture tradition and log house context and its common roof.

breezeways
SN Use for roofed passages connecting two parts of a house or a house and a garage; common after 1930. Distinct from "dog-trots," which occur in folk architecture log houses.

4.1.6.2 Definitional Scope Notes It is not usual for dictionary-style definitions to be included in a thesaurus. However, because of the specificity of the terminology contained in the *AAT*, and our wish to clarify the meaning of imprecise or controversial terms, definitional scope notes have been liberally provided to supplement meanings conveyed by hierarchical placement or qualifiers.

EXAMPLE:

conceptual drawings
SN Designates architectural drawings done early in the design process; often not to scale and may include diagrammatic elements.

4.1.6.3 Source of Scope Notes A code indicating the source from which a definitional scope note was derived is given in parentheses at the end of the portion of the scope note that cites the source used.

EXAMPLE:

finding aids
SN Documents, published or unpublished, listing or describing a body of records within a record center or archives, making them more readily accessible and comprehensible to the user. (ICA)

Full citations for all codes can be found in the list of sources following this guide. When scope notes have been composed by the *AAT* editorial staff, no source is indicated. The format of scope notes has been developed according to *AAT* editorial conventions to ensure consistency and grammatical correctness. Therefore, when a source is indicated, it does not necessarily mean that the scope note is listed verbatim in the cited source. More than one citation may appear in a scope note.

4.1.7 Parenthetical Qualifiers Parenthetical qualifiers (words in parentheses), sometimes called glosses, are employed to distinguish between homographs, that is, terms that are spelled alike but that are different in meaning, such as *bonds* (*masonry*) and *bonds* (*legal records*). Qualifiers are considered integral parts of terms and are "bound" to them in indexing and retrieval. If one of two homographs is a lead-in term and the other is a descriptor, only the lead-in term is qualified (*charts* (*maps*) is a lead-in term to *maps; charts* is a descriptor).

4.1.8 Lead-in References Synonyms and spelling variants are called lead-in terms or Use For terms (UF). In the alphabetical display these appear as individual entries with cross-references to a descriptor.

EXAMPLE: concept sketches
USE
conceptual drawings

Synonyms and spelling variants for each descriptor also appear collectively, preceded by the code UF, under the entry for the descriptor.

EXAMPLE: **conceptual drawings**
UF concept drawings
concept sketches
conceptual sketches
drawings, conceptual
sketches, conceptual

Some spelling variants of a descriptor, such as hyphenated forms or forms with different plural endings, are excluded from the alphabetical display when they file close to the descriptor. For example, a reference from *audio-visual centers* to *audiovisual centers* is not given in the alphabetical display. Access by these variant spellings is provided in some online versions of the *AAT.*

Lead-in terms are, as far as possible, considered to be true synonyms of a descriptor. Close synonyms and narrower concepts to a descriptor are never listed as UFs, but they are themselves available as descriptors, often with scope notes that clarify their usage.

4.1.9 Related Terms Cross-references to related terms (RT), used to indicate terms associated with a given descriptor, are not included in this edition. The hierarchical displays obviate the need for many of the cross-references that would ordinarily be made between siblings in a strictly alphabetical thesaurus. In the next edition of the *AAT,* citation of related terms will generally be limited to relationships from a descriptor in one hierarchy to a descriptor in another hierarchy. Thesaurus users should review the hierarchy scope statements for explanations of the relationships between hierarchies.

4.2 Hierarchical Display In the hierarchical display, descriptors are organized in a graphic arrangement that allows for browsing closely related terms and for selecting terms at appropriate levels of specificity.

AAT hierarchies are not intended to show the definitive way in which terms in a particular area should be classified. It would be possible to conceive of other versions of hierarchical structures. In the *AAT,* the structure of each hierarchy is based on the most generally accepted organization of concepts in each field as determined by the *AAT* editorial process in consultation with subject scholars and information handlers such as collections managers, archivists, catalogers, and indexers.

The *AAT* hierarchies also do not provide an exhaustive listing of all terms within their scope. Our intention has been to enumerate a sufficient number of terms to be useful to current users and to develop a classificatory structure that will accommodate additional terms as required in the future by *AAT* users.

4.2.1 Classification of Terms The hierarchical display shows genus-species, or class-subclass, relationships between terms. Broader terms and narrower terms are not explicitly labeled with the conventional abbreviations BT and NT. Instead, the relationship of broader term to narrower term is shown graphically by successive levels of indentation. A term is broader than those that are indented below it and narrower than the term below which it itself is indented.

A broader term gives the immediate class, or genus, to which the descriptor belongs in a hierarchy and serves to clarify its meaning. If a term is always a type of, kind of, example of, or manifestation of another term, then a true genus-species relationship exists and that genus is assigned as the broader term. For example, houses are always types of dwellings, but not all dwellings are houses. Dwellings also include cave dwellings and apartment houses. Therefore, *dwellings* is broader than the sibling terms *houses, cave dwellings*, and *apartment houses*.

AAT descriptors have only one broader term. This means that descriptors are placed in their most generic location. For example, plans are sometimes, but not always, types of architectural drawings. The descriptor *plans* therefore is found as a narrower term to *orthographic drawings*, since plans are always orthographic.

As stated above, descriptors that have the same broader term are called siblings. Siblings are usually arranged alphabetically; however, they may occasionally be found arranged in chronological order or by size, if such an arrangement appears the more logical.

4.2.1.1 Guide Terms Terms that do not meet the criteria for descriptors but that are nevertheless useful in demonstrating the hierarchical structure of a vocabulary are called guide terms. They are also called node labels or facet indicators in some thesauri. In the *AAT* they are used as broader terms of some descriptors when no real term exists. To indicate that they cannot be used as indexing terms, they are printed in italics and enclosed in angle brackets (*<document genres>, <chairs by form>*).

In addition to serving as broader terms, many guide terms define the characteristics of division by which a listing of narrower terms is clustered. For example, the term *high-rise buildings* is listed under the guide term *single built works by form*, whereas the term *agricultural buildings* appears under the guide term *single built works by function*.

Certain types of guide terms are consistently applied throughout the thesaurus since particular characteristics of division, such as form and function, are applicable to many classes of terms. For example, chairs as well as buildings can be classified according to form (*cabriole chairs*) and function (*nursing chairs*). Three recurrent guide terms are *by form, by function*, and *by location or context*:

<by form> This guide term is used to collocate terms for images and objects that are distinguishable by their physical form or by the manner in which they are presented. In general, if an image or an object is identifiable by sight, then it is cited under a *by form* guide term.

<by function> This guide term is used to collocate terms for images and objects that are distinguishable by the particular purpose for which they are designed or used. If an image or an object is identifiable by its intended use, it is cited under a *by function* guide term.

<by location or context> This guide term is used to collocate terms for images and objects that are distinguishable by their use or application within a particular physical location. If an image or an object is identifiable by association with specific surroundings, it is cited under a *by location* guide term.

The nature of certain subject areas requires the use of subject-specific guide terms to structure the vocabulary, such as *by method of representation* in the Drawings hierarchy.

4.2.1.2 Whole-Part Relationships In accordance with ANSI and ISO thesaurus construction standards, the *AAT* does not exhibit whole-part (partitive) relationships between terms in the hierarchies. *Columns*, for example, is classified under *architectural elements* and not under *temples*. An exception has been made for some hierarchies in the Objects facet, where component terms relevant to a particular type of object may appear in the same hierarchy, although in separate sections. The Furniture hierarchy, for example, contains two major sections, *furniture* and *furniture components*.

4.2.2 Synthesis Notes At the foot of each page of the hierarchical display, a brief note suggesting ways in which descriptors from a particular hierarchy may be combined or synthesized with other descriptors is provided. The synthesis note for the Drawings hierarchy states, for example:

> May be used in combination with other descriptors, (e.g., *Japanese + watercolors; ink + drawings; brush + drawings; landscape + drawings*).

5. How to Use the *AAT*

The *AAT* is appropriate for a variety of applications:

1. Physical description of museum objects, slides, photographs, archival materials, books, drawings
2. Subject cataloging and keyword indexing of books, images of architecture, images of art, periodical literature
3. Database searching by scholars, researchers, students, practitioners, librarians, and other information intermediaries

Because of the diversity of applications using the *AAT*, it is expected that thesaurus users will develop and document local *AAT* application rules. An example of a local application rule is limiting database field values to terms found in certain *AAT* hierarchies (e.g., only terms from the *AAT* Activities facet would be allowed in a field for Technique).

What follows are general guidelines for selecting terms from the *AAT* and an explanation of how the *AAT* facets can be used to create multiword expressions or complex subject statements. The *AAT* project staff will continue to work with users as the remaining portions of the thesaurus are developed to refine application guidelines.

5.1 Hierarchy Selection Users may have need to employ all or only some of the *AAT* hierarchies, depending on the scope of each user's discipline or collection. Hierarchies of primary interest to archivists, for example, may include Document Types, People and Organizations, and a select number of hierarchies from the Activities facet, while architectural librarians might require extensive use of terminology from all facets of the thesaurus. However, since descriptors are classified at the most generic location possible, and because it is often necessary to use multiple hierarchies to build indexing strings, individual applications should probably not restrict thesaurus usage solely to a particular set of hierarchies.

5.2 Term Selection The following is a general procedure for selecting a term from the thesaurus:

1. Determine a set of words or phrases that characterizes the concept being sought.
2. Check the alphabetical display to see if the term can be found there.
3. Examine the scope note for the term to see if its meaning applies.
4. Examine the synonyms under the term.
5. If there is an alternate term, decide whether it is more appropriate for the application at hand.
6. Check the hierarchical display to see if there is another, more appropriate term at a different level of specificity.
7. Check the guide terms to see if any other aspects of the hierarchy are relevant.

For accuracy in indexing and compatibility between users, a concept should never be "forced" from the existing vocabulary by using a broader term or by artificially creating a term from two or more *AAT* descriptors when it is fairly certain that a specific word exists. Instead, the problem should be called to the attention of the *AAT* staff with the submission of a Candidate Term Form. This procedure is described in section 6 below.

5.2.1 Specificity of Term Selection The *AAT* vocabulary has been developed to a considerable level of specificity. Users may apply the level of specificity provided or adjust their indexing to a more general level. Several factors affect a decision on specificity:

1. Level of indexer's expertise. Terminology for image and object description is usually supplied by the indexers who must rely on their own expertise in identifying the appropriate descriptors.
2. Research time and cost. Local practice determines to what extent an item is researched to identify unknown or uncertain aspects of its creation, such as composition or style. This must be weighed against staff time and costs. There may be instances where an institution chooses to use broader, more encompassing descriptors instead of researching the item to determine more specific identification.
3. The scope of the collection. An index term should be neither too broad nor too narrow; that is, a balance should be struck so that neither too many nor too few items are indexed under it. The size of a collection and policies regarding indexing depth will affect the specificity level. Within one collection, the use of varying specificity levels may be appropriate. For instance, so-called fringe areas of a collection may be indexed to a broader level than its core areas.

As a general rule, the most specific terms should be assigned in indexing and as many descriptors as necessary used. For example, if one were cataloging an orthographic drawing of an apartment house the descriptors *architectural drawings, orthographic drawings*, and *apartment houses* should be assigned in the catalog entry.

5.3 Constructing Indexing Statements Appendix D gives procedures for constructing indexing statements from *AAT* descriptors.

5.4 Using the *AAT* in MARC *AAT* terms are appropriate for use in the subject and physical characteristics fields of the MARC format. Terms from some hierarchies are more appropriate to a given MARC field than others, but since any term could theoretically occur in any field, MARC tags are not preassigned to *AAT* terms. Instead, the following guidelines are given to provide general statements and examples on the use of *AAT* hierarchies in MARC. (Figure 3 displays a summary of MARC tags and corresponding *AAT* hierarchies.) Each user should customize these rules and should review the field content standards that may exist for particular disciplines.

MARC TAG	Field Name	Applicable *AAT* Hierarchies
650	Subject Added Entry—Topical Term	all hierarchies
654	Subject Added Entry—Faceted Topical Terms	all hierarchies
655	Index Term—Genre/Form	Image and Object Genres Drawings Photographs Document Types
656	Index Term—Occupation	People and Organizations
657	Index Term—Function	Disciplines Functions Processes and Techniques
755	Added Entry—Physical Characteristics	Design Attributes Design Elements Processes and Techniques Materials

FIGURE 3. *MARC fields with Corresponding* AAT *Hierarchies*

5.4.1 Subject Added Entry—Topical Subject (650) Any *AAT* descriptor may be used to indicate the subject of a work and is available for use in 650. Descriptors may be used as they appear in the thesaurus or precoordinated according to an LCSH-type syntax that allows for geographical and topical subdivision. However, since the *AAT* is a faceted thesaurus, the use of 654 is recommended over 650.

5.4.2 Subject Added Entry—Faceted Topical Terms (654) Appendix D gives procedures for coding *AAT* descriptors in the 654 field.

5.4.3 Index Term—Genre/Form Heading (655) The 655 field should be used for terms describing what a cataloged or indexed item *is* as opposed to what it is *about*. For example, when indexing a bibliography of works on painting techniques, the term for genre/form is *bibliographies*, while the term for the subject is *painting techniques*. In another example, an architectural drawing of an apartment house could be described in MARC by the descriptors *architectural drawings* in 655 and *apartment houses* in 65Ø. In this case, the depiction is the "subject" of the drawing.

The *AAT* contains many descriptors for genre/form designation. These appear primarily in the Visual and Verbal Communication hierarchies of the Objects facet (*portraits, relief maps, plans, photographs*).

5.4.4 Index Term—Occupation (656) This field contains terms for the generic roles, occupations, or groups associated with the material being cataloged. Terms appropriate for use in the 656 field are found primarily in the People and Organizations hierarchy of the Agents facet.

5.4.5 Index Term—Function (657) The 657 field is used primarily for the description of archival materials in order to provide access to these materials by the activity of the organization that produced them. For example, the MARC record for a group of documents generated by the Department of Environmental Conservation might contain the function descriptors *regulating* or *licensing* in the 657 field.

Descriptors for use in 657 are found primarily in the Functions hierarchy, which contains descriptors denoting activities and methodologies associated with specific disciplines or other areas of endeavor (*inspecting, counseling, bidding, accessioning, maintaining*). In some cases, users may find that descriptors from the other hierarchies in the Activities facet are also appropriate as entries in 657 (*engineering* in the Disciplines hierarchy, *transporting* in the Processes and Techniques hierarchy).

5.4.6 Added Entry—Physical Characteristics (755) This field contains terms describing the physical aspects of the cataloged item as distinct from terms that describe the genre/form heading, which are entered in 655. The kinds of term entered in 755 will thus be adjectival terms denoting physical characteristics such as color (*blue*), condition (*warped*), and material (*charcoal*). These descriptors may be found in the hierarchies listed below:

Processes and Techniques: *etched, painted, discolored*
Materials: *charcoal, ink, porcelain*
Design Elements: *festoons, chevrons, grotesques*
Design Attributes: *exterior, round, diagonal*
Tools and Equipment: *pen, brush, metal point*

6. User Interaction and Thesaurus Maintenance

In order to accommodate new terminology and respond to questions regarding the vocabulary, users may participate in a formal procedure of communication with the *AAT* office. This process allows thesaurus users to contribute to the updating and long-term maintenance of the thesaurus via submission of candidate terms and comments. The *AAT* staff hopes to decentralize *AAT* vocabulary development by having institutions submit terms for inclusion on a regular basis.

6.1 Candidate Terms If a descriptor is not found in the thesaurus, and the term sought is not one that can be precoordinated (i.e., created by the indexer combining two or more existing *AAT* descriptors), a Candidate Term Form should be completed and submitted to the *AAT* office. A blank Candidate Term Form, intended for reproduction and use, can be found in Appendix B.

When a completed Candidate Term Form is submitted to the *AAT* office, the staff follows a vocabulary development procedure. Candidate terms are evaluated for sufficient literary warrant and clear definition. In addition, candidate terms are evaluated in relation to other descriptors in the thesaurus to see if the concept is already represented. The form of the term and its thesaurus relationships are also researched by *AAT* staff members. The form is then sent back to the contributor with notification of the disposition of the term. New descriptors resulting from this process are integrated into the *AAT* database and distributed through periodic thesaurus supplements. This system of user interaction allows thesaurus users to apply descriptors they feel are appropriate rather than trying to work within the confines of a static vocabulary. It also ensures that current terminology emerging in the field is covered by the thesaurus.

6.2 Comments on Existing Descriptors In addition to finding gaps in the terminology, thesaurus users may encounter problems or have questions relating to existing *AAT* descriptors. Like candidate terms, these concerns may also be submitted to the *AAT* office on a report sheet called a Comment Form. This form may be used to suggest synonyms, to question terms, to ask for definitions of terms, and so on. A blank Comment Form, intended for reproduction and use, can be found in Appendix C.

6.3 Thesaurus Updates Changes resulting from the submission of Candidate Term Forms and Comment Forms will be included in future editions of the *AAT* and in any supplements that may be issued in the interim. Supplements will include new descriptors and notices of all changes in the form, status, or hierarchical location of existing descriptors. If the status or form of a descriptor has been changed, a History Note (HN) will be provided to indicate the type of change and the date the descriptor was changed.

7. Machine-readable Formats

In addition to the printed edition, some users may desire a machine-readable form of the thesaurus. A machine-readable version of the *AAT* could be imported into existing or developing applications so that the thesaurus may be used as part of an integrated system, rather than an independent tool for data entry and searching.

Since no single data format could be expected to be compatible with the diversity of *AAT* users' means of access, ranging from MARC-based applications to microcomputer database-management systems, the *AAT* database has been designed to provide users with certain options, as explained in sections 7.1 and 7.2.

7.1 Electronic Edition An electronic edition containing ASCII text files of the hierarchical and alphabetical displays on floppy diskettes is available. In the electronic edition, descriptors are distributed as individual term records in which every element of term data, such as nonpreferred synonyms, scope notes, and sources, is explicitly labeled. Hierarchical displays can be built from data in the Classification Notation supplied with each record, or can be built from the hierarchical text files accompanying the fielded records.

7.2 USMARC Authority Records *AAT* term data formatted according to the USMARC Authorities Format is available by request from the *AAT* office. In these records, each element of term data is labeled through the use of tags (e.g., 150) and subfield codes (e.g., #x). Field 072 (Subject Category Code) contains the classification notation for each *AAT* descriptor necessary to display the vocabulary in hierarchical order.

AAT USMARC authority records have been implemented as an authority file in the Research Libraries Information Network (RLIN) established by the Research Libraries Group (RLG). In this implementation, an *AAT* term-record display and a hierarchical display are provided.

7.3 Implementation Local programming is required to implement the machine-readable versions of the *AAT*. While the *AAT* staff cannot offer direct programming help, it can offer advice on displaying the hierarchies and updating the vocabulary. Through periodically surveying its user community, the *AAT* staff will facilitate communication among institutions using the same software so that they can learn from each other's experience.

8. *AAT* and Local Authority Files

Although the *AAT* is a source of authoritative subject descriptors, it is not in itself an authority file, which is commonly thought of as a record of terms used in a particular database and which may reflect local usage. Users may choose to maintain their own authority file based on the *AAT* to record those single descriptors and combinations of descriptors (i.e., subject headings) that have been used in their systems, as well as notes on local practice and cross-references.

9. Glossary

alternate term A variant form of a descriptor available for use; usually a singular form or a different part of speech; abbreviated ALT

authority file A record of terms used in a particular database, with accompanying cross-references; may include notes on local usage

bound term A compound term that represents a single concept

classification notation A unique code assigned to each descriptor; may be used as a surrogate for a descriptor; abbreviated CN

descriptor A term recommended for use in indexing; also called main term, postable term, preferred term

facet A homogeneous category of terms whose members share characteristics that distinguish them from the members of another facet

facet indicator See **guide term**

guide term A term or phrase used to indicate the principle by which an array of siblings is classified; printed in italics and enclosed by angle brackets; also called node label, facet indicator

hierarchy A graphic arrangement of terms showing genus-species or broader-narrower relationships between the terms

homographs Terms that are spelled alike but that have different meanings

lead-in term See **Use For**

main term See **descriptor**

node label See **guide term**

nonpreferred term See **Use For**

potable term See **descriptor**

postcoordination Combining two or more descriptors at the time of retrieval, usually using Boolean operators (*Victorian* and *houses*), in order to formulate a query

precoordination Combining two or more descriptors at the time of indexing (*Victorian houses*), in order to formulate a subject statement or object description

preferred term See **descriptor**

qualifier A term used to distinguish between homographs; enclosed in parentheses

scope note A note explaining coverage or specialized usage of a descriptor

siblings Descriptors that are subordinate to the same broader term and that are at the same hierarchical level

term A word or group of words designating a concept

Use For A synonym or spelling variant of a descriptor; also called lead-in term, nonpreferred term; abbreviated UF

10. Bibliography

Aitchison, Jean, and Alan Gilchrist. *Thesaurus Construction: A Practical Manual.* 2d ed. London: Aslib, 1987.

American National Standards Institute. *Guidelines for Thesaurus Structure, Construction, and Use*. New York: American National Standards Institute, 1980. (ANSI Z39.19)

Austin, Derek William. *PRECIS: A Manual of Concept Analysis and Subject Indexing*. 2d ed. London: British National Library, 1984.

British Standards Institution. *Guidelines for the Establishment and Development of Monolingual Thesauri.* 2d ed. London: British Standards Institute, 1987. (BS 5273)

Cataloging Service Bulletin. Washington, D.C.: Library of Congress, 1945-.

Foskett, A. C. *The Subject Approach to Information*. 4th ed. London: Clive Bingley, 1982.

International Organization for Standardization. *Methods for Examining Documents, Determining Their Subject, and Selecting Indexing Terms*. Geneva: International Organization for Standardization, 1978. (ISO TC46 SC5)

Soergel, Dagobert. *Indexing Languages and Thesauri: Construction and Maintenance.* Los Angeles: Melville Publishing Co., 1974.

UNISIST Guidelines for the Establishment and Development of Monolingual Thesauri. 2nd ed. Paris: United Nations Educational, Scientific, and Cultural Organization, 1986. (PGI-81/ws/15)

Appendix A.

Projected *AAT* Hierarchies

AAT Facets and Hierarchies

Associated Concepts Facet
- Associated Concepts

Physical Attributes Facet
- Design Attributes
- Design Elements
- Colors

Styles and Periods Facet
- Styles and Periods

Agents Facet
- People and Organizations

Activities Facet
- Disciplines
- Functions
- Events
- Processes and Techniques

Materials Facet
- Materials

Objects Facet

Built Environment
- Settlements, Systems and Landscapes
- Built Complexes and Districts
- Single Built Works and Open Spaces
- Building Divisions and Site Elements
- Built Works Components

Furnishings and Equipment
- Tools and Equipment
- Measuring Devices
- Hardware and Joints
- Furniture
- Furnishings
- Personal Artifacts
- Containers
- Culinary Artifacts
- Musical Instruments
- Recreational Artifacts
- Armament
- Transportation Artifacts
- Communication Artifacts

Visual and Verbal Communication
- Image and Object Genres
- Drawings
- Paintings
- Prints
- Photographs
- Sculpture
- Multi-Media Art Forms
- Communication Design
- Exchange Media
- Book Arts
- Document Types

APPENDIX B.
Candidate Term Form

Please copy this form to submit Candidate Terms to the AAT office at 62 Stratton Road, Williamstown, MA 01267, 413-458-2151, FAX 413-458-3757. Be sure to complete section I. Section II is optional. Section III is for AAT staff use.

Submitting organization: ____________________

Contact person: ____________________ Date: ____________

SECTION I

Suggested Term:

____

Source of Term: (please give specific indication of at least one place where the term was found; if in text, give full citation, including page numbers; include photocopy if possible.)

____

SECTION II [Optional]

Suggested definition:

____

Suggested Lead-in Term(s): ____________________

Suggested Broader Term: ____________________

Suggested Related Term(s): ____________________

Comments: (continue on reverse or attach sheet if necessary)

____

SECTION III [For AAT Office Use]

AAT Editor(s): ____________________ Date: ____________

☐ Accepted form of term: ____________________ AAT hier.: ____________

AAT Broader Term: ____________________ Spc. Thes.: ____________

AAT Scope Note:

☐ Accepted as Lead-in Term to AAT Term: ____________________

☐ Not accepted: ☐ Use existing AAT Term(s): ____________________

☐ Postcoordinate from AAT Term(s): ____________________

☐ Sufficient literary warrant not found. Please supply further information.

☐ Term is outside scope of AAT ☐ Other

AAT Comments:

rev. 10/88

APPENDIX C.

Comment Form

Please use this form to submit Comments on existing terms to the AAT office at 62 Stratton Road, Williamstown, MA 01267, 413-458-2151, FAX 413-458-3757. Be sure to complete section I. Section II is for AAT staff use.

SECTION I

Submitting project: ______________________ Date: __________

Name of Contact: ______________________

AAT Term: ______________________ Status in AAT: ___ MT ___ Lead-in

Suggested Change:

☐ Add or Change Scope Note

☐ Change form of term to ______________________

☐ Move to different Broader Term ______________________

☐ Add Related Term(s) ______________________

☐ Delete term because ______________________

☐ Question relationship to AAT Term(s) ______________________

☐ Revise structure as noted on reverse or attached sheet

☐ Add qualifier ☐ Delete qualifier

☐ Other

Comments: ______________________

SECTION II (For AAT Office Use]

AAT Editor(s): ______________________ Date: __________

☐ Accepted

☐ New Term Form: ______________________

☐ New AAT Broader Term: ______________________

☐ Add/Change Scope Note:

☐ Not accepted

☐ Other

AAT Comments:

rev. 10/88

APPENDIX D.

AAT Application Protocol and Indexer's Guide

This document has been produced by the AAT *Implementation Subcommittee of the Art and Architecture Program Committee (AAPC) of the Research Libraries Group (RLG), aided by Mary Dykstra, who revised the subcommittee's draft into this present form. Like the* AAT *Field Guide to Coding that follows, this is a working document that will be augmented with changes resulting from testing the* AAT *vocabulary according to the guidelines for indexing given herein.*

Subject indexing consists of two interrelated intellectual steps: (1) conceptual analysis and (2) translation of that analysis into a particular indexing vocabulary. In other words, the indexer's first step is to determine what an item to be indexed is *about* or, in the case of art objects, what the item *is*. The second step is to translate that "aboutness" into the terminology of the indexing vocabulary. In addition to an indexing vocabulary, a complete indexing system may provide rules for the coordination, or stringing together, of vocabulary terms into meaningful syntactic expressions.

The *AAT* vocabulary has been designed for use in either a postcoordinate or a precoordinate fashion. Applying the vocabulary in a postcoordinate fashion means that as many individual descriptors as necessary are assigned to a record without making any semantic or syntactic linkages between them. At the time of searching, the terms are combined, or coordinated, using Boolean search techniques (e.g., AND, OR, NOT). Normally, more index entries are required in postcoordinate systems.

In precoordinate systems of indexing, individual descriptors are used as building blocks of headings for the physical description of objects, images, or subjects of documents. Because descriptors are combined in one heading, fewer index entries are required in precoordinate systems.

Guidelines for Use of the *AAT* Vocabulary

Depending upon the complexity of a subject to be specified or an item to be described, users may need to use *AAT* descriptors in any one of the following configurations:

descriptors	=	units in the *AAT* hierarchies
modified descriptors	=	combinations of two or more *AAT* descriptors into an adjectival phrase
strings	=	syntactic constructions of *AAT* descriptors and/or modified descriptors

Guidelines for use of the *AAT* vocabulary in these three ways are given below.

Descriptors A descriptor in the *AAT* is a single unit from any hierarchy. *AAT* descriptors many be single or multiword terms, but in all cases they signify a single concept.

EXAMPLES: *chairs, bowls, limestone, brushwork, restoration, furniture making, ribbed vaults*

Descriptors may be used alone when nothing more is required to specify a subject or item description. If an item is simply about chairs, for example, use just the term *chairs*. When descriptors are used alone in this way, they must be used in the form found in the thesaurus. Note that alternate forms are provided (*painting*; *painted*). Use of these depends on the application.

Descriptors are also used alone when a postcoordinate system of indexing has been chosen. In this case, as many single descriptors as necessary may be applied to a single description. When a subject cannot be specified by one or more descriptors from the *AAT*, or when a precoordinate indexing system has been chosen, use a modified descriptor or a string of descriptors, as appropriate.

Modified Descriptors Guidelines for building modified descriptors are as follows:

1. A modified descriptor consists of a descriptor from the *AAT*, chosen as the focus term, and other descriptors modifying it, called modifiers.
2. A modified descriptor may include only one focus term. As many modifiers as needed may be used.
3. Modifiers should normally precede the focus term, as in natural language.
4. When more than one modifier is required for use with a focus term, the order of the modifiers usually reflects the order of the facets in the *AAT*. (For two exceptions, see 4(e) and 4(h) below.) Thus modifiers should normally be placed in the following order preceding a focus term:
   (a) descriptor from facet 1, Associated Concepts
   (use alternate adjectival form)
   (b) descriptor from facet 2, Physical Attributes
   (use alternate adjectival form)
   (c) descriptor from facet 3, Styles and Periods
   (d) descriptor from facet 4, Agents
   (e) descriptor from one of various facets
   (e.g., Materials, or Objects, when the subject is an instrument in an activity [e.g., *charcoal sketching* = the activity of sketching with charcoal]; descriptors from other facets may also apply to similar instances)
   (f) descriptor from facet 5, Activities
   (use alternate past tense form; these terms describe activities or processes that have already or previously been performed upon the focus)
   (g) descriptor from facet 6, Materials
   (h) descriptor from one of various facets
   (e.g., Agents, or Activities, denoting use or function of the focus; use gerund form for Activities [e.g., *carving knives* = knives for carving])

(i) descriptor from facet 7, Objects
(use only if the whole of an object part must be specified, in which case use alternate singular form [e.g., *church doors*])

5. The focus term, following as many modifiers as required, will then be the final element of the modified descriptor. The focus term of a modified descriptor will usually be found in the Objects facet (facet 7), although it may appear in any earlier facet in the *AAT*. In all cases, except when 4(e) and 4(h) above apply, a focus term will be preceded by modifiers from facets appearing earlier in the *AAT* than the facet of the focus term itself. For example, a focus term from the Activities facet (facet 5) may not have modifiers from the Materials facet (facet 6), except as specified in 4(e) above, or from the Objects facet (facet 7).
6. When it is necessary to use two modifiers from the same facet (e.g., both *carved* and *gilded* from the Activities facet, as in *carved gilded chairs*), the modifiers should be placed in alphabetical order unless they are from a facet where other criteria apply.
7. No punctuation is required between a focus term and any of its modifiers.

For examples of modified descriptors, showing order of modifiers, see Figure D1.

Strings Firm linguistic or grammatical rules limit the way in which *AAT* terms may be strung together to create modified descriptors. For example, the topic "the restoration of Renaissance oil paintings" cannot be expressed as "Renaissance oil paintings restoration." This is so because such an expression contains both a noun (*restoration*) and a prepositional phrase containing a second noun (*paintings*) modified by two adjectives (*Renaissance, oil*). In other words, the expression is more than a single term with adjectival modifiers. It thus consists of a descriptor and a modified descriptor. It can also be said to contain two focus terms (*restoration, paintings*).

Indexers perplexed by whether a subject expression contains more than one focus term can find their best clues in the prepositions in the expression in question. In "the restoration of Renaissance oil paintings," the preposition *of* preceding *Renaissance oil paintings* provides the clue that a second focus term is present and is functioning as the object of the preposition. The most common prepositions in subject expressions and the clues they provide are as follows:

of - usually precedes a noun naming an object
by - usually precedes a noun naming an agent
in - usually precedes a noun naming a place (e.g., a geographic location) or a time period

When an indexer must use one or more of these prepositions in the formulation of a subject expression, chances are good that the expression is too complex syntactically to be handled as a modified descriptor.

In all such cases, when neither a single descriptor nor a modified descriptor is adequate to specify a subject, terms may be combined into more complex syntactic configurations called strings. Like "the restoration of Renaissance oil paintings," the following subject expressions are typical candidates for strings:

nineteenth-century Canadian manuscripts cataloged in England in 1980

the renovation of Victorian houses
the design of gazebos by landscape architects

These and similar subject expressions must be analyzed fully into their component parts. Then the components must be placed in a syntactic order that is both consistent and unambiguous.

Guidelines for the Construction of Strings

Guidelines for the syntactic construction of strings using the *AAT* vocabulary are based on use of the passive voice and reverse facet order. In natural language, words in sentences are often strung together by means of syntactic devices such as prepositions. The syntactic device used to separate the various components of string is a long dash (—).

Passive Voice Experience with natural language has shown that the most unambiguous syntactic constructions are those in which the passive voice is used. Accordingly, the *AAT* Application Protocol specifies that strings should be constructed so that descriptors or modified descriptors are placed in an order that reflects the passive voice.

For example, an item about antique dealers appraising tables should be expressed as "the appraisal of tables by antique dealers" or simply as "tables appraised by antique dealers." It can be seen that the preposition *by*—which is the indexer's clue that a second focus term, a noun naming an agent, is present—shows up clearly when the subject is expressed in the passive voice. Stripped of extraneous, natural-language parts of speech (articles, prepositions, etc.), this expression translates into the following string: *tables—appraisal—antique dealers*.

Consistent use of the passive voice helps to ensure consistency in the placement of descriptors in strings.

Reverse Facet Order When the passive voice is used, it is important to note that, whereas in the construction of modified descriptors the order of the modifiers reflects the order of the *AAT* facets, in the construction of strings the order of modifiers is almost completely reversed. The most useful and unambiguous term order for strings is one that generally reflects a reverse facet order, as follows:

descriptor from facet 7, Objects
descriptor from facet 6, Materials
descriptor from facet 5, Activities
descriptor from facet 4, Agents

Dates and place names, representing the Chronological facet and the Geographic facet respectively, may be interposed at any point in this order, as required.

Examples of strings constructed from descriptors from facets 7–4 are as follows:

SUBJECT EXPRESSION: the bonding of wood onto tables by manufacturers
STRING: tables—wood—bonding—manufacturers
(facets 7, 6, 5, and 4)

Subject expression: the restoration of paper by archivists
String: paper—restoration—archivists
(facets 6, 5, and 4)

Subject expression: collecting paintings [no agent specified]
String: paintings—collecting
(facets 7 and 5)

Examples of strings constructed from descriptors and modified descriptors are as follows:

Subject expression: the evaluation of wood tables by antique dealers
String: wood tables—evaluation—antique dealers
(modified descriptor from facets 6 and 7;
descriptors from facets 5 and 4)

Figure D1. *Examples of modified descriptors, constructed in an order that reflects the facets of the AAT. Entries should read downward in each column. The focus term in each of these examples is the final underlined word in the modified descriptor.*

Facet/descriptor order	Facet no.							
Associated Concepts (Adjectival)	1	functional			asymmetrical			
Physical Attributed (Adjectival)	2				blue			large
Styles and Periods	3	Victorian	Renaissance					Baroque
Agents (Possessive)	4					authors		
Term denoting Instrument				oil				
Activities (Past tense)	5	painted		painting	pressed	inscribed	galvanized	
Materials	6	wood	oil		glass		metal	
Term denoting Use or Function		children's			serving			hunting
Objects (Whole) (Singular if acc. by Part)	7	bedroom	paintings		bowls	book		lodges
Objects (Part)	7	furniture				copies		

SUBJECT EXPRESSION: the restoration of Renaissance oil paintings
STRING: Renaissance oil paintings—restoration (modified descriptor from facets 3, 6, and 7; descriptor from facet 5)

SUBJECT EXPRESSION: the renovation of Victorian houses
STRING: Victorian houses—renovation (modified descriptor from facets 3 and 7; descriptor from facet 5)

Examples of strings constructed from descriptors and modified descriptors from facets 7–4, with interposed dates and place names from the Chronological and/or Geographic facets, are as follows:

SUBJECT EXPRESSION: the restoration of nineteenth-century Massachusetts wood chairs in New York in 1980
STRING: wood chairs—Massachusetts—1800-1900—restoration—New York—1980

SUBJECT EXPRESSION: the cataloging of nineteenth-century Canadian manuscripts in England in 1980
STRING: Canadian manuscripts—1800-1900—cataloging—England—1980

Note that place names and time concepts from the Geographic and Chronological facets must be interposed immediately after the term (or terms) in the string that they most logically modify.

APPENDIX E.

AAT Field Guide to Coding

This document has been produced by the AAT *Implementation Subcommittee of the Art and Architecture Program Committee (AAPC) of the Research Libraries Group (RLG), aided by Mary Dykstra, who revised the subcommittee's draft into this present form. Like the Application Protocol and Indexer's Guide that precedes it, this is a working document that will be augmented with changes resulting from testing the* AAT *vocabulary according to the guidelines for indexing given herein.*

The *AAT* Field Guide to Coding has been designed to accompany the USMARC Format description for field 654 (see Figure E1). Together these may be used with the *AAT* Application Protocol and Indexer's Guide (Appendix D) as a set of procedures for combining descriptors from the *Art and Architecture Thesaurus* into specific item descriptions or subject index entries.

Once the indexing function has been completed according to the rules outlined in the *AAT* Application Protocol and Indexer's Guide, this Field Guide to Coding specifies how the index entry should be coded so as to conform with the USMARC Format for field 654.

Indicators

First Indicator (Mandatory) The first position in the coded index entry must contain a value that indicates the level of the subject indexed. Since 654 is a repeatable field, indexers may wish to provide more than one index entry per item. If so, they may also wish to specify primary entries (those that cover the main subject content of the item) and secondary entries (those that represent less important content). Use values 0-2 as outlined on page 2. Or, if no level information is available, use ƀ. Use value 0 as the default, or value assigned to indicate all index entries for which the primary/secondary distinction is not applicable.

Second Indicator (Mandatory) Place a ƀ in the second indicator position, as instructed on page 2. This position is presently undefined.

Subfield Codes

Data elements (descriptors) following the two mandatory indicator positions in field 654 may be preceded by any of several subfield codes, as appropriate. An index entry may consist of only one data element, as is the case when a single descriptor is sufficient to express a subject. Or, in cases where the index entries consist of modified descriptors or strings, several data elements may be required. Each separate data element, or term component of the index entry, is preceded by its own subfield code. By studying the examples given in this field guide, together with those given in the USMARC Format description for field 654, indexers will become familiar with the various subfield coding possibilities.

Because subfield code #c must precede either #a or #b, it is considered first.

#c Facet Designation (Repeatable) The coding that introduces each term or data element must begin with a 1-position code that designates the *AAT* facet to which that term belongs. The 1-position designation codes for the *AAT* facets are as follows:

	AAT FACET	DESIGNATION
1	Associated Concepts	b
2	Physical Attributes	d
3	Styles and Periods	f
4	Agents	h
5	Activities	k
6	Materials	m
7	Objects	r, t, or v

In addition, time and place terms have 1-position designations as follows:

Time (Dates)	y
Places	z

The *AAT* Application Protocol and Indexer's Guide specifies that USMARC field 655 should be used to record information concerning the genre/form of an item (i.e., what the item *is* as opposed to what it is *about*). However, should an indexing agency feel strongly about including genre/form information with the subject index entry itself, it seems possible to use the 1-position designation "x" (as used in other 600 fields) for this information. Indexers opting for this alternative should place this information at the end of the entry; it should immediately precede #2aat.

Each designation code is immediately preceded by #c. Thus a term coded "m," for example, must appear as "#cm."

#a Focus Term (Nonrepeatable) If indexers in a particular library or agency believe that it will serve a useful purpose in their system, it is possible to use #a immediately following the #c facet designation to identify a particular term as a focus term. Each single-term index entry is of course a focus term. Normally, the final element in a modified descriptor is the focus term. Whether or not to code a focus as such will depend upon the searching and retrieval capabilities of a given automated system, whether or not a printed index with specified main or lead terms is required, and other factors.

#b Term (i.e., Descriptor; Repeatable) For all terms not coded #a after the #c facet designation, #b must be used. Subfield code #b indicates simply that the data element is a descriptor. In those systems that do not require focus terms to be distinguished, it is possible to ease the coding drudgery simply by assigning #b after the #c facet designator to *all* terms or data elements in the index entry.

All that would then remain to be filled in by the indexer would be the facet designation and the descriptor.

#2 Source of Heading or Term (Nonrepeatable) For all agencies using the *Art and Architecture Thesaurus* as the source of their indexing vocabulary, their fully coded index entries in field 654 must each conclude with the characters #2aat.

#3 Materials Specified This subfield is not known to be in use or required by a participating *AAT* user at the present time.

Capitalization

The use of lowercase or capital letters in index entries is a matter of individual indexer policy; no one system of capitalization is mandated by the USMARC Format description for field 654. Nor do the codes carry any instructions for changing from one type of letter to the other. Indexers must capitalize terms themselves if they want them to appear that way in the index entry. The *AAT* uses lowercase letters throughout, with the exception of proper nouns and adjectives which are capitalized.

Output and Display

Indexers using the *AAT* Application Protocol and Indexer's Guide in conjunction with USMARC field 654 will need to pay attention to punctuation in order to be able to generate consistent and readable index entries as output, either for on-screen display or in printed products. The output or display will vary according to the systrem being used.

Most systems should automatically supply a long (—), preceding the value of the next subfield #a or subfield #b when the value of a subfield #c is #z (place) or #y (date).

EXAMPLE 1:
Output: feminism—1950-1980
Input: #cb#afeminism#cy#b1950-1980

In order to separate other elements of a string, indexers must insert a code for which punctuation will be generated. It is recommended that a hypen (-) following the last character in subfield #c (the facet code) be input when a long dash is to precede the value of the next #a or #b.

EXAMPLE 2:
Output: furniture—restoration
Input: #ct#afurniture#ck–#brestoration

In the example above, a hyphen follows the one-letter facet code "k."

The examples below are provided to illustrate the use of field 654. For each indexing example, remember that the first presentation gives the index entry itself, that is, the expected output. The second presentation gives the coded input data required to generate that index entry.

EXAMPLE 3:
Output: chairs
Input: #ct#achairs#2aat

EXAMPLE 4:
Output: ribbed vaults
Input: #cr#aribbed vaults#2aat

EXAMPLE 5:
Output: romanticism—Europe
Input: #cb#aromanticism#cz#bEurope

EXAMPLE 6:
Output: Rococo gilded wood chairs
Input: #cf#bRococo#ck#bgilded#cm#bwood#ct#achairs#2aat

654

		Formats/NLR						
		BK	AM	CF	MP	MU	VM	SE
654 Subject Added Entry—Faceted Topical Terms (R)		*A*	*A*	*A*	*A*	*A*	*A*	*A*
Indicators								
First	Level of subject	*M*	*M*	*M*	*M*	*M*	*M*	*M*
ƀ	No information available	*A*	*A*	*A*	*A*	*A*	*A*	*A*
0	No level specified	*A*	*A*	*A*	*A*	*A*	*A*	*A*
1	Primary	*A*	*A*	*A*	*A*	*A*	*A*	*A*
2	Secondary	*A*	*A*	*A*	*A*	*A*	*A*	*A*
Second	Undefined	*M*	*M*	*M*	*M*	*M*	*M*	*M*
ƀ	Undefined	*M*	*M*	*M*	*M*	*M*	*M*	*M*
Subfield Codes								
ǂa	Focus term (NR)	*A*	*A*	*A*	*A*	*A*	*A*	*A*
ǂb	Term (R)	*A*	*A*	*A*	*A*	*A*	*A*	*A*
ǂc	Facet/hierarchy designation (R)	*M*	*M*	*M*	*M*	*M*	*M*	*M*
ǂ2	Source of heading or term (NR)	*M*	*M*	*M*	*M*	*M*	*M*	*M*
ǂ3	Materials specified (NR)	*O*	*O*	*O*	*O*	*O*	*O*	*O*

FIELD DEFINITION AND SCOPE

This field contains a topical subject constructed from a faceted vocabulary. For each term found in the field, an identification is given as to the facet/hierarchy in the thesaurus from which the term came. In addition, identification is given as to which term is the focus term of the expression.

GUIDELINES FOR APPLYING CONTENT DESIGNATORS

■ INDICATORS

First Indicator - Level of subject

The first indicator position contains a value that specifies the level of the subject expression or string. This indicator is used to distinguish primary and secondary descriptors.

ƀ - No information available

Value ƀ indicates that no information as to the level of the subject expression is available.

FIGURE E1. *Field 654 from* USMARC Format for Bibliographic Data

EXAMPLE 7:

Output: Japanese papermaking

Input: #cf#bJapanese#ck#apapermaking#2aat

EXAMPLE 8:

Output: realism—Baroque architecture

Input: #cb#arealism#cf–#bBaroque#ck#barchitecture

EXAMPLE 9:

Output: wood tables—evaluation—antique dealers

Input: #cm#bwood#ct#atables#ck–#bevaluation#ch–#bantique dealers#2aat

654

0 - No level specified
Value 0 indicates that the level could be determined but is not specified.

Heading: Landscape gardens--18th century--England

654 0ƀ‡cob‡aLandscape gardens‡cy‡b18th century‡cz‡bEngland‡2aat

1 - Primary
Value 1 indicates that the entry is a primary expression or string. A subject is considered primary if it covers the main subject content of the material.

Heading: Architectural design

654 1ƀ‡cac‡aArchitectural design‡2aat

2 - Secondary
Value 2 indicates that the entry is a secondary subject. A subject is considered secondary if it represents a less important content of the material.

Heading: Housing

654 2ƀ‡cob‡aHousing‡2aat

Second Indicator - Undefined
The second indicator position is undefined; it contains a blank (ƀ).

■ SUBFIELD CODES

‡a - Focus term
Subfield ‡a contains a term which is considered the focus term. A focus term is the concrete thing, being, idea, or activity forming the basis of the indexing entry.

Heading: Limestone

654 ƀƀ‡cmt‡aLimestone‡2aat

Heading: French Colonial Landscapes--United States--New Jersey

654 ƀƀ‡csp‡bFrench Colonial‡cob‡aLandscapes‡cz‡bUnited States‡cz ‡bNew Jersey‡2aat
[The focus term in the AAT expression is "Landscapes."]

‡b - Term
Subfield ‡b contains a term other than that considered the focus.

Heading: Charcoal drawings--Great Britain--18th century

654 ƀƀ‡cmt‡bCharcoal‡cob‡adrawings‡cz‡bGreat Britain‡cy ‡b18th century‡2aat

FIGURE E1. *(continued)*

EXAMPLE 10:

Output: wood chairs—Massachusetts—1800-1900—restoration—New York—1980

Input: #cm#bwood#ct#achairs#cz#bMassachusetts#cy#b1800–1900#ck–#brestoration#cz#bNew York#cy#b1980#2aat

654

ǂc - Facet/hierarchy designation

Subfield ǂc contains a designation identifying the facet/hierarchy for each term found in subfields ǂa and ǂb. The designations differ, depending on the subject heading thesaurus used (as specified by the code found in subfield ǂ2). The designations and their associated facets/hierarchies can be found in the thesaurus identified by subfield ǂ2. Subfield ǂc always precedes the data to which it is associated.

Heading: Housing--United States

654 ƀƀǂcobǂaHousingǂczǂbUnited Statesǂ2aat

Heading: Baroque blue bowls

654 ƀƀǂcspǂbBaroqueǂcpaǂbblueǂcobǂabowlsǂ2aat

ǂ2 - Source of heading or term

Subfield ǂ2 contains a USMARC code that identifies the source list from which the subject expression was assigned. The source code is an authoritative-agency data element. (The Library of Congress maintains the *USMARC Code List for Relators, Sources, Description Conventions* and is the authoritative agency.)

Headings: Country houses--Great Britain--18 century
Guidebooks
Bibliographies

654 ƀƀǂcobǂaCountry housesǂczǂbGreat Britainǂcyǂb18th centuryǂ2aat
654 ƀƀǂcobǂaGuidebooksǂ2aat
654 ƀƀǂcobǂaBibliographiesǂ2aat

ǂ3 - Materials specified

Subfield ǂ3 contains information which indicates the part of the collection, etc. to which the field applies.

Heading: Letters: Housing--United States

654 ƀƀǂ3LettersǂcobǂaHousingǂczǂbUnited Statesǂ2aat

RELATED USMARC DOCUMENT/FIELD

USMARC Code List for Relators, Sources, Description Conventions

FIGURE E1. *(continued)*

Sources

The following sources cite the works consulted to validate the choice of descriptors in this edition of the Art and Architecture Thesaurus. *Each source is represented by a one to six letter code and arranged alphabetically by that code.*

The codes are found in parentheses at the end of some scope notes in the alphabetical section of the Thesaurus.

This list, therefore, serves a dual purpose. It provides citations of the sources used to establish the descriptors and identifies the codes that appear in the alphabetical index.

A-L Francis Ames-Lewis. *Drawing in Early Renaissance Italy*. New Haven, Conn.: Yale University Press, 1981.

A-Z James S. Pierce. *From Abacus to Zeus: A Handbook of Art History*. Englewood Cliffs, N.J.: Prentice Hall, 1987.

AA *American Archivist*. Chicago: Society of American Archivists. 1938-.

AAC71 Laurence Sickman and Alexander Soper. *The Art and Architecture of China*. 4th ed. Harmondsworth, England: Penguin Books, 1971.

AACR2 Michael Gorman and Paul W. Winkler, eds. *Anglo-American Cataloguing Rules*. 2d ed. Chicago: American Library Association, 1978.

AAD *American Art Directory*. 49th ed. New York: R. R. Bowker Co., 1982.

AAF82 Anthony Blunt. *Art and Architecture in France 1500-1700*. 4th rev. ed. Harmondsworth, England: Penguin Books, 1982.

AAI70 Benjamin Rowland. *Art and Architecture of India: Buddhist, Hindu, and Jain*. Harmondsworth, England: Penguin Books, 1970.

AANDG Willy Rotzler. *Art and Graphics*. Zurich: ABC Edition, 1983.

AASAM Henry Trubner, William J. Rathbun, and Catherine A. Kaputa. *Asiatic Art in the Seattle Art Museum*. Seattle: Seattle Art Museum, 1973.

AASHOP Alison Adburgham. *Shopping in Style: London from the Restoration to Edwardian Elegance*. London: Thames & Hudson, 1979.

AATA *Art and Archaeology Technical Abstracts*. Marina del Rey, Calif.: Getty Conservation Institute, 1955-.

AAWMAA Whitney Museum of American Art. *American Art 1936-1956*. Montgomery, Ala.: Montgomery Museum of Fine Arts, 1978.

ABB Anthony Blunt. *Borromini*. Cambridge, Mass.: Harvard University Press, 1979.

ABCB Eric Sloane. *American Barns and Covered Bridges*. New York: Funk & Wagnalls Co., 1954.

SOURCES

ABM *Art Bibliographies Modern*. Santa Barbara, Calif.: Clio Press, 1971-.

ABSA Albert Boime. *Strictly Academic: Life Drawing in the Nineteenth Century*. Binghamton, N.Y.: University Art Gallery, 1974.

ACLAND James H. Acland. *Medieval Structure: The Gothic Vault*. Toronto: University of Toronto Press, 1972.

ACME American Association of Cost Engineers. *ACME: Glossary of Terms*. Morgantown, W.Va.: American Association of Cost Engineers, 1979.

ACRIV Allan H. Cullen. *Rivers in Harness: The Story of Dams*. Philadelphia: Chilton Books, 1962.

AD Arthur Drexler. *The Architecture of the Ecole des Beaux-Arts*. New York: Museum of Modern Art, 1977.

ADAG Architectural Drawings Advisory Group. "Glossary for Technique, Medium, and Support." Document prepared for internal distribution. Architectural Drawings Advisory Group, Washington, D.C., 1984.

ADAJ Arthur Drexler. *Architecture of Japan*. New York: Museum of Modern Art, 1955.

ADAMS Thomas Adams. *Outline of Town and City Planning*. New York: Russell Sage Foundation, 1935.

ADCAD Yvon Gordon, ed. *Architectural Design and CAD*. New York: Nichols Publishing Co., 1986.

ADEL Jules Adeline. *Adeline's Art Dictionary*. New York: D. Appleton & Co., 1891.

ADIE Donald W. Adie. *Marinas: A Working Guide to Their Development and Design*. London: Architectural Press, 1975.

ADKINS Lesley Adkins and Roy A. Adkins. *A Thesaurus of British Archaeology*. Newton Abbot, England: David & Charles, 1982.

ADLR Keith Crim, ed. *Abingdon Dictionary of Living Religions*. Nashville, Tenn.: Abingdon Press, 1981.

AEGCAT Metropolitan Museum of Art. *Greek Art of the Aegean Islands*. New York: Metropolitan Museum of Art, 1979.

AEOLIC Philip P. Betancourt. *The Aeolic Style in Architecture*. Princeton, N.J.: Princeton University Press, 1977.

AESTH Harold Osborne. *Aesthetics and Art Theory*. London: Longmans, Green & Co., 1968.

AFBA American Face Brick Association. *Industrial Building and Housing*. New York: Architectural Forum, 1926.

AFTP Otto G. Ocvirk, Robert O. Bone, Robert E. Stinson, and Philip R. Wigg. *Art Fundamentals: Theory and Practice*. 5th ed. Dubuque, Iowa: William C. Brown Publishers, 1981.

AGEOFB Eric Sloan. *An Age of Barns*. New York: Funk & Wagnalls Co., 1966.

AGEOFS Kurt Weitzmann, ed. *Age of Spirituality: Late Antique and Early Christian Art, Third to Seventh Century*. New York: Metropolitan Museum of Art in association with Princeton University Press, 1979.

AGI American Geological Institute. *Dictionary of Geological Terms*. 3d ed. New York: Doubleday & Co., 1984.

AGIUS Pauline Agius. *British Furniture 1880-1915*. Woodbridge, Suffolk, England: Antique Collectors' Club, 1978.

AGORA American School of Classical Studies at Athens. *The Athenian Agora*. 24 vols. Princeton, N.J.: American School of Classical Studies at Athens, 1953-1988.

AGRBLD James H. Whitaker. *Agricultural Buildings and Structures*. Reston, Va.: Reston Publishing Co., 1979.

AGS6 Charles G. Ramsey and Harold R. Sleeper. *Architectural Graphics Standards*. 6th ed. Edited by Harold D. Hauf and Joseph N. Boaz. New York: John Wiley & Sons, 1970.

AGS7 Charles G. Ramsey and Harold R. Sleeper. *Architectural Graphics Standards*. 7th ed. Edited by Robert T. Packard. New York: John Wiley & Sons, 1981.

AGS8 Charles G. Ramsey and Harold R. Sleeper. *Architectural Graphics Standards*. 8th ed. Edited by John R. Hoke, Jr. New York: John Wiley & Sons, 1988.

AHD *American Heritage Dictionary*. New York: American Heritage Publishing Co., 1969.

AHMT Ralph Mayer. *The Artist's Handbook of Materials and Techniques*. 4th ed. New York: Viking Press, 1981.

AI *Art Index*. New York: H. W. Wilson Co., 1929-.

AIABPR American Institute of Architects. *Building Products Register*. 3d ed. Washington, D.C.: American Institute of Architects, 1964.

AIACD American Institute of Architects. *Architect's Handbook of Professional Practice*. Vol. 12, *Construction Documents*. Washington, D.C.: American Institute of Architects, 1970.

AIAENC Joseph A. Wilkes and Robert T. Packard, eds. *Encyclopedia of Architecture: Design, Engineering, and Construction*. 4 vols. New York: John Wiley & Sons, 1988-1989.

AIAJ *Architecture*. Washington, D.C.: American Institute of Architects, 1913-.

AITECR *Archival Informatics Technical Report*. Pittsburgh: Archives & Museum Informatics. 1987-.

AITGIL Jean Aitchison and Alan Gilchrist. *Thesaurus Construction: A Practical Manual*. 2d ed. London: Aslib, 1987.

AIW George Michell, ed. *Architecture of the Islamic World*. New York: William Morrow & Co., 1978.

AJA *American Journal of Archaeology*. Boston: Archaeological Institute of America, 1885-.

AK Aga Khan Program Documentation Center. "Aga Khan Glossary." Cambridge, Mass., 1984.

AKURGA Ekrem Akurgal, ed. *Art and Architecture of Turkey*. New York: Rizzoli International Publications, 1980.

ALAG Heartsill Young, ed. *ALA Glossary of Library and Information Science*. Chicago: American Library Association, 1983.

ALDOW2 Andrew J. Downing. *Cottage Residences, or a Series of Designs for Rural Cottages and Cottage-Villas and Their Gardens and Grounds Adapted to North America*. New York: Wiley & Putnam, 1842.

ALDOWN Andrew J. Downing. *The Architecture of Country Houses: Including Designs for Cottages, Farm-Houses, and Villas, with Remarks on Interiors, Furniture, and the Best Modes of Warming and Ventilating*. New York: D. Appleton & Co., 1859.

ALLABY Michael Allaby. *A Dictionary of the Environment*. 2d ed. New York: New York University Press, 1983.

ALLEN Edward M. Allen. *Harper's Dictionary of the Graphic Arts*. New York: Harper & Row Publishers, 1963.

ALMEID Oscar Almeida. *Metalworking for Schools, Colleges, and Home Craftsmen*. New York: Drake Publishers, 1971.

ALPERS Svetlana Alpers. *The Art of Describing: Dutch Art in the Seventeenth Century*. Chicago: University of Chicago Press, 1983.

ALTMAN Irwin Altman. *The Environment and Social Behavior: Privacy, Personal Space, Territory, Crowding*. Monterey, Calif.: Brooks/Cole Publishing Co., 1975.

AMC H. Thomas Hickerson and Elaine D. Engst. "Terms for Use in Field 655 of the USMARC Format for Archival and Manuscript Control." Produced by the Research Libraries Group Task Force on Special Formats, Mountain View, Calif., 1984.

AMCAR Automobile Quarterly. *The American Car since 1775*. New York: Automobile Quarterly, 1971.

AMCRAF *American Craft*. New York: American Craft Council, 1941-.

AMERPR Blake McKelvey. *American Prisons: A History of Good Intentions*. Montclair, N.J.: Patterson Smith Publishing Corp., 1977.

AMES Kenneth L. Ames, ed. *Victorian Furniture*. Philadelphia: Victorian Society in America, 1982.

AMMI American Museum of the Moving Image. "Collections Categories and Definitions." Document prepared for internal distribution. American Museum of the Moving Image: Astoria, N.Y., 1980s.

AMWING Marshall B. Davidson and Elizabeth Stillinger. *The American Wing at the Metropolitan Museum of Art*. New York: Metropolitan Museum of Art and Alfred A. Knopf, 1985.

ANDIR Judith Miller and Martin Miller, eds. *The Antiques Directory: Furniture*. New York: Portland House, 1988.

ANRW *Aufstieg und Niedergang der Römischen Welt*. 36 vols. New York: De Gruyter, 1972-1989.

ANTIQS *The Magazine Antiques*. New York: Brant Publications, 1922-.

AO Gerald Allen and Richard Oliver. *Architectural Drawings: The Art and the Process*. New York: Whitney Library of Design, 1981.

AOFIRE Maurice Craig. *The Architecture of Ireland*. London: B. T. Batsford, 1982.

APG78 Sinclair Hood. *The Arts in Prehistoric Greece*. Harmondsworth, England: Penguin Books, 1978.

API American Petroleum Institute. *American Petroleum Institute Thesaurus*. 22d ed. Washington, D.C.: American Petroleum Institute, 1985.

APOSTS Tom Scanlan, ed. *Army Times Guide to Army Posts*. Harrisburg, Pa.: Stackpole Co., 1963.

AR Amos Rapoport. *House Form and Culture*. Englewood Cliffs, N.J.: Prentice Hall, 1969.

ARBA *American Reference Books Annual*. Littleton, Colo.: Libraries Unlimited, 1970-.

ARBOR Marilyn Arbor. *Tools and Trades of America's Past: The Mercer Collection*. Doylestown, Pa.: Buck's County Historical Society, 1981.

ARC Kathleen R. Cummings. *Architectural Records in Chicago*. Chicago: Art Institute of Chicago, 1981.

ARCHEO *Archeologia*. Paris: A. Santon, 1964-.

ARCHER George Archer & Co. *Price List of Store or Counter Stools*. Furniture catalog. Rochester, N.Y.: George Archer & Co., 1880.

ARCHMV Francis Salet and Sylvain Stym-Popper, eds. *Architecture: méthode et vocabulaire*. Paris: Imprimerie Nationale, 1972.

ARCHTJ *Architects' Journal*. London: Architectural Press, 1895-.

ARCRMA Robert J. Clark. *Arts and Crafts Movement in America: 1876-1916*. Princeton University Press, 1972.

ARDM Alexander Ratensky. *Drawing and Modelmaking*. New York: Whitney Library of Design, 1983.

ARENDT Rudy H. Arendt. *Test Site Instrumentation Study*. Washington, D.C.: U.S. Department of Transportation, National Highway Traffic Safety Administration, 1980s.

ARGGR Charles J. Adams, ed. *A Reader's Guide to the Great Religions*. 2d ed. New York: Free Press, 1977.

ARIST *Annual Review of Information Science and Technology*. New York: Elsevier Science Publishers, 1965-.

ARMS John T. Arms. *Handbook of Print Making and Print Makers*. New York: Macmillan Publishing Co., 1934.

ARNASO H. H. Arnason. *History of Modern Art*. New York: Harry N. Abrams, 1977.

ARON Joseph Aronson. *Encyclopedia of Furniture*. New York: Crown Publishers, 1959.

ARONS Joseph Aronson. *The Book of Furniture and Decoration: Period and Modern*. rev. ed. New York: Crown Publishers, 1952.

ARPARK Richard G. Kraus and Joseph E. Curtis. *Creative Administration in Recreation and Parks*. 2d ed. St. Louis: C. V. Mosby Co., 1977.

ARPM Richard E. W. Adams. *Prehistoric Mesoamerica*. Boston: Little, Brown & Co., 1977.

ARREC *Architectural Record*. New York: McGraw-Hill Information Systems, 1891-.

ARTBUL *Art Bulletin*. New York: College Art Association of America, 1912-.

ARTCFT *Artcraft for the Home*. Furniture catalog. New York, 1928.

ARTDOC *Art Documentation*. Tucson, Ariz.: Art Libraries Society of North America, 1982-.

ARTISL Arts Council of Great Britain. *The Arts of Islam*. London: Arts Council of Great Britain, 1976.

ARTSMA *Arts Magazine*. New York: Art Digest Co., 1926-.

ASA Hans-Georg Bandi. *The Art of the Stone Age: Forty Thousand Years of Rock Art*. New York: Crown Publishers, 1961.

ASC Alfred E. Zapf. *Cyclopedia of Drawing*. Chicago: American School of Correspondence, 1907.

ASH87 American Society of Heating, Refrigeration, and Air Conditioning Engineers. *ASHRAE Handbook: HVAC Systems*. Atlanta: American Society of Heating, Refrigeration, and Air Conditioning Engineers, 1987.

ASHR-E American Society of Heating, Refrigeration, and Air Conditioning Engineers. *ASHRAE Handbook: Equipment*. Atlanta: American Society of Heating, Refrigeration, and Air Conditioning Engineers, 1983.

ASHR-S American Society of Heating, Refrigeration, and Air Conditioning Engineers. *ASHRAE Handbook: Systems*. Atlanta: American Society of Heating, Refrigeration, and Air Conditioning Engineers, 1984.

ASHRAE American Society of Heating, Refrigeration, and Air Conditioning Engineers. *ASHRAE Handbook: Heating, Ventilating, and Air Conditioning Systems and Applications*. Atlanta: American Society of Heating, Refrigeration, and Air Conditioning Engineers, 1967.

ASLAN Oktay Aslanapa. *Turkish Art and Architecture*. New York: Praeger Publishers, 1971.

ASLIN Elizabeth Aslin. *Nineteenth-Century English Furniture*. London: Faber & Faber, 1962.

ASP Guitty Azarpay. *Sogdian Painting: The Pictorial Epic in Oriental Art*. Berkeley and Los Angeles: University of California Press, 1981.

ASR *Architectural Science Review*. Sydney, Australia: University of Sydney, Department of Architectural Science, 1958-.

ASRH Centre Georges Pompidou. *All Stations: A Journey through One Hundred and Fifty Years of Railway History*. London: Thames & Hudson, 1981.

ASTM American Society for Testing and Materials: *1980 ASTM Standards*. Philadelphia: American Society for Testing and Materials, 1980.

ATILTA Esin Atil, ed. *Turkish Art*. Washington, D.C.: Smithsonian Institution Press. New York: Harry N. Abrams, 1980.

ATTW Donald Attwater, ed. *A Catholic Dictionary*. 2d ed. New York: Macmillan Publishing Company, 1949.

AV William R. Ware. *The American Vignola*. Scranton, Pa.: International Textbook Co., 1904.

AVERY *Avery Index to Architectural Periodicals*. Boston: G. K. Hall & Co., 1979-.

AVISO *Aviso*. Washington, D.C.: American Association of Museums, 1968-.

AVP Rudolph Arnheim. *Art and Visual Perception*. Berkeley and Los Angeles: University of California Press, 1969.

AWTS *Management of Former U.K. Atomic Weapons Test Sites in Australia*. Canberra, Australia: Department of National Development and Energy, 1980s.

B&L Samuel W. Boggs and Dorothy L. Lewis. *Classification and Cataloging of Maps and Atlases*. New York: Special Libraries, 1945.

BAAA Wendell C. Bennett. *Ancient Arts of the Andes*. New York: Museum of Modern Art, 1954.

BAACP William R. Bascom. *African Art in Cultural Perspective: An Introduction*. New York: W. W. Norton & Co., 1973.

BACH Wendell C. Bennett and Junius B. Bird. *Andean Cultural History*. 2d ed. Garden City, N.Y.: Natural History Press, 1964.

BACKST Christopher Gilbert. *Back-Stairs Furniture: An Exhibition of Back-Stairs Furniture from Country Houses*. Leeds, England: Temple Newsam, 1977.

BADGLE Peter C. Badgley. *Structural and Tectonic Principles*. New York: Harper & Row Publishers, 1965.

BAER Kurt Baer. *Architecture of the California Missions*. Berkeley and Los Angeles: University of California Press, 1958.

BAGBY Bagby Furniture Co. *Illustrations of Furniture*. Baltimore, Md.: Bagby Furniture Co., ca. 1885.

BAGBY2 Bagby & Rivers Manufacturers. *Illustrations of Furniture, Mattresses, and Chairs*. Baltimore, Md.: Bagby & Rivers Manufacturers, 1895.

BAILM Titus Burckhardt. *Art of Islam: Language and Meaning*. Translated by J. Peter Hobson. [London]: World of Islam Festival Publishing Co., 1976.

BAINES Ambrose Baines & Co. *Chairs and Bedroom Furniture*. Furniture catalog. New York: Ambrose Baines & Co., 1871.

BALAN George Balandier and Jacques Maquet, eds. *Dictionary of Black African Civilization*. Secaucus, N.J.: Leon Amiel Publishing, 1974.

BALL Conant Ball Co. Furniture catalog. Gardner, Mass.: Conant Ball Co., 1937.

BANDI Hans-Georg Bandi. *Eskimo Prehistory*. Fairbanks: University of Alaska Press, 1969.

BANHAM Martin Banham, ed. *Cambridge Guide to the World Theatre*. Cambridge: Cambridge University Press, 1988.

BARA Moshe Barasch. *Theories of Art from Plato to Winckelmann*. New York: New York University Press, 1985.

BARLEY Maurice Barley. *Houses and History*. London: Faber & Faber, 1986.

BARNST Howard Barnstone. *Architecture of John F. Staub: Houston and the South*. Austin: University of Texas Press, 1979.

BASSI Alfred Buehler, Terry Barrow, and Charles P. Mountford. *Art of the South Sea Islands*. New York: Crown Publishers, 1962.

BAUM Hermann Baumann. *Die Völker Afrikas und ihre traditionellen Kulturen*. Pt. 2, *Ost-, West-, und Nordafrica*. Wiesbaden: Franz Steiner, 1979.

BAUMAN Bauman & Co. *Ludwig Bauman & Co. Catalogue*. Furniture catalog. New York: Bauman & Co., 1895.

BBRSS *Records Control and Storage Handbook*. Itasca, Ill.: Bankers Box, 1977.

BBSJ Donald S. Berry, George W. Blomme, Paul W. Shuldiner, and John H. Jones. *The Technology of Urban Transportation*. Evanston, Ill.: Northwestern University Press, 1963.

BCGCC Cécile Beurdeley and Michel Beurdeley. *A Connoisseur's Guide to Chinese Ceramics*. Secaucus, N.J.: Leon Amiel Publishers, 1974.

BCI Francis Ching. *Building Construction Illustrated*. New York: Van Nostrand Reinhold, 1975.

BCM Gary Moselle, ed. *Building Cost Manual*. Carlsbad, Calif.: Craftsman Book Co., 1979.

BCMTC Whitney C. Huntington and Robert E. Mickadeit. *Building Construction Materials and Types of Construction*. 4th ed. New York: John Wiley & Sons, 1975.

BD&C *Building Design & Construction*. Des Plaines, Ill.: Cahner Publishing Co., 1958-.

BDT Arthur Burke, J. Ralph Dalzell, and Gilbert Townsend. *Architectural and Building Trades Dictionary*. Chicago: American Technical Society, 1950.

BEAA *The Britannica Encyclopaedia of American Art*. Chicago: Encyclopaedia Britannica Educational Corp., 1973.

BEAK George C. Beakley. *Architectural Drawing and Design*. New York: Macmillan Publishing Co., 1984.

BEARD Geoffrey Beard and Judith Goodison. *English Furniture 1500-1840*. Oxford: Phaidon Christie's, 1987.

BEARD2 Geoffrey Beard. *The National Trust Book of English Furniture*. London: Viking & National Trust, 1985.

BEAUJ J. Beaujeu-Garnier and G. Chabot. *Urban Geography*. New York: John Wiley & Sons, 1967.

BECKW John Beckwith. *The Art of Constantinople*. London: Phaidon Press, 1961.

BEEDLE Lynn S. Beedle, ed. *Second Century of the Skyscraper*. New York: Van Nostrand Reinhold, 1988.

BEGUIN Andre Beguin. *Technical Dictionary of Printmaking*. 3 vols. Translated by Allen J. Grieco. Brussels: A. Beguin, 1981.

BELLMN Willard F. Bellman. *Scenography and Stage Technology: An Introduction*. New York: Thomas Y. Crowell Co., 1977.

BENDIN Kenneth Bendiner. *An Introduction to Victorian Painting*. New Haven, Conn.: Yale University Press, 1985.

BERFOX George Berkeley and Douglas Fox. *Eighty Thousand Governments: The Politics of Subnational America*. Boston: Allyn & Bacon, 1978.

BERK Visual Aids Library, Department of Architecture, University of California, Berkeley. "Classification Manual." Document prepared for internal distribution. University of California, Berkeley.

BESD Frederick S. Merritt. *Building Engineering and Systems Designs*. New York: Van Nostrand Reinhold, 1979.

BETTI Claudia Betti and Teel Sale. *A Contemporary Approach to Drawing*. New York: Holt, Rinehart & Winston, 1980.

BEVAN Bernard Bevan. *History of Spanish Architecture*. New York: Charles Scribner's Sons, 1939.

BF Bernard M. Feilden. *Conservation of Historic Buildings*. London: Butterworths, 1982.

BFORI *Buildings for Industry.* New York: F. W. Dodge Corp., 1957.

BFSD American Society of Landscape Architects Foundation. *Barrier Free Site Design.* Washington, D.C.: U.S. Department of Housing and Urban Development, 1974.

BFTPS Fred W. Billmeyer. *Textbook of Polymer Science.* 3d ed. New York: John Wiley & Sons, 1984.

BGPBA A. A. Bronson and Peggy Gale. *Performance By Artists.* Toronto: Art Metropole, 1979.

BH Lisbeth Mark. *Book of Hierarchies.* New York: William Morrow & Co., 1984.

BHFPEP Robert Bartholomew. *Human Factors in Physical Environment Planning.* Monticello, Ill.: Council of Planning Librarians, 1976.

BHSC Wilson Bently and William Humphreys. *Snow Crystals.* New York: McGraw-Hill Book Co., 1931.

BIBBY Geoffrey Bibby. *Looking for Dilmun.* New York: Alfred A. Knopf, 1969.

BIBIAP U.S. Environmental Protection Agency. Headquarter Library. *Bibliography on Indoor Air Pollution.* Washington, D.C.: U.S. Environmental Protection Agency, 1985.

BIEBER Margaret Bieber. *The History of the Greek and Roman Theater.* Princeton, N.J.: Princeton University Press, 1961.

BIGHSE Thomas C. Hubka. *Big House, Little House, Back House, Barn: The Connected Farm Buildings of New England.* Hanover, N.H.: University Press of New England, 1984.

BIH Raymond Bushell. *Inro Handbook: Studies of Netsuke, Inro, and Lacquer.* New York: John Weatherhill, 1979.

BILESJ John H. Biles. *The Design and Construction of Ships.* London: Griffin, 1908.

BINNEY Marcus Binney and David Pearce, eds. *Railway Architecture.* New York: Van Nostrand Reinhold, 1980.

BIP *Books in Print.* New York: R. R. Bowker Co., 1947-.

BIRREL Verla Birrell. *The Textile Arts. A Handbook of Fabric Structure and Design Processes: Ancient and Modern Weaving, Braiding, Printing, and Other Textile Techniques.* New York: Harper-Brothers Publishers, 1959.

BISANZ *Konsthistorisk Tidskrift.* Stockholm: University of Stockholm, Institute of the History of Art, 1932-.

BISH10 Bishop Furniture Co. *Catalogue Number Fifty.* Grand Rapids, N.Dak.: Bishop Furniture Co., ca. 1910.

BISHOP Robert Bishop. *Centuries and Styles of the American Chair, 1640-1970.* New York: E. P. Dutton, 1972.

BJHTS Jean Boisselier. *Heritage of Thai Sculpture.* New York: John Weatherhill, 1975.

BLACK Blackie & Son. *The Victorian Cabinet-Maker's Assistant.* Reprint. New York: Dover Publications, 1970.

BLACKB Graham Blackburn. *Illustrated Encyclopedia of Woodworking Handtools, Instruments, and Devices.* New York: Simon & Schuster, 1974.

BLACKS Henry C. Black. *Black's Law Dictionary.* 4th ed. St. Paul, Minn.: West Publishing Co., 1951.

BLAIR John Murray and H. Blairman and Son. *George Bullock: Cabinetmaker.* London: John Murray Publishers, 1988.

BLAKE Peter Blake. *Marcel Breuer: Architect and Designer.* New York: Museum of Modern Art, 1949.

BLAKE1 Marion E. Blake. *Ancient Roman Construction in Italy from the Prehistoric Period to Augustus.* Washington, D.C.: Carnegie Institution of Washington, 1947.

BLAKE2 Marion E. Blake. *Roman Construction in Italy from Tiberius through the Flavians.* Washington, D.C.: Carnegie Institution of Washington, 1959.

BLAKE3 Marion E. Blake. *Roman Construction in Italy from Nerva through the Antonines.* Edited and completed by Doris T. Bishop. Philadelphia: American Philosophical Society, 1973.

BLCT Harold Kueppers. *The Basic Law of Color Theory.* New York: Barron's Educational Series, 1982.

BLDG *Building.* London: Building, 1842-.

BLODG Richard Blodgett. *Photographs: A Collector's Guide.* New York: Ballantine Books, 1979.

BLUNT Anthony Blunt, ed. *Baroque and Rococo: Architecture and Decoration.* New York: Harper & Row Publishers, 1982.

BMDWG J. A. Gere and P. Pouncey. *Italian Drawings in the Department of Prints and Drawings in the British Museum: Artists Working in Rome c.1550-c.1640.* London: British Museum, 1962.

BMDWG2 J. A. Gere and P. Pouncey. *Italian Drawings in the Department of Prints and Drawings in the British Museum: Raphael and His Circle.* London: British Museum, 1962.

BMDWG3 J. A. Gere and P. Pouncey. *Italian Drawings in the Department of Prints and Drawings in the British Museum: Artists Working in Parma in the Sixteenth Century.* London: British Museum, 1967.

BMT Paul Bianchina. *Illustrated Dictionary of Building Materials and Techniques.* Blue Ridge Summit, Pa.: Tab Books, 1986.

BNAOP Gregory Battock and Robert Nickas, eds. *The Art of Performance: A Critical Anthology.* New York: E. P. Dutton, 1984.

BOCOBA Boston Co-operative Buyers Association. *Catalogue of the Boston Co-operative Buyers Association.* Furniture catalog. Boston: Boston Co-operative Buyers Association, 1895.

BODE Wilhelm von Bode. *Italian Renaissance Furniture.* Translated by Mary E. Herrick. New York: William Helburn, 1921.

BOETH Axel Boethius. *Etruscan and Early Roman Architecture.* 2d ed. Harmondsworth, England: Penguin Books, 1978.

BOIME Albert Boime. *The Academy and French Painting in the Nineteenth Century.* London: Phaidon Press, 1971.

BOKRU Constance M. Boris and John V. Krutilla. *Water Rights and Energy Development in the Yellowstone River Basin: An Integrated Analysis.* Baltimore, Md.: Johns Hopkins University Press, 1980.

BONMAR Michael B. Miller. *The Bon Marché: Bourgeois Culture and the Department Store, 1869-1920.* Princeton, N.J.: Princeton University Press, 1981.

BONYED Jean Bony. *The English Decorated Style: Gothic Architecture Transformed, 1250-1350*. Oxford: Phaidon Press, 1979.

BOSS Richard W. Boss. *Library Manager's Guide to Automation*. 2d ed. White Plains, N.Y.: Knowledge Industry Publications, 1984.

BOSWOR Clifford E. Bosworth. *The Islamic Dynasties: A Chronological and Genealogical Handbook*. rev. ed. Edinburgh: Edinburgh University Press, 1980.

BOTKIN Daniel Botkin and Edward Keller. *Environmental Studies*. Columbus, Ohio: Charles E. Merrill Publishing Co., 1982.

BOVAY H. E. Bovay, Jr., ed. *Handbook of Mechanical and Electrical Systems for Buildings*. New York: McGraw-Hill Book Co., 1981.

BOXCF Liz-Anne Bawden, ed. *Oxford Companion to Film*. New York: Oxford University Press, 1976.

BOYCE Charles Boyce. *Dictionary of Furniture*. New York: Henry Holt & Co., 1985.

BPCA Mario Bussagli. *Treasures of Asia*. Vol. 6, *Painting of Central Asia*. Translated by Lothian Small. Geneva: Skira, 1963.

BPGIM Henry S. Borneman. *Pennsylvania German Illuminated Manuscripts*. Reprint. New York: Dover Publications, 1973.

BPI *Business Periodicals Index*. New York: H. W. Wilson Co., 1958-.

BRAAH Ronald Berndt and E. S. Phillips, eds. *Australian Aboriginal Heritage*. 2d ed. Sydney: Australian Society for Education Through the Arts, 1978.

BRAD Morton C. Bradley. *The Treatment of Pictures*. Cambridge, Mass.: Art Technology, 1950.

BRAY Warwick Bray and David Trump. *The Penguin Dictionary of Archeology*. 2d ed. Harmondsworth, England: Penguin Books, 1972.

BRE Building Research Establishment. *Building Defects and Maintenance*. Lancaster, England: Construction Press, 1977.

BREGAZ Breeder's Gazette. *Farm Buildings*. 2d ed. Chicago: Breeder's Gazette, 1916.

BRENDL Otto Brendl. *Etruscan Art*. Harmondsworth, England: Penguin Books, 1978.

BRGLND Abraham Berglund. *Ocean Transportation*. New York: Longman's Green, 1931.

BRHCI Ronald M. Baecker and William A. S. Buxton. *Readings in Human-Computer Interaction: A Multidisciplinary Approach*. Los Altos, Calif.: Morgan Kaufmann Publishers, 1987.

BRLLNT Richard Brilliant. *Roman Art from the Republic to Constantine*. London: Phaidon Press, 1974.

BRO Lu Bro. *Drawing: A Studio Guide*. New York: W. W. Norton & Co., 1978.

BROCK Oscar Brockett. *History of the Theater*. Boston: Allyn & Bacon, 1974.

BROLAY James Penderel-Brodhurst and Edwin J. Layton. *A Glossary of English Furniture of the Historic Periods*. New York: R. M. McBride, 1925.

BROOKS Hugh Brooks. *Encyclopedia of Building and Construction Terms*. Englewood Cliffs, N.J.: Prentice Hall, 1983.

BROTH Alfred Brothers. *Photography: Its History, Processes, Apparatus, and Materials*. London: Charles Griffin & Co., 1899.

BROWN Milton W. Brown. *American Art: Painting, Sculpture, Architecture, Decorative Arts, Photography*. New York: Harry N. Abrams, 1979.

BROWNL Adon H. Brownell. *Hardware Age. Builders' Hardware Handbook*. Philadelphia: Chilton Co., 1956.

BRPS John White. *The Birth and Rebirth of Pictorial Space*. London: Faber & Faber, 1967.

BRUNS Roland W. Brunskill and Alec Clifton-Taylor. *English Brickwork*. London: Wardlock, 1977.

BRUNT Andrew Brunt. *Phaidon Guide to Furniture*. Oxford: Phaidon Press, 1978.

BS5723 British Standards Institution. *Guidelines for the Establishment and Development of Monolingual Thesauri*. London: British Standards Institution, 1979.

BSDSL Willard F. Bellman. *Scene Design, Stage Lighting, Sound, Costume, and Makeup: A Scenographic Approach*. New York: Harper & Row Publishers, 1983.

BSNC U.S. Department of the Interior. *Building Stones of Our Nation's Capital*. Washington, D.C.: Government Printing Office, 1975.

BSSF R. Barry. *Construction of Buildings: Single Storey Frames, Shells, and Lightweight Coverings*. London: Granada, 1984.

BUBKIP Bub & Kipp. *Bub & Kipp's Illustrated Catalogue*. Furniture catalog. Milwaukee, Wis.: Bub & Kipp, 1885.

BUDIAG *Architectural Technology*. Washington, D.C.: American Institute of Architects Service Corp, 1983-.

BUENO Rafael Domenech and Luis P. Bueno. *Antique Spanish Furniture*. Translated by Grace H. Burr. New York: Archive Press, 1965.

BURDEN Ernest Burden. *Living Barns: How to Find and Restore a Barn of Your Own*. New York: Bonanza, 1984.

BURGER Robert H. Burger. *Authority Work: The Creation, Use, Maintenance, and Evaluation of Authority Records and Files*. Littleton, Colo.: Libraries Unlimited, 1985.

BURL *Burlington Magazine*. London: Burlington Magazine Publications, 1903-.

BURR Grace H. Burr. *Hispanic Furniture from the Fifteenth to Eighteenth Centuries*. 2d ed. New York: Archives Press, 1964.

BURR2 Grace H. Burr. *Hispanic Furniture: Notes and Monographs*. New York: Hispanic Society of America, 1941.

BURT Eugene C. Burt. *An Annotated Bibliography of the Visual Arts of East Africa*. Bloomington: Indiana University Press, 1980.

BUSHNE G. H. S. Bushnell. *Ancient Arts of the Americas*. New York: Praeger Publishers, 1965.

BUSS Truman C. Buss. *Simplified Architectural Drawings with Examples and Problems*. Chicago: American Technical Society, 1946.

BYNE Arthur Byne and Mildred Stapley. *Spanish Interiors and Furniture*. 2 vols. New York: William Helburn, 1921-22.

BYZAN *Byzantion*. Brussels: Foundation Byzantine, 1924-.

CA *Classical America*. Long Island City, N.Y.: Classical America Society, 1971-.

CAB Graham Connah. *Architecture of Benin*. Oxford: Clarendon Press, 1975.

CABDIC Thomas Sheraton. *The Cabinet Dictionary.* 2 vols. Reprint. New York: Praeger Publishers, 1970.

CABDRA Thomas Sheraton. *The Cabinet-makers and Upholster's Drawing-Book.* London: T. Bensley, 1802.

CACIC Ananda K. Coomaraswamy. *Arts and Crafts of India and Ceylon.* New York: Farrar, Straus & Co., 1964.

CAD *Chicago Architects Design: A Century of Architectural Drawings from the Art Institute of Chicago.* Chicago: Art Institute of Chicago, 1982.

CADEN *Cadence.* Austin, Tex.: Ariel Communications, 1986-.

CAH71A I. E. S. Edwards, C. J. Gadd, and N. G. L. Hammond, eds. *Cambridge Ancient History.* Vol. 1, Pt. 2, *Early History of the Middle East.* Cambridge: Cambridge University Press, 1971.

CAH80A I. E. S. Edwards, C. J. Gadd, N. G. L. Hammond, and E. Sollberger, eds. *Cambridge Ancient History.* Vol. 2, Pt. 1, *History of the Middle East and the Aegean Region C.1800-1380 B.C.* Cambridge: Cambridge University Press, 1980.

CAH80B I. E. S. Edwards, C. J. Gadd, N. G. L. Hammond, and E. Sollberger, eds. *Cambridge Ancient History.* Vol. 2, Pt. 2, *History of the Middle East and Aegean Region C.1380-1000 B.C.* Cambridge: Cambridge University Press, 1980.

CALK Robert G. Calkins. *Illuminated Books of the Middle Ages.* Ithaca, N.Y.: Cornell University Press, 1983.

CALMIS Paul C. Johnson, ed. *The California Missions: A Pictorial History.* Menlo Park, Calif.: Lane, 1964.

CAMARC Andrew Sherratt, ed. *The Cambridge Encyclopedia of Archaeology.* New York: Cambridge University Press, 1980.

CAMLAC *Cambridge Encyclopedia of Latin America and the Caribbean.* Cambridge: Cambridge University Press, 1985.

CAMPLN Richard Dober. *Campus Planning.* New York: Reinhold Publishing Co. 1963.

CANAD John Canaday. *Mainstreams of Modern Art.* 2d ed. New York: Holt, Rinehart & Winston, 1981.

CANENC *Canadian Encyclopedia.* 3 vols. Edmonton, Alta.: Hartig, 1985.

CAPOT Rosario Capotosto. *Complete Book of Woodworking.* New York: Harper & Row Publishers, 1975.

CARCH *Canadian Architect.* Don Mills, Ont.: Southam Communications. 1956-.

CARDVR *Car and Driver.* New York: Diamandis Communications, 1956-.

CARK Joseph Cornet. *Art Royal Kuba.* Milan: Edizioni Sipiel, 1982.

CAS *Ceramic Art of Japan: One Hundred Masterpieces from Japanese Collections.* Seattle: Seattle Art Museum, 1972.

CASAB *Casabella.* Milan: Electa Periodici, 1928-.

CASCLD D. P. Simpson, comp. *Cassell's New Compact Latin-English Dictionary.* New York: Dell Publishing Co., 1963.

CASSON Lionel Casson. *Travel in the Ancient World.* Toronto: Hakkert, 1974.

CASTAG Ferdinando Castagnoli. *Orthogonal Town Planning In Antiquity.* Cambridge: Massachusetts Institute of Technology Press, 1971.

CASTED Leopoldo Castedo. *A History of Latin American Art and Architecture, from Pre-Columbian Times to the Present*. New York: Praeger Publishers, 1969.

CATHER David M. Cathers. *Furniture of the American Arts and Crafts Movement: Stickley and Roycroft Mission Oak*. New York: New American Library, 1981.

CBC3 John L. Ferrer and Gilbert R. Hutchings. *Carpentry and Building Construction*. 3d ed. Encino, Calif.: Glencoe, 1986.

CBD John Harris. *A Catalogue of British Drawings for Architecture, Decoration, Sculpture, and Landscape Gardening, 1550-1900, in American Collections*. Boston: Gregg Press, 1971.

CBPP Warren E. Cox. *The Book of Pottery and Porcelain*. 2 vols. New York: Crown Publishers, 1944.

CBTW *Campus Buildings that Work*. Philadelphia: North American Publishing Co., 1972.

CC Claudius Coulin. *Step-By-Step Perspective Drawings*. New York: Van Nostrand Reinhold, 1966.

CCDP Center for Community Development and Preservation. *Affordable Housing: Public and Private Partnerships for Constructing Middle and Moderate Income Housing*. New York: Center for Community Development and Preservation, 1980.

CCE Judith S. Levey and Agnes Greenhall. *Concise Columbia Encyclopedia*. New York: Columbia University Press, 1983.

CCOFE George Gilbert. *Cathedral Cities of England*. New York: Dodd, Mead, 1905.

CE Colin T. Eisler. *Sculptors' Drawings Over Six Centuries, 1400-1950*. New York: Agrinde Publications, 1981.

CEDEL *Comprehensive Etymological Dictionary of the English Language*. New York: Elsevier Science Publishing Co., 1966-1967.

CEDPS Cesare Emiliani. *Dictionary of the Physical Sciences*. New York: Oxford University Press, 1987.

CEEB College Entrance Examination Board. *Index of Majors: 1985-1986*. 8th ed. New York: College Entrance Examination Board, 1985.

CELENK Theodore Celenko. *A Treasury of African Art from the Harrison Eiteljorg Collection*. Bloomington: Indiana University Press, 1983.

CENSUS U.S. Department of Commerce. *1980 Census of Population and Housing: Census Tracts, United States Summary*. Washington, D.C.: Government Printing Office, 1984.

CESCIN Herbert Cescinsky. *English Furniture: From Gothic to Sheraton*. Grand Rapids, Mich.: Dean-Hicks Co., 1929.

CFCHAP Charles F. Chapman. *Piloting, Seamanship, and Small Boat Handling*. 51st ed. New York: Hearst Books, 1974.

CGSW Timothy Champion, Clive Gamble, Stephan Shennan, and Alasdair Whittle. *Prehistoric Europe*. London: Academic Press, 1984.

CGWRV Wanda M. Corn. *Grant Wood: The Regionalist Vision*. New Haven, Conn.: Yale University Press, 1983.

CHA Roland A. Oliver and J. D. Fage, eds. *Cambridge History of Africa*. 5 vols. Cambridge: Cambridge University Press, 1978.

CHAMB *Chamber's Encyclopaedia*. rev. ed. London: International Learning Systems Corp., 1968.

CHANG Kwang-Chih Chang. *The Archaeology of Ancient China*. New Haven, Conn.: Yale University Press, 1963.

CHARLS Robert J. Charleston. *English Porcelain*. London: Ernest Benn, 1965.

CHIEFF Clifford T. Chieffo. *The Contemporary Oil Painter's Handbook*. Englewood Cliffs, N.J.: Prentice Hall, 1976.

CHING Frank Ching. *Architectural Graphics*. New York: Reinhold Publishing Co., 1975.

CHINNE Victor Chinnery. *Oak Furniture: The British Tradition*. Woodbridge, England: Antique Collectors' Club, 1979.

CHINPT Torao Miyagawa, ed. *Chinese Painting*. New York: John Weatherhill. Kyoto: Tankosha, 1983.

CHIPP Thomas Chippendale. *The Gentleman and Cabinet-Maker's Director*. London: Thomas Chippendale, 1754.

CHIPP3 Thomas Chippendale. *The Gentleman and Cabinet-Maker's Director*. Reprint of 3d ed. New York: Dover Publications, 1966.

CHRST Edwin Christensen. *The Index of American Design*. Washington, D.C.: National Gallery of Art, 1950.

CHWMS Charles Williams. *Your Bargain Store*. Furniture catalog. New York: Charles Williams, 1923.

CICMFA Boston Museum of Fine Arts. *Catalogue of the Indian Collections in the Museum of Fine Arts, Boston*. Pts. 1-6. Delhi, India: Bharatiya, 1978-1981.

CIF Robert F. Cushman, Michael S. Simon, and McNeill Stoker. *Construction Industry Formbook*. New York: McGraw-Hill Book Co., 1979.

CIHBE Canadian Inventory of Historic Building. *Exterior Recorded Training Manual*. Ottawa: Minister of the Environment, 1979.

CINFUR Cincinnati Furniture World. *The Cincinnati Furniture World*. Cincinnati: Cincinnati Furniture World, 1885.

CINPRI Master Carpenters' & Joiners' Society of Cincinnati. *Book of Prices of the United Society of Journeymen Cabinet Makers of Cincinnati for the Manufacture of Cabinet Ware*. Cincinnati: Master Carpenters' & Joiners' Society of Cincinnati, 1836.

CIT Michael J. Roberts. *Construction Industry Thesaurus*. 2d ed. London: Property Services Agency, Department of the Environment, 1976.

CLARKB Clark Brothers & Co. *Illustrated Catalogue of Fancy Cabinet Ware*. Cincinnati: Clark Brothers & Co., 1875.

CLFFRD Derek Clifford. *A History of Garden Art*. London: Faber & Faber, 1966.

CM Hugo L. P. Stibbe. *Cartographic Materials: A Manual of Interpretation for AACR2*. Chicago: American Library Association, 1982.

CMA Sara J. Pearman. "Cleveland Museum of Art Slide Library Classification Scheme, Chronologies and Sub-Divisions." Document prepared for internal distribution. Cleveland Museum of Art, 1980s.

CMM William R. Hawken. *Copying Methods Manual*. Chicago: American Library Association, 1966.

CMMPP William Chaffers. *Marks and Monograms on Pottery and Porcelain*. London: Bickers & Sons, 1876.

COCHRA Pauline A. Cochrane. *Redesign of Catalogs and Indexes for Improved Online Subject Access: Selected Papers of Pauline A. Cochrane*. Phoenix, Ariz.: Oryx Press, 1985.

COCKE Richard Cocke. *The Drawings of Raphael*. London: Hamlyn Publishing Group, 1969.

COFC Lewis Mumford. *The Culture of Cities*. New York: Harcourt, Brace & Co., 1938.

COLEMA William E. Coleman. *Grants in the Humanities; A Scholar's Guide to Funding Sources*. New York: Neal-Schuman Publishers, 1980.

COLENC William Bridgewater and Seymour Durtz, eds. *Columbia Encyclopedia*. New York: Columbia University Press, 1963.

COLERI Anthony Coleridge. *Chippendale Furniture*. London: Faber & Faber, 1968.

COLGAN Susan Colgan. *Restaurant Design: Ninety-Five Spaces that Work*. New York: Whitney Library of Design, 1987.

COLGT Sandra Dallas. *Colorado Ghost Towns and Mining Camps*. Norman: University of Oklahoma Press, 1985.

COLIE Colie & Son. *Parlor Furniture*. Buffalo, N.Y.: Colie & Son, 1885.

COLLAR Frances Collard. *Regency Furniture*. Woodbridge, Suffolk, England: Antique Collectors' Club, 1985.

COLLEC Phoebe Phillips, ed. *The Collectors' Encyclopedia of Antiques*. New York: Crown Publishers, 1973.

COLLED Malcolm A. R. Colledge. *Parthian Art*. Ithaca, N.Y.: Cornell University Press, 1977.

COLLEY B. C. Colley. *Practical Manual of Site Development*. New York: McGraw-Hill Book Co., 1986.

COLLIE Emanuel Friedman, ed. *Collier's Encyclopedia*. New York: Macmillan Educational Co., 1983.

COLORN U.S. Department of Commerce. *Color: Universal Language and Dictionary of Names*. Washington, D.C.: National Bureau of Standards, 1976.

COMBAS *Computer Basics*. Chicago: Time-Life Books, 1985.

COMBLD *Commercial Buildings: An Architectural Record Book*. New York: Dodge, 1953.

COMEPA Come-Packt Furniture Co. *Come-Packt Furniture Company Catalogue*. Toledo, Ohio: Come-Packt Furniture Co., 1911.

COMMFR Christopher Gilbert. *An exhibition of Common Furniture Illustrating Sub-Groups Within the Vernacular Tradition*. Leeds, England: Temple Newsam, 1982.

COMST Helen Comstock. *American Furniture: Seventeenth-Eighteenth-, and Nineteenth-Century Styles*. Exton, Pa.: Schiffer Publishing, 1962.

COMSTK Helen Comstock, ed. *The Concise Encyclopedia of American Antiques*. New York: Hawthorn Books, 1958.

CONANT Kenneth J. Conant. *Carolingian and Romanesque Architecture, 800-1200*. Harmondsworth, England: Penguin Books, 1973.

CONK Margo A. Conk. *The U.S. Census and Labor Force Change*. Ann Arbor: University of Michigan Research Press, 1980.

CONNEL Will Connell. *The Missions of California*. New York: Hastings House, 1941.

CONNS *Connoisseur*. New York: Hearst Corp., 1901-.

CONRAD Lynn Conrad. *The Complete Grants Sourcebook*. San Francisco: Institute for Fund Raising, 1978.

CONRDS Conrades Chair & Parlor Furniture Co. *Illustrated Catalogue*. Chicago: Conrades Chair & Parlow Furniture Co., 1891.

COOKCO *Kennilworth and Phillippine Fiber*. Michigan City, Ind.: Cook Co., 1902.

COOM Ananda K. Coomaraswamy. *History of Indian and Indonesian Art*. New York: E. Weyhe, 1927.

COOPER Wendy A. Cooper. *In Praise of America: American Decorative Arts, 1650-1830*. New York: Alfred A. Knopf, 1980.

COPENH Emily D. Copenhaver and Benita K. Wilkonson. *Movement of Hazardous Substances in Soil: A Bibliography*. Cincinnati: Environmental Protection Agency, 1979.

COPPLE Trewin Copplestone, ed. *World Architecture: An Illustrated History*. rev. ed. London: Hamlyn Publishing Group, 1972.

CORKH T. Corkhill. *Concise Building Encyclopedia*. London: Pitman Publishing, 1945.

CORMA Malcolm Cormack. *The Drawings of Watteau*. London: Hamlyn Publishing Group, 1970.

COTT Leonard Cottrell. *The Concise Encyclopedia of Archaeology*. New York: Hawthorn Press, 1960.

COVARR Miguel Covarrubias. *Indian Art of Mexico and Central America*. New York: Alfred A. Knopf, 1966.

COWAN Henry J. Cowan and Peter R. Smith. *Dictionary of Architectural and Building Technology*. New York: Elsevier Science Publishing Co., 1986.

COXBPP Warren E. Cox. *Book of Pottery and Porcelain*. 2 vols. New York: Crown Publishers, 1944.

CPA John D. Clark. *The Prehistory of Africa*. London: Thames & Hudson, 1970.

CPD A. H. Christie. *Pattern Design: An Introduction to the Study of Formal Ornament*. Reprint. New York: Dover Publications, 1969.

CPEK Eastman Kodak Company. *Conservation of Photographs*. Rochester, N.Y.: Eastman Kodak Co., 1985.

CPL176 John S. Marsh. *Marine Parks: An Annotated Bibliography*. Council of Planning Librarians Exchange Bibliography No. 176. Monticello, Ill.: Council of Planning Librarians, 1971.

CPL681 James C. Starbuck. *Stadiums: A Bibliography*. Council of Planning Librarians Exchange Bibliography No. 681. Monticello, Ill.: Council of Planning Librarians, 1974.

CRANE Michael Crane and Mary Stofflet, eds. *Correspondence Art: Source Book for the Network of International Postal Art Activity*. San Francisco: Contemporary Arts Press, 1984.

CRAVEN David Craven. *The New Concept of Popular Culture in Nicaragua since the Revolution in 1979: An Analytic Essay and Compendium of Illustrations*. Lewiston, N.Y.: Edwin Mellen Press, 1989.

CRAWF William Crawford. *The Keepers of Light: A History and Working Guide to Early Photographic Processes*. Dobbs Ferry, N.Y.: Morgan & Morgan, 1979.

CRAWFO Walt Crawford. *Technical Standards: An Introduction for Librarians*. White Plains, N.Y.: Knowledge Industry Publications, 1986.

CRBOOK Pauline Johnson. *Creative Bookbinding*. Seattle: University of Washington Press, 1984.

CREATE Terence Pitts and Sharon Denton. *Create: A Procedure Manual for Cataloging Photographs*. 2d ed. Tucson: Center for Creative Photography, University of Arizona, 1984.

CRI2 Thomas V. Atkins and Rona Ostrow, eds. *Cross-Reference Index: A Guide to Search Terms*. New York: R. R. Bowker Co., 1989.

CRIBA Sir Banister Fletcher Library. *Catalogue of the Drawings Collection of the Royal Institute of British Architects*. Farnborough, England: Gregg, 1977.

CRNA *Guide to Cartographic Records in the National Archives*. Washington , D.C.: Government Printing Office, 1971.

CRTHE Alphonse Chapanis. *Research Techniques in Human Engineering*. Baltimore, Md.: Johns Hopkins University Press, 1959.

CSC Ralph T. Coe. *Sacred Circles: Two Thousand Years of North American Indian Art*. London: Arts Council of Great Britain, 1976.

CSID *Collins-Sansoni Italian Dictionary*. 2d ed. Florence, Italy: G. C. Sansoni Editore, 1981.

CTPB92 Hartford Cabinetmakers. Furniture price list. Hartford Cabinetmakers, Hartford, Conn., 1792.

CTSB Marvin D. Schwartz. *Chairs, Tables, Sofas, and Beds*. New York: Alfred A. Knopf, 1982.

CUA Richard Strasberg, ed. *Glossary of Record Types*. Ithaca, N.Y.: Cornell University Press, 1974.

CUT Ministry of State for Urban Affairs. *Canadian Urban Thesaurus*. Montreal: University of Montreal, 1979.

CUTNP Charles D. Cuttler. *Northern Painting from Pucelle to Bruegel*. New York: Holt, Rinehart & Winston, 1968.

CWC Carl W. Condit. *Chicago, 1930-1970*. Chicago: University of Chicago Press, 1974.

CWPNP Grahame Clark. *World Prehistory in New Perspective*. 3d ed. Cambridge: Cambridge University Press, 1977.

D20CA Bernard S. Myers and Shirley D. Myers, eds. *Dictionary of Twentieth Century Art*. New York: McGraw-Hill Book Co., 1974.

DAAPS T. Richards. *Dictionary of Architecture*. London: Architecture Publishing Society, 1892.

DAC Cyril M. Harris. *Dictionary of Architecture and Construction*. New York: McGraw-Hill Book Co., 1975.

DADA Louise A. Boger and H. Batterson Boger, eds. *The Dictionary of Antiques and the Decorative Arts*. New York: Charles Scribner's Sons, 1957.

DAGO Frank Dagostino. *Materials of Construction*. Reston, Va.: Reston Publishing Co., 1982.

DAHC Basil Davidson. *Africa: History of a Continent*. London: Weidenfeld & Nicolson, 1972.

DAHTO Basil Davidson. *Africa in History: Themes and Outlines*. New York: Macmillan Publishing Co., 1974.

DAIDAL *Daidalos*. Geutersloh, West Germany: Bertelsmann Fachzeitschriften, 1981-.

DALLI W. Dallimore and A. Bruce Jackson. *A Handbook of Coniferae Including Ginkoacea*. London: Edward Arnold, 1923.

DAMR *Dictionary of Archives and Manuscripts*. Washington, D.C.: National Historical Publications & Records Committee, 1978.

DARIS Detroit Institute of Arts. *Detroit Art Registration and Information System Glossary*. Detroit: Founders Society, Detroit Institute of Arts, 1980.

DARLIN Sharon Darling. *Chicago Furniture: Art, Craft, and Industry, 1833-1983*. New York: Chicago Historical Society in association with W. W. Norton Co., 1984.

DARYAN Sital Daryanani. *Buildings Systems Design with Programmable Calculators*. New York: McGraw-Hill Book Co., 1980.

DASHIP Charles G. Davis. *Ships of the Past*. Salem, Mass.: Marine Research Society, 1929.

DATPRO *Series Report One*. Delran, N.J.: Datapro Research Corp., 1987.

DAUM Jeanne L. Wasserman. *Daumier Sculpture: A Critical and Comparative Study*. Cambridge, Mass.: Fogg Museum, Harvard University, 1969.

DAYPD Lewis F. Day. *Pattern Design: A Book for Students, Treating in a Practical Way of the Anatomy, Planning, and Evolution of Repeated Ornament*. New York: Taplinger Publishing Co., 1979.

DCA William Smith and Samuel Cheetham, eds. *A Dictionary of Christian Antiquities*. 2 vols. London: John Murray Publishers, 1880.

DCART V. Babington Smith. *Dictionary of Contemporary Artists*. Santa Barbara, Calif.: Clio Press, 1981.

DCE John S. Scott. *Dictionary of Civil Engineering*. New York: Halsted Press, 1982.

DCP Wai-Kam Ho, Sherman E. Lee, Laurence Sickman, and Marc F. Wilson. *Eight Dynasties of Chinese Painting: The Collections of the Nelson Gallery-Atkins Museum, Kansas City, and the Cleveland Museum of Art*. Cleveland: Cleveland Museum of Art, 1980.

DDA John Fleming and Hugh Honour. *Dictionary of the Decorative Arts*. New York: Harper & Row Publishers, 1977.

DDD Robert Harling, ed. *Dictionary of Design and Decoration*. New York: Viking Press, 1973.

DDT Robert J. Dumouchel. *Dictionary of Development Terminology*. New York: McGraw-Hill Book Co., 1975.

DEF Ralph Edwards. *The Dictionary of English Furniture*. 2d ed. Barra Books, 1983.

DEGENS John D. Rosecrance. *The Degenerates of Lake Tahoe*. New York: Lang, 1985.

DEISS William A. Deiss. *Museum Archives: An Introduction*. Chicago: Society of American Archivists, 1984.

DENYER Susan Denyer. *African Traditional Architecture: An Historical and Geographical Perspective*. New York: Africana Publishing Co., 1978.

DEPA Edward Dodd. *Polynesian Art*. New York: Dodd, Mead & Co., 1967.

DERBY Derby & Co. Furniture catalog. Boston: Derby & Co., 1915.

DESAJ *Design Arts*. New York: Cooper Union for the Advancement of Science and Art, 1980-.

DESWLD *Design World*. Victoria, Australia: Design Editorial, 1983-.

DEVA John F. A. Taylor. *Design and Expression in the Visual Arts*. New York: Dover Publications, 1964.

DH David Haberstich. "Photographs Thesaurus for SIBIS, Including Research by the Smithsonian Photographic Survey Project, with Terms Compiled by Diane Vogt-O'Connor and Constance McCabe." Archives Center, National Museum of American History, Washington, D.C., 1988.

DICMUS International Commission For Documentation. *Dictionarium Museologicum*. Budapest: International Council of Museums, 1986.

DICWPP Louise A. Boger. *The Dictionary of World Pottery and Porcelain*. New York: Charles Scribner's Sons, 1971.

DIETZ Al Dietz. Plastics terminology. Document prepared for internal distribution. Unpublished manuscript. 1986.

DIJK T. A. van Dijk. *Some Aspects of Text Grammars: A Study in Theoretical Linguistics and Poetics*. The Hague: Mouton, 1972.

DIMAND Maurice S. Dimand. *Handbook of Mahammadan Art*. 2d ed. New York: Metropolitan Museum of Art, 1944.

DINSMR William B. Dinsmoor. *The Architecture of Ancient Greece*. 3d rev. ed. New York: W. W. Norton & Co., 1975.

DIRDIR James M. Ethridge. *The Directory of Directories*. 3d ed. Detroit: Gale Research Co., 1984.

DISD Elizabeth A. McCauley. *A. A. E. Disderi and the Carte De Visite Portrait Photograph*. New Haven, Conn.: Yale University Press, 1985.

DISSEL Hans-Dietrich Disselhoff and Sigvald Liune. *The Art of Ancient America*. New York: Crown Publishers, 1961.

DISSTO Henry Disston. *The Saw in History*. 9th ed. Philadelphia: Early American Industries Association and Mid-West Tool Collectors Association, 1978.

DIT Dennis Longley and Michael Shain. *Dictionary of Information Technology*. New York: John Wiley & Sons, 1982.

DITTRI Mark Dittrick and Diane K. Dittrick. *Decorative Hardware*. New York: Hearst Books, 1982.

DL Douglas Lewis. *The Drawings of Andrea Palladio*. Washington, D.C.: International Exhibitions Foundation, 1981.

DLA Baker H. Morrow. *A Dictionary of Landscape Architecture*. Albuquerque: University of New Mexico Press, 1987.

DLAC Vishakha N. Desai. *Life at Court: Art for India's Rulers, Sixteenth to Nineteenth Centuries*. Boston: Museum of Fine Arts, 1985.

DLCA Basil Davidson. *Lost Cities of Africa*. Boston: Little, Brown & Co., 1959.

DLI Winterthur Museum. "Downs Library Index: Section Five, Type of Record." Document prepared for internal distribution. Henry du Pont Winterthur Museum, Winterthur, Del.

DMA John R. Strayer, ed. *Dictionary of the Middle Ages*. 12 vols. New York: Charles Scribner's Sons, 1982-1989.

DMCT Roger Fowler, ed. *A Dictionary of Modern Critical Terms*. rev. ed. New York: Routledge & Kegan Paul, 1987.

DN Ian L. McHarg. *Design with Nature*. New York: Doubleday & Co., 1971.

DNCR Geoffrey Parrinder. *A Dictionary of Non-Christian Religions*. London: Hulton Educational Publications, 1971.

DNE F. J. Monkhouse and John Small. *A Dictionary of the Natural Environment*. London: Edward Arnold, 1978.

DNIT A. J. Meadows, M. Gordon, and A. Singleton. *Dictionary of New Information Technology*. New York: H. W. Wilson Co., 1968.

DOAP Edward C. Smith and Arnold J. Zurcher. *Dictionary of American Politics*. 2d ed. New York: Barnes & Noble Books, 1968.

DOC *Dictionary of Computing*. New York: Oxford University Press, 1986.

DOCR U.S. Department of Commerce. *Report on Statistical Uses of Administrative Records*. Washington, D.C.: Government Printing Office, 1980.

DOD U.S. Department of Defense. *Glossary of Mapping, Charting, and Geodetic Terms*. Washington, D.C.: U.S. Department of Defense, 1973.

DODDIC Joint Chiefs of Staff. *Department of Defense Dictionary of Military and Associated Terms*. Washington, D.C.: Government Printing Office, 1987.

DODW C. R. Dodwell. *Painting in Europe, 800-1200*. Harmondsworth, England: Penguin Books, 1971.

DOFCJ George E. Rush. *The Dictionary of Criminal Justice*. 2d ed. Guilford, Conn.: Dushkin Publishing Group, 1986.

DOHR U.S. Department of Health and Human Services. *Where to Write for Vital Records*. Hyattsville, Md.: U.S. Department of Health and Human Services, 1982.

DOP Walter J. Raymond. *Dictionary of Politics*. 6th ed. Lawrenceville, Va.: Brunswick Publishing Corp., 1978.

DOS Parke Cummings, ed. *Dictionary of Sports*. New York: A. S. Barnes & Co., 1949.

DOT U.S. Employment Service. *Dictionary of Occupational Titles*. 4th ed. Washington, D.C.: U.S. Department of Labor, 1977.

DOWNS Joseph Downs. *American Furniture: Queen Anne and Chippendale Periods in the Henry Francis du Pont Winterthur Museum*. New York: Macmillan Publishing Co., 1952.

DRAGE David Drage & Sons. Furniture catalog. David Drage & Sons, ca. 1911.

DS Daniel Schodek. *Structures*. Englewood Cliffs, N.J.: Prentice Hall, 1980.

DSE H. E. Reineck and L. B. Singh. *Depositional Sedimentary Environments*. Berlin: Springer-Verlag, 1973.

DTE *Down to Earth: Adobe Architecture—An Old Idea, A New Future*. New York: Facts on File, 1983.

DTLCOM Joseph Dechiara. *Handbook of Architectural Details for Commercial Buildings*. New York: McGraw-Hill Book Co., 1980.

DUCK Kenneth W. Duckett. *Modern Manuscripts: A Practical Manual for Their Management, Care, and Use*. Nashville, Tenn.: American Association for State and Local History, 1975.

DUCKW John E. Duckworth. *Forensic Photography*. Springfield, Ill.: Charles C. Thomas Publishing, 1983.

DUDEN *Oxford-Duden Pictorial French-English Dictionary*. Oxford: Clarendon Press, 1983.

DUDWIL Dorothy H. Dudley and Irma B. Wilkinson. *Museum Registration Methods*. Washington, D.C.: American Association of Museums, 1979.

DUGGAR John F. Duggar III. *Checking and Coordinating Architectural and Engineering Working Drawings*. New York: McGraw-Hill Book Co., 1984.

DUMOND Don E. Dumond. *The Eskimos and Aleuts*. New York: Thames & Hudson, 1987.

DURY Carel J. Du Ry. *Art of Islam*. New York: Harry N. Abrams, 1970.

DUTCH Jakob Rosenberg, Seymour Slive, and E. H. ter Kuile. *Dutch Art and Architecture, 1600-1800*. rev. ed. Harmondsworth, England: Penguin Books, 1972.

DWELL Paul Oliver. *Dwellings: Houses across the World*. Austin: University of Texas Press, 1987.

E&G Richard Ettinghausen and Oleg Grabar. *Art and Architecture of Islam, 650-1250*. Harmondsworth, England: Penguin Books, 1987.

EAA William D. Hunt, Jr. *Encyclopedia of American Architecture*. New York, McGraw-Hill Book Co., 1980.

EAMES Penelope Eames. *Medieval Furniture: Furniture in England, France, and the Netherlands from the Twelfth to the Fifteenth Century*. London: Furniture History Society, 1977.

EARE Charles H. Lippy and Peter W. Williams, eds. *Encyclopedia of the American Religious Experience: Studies of Traditions and Movements*. New York: Charles Scribner's Sons, 1988.

EASTMA International Museum of Photography at George Eastman House. List of cataloging terms. Document prepared for internal distribution. George Eastman House, Rochester, N.Y., 1989.

EATAVS Kym S. Rice. *Early American Taverns: For the Entertainment of Friends and Strangers*. Chicago: Regnery Gateway, 1983.

EB Ernest Burden. *Design Presentation: Techniques for Marketing and Project Proposals*. New York: McGraw-Hill Book Co., 1984.

EBAD R. S. Odingo, ed. *African Dam: An Ecological Survey of the Kamburu/Gtaru*

Hydro-Electric Dam Area, Kenya. Stockholm: Swedish Natural Sciences Research Council, Editorial Service, 1979.

EBERLE Harold D. Eberlein and R. W. Ramsdell. *The Practical Book of Italian, Spanish, and Portuguese Furniture*. Philadelphia: J. B. Lippincott Co., 1927.

EBERLN Harold D. Eberlein. *Interiors, Fireplaces, and Furniture of the Italian Renaissance*. New York: Architectural Book Publishing Co., 1916.

EBMAC *New Encyclopaedia Britannica: Macropaedia*. Chicago: Encyclopaedia Britannica, 1984.

EBMIC *New Encyclopaedia Britannica: Micropaedia*. Chicago: Encyclopaedia Britannica, 1984.

EDER Josef M. Eder. *History of Photography*. Reprint. Translated by Edward Epstean. New York: Dover Publications, 1978.

EDUDEN *The English Duden*. 2d ed. Mannheim, West Germany: Bibliographisches Institut, 1960.

EDWARD Ralph Edwards and L. G. G. Ramsey. *The Conoisseur's Complete Period Guides to the Houses, Decoration, Furnishing, and Chattels of the Classic Periods*. London: Connoisseur Publications, 1968.

EGAN M. David Egan. *Concepts in Thermal Comfort*. Englewood Cliffs, N.J.: Prentice Hall, 1975.

EGANAA M. David Egan. *Architectural Acoustics*. New York: McGraw-Hill Book Co., 1988.

EGATM Sir Charles J. Jackson. *English Goldsmiths and Their Marks*. 2d ed. New York: Dover Publications, 1964.

EHR65 Robert W. Ehrich, ed. *Chronologies in Old World Archaeology*. Chicago: University of Chicago Press, 1965.

EHR71 Robert W. Ehrich, ed. *Chronologies in Old World Archaeology*. Reprint of 2d ed. Chicago: University of Chicago Press, 1971.

EHREN Ralph E. Ehrenberg. *Archives and Manuscripts: Maps and Architectural Drawings*. Chicago: Society of American Archivists, 1982.

EISLER Colin T. Eisler. *The Seeing Hand*. New York: Harper & Row Publishers, 1975.

EISS Amy Lucas, ed. *Encyclopedia of Information Systems and Services*. 9th ed. Detroit: Gale Research Co., 1989.

EIT Manly Banister. *Etching and Other Intaglio Techniques*. New York: Sterling Publishing Co., 1969.

EJ Cecil Roth and Geoffrey Wigoder, eds. *Encyclopaedia Judaica*. Jerusalem: Keter Publishing House. New York: Macmillan Publishing Co., 1971-72.

EJM Edward J. Muller. *Reading Architectural Working Drawings*. 2d ed. Englewood Cliffs, N.J.: Prentice Hall, 1981.

EJTOWN Emrys Jones. *Towns and Cities*. New York: Oxford University Press, 1966.

ELIAS Thomas S. Elias. *The Complete Trees of North America*. New York: Van Nostrand Reinhold, 1980.

ELITE *Furniture Originations*. Furniture catalog. Jamestown, N.Y., 1939-1940.

ELSDLS W. E. Clason, comp. *Elsevier's Dictionary of Library Science, Information, and Documentation*. New York: Elsevier Science Publishing Co., 1976.

ELSEN Albert Elsen. *Purposes of Art*. New York: Holt, Rinehart & Winston, 1972.

ELSEVI C. J. van Mansum, ed. *Elsevier's Dictionary of Building Construction*. Amsterdam: Elsevier Science Publishing Co., 1959.

ELSLAT *Elsevier's Lexicon of Archive Terminology*. Amsterdam: Elsevier Science Publishing Co., 1964.

EMA John Beckwith. *Early Medieval Art*. New York: Praeger Publishers, 1964.

EMBURY Aymar Embury. *Roofs: The Varieties Commonly Used in the Architecture of the American Colonies*. Monograph Series, Vol. 18, No. 1. New York: Pencil Points, 1932.

EMCL Harold D. Eberlein and Abbott McClure. *The Practical Book of Period Furniture*. Philadelphia: J. B. Lippincott Co., 1914.

EMERY Irene Emery. *The Primary Structures of Fabrics: An Illustrated Classification*. Washington, D.C.: Textile Museum, 1980.

EMILLS Edward D. Mills, ed. *Planning: Buildings for Education, Culture, and Science*. London: Newnes-Butterworths, 1976.

EMVILL Kent V. Flannery, ed. *The Early Mesoamerican Village*. New York: Academic Press, 1976.

ENCASS *Encyclopedia of Associations*. Detroit: Gale Research Co., 1988.

ENCDA Philippe Garner, ed. *The Encyclopedia of Decorative Arts, 1890-1940*. New York: Galahad Books, 1978.

ENCREL Mircea Eliade, ed. *Encyclopedia of Religion*. New York: Macmillan Publishing Co., 1987.

ENCYAM *The Encyclopedia Americana*. Danbury, Conn.: Grolier, 1985.

ENCYB *Encyclopaedia Britannica*. Chicago: Encyclopaedia Britannica, 1973.

ENCYHO Thomas H. Everett, ed. *The New York Botanical Gardens Illustrated Encyclopedia of Horticulture*. New York: Garland Publishing, 1980.

ENCYUP Arnold Whittick, ed. *Encyclopedia of Urban Planning*. New York: McGraw-Hill Book Co., 1974.

ENGCH John Gloag. *The Englishman's Chair: Origins, Design, and Social History of Seating Furniture in England*. London: Allen & Unwin Publishers, 1964.

ENGEL David H. Engel. *Creating a Chinese Garden*. Portland, Oreg.: Timber Press, 1986.

ENK W. A. McEwen and A. H. Lewis. *Encyclopedia of Nautical Knowledge*. Cambridge, Md.: Cornell Maritime, 1950s.

ENRGYE *Energy Engineering*. Atlanta: Association of Energy Engineers, 1904-.

ENVHBK Robert W. Burchell. *The Environmental Impact Handbook*. New Brunswick, N.J.: Rutgers University Press, 1975.

ENVRSK Richard E. Conway, ed. *Environmental Risk Analysis for Chemicals*. New York: Van Nostrand Reinhold, 1982.

ENVTEC Charles N. Ehler. *Environmental Impacts of New Technology: An Annotated Bibliography*. Ann Arbor: University of Michigan Press, 1969.

ENVWAT Larry Canter. *Environmental Impact of Water Resources Projects*. Chelsea, Mich.: Lewis Publishers, 1985.

EOT American Fabrics Magazine. *Encyclopedia of Textiles*. Englewood Cliffs, N.J.: Prentice Hall, 1972.

EPHEM *Ephemera News*. Peterborough, N.H.: Ephemera Society of America, 1981-.

EPST Robert Meyers, ed. *Encyclopedia of Physical Science and Technology*. Orlando, Fla.: Academic Press, 1987.

ERIC *Thesaurus of ERIC Descriptors*. 9th ed. Phoenix, Ariz.: Oryx Press, 1982.

ERIK Svend Eriksen. *Early Neo-Classicism in France*. Translated by Peter Thornton. London: Faber & Faber, 1974.

ERIKSN Aase Erikson. *Playground Design*. New York: Van Nostrand Reinhold, 1985.

ESPEC H. Griffith Edwards. *Specifications*. 2d ed. New York: Van Nostrand Reinhold, 1961.

ESPISA Instrument Society of America. *Electrical Safety Practices*. Pittsburgh: Instrument Society of America, 1972.

ESTCON Albert D. Parker, Donald S. Barrie, and Robert M. Snyder. *Planning and Estimating Heavy Construction*. New York: McGraw-Hill Book Co., 1984.

ETHGEN Jessie C. Smith, ed. *Ethnic Genealogy: A Research Guide*. Westport, Conn.: Greenwood Press, 1983.

EVANS Nancy G. Evans. "American Windsor Furniture." Unpublished manuscript. 1989.

EVP Joan Evans. *Pattern: A Study of Ornament in Western Europe from 1180-1900*. Oxford: Clarendon Press, 1931.

EW Ernest R. Wiedhass. *Architectural Drafting and Design*. 5th ed. Boston: Allyn & Bacon, 1981.

EWA *Encyclopedia of World Art*. New York: McGraw-Hill Book Co., 1961.

EYPK *Introduction to Building Plans and Working Drawings and How to Read Them*. New York: F. W. Dodge Div., McGraw-Hill Information Systems, 1981.

F Thomas E. French and Charles Vierck. *Engineering Drawing and Graphic Technology*. 12th ed. New York: McGraw-Hill Book Co., 1978.

F&F Karl G. P. Hulton. *Futurism and Futurisms*. New York: Abbeville Press, 1986.

F&P Frost & Petersen. *1887 Illustrated Catalogue*. Furniture catalog. New York: Frost & Petersen, 1887.

FAAI Laurence Urdang and Frank R. Abate, eds. *Fine and Applied Arts Index*. Detroit: Gale Research Co., 1983.

FACBWE Linda C. Franklin. *Antiques and Collectibles: A Bibliography of Works in English, Sixteenth Century to 1976*. Methuchen, N.J: Scarecrow Press, 1978.

FAEGRE Torvald Faegre. *Tents: Architecture of the Nomads*. New York: Anchor Books, 1979.

FAIRB Jonathan Fairbanks and Elizabeth Bates. *American Furniture: 1620 to the Present*. New York: Marek Press, 1981.

FALES Dean A. Fales, Jr. *American Painted Furniture, 1660-1880*. New York: E. P. Dutton, 1972.

FAMP75 Paul Cummings. *Fine Arts Market Place: 1975-1976 Edition*. New York: R. R. Bowker Co., 1975.

FARNH Alexander Farnham. *Tool Collectors' Handbook of Prices Paid at Auction for Early American Tools*. [Stockton, N.J.], ca. 1970.

FASH85 American Society of Heating, Refrigeration, and Air Conditioning Engineers. *ASHRAE Handbook: Fundamentals*. Atlanta: American Society of Heating, Refrigeration, and Air Conditioning Engineers, 1985.

FASTN Ralph Fastnedge. *Sheraton Furniture*. London: Faber & Faber, 1962.

FDM *Facilities Design and Management*. New York: Gralla Publications, 1982-.

FEHER Geza Fehervari. *Islamic Pottery: A Comprehensive Study Based on the Barlow Collection*. London: Faber & Faber, 1973.

FEHR Cherie Fehrman and Kenneth Fehrman. *Postwar Interior Design, 1945-1960*. New York: Van Nostrand Reinhold, 1987.

FELLER Robert Feller, ed. *Artists' Pigments: A Handbook of Their History and Characteristics*. Cambridge: Cambridge University Press, 1986.

FENA S. David Freeman. *Energy: The New Era*. New York: Walker & Co., 1974.

FENHOG Carol H. Fenichel and Thomas H. Hogan. *Online Searching: A Primer*. 2d ed. Medford, N.J.: Learned Information, 1984.

FF Talbot Hamlin. *Forms and Functions of Twentieth Century Architecture*. 4 vols. New York: Columbia University Press, 1952.

FFF Arts Council of Great Britain. *Frescos from Florence*. London: Arts Council of Great Britain, 1969.

FFG-DO Elisabeth B. MacDougall and F. Hamilton Hazlehurst, eds. *The French Formal Gardens*. Washington, D.C.: Dumbarton Oaks, 1974.

FGAH Virginia McAllister and Lee McAllister. *A Field Guide to American Houses*. New York: Alfred A. Knopf, 1984.

FGN Brian Fagan. *People of the Earth: An Introduction to World Prehistory*. 4th ed. Boston: Little, Brown & Co., 1983.

FHCMO Joseph P. Frein, ed. *Handbook of Construction Management and Organization*. New York: Van Nostrand Reinhold, 1980.

FHSJ *Furniture History*. London: Furniture History Society, Victoria and Albert Museum, 1965-.

FIBERR Milwaukee Art Museum and University Art Museum, University of Wisconsin. *Fiber R/Evolution: John Porter Retzer and Florence Horn Retzer Exhibition*. Milwaukee: University of Wisconsin, 1986.

FIBERW Cleveland Museum of Art. *Fiberworks: 15 October-20 November, 1977*. Cleveland: Cleveland Museum of Art, 1977.

FIEDEL Stuart J. Fiedel. *Prehistory of the Americas*. Cambridge: Cambridge University Press, 1987.

FITCH James M. Fitch. *Historic Preservation*. New York: McGraw-Hill Book Co., 1982.

FLAMAR Kent V. Flannery and Joyce Marcus. *Evolution of the Public Building in Formative Oaxaca*. New York: Academic Press, 1976.

FLETCH Sir Banister Fletcher. *History of Architecture*. 18th ed. New York: Charles Scribner's Sons, 1975.

FOCAL *Focal Encyclopedia of Photography*. New York: Focal Press, 1965.

FOFDA Ruth D. Whitehouse, ed. *The Facts on File Dictionary of Archaeology*. New York: Facts on File, 1983.

FOFDMC Anthony Chander. *Facts on File Dictionary of Microcomputers*. New York: Facts on File, 1981.

FOFVD Jean-Claude Corbeil. *The Facts on File Visual Dictionary*. New York: Facts on File, 1986.

FOGG Fogg Museum. "Photograph and Slide Classification for Western Art." Revised. Fine Arts Library, Harvard University. 1973.

FOLKEU Jane Kallir. *The Folk Art Tradition: Naive Painting in Europe and the United States*. New York: Viking Press, 1981.

FOLKGL Alexandra de Lallier. "A Basic Glossary of American Folk Art Terms." Museum of Folk Art, New York. 1983.

FONG Wen Fong. *The Great Bronze Age of China: An Exhibition from the People's Republic of China*. New York: Metropolitan Museum of Art and Alfred A. Knopf, 1980.

FORCIT Forest City Furniture Co. *Forest City Furniture Company*. Rockford, Ill.: Forest City Furniture Co., 1891.

FORMAN Benno M. Forman. *American Seating Furniture, 1630-1730: An Interpretive Catalogue*. New York: W. W. Norton & Co., 1987.

FOSKET A. C. Foskett. *The Subject Approach to Information*. 4th ed. London: Clive Bingley, 1982.

FOSTER William A. Foster and Deane G. Carter. *Farm Buildings*. New York: John Wiley & Sons, 1922.

FOURN Robert Fournier. *Illustrated Dictionary of Practical Pottery*. New York: Van Nostrand Reinhold, 1973.

FPG Thomas Frejka. *The Future of Population Growth*. New York: John Wiley & Sons, 1973.

FRANKL Bud Frankel and H. W. Phillips. *Your Advertising's Great... How's Business?: The Revolution in Sales Promotion*. Homewood, Ill.: Dow Jones-Irwin, 1986.

FRASER Douglas Fraser. *Village Planning in the Primitive World*. New York: George Braziller, 1968.

FRESCO Gardner Hale. *The Technique of Fresco Painting*. New York: Dover Publications, 1966.

FREWAY Lawrence Halprin. *Freeways*. New York: Reinhold Publishing Co., 1966.

FRKFRT Henri Frankfort. *The Art and Architecture of the Ancient Orient*. 4th rev. ed. Harmondsworth, England: Penguin Books, 1970.

FURN2 William C. Ketchum. *Furniture Two: Neoclassic to the Present*. New York: Cooper-Hewitt Museum, 1981.

FV Thomas E. French and Charles J. Vierck. *Engineering Drawing: Manual for Students and Draftsmen*. New York: McGraw-Hill Book Co., 1947.

G&EP Tony Spiteris. *Greek and Etruscan Painting*. Translated by Janet Sondheimer. New York: Funk & Wagnalls Co., 1965.

GA Rudolph Huber and Renate Rieth, eds. *Glossarium Artis*. 9 vols. Vols. 1 and 8: Tübingen, West Germany: Max Niemeyer Verlag, Vols. 2-7 and 9: Munich: K. G. Saur, 1977-87.

GABKT Alexander B. Griswald, Chewon Kim, and Peter H. Pott. *Art of Burma, Korea, and Tibet*. New York: Crown Publishers, 1964.

GAE George A. Stevenson, ed. *Graphic Arts Encyclopedia*. New York: McGraw-Hill Book Co., 1968.

GAHLM Edwin A. Thompson, comp. "A Glossary of American Historical and Literary Manuscript Terms." Washington, D.C., 1965.

GALAW *The Guide to American Law: Everyone's Legal Encyclopedia*. 12 vols. St. Paul, Minn.: West Publishing Co., 1983.

GARD Horst de La Croix and Richard G. Tansey. *Gardner's Art through the Ages*. 7th ed. New York: Harcourt Brace Jovanovich, 1980.

GARD86 Horst de La Croix and Richard G. Tansey. *Gardner's Art through the Ages*. 8th ed. New York: Harcourt Brace Jovanovich, 1986.

GARNER H. F. Garner. *The Origin of Landscapes: A Synthesis of Geomorphology*. New York: Oxford University Press, 1974.

GASCO Bamber Gascoigne. *How to Identify Prints: A Complete Guide to Manual and Mechanical Processes from Woodcut to Ink Jet*. New York: Thames & Hudson, 1986.

GBPP Basil Gray. *Persian Painting*. New York: Skira, 1961.

GC George R. Collins. *Visionary Drawings of Architecture and Planning: Twentieth Century through the 1960s*. Cambridge: Massachusetts Institute of Technology Press, 1979.

GCIT American Institute of Architects. *Glossary of Construction Industry Terms*. Washington, D.C.: American Institute of Architects, 1982.

GCK James Graham-Campbell and Dafydd Kidd. *The Vikings*. London: British Museum, 1980.

GCSIP Ernst J. Grube. *Classical Style in Islamic Painting: The Early School of Herat and Its Impact on Islamic Painting of the Later Fifteenth, the Sixteenth, and Seventeenth Centuries*. Edizioni Oriens, 1968.

GCT Federation of Societies for Coating Technology. *Glossary of Color Terms*. Philadelphia: Federation of Societies for Coating Technology, 1981.

GEIP Ernst J. Grube. *Islamic Pottery of the Eighth to Fifteenth Century in the Keir Collection*. London: Faber & Faber, 1976.

GENTHF Society of Upholsterers, Cabinetmakers, etc. *Genteel Household Furniture in the Present Taste*. Reprint. West Yorkshire, England: E. P. Publishing, 1978.

GEO&M *Geoscience and Man*. Dallas: American Association of Stratigraphic Palynologists Foundation, 1977-.

GEOLEE George N. Lee. *Mouldings, Mirrors, Pictures, and Frames*. Chicago: Colbert & Co., 1883.

GERE J. A. Gere. *Drawings by Raphael and His Circle*. New York: Pierpont Morgan Library, 1987.

GERFOC Helmut Gernsheim. *Focus on Architecture and Sculpture: An Original Approach to the Photography of Architecture and Sculpture*. London: Fountain Press, 1949.

GERN Helmut Gernsheim. *The History of Photography*. New York: McGraw-Hill Book Co., 1969.

GETA Nelson H. H. Graburn, ed. *Ethnic and Tourist Arts: Cultural Expressions from the Fourth World*. Berkeley and Los Angeles: University of California Press, 1976.

GETTEN Rutherford Gettens and George Stout. *Painting Materials: A Short Encyclopedia*. New York: Van Nostrand Reinhold, 1942.

GETTIN Frank Gettings. *Drawings*. Washington, D.C.: Smithsonian Institution Press, 1984.

GETZ Lowell Getz and Frank Stasiowski. *Financial Management for the Design Professional*. New York: Whitney Library of Design, 1984.

GEWARD Gerald W. R. Ward. *American Case Furniture in The Mabel Brady Garvan and Other Collections at Yale University*. New Haven, Conn.: Yale University Art Gallery, 1987.

GFIA Oleg Grabar. *Formation of Islamic Art*. rev. ed. New Haven, Conn.: Yale University Press, 1987.

GGCA U.S. Copyright Office. *General Guide to the Copyright Act of 1976*. Washington, D.C.: Library of Congress, 1977.

GGHOA Godfrey Goodwin. *History of Ottoman Architecture*. Baltimore, Md.: Johns Hopkins University Press, 1971.

GGT Sir Dudley Stamp and Audrey N. Clark. *Glossary of Geographical Terms*. London: Longman, 1979.

GHOMCL Auijit Ghosh and Sara L. McLafferty. *Location Strategies for Retail and Service Firms*. Lexington, Mass.: Lexington Books, 1987.

GIBBON Guy E. Gibbon. *Anthropological Archaeology*. New York: Columbia University Press, 1984.

GICAM Bernard P. Groslier. *Indo-China: Art in the Melting-Pot of Races*. London: Methuen & Co., 1962.

GIESEC Frederick E. Giesecke, Alva Mitchell, and Henry C. Spenser. *Technical Drawing*. New York: Macmillan Publishing Co., 1937.

GILBOR Craig Gilborn. *Adirondack Furniture and the Rustic Tradition*. New York: Harry N. Abrams, 1987.

GILBR1 Christopher Gilbert. *The Life and Work of Thomas Chippendale*. 2 vols. New York: Macmillan Publishing Co., 1978.

GILBR2 Christopher Gilbert. *Furniture at Temple Newsam House and Lutherton Hall*. Leeds, England: National Art Collection Fund and Leeds Art Collection Fund, 1978.

GILL Werner Gillon. *Collecting African Art*. New York: Rizzoli International Publications, 1979.

GILLT A. S. Gillette and J. Michael Gillette. *Stage Scenery: Its Construction and Rigging*. 3d ed. New York: Harper & Row Publishers, 1981.

GIRCIT Mark Girouard. *Cities and People*. New Haven, Conn.: Yale University Press, 1985.

GJF Gordon J. Fielding. *Managing Public Transit Strategically*. San Francisco: Jossey-Bass, 1987.

GJOC Hazel H. Gorham. *Japanese and Oriental Ceramics*. Rutland, Vt.: Charles E. Tuttle Co., 1971.

GKA Peter Garlake. *Kingdoms of Africa*. Oxford: Elsevier-Phaidon, 1978.

GL *Grand Larousse de la langue française*. 6 vols. Paris: Libraire Larousse, 1972.

GLAIST Geoffrey A. Glaister. *Glaister's Glossary of the Book*. 2d ed. Berkeley and Los Angeles: University of California Press, 1979.

GLANZ V. M. Glanzman. *Bibliography of Reports by U.S. Geological Survey Personnel on Studies of Underground Nuclear Test Sites and on Waste Management Studies at the Nevada Test Site and the Waste Isolation Pilot Plant Site, New Mexico, January 1, 1983-December 31, 1984*. Denver, Colo.: U.S. Department of the Interior, Geological Survey, 1985.

GLASF Alexander L. Glasfurd. *Siena and the Hill Towns*. London: E. Benn, 1962.

GLOAG John Gloag. *A Short Dictionary of Furniture*. New York: Holt, Rinehart & Winston, 1965.

GMBSO E. H. Gombrich. *Sense of Order: A Study in the Psychology of Decorative Arts*. Ithaca, N.Y.: Cornell University Press, 1979.

GMF John M. Robinson. *Georgian Model Farms: A Study of Decorative and Model Farm Buildings in the Age of Improvement, 1700-1846*. Oxford: Clarendon Press, 1983.

GMGPC Helena Zinkham and Elisabeth B. Parker. *Descriptive Terms for Graphic Materials: Genre and Physical Characteristic Headings*. Washington, D.C.: Library of Congress, 1986.

GN David Gebhard and Deborah Nevins. *Two Hundred Years of American Architectural Drawing*. New York: Watson-Guptill Publications, 1977.

GOELLR Carl Goeller. *Writing and Selling Greeting Cards*. Boston: The Writer, 1980.

GOG Margaret Gary, Robert H. McAfee, and Carol L. Wolf, eds. *Glossary of Geology*. Washington, D.C.: American Geological Institute, 1972.

GOLDST Nathan Goldstein. *The Art of Responsive Drawing*. Englewood Cliffs, N.J.: Prentice Hall, 1984.

GOODAD Goodad Co. *White Mountain Hammock Chair*. Andrim, N.H.: Goodad Co., ca. 1882.

GOTHIC Paul Frankl. *Gothic Architecture*. Baltimore, Md.: Penguin Books, 1962.

GOTTS Mark D. Gottsegen. *Manual of Painting Materials and Techniques*. New York: Harper & Row Publishers, 1987.

GOVSPT Arthur T. Johnson and James H. Frey, eds. *Government and Sport: The Public Policy Issues*. Totowa, N.J.: Rowman & Allanheld, 1985.

GPM George P. Merrill. *Stones for Building and Decoration*. New York: John Wiley & Sons, 1891.

GRAAI Roman Ghirshman. *Arts of Ancient Iran: From Its Origins to the Time of Alexander the Great*. New York: Golden Press, 1964.

GRAB Andre Grabar and Carl Nordenfalk. *Early Medieval Painting from the Fourth to the Eleventh Century*. Lausanne, Switzerland: Skira, 1957.

GRACY David B. Gracy. *Archives and Manuscripts: Arrangement and Description*. Chicago: Society of American Archivists, 1977.

GRANDJ Serge Grandjean. *Empire Furniture, 1800-1825*. London: Faber & Faber, 1966.

GRAVES H. B. Graves Co., *Suggestions for the Home*. Rochester, N.Y.: H. B. Graves Co., ca. 1915.

GRCA Deborah F. Jewett. *A Glossary for Recording the Condition of an Artifact*. Ottawa: Canadian Heritage Information Network, 1980s.

CRCAT6 Grand Rapids Bookcase & Chair Co. *Catalogue No. 6*. Furniture catalog. Hastings, Mich.: Grands Rapids Bookcase & Chair Co., 1911.

GREGOR Ruth Gregory, ed. *Anniversaries and Holidays*. Chicago: American Library Association, 1983.

GRIMMR Anne E. Grimmer. *Glossary of Historic Masonry Deterioration Problems and Preservation Treatments*. Washington, D.C.: Government Printing Office, 1984.

GRIPS Roman Ghirshman. *Iran: Parthians and Sassanians*. London: Thames & Hudson, 1962.

GRKART John Boardman. *Greek Art*. rev. ed. New York: Praeger Publishers, 1973.

GRLIFU Grand Rapids Bookcase & Chair Co. *Lifetime Furniture*. Grands Rapids, Mich.: Grand Rapids Bookcase & Chair Co., 1910.

GROER Leon de Groer. *Decorative Arts in Europe, 1790-1850*. New York: Rizzoli International Publications, 1986.

GROS Grosfeld House. Furniture catalogs. Chicago: Grosfeld House, 1930s.

GROS31 Albert Grosfeld. *Fine Furniture Catalog*. New York: Albert Grosfeld, 1931.

GROS35 Grosfeld House. *Manufacturers of Fine Furniture*. Chicago: Grosfeld House, ca. 1935.

GROSCH Audrey N. Grosch. *Distributed Computing and the Electronic Library: Micros to Superminis*. White Plains, N.Y.: Knowledge Industry Publications, 1985.

GROVE Stanley Sadie. *New Grove Dictionary of Music and Musicians*. 20 vols. London: Macmillan Publishing Co., 1980.

GRUBE Oswald W. Grube. *Industrial Buildings and Factories*. New York: Praeger Publishers, 1971.

GRUWOR Ernst J. Grube. *World of Islam*. New York: McGraw-Hill Book Co., 1967.

GRYAZ Mikhail P. Gryaznov. *Ancient Civilization of Southern Siberia*. New York: Cowles Book Co., 1969.

GSCMUG George Smith. *Cabinet-Maker and Upholsterer's Guide*. London: Jones & Co., 1826.

GSDHF George Smith. *Collection of Designs for Household Furniture and Interior Decoration*. Reprint. Edited by Charles T. Montgomery and Benno M. Forman. New York: Praeger Publishers, 1970.

GTOWNS James E. Sherman and Barbara H. Sherman. *Ghost Towns and Mining Camps of New Mexico*. Norman: University of Oklahoma Press, 1977.

GTTC National Committee for Geography, London. *Glossary of Technical Terms in Cartography*. London: Royal Society, 1966.

GUIART Jean Guiart. *Arts of Mankind*. Vol. 4, *Arts of the South Pacific*. Translated by Anthony Christie. London: Thames & Hudson, 1963.

GUIDON Enrico Guidoni. *Primitive Architecture*. New York: Harry N. Abrams, 1978.

GUSMR U.S. Department of Commerce. *Guide to U.S. Government Information in Machine-Readable Form*. Washington, D.C.: U.S. Department of Commerce, 1988.

GUTKND E. A. Gutkind. *International History of City Development*. 8 vols. New York: Free Press, 1964-72.

GWILT Joseph Gwilt. *Encyclopedia of Architecture: Historical, Theoretical, and Practical*. London: Longmans, Green & Co., 1888.

GWM Jennifer Tann. *Gloucestershire Woolen Mills*. Newton Abbot, England: David & Charles, 1967.

GZMHO Richard Glazier. *Manual of Historic Ornament*. 5th ed. London: B. T. Batsford, 1933.

HAAIS James C. Harle. *Art and Architecture of the Indian Subcontinent*. Harmondsworth, England: Penguin Books, 1986.

HABERK C. H. Haberkorn & Co. *High Grade Table and Furniture Novelties Catalogue No. 72*. C. H. Haberkorn & Co., ca. 1925.

HABS Alicia Stamm and C. Ford Peatross. *Historic America: Buildings, Structures, and Sites*. Washington, D.C.: Library of Congress, 1983.

HAFTM Werner Haftmann. *Painting in the Twentieth Century*. 2 vols. New York: Praeger Publishers, 1965.

HAIST Grant Haist. *Modern Photographic Processing*. New York: John Wiley & Sons, 1979.

HAM Thomas Hickerson. *Archives and Manuscripts: An Introduction to Automated Access*. Chicago: Society of American Archivists, 1981.

HAMILT George H. Hamilton. *Painting and Sculpture in Europe: 1880-1940*. Harmondsworth, England: Penguin Books, 1984.

HANA Wolfgang Haberland. *The Art of North America*. New York: Crown Publishers, 1964.

HAND The Diagram Group and Ruth Midgley, eds. *Handtools of Arts and Crafts: The Encyclopedia of the Fine, Decorative, and Applied Arts*. New York: St. Martin's Press, 1981.

HANDY *Family Handyman*. Minneapolis, Minn.: Home Service Publications, 1951-.

HANSON A. C. Hanson & Co. *Furniture Catalogue*. Racine, Wis.: A. C. Hanson & Co., 1907.

HARCAN Robert Harris. *Canals and Their Architecture*. New York: Praeger Publishers, 1969.

HARTMR Hartmeier & Sons. *Children's Chairs, Rockers, Etc.* Paterson, N.J.: Hartmeier & Sons, ca. 1900.

HAS Cyril M. Harris, *Historic Architecture Sourcebook*. New York: McGraw-Hill Book Co., 1977.

HAUF Harold D. Hauf. *Building Contracts for Design and Construction*. New York: John Wiley & Sons, 1968.

HAYKIR Helena Hayward and Patricia Kirkham. *William and John Linnell: Eighteenth-Century London Furniture Makers*. 2 vols. London: Studio Vista, Christie's, 1980.

HAYWAR Helena Hayward, ed. *World Furniture*. New York: McGraw-Hill Book Co., 1965.

HBEAUT *House Beautiful*. New York: Hearst Magazines, 1896-.

HCAC William B. Honey. *Ceramic Art of China and Other Countries of the Far East*. New York: Beechhurst Press, 1954.

HCAGE Norman Johnston. *The Human Cage: A Brief History of Prison Architecture*. New York: Walker & Co., 1973.

HCDM Michael Randel, ed. *Harvard Concise Dictionary of Music*. Cambridge, Mass.: Belknap Press, 1978.

HCIP R. C. Majumdar, ed. *History and Culture of the Indian People*. No. 3, *The Classical Age*. Bombay, India: Bharatiya Vidya Bhavan, 1954.

HCOP Margaret Haller. *Collecting Old Photographs*. New York: Arco Publishing, 1978.

HEALS *Furniture of the Middle Class*. Reprint. London: Heals & Co., 1972.

HECFS The Hydrologic Engineering Center and The Institute for Water Resources, U.S. Army Corps of Engineers. *Feasibility Studies for Small Scale Hydropower Additions: A Guide Manual*. Davis, Calif.: Hydrologic Engineering Center, 1979.

HEIDER Karl G. Heider. *The Dugum Dani: Papuan Culture in the Highlands of West New Guinea*. Chicago: Aldine Publishing Co., 1970.

HELDPR Julius Held. *The Oil Sketches of Peter Paul Rubens: A Critical Catalogue*. Washington, D.C.: National Gallery of Art, 1980.

HELLER Julius Heller. *Papermaking: The White Art*. Scottsdale, Ariz.: Scorpio Press, 1980.

HEMPEL Eberhard Hempel. *Baroque Art and Architecture in Central Europe*. Harmondsworth, England: Penguin Books, 1965.

HENSHW George Henshaw & Sons. *All Kinds of Chairs*. Cincinnati: George Henshaw & Sons, 1885.

HEPP William B. Honey. *English Pottery and Porcelain*. London: A. & C. Black, 1933.

HEPPLE George Hepplewhite. *Cabinet-Maker and Upholsterer's Guide*. Reprint. Dover Publications, 1969.

HERVEY W. H. Hervey & Co. *Condensed Price List of House Furnishings Goods*. Boston: W. H. Hervey & Co., 1898.

HESS Thomas B. Hess and John Ashbery, eds. *Painterly Painting*. New York: Macmillan Publishing Co., 1971.

HEYD Heywood Brothers & Wakefield Co. Furniture catalogs. Gardner, Mass.: Heywood Brothers & Wakefield Co.

HEYD20 Heywood Brothers & Wakefield Co. *Catalogue No. 8*. Furniture catalog. Gardner, Mass.: Heywood Brothers & Wakefield Co., ca. 1920.

HEYD38 Heywood Brothers & Wakefield Co. *Summer Furniture*. Gardner, Mass.: Heywood Brothers & Wakefield Co., 1938.

HFE *Harrap's New College French and English Dictionary*. Lincolnwood, Ill.: National Textbook Co., 1982.

HGA Marie L. Gothein. *A History of Garden Art*. Reprint. New York: Hacker Art Books, 1979.

HGMBLC H. Hagiwara and D. J. Green. *Mechanical Behavior of Lightweight Cellular Ceramics*. Essex, England: Elsevier Science Publishers, 1988.

HHR James F. O'Gorman. *Henry Hobson Richardson and His Office: Selected Drawings*. Boston: David R. Godine Publishing, 1974.

HIA John D. Hoag. *Islamic Architecture*. New York: Harry N. Abrams, 1975.

HIDENS Rolf Jensen. *High Density Living*. New York: Praeger Publishers, 1966.

HIGGNS Reynold Higgins. *Minoan and Mycenaean Art*. New York: Praeger Publishers, 1974.

HIMME Georg Himmelheber. *Biedermeier Furniture*. Translated and edited by Simon Jervis. London: Faber & Faber, 1974.

HIND Arthur M. Hind. *The Processes and Schools of Engraving: A Guide*. London: British Museum, 1952.

HISNEW *History News*. Nashville Tenn.: American Association for State and Local History, 1940-.

HISS James E. Hiss. *Perspective: An Effective Design Tool*. Washington, D.C.: American Society of Landscape Architects, 1985.

HISTSO Donna McDonald, ed. *Dictionary of Historical Societies and Agencies in the United States and Canada*. 11th ed. Nashville, Tenn.: American Association for State and Local History, 1978.

HIXGHS John Hix. *The Glass House*. Cambridge: Massachusetts Institute of Technology Press, 1981.

HJA National Sheriffs' Association. *A Handbook on Jail Architecture*. Washington, D.C.: National Sheriffs' Association, 1975.

HMAI Robert Wauchope, ed. *Handbook of Middle American Indians*. 16 vols. Austin: University of Texas Press, 1964-76.

HMAIS1 Jeremy A. Sabloff, ed. *Supplement to the Handbook of Middle American Indians*. Vol. 1, *Archaeology*. Austin: University of Texas Press, 1981.

HMHO Alfred D. F. Hamlin. *History of Ornament*. New York: Cooper Square, 1973.

HNAI William C. Sturtevant, ed. *Handbook of North American Indians*. Washington, D.C.: Smithsonian Institution, 1984.

HOAD R. Bruce Hoadley. *Understanding Wood: A Craftsman's Guide to Wood Technology*. Newton, Conn.: The Tounton Press, 1980.

HOFGLS Georg Kohlmaier and Barna von Sartory. *Houses of Glass*. Translated by John C. Harvey. Cambridge: Massachusetts Institute of Technology Press, 1986.

HOGG Ian Hogg. *Fortress: A History of Military Defense*. New York: St. Martin's Press, 1977.

HOLHZR Frank Hole and Robert F. Heizer. *Prehistoric Archaeology: A Brief Introduction*. New York: Holt, Rinehart & Winston, 1977.

HOLMQ Wilhelm Holmquist. *Germanic Art During the First Millennium A.D.* Stockholm: Almquist & Wiksell, 1955.

HOPE Thomas Hope. *Household Furniture and Interior Decoration*. Reprint. London: Alec Tiranti, 1970.

HORA Bayard Hora. *The Oxford Encyclopedia of Trees of the World*. Oxford: Oxford University Press, 1981.

HORN Clarence P. Hornung. *Handbook of Designs and Devices*. New York: Dover Publications, 1946.

HORNB Caleb Hornbostel. *Construction Materials*. New York: John Wiley & Sons, 1978.

HORNOR William M. Hornor, Jr. *Blue Book of Philadelphia Furniture: William Penn to George Washington*. Washington, D.C.: Highland House Publishers, 1977.

HOWSON Henry F. Howson. *The Rapid Transit Railways of the World*. London: Allen & Unwin, 1971.

HPG Arnold L. Markowitz. *Art and Architecture Information Guide Series*. Vol. 13, *Historic Preservation: A Guide to Information Sources*. Detroit: Gale Research Co., 1980.

HPRES *Historic Preservation*. Washington, D.C.: National Trust for Historic Preservation, 1949-.

HRBAS Milos Hrbas and Edgar Knoblock. *Art of Central Asia*. London: Paul Hamlyn, 1965.

HRGAJ Rose Hempel. *Golden Age of Japan, 794-1192*. Translated by Katherine Watson. New York: Rizzoli International Publications, 1983.

HRH Henry R. Hitchcock. *Architecture: Nineteenth and Twentieth Centuries*. 4th ed. New York: Penguin Books, 1977.

HRH71 Henry R. Hitchcock. *Architecture: Nineteenth and Twentieth Centuries*. Harmondsworth, England. Penguin Books, 1971.

HRUSS George H. Hamilton. *The Art and Architecture of Russia*. 2d ed. Harmondsworth, England: Penguin Books, 1963.

HS Howard Saalman. *Medieval Cities*. New York: George Braziller, 1968.

HSAI Julian H. Steward, ed. *Handbook of South American Indians*. New York: Cooper Square, 1963.

HSJ *Heibonsha Survey of Japanese Art*. 31 vols. Tokyo: Heibonsha. New York: John Weatherhill, 1972-1980.

HSRBD Jon Geraint and Helen Heard, eds. *Handbook of Sports and Recreation Building Design*. London: Architectural Press, 1981.

HT Joan Kron and Suzanne Slesin. *High-Tech: The Industrial Style and Sourcebook for the Home*. New York: Clarkson N. Potter Books, 1978.

HTOWNS Egerton R. Williams. *Hill Towns of Italy*. Boston: Houghton Mifflin Co., 1903.

HTSC Tom Harrisson. *Savage Civilization*. New York: Alfred A. Knopf, 1937.

HUBERT Jean Hubert, Jean Porcher, and W. F. Volbach. *Europe of the Invasions*. New York: George Braziller, 1969.

HUD HUD USER, comp. *HUD Research Thesaurus*. Germantown, Md.: U.S. Department of Housing and Urban Development, 1980.

HUD-AH HUD USER. *Affordable Housing*. Germantown, Md.: U.S. Department of Housing and Urban Development, 1982.

HUMMEL Charles F. Hummel. *With Hammer in Hand: The Dominy Craftsmen of East Hampton, New York*. Charlottesville: University Press of Virginia, 1968.

HUNT George L. Hunter. *Italian Furniture and Interiors*. 2 vols. New York: W. Helburn, 1918.

HUNTED V. Daniel Hunt. *Energy Dictionary*. New York: Van Nostrand Reinhold, 1979.

HUNTER Dard Hunter. *Papermaking: The History and Technique of an Ancient Craft*. New York: Alfred A. Knopf, 1947.

HUNZ George Hunzinger and Son. Furniture catalog. New York: George Hunzinger and Son, ca. 1915.

HUTTER Herbert Hutter. *Drawing: History and Technique*. London: Thames & Hudson, 1968.

HWA David Watkin. *A History of Western Architecture*. London: Thames & Hudson, 1986.

HWP Henry W. Pullen. *Handbook of Ancient Roman Marbles*. London: J. Murray, 1894.

IAA John J.-G. Blumenson. *Identifying American Architecture*. 2d ed. New York: W. W. Norton & Co., 1981.

IAB Edgar Jones. *Industrial Architecture in Britain: 1750-1939*. London: B. T. Batsford, 1985.

IAF Milo M. Naeve. *Identifying American Furniture: A Pictorial Gude to Styles and Terms, Colonial to Contemporary*. Nashville, Tenn.: American Association for State and Local History, 1982.

IAF2 Milo M. Naeve. *Identifying American Furniture: A Pictorial Guide to Styles and Terms, Colonial to Contemporary*. 2d ed. Nashville, Tenn.: American Association for State and Local History, 1989.

IAIAA *African Abstracts*. London: International African Institute, 1950-1972.

IB Louis G. Redstone. *Institutional Buildings: Architecture of the Controlled Environment*. New York: McGraw-Hill Book Co., 1980.

IBOW *The International Book of Wood*. London: Mitchell Beazley Publishers, 1976.

ICA Frank B. Evans, Francois J. Himley, and Peter Walne, eds. and comps. *ICA Handbook Series*. Vol. 3, *Dictionary of Archival Terminology: English and French, with Equivalents in Dutch, German, Italian, Russian, and Spanish*. New York: K. G. Saur, 1984.

ICAMN *ICAM News*. Montreal: International Confederation of Architectural Museums, 1980-.

ICCRSP International Centre for the Study of the Preservation and the Restoration of Cultural Property. ICCROM geographic name authority files (subject headings). Document prepared for internal distribution. Rome, Italy.

ICEPAL Fred Anderes and Ann Agranoff. *Ice Palaces*. New York: Abbeville Press, 1983.

ICOMN *ICOM NEWS*. Paris: International Council of Museums, 1948-.

ICON H. van de Waal. *ICONCLASS: An Iconographic Classification System*. 17 vols. Amsterdam: North-Holland Publishing Co., 1975.

ICPEP *International Center of Photography Encyclopedia of Photography.* New York: Crown Publishers, 1984.

IDEA Veronica B. Smith. *International Directory of Exhibiting Artists.* Vol. 2. Santa Barbara, Calif.: Clio Press, 1983.

IDO Dora Ware and Maureen Stafford. *Illustrated Dictionary of Ornament.* London: Allen & Unwin Publishers, 1974.

IDTL Joel Trapido, ed. *An International Dictionary of Theatre Language.* Westport, Conn.: Greenwood Press, 1985.

IFLA Ian Sheridan. *An Art Librarian's Glossary.* Bristol, England: International Federation of Library Associations, Section of Art Libraries, 1984.

IGA John Harris and Jill Lever. *Illustrated Glossary of Architecture, 850-1830.* New York: Clarkson N. Potter Books, 1966.

IHVA Roland W. Brunskill. *Illustrated Handbook of Vernacular Architecture.* London: Faber & Faber, 1978.

ILDIGL Harold Newman. *An Illustrated Dictionary of Glass.* London: Thames & Hudson, 1977.

ILLLIB *Illinois Libraries.* Springfield, Ill.: State Library, 1919-.

ILO International Labour Office. *International Standard Classification of Occupations.* rev. ed. Geneva: International Labour Office, 1969.

ILOTH International Labour Office. *ILO Thesaurus: Labour, Employment and Training Terminology.* 2d ed. Geneva: International Labour Office, 1978.

IMAP Kenneth L. Winch, ed. *International Maps and Atlases in Print.* 2d ed. New York: R. R. Bowker Co., 1976.

INCART International Cartographic Association, Commission II. *Multilingual Dictionary of Technical Terms in Cartography.* Wiesbaden, West Germany: Franz Steiner, 1973.

INCE William Ince and John Mayhew. *The Universal System of Household Furniture.* Reprint. London: Alec Tiranti, 1960.

INDARC John Winter. *Industrial Architecture: A Survey of Factory Building.* London: Studio Vista, 1970.

INFOD British Standards Institution. *Definitions of Construction Terms, 1984.* London: Infodoc Services, 1984.

INGLE Marjorie Ingle. *Mayan Revival Style: Art Deco Mayan Fantasy.* Layton, Utah: Gibbs Smith Publishing, 1984.

INNO David A. Hanks. *Innovative Furniture in America from 1800 to the Present.* New York: Horizon Press, 1981.

INOUE Mitsuo Inoue. *Space in Japanese Architecture.* Translated by Hiroshi Watanabe. New York: John Weatherhill, 1985.

INTDES *Interior Design.* New York: Cahners Publishing Society, 1932.-

INVASC National Museum of American Art. Inventory of Sculpture. "Media Thesaurus." Document prepared for internal distribution. Smithsonian Institution, Washington, D.C., 1980s.

INVEN Inventaire général des monuments et des richesses artistiques de la France. *Le Mobilier Domestique: Vocabularie Typologique.* Par Nicole de Reyniés. 2 vols. Paris: Imprimerie Nationale, 1987.

IRCD *International Research Centers Directory.* Detroit: Gale Research Co., 1982.

IRRD Organization for Economic Cooperation and Development. *International Road Research Documentation Thesaurus.* Paris: Organization for Economic Cooperation and Development, 1975.

IRRIG Theodore E. Downing and McGuire Gibson, eds. *Anthropological Papers of the University of Arizona.* No. 25, *Irrigation's Impact on Society.* Tucson: University of Arizona Press, 1974.

IRST Henry Irving and Edward F. Strange. *Flowers and Plants for Designers and Schools.* London: Hodder & Stoughton, 1907.

ISA Valerie Bradfield. *Information Sources in Architecture.* London: Butterworths, 1979.

ITHILL Norman F. Craver. *Italian Hilltowns.* Kalamazoo, Mich.: Documan Press, 1985.

ITREN Frederick Hartt. *History of Italian Renaissance Art: Painting, Sculpture, Architecture.* 2d ed. New York: Harry N. Abrams, 1979.

IVINS William M. Ivins, Jr. *Prints and Visual Communication.* Cambridge, Mass.: Harvard University Press, 1953.

IWP David R. Inglis. *Wind Power and Other Energy Options.* Ann Arbor: University of Michigan Press, 1980.

JACAES Lee A. Jacobus. *Aesthetics and the Arts.* New York: McGraw-Hill Book Co., 1968.

JAFH *Journal of African History.* New York: Cambridge University Press, 1960-.

JAHN Hugo Jahn. *Dictionary of Graphic Arts Terms.* Chicago: Committee on Education, United Typothetae of America, 1928.

JAKROS Jakob Rosenberg. *Great Draughtsmen.* Cambridge, Mass.: Harvard University Press, 1984.

JANA Jesse D. Jennings, ed. *Ancient Native Americans.* San Francisco: W. H. Freeman, 1978.

JANSON H. W. Janson. *History of Art.* 3d ed. New York: Harry N. Abrams, 1986.

JAO Jeannie Auboyer, Michel Beurdeley, Jean Boisselier, Huguette Rousset, and Chantal Massonaud. *Oriental Art: A Handbook of Styles and Forms.* New York: Rizzoli International Publications, 1980.

JAPA *American Planning Association Journal.* Chicago: American Planning Association, 1925-.

JBW-P J. B. Ward-Perkins. *Roman Imperial Architecture.* Harmondsworth, England: Penguin Books, 1985.

JCCOP Bernard E. Jones, ed. *Cassell's Cyclopedia of Photography.* London: Cassell & Co., 1911.

JCM James C. Morehead. *A Handbook of Perspective Drawing.* Jacksonville, Fla.: Drew, 1971.

JCWOOL John C. Wooley. *Farm Buildings.* New York: McGraw-Hill Book Co., 1946.

JCYU Jason C. Yu. *Transportation Engineering: Introduction to Planning, Design, and Operation.* New York: Elsevier Science Publishing Co., 1982.

JEFFER Louise Jefferson. *The Decorative Arts of Africa.* New York: Viking Press, 1973.

JENORB Jesse D. Jennings and Edward Norbeck, eds. *Prehistoric Man in the New World.* Chicago: University of Chicago Press, 1964.

JENSEN David E. Jensen. *Minerals of New York State.* Rochester, N.Y.: Ward Press, 1978.

JETTM Karl Jettmar. *Art of the Steppes.* New York: Crown Publishers, 1964.

JFINGN Jack Finegan. *Archaeological History of the Ancient Middle East.* Boulder, Colo.: Westview Press, 1979.

JFRIED Jurgen Friedrichs, ed. *Affordable Housing and the Homeless.* Berlin: De Gruyter, 1988.

JH John Harris and A. A. Tait. *Catalogue of the Drawings by Inigo Jones, John Webb, and Issac Decaus at Worcester College.* Oxford: Oxford University Press, 1979.

JIJAGL Ruth Jacoby and Rina Talgam. *Architectural Glossary.* Jerusalem: Centre for Jewish Art, Hebrew University, 1988.

JJC J. J. Coulton. *Ancient Greek Architects at Work: Problems of Structure and Design.* Ithaca, N.Y.: Cornell University Press, 1972.

JMAPCO Jimapco. List of maps published. Burnt Hills, N.Y.: Jimapco, 1980s.

JMRICH James M. Richards. *Introduction to Modern Architecture.* Harmondsworth, England: Penguin Books, 1948.

JO James F. O'Gorman. *Drawing Towards Building: Philadelphia Architectural Graphics, 1732-1986.* Philadelphia: University of Pennsylvania Press, 1986.

JOHNSO Hugh Johnson. *The International Book of Trees.* New York: Simon & Schuster, 1973.

JOHNUG James H. Johnson. *Urban Geography: An Introductory Analysis.* Oxford: Pergamon Press, 1969.

JONES Bernard E. Jones, ed. *Cassell's Cyclopedia of Photography.* New York: Arno Press, 1973.

JONESC C. R. Jones. *Momento Mori: Two Hundred Years of Funerary Art and Customs of Concord, Massachusetts.* Concord, Mass.: Concord Antiquarian Society, 1967.

JORDMO Jordan & Moriarty. *Furniture and Carpets.* New York: Jordan & Moriarty, 1883.

JOUSS Roger Joussaume. *Dolmens for the Dead: Megalithic Building throughout the World.* Translated by Anne and Christopher Chippindale. Ithaca, N.Y.: Cornell University Press, 1988.

JPNA Jesse D. Jennings. *Prehistory of North America.* 2d ed. New York: McGraw-Hill Book Co., 1974.

JSAH *Journal of the Society of Architectural Historians.* Philadelphia: Society of Architectural Historians, 1940-.

JSAHX Shirley P. Branner. *Index to the Journal of the Society of Architectural Historians, Vols. 1-20, 1941-1961.* Philadelphia: Society of Architectural Historians, 1974.

JSFORD J. S. Ford, Johnson & Co. *Chairs.* Chicago: J. S. Ford, Johnson & Co., 1882.

JTANN Jennifer Tann. *The Development of the Factory*. London: Cornmarket Press, 1970.

JTBENT James T. Bent. *The Ruined Cities of Mashonaland*. 2d ed. London: Longmans, Green, 1895.

JULL Philippe Jullian. *Dreamers of the Decadence: Symbolist Painters of the 1890s*. Translated by R. Baldick. New York: Praeger Publishers, 1971.

KAAA George Kubler. *The Art and Architecture of Ancient America: The Mexican, Maya, and Andean Peoples*. New York: Viking Penguin, 1975.

KADISH Sanford H. Kadish, ed. *Encyclopedia of Crime and Justice*. New York: Free Press, 1983.

KALMAN Harold D. Kalman. *The Railway Hotels and the Development of the Chateau Style in Canada*. Victoria, B.C.: University of Victoria, Maltwood Museum, 1968.

KALNEI Wend G. Kalnein and Michael Levey. *Art and Architecture of the Eighteenth Century in France*. Harmondsworth, England: Penguin Books, 1972.

KANE Patricia E. Kane. *Three Hundred Years of American Seating Furniture: Chairs and Beds from the Mabel Brady Garvan and Other Collections at Yale University*. Boston: New York Graphic Society, 1976.

KARP Karpen & Brothers. Furniture catalogs. Chicago: Karpen & Brothers.

KARP09 Karpen & Brothers. *Twenty-ninth Annual Catalogue, S. Karpen & Brothers*. Chicago: Karpen & Brothers, 1909.

KASSAY John Kassay. *The Book of Shaker Furniture*. Amherst: University of Massachusetts Press, 1980.

KATZ William A. Katz. *Introduction to Reference Work*. 3d ed. New York: McGraw-Hill Book Co., 1978.

KAUMED Edward Kaufman and Sharon Irish. *Medievalism: An Annotated Bibliography of Recent Research in the Architecture and Art of Britain and North America*. New York: Garland Publishing, 1988.

KAUP Robert Kaupelis. *Experimental Drawing*. New York: Watson-Guptill Publications, 1980.

KBO Edgar Knoblock. *Beyond the Oxus: Archaeology, Art, and Architecture of Central Asia*. London: Ernest Benn, 1972.

KC Alan Doig. *The Architectural Drawings of King's College, Cambridge*. Cambridge: Avebury Publishing Co., 1979.

KCNA A. L. Kroeber. *Culture and Natural Areas of Native North America*. Berkeley and Los Angeles: University of California Press, 1963.

KEBABI Paul B. Kebabian. *American Woodworking Tools*. Boston: New York Graphic Society, 1978.

KECK Caroline K. Keck. *How to Take Care of Your Pictures: A Primer of Practical Information*. New York: Museum of Modern Art and Brooklyn Museum, 1954.

KEHOE Alice B. Kehoe. *North American Indians: A Comprehensive Account*. Englewood Cliffs, N.J.: Prentice Hall, 1981.

KEJ *Kodansha Encyclopedia of Japan*. 9 vols. Tokyo: Kodansha International, 1983.

KELEM Pal Kelemen. *Art of the Americas: Ancient and Hispanic*. New York: Thomas Y. Crowell Co., 1969.

KEMPER A. J. B. Kempers. *Ancient Indonesian Art*. Cambridge, Mass.: Harvard University Press, 1959.

KENSIN Kenneth M. Kensinger. *Studies in Anthropology and Material Culture*. Vol. 1, *The Cashinahua of Eastern Peru*. Providence, R.I.: Brown University Press, 1975.

KERRGH Robert Kerr. *The Gentleman's House*. London: J. Murray, 1871.

KETCH William K. Ketchum. *Chests, Cupboards, Desks, and Other Pieces*. New York: Alfred A. Knopf, 1982.

KIRK John T. Kirk. *American Furniture and the British Tradition to 1830*. New York: Alfred A. Knopf, 1982.

KLAM Charles Klamkin. *Barns*. New York: Hawthorn Press, 1973.

KLAWIS Charles Z. Klauder and Herbert C. Wise. *College Architecture in America*. New York: Charles Scribner's Sons, 1929.

KNAPP Ronald G. Knapp. *China's Traditional Rural Architecture: A Cultural Geography of the Common House*. Honolulu: University of Hawaii Press, 1986.

KNIGHT Edward H. Knight. *Knight's American Mechanical Dictionary*. 3 vols. New York: J. B. Ford & Co., 1874.

KNJBS Nishikawa Kyotaro and Emily J. Sano. *Great Age of Japanese Buddhist Sculpture: A.D. 600-1300*. Forth Worth, Tex.: Kimball Art Museum. New York: Japan Society, 1983.

KNOPGP William C. Ketchum, Jr. *The Knopf Collectors' Guides to American Antiques: Pottery and Porcelain*. New York: Alfred A. Knopf, 1983.

KNOWLE Morris Knowles. *Industrial Housing*. Reprint. New York: Arno Press, 1974.

KOHLER Eric L. Kohler. *A Dictionary for Accountants*. Englewood Cliffs, N.J.: Prentice Hall, 1975.

KOSAR Jaromir Kosar. *Light-Sensitive Systems: Chemistry and Application of Non-silver Halide Photographic Processes*. New York: John Wiley & Sons, 1965.

KOSTOF Spiro Kostof. *History of Architecture: Settings and Rituals*. New York: Oxford University Press, 1985.

KOVEL Ralph M. Kovel and Terry H. Kovel. *Directory of American Silver, Pewter, and Silver Plate*. New York: Crown Publishers, 1961.

KPD Alfred Kemper, comp. *Presentation Drawings by American Architects*. New York: John Wiley & Sons, 1977.

KPDAF H. Kauffman. *Pennsylvania Dutch American Folk Art*. New York: Dover Publications, 1964.

KS Keith Styles. *Working Drawings Handbook*. London: Architectural Press, 1982.

KUBSOR George Kubler and Martin Soria. *Art and Architecture in Spain, Portugal and Their American Dominions, 1500-1800*. Harmondsworth, England: Penguin Books, 1959.

KUHNEL Ernst Kuhnel. *The Minor Arts of Islam*. Translated by Katherine Watson. Ithaca, N.Y.: Cornell University Press, 1970.

KURZIG Carol M. Kurzig. *Foundation Fundamentals: A Guide for Grantseekers*. New York: Foundation Center, 1980.

KUTHAR David Kut and Gerard Hare. *Waste Recycling for Energy Conservation.* London: Architectural Press, 1981.

KWONG Peter Kwong. *The New Chinatown.* New York: Hill & Wang, 1987.

LA *Landscape Architecture.* Washington, D.C.: American Society of Landscape Architects, 1910-.

LAANP Elsy Leuzinger. *Africa: The Art of the Negro Peoples.* New York: Greystone, 1967.

LAB Carlos Lemos, Jose R. T. Leite, and Pedro M. Gismonti. *Art of Brazil.* New York: Harper & Row Publishers, 1983.

LABA Elsy Leuzinger. *Art of Black Africa.* Translated by R. A. Wilson. Greenwich, Conn.: New York Graphic Society, 1972.

LACS Sherman E. Lee. *Ancient Cambodian Sculpture.* New York: Asia Society, 1969.

LAD Paul Goldman. *Looking at Drawings: A Guide to Technical Terms.* London: British Museum, 1979.

LANDSP *Landscape.* Berkeley, Calif.: Landscape, 1951-.

LANE Arthur Lane. *Later Islamic Pottery: Persia, Syria, Egypt, Turkey.* 2d ed. London: Faber & Faber, 1971.

LANG Michael Langford.. *The Master Guide to Photography.* New York: Alfred A. Knopf, 1982.

LARMIL Larry Millet. *The Curve of the Arch.* St. Paul: Minnesota Historical Society Press, 1985.

LATIX Bell & Howell. *Bell & Howell Newspaper Index to the Los Angeles Times, 1985.* Wooster, Ohio: Bell & Howell, 1986.

LAUD Jean Laude. *The Arts of Black Africa.* Translated by Jean Decock. Berkeley and Los Angeles: University of California Press, 1971.

LAUTPA Carl Lauterbach. *Postcard Albums.* New York: Universe Books, 1961.

LAWR73 A. W. Lawrence. *Greek Architecture.* Harmondsworth, England: Penguin Books, 1973.

LBIER Lionel Bier. *Sarvistan: A Study in Early Iranian Architecture.* University Park: Pennsylvania State University Press, 1986.

LCIAP Library of Congress, Science and Technology Division, Reference Section. *Indoor Air Pollution.* Washington, D.C.: Library of Congress, 1986.

LCMD Library of Congress, Map Division. *United States Atlas.* Washington, D.C.: Library of Congress, 1953.

LCSH Library of Congress. *Subject Headings.* 11th ed. 3 vols. Washington, D.C.: Library of Congress, 1988.

LDDO Philippa Lewis and Gillian Darley. *Dictionary of Ornament.* New York: Pantheon Books, 1986.

LEAVNS William Leavins & Co. *Trade Catalog.* Boston: William Leavins & Co., ca. 1900.

LEDE Michel Leiris and J. Delange. *African Art.* New York: Golden Press, 1968.

LEH Robert L. Loftness. *Energy Handbook.* New York: Van Nostrand Reinhold Co., 1978.

LEMAY Reginald LeMay. *Concise History of Buddhist Art in Siam*. 2d ed. Rutland, Vt.: Charles E. Tuttle Co., 1963.

LEOP Luna B. Leopold, M. Gordon Wolman, and John P. Miller. *Fluvial Processes in Geomorphology*. San Francisco: W. H. Freeman & Co., 1964.

LERSCH Charles Lersch. Furniture catalog. New York: Sinclair & Co., ca. 1880.

LEVER Jill Lever and Margaret Richerson. *The Architect as Artist*. New York: Rizzoli International Publications, 1984.

LFMAH Sir Ambrose Heal. *The London Furniture Makers from the Restoration to the Victorian Era, 1660-1840*. New York: Dover Publications, 1972.

LG Leonard M. Harrod. *Librarians' Glossary and Reference Book*. London: Andre Deutsch, 1977.

LHFEA Sherman E. Lee. *History of Far Eastern Art*. 4th ed. New York: Harry N. Abrams, 1982.

LIA Frank Seiberling. *Looking into Art*. New York: Henry Holt & Co., 1959.

LIBJRN *Library Journal*. New York: R. R. Bowker Co., 1876-.

LIBLIT *Library Literature*. New York: H. W. Wilson Co., 1921-.

LICHT Frances Lichten. *Decorative Art of Victoria's Era*. New York: Alfred A. Knopf, 1950.

LIFE *Life Magazine: Anniversary Issue; One Hundred and Fifty Years of Photography*. New York: Time, 1988.

LIFW Richard Lane. *Images from the Floating World: The Japanese Print*. New York: Dorset Press, 1982.

LIMPD Linda Y. Leach. *Indian Miniature Paintings and Drawings*. Bloomington, Ind.: Cleveland Museum of Art in cooperation with Indiana University Press, 1986.

LING T. O. Ling. *A Dictionary of Buddhism*. New York: Charles Scribner's Sons, 1972.

LIS Karen S. Jones and Martin Kay. *Linguistic and Information Science*. New York: Academic Press, 1973.

LIVABL Donald Appleyard. *Livable Streets*. Berkeley and Los Angeles: University of California Press, 1981.

LNDECO Richard T. T. Forman and Michel Godron. *Landscape Ecology*. New York: John Wiley & Sons, 1986.

LOC Charles Abrams. *The Language of Cities: A Glossary of Terms*. New York: Viking Press, 1971.

LOCDIA Arthur Lockwood. *Diagrams: A Visual Survey of Graphs, Maps, Charts, and Diagrams for the Graphic Designer*. New York: Watson-Guptill Publications, 1969.

LOCK Luke V. Lockwood. *The Furniture Collectors' Glossary*. Reprint. New York: De Capo Press, 1967.

LOFZ Michael J. Meshenberg. *The Language of Zoning: A Glossary of Words and Phrases*. Chicago: American Society of Planning Officials, 1976.

LOG L. S. B. Leakey and M. D. Leakey. *Olduvai Gorge*. 3 vols. Cambridge: Cambridge University Press, 1971.

LONPR1 Ralph Fastnedge, ed. *Shearer Furniture Designs from the Cabinet-Makers' London Book of Prices, 1788*. London: Alec Tiranti, 1962.

LONPR2 *London Cabinet Book of Prices*. London, 1788.

LONPR3 *London Cabinet-Makers' Book of Prices*. 2d ed. London, 1863.

LOTEN H. Stanly Loten and David M. Pendergast. *A Lexicon For Maya Architecture*. Toronto: Royal Ontario Museum, 1984.

LOUAM American Assembly. *On Understanding Art Museums*. Edited by Sherman E. Lee. Englewood Cliffs, N.J.: Prentice Hall, 1975.

LOUDON John C. Loudon. *Loudon Furniture Designs from the Encyclopedia of Cottage, Farmhouse and Villa Architecture and Furniture, 1839*. London: R. S. Publishers, 1970.

LOWEN Sharon R. Lowenstein. *Token Refuge: The Story of the Jewish Refugee Shelter at Oswego, 1944-1946*. Bloomington: Indiana University Press, 1986.

LP Ralph W. Liebing and Mimi F. Paul. *Architectural Working Drawings*. New York: John Wiley & Sons, 1983.

LPSL Rose DeMarr and Hyman Rosenberg. *Legal and Professional Secretary's Lexicon*. Brooklyn, N.Y.: Central Book Co., 1966.

LRD Laurance P. Roberts. *A Dictionary of Japanese Artists: Painting, Sculpture, Ceramics, Prints, Lacquer.* New York: John Weatherhill, 1976.

LRKN Larkin Co. Furniture catalogs. Buffalo, N.Y.: Larkin Co.

LRKN22 Larkin Co. *The Larkin Book of Better Homes*. Buffalo, N.Y.: Larkin Co., 1922.

LRKN39 Larkin Co. *The Larkin Catalog for 1939*. Furniture catalog. Buffalo, N.Y.: Larkin Co., 1939.

LSAS Edward Luci-Smith. *Art in the Seventies*. Ithaca, N.Y.: Cornell University Press, 1980.

LSLM Edward Lucie-Smith. *Late Modern: The Visual Arts since 1945*. rev. ed. New York: Oxford University Press, 1975.

LTEMK Allen Temk. *Eero Saarinen*. New York: George Braziller, 1962.

LUPTON David W. Lupton. *Zoo and Aquarium Design*. Council of Planning Librarians Exchange Bibliographies No. 1484. Monticello, Ill.: Council of Planning Librarians, 1978.

LUZZAD Warren J. Luzzader. *Basic Graphics*. Englewood Cliffs, N.J.: Prentice Hall, 1968.

LWASS Ralph Linton and Paul S. Wingert. *Arts of the South Seas*. New York: Museum of Modern Art, 1946.

LWOA Michael L. Levey. *World of Ottoman Art*. London: Thames & Hudson, 1975.

MA H. J. Cowan and J. T. Gero. *Models in Architecture*. Amsterdam: Elsevier Science Publishing Co., 1968.

MAA U.S. Commission on Fine Arts. *Massachusetts Avenue Architecture*. Washington, D.C.: Government Printing Office, 1975.

MACE L. H. Mace & Co. *Mace & Company Catalogue of 1890*. Furniture catalog. New York: L. H. Mace & Co., 1890.

MACELW Roy S. MacElwee. *Ports and Terminal Facilities*. New York: McGraw-Hill Book Co., 1918.

MACKAY James MacKay. *The Animaliers*. New York: E. P. Dutton, 1973.

MACU84 John Thompson, ed. *Manual of Curatorship: A Guide to Museum Practice*. Boston: Butterworths, 1984.

MAES J. Maes and O. Boone. *Les Peuplades Du Congo Belge*. Brussels: Veuve Monnom, 1935.

MALLAM William S. Kowinski. *The Malling of America*. New York: William Morrow & Co., 1985.

MANDLB Benoit B. Mandelbrot, ed. *Extended Abstracts: Fractal Aspects of Materials—Metal and Catalyst Surfaces, Powders and Aggregates*. Pittsburgh: Materials Research Society, 1984.

MANG Karl Mang. *History of Modern Furniture*. New York: Harry N. Abrams, 1979.

MANGO Cyril A. Mango. *Byzantine Architecture*. New York: Harry N. Abrams, 1976.

MAOAA Museum of Primitive Art. *Art of Oceania, Africa, and the Americas from the Museum of Primitive Art*. New York: Metropolitan Museum of Art, 1969.

MAPCH George P. Murdock. *Africia: Its Peoples and Their Culture History*. New York: McGraw-Hill Book Co., 1959.

MARIET Marietta Chair Co. *Illustrated Catalogue of the Marietta Chair Company*. Marietta, Ohio: Marietta Chair Co., ca. 1885.

MARIN Richard Finnie, ed. *Marinship: The History of a Wartime Shipyard*. San Francisco: Marinship Corp., 1947.

MARSH Paul Marsh. *Illustrated Dictionary of Building*. London: Construction Press, 1982.

MARTEN Charles R. Martens. *Technology of Paints, Varnishes, and Lacquers*. Huntington, N.Y.: R. E. Kreiger, 1974.

MARTIN Leslie Martin. *Architectural Graphics*. New York: Macmillan Publishing Co., 1964.

MATENG *Materials Engineering*. Cleveland: Penton-IPC, 1929-.

MAYALL David Mayall. *Gypsy-Travellers in Nineteenth-Century Society*. New York: Cambridge University Press, 1988.

MAYER Ralph Mayer. *Dictionary of Art Terms and Techniques*. New York: Barnes & Noble Books, 1969.

MBAR John R. Martin. *Baroque*. New York: Harper & Row Publishers, 1977.

MBLOCK Martin Block. *Gypsies: Their Life and Their Customs*. Translated by Barbara Kuczynski and Duncan Taylor. New York: Appleton-Century, 1939.

MBRICE Martin H. Brice. *Stronghold: A History of Military Architecture*. New York: Shocken Books, 1985.

MCATBA V. M. Masson, V. I. Sarianidi, and Ruth Tringham, eds. *Central Asia: Turkmenia Before the Achaemenids*. New York: Praeger Publishers, 1972.

MCAVAL *The Americas*. West Bethesda, Md.: Academy of American Franciscan History, 1944-.

MCCLEL Nancy V. McClelland. *Historic Wall-Papers From Their Inception to the Introduction of Machinery*. Philadelphia: L. B. Lippincott Co., 1924.

MCCUL Niall McCullough and Valerie Mulvin. *A Lost Tradition: The Nature of Architecture in Ireland*. Dublin: Gandon Editions, 1987.

MCFAD Dennis McFadden. "A Glossary of Terms for Use in Describing Architectural Records." Paper presented at conference: "Towards Standards for Architectural Archives." American Institute of Architects, Washington, D.C., February, 1981.

MCGRAT Raymond McGrath and A. C. Frost. *Glass in Architecture and Decoration*. rev. ed. London: Architectural Press, 1961.

MCKEE Harley J. McKee. *Introduction to Early American Masonry, Stone, Brick, Mortar, and Plaster*. Washington, D.C.: National Trust for Historic Preservation, 1973.

MCML97 Committee of Master Cabinet Makers. *The Prices of Cabinet Work, with Tables and Designs, Illustrating the Various Articles of Manufacture*. rev. ed. London: S. Low, 1797.

MCPAR Massachusetts Committee for the Preservation of Architectural Records. *Architectural Records in Boston*. New York: Garland Publishing, 1983.

MCQEEN James G. MacQueen. *The Hittites and Their Contemporaries in Asia Minor*. Boulder, Colo.: Westview Press, 1975.

MCRVN Charles McCraven. *Building the Hewn Log House*. Hollister, Mont.: Mountain Publishing Services, 1978.

MDWG Guggenheim Museum. *The Nineteenth Century: One Hundred and Twenty-Five Master Drawings*. New York: Guggenheim Museum, 1962.

MEA Adolf K. Placzek, ed. *Macmillan Encyclopedia of Architects*. New York: Free Press, 1982.

MEADER Robert F. Meader. *Illustrated Guide to Shaker Furniture*. New York: Dover Publications, 1972.

MEANS Kornelis Smith, ed. *Means Illustrated Construction Dictionary*. Kingston, Mass.: R. S. Means Co., 1985.

MEBNA George P. Murdock and T. J. O'Leary. *Ethnographic Bibliography of North America*. 4th ed. New Haven, Conn.: Human Relations Area Files Press, 1975.

MECHIM Arts Council of Great Britain. *The Mechanized Image: Historical Perspective on Twentieth Century Prints*. London: Arts Council of Great Britain, 1978.

MEDER Joseph Meder. *The Mastery of Drawing*. New York: Abaris Books, 1978.

MEDLEY Margaret Medley. *Chinese Pottery: A Practical History of Chinese Ceramics*. 2d ed. Oxford: Phaidon Press, 1980.

MEEKS Carroll L. V. Meeks. *Italian Architecture, 1750-1914*. New Haven, Conn.: Yale University Press, 1966.

MEGAST Reyner Banham. *Megastructures: Urban Futures of the Recent Past*. London: Thames & Hudson, 1978.

MELIM Minnesota Museum of Modern Art. *Melanesian Images*. St. Paul: Minnesota Museum of Modern Art, 1981.

MELL78 James Mellaart. *The Archaeology of Ancient Turkey*. Totowa, N.J.: Rowman & Littlefield, 1978.

MERCER Henry C. Mercer. *Ancient Carpenters' Tools*. Doylestown, Pa.: Bucks County Historical Society, 1960.

MERD Society of Naval Architects and Marine Engineers (U.S.), Committee on Maritime Energy Research and Development. *Maritime Energy Research and Development*. New York: Society of Naval Architects and Marine Engineers, 1983.

MESH National Library of Medicine. *Medical Subject Headings*. Springfield, Va.: U.S. Department of Commerce, 1979.

METAMO Jeanne L. Wasserman, ed. *Metamorphosis in Nineteenth-Century Sculpture*. Cambridge, Mass.: Fogg Museum, Harvard University, 1975.

METD Jacob Bean. *One Hundred European Drawings in the Metropolitan Museum of Art*, New York: Metropolitan Museum of Art, 1964.

METRO *Metropolis*. New York: Bellerophon Publications, 1981-.

MEYER Franz S. Meyer. *Handbook of Ornament*. New York: Dover Publications, 1957.

MFA Museum of Fine Arts. Object names. Document prepared for internal distribution. Boston: Museum of Fine Arts.

MFF Samuel Muller, Johan A. Feith, and Robert Fruin. *Manual for the Arrangement and Description of Archives: Drawn Up by Direction of the Netherlands Association of Archivists*. New York: H. W. Wilson Co., 1968.

MGHDIC Bernard S. Myers, ed. *McGraw-Hill Dictionary of Art*. 5 vols. New York: McGraw-Hill Book Co., 1969.

MGHDME *McGraw-Hill Dictionary of Modern Economics*. 3d ed. New York: McGraw-Hill Book Co., 1983.

MGOLF John Margolies, Nina Garfinkel, and Maria Reidelbach. *Miniature Golf*. New York: Abbeville Press, 1987.

MGWD Montgomery Ward. *Catalogue No. 99*. Chicago: Montgomery Ward, 1923-1924.

MH George S. Brady and Henry R. Clauser. *Materials Handbook*. New York: McGraw-Hill Book Co., 1977.

MH12 George S. Brady and Henry R. Clauser. *Materials Handbook*. 12th ed. New York: McGraw-Hill Book Co., 1986.

MHDSTT Daniel N. Lapedes, ed. *McGraw-Hill Dictionary of Scientific and Technical Terms*. 2d ed. New York: McGraw-Hill Book Co., 1978.

MHENCE Sybil Parker, ed. *McGraw-Hill Encyclopedia of Energy*. 2d ed. New York: McGraw-Hill Book Co., 1981.

MHEST *McGraw-Hill Encyclopedia of Science of Technology*. 6th ed. New York: McGraw-Hill Book Co., 1987.

MHJPHG Hugo Munsterberg. *Japanese Prints: A Historical Guide*. New York. John Weatherhill, 1982.

MIGAA N. G. L. Hammond. *Migrations and Invasions in Greece and Adjacent Areas*. Park Ridge, N.J.: Noyes Press, 1976.

MILLER Edgar C. Miller, Jr. *American Antique Furniture*. New York: M. Barrows & Co., 1937.

MILLS Edward D. Mills, ed. *Planning: The Architect's Handbook*. London: Butterworths, 1985.

MIM Martha M. Yee, comp. *Moving Image Materials: Genre Terms*. Washington, D.C.: Library of Congress, 1988.

MIMAR *Mimar: Architecture in Development Quarterly*. Cambridge: Massachusetts Institute of Technology Press, 1981-.

MINPNT Karl Khandalavala, Moti Chandra, and Pramod Chandra. *Miniature Painting*. New Delhi, India: Lalit Kala Akademi, 1960.

MIRAMS D. G. Mirams. *A Brief History of Chinese Architecture*. Shanghai: Kelly & Walsh, 1940.

MITCH William J. Mitchell and Robin S. Liggett. *The Art of Computer Graphics Programming*. New York: Van Nostrand Reinhold, 1987.

MITDME David W. Pearce. *MIT Dictionary of Modern Economics*. 3d ed. Cambridge: Massachusetts Institute of Technology Press, 1986.

MIUSPD Joe Morehead. *Introduction to United States Public Documents*. Englewood, Colo.: Libraries Unlimited, 1975.

MKSS Karen Markey. *Subject Searching in Library Catalogs: Before and After the Introduction of Online Catalogs*. Dublin, Ohio: Online Computer Library Center, 1984.

MLT Marvin L. Thomas. *Architectural Working Drawings: A Professional Technique*. New York: McGraw-Hill Book Co., 1978.

MMA Metropolitan Museum of Art. *Library Catalog of the Metropolitan Museum of Art*. Boston: G. K. Hall & Co., 1980.

MMAC Harry Parker. *Materials and Methods of Architectural Construction*. 3d ed. New York: John Wiley & Sons, 1958.

MMF Mary M. Foley. *The American House*. New York: Harper & Row Publishers, 1980.

MMMT Harry Sternberg. *Modern Methods and Materials of Etching*. New York: McGraw-Hill Book Co., 1949.

MNBH Massismo Marafatto. *Nigerian Brazilian Houses*. Lagos, Nigeria: Instituto Italian Di Luttura, 1983.

MOBHOM L. C. Michelon and Herbert Behrend. *How to Build and Operate a Mobile Home Park*. 3d ed. Chicago: Mobile Homes Manufacturers Association, 1970.

MODFRM Alfred Hopkins. *Modern Farm Buildings*. rev. ed. New York: McBride, 1916.

MOHL *Nigeria*. Lagos, Nigeria: Cultural Division of the Federal Ministry of Information, 1937-.

MOLLA Molla. Furniture catalog. New York: Molla.

MOLNAR John Molnar. *Building Construction, Drafting and Design*. New York: Holt, Rinehart & Winston, 1986.

MOMA Museum of Modern Art. *The Architecture of Bridges*. New York: Museum of Modern Art, 1949.

MOMAWL Museum of Modern Art. Word list. Document prepared for internal distribution. Museum of Modern Art, New York.

MONKAN Charles F. Montgomery and Patricia Kane, eds. *American Art, 1750-1800: Towards Independence*. Boston: New York Graphic Society for the Yale

University Art Gallery and the Victoria and Albert Museum, 1976.

MONTGO Charles F. Montgomery. *American Furniture: The Federal Period in the Henry Francis Du Pont Winterthur Museum*. New York: Viking Press, 1966.

MORLEY Sylvanus G. Morley. *The Ancient Maya*. Stanford, Calif.: Stanford University Press, 1956.

MORROW Anne Charlish, ed. *The History of Furniture*. New York: William Morrow & Co., 1976.

MORS Ethel Auster, ed. *Managing Online Reference Services*. New York: Neal-Schuman Publishers, 1986.

MOSAC George P. Murdock. *Behavior Science Outlines*. Vol. 2, *Outline of South American Cultures*. New Haven, Conn.: Human Relations Area Files Press, 1951.

MOWC George P. Murdock. *Outline of World Cultures*. New Haven, Conn.: Human Relations Area Files Press, 1975.

MOYER Frederic D. Moyer, Edith E. Flynn, Fred A. Powers, and Michael J. Plautz. *Guidelines for the Planning and Design of Regional and Community Correctional Centers for Adults*. Urbana, Ill.: University of Illinois, Department of Architecture, 1971.

MPE Joan Agranoff, ed. *Modern Plastics Encyclopedia, 1984-1985*. New York: McGraw-Hill Book Co., 1984.

MPT Revil Mason. *Prehistory of the Transvaal: A Record of Human Activity*. Johannesburg: University of the Witwatersrand Press, 1962.

MSAC Robert Moes. *Southeast Asian Ceramics*. Brooklyn, N.Y.: Brooklyn Museum, 1975.

MSD Adelaide Hechtlinger. *Modern Science Dictionary*. Indianapolis, Ind.: Bobbs-Merrill Co., 1959.

MSR William J. McGuinness, Benjamin Stein, and John S. Reynolds. *Mechanical and Electrical Equipment for Buildings*. 6th ed. New York: John Wiley & Sons, 1980.

MSR-86 William J. McGuinness, Benjamin Stein, and John S. Reynolds. *Mechanical and Electrical Equipment for Buildings*. 7th ed. New York: John Wiley & Sons, 1986.

MSTOMM Chester H. Liebs. *Main Street to Miracle Mile: American Roadside Architecture*. Boston: Little, Brown & Co., 1985.

MSY Samuel Martin, Yang Ha Lee, and Sung-Un Chang. *A Korean-English Dictionary*. New Haven, Conn.: Yale University Press, 1967.

MTINFR Alan H. Molof and Carl J. Turkstra. *Infrastructure: Maintenance and Repair of Public Works*. Annals of the New York Academy of Sciences, Vol. 431. New York: New York Academy of Sciences, 1984.

MULSCU Theodor Muller. *Sculpture in the Netherlands, Germany, France, and Spain: 1400-1500*. Translated by Elaine and William Robson Scott. Harmondsworth, England: Penguin Books, 1966.

MUQARN *Muqarnas*. New Haven, Conn.: Yale University Press, 1983-.

MURRAY Peter Murray and Linda Murray. *A Dictionary of Art and Artists*. Harmondsworth, England: Penguin Books, 1971.

MUSER Curt Muser. *Facts and Artifacts of Ancient Middle America: A Glossary of Terms and Words Used in the Archaeology and Art History of Pre-Columbian Mexico and Central America*. New York: E. P. Dutton, 1978.

MUSGR1 Clifford Musgrave. *Regency Furniture, 1800-1830*. London: Faber & Faber, 1961.

MUSGR2 Clifford Musgrave. *Adam and Hepplewhite and Other Neo-Classical Furniture*. London: Faber & Faber, 1966.

MUSNEW *Museum News*. Washington, D.C.: American Association of Museums, 1924-.

MUTSCH Mutschler Brothers Co. *Porce-Namel Kitchen Furniture*. Nappance, Ind.: Mutschler Brothers Co., 1930.

MWCAB Northwestern Cabinet Co. *Catalogue No. 36*. Furniture catalog. Boston: Northwestern Cabinet Co., 1936.

MWH Mark W. Huth. *Basic Construction Blueprint Reading*. Albany: Delmar Publishers, 1980.

MXDS Robert E. Witherspoon, Jon P. Abbett, and Robert M. Gladstone, eds. *Mixed-Use Developments: New Ways of Land Use*. Washington, D.C.: Urban Land Institute, 1976.

MYSTIC Mystic Seaport Museum. Term List. Document prepared for internal distribution. Mystic Seaport Museum, Mystic, Conn., 1989.

NACEGL National Association of Corrosion Engineers. "Glossary of Terms: Conservation of Metallic Artistic and Historic Works." Houston, Texas, 1988.

NARA Society of American Archivists Functions Committee. Draft list of functions terms. Document prepared for internal distribution. Chicago: Society of American Archivists, 1987.

NARS National Archives and Records Service. *Guide to the National Archives of the United States*. Washington, D.C.: National Archives and Records Service, 1974.

NASPG Douglas Newton. *Art Styles of the Papuan Gulf*. New York: Museum of Primitive Art, 1961.

NATGAL National Gallery of Art. Medium table. Document prepared for internal distribution. National Gallery of Art, Washington, D.C.

NB Richard Fothergill and Ian Butchart. *Non-Book Materials in Libraries: A Practical Guide*. London: Clive Bingley, 1984.

NBCT Bureau of Navy Personnel. *Basic Construction Techniques for Houses and Small Buildings Simply Explained*. New York: Dover Publications, 1972.

NBMRSE National Building Museum. *James Wilson Rouse, Urban Visionary*. Washington, D.C.: National Building Museum, 1988.

NCD Conde B. Pallen and John J. Wynne, eds. *New Catholic Dictionary*. New York: Universal Knowledge Foundation, 1929.

NCE Catholic University of America. *New Catholic Encyclopedia*. New York: McGraw-Hill Book Bo., 1967.

NCR Horace L. Friess, ed. *Non-Christian Religions*. New York: Grosset & Dunlap, 1963.

ND Norman Davey. *A History of Building Materials*. New York: Drake Publishers, 1971.

NDIBA David N. Freedman and Jonas C. Greenfield, eds. *New Directions in Biblical Archaeology*. Garden City, N.Y.: Doubleday & Co., 1971.

NDSA *The National Directory of State Agencies*. Arlington, Va.: Information Resources Press, 1980.

NEARMU S. Lane Faison, Jr. *A Guide to the Art Museums of New England*. New York: Harcourt, Brace & Co., 1958.

NEBL62 C. B. Neblette. *Photography: Its Materials and Processes*. 6th ed. New York: D. Van Nostrand Co., 1962.

NEBLET C. B. Neblette. *Photography: Its Materials and Processes*. 5th Ed. New York: D. Van Nostrand Co., 1952.

NEF Brock Jobe and Myrna Kaye. *New England Furniture: The Colonial Era: Selections from the Society for the Preservation of New England Antiquities*. Boston: Houghton Mifflin Co., 1984.

NEO-NE James Mellaart. *The Neolothic of the Near East*. New York: Charles Scribner's Sons, 1975.

NES Ralph Hickok. *New Encyclopedia of Sports*. New York: McGraw-Hill Book Co., 1977.

NEWEB *New Encyclopaedia Britannica*. Chicago: Encyclopaedia Britannica, 1984.

NEWENG Boston Museum of Fine Arts. *New England Begins: The Seventeenth Century*. 3 vols. Boston: Museum of Fine Arts, 1982.

NEWHA Beaumont Newhall. *The History of Photography: From 1839 to the Present*. New York: Museum of Modern Art, 1982.

NEWMAN Oscar Newman. *Defensible Space: Crime Prevention through Urban Design*. New York: Macmillan Publishing Co., 1972.

NGA National Gallery of Art. List of object names. Document prepared for internal distribution. Washington, D.C.: National Gallery of Art.

NICH Peter Nicholson. *Encyclopaedia of Architecture*. 2 vols. Edited by Edward Lomax and Thomas Gunion. New York: Johnson, Fry & Co., 1850s.

NICOLA Kimon Nicolaides. *The Natural Way to Draw*. Boston: Houghton, Mifflin Co., 1941.

NISHI Kazuo Nishi and Kazuo Hozumi. *What is Japanese Architecture?* Translated by H. Mack Horton. New York: Kodansha International, 1983.

NLLOYD Nathaniel Lloyd. *A History of the English House*. London: Architectural Press, 1949.

NMK Sun-u Choe. *Five Thousand Years of Korean Art*. Seoul, South Korea: Hyonam Publishing Co., 1979.

NMP John Bickford. *New Media in Printmaking*. New York: Watson-Guptill Publications, 1976.

NNGA Douglas Newton. *New Guinea Art in the Collection of the Museum of Primitive Art*. New York: Museum of Primitive Art, 1967.

NOLANS Mary L. Nolan and Sidney Nolan. *Christian Pilgrimage in Modern Western Europe*. Chapel Hill: University of North Carolina Press, 1989.

NOM *The Revised Nomenclature for Museum Cataloging: A Revised and Expanded Version of Robert G. Chenhall's System for Classifying Man-Made Objects*. Nashville, Tenn.: American Association for State and Local History, 1988.

NOOTE C. Nooteboom. *Unbuilt Netherlands: Visionary Projects by Berlage, Oud, Duiker, Van Den Brock, Van Eyck, Herzegerger and Others*. New York: Rizzoli International Publications, 1985.

NORARC Margaret Cross Norton. *Norton on Archives: The Writing of M. Cross Norton on Archival and Records Management*. Chicago: Society of American Archivists, 1975.

NOSS John B. Noss. *Man's Religions*. 3d ed. New York: Macmillan Publishing Co., 1963.

NOXCM Dennis Arnold, ed. *New Oxford Companion to Music*. New York: Oxford University Press, 1983.

NPALG *New Palgrave: A Dictionary of Economics*. New York: Stockton Press, 1987.

NS Deborah Nevis and Robert A. M. Stern. *The Architect's Eye: American Architectural Drawings from 1799-1978*. New York: Pantheon Books, 1979.

NTBEA J. M. Richards. *National Trust Book of English Architecture*. New York: W. W. Norton & Co., 1981.

NTBOFB J. M. Richards. *The National Trust Book of Bridges*. London: Jonathan Cape, 1984.

NTHP85 Diane Maddex, ed. *All About Buildings: The Whole Preservation Catalog*. Washington, D.C.: Preservation Press, 1985.

NUCMC Library of Congress. National Union Catalog of Manuscript Collections. List of occupations. Document prepared for internal distribution. Library of Congress, Washington, D.C., 1980s.

NWCAB Northwestern Cabinet Co. *Catalog No. 36*. Furniture catalog. Boston: Northwestern Cabinet Co., 1936.

NWDB John Fitchen. *The New World Dutch Barn*. Syracuse, N.Y.: Syracuse University Press, 1968.

NWHOW Nancy W. Howard. *Variation of Properties of Nuclear Test Areas and Media at the Nevada Test Site*. Livermore, Calif.: Lawrence Livermore National Laboratory, University of California, 1985.

NYLAN Jane Nylander. *Fabrics for Historic Buildings*. Washington, D.C.: Preservation Press, 1983.

NYPB10 Southwick & Peluse. *New York Revised Prices for Manufacturing Cabinet and Chair Work, June 1810*. Furniture catalog. New York: Southwick & Peluse, 1810.

NYPB15 Society of Journeymen Cabinet Makers. *Additional Prices Agreed Upon by the New York Society of Journeymen Cabinet Makers*. New York: Society of Journeymen Cabinet Makers, 1815.

NYT *New York Times*. New York: New York Times Co., 1851.-

NYWALL Richard C. Nylander. *Wallpapers for Historic Buildings*. Washington, D.C.: Preservation Press, 1983.

OATES1 Joan Oates. *Babylon*. London: Thames & Hudson, 1970.

OCA Harold Osborne, ed. *The Oxford Companion to Art*. New York: Oxford University Press, 1984.

OCD N. G. L. Hammond and H. H. S. Scullard, eds. *Oxford Classical Dictionary*. 2d ed. New York: Oxford University Press, 1970.

OCDA Harold Osborne, ed. *Oxford Companion to the Decorative Arts.* Oxford: Clarendon Press, 1975.

OCG Patrick Goode and Michael Lancaster, eds. *The Oxford Companion to Gardens.* Oxford: Oxford University Press, 1986.

OCLD John Burke. *Osborn's Concise Law Dictionary.* 6th ed. London: Sweet & Maxwell, 1976.

OCM John Walton, Paul B. Beeson, and Ronald B. Scott, eds. *Oxford Companion to Medicine.* Oxford: Oxford University Press, 1986.

OCSS Peter Kemp, ed. *Oxford Companion to Ships and the Sea.* London: Oxford University Press, 1976.

OCTCA Harold Osborne, ed. *Oxford Companion to Twentieth-Century Art.* New York: Oxford University Press, 1981.

OCULUS *Oculus.* Amsterdam: Nederlandse Unie van Opticiens, 1939-.

ODA Ian Chilvers and Harold Osborne, eds. *The Oxford Dictionary of Art.* New York: Oxford University Press, 1988.

ODCC F. L. Cross and E. A. Livingstone. *Oxford Dictionary of the Christian Church.* New York: Oxford University Press, 1983.

ODOM William M. Odom. *A History of Italian Furniture from the Fourteenth to the Early Nineteenth Centuries.* 2d ed. 2 vols. New York: Archive Press, 1966-1967.

OED *Oxford English Dictionary.* New York: Oxford University Press, 1961.

OEDSUP *A Supplement to the Oxford English Dictionary.* Oxford: Clarendon Press, 1972-1986.

OFFAUT Nancy M. Edwards, ed. *Office Automation: A Glossary and Guide.* White Plains, N.Y.: Knowledge Industry Publications, 1982.

OHINTL *Open House International.* Eindhoven, Netherlands: Stichting Architecten Research, 1982-.

OJO G. J. Afolabi Ojo. *Yoruba Palaces: A Study of Afins of Yorubaland.* London: University of London Press, 1967.

OLBR Frans M. Olbrechts. *Congolese Sculpture.* Translated by Daniel J. Crowley and Pearl Ramchoran-Crowley. New Haven, Conn.: Human Relations Area Files Press, 1982.

OLD *Oxford Latin Dictionary.* Oxford: Clarendon Press, 1968.

OLEAR Timothy J. O'Leary. *Ethnographic Bibliography of South America.* New Haven, Conn.: Human Relations Area Files Press, 1963.

OLES Paul S. Oles. *Architectural Illustration.* New York: Van Nostrand Reinhold, 1979.

OLGR Thomas H. Ohlgren, ed. *Insular and Anglo-Saxon Illuminated Manuscripts: An Iconographic Catalogue, c. A.D. 625 to 1100.* New York: Garland Publishing, 1986.

OLIVER Paul Oliver, ed. *Shelter in Africa.* New York: Overlook Press, 1971.

OMAAT Blanche C. Oschak. *Mystic Art of Ancient Tibet.* New York: McGraw-Hill Book Co., 1973.

OMD American Association of Museums. *Official Museum Directory.* Washington, D.C.: American Association of Museums and National Register Publishing Co., 1989.

ONLINE *Online*. Weston, Conn.: Online, 1976-.

OOH U.S. Department of Labor. Bureau of Labor Statistics. *Occupational Outlook Handbook*. 1984-1985 ed. Washington, D.C.: Government Printing Office, 1984.

OPPOSI *Oppositions: A Journal for Ideas and Criticism*. New York: Rizzoli International Publications. 1973-1984.

ORCH Dennis F. Orchard. *Concrete Technology*. 4th ed. London: Applied Science Publishers, 1979.

ORGINF Dagobert Soergel. *Organizing Information: Principles of Data Base and Retrieval Systems*. Orlando, Fla.: Academic Press, 1985.

OSTE Derek E. Ostergard, ed. *Bentwood and Metal Furniture, 1850-1946*. Seattle: University of Washington Press in association with American Federation of Arts, 1987.

OSTIA Gustav Hermansen. *Ostia: Aspects of Roman City Life*. Edmonton, Alta.: University of Alberta Press, 1981.

OTA U.S. Congress. Office of Technology Assessment. *Intellectual Property Rights in an Age of Electronics and Automation*. Washington, D.C.: Government Printing Office, 1986.

OTTO Christian F. Otto. *Space Into Light: The Church Architecture of Balthasar Neumann*. New York: Architectural Historical Foundation, 1979.

OTTOTS Frei Otto. *Tensile Structures*. Translated by D. Ben-Yaakov and T. Pelz. Cambridge: Massachusetts Institute of Technology Press, 1967.

OUTBK John B. Brimer. *Homeowner's Complete Outdoor Building Book*. New York: Popular Science Books, 1985.

OVRMAN Michael Overman. *Roads, Bridges, and Tunnels: Modern Approaches to Road Engineering*. London: Aldus, 1968.

P&H Peck & Hill. *1912 Catalog No. 52: Wholesale Furniture*. Brooklyn, N.Y.: Peck & Hill, 1912.

PA *Progressive Architecture*. Stamford, Conn.: Penton-IPC. 1920-.

PAC Public Archives of Canada. "Architecture and Engineering." Document prepared for internal distribution. Public Archives of Canada, Ottawa, Canada.

PACHT Otto Pacht. *Book Illumination in the Middle Ages: An Introduction*. London: Harvey Miller Publishers, 1986.

PAE85 N. K. Sandars. *Prehistoric Art in Europe*. 2d ed. Harmondsworth, England: Penguin Books, 1985.

PAF National Facilities Conference. *Planning Areas and Facilities for Health, Physical Education, and Recreation*. Chicago: Athletic Institute, 1965.

PAGE Marian Page. *Furniture Designed by Architects*. New York: Whitney Library of Design, 1980.

PAIN Howard Pain. *The Heritage of Country Furniture: A Study in the Survival of Formal and Vernacular Styles from the U.S., Britain, and Europe Found in Upper Canada, 1780-1900*. Toronto: Van Nostrand Reinhold, 1978.

PAINE1 Robert T. Paine and Alexander Soper. *The Art and Architecture of Japan*. Baltimore, Md.: Penguin Books, 1955.

PAINE2 Robert T. Paine and Alexander Soper. *The Art and Architecture of Japan*. 2d ed. Harmondsworth, England: Penguin Books, 1974.

PAINE3 Robert T. Paine and Alexander Soper. *The Art and Architecture of Japan*. 3d ed. Harmondsworth, England: Penguin Books, 1981.

PAIS *Public Affairs Information Service Bulletin*. New York: Public Affairs Information Service, 1915-.

PALAN Pratapaditya Pal. *Art of Nepal*. Los Angeles: Los Angeles County Museum of Art, 1985.

PALARD Jean Palardy. *The Early Furniture of French Canada*. New York: St. Martin's Press, 1963.

PALAT Pratapaditya Pal. *Art of Tibet*. Los Angeles: Los Angeles County Museum of Art, 1983.

PAN Pratapaditya Pal. *Arts of Nepal*. 2 vols. Leiden, Netherlands: E. J. Brill, 1974.

PANDI Lauro Martines. *Power and Imagination: City-States in Renaissance Italy*. New York: Alfred A. Knopf, 1979.

PANENP Erwin Panofsky. *Early Netherlandish Painting*. 2 vols. New York: Harper & Row Publishers, 1971.

PAPA Arthur U. Pope. *Persian Architecture*. Shiraz, Iran: Asia Institute, 1969.

PARKER John H. Parker. *Glossary of Terms Used in Grecian, Roman, Italian and Gothic Architecture*. 4th ed. London: David Bogue, 1845.

PARROT Andre Parrot. *The Arts of Assyria*. Translated by Stuart Gilbert and James Emmons. New York: Golden Press, 1961.

PAYNE Christopher Payne. *Nineteenth-Century European Furniture (Excluding British)*. Woodbridge, Suffolk, England: Antique Collector's Club, 1981.

PBCD Robert Putnam. *Builders' Comprehensive Dictionary*. Reston, Va.: Prentice Hall, 1984.

PBE Wolfgang F. E. Preiser, ed. *Programming the Built Environment*. New York: Van Nostrand Reinhold, 1985.

PBPB30 Joseph Snowden. *The Pittsburgh Cabinet Makers' Book of Prices*. Pittsburgh: Joseph Snowden, 1830.

PBROWN Percy Brown. *Indian Architecture*. 2 vols. Bombay, India: Taraporevala, 1956.

PC Personal communication.

PCA Portland Cement Association. *Modern Plans for Modern Farms*. Chicago: Portland Cement Association, 1960.

PCI Prestressed Concrete Institute. Committee on Architectural Precast Concrete Shop Drawings. *PCI Architectural Precast Concrete Drafting Handbook*. Englewood Cliffs, N.J.: Prentice Hall, 1975.

PCIT Richard Pearce-Moses, comp. *Photographic Collections in Texas: A Union Guide*. College Station: Texas A & M University Press for Texas Historical Foundation, 1987.

PCMAG *PC Magazine*. New York: Ziff-Davis Publishing Co., 1982-.

PCMC Raymond D. Caravaty and Harry C. Plummer. *Principles of Clay Masonry Construction*. Washington, D.C.: Structural Clay Products Institution, 1960.

PCPI Pratapaditya Pal. *Court Paintings of India*. New York: Navin Kumar, 1983.

PDAC Woodmere Art Gallery. *Pennsylvania Dutch Arts and Crafts*. Philadelphia: Woodmere Art Gallery, 1952.

PDARC John Fleming, Hugh Honour, and Nikolaus Pevsner. *Penguin Dictionary of Architecture*. Harmondsworth, England: Penguin Books, 1981.

PDAT Julia Ehresmann. *The Pocket Dictionary of Art Terms*. Boston: Little, Brown & Co., 1979.

PEABOD H. S. Cosgrove and C. B. Cosgrove. *Papers of the Peabody Museum of American Archaeology and Ethnology*. Vol. 15, No. 1, *The Swarts Ruin: A Typical Mimbres Site in Southwestern New Mexico*. Cambridge, Mass.: Peabody Museum, Harvard University, 1932.

PEAPOT D. P. S. Peacock. *Pottery in the Roman World*. London: Longman, 1982.

PEB Alec Clifton-Taylor. *Pattern of English Building*. London: Faber & Faber, 1972.

PECS Richard Stillwell, ed. *The Princeton Encyclopedia of Classical Sites*. Princeton: Princeton University Press, 1976.

PENN University of Pennsylvania. University Museum. "Approved Terms for Object Materials." Document prepared for internal distribution. University of Pennsylvania, Philadelphia, 1980.

PEROUS Gabriel A. Perouse. *Nouvelles francaises du XVIème siecle: Images de la vie du temps*. Geneva: Droz, 1977.

PERSP *Perspecta: The Yale Architectural Journal*. New Haven, Conn.: Yale University, Schools of Architecture and Design, 1952-.

PETERS Joseph Peters Furniture Co. *Illustrated Catalogue*. Furniture catalog. Chicago: Joseph Peters Furniture Co., 1891.

PEVAC Nikolaus Pevsner. *Academies of Art: Past and Present*. Cambridge: Cambridge University Press. New York: Macmillan Publishing Co., 1940.

PFEIF Bruce B. Pfeiffer. *Frank Lloyd Wright, Treasures of Taliesin: Seventy-six Unbuilt Designs*. Fresno, Calif.: Press at California State University. Carbondale, Ill.: Southern Illinois University Press, 1985.

PFOFA Nathan Glazer and Mark Lilla, eds. *The Public Face of Architecture*. New York: Free Press, 1987.

PG Amy Goldstein, ed. *Peterson's Annual Guides to Graduate Study*. 20th ed. Princeton, N.J.: Peterson's Guides, 1986.

PGS U.S. Geological Survey. *Publications of the Geological Survey, 1962-1970*. Washington, D.C.: Government Printing Office, 1972.

PHCA Liang Ssu-Ch'Eng. *A Pictorial History of Chinese Architecture*. Cambridge, Massachusetts Institute of Technology Press, 1984.

PHCHES Nikolaus Pevsner and Edward Hubbard. *Cheshire*. Harmondsworth, England: Penguin Books, 1971.

PHLPI Herbert Philippi. *Stage Craft and Scenery Design*. Boston: Houghton Mifflin Co., 1953.

PHPB11 *The Journeymen Cabinet and Chairmakers' Pennsylvania Book of Prices*. Philadelphia, 1811.

PIDWA Labelle Prussin. *Hatuinere: Islamic Design in West Africa*. Berkeley and Los Angeles: University of California Press, 1986.

PIEDMT Piedmont Co. *Piedmont Red Cedar Chests*. Statesville, N.C.: Piedmont Co., 1915.

PIMA Alexandre Papadopoulo. *Islam and Muslim Art*. New York: Harry N. Abrams, 1979.

PINGP E. B. French and K. A. Wardle, eds. *Problems in Greek Prehistory*. Bristol, England: Bristol Classical Press, 1988.

PINP Lawrence Wright. *Perspective in Perspective*. London: Routledge & Kegan Paul, 1983.

PINYON Wu Jingrong, ed. *The Pinyon Chinese-English Dictionary*. New York: John Wiley & Sons, 1979.

PIP *Polynesia: The Iconography of the Pacific*. Northridge, Calif.: San Fernando Valley State College, 1960s.

PIS Pratapaditya Pal. *Indian Sculpture: A Catalogue of the Los Angeles County Museum of Art Collection*. Vol. 1, *Circa 500 B.C.-A.D. 700*. Los Angeles: Los Angeles County Museum of Art in association with University of California Press, Berkeley, 1986-1988.

PLANC Nilolaus Pevsner. *Lancashire*. Harmondsworth, England: Penguin Books, 1969.

PLANN *Planning*. Chicago: American Planning Association, 1972-.

PLENDE Harold J. Plenderleith. *The Conservation of Antiquities and Works of Art*. Oxford: Oxford University Press, 1956.

PLOWDN Anne Plowden. "Products/Materials: A Classification for the Construction Industry." Watsford, England, 1969.

PLPB96 Snowden & McCorkle. *The Cabinet-Makers' Philadelphia and London Book of Prices*. Philadelphia: Snowden & McCorkle, 1796.

PMAALA Robert Smith. *Periodic Markets in Africa, Asia, and Latin America*. Monticello, Ill.: Council of Planning Librarians, 1972.

PNFU Paine's Furniture Co. Furniture catalogs. Boston: Paine's Furniture Co.

PNFU95 Paine's Furniture Co. *Paine's Furniture Company Catalogue*. Boston: Paine's Furniture Co., ca. 1895.

PNTDEL Stella Kramrisch. *Painted Delight: Indian Paintings from Philadelphia Collections*. Philadelphia: Philadelphia Museum of Art, 1986.

PNYATS Port of New York Authority. *The Port of New York Authority Treaties and Statutes*. New York: Port of New York Authority, 1948.

PODS Fred Dubery and John Willats. *Perspective and Other Drawing Systems*. New York: Van Nostrand Reinhold, 1983.

POEWB Institute for Environmental Education. *Post-Occupancy Evaluation of the Wentworth Building*. Albuquerque, N.Mex.: Institute for Environmental Education, School of Architectural Planning, University of New Mexico, 1981.

POLLIT J. J. Pollitt. *Art and Experience in Classical Greece*. Cambridge: Cambridge University Press, 1980.

POMPEI Lawrence Richardson, Jr. *Pompeii: An Architectural History*. Baltimore, Md.: Johns Hopkins University Press, 1988.

POPPAR A. E. Popham. *The Drawings of Parmigianino*. London: Faber & Faber, 1953.

PORADA Edith Porada. *Art of Ancient Iran: Pre-Islamic Cultures*. New York: Crown Publishers, 1965.

PORT Stanley Port. *Computer-Aided Design for Construction*. New York: John Wiley & Sons, 1984.

PORTER Mary W. Porter. *What Rome was Built With: A Description of the Stones Employed in Ancient Times for its Building and Decoration*. London: Henry Frowde, 1907.

POSTSP Chandler R. Post. *A History of Spanish Painting*. Cambridge, Mass.: Harvard University Press, 1933.

POTDIC Frank Hammer and Janet Hammer. *The Potter's Dictionary of Materials and Techniques*. rev. ed. New York: Watson-Guptill Publications, 1986.

POUGH Frederick H. Pough. *Field Guide to Rocks and Minerals*. Boston: Houghton Mifflin Co., 1955.

POWGOL Susan Rogers. *Power and Gold: Jewelry from Indonesia, Malaysia, and the Philippines*. Geneva: Barbier-Muller Museum. New York: Asia Society, 1985.

PPD T. O. McCartney. *Precision Perspective Drawing*. New York: McGraw-Hill Book Co., 1963.

PPI National Recreation and Park Association. *Park Practice Index*. Arlington, Va.: National Park Service, 1978.

PPSD Kam W. Li and A. Paul Priddy. *Power Plant System Design*. New York: John Wiley & Sons, 1985.

PRA Museum of Fine Arts. *Paris, Rome, Athens: Travels in Greece by French Architects in the Nineteenth and Twentieth Centuries*. Houston: Museum of Fine Arts, 1983.

PRAHOM *Practical Homeowner*. New York: Practical Homeowner Publishing Co., 1979-.

PRAKK Sarah L. Prakken. *Readers' Advisor*. 12 ed. New York: R. R. Bowker Co., 1974.

PREBLE Duane Preble and Sarah Preble. *Artforms*. 4th ed. New York: Harper & Row Publishers, 1989.

PRESTO *The Preston Cabinet and Chair-Makers Book of Prices*. London, 1802.

PRIMAC Alice L. Primac. *Finding Answers in Science and Technology*. New York: Van Nostrand Reinhold, 1984.

PRIPO Charles Komano, Holly Miller, and Sandy Noyes. *The Price of Power: Electric Utilities and the Environment*. New York: Council on Economic Priorities, 1972.

PRNEWS *Preservation News*. Washington, D.C.: National Trust for Historic Preservation, 1961-.

PROG William A. McDonald. *Progress into the Past*. New York: Macmillan Publishing Co., 1967.

PRP Jay S. Shivers and George Hjelte. *Planning Recreational Places*. Rutherford, N.J.: Fairleigh Dickinson University Press, 1971.

PRTT Jules Heller. *Printmaking Today*. 2d ed. New York: Holt, Rinehart & Winston, 1973.

PSINA Richard Woodbury. *Papers of the Peabody Museum of American Archaeology and Ethnology, Harvard University.* Vol. 34, *Prehistoric Stone Implements of North-eastern Arizona: Reports on the Awatovi Expedition.* Cambridge, Mass.: Peabody Museum, 1954.

PSMITH Peter C. Smith. *Design and Construction of Stables.* London: J. A. Allen & Co., 1967.

PUD Seishiro Tomioka. *Planned Unit Developments: Design and Regional Impact.* New York: John Wiley & Sons, 1984.

PUR Stuart R. Purser. *The Drawing Handbook.* Gainesville, Fla.: Purser, 1976.

PUTNAM Robert E. Putnam and G. E. Carlson. *Architectural and Building Trades Dictionary.* 3d ed. Chicago: American Technical Publishers, 1974.

PWFE Wolfgang F. E. Preiser. *Post-Occupancy Evaluation.* New York: Van Nostrand Reinhold, 1988.

PWPM Robert Pincus-Witten. *Postminimalism.* New York: Out of London Press, 1977.

PZC Boris S. Pushkarev, Jeffrey M. Zupan, and Robert S. Cumella. *Urban Rail in America: An Exploration of Criteria for Fixed-Guideway Transit.* Bloomington: Indiana University Press, 1982.

QCRS Robert Bishop. *Quilts, Coverlets, Rugs and Samplers.* New York: Alfred A. Knopf, 1982.

QUICK John Quick. *Artists' and Illustrators' Encyclopedia.* New York: McGraw-Hill Book Co., 1978.

QUIMBY Ian M. G. Quimby. *Material Culture and the Study of the American Life.* New York: W. W. Norton & Co., 1978.

R&H Rohmann & Hillman. *Illustrated Catalogue.* Furniture catalog. Brooklyn, N.Y.: Rohmann & Hillman, 1885.

RA80 Donald Strong. *Roman Art.* 2d ed. Harmondsworth, England: Penguin Books, 1980.

RAA Mortimer Wheeler. *Roman Art and Architecture.* New York: Praeger Publishers, 1973.

RAACA Tamara T. Rice. *Ancient Arts of Central Asia.* New York: Praeger Publishers, 1965.

RACA Benjamin Rowland. *Art of Central Asia.* New York: Crown Publishers, 1974.

RAND Paul Rand. *A Designer's Art.* New Haven, Conn.: Yale University Press, 1985.

RAST Oliver Ransford and Peter Steyn. *Historic Rhodesia.* Salisbury, Rhodesia: Longman Rhodesia, 1975.

RAWS Jessica Rawson. *Chinese Ornament: The Lotus and the Dragon.* London: British Museum, 1983.

RBDUNN R. B. Dunning & Co. *Illustrated 1913 Catalogue.* Furniture catalog. Bangor, Maine: R. B. Dunning & Co., 1913.

RBTSON D. S. Robertson. *A Handbook of Greek and Roman Architecture.* Cambridge: Cambridge University Press, 1929.

RC&B Fred Lawson. *Restaurants, Clubs and Bars.* London: Architectural Press, 1987.

RCI Records Control. *Guide to the Retention and Preservation of Records with Destruction Schedules*. Chicago: Records Control, 1978.

RDBM Jerry M. Rosenberg. *Dictionary of Business and Management*. New York: John Wiley & Sons, 1978.

RDKC Dawn Rooney. *Khmer Ceramics*. New York: Oxford University Press, 1984.

RDLA Dennis Reynolds. *Library Automation: Issues and Application*. New York: R. R. Bowker Co., 1985.

READSC Herbert Read. *A Concise History of Modern Sculpture*. New York: Oxford University Press, 1964.

RECORD Samuel J. Record and Robert W. Hess. *Timbers of the New World*. New Haven, Conn.: Yale University Press, 1943.

RECPE Anthony Ralston and Edwin D. Reilly, Jr., eds. *Encyclopedia of Computer Science and Engineering*. 2d ed. New York: Van Nostrand Reinhold, 1983.

RECY Jerome Goldstein. *Recycling*. New York: Schocken Books, 1979.

REDMAN Charles L. Redman. *The Rise of Civilization*. San Francisco: W. H. Freeman & Co., 1978.

REFW David Ross. *Energy From the Waves*. 2d ed. Oxford: Pergamon Press, 1981.

REILLY James M. Reilly. *Care and Identification of Nineteenth-Century Photographic Prints*. Rochester, N.Y.: Eastman Kodak Co., 1986.

RELPH Edward Relph. *The Modern Urban Landscape*. Baltimore, Md.: Johns Hopkins University Press, 1987.

RENEW Daniel Deudney and Christopher Flavin. *Renewable Energy: The Power to Choose*. New York: W. W. Norton & Co., 1985.

RENSTY Joanna L. Krotz. *Metropolitan Home Renovation Style*. New York: Villard Books, 1986.

REPS John W. Reps. *Views and Viewmakers of Urban America*. Columbia: University of Missouri Press, 1984.

REPSTP John W. Reps. *Town Planning in Frontier America*. Princeton, N.J.: Princeton University Press, 1969.

REW R. E. Wycherley. *The Stones of Athens*. Princeton, N.J.: Princeton University Press, 1978.

RGAG Val D. Greenwood. *The Researcher's Guide to American Genealogy*. Baltimore, Md.: Genealogical Publishing Co., 1973.

RGBR Frank Reynolds. *Guide to Buddhist Religion*. Boston: G. K. Hall & Co., 1981.

RGNOLL Roger G. Noll, ed. *Government and the Sports Business*. Washington, D.C.: Brookings Institution, 1974.

RGPL *Readers' Guide to Periodical Literature*. New York: H. W. Wilson Co., 1900-.

RGRS J. M. Rogers. *Islamic Art and Design, 1500-1700*. London: British Museum, 1983.

RGSYMB Robert Goldwater. *Symbolism*. New York: Harper & Row Publishers, 1979.

RHDEL1 *Random House Dictionary of the English Language*. New York: Random House, 1983.

RHDEL2 *Random House Dictionary of the English Language*. 2d ed. New York: Random House, 1987.

RHLPS *The Random House Library of Painting and Sculpture*. 4 vols. New York: Random House, 1981.

RHONER Rhoner & Co. *Trade Catalogue*. Furniture catalog. New York: Rhoner & Co., 1878.

RI William H. Jordy and Christopher P. Monkhouse. *Buildings on Paper: Rhode Island Architectural Drawings, 1825-1945*. Providence, R.I.: Brown University Press, 1982.

RIA David T. Rice. *Islamic Art*. New York: Praeger Publishers, 1965.

RIBA Royal Institute of British Architects. *Architectural Keywords*. London: Royal Institute of British Architects Publications, 1982.

RIBAJ *RIBA Journal*. London: Royal Institute of British Architects Publications, 1893-.

RICE David T. Rice. *Art of the Byzantine Era*. London: Thames & Hudson, 1963.

RICH Jack C. Rich. *The Materials and Methods of Sculpture*. New York: Oxford University Press, 1959.

RICHAR Milton T. Richardson. *Practical Blacksmithing*. 4 vols. New York: Richardson, 1889.

RICHTE Gisela M. A. Richter. *Furniture of the Greeks, Etruscans and Romans*. London: Phaidon Press, 1966.

RICHTR Gisela M. A. Richter. *A Handbook of Greek Art*. 7th ed. London: Phaidon Press, 1974.

RICONS David T. Rice and Tamara T. Rice. *Icons and Their Dating*. London: Thames & Hudson, 1974.

RIDDLS Richard Muir. *Riddles in the British Landscape*. London: Thames & Hudson, 1981.

RILA *International Repertory of the Literature of Art*. Williamstown, Mass.: J. Paul Getty Trust, 1975-.

RILAVM International Repertory of the Literature of Art. "RILA Verification Manual." Document prepared for internal distribution. J. Paul Getty Trust, Williamstown, Mass.

RIMBRG David Rimberg. *Utilization of Waste Heat From Power Plants*. Park Ridge, N.J.: Noyes Data Corp., 1974.

RIPAB B. W. Robinson, ed. *Islamic Painting and the Arts of the Book*. London: Faber & Faber, 1976.

RISCIV David Oates and Joan Oates. *The Rise of Civilization*. Lusanne, Switzerland: Elsevier-Phaidon, 1976.

RJAC Jessica Rawson. *Ancient China*. New York: Harper & Row Publishers, 1980.

RK Richard Krautheimer. *Early Christian and Byzantine Architecture*. New York: Pelican Books, 1979.

RLG7 Research Libraries Group Seven State Project. "Function Vocabulary: Processes List." Document prepared for internal distribution. New York State Archives, Albany, N.Y., 1987.

RMBA Robin Middleton, ed. *The Beaux-Arts and Nineteenth Century French Architecture*. London: Thames & Hudson, 1982.

RMEGFF Peter G. Robinson. *Marine Engineer's Guide to Fluid Flow*. Cambridge, Md.: Cornell Maritime Press, 1975.

RMITCH Robert Mitchell Furniture Co. *Robert Mitchell Furniture Company*. Cincinnati: Robert Mitchell Furniture Co., 1885.

ROBERT Kenneth D. Roberts. *Tools of the Trades and Crafts: An Eighteenth Century Pattern Book*. Fitzwilliam, N.H.: Roberts Publishing Co., 1976.

ROGET2 *Roget's II: The New Thesaurus*. New York: Berkeley Books, 1984.

ROMPOT R. J. Charleston. *Roman Pottery*. New York: Pitman, 1956.

ROMRDS Raymond Chevallier. *Roman Roads*. Translated by N. H. Fields. Berkeley and Los Angeles: University of California Press, 1976.

ROOT British Standards Institution. *BSI Root Thesaurus*. Hemel Hempstead, England: British Standards Institution, 1981.

ROSENB Robert Rosenblum. *Transformations in Late Eighteenth Century Art*. Princeton, N.J.: Princeton University Press, 1967.

ROSJAN Robert Rosenblum and H. W. Janson. *Nineteenth-Century Art*. New York: Harry N. Abrams, 1984.

ROST United Nations. *Railway Operating and Signalling Techniques in Europe, Japan and the United States of America*. New York: United Nations, 1954.

ROUX Georges Roux. *Ancient Iraq*. 2d ed. Harmondsworth, England: Penguin Books, 1972.

ROWLND Benjamin Rowland. *Drawings of the Masters: Cave to Renaissance*. New York: Shorewood Fine Arts Books, 1965.

ROYCRT Roycraft. *Roycraft Furniture*. East Aurora, N.Y.: Roycraft, 1912.

RP Roland Palmquist. *Answers on Blueprint Reading*. Indianapolis, Ind.: Audel, 1979.

RPD Seymour M. Gold. *Recreation Planning Design*. New York: McGraw-Hill Book Co., 1980.

RRCAMP Raymond R. Camp. *The Hunter's Encyclopedia*. 3d ed. Harrisburgh, Pa.: Stackpole Books, 1951.

RRLP Samuel Edgerton. *Renaissance Rediscovery of Linear Perspective*. New York: Basic Books, 1975.

RS Russell Sturgis. *Dictionary of Architecture and Building*. New York: Macmillan Publishing Co., 1902.

RTIA George N. Roerich. *Trails to Inmost Asia*. New Haven, Conn.: Yale University Press, 1931.

RTR Fogg Art Museum. *Turkoman Rugs*. Cambridge, Mass.: Fogg Art Museum, Harvard University, 1966.

RUBIRA Jose C. Rubira. *Encyclopedia of Spanish Period Furniture Designs*. New York: Sterling Publishing Co., 1984.

RUDIN Alfred Rudin. *Elements of Polymer Science and Engineering: An Introductory Text for Engineers and Chemists*. New York: Academic Press, 1982.

RUFFLE John Ruffle. *The Egyptians: An Introduction to Egyptian Archaeology*. Ithaca, N.Y.: Cornell University Press, 1977.

RUHEMA Helmut Ruhemann. *Cleaning of Paintings*. New York: Praeger Publishers, 1968.

RUSERW Russell & Erwin Manufacturing Co. *Illustrated Catalogue of American Hardware of the Russell & Erwin Manufacturing Company: An Unabridged Reprint of the 1865 Edition*. Ottawa: Association for Preservation Technology, 1980.

RUSSEL Frank Russell, ed. *A Century of Chair Design*. New York: Rizzoli International Publications, 1980.

RUSTIC Sue H. Stephenson. *Rustic Furniture*. New York: Van Nostrand Reinhold Co., 1979.

S&J Robert F. Spencer and Jesse D. Jennings. *The Native Americans: Ethnology and Backgrounds of the North American Indians*. 2d ed. New York: Harper & Row Publishers, 1977.

S&S Alison Sky and Michelle Stone. *Unbuilt America*. New York: McGraw-Hill Book Co., 1976.

SAA Frank B. Evans, Donald F. Harrison, and Edwin A. Thompson, comps.; William L. Rolfs, ed. *Basic Glossary for Archivists, Manuscript Curators, and Records Managers*. Reprint. Chicago: Society of American Archivists, 1974.

SAC Michael Sullivan. *The Arts of China*. rev. ed. Berkeley and Los Angeles: University of California Press, 1973.

SACK Albert Sack. *Fine Points of Furniture: Early American*. New York: Crown Publishers, 1950.

SAF6BU *Library Technical Reports*. Chicago: American Library Association, 1965-.

SAFF Donald Saff and Deli Sacilotto. *Printmaking: History and Process*. New York: Holt, Rinehart & Winston, 1948.

SAGINA Brooks Manufacturing Co. *Brooks Manufacturing Company Knock-Down Furniture*. Saginaw, Mich.: Brooks Manufacturing Co., 1910.

SAH Society of Architectural Historians. Subject headings cumulative index. Document prepared for internal distribution. Philadelphia.

SALAM R. A. Salaman. *Dictionary of Tools Used in Woodworking and Allied Trades, c.1700-1970*. New York: Charles Scribner's Sons, 1975.

SALOON Perry R. Duis. *The Saloon: Public Drinking in Chicago and Boston, 1880-1920*. Urbana: University of Illinois Press, 1983.

SALVA Mario Salvadori. *Why Buildings Stand Up*. New York: McGraw-Hill Book Co., 1980.

SAMPLE Palm Letter Co. *Illustrated Sample Book and Price List of Palm's Patent Transfer Letters, Ornaments and Trade Designs for Signs, Wagons, Cars, Machines, Etc*. Cincinnati: Palm Letter Co., 1901.

SANTO Charles Santore. *The Windsor Style in America: A Pictorial Study of the History and Regional Characteristics of the Most Popular Furniture Form of Eighteenth-Century America, 1730-1830*. Philadelphia: Running Press, 1981.

SAPSP Diane V. O'Connor. "Smithsonian Archives Photo Survey Project: A Draft Photographic Thesaurus." Document prepared for internal distribution. Smithsonian Institution, Washington, D.C., 1987.

SARNOF Paul Sarnoff. *The New York Times Encyclopedic Dictionary of the Environment*. New York: Quadrangle Books, 1971.

SATISH Satish Grover. *The Architecture of India: Islamic 727-1707 A.D.* New Delhi, India: Vikas Publishing House, 1981.

SAVA George Savage. *Dictionary of Antiques*. London: Barrie & Jenkins, 1970.

SAVAGE George Savage and Harold Newman. *An Illustrated Dictionary of Ceramics Defining Three Thousand Fifty-Four Terms Relating to Wares, Materials, Processes, Styles, Patterns and Shapes from Antiquity to the Present Day*. New York: Van Nostrand Reinhold, 1974.

SAXONH George E. Burcaw. *The Saxon House*. Moscow, Idaho: University Press of Idaho, 1979.

SAYLOR Henry H. Saylor. *Dictionary of Architecture*. New York: John Wiley & Sons, 1952.

SBBAC Thomas K. Seligman and Kathleen Berrin. *The Bay Area Collects: Art from Africa, Oceana, and the Americas*. San Francisco: Fine Arts Museums of San Francisco, 1982.

SBT Joseph de Chiara and John H. Callender, eds. *Time-Saver Standards for Building Types*. New York: McGraw-Hill Book Co., 1973.

SCHIF Herbert E. Schiffer and Nancy Schiffer. *The Woods We Live With: A Guide to the Identification of Wood in the Home*. Exton, Pa.: Schiffer Publishing, 1977.

SCHNEI Mary J. Schneider, ed. *Guide to Inventorying Ethnological Collections*. Columbia: Museum of Anthropology, University of Missouri, 1970.

SCHORV Raymond V. Schoder. *Wings over Hellas: Ancient Greece from the Air*. New York: Oxford University Press, 1974.

SCHOT2 Frieda Schottmuller. *Furniture and Interior Decoration of the Italian Renaissance*. 2d rev. ed. New York: B. Westerman Co., 1928.

SCHOTT Frieda Schottmuller. *Furniture and Interior Decoration of the Italian Renaissance*. New York: Brentano's, 1921.

SCHREN M. & H. Schrenkeisen. *Illustrated Catalogue of Parlor Furniture*. New York: M. & K. Schrenkeisen, 1881.

SCHUTZ Herbert Schutz. *The Prehistory of Germanic Europe*. New Haven, Conn.: Yale University Press, 1983.

SCHWZ Marvin D. Schwartz. *The Furniture of John Henry Belter and the Rococo Revival*. New York: E. P. Dutton, 1981.

SCIENC *Science*. Washington, D.C.: American Association for the Advancement of Science, 1880-.

SCOTT John S. Scott. *A Dictionary of Building*. Baltimore, Md.: Penguin Books, 1964.

SEA William Sorsby. *South-East Asian and Early Chinese Export Ceramics*. London: William Sorsby, 1974.

SEAR Sears & Roebuck. Catalogs. Chicago: Sears & Roebuck.

SELTZ Ralph Seletizer. *The Dairy Industry in America*. New York: Dairyfield, 1976.

SELZAN Peter Selz, ed. *Art Nouveau*. New York: Museum of Modern Art, 1960.

SEMBA Klaus-Jurgen Sembach. *Style 1930*. Translated by Judith Filson. New York: University Books, 1971.

SEMENW Robert W. Semenow. *Questions and Answers on Real Estate*. 9th ed. Englewood Cliffs, N.J.: Prentice Hall, 1978.

SERBY Myron W. Serby. *The Stadium: A Treatise on the Design of Stadiums and Their Equipment*. New York: American Institute of Steel Construction, 1930.

SEREDW Alastair Service. *Edwardian Architecture and Its Origins*. London: Architectural Press, 1975.

SERIOA Ann M. Serio. *Political Cartoons in the 1848 Election Campaign*. Washington, D.C.: Smithsonian Institution, 1972.

SEXD Thurstan Shaw. *Excavation at Dawu: Report on an Excavation in a Mound at Dawu, Akuapim, Ghana*. London: T. Nelson, on behalf of University College of Ghana, 1961.

SEXTON R. W. Sexton. *American Commercial Buildings Today*. New York: Architectural Book Publishing Co., 1928.

SFB Alan Ray-Jones and David Clegg. *CI/SFB: Construction Indexing Manual*. London: Royal Institute of British Architects Publications, 1976.

SFBAA1 Royal Australian Institute of Architects. *Alphabetical Subject Index to the SFB Classification System for Use in Australia*. North Sydney, Australia: Royal Australian Institute of Architects, 1970s.

SHADOW Sarah Greenough, Joel Snyder, David Travis, and Colin Westerbeck. *On the Art of Fixing a Shadow: One Hundred and Fifty Years of Photography*. Washington, D.C.: National Gallery of Art, 1989.

SHAFF Maura Shaffrey and Patrick Shaffrey. *Irish Countryside Buildings*. Dublin: O'Brien, 1985.

SHAW *Country Living*. New York: Hearst Magazines, 1978-.

SHEA John G. Shea. *Pennsylvania Dutch and Their Furniture*. New York: Simon & Schuster, 1980.

SHEARM John Shearman. *Mannerism*. Harmondsworth, England: Penguin Books, 1967.

SHEEHY Eugene P. Sheehy. *Guide to Reference Books*. Chicago: American Library Association, 1976.

SHELLE Marjorie Shelley. *The Care and Handling of Art Objects: Practices in the Metropolitan Museum of Art*. New York: Metropolitan Museum of Art, 1987.

SHEPAR Anna O. Shepard. *Ceramics for the Archaeologist*. Washington, D.C.: Carnegie Institution of Washington, 1965.

SHHF Gavriel Salvendy, ed. *Handbook of Human Factors*. New York: John Wiley & Sons, 1987.

SHHP National Trust fof Historic Preservation. *Subject Headings for Historic Preservation*. 3d ed. Washington, D.C.: National Trust for Historic Preservation, 1981.

SHIC *Social History and Industrial Classification (SHIC): A Subject Classification for Museum Collections*. 2 vols. Sheffield, England: Published for the SHIC Working Group by the Centre for English Cultural Traditions and Language, 1983.

SHOTC *Shop of the Crofters*. Furniture catalog. Cincinnati, 1906.

SHUPE Barbara Shupe and Colette O'Connell. *Mapping Your Business*. New York: Special Libraries Association, 1983.

SHYDRO Charles Simeons. *Hydro-Power: The Use of Water as an Alternative Source of Energy.* Elmsford, N.Y.: Pergamon Press, 1980.

SIC Office of Management and Budget. *Standard Industrial Classification Manual.* Washington, D.C.: Executive Office of the President, Office of Management and Budget, 1987.

SIEBER Roy Sieber. *African Textiles and Decorative Arts.* New York: Museum of Modern Art, 1972.

SIEGAN Bernard H. Siegan. *Land Use without Zoning.* Lexington, Mass.: Lexington Books, 1972.

SIMMO Harold C. Simmons. *Archaeological Photography.* New York: New York University Press, 1969.

SIMOND John O. Simonds. *Landscape Architecture: The Shaping of Man's Natural Environment.* New York: F. W. Dodge, 1961.

SINGLE Esther Singleton. *The Furniture of Our Forefathers.* New York: Doubleday & Co., 1922.

SIPPL Charles J. Sippl. *Essential Computer Dictionary and Speller.* Englewood Cliffs, N.J.: Prentice Hall, 1980.

SIPPS L. H. Sperling. *Introduction to Physical Polymer Science.* New York: John Wiley & Sons, 1986.

SIREN Osvold Siren. *The Chinese on the Art of Painting.* New York: Shocken Books. Hong Kong: Hong Kong University Press, 1963.

SJMAPA Stephen J. Mapa. *The Naval Land-Based Test Site Inertial Navigation Set Simulator.* King of Prussia, Pa.: Pennsylvania State University, Graduate Center, 1987.

SLIGH Charles R. Sligh Co. *Furniture by Sligh, Catalogue no. 5.* Holland, Mich.: Charles R. Sligh Co., 1938.

SLOANE Eric Sloane. *A Museum of Early American Tools.* New York: Ballantine Books, 1964.

SMAI George Savage. *The Market in Art.* London: Institute for Economic Affairs, 1969.

SMHA Madanjeet Singh. *Himalayan Art. Wall-Painting and Sculpture in Ladakh, Lahaul Andspiti, The Siwalik Ranges, Nepal, Sikkim, and Bhutan.* Greenwich, Conn.: New York Graphic Society, 1968.

SMITH H. R. Bradley Smith. *Blacksmiths' and Farriers' Tools at the Shelburne Museum.* Shelburne, Vt.: Shelburne Museum, 1966.

SMMA Laurence Schmeckebier. *Modern Mexican Art.* Minneapolis: University of Minnesota Press, 1939.

SMPJ Harold P. Stern. *Master Prints of Japan: Ukiyo-E Hanga.* New York: Harry N. Abrams, 1960s.

SNAEH Thurstan Shaw. *Nigeria: Its Archaeology and Early History.* London: Thames & Hudson, 1978.

SNC Roy Sieber, Douglas Newton, and Michael D. Coe. *African, Pacific, and Pre-Columbian Art in the Indiana University Art Museum.* Bloomington: Indiana University Art Museum in association with Indiana University Press, 1986.

SNYDER James Snyder. *Medieval Art: Painting, Sculpture, Architecture, Fourth to Fourteenth Century*. New York: Harry N. Abrams, 1989.

SOCH R. C. Green and M. Kelly, eds. *Wenner-Gren Symposium on Oceanic Culture History (1969: Singatoka, Fiji). Studies in Oceanic Culture History; Papers*. Honolulu: Department of Anthropology, Bernice P. Bishop Museum, 1970-72.

SONF Alan Sonfist, ed. *Art in the Land: A Critical Anthology of Environmental Art*. New York: E. P. Dutton, 1983.

SOTHEB Sotheby-Parke Bernet Co. Auction catalogs. New York and London: Sotheby-Parke Bernet Co.

SPDES *Space Design*. Tokyo: Kajima Institute Publishing Co., 1965.-

SPENCE L. Andrew Mannheim and Viscount Hanworth, eds. *D. A. Spencer's Colour Photography in Practice*. rev. ed. London: Focal Press, 1966.

SPICER Dorothy G. Spicer. *Festivals of Western Europe*. New York: H. W. Wilson Co., 1958.

SPICT Friedrich Spuhler. *Islamic Carpets and Textiles in the Keir Collection*. London: Faber & Faber, 1978.

SPIEGL Spiegel & Co. *Catalogue of Spiegel & Company*. Chicago: Spiegel & Co., ca. 1890.

SPILLM Jane S. Spillman. *Glass Tableware, Bowls, and Vases*. New York: Alfred A. Knopf, 1982.

SPIPEH Society of the Plastics Industry. *Plastics Engineering Handbook of the Society of the Plastics Industry*. 4th ed. New York: Van Nostrand Reinhold, 1976.

SSCI *Social Science Citation Index*. Philadelphia: Institute for Scientific Information. 1969-.

SSENRG Robert L. Seale and Raymond A. Sierka, eds. *Energy Needs and the Environment*. Tucson: University of Arizona Press, 1973.

SSN Derrick Stenning. *Savannah Nomads: Study of the Wodaabe Pastoral Fulani of Western Banu Province*. New York: Oxford University Press, 1959.

ST&JO Paul J. Strand and Woodrow Jones, Jr. *Indochinese Refugees in America*. Durham, N.C.: Duke University Press, 1985.

STAMB John E. Stambaugh. *The Ancient Roman City*. Baltimore, MD.: Johns Hopkins University Press, 1988.

STEIN J. Stewart Stein. *Construction Glossary: An Encyclopedic Reference and Manual*. New York: John Wiley & Sons, 1980.

STEINE Carol E. Steinhart and John S. Steinhart. *Energy: Sources, Use, and Role in Human Affairs*. North Scituate, Mass. : Duxbury Press, 1974.

STEW Hilary Stewart. *Indian Artifacts of the Northwest Coast*. Seattle: University of Washington Press, 1973.

STIC79 Gustav Stickley. *Craftsman Homes: Architecture and Furnishings of the American Arts and Crafts Movement*. New York: Dover Publications, 1979.

STIK Stickely Brothers Co. Furniture catalogs. Grand Rapids, Mich.: Stickely Brothers Co.

STILGO John R. Stilgoe. *Common Landscape of America, 1580-1845*. New Haven, Conn.: Yale University Press, 1982.

STOD Whitney S. Stoddard. *Art and Architecture in Medieval France*. New York: Harper & Row Publishers, 1966.

STOEHR C. Eric Stoehr. *Bonanza Victorian: Architecture and Society in Colorado Mining Towns*. Albuquerque: University of New Mexico Press, 1975.

STOK Marilyn Stokstad. *Medieval Art*. New York: Harper & Row Publishers, 1986.

STONE Lawrence Stone. *Sculpture in Britain in the Middle Ages*. Harmondsworth, England: Penguin Books, 1955.

STRAAT J. F. van Straaten. *Thermal Performance of Buildings*. Amsterdam: Elsevier Publishing Co., 1967.

STRONG Strong Museum. List of object names. Document prepared for internal distribution. Strong Museum, Rochester, N.Y., 1984.

SUEME Charles Sueme. *Illustrated Catalogue*. Furniture catalog. Chicago: Charles Sueme, 1891.

SUMMER John Summerson. *Architecture in Britain, 1530-1830*. Harmondsworth, England: Penguin Books, 1953.

SWAC Werner Speiser. *The Art of China*. New York: Crown Publishers, 1960.

SWAN Peter C. Swann. *Art of China, Korea, and Japan*. New York: Praeger Publishers, 1963.

SWED Charles Swedlund. *Photography: A Handbook of History, Materials, and Processes*. New York: Holt, Rinehart & Winston, 1974.

SWEET Justin Sweet. *Legal Aspects of Architecture and the Construction Process*. St. Paul, Minn.: West Publishing Co., 1977.

SWEETS *Sweet's Catalog-file: Products for General Building and Renovation*. New York: McGraw-Hill Book Co., 1987.

SYMOND Robert W. Symond and B. B. Whineray. *Victorian Furniture*. London: Country Life, 1965.

SYRBAM Syracuse Bamboo Furniture Co. *Illustrated Catalogue*. Furniture catalog. Syracuse, N.Y.: Syracuse Bamboo Furniture Co., ca. 1890.

T&D Trorlight-Dunker Carpet Co. *Wholesale Furniture*. St. Louis: Trorlight-Duncker Carpet Co., 1917.

TA John L. Andriot. *Township Atlas of the United States*. McLean, Va.: Andriot Associates, 1979.

TANP Vilsoni Tausie. *Art in the New Pacific*. Suva, Fiji: Institute of Pacific Studies, 1979.

TANSAM A. G. Tansley and T. F. Chipp. *Aims and Methods in the Study of Vegetation*. London: British Empire Vegetation Commission and Crown Agents for the Colonies, 1926.

TAO Alastair Couper, ed. *The Times Atlas of the Oceans*. New York: Van Nostrand Reinhold, 1983.

TAPA Honolulu Academy Symposium. *Tapi, Washi, and Western Handmade Paper*. Honolulu: Honolulu Academy Symposium, 1980.

TATEMT Tate Gallery. *Completing the Picture: Materials and Techniques of Twenty-six Paintings in the Tate Gallery*. London: Tate Gallery, 1982.

TAYLOR Robert R. Taylor. *Word in Stone: The Role of Architecture in the National Socialist Ideology*. Berkeley and Los Angeles: University of California Press, 1974.

TBL Gara Antreasian and Clinton Adams. *The Tamarind Book of Lithography: Art & Techniques*. New York: Harry N. Abrams, 1971.

TC *Technology and Conservation of Art, Architecture, and Antiquities*. Boston: Technology Organization, 1976-.

TCCS IF Research Group, University of Montreal. *Canadian Thesaurus of Construction Science and Technology*. Ottawa: Canadian Department of Industry, Trade, and Commerce, 1978.

TEH Wolfgang S. Hornberger, Louis E. Keefer, and William R. McGrath. *Transportation and Traffic Engineering Handbook*. 2d ed. Englewood Cliffs, N.J.: Prentice Hall, 1982.

TEMIZR Raci Temizer. *Museum of Anatolian Civilizations*. Ankara, Turkey: Ankara Society for Promotion of Tourism, Antiquities, and Museums, 1960s.

TERU61 Akiyma Terukazu. *Japanese Painting*. Geneva: Editions d'art Albert Skira, 1961.

TERU77 Akiyma Terukazu. *Japanese Painting*. 2d ed. Geneva: Editions d'art Albert Skira. New York: Rizzoli International Publications, 1977.

TEXARC *Texas Architect*. Austin: Texas Society of Architects, 1950-.

TEXFUR Lonn Taylor and David B. Warren. *Texas Furniture: The Cabinetmakers and Their Work, 1840-1880*. Austin: University of Texas Press, 1975.

TEXLOG Terry G. Jordan. *Texas Log Buildings: A Folk Architecture*. Austin: University of Texas Press, 1978.

TFCZ Filia C.-Z. Tanindi. *Islamic Miniature Painting*. Istanbul: Ali Riza Baskan, 1979.

TGT Giuseppe Tucci. *Transhimalaya*. Translated by James Hogarth. Geneva: Nagel Publishers, 1973.

THAC Friedrich W. Schwerdtfeger. *Traditional Housing in African Cities: A Comparative Study of Houses in Zaria, Ibadan, and Marrakech*. New York: John Wiley & Sons, 1982.

THACK Christopher Thacker. *The History of Gardens*. Berkeley and Los Angeles: University of California Press, 1979.

THAPAR Romila Thapar. *History of India*. 2 vols. Baltimore, Md.: Penguin Books, 1966.

THDAT Edward Lucie-Smith. *Thames & Hudson Dictionary of Art Terms*. New York: Thames & Hudson, 1986.

THEFAC Jean Aitchison, Alan Gomersall, Ralph Ireland, and Patricia Day, eds. and comps. *Thesaurofacet: A Thesaurus and Faceted Classification for Engineering and Related Subjects*. Whetstone, England: English Electric Co., 1969.

THOA Herbert Tischner. *Oceanic Art*. New York: Pantheon Books, 1954.

THONET Gebruder Thonet. *Thonet Bentwood and Other Furniture: The 1904 Illustrated Catalogue*. Reprint. New York: Dover Publications, 1980.

THONTC Thonet. *Thonet Trade Catalogue*. New York: Thonet, 1925.

THORN1 Peter Thornton. *Authentic Decor: The Domestic Interior, 1620-1920*. New York: Viking Press, 1984.

THORN2 Peter Thornton. *Seventeenth Century Interior Decoration in England, France, and Holland*. New Haven, Conn.: Yale University Press, 1978.

THRBG *Thomas Register of American Manufacturers and Thomas Register Catalog File*. New York: Thomas Publishing Co., 1985.

TIMP Raj K. Tandan. *Indian Miniature Painting: Sixteenth through Nineteenth Centuries*. Bangalore, India: Natesan Publishers, 1982.

TITMUS F. H. Titmuss. *Commercial Timbers of the World*. London: Technical Press, 1965.

TKOCL B. G. Trigger, B. G. Kemp, D. O'Connor, and A. B. Lloyd, *Ancient Egypt: A Social History*. Cambridge: Cambridge University Press, 1983.

TL Walter P. Bowman and Robert H. Ball. *Theatre Language*. New York: Theatre Arts Books, 1961.

TOK Sadao Kikuchi. *A Treasury of Japanese Wood Block Prints: Ukiyo-E*. New York: Crown Publishers, 1969.

TOLDWG Charles de Tolnay. *History and Technique of Old Master Drawings*. New York: Bittner, 1943.

TOMLAN Michael A. Tomlan. *Popular and Professional American Architectural Literature in the Late Nineteenth Century*. Ithaca, N.Y.: Cornell University Press, 1983.

TOMLIN Maurice Tomlin. *English Furniture: An Illustrated Handbook*. London: Faber & Faber, 1972.

TOXSUB David D. Doniger. *The Law and Policy of Toxic Substances Control: A Case Study of Vinyl Chloride*. Baltimore, Md.: Johns Hopkins University Press, 1978.

TOYNBE J. M. C. Toynbee. *Death and Burial in the Roman World*. Ithaca, N.Y.: Cornell University Press, 1971.

TPIT American Psychological Association. *Thesaurus of Psychological Index Terms*. 2d ed. Washington, D.C.: American Psychological Association, 1977.

TPPI John Terrell. *Prehistory in the Pacific Islands*. Cambridge: Cambridge University Press, 1986.

TQ *Transportation Quarterly*. Westport, Conn.: Eno Foundation for Transportation, 1947-.

TRADHM *Traditional Homes*. Watford, England: C. F. E. Publishing, 1984-.

TRCVD Chogyam Trungpa, Rinpoche. *Visual Dharma: The Buddhist Art of Tibet*. Berkeley, Calif.: Shambhala Publications, 1975.

TRENT Robert F. Trent. *Hearts and Crowns: Folk Chairs of the Connecticut Coast, 1720-1840, as Viewed in the Light of Henri Focillon's Introduction to Art Populaire*. New Haven, Conn.: New Haven Colony Historical Society, 1977.

TSIT Barbara Booth. *Thesaurus of Sociological Indexing Terms*. San Diego, Calif.: Sociological Abstracts, 1986.

TURNER Victor Turner, ed. *Celebration: Studies in Festivity and Ritual*. Washington, D.C.: Smithsonian Institution, 1982.

TWA *The Weather Almanac*. Detroit: Gale Research Co., 1974-.

TWP Richard A. Martin. *The Wooden Plane*. South Burlington, Vt.: Early American Industries Association, 1977.

TY1200 Konrad Hoffman, ed. *The Year 1200*. New York: Metropolitan Museum of Art, 1970.

TYR Henry G. Tyrrell. *Engineering of Shops and Factories*. New York: McGraw-Hill Book Co., 1912.

UBC International Conference of Building Officials. *Uniform Building Code*. Whittier, Calif.: International Conference of Building Officials, 1976.

UDAPP Jonathan Barnett. *Urban Design as Public Policy*. New York: Architectural Press, 1974.

UDINWE Wolfgang Braunfels. *Urban Design in Western Europe*. Translated by Kenneth J. Northcott. Chicago: University of Chicago Press, 1988.

ULANDU F. Stuart Chapin, Jr. *Urban Land Use Planning*. 2d ed. Urbana: University of Illinois Press, 1972.

UMD George Smith. *Universal Military Dictionary*. Reprint. Ottawa: Museum Restoration Service, 1969.

UMSC Slide and Photograph Collection, Department of Art History, University of Michigan. "University of Michigan Slide Classification." Document prepared for internal distribution. Ann Arbor, Mich.

UNESCO *UNESCO Theasurus: A Structured List of Descriptors for Indexing and Retrieving Literature in the Fields of Education, Science, Social Science, Culture, and Communication*. Paris: United Nations Educational, Scientific, and Cultural Organization, 1977.

UNIQUE Wood Products Corp. *Unique Furniture Price List*. Grand Rapids, Mich.: Wood Products Corp., 1936.

UPDC Joseph de Chiara and Lee Koppelmann. *Urban Planning and Design Criteria*. 2d ed. New York: Van Nostrand Reinhold, 1975.

UPTON Barbara Upton and John Upton. *Photography*. Boston: Little, Brown & Co., 1975.

URBAN John E. Rickert. *Urban Thesaurus: A Vocabulary for Indexing and Retrieving Urban Literature*. Kent, Ohio: Center for Urban Regionalism, Kent State University, 1968.

URBFOR Robert W. Miller. *Urban Forestry; Planning and Managing Urban Green Spaces*. Englewood Cliffs, N.J.: Prentice Hall, 1988.

USBP U.S. Bureau of Prisons. *Handbook of Correctional Institution Design and Construction*. Washington, D.C.: U.S. Bureau of Prisons, 1949.

USGS U.S. Geological Survey. *Guide to U.S.G.S. Geologic and Hydraulic Maps*. McLean, Va.: Documents Index, 1983.

USGSMA U.S. Geological Survey. *Maps for America*. Washington, D.C.: Government Printing Office, 1979.

USMREL Network Development and MARC Standards Office. *USMARC Code List for Relators, Sources, Description Conventions*. Washington, D.C.: Library of Congress, 1988.

USPOST U.S. Postal Service. *National Five Digit Zip Codes and Post Office Directory*. Washington, D.C.: Government Printing Office, 1985.

UTIASO Behcet Unsal. *Turkish Islamic Architecture in Seljuk and Ottoman Times, 1071-1923*. London: Alec Tiranti, 1970.

UTSEY Michael D. Utsey. *Media Handbook: Introduction to Architectural Media*. 2d ed. Eugene, Oreg.: University of Oregon, School of Architecture and Allied Arts, 1974.

UWMSC Christine L. Sundt. "Outline of the Classification Scheme Used for the Circulating Slide Collection of the University of Wisconsin—Madison." Document prepared for internal distribution. University of Wisconsin, Madison, 1982.

V1025 Anthony G. White. *Experimental Buildings: A Selected Bibliography*. Monticello, Ill.: Vance Bibliographies, 1983.

V1548 Mary A. Vance. *Hillside Architecture*. Monticello, Ill.: Vance Bibliographies, 1986.

V16 Carole Cable. *The Architectural Drawing: Its Development and History, 1300-1950*. Monticello, Ill.: Vance Bibliographies, 1978.

V5 Carole Cable. *Current Techniques in the Production and Retrieval of Architectural Drawings and Contract Documents: An Annotated Bibliography of Articles, 1960-1977*. Monticello, Ill.: Vance Bibliographies, 1978.

V706 Carole Cable. *Architecture of the Olympics, 1960-1980*. Monticello, Ill.: Vance Bibliographies, 1982.

VACHAI Victoria and Albert Museum. *English Chairs*. 3d ed. London: Her Majesty's Stationery Office, 1970.

VACI James M. Carpenter. *Visual Art: A Critical Introduction*. New York: Harcourt Brace Jovanovich, 1982.

VAHA Jan Vansina. *Art History in Africa: An Introduction to Method*. New York: Longman, 1984.

VANDER Frederick van der Meer. *Apocalypse: Visions from the Book of Revelation in Western Art*. New York: Alpine Fine Art Collection, 1978.

VATABL Victoria and Albert Museum. *Tables in the Victoria and Albert Museum*. London: Her Majesty's Stationery Office, 1968.

VAUTOA Dave Brownell, ed. *The Vintage Auto Almanac*. Bennington, Vt.: Hemmings Motor News, 1976.

VBAT Steve van Beek. *An Introduction to the Arts of Thailand*. Hong Kong: Luca Invernizzi Tettoni, 1985.

VERGAR Lisa Vergara. *Rubens and the Poetics of Landscape*. New Haven, Conn.: Yale University Press, 1982.

VERGBA Emily Vermeule. *Greece in the Bronze Age*. Chicago: University of Chicago Press, 1964.

VERLAN John B. Jackson. *Discovering the Vernacular Landscape*. New Haven, Conn.: Yale University Press, 1984.

VERLET Pierre Verlet. *Eighteenth Century in France: Society, Decoration, and Furniture*. Translated by George Savage. Rutland, Vt.: Charles E. Tuttle Co., 1967.

VERNAC *Vernacular Architecture*. York, England: Vernacular Architecture Group, 1971-.

VERNFR Christopher Gilbert. *An Exhibition of School Furniture in the Vernacular Tradition*. Leeds, England: Temple Newsam.

VHFICS Yannis Vassiliov, ed. *Human Factors and Interactive Computer Systems: Proceedings of the New York University Symposium on User Interfaces*. Norwood, N.J.: Ablex Publishing Corp., 1982.

VHINMA Jean Chapelot and Robert Fossier. *The Village and House in the Middle Ages*. Translated by Henry Cleere. Berkeley and Los Angeles: University of California Press, 1985.

VICPUB Mark Girouard. *Victorian Pubs*. New Haven, Conn.: Yale University Press, 1984.

VICTOR Victor Manufacturing Co. *Up-To-Date Furniture*. Chicago: Victor Manufacturing Co., 1899.

VIECER Southeast Asia Ceramic Society. *Vietnamese Ceramics*. Singapore: Southeast Asia Ceramic Society, 1982.

VIENNA Cooper-Hewitt Museum. *Vienna Moderne: 1898-1918*. Houston: Sarah Campbell Blaffer Gallery, University of Houston, 1978.

VKS Jan Vansina. *Kingdoms of the Savanna: A History of Central African States until European Occupation*. Madison: University of Wisconsin Press, 1966.

VNCP Nicole Vandier-Nicolas. *Chinese Painting: An Expression of a Civilization*. New York: Rizzoli International Publications, 1983.

VNSE Douglas Considine, ed. *Van Nostrand's Scientific Encyclopedia*. 6th ed. New York: Van Nostrand Reinhold, 1983.

VOGEL J. Ph. Vogel. *Buddhist Art in India, Ceylon, and Java*. Translated by A. J. Barnouw. Oxford: Clarendon Press, 1936.

VONWIN Hasso von Winning. *Pre-Columbian Art of Mexico and Central America*. New York: Harry N. Abrams, 1968.

VORNBK Vornbeck Furniture Co. *Illustrated Catalogue*. Chicago: Vornbeck Furniture Co., 1891.

VR *Visual Resources: An International Journal of Documentation*. New York: Gordon & Breach Science Publishers, 1980-.

VZANT David van Zanten. *Designing Paris: The Architecture of Duban, Labrouste, Duc, and Vaudoyer*. Cambridge: Massachusetts Institute of Technology Press, 1987.

W *Webster's Third New International Dictionary of the English Language, Unabridged*. Springfield, Mass.: G. & C. Merriam Co., 1961.

W&P Gordon R. Willey and Philip Phillips. *Method and Theory in American Archaeology*. Chicago: University of Chicago Press, 1958.

WAA *World Atlas of Archaeology*. Boston: G. K. Hall & Co., 1985.

WAASG Marcus Whiffen. *American Architecture since 1780: A Guide to the Styles*. Cambridge: Massachusetts Institute of Technology Press, 1969.

WADDEN R. A. Wadden. *Indoor Air Pollution*. New York: John Wiley & Sons, 1982.

WAEGMN Peter C. Waegemann. *Handbook of Record Storage and Space Management*. Westport, Conn.: Quorum Books, 1983.

WAJ *Woman's Art Journal*. Knoxville, Tenn.: Woman's Art, 1980-.

WAKITA Osamu A. Wakita and Richard M. Linde. *The Professional Handbook of Architectural Working Drawings*. New York: John Wiley & Sons, 1984.

WALDS Ernst Waldschmidt and Rose L. Waldschmidt. *Nepal: Art Treasures from the Himalayas*. Translated by David Wilson. London: Elek Books, 1969.

WALKER John A. Walker. *Glossary of Art, Architecture, and Design since 1945*. 2d ed. London: Clive Bingley, 1977.

WALNUT Wallace Nutting. *The Great American Idea*. Ashland, Mass.: Wallace Nutting Inc., 1921.

WALTON James Walton. *African Village*. Pretoria: J. L. van Schaik, 1956.

WARDJ Peter Ward-Jackson. *English Furniture Designs of the Eighteenth Century*. London: Her Majesty's Stationery Office, 1958.

WASS Rene S. Wassing. *African Art: Its Background and Traditions*. New York: Harry N. Abrams, 1968.

WATCH F. J. Britten. *The Watch and Clock Makers' Handbook, Dictionary and Guide*. 11th ed. London: E. & F. N. Spon, 1915.

WATKIN David Watkin. *The Rise of Architectural History*. London: Architectural Press, 1980.

WATROU James Watrous. *The Craft of Old Master Drawings*. Madison: University of Wisconsin Press, 1957.

WATS Francis J. Watson. *The History of Furniture*. New York: William Morrow Co., 1976.

WATSON Don A. Watson. *Construction Materials and Processes*. 2d ed. New York: McGraw-Hill Book Co., 1978.

WATWAL Francis J. Watson. *Wallace Collection Catalogues, Furniture: Text with Historical Notes and Illustrations*. London: W. Clowes, 1956.

WATWRI Francis J. Watson. *The Wrightsman Collection*. 5 vols. New York: Metropolitan Museum of Art, 1966-1973.

WAYTA Douglas S. Way. *Terrain Analysis: A Guide to Site Selection Using Aerial Photographic Interpretation*. Stroudsburg, Pa.: Dowden, Hutchinson & Ross, 1973.

WB *The World Book Encyclopedia*. Chicago: World Book-Childcraft International, 1982.

WB&S Allen G. Noble. *Wood, Brick, and Stone: The North American Settlement Landscape*. 2 vols. Amherst: University of Massachusetts Press, 1984.

WBFHP *Metal Powder Report*. Shrewsbury, England: MPR Publishing Services, 1946-.

WBLUNT Wilfrid Blunt. *The Art of Botanical Illustration*. London: Collins, 1967.

WCOL *Webster's Ninth New Collegiate Dictionary*. Springfield, Mass.: G. & C. Merriam Co., 1985.

WEBBAB Geoffrey Webb. *Architecture in Britain: The Middle Ages*. Harmondsworth, England: Penguin Books, 1956.

WEHLTE Kurt Wehlte. *The Materials and Techniques of Painting*. New York: Van Nostrand Reinhold, 1982.

WEIDHS Ernest R. Weidhaas. *Architectural Drafting and Construction*. Boston: Allyn & Bacon, 1972.

WENA Oto Bihalji-Merin and Tomasevic Nebojsa-Bato, eds. *The World Encyclopedia of Naive Art*. London: Frederic Muller, 1984.

WESTRN Western Furniture Co. *Illustrated Catalogue*. Chicago: Western Furniture Co., 1891.

WESTRS Richard S. West. *Satire on Stone: The Political Cartoons of Joseph Keppler*. Urbana: University of Illinois Press, 1988.

WFALB W. F. Albright. *The Archaeology of Palestine*. Harmondsworth, England: Penguin Books, 1961.

WFIA Frits A. Wagner. *Indonesia: The Art of an Island Group*. New York: McGraw-Hill Book Co., 1959.

WGE W. G. Ernst. *Earth Materials*. Englewood Cliffs, N.J.: Prentice Hall, 1969.

WHADMS William H. Adams. *The French Garden, 1500-1800*. New York: George Braziller, 1979.

WHATS Reginald Bragonier, Jr. and David Fisher. *What's What: A Visual Glossary of the Physical World*. Maplewood, N.J.: Hammond, 1981.

WHEEL Sir Mortimer Wheeler. *The Indus Civilization*. Cambridge: Cambridge University Press, 1953.

WHIRA Paul Barolsky. *Infinite Jest: Wit and Humor in Italian Renaissance Art*. Columbia: University of Missouri Press, 1978.

WHP Naomi Rosenblum. *A World History of Photography*. New York: Abbeville Press, 1981.

WIA John D. Hoag. *Western Islamic Architecture*. New York: George Braziller, 1963.

WIAA Gordon R. Willey. *Introduction to American Archaeology*. 2 vols. New York: Prentice Hall, 1971.

WIEDEN Ronald V. Wiedenhoeft. *Workers' Housing in Berlin in the 1920s*. Ann Arbor, Mich.: University Microfilms, 1971.

WIFSON Wifson & Sons. *Eagle Furniture Works*. Baltimore, Md.: Wifon & Sons, 1891.

WILHOG Martha E. Williams and Thomas N. Hogan, comps. *National Online Meeting: Proceedings of the Ninth National Online Meeting*. Medford, N.J.: Learned Information, 1988.

WILIFE Frank Willett. *Ife in the History of West African Sculpture*. New York: McGraw-Hill Book Co., 1967.

WILLIS Charles D. Willis. *Blueprint Reading for Commercial Construction*. Albany, N.Y.: Delmar Publishers, 1979.

WINGT Isabel Wingate. *Textile Fabrics and Their Selection*. New York: Prentice Hall, 1947.

WINICK Charles Winick. *Dictionary of Anthropology*. New York: Philosophical Library, 1956.

WINTER Winterthur Museum. Object name list. Document prepared for internal distribution. Winterthur Museum, Winterthur, Del., 1987.

WINTRP Winthrop Furniture Co. *Winthrop Furniture Company Antique Reproductions*. Boston: Winthrop Furniture Co., ca. 1915.

WITTK Rudolf Wittkower. *Art and Architecture in Italy, 1600-1750*. 2d ed. Harmondworth, England: Penguin Books, 1965.

WJSTP Langdon Warner. *Japanese Sculpture of the Tempyo Period: Masterpieces of the Eighth Century*. Cambridge, Mass.: Harvard University Press, 1964.

WKL William K. Lockard. *Drawing as a Means to Architecture*. New York: Van Nostrand Reinhold, 1968.

WLT Frank Willett. *African Art: An Introduction*. New York: Praeger Publishers, 1971.

WMILLS John Reynolds. *Windmills and Watermills*. New York: Praeger Publishers, 1970.

WNAM Winsor & Newton. *Artists' Materials*. Secaucus, N.J.: Winsor & Newton, 1980s.

WOLOCH Pierre Grimal. *Roman Cities*. Translated by G. Michael Woloch. Madison: University of Wisconsin Press, 1983.

WOODB Walter E. Woodbury. *The Encyclopaedic Dictionary of Photography*. Reprint. New York: Arno Press, 1979.

WOOTON Betty L. Walters. *The King of Desks: Wooton's Patent Secretary*. Washington, D.C.: Smithsonian Institution, 1969.

WORMUS Worcester Art Museum Library. List of subject headings. Document prepared for internal distribution. Worcester Art Museum Library, Worcester, Mass., 1976.

WPATS Paul S. Wingert. *Primitive Art: Its Traditions and Styles*. New York: Oxford University Press, 1962.

WPNCA Kenneth D. Roberts. *Wooden Planes in Nineteenth Century America*. 2d ed. 2 vols. Fitzwilliam, N.H.: K. Roberts Publishing Co., 1978-1983.

WRAA A. R. Willcox. *The Rock Art of Africa*. New York: Holmes & Meier Publishers, 1984.

WRS *World Refugee Survey*. New York: Council for Nationalities Service, 1961-.

WWAA *Who's Who in American Art*. 17th ed. New York: R. R. Bowker Co., 1986.

WWCON Paul Wasserman and Janice McLean, eds. *Who's Who in Consulting*. 2d ed. Detroit: Gale Research Co., 1973.

WYNAR Bohdan S. Wynar. *Introduction to Cataloging and Classification*. 17th ed. Englewood, Colo.: Libraries Unlimited, 1985.

YMG Yutaka Mino. *The Great Eastern Temple: Treasures of Japanese Buddhist Art from Todai-Ji*. Chicago: Art Institute of Chicago in association with Indiana University Press, Bloomington, 1986.

YSM Yoshiaki Shimizu and John M. Rosenfield. *Masters of Japanese Calligraphy: Eighth to Nineteenth Centuries*. New York: Asia Society Galleries and Japan House Gallery, 1984.

YTB Utaka Tazawa. *The Biographical Dictionary of Japanese Art*. New York: Kodansha International, 1981.

YUD E. Haverkamp-Begemann and A. M. S. Logan. *European Drawings and Watercolors in the Yale University Art Gallery, 1500-1900*. 2 vols. New Haven, Conn.: Yale University Press for the Yale Art Gallery, 1970.

Z&P Zanerle & Peterson Co. *Occasional Furniture Net Price List*. Chicago: Zanerle & Peterson Co., 1938.

ZARN George Zarnecki. *Art of the Medieval World: Architecture, Sculpture, Painting, the Sacred Arts*. New York: Harry N. Abrams, 1975.

ZIEGLR Philip C. Ziegler. *Storehouses of Time: Historic Barns of the Northeast*. Camden, Maine: Down East Books, 1985.

ZOOS Lord Zucherman, ed. *Great Zoos of the World: Their Origins and Significance*. London: Weidenfeld & Nicolson, 1980.

ZPCS Fernando Zob el de Ayala. *Philippine Colonial Sculpture*. Manila: [private publication], 1958. Reprint from *Philippine Studies*. Manila, Philippines: Ateneo de Manila University Press. 1953-.

ZWIRN Jerrold Zwirn. *Congressional Publications: A Research Guide to Legislation, Budgets, and Treaties*. Littleton, Colo.: Libraries Unlimited, 1983.

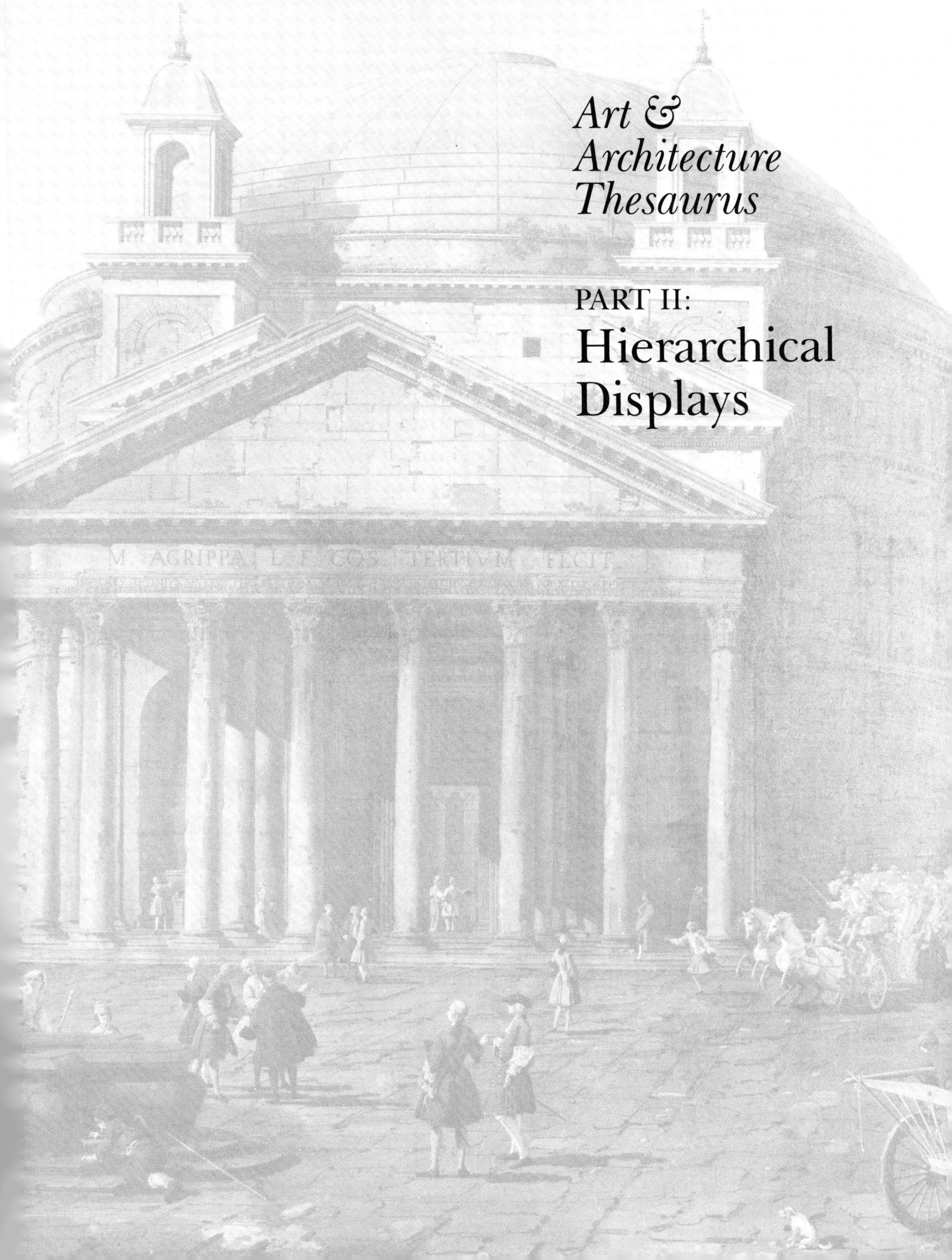

Art & Architecture Thesaurus

PART II: Hierarchical Displays

Thumb Index to the Hierarchies

Associated Concepts facet

The Associated Concepts facet brings together abstract concepts, qualities, and phenomena that relate directly to the study and execution of art and architecture, as well as those associated with other disciplines that are not specifically in the scope of the thesaurus but are often relevant to art or architecture. Also covered here are theoretical and critical concerns, ideologies, attitudes, and social or cultural movements.

The Associated Concepts facet consists of the following hierarchy:

Associated Concepts (BM)

Associated
Concepts
Hierarchy

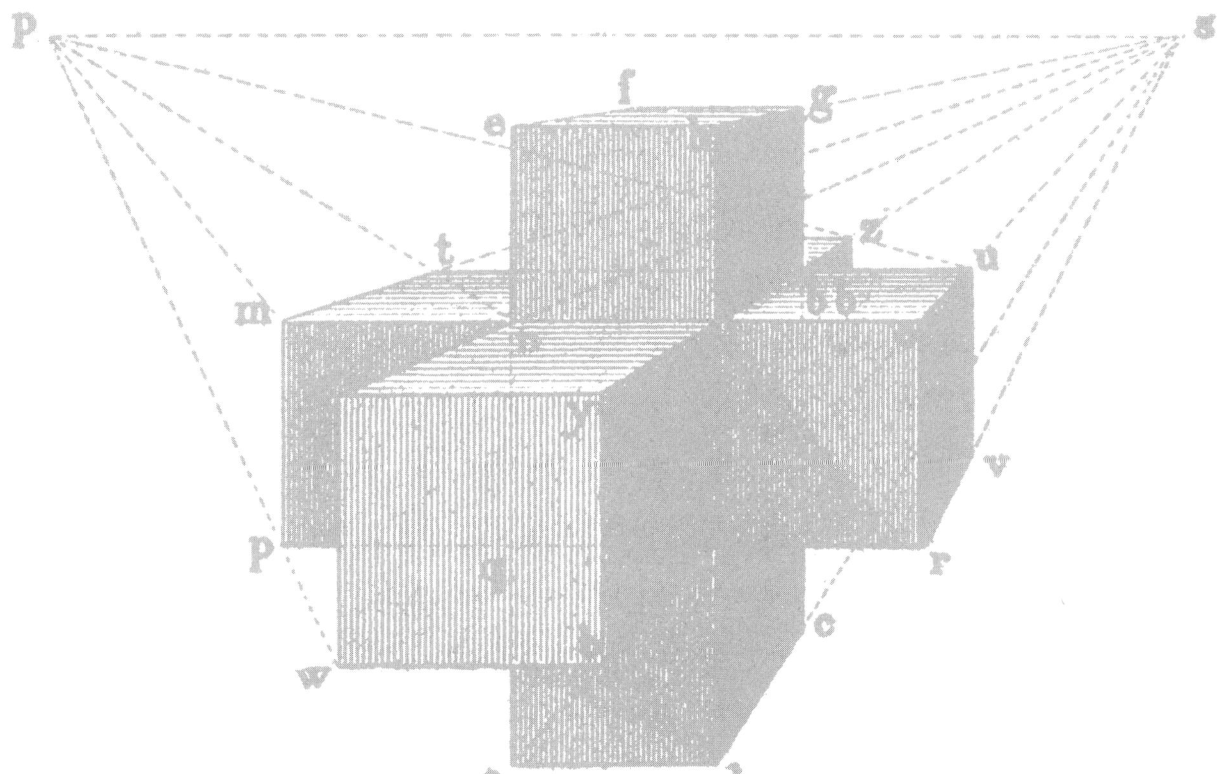

ASSOCIATED CONCEPTS

Scope The Associated Concepts hierarchy consists of descriptors for concepts, properties, and phenomena relating to a wide range of subjects, some of which are not within the primary scope of the *AAT*, such as philosophical concepts, but which affect subjects within that scope.

Organization Descriptors are arranged according to the field of study or activity to which they relate, such as *<concepts in the arts>* (e.g., **iconography**), *<legal concepts>* (e.g., **liability**), *<psychological concepts>* (e.g., **perception**). Concepts that relate to many fields of study (e.g., **methodology**) are found under *<multidisciplinary concepts>*.

Relation to Other Hierarchies Descriptors for branches of learning and areas of specialization, as well as professions and professional specialties, (e.g., **philosophy**) are found in the Disciplines hierarchy, while concepts associated with these disciplines (e.g., **positivism**) appear here. Descriptors for styles and for art and architecture movements (e.g., **Neoclassicist**, **Impressionist**) are found in the Styles and Periods hierarchy, while forms of expression (e.g., **abstraction**) and broad categories of art and architecture (e.g., **organic architecture**, **computer art**) appear here. Descriptors for processes associated with materials (e.g., **expansion**) appear in the Processes and Techniques hierarchy, while properties of materials (e.g., **elasticity**) appear here.

Descriptor Form and Use Descriptors appear as nouns. Use of the singular or plural has been decided on the basis of literary warrant and common usage. Some adjectival forms have been supplied as alternate terms (e.g., **Buddhism**, alternate: **Buddhist**). These alternate terms may be used as modifiers of descriptors in other hierarchies (e.g., **Buddhist** + **monasteries**).

Number of Descriptors 1073

Synopsis

BM.1 *<concepts in the arts>*
BM.2 *<artistic concepts>*
BM.198 *<functional concepts>*
BM.216 *<genres in the arts>*
BM.285 *<historical, theoretical and critical concepts>*
BM.325 *<culture and related concepts>*
BM.368 *<economic concepts>*
BM.416 *<environmental sciences concepts>*
BM.442 *<legal concepts>*
BM.486 *<philosophical concepts>*
BM.530 *<political concepts>*
BM.568 *<psychological concepts>*
BM.608 *<religions and religious concepts>*
BM.714 *<scientific concepts>*
BM.1041 *<social and economic geography concepts>*
BM.1087 *<sociological concepts>*
BM.1132 *<technology and related concepts>*
BM.1145 *<transportation and related concepts>*
BM.1153 *<multi-disciplinary concepts>*

ASSOCIATED CONCEPTS (BM)

BM.1 *<concepts in the arts>*
BM.2   *<artistic concepts>*
BM.3   *<artistic devices>*
BM.4   **allusion**
BM.5   **humor**
BM.6   **imagery**
BM.7   **mimesis**
BM.8   **parody**
BM.9   **narrative**
BM.10   **personification**
BM.11   **satire**
BM.12   **stylization**
BM.13   **symbolism**
BM.14   **allegory**
BM.15   **number symbolism**
BM.16   **religious symbolism**
BM.17   **symbolic color**
BM.18   *<artistic devices: literature>*
BM.19   **analogy**
BM.20   **ekphrasis**
BM.21   **irony**
BM.22   **metaphor**
BM.23   **metonymy**
BM.24   **synecdoche**
BM.25   *<concepts relating to the creative process>*
BM.26   **authorship**
BM.27   **craftsmanship**
BM.28   **creativity**
BM.29   **imagination**
BM.30   **fantasy**
BM.31   **inspiration**
BM.32   **designs**
BM.33   **unexecuted designs**
BM.34   **execution**
BM.35   **expression**
BM.36   **self-expression**
BM.37   **genius**
BM.38   **influence**
BM.39   **invention**
BM.40   **originality**
BM.41   **projects**
BM.42   **student projects**
BM.43   **unbuilt projects**
BM.44   **sprezzatura**
BM.45   *<formal concepts>*
BM.46   *<form and composition concepts>*
BM.47   **alignment**
BM.48   **articulation**
BM.49   **asymmetry**

May be used in combination with other descriptors, especially in the Objects facet (e.g., **hemispherical** + **domes**; **Buddhist** + **monasteries**)

BM.50	balance
BM.51	*<composition and compositional elements>*
BM.52	composition
BM.53	closed composition
BM.54	open composition
BM.55	*<compositional elements>*
BM.56	background
BM.57	coulisses
BM.58	focal point
BM.59	foreground
BM.60	middle ground
BM.61	pentimenti
BM.62	repoussoir
BM.63	disproportion
BM.64	enfilade
BM.65	form
BM.66	frontality
BM.67	horizontality
BM.68	line
BM.69	contour
BM.70	Hogarth's line
BM.71	outline
BM.72	phantom line
BM.73	linearity
BM.74	massing
BM.75	monumentality
BM.76	morbidezza
BM.77	optical correction
BM.78	entasis
BM.79	orientation (architecture)
BM.80	solar orientation
BM.81	painterliness
BM.82	plan (formal concept)
BM.83	grid plan
BM.84	radial plan
BM.85	proportion
BM.86	golden section
BM.87	scale
BM.88	setback (formal concept)
BM.89	shape
BM.90	space
BM.91	negative space
BM.92	pictorial space
BM.93	symmetry
BM.94	approximate symmetry
BM.95	axial symmetry
BM.96	bilateral symmetry
BM.97	radial symmetry
BM.98	verticality

May be used in combination with other descriptors, especially in the Objects facet (e.g., **hemispherical** + **domes**; **Buddhist** + **monasteries**)

- BM.99 complexity
- BM.100 harmony
  - BM.101 concinnity
- BM.102 rhythm
- BM.103 simplicity
- BM.104 unity
- BM.105 *<visual and representational concepts>*
  - BM.106 camouflage
  - BM.107 *<color and related concepts>*
    - BM.108 color
      - BM.109 complementary colors
      - BM.110 cool colors
      - BM.111 film color
      - BM.112 local color
      - BM.113 luminous color
      - BM.114 mass color
      - BM.115 primary colors
      - BM.116 reflected color
      - BM.117 secondary colors
      - BM.118 structural colors
      - BM.119 undertone
      - BM.120 volume color
      - BM.121 warm colors
    - BM.122 *<color-related concepts>*
      - BM.123 *<color effects>*
        - BM.124 assimilation (color)
        - BM.125 color mixture
          - BM.126 additive mixture
          - BM.127 subtractive mixture
        - BM.128 simultaneous contrast
      - BM.129 *<color properties>*
        - BM.130 constancy
        - BM.131 hue
        - BM.132 intensity
        - BM.133 key (color)
        - BM.134 tint
        - BM.135 tone
        - BM.136 value (color)
      - BM.137 metamerism
      - BM.138 palette
      - BM.139 polychromy
      - BM.140 spectrum
  - BM.141 continuous representation
  - BM.142 depth of field
  - BM.143 distortion
  - BM.144 figure-ground perception
  - BM.145 gesture
  - BM.146 illusionism
    - BM.147 trompe-l'oeil

BM.148 optical illusion
BM.149 afterimages
BM.150 false perspective
BM.151 moiré effect
BM.152 *<perspective-related concepts>*
BM.153 center of projection
BM.154 horizon line
BM.155 orthogonals
BM.156 picture plane
BM.157 station point
BM.158 vanishing area
BM.159 vanishing axis
BM.160 vanishing point
BM.161 plasticity
BM.162 pose
BM.163 contrapposto
BM.164 quotations (visual)
BM.165 sight lines
BM.166 simultaneous representation
BM.167 sotto in su
BM.168 texture
BM.169 tactile values
BM.170 viewpoint
BM.171 *<forms of expression>*
BM.172 classicism
BM.173 eclecticism
BM.174 formalism
BM.175 functionalism
BM.176 historicism
BM.177 occultism
BM.178 realism (form of expression)
BM.179 social realism
BM.180 verism
BM.181 regionalism (form of expression)
BM.182 romanticism (form of expression)
BM.183 simultaneism
BM.184 *<forms of expression: visual arts>*
BM.185 abstraction
BM.186 biomorphic abstraction
BM.187 geometric abstraction
BM.188 adhocism
BM.189 anti-art
BM.190 dynamism
BM.191 ideism
BM.192 machine aesthetic
BM.193 Poussinism
BM.194 primitivism
BM.195 rationalism (architecture)
BM.196 representation

May be used in combination with other descriptors, especially in the Objects facet (e.g., **hemispherical** + **domes**; **Buddhist** + **monasteries**)

BM.197 **Rubenism**
BM.198 *<functional concepts>*
BM.199 **access**
BM.200 **adaptability**
BM.201 **flexibility**
BM.202 **air quality**
BM.203 **indoor air quality**
BM.204 **barrier-free design**
BM.205 **circulation (architecture)**
BM.206 **joint occupancy**
BM.207 **safety**
BM.208 **electrical safety**
BM.209 **fire safety**
BM.210 **space utilization**
BM.211 **storage**
BM.212 **use**
BM.213 **adaptive reuse**
BM.214 **mixed use**
BM.215 **multi-use**
BM.216 *<genres in the arts>*
BM.217 **erotica**
BM.218 **pornography**
BM.219 **propaganda**
BM.220 **agitprop**
BM.221 *<architecture genres>*
BM.222 **academic architecture**
BM.223 **fantastic architecture**
BM.224 **visionary architecture**
BM.225 **fictive architecture**
BM.226 **organic architecture**
BM.227 **vernacular architecture**
BM.228 **primitive architecture**
BM.229 *<art genres>*
BM.230 **academic art**
BM.231 **amateur art**
BM.232 **apocalyptic art**
BM.233 **art brut**
BM.234 **cave art**
BM.235 **children's art**
BM.236 **commercial art**
BM.237 **community art**
BM.238 **court art**
BM.239 **crafts**
BM.240 **didactic art**
BM.241 **dissident art**
BM.242 **ethnic art**
BM.243 **fantastic art**
BM.244 **figurative art**
BM.245 **folk art**

May be used in combination with other descriptors, especially in the Objects facet (e.g., **hemispherical** + **domes**; **Buddhist** + **monasteries**)

BM.246 funerary art
BM.247 monumental art
BM.248 naive art
BM.249 nonrepresentational art
BM.250 primitive art
BM.251 public art
BM.252 serial art
BM.253 street art
BM.254 *<art genres by medium>*
BM.255 air art
BM.256 computer art
BM.257 copy art
BM.258 correspondence art
BM.259 environmental art
BM.260 land art
BM.261 laser art
BM.262 light art
BM.263 performance art
BM.264 video art
BM.265 *<literary and oral genres>*
BM.266 comedy
BM.267 commedia dell'arte
BM.268 fiction
BM.269 science fiction
BM.270 folklore
BM.271 fables
BM.272 folk tales
BM.273 legends
BM.274 juvenilia
BM.275 mythology
BM.276 nonfiction
BM.277 biography
BM.278 autobiography
BM.279 hagiography
BM.280 poetry
BM.281 religious drama
BM.282 mystery plays
BM.283 passion plays
BM.284 tragedy
BM.285 *<historical, theoretical and critical concepts>*
BM.286 Antique, the
BM.287 attribution
BM.288 connoisseurship
BM.289 *<critical theories>*
BM.290 deconstruction
BM.291 psychologism
BM.292 structuralism
BM.293 criticism
BM.294 decorum

May be used in combination with other descriptors, especially in the Objects facet (e.g., **hemispherical** + **domes**; **Buddhist** + **monasteries**)

BM.295	**Gesamtkunstwerk**
BM.296	**hermeneutics**
BM.297	**kitsch**
BM.298	**masterpiece**
BM.299	**oeuvre**
BM.300	**paragone**
BM.301	**period**
BM.302	**provenance**
BM.303	**revival**
BM.304	**school**
BM.305	**style**
BM.306	**court style**
BM.307	**technique**
BM.308	*<historical, theoretical and critical concepts: literature>*
BM.309	**analytical bibliography**
BM.310	**exegesis**
BM.311	*<literary movements>*
BM.312	**concrete poetry**
BM.313	**imagism**
BM.314	**literary theory**
BM.315	*<historical, theoretical and critical concepts: visual arts>*
BM.316	**architectural theory**
BM.317	**contextualism**
BM.318	**tectonics**
BM.319	**art theory**
BM.320	**disegno**
BM.321	**iconography**
BM.322	**iconology**
BM.323	**Kunstwollen**
BM.324	**ut pictura poesis**
BM.325	*<culture and related concepts>*
BM.326	**culture**
BM.327	*<culture-related concepts>*
BM.328	**civilization**
BM.329	**customs**
BM.330	**etiquette**
BM.331	**fashion**
BM.332	**leisure**
BM.333	**mass media**
BM.334	**recreation**
BM.335	**sports**
BM.336	**travel**
BM.337	**Volksgeist**
BM.338	**Zeitgeist**
BM.339	*<cultural movements and attitudes>*
BM.340	**amateurism**
BM.341	**dilettantism**
BM.342	**aniconism**
BM.343	**antiquarianism**

May be used in combination with other descriptors, especially in the Objects facet (e.g., **hemispherical** + **domes**; **Buddhist** + **monasteries**)

BM.344	archaism
BM.345	avant-garde
BM.346	Bohemianism
BM.347	dandyism
BM.348	elitism
BM.349	ethnocentrism
BM.350	exoticism
BM.351	Orientalism
BM.352	Japonism
BM.353	feminism
BM.354	golden age
BM.355	Hellenism
BM.356	hermetism
BM.357	humanism
BM.358	iconoclasm
BM.359	illuminism
BM.360	materialism
BM.361	Medievalism
BM.362	new wave
BM.363	popular culture
BM.364	provincialism
BM.365	punk culture
BM.366	radicalism
BM.367	traditionalism
BM.368	*<economic concepts>*
BM.369	amortization
BM.370	art market
BM.371	capital
BM.372	compensation
BM.373	fees
BM.374	pensions
BM.375	salaries
BM.376	wages
BM.377	costs
BM.378	credit
BM.379	depreciation
BM.380	*<economic ideologies>*
BM.381	capitalism
BM.382	communism
BM.383	employment
BM.384	unemployment
BM.385	equity
BM.386	finance
BM.387	municipal finance
BM.388	*<financial aid>*
BM.389	grants
BM.390	subventions
BM.391	subsidies
BM.392	federal aid

BM.393   fellowships
BM.394   student aid
BM.395   scholarships
BM.396   tax incentives
BM.397   industry
BM.398   tourism
BM.399   insurance
BM.400   investments
BM.401   joint ventures
BM.402   mass production
BM.403   monopolies
BM.404   patronage
BM.405   prices
BM.406   prosperity
BM.407   rent
BM.408   economic rent
BM.409   ground rent
BM.410   rent control
BM.411   tariff
BM.412   trade
BM.413   art trade
BM.414   value
BM.415   wealth
BM.416 <*environmental sciences concepts*>
BM.417   drainage
BM.418   land drainage
BM.419   runoff
BM.420   soil percolation
BM.421   environment
BM.422   noise
BM.423   city noise
BM.424   traffic noise
BM.425   transportation noise
BM.426   environmental impact
BM.427   natural resources
BM.428   pollution
BM.429   <*pollution by location or context*>
BM.430   air pollution
BM.431   indoor air pollution
BM.432   smog
BM.433   soil pollution
BM.434   water pollution
BM.435   marine pollution
BM.436   <*pollution by agent*>
BM.437   acid rain
BM.438   chemical pollution
BM.439   noise pollution
BM.440   radioactive pollution
BM.441   thermal pollution

BM.442 *<legal concepts>*
BM.443   air rights
BM.444   artists' rights
BM.445   dedication to public use
BM.446   development rights transfer
BM.447   easement
BM.448   eminent domain
BM.449   encumbrances
BM.450   covenants
BM.451   restrictive covenants
BM.452   liens
BM.453   legislation
BM.454   liability
BM.455   malpractice
BM.456   negligence
BM.457   partnership
BM.458   *<property and related concepts>*
BM.459   property
BM.460   cultural property
BM.461   estates (law)
BM.462   gifts
BM.463   bequests
BM.464   donations
BM.465   intellectual property
BM.466   copyright
BM.467   personal property
BM.468   real estate
BM.469   *<property-related concepts>*
BM.470   boundaries
BM.471   *<property rights>*
BM.472   ownership
BM.473   home ownership
BM.474   title
BM.475   public domain
BM.476   right of way
BM.477   water rights
BM.478   riparian rights
BM.479   *<zoning concepts>*
BM.480   building envelopes
BM.481   building lines
BM.482   frontages
BM.483   height restrictions
BM.484   property lines
BM.485   setback (zoning law)
BM.486 *<philosophical concepts>*
BM.487   *<aesthetic concepts>*
BM.488   beauty
BM.489   empathy
BM.490   grandeur

BM.491	**Ideal, the**
BM.492	**Picturesque, the**
BM.493	**significant form**
BM.494	**Sublime, the**
BM.495	**taste (aesthetics)**
BM.496	**ugliness**
BM.497	**ethics**
BM.498	**professional ethics**
BM.499	**social ethics**
BM.500	*<metaphysical concepts>*
BM.501	**dialectic**
BM.502	**supernatural**
BM.503	*<philosophical movements and attitudes>*
BM.504	**academicism**
BM.505	**aestheticism**
BM.506	**anthropomorphism**
BM.507	**Aristotelianism**
BM.508	**determinism**
BM.509	**dualism**
BM.510	**Enlightenment**
BM.511	**existentialism**
BM.512	**idealism**
BM.513	**individualism**
BM.514	**mysticism**
BM.515	**naturalism**
BM.516	**nihilism**
BM.517	**nominalism**
BM.518	**Platonism**
BM.519	**Neo-Platonism**
BM.520	**positivism**
BM.521	**pragmatism**
BM.522	**rationalism (philosophy)**
BM.523	**scholasticism**
BM.524	**spiritualism**
BM.525	**stoicism**
BM.526	**syncretism**
BM.527	**transcendentalism**
BM.528	**utilitarianism**
BM.529	**truth**
BM.530	*<political concepts>*
BM.531	**church and state**
BM.532	**citizen participation**
BM.533	**civil rights**
BM.534	**decentralization**
BM.535	**expatriation**
BM.536	**freedom**
BM.537	**government**
BM.538	*<government by form>*
BM.539	**democracy**

May be used in combination with other descriptors, especially in the Objects facet (e.g., **hemispherical** + **domes**; **Buddhist** + **monasteries**)

BM.540 dictatorship
BM.541 monarchy
BM.542 theocracy
BM.543 *<government by location or context>*
BM.544 local government
BM.545 municipal government
BM.546 provincial government
BM.547 state government
BM.548 federal government
BM.549 government policy
BM.550 environmental policy
BM.551 land reform
BM.552 *<political ideologies and attitudes>*
BM.553 anarchism
BM.554 conservatism
BM.555 despotism
BM.556 totalitarianism
BM.557 fascism
BM.558 National Socialism
BM.559 feudalism
BM.560 liberalism
BM.561 nationalism
BM.562 patriotism
BM.563 populism
BM.564 socialism
BM.565 politics
BM.566 taxes
BM.567 utopias
BM.568 *<psychological concepts>*
BM.569 automatism
BM.570 cognition
BM.571 emotion
BM.572 anger
BM.573 anxiety
BM.574 awe
BM.575 envy
BM.576 fear
BM.577 grief
BM.578 hate
BM.579 joy
BM.580 love
BM.581 melancholy
BM.582 human behavior
BM.583 deviant behavior
BM.584 voyeurism
BM.585 spatial behavior
BM.586 knowledge
BM.587 language
BM.588 perception

May be used in combination with other descriptors, especially in the Objects facet (e.g., **hemispherical** + **domes**; **Buddhist** + **monasteries**)

BM.589 intuition
BM.590 space perception
BM.591 personal space
BM.592 privacy
BM.593 reason
BM.594 sensation
BM.595 comfort
BM.596 pain
BM.597 pleasure
BM.598 suffering
BM.599 synesthesia
BM.600 sensuality
BM.601 sexuality
BM.602 bisexuality
BM.603 heterosexuality
BM.604 homosexuality
BM.605 speech
BM.606 territoriality
BM.607 unconscious
BM.608 *<religions and religious concepts>*
BM.609 religions
BM.610 Buddhism
BM.611 Hinayana
BM.612 Theravada
BM.613 Lamaism
BM.614 Mahayana
BM.615 Vajrayana
BM.616 *<Chinese Buddhism>*
BM.617 Ch'an
BM.618 Chen-Yen
BM.619 Ching-T'u
BM.620 T'ien-T'ai
BM.621 *<Japanese Buddhism>*
BM.622 Jodo
BM.623 Shin
BM.624 Shingon
BM.625 Tendai
BM.626 Zen
BM.627 Christianity
BM.628 Catholicism
BM.629 Orthodox Eastern
BM.630 Protestantism
BM.631 Amish
BM.632 Anglican
BM.633 Baptist
BM.634 Congregational
BM.635 Episcopal
BM.636 Huguenot
BM.637 Lutheran

May be used in combination with other descriptors, especially in the Objects facet (e.g., **hemispherical** + **domes**; **Buddhist** + **monasteries**)

BM.638	Mennonite
BM.639	Methodist
BM.640	Moravian
BM.641	Presbyterian
BM.642	*<Christian sects>*
BM.643	Coptic
BM.644	Jacobite
BM.645	Maronite
BM.646	Melchite
BM.647	Nestorian
BM.648	Quaker
BM.649	Shaker
BM.650	*<Christian orders>*
BM.651	Basilian
BM.652	Benedictine
BM.653	Cluniac
BM.654	Carthusian
BM.655	Cistercian
BM.656	Dominican
BM.657	Franciscan
BM.658	Jesuit
BM.659	Confucianism
BM.660	Hinduism
BM.661	Brahmanism
BM.662	Sivaism
BM.663	Vaisnavism
BM.664	Islam
BM.665	Shi'a
BM.666	Sufism
BM.667	Sunni
BM.668	Jainism
BM.669	Judaism
BM.670	Conservative Judaism
BM.671	Orthodox Judaism
BM.672	Reform Judaism
BM.673	Manichaeism
BM.674	Mithraism
BM.675	Shinto
BM.676	Sikhism
BM.677	Taoism
BM.678	Zoroastrianism
BM.679	*<religious concepts>*
BM.680	*<doctrinal concepts>*
BM.681	creation
BM.682	divinity
BM.683	faith
BM.684	Immaculate Conception
BM.685	indulgence
BM.686	Paradise

May be used in combination with other descriptors, especially in the Objects facet (e.g., **hemispherical** + **domes**; **Buddhist** + **monasteries**)

BM.687 — reincarnation
BM.688 — salvation
BM.689 — stigmatization
BM.690 — theophany
BM.691 — transubstantiation
BM.692 — monasticism
BM.693 — *<religious ideologies>*
BM.694 — Adoptionism
BM.695 — agnosticism
BM.696 — animism
BM.697 — atheism
BM.698 — gnosticism
BM.699 — Hasidism
BM.700 — millenarianism
BM.701 — monotheism
BM.702 — paganism
BM.703 — pantheism
BM.704 — pietism
BM.705 — polytheism
BM.706 — quietism
BM.707 — shamanism
BM.708 — tantrism
BM.709 — theosophy
BM.710 — anthroposophy
BM.711 — totemism
BM.712 — worship
BM.713 — liturgy
BM.714 — *<scientific concepts>*
BM.715 — *<biological concepts>*
BM.716 — disease
BM.717 — mental illness
BM.718 — insanity
BM.719 — sick building syndrome
BM.720 — evolution
BM.721 — health
BM.722 — life
BM.723 — growth
BM.724 — senses
BM.725 — hearing
BM.726 — sight
BM.727 — blindness
BM.728 — smell
BM.729 — taste (senses)
BM.730 — touch
BM.731 — sex
BM.732 — *<earth sciences concepts>*
BM.733 — soil mechanics
BM.734 — soil structure
BM.735 — tides

May be used in combination with other descriptors, especially in the Objects facet (e.g., **hemispherical** + **domes**; **Buddhist** + **monasteries**)

BM.736 topography
BM.737 *<weather and related phenomena>*
BM.738 weather
BM.739 *<weather-related phenomena>*
BM.740 climate
BM.741 desert climate
BM.742 polar climate
BM.743 temperate climate
BM.744 tropical climate
BM.745 dew point
BM.746 drought
BM.747 humidity
BM.748 lightning
BM.749 precipitation
BM.750 hail
BM.751 rain
BM.752 sleet
BM.753 snow
BM.754 wind
BM.755 *<mathematical concepts>*
BM.756 algorithms
BM.757 formulas
BM.758 fractals
BM.759 equations
BM.760 functions (mathematics)
BM.761 *<geometric concepts>*
BM.762 angles (mathematics)
BM.763 axes (mathematics)
BM.764 centers
BM.765 distance
BM.766 *<geometric figures>*
BM.767 plane figures
BM.768 circles
BM.769 ellipses
BM.770 hyperbolas
BM.771 ovals
BM.772 parabolas
BM.773 polygons
BM.774 triangles
BM.775 quadrilaterals
BM.776 parallelograms
BM.777 rectangles
BM.778 squares (geometric figures)
BM.779 rhombuses
BM.780 trapezoids
BM.781 pentagons
BM.782 hexagons
BM.783 octagons
BM.784 decagons

May be used in combination with other descriptors, especially in the Objects facet (e.g., **hemispherical** + **domes**; **Buddhist** + **monasteries**)

BM.785	dodecagons
BM.786	trapeziums
BM.787	semicircles
BM.788	semiellipses
BM.789	solids (geometric)
BM.790	cones
BM.791	cylinders
BM.792	hemispheres
BM.793	polyhedra
BM.794	cubes
BM.795	pyramids (geometric figures)
BM.796	tetrahedrons
BM.797	spheres
BM.798	spirals
BM.799	planes (mathematics)
BM.800	radius
BM.801	size
BM.802	area
BM.803	circumference
BM.804	depth
BM.805	diameter
BM.806	height
BM.807	length
BM.808	thickness
BM.809	volume
BM.810	width
BM.811	slope
BM.812	infinity
BM.813	logarithms
BM.814	mathematical models
BM.815	numbers
BM.816	roots (mathematics)
BM.817	scalars
BM.818	series (mathematics)
BM.819	arithmetic progressions
BM.820	Fibonacci numbers
BM.821	summations
BM.822	*<statistics and related concepts>*
BM.823	statistics
BM.824	*<statistics-related concepts>*
BM.825	correlation
BM.826	distribution (statistics)
BM.827	mean
BM.828	median
BM.829	probability
BM.830	standard deviation
BM.831	vectors
BM.832	*<physical sciences concepts>*
BM.833	electricity

May be used in combination with other descriptors, especially in the Objects facet (e.g., **hemispherical** + **domes**; **Buddhist** + **monasteries**)

BM.834 *<energy and related concepts>*
BM.835 energy
BM.836 *<heat and related concepts>*
BM.837 heat
BM.838 *<heat-related concepts>*
BM.839 heat gain
BM.840 heat loss
BM.841 heat transmission
BM.842 temperature
BM.843 cold
BM.844 thermal efficiency
BM.845 *<light and related concepts>*
BM.846 light
BM.847 artificial light
BM.848 daylight
BM.849 sunlight
BM.850 reflected light
BM.851 transmitted light
BM.852 *<light-related concepts>*
BM.853 brightness
BM.854 darkness
BM.855 glare
BM.856 highlights
BM.857 luminescence
BM.858 thermoluminescence
BM.859 reflections
BM.860 refraction
BM.861 shade
BM.862 shadows
BM.863 cast shadows
BM.864 radiation
BM.865 solar radiation
BM.866 ultraviolet radiation
BM.867 x-rays
BM.868 *<energy-related concepts>*
BM.869 energy conservation
BM.870 energy consumption
BM.871 fuel consumption
BM.872 fuel economy
BM.873 energy resources
BM.874 geothermal power
BM.875 hydroelectric power
BM.876 nuclear power
BM.877 solar power
BM.878 wind power
BM.879 power supply
BM.880 electric power production
BM.881 entropy
BM.882 *<fire and related concepts>*

May be used in combination with other descriptors, especially in the Objects facet (e.g., **hemispherical** + **domes**; **Buddhist** + **monasteries**)

BM.883 fire
BM.884 *<fire-related concepts>*
BM.885 flame spread ratings
BM.886 flashover
BM.887 mass
BM.888 *<mechanics-related concepts>*
BM.889 dynamics
BM.890 aerodynamics
BM.891 kinematics
BM.892 kinetics
BM.893 motion
BM.894 acceleration
BM.895 centrifugal force
BM.896 centripetal force
BM.897 inertia
BM.898 momentum
BM.899 rotation
BM.900 torque
BM.901 speed
BM.902 thermodynamics
BM.903 statics
BM.904 force
BM.905 graphic statics
BM.906 funicular lines
BM.907 funicular polygons
BM.908 influence lines
BM.909 strength of materials
BM.910 deformations
BM.911 deflections
BM.912 moment of inertia
BM.913 radius of gyration
BM.914 section modulus
BM.915 strains
BM.916 stress
BM.917 axial stress
BM.918 bearing stress
BM.919 bending stress
BM.920 combined stress
BM.921 shear stress
BM.922 thermal stress
BM.923 torsional stress
BM.924 moisture
BM.925 condensation
BM.926 dew
BM.927 fog
BM.928 frost
BM.929 dampness
BM.930 pressure
BM.931 air pressure

May be used in combination with other descriptors, especially in the Objects facet (e.g., **hemispherical** + **domes**; **Buddhist** + **monasteries**)

BM.932 atmospheric pressure
BM.933 earth pressure
BM.934 vapor pressure
BM.935 water pressure
BM.936 *<properties of materials>*
BM.937 acid resistance
BM.938 acoustical properties
BM.939 chemical properties
BM.940   acidity
BM.941   solubility
BM.942 density
BM.943   specific gravity
BM.944 electrical properties
BM.945   electrical conductivity
BM.946 magnetic properties
BM.947 mechanical properties
BM.948   brittleness
BM.949   compressibility
BM.950   creep
BM.951   ductility
BM.952   elastic limit
BM.953   elasticity
BM.954   malleability
BM.955   modulus of elasticity
BM.956   rigidity
BM.957   stiffness
BM.958   *<strength properties>*
BM.959   bursting strength
BM.960   fatigue strength
BM.961   hardness
BM.962   impact strength
BM.963   shear strength
BM.964   tensile strength
BM.965   ultimate strength
BM.966   yield strength
BM.967 optical properties
BM.968   fluorescence
BM.969   iridescence
BM.970   opalescence
BM.971   opacity
BM.972   covering power
BM.973   phosphorescence
BM.974   translucency
BM.975   transparency
BM.976 surface properties
BM.977   airtightness
BM.978   permeability
BM.979   soil permeability
BM.980   porosity

May be used in combination with other descriptors, especially in the Objects facet (e.g., **hemispherical** + **domes**; **Buddhist** + **monasteries**)

BM.981 weathertightness
BM.982 thermal properties
BM.983 boiling point
BM.984 fire resistance
BM.985 flash point
BM.986 freezing point
BM.987 fusibility
BM.988 melting point
BM.989 specific heat
BM.990 thermal conductivity
BM.991 vibration
BM.992 weight
BM.993 *<sound and related concepts>*
BM.994 sound
BM.995 *<sound-related concepts>*
BM.996 echo
BM.997 sound absorption
BM.998 sound transmission
BM.999 *<structural analysis and related concepts>*
BM.1000 structural analysis
BM.1001 *<structural analysis-related concepts>*
BM.1002 equilibrium
BM.1003 flutter
BM.1004 loads
BM.1005 axial loads
BM.1006 combined loads
BM.1007 concentrated loads
BM.1008 construction loads
BM.1009 dead loads
BM.1010 distributed loads
BM.1011 eccentric loads
BM.1012 impact loads
BM.1013 lateral loads
BM.1014 earthquake loads
BM.1015 wind loads
BM.1016 live loads
BM.1017 moving loads
BM.1018 snow loads
BM.1019 traffic loads
BM.1020 uniform loads
BM.1021 moments
BM.1022 plastic design
BM.1023 plastic hinges
BM.1024 shape factors
BM.1025 seismic design
BM.1026 resonance (seismic design)
BM.1027 settlement of structures
BM.1028 span
BM.1029 structural failures

BM.1030 bridge failures
BM.1031 building failures
BM.1032 structural stability
BM.1033 time
BM.1034 day
BM.1035 night
BM.1036 seasons
BM.1037 autumn
BM.1038 spring
BM.1039 summer
BM.1040 winter
BM.1041 *<social and economic geography concepts>*
BM.1042 demographics
BM.1043 land use
BM.1044 land settlement
BM.1045 colonization
BM.1046 rural land use
BM.1047 urban land use
BM.1048 migration
BM.1049 emigration
BM.1050 immigration
BM.1051 internal migration
BM.1052 labor mobility
BM.1053 residential mobility
BM.1054 rural-urban migration
BM.1055 student mobility
BM.1056 urban-rural migration
BM.1057 population
BM.1058 population change
BM.1059 population decline
BM.1060 population growth
BM.1061 population density
BM.1062 resettlement
BM.1063 *<development concepts>*
BM.1064 civic improvement
BM.1065 beautification
BM.1066 urban beautification
BM.1067 roadside improvement
BM.1068 economic development
BM.1069 community development
BM.1070 rural development
BM.1071 urban development
BM.1072 gentrification
BM.1073 infill
BM.1074 slum clearance
BM.1075 urban renewal
BM.1076 real estate development
BM.1077 land subdivision
BM.1078 linear development

May be used in combination with other descriptors, especially in the Objects facet (e.g., **hemispherical** + **domes**; **Buddhist** + **monasteries**)

BM.1079 linkage
BM.1080 ribbon development
BM.1081 industrialization
BM.1082 urbanization
BM.1083 suburban growth
BM.1084 urban blight
BM.1085 urban sprawl
BM.1086 industrial location
BM.1087 *<sociological concepts>*
BM.1088 critical theory
BM.1089 defensible space
BM.1090 Marxism
BM.1091 dialectical materialism
BM.1092 Social Darwinism
BM.1093 social issues
BM.1094 censorship
BM.1095 crime
BM.1096 fraud
BM.1097 forgery
BM.1098 theft
BM.1099 plagiarism
BM.1100 vandalism
BM.1101 defacement
BM.1102 mutilation
BM.1103 discrimination
BM.1104 age discrimination
BM.1105 antisemitism
BM.1106 housing discrimination
BM.1107 race discrimination
BM.1108 sex discrimination
BM.1109 homelessness
BM.1110 obscenity
BM.1111 overcrowding
BM.1112 poverty
BM.1113 public health
BM.1114 quality of life
BM.1115 slavery
BM.1116 social conflict
BM.1117 revolution
BM.1118 terrorism
BM.1119 war
BM.1120 civil war
BM.1121 guerilla warfare
BM.1122 nuclear war
BM.1123 urban decay
BM.1124 social mobility
BM.1125 social status
BM.1126 social structure
BM.1127 caste

May be used in combination with other descriptors, especially in the Objects facet (e.g., **hemispherical** + **domes**; **Buddhist** + **monasteries**)

BM.1128 communal living
BM.1129 kinship
BM.1130 marriage
BM.1131 sex role
BM.1132 *<technology and related concepts>*
BM.1133 technology
BM.1134 appropriate technology
BM.1135 biotechnology
BM.1136 information technology
BM.1137 *<technology-related concepts>*
BM.1138 automation
BM.1139 office automation
BM.1140 infrastructure
BM.1141 mechanization
BM.1142 standardization
BM.1143 modular coordination
BM.1144 tolerances
BM.1145 *<transportation and related concepts>*
BM.1146 transportation
BM.1147 air transport
BM.1148 urban transportation
BM.1149 water transport
BM.1150 *<transportation-related concepts>*
BM.1151 parking
BM.1152 traffic
BM.1153 *<multi-disciplinary concepts>*
BM.1154 authenticity
BM.1155 chronology
BM.1156 methodology
BM.1157 case method
BM.1158 simulation methods
BM.1159 standards
BM.1160 professional standards
BM.1161 systems
BM.1162 terminology
BM.1163 theory
BM.1164 typology

May be used in combination with other descriptors, especially in the Objects facet (e.g., **hemispherical** + **domes**; **Buddhist** + **monasteries**)

Physical Attributes facet

The Physical Attributes facet concerns the appearance or qualities of artifacts, especially relating to their design or decoration, such as shape and color. Other aspects of design covered here include elements of decoration schemes, such as patterns and borders.

The Physical Attributes facet consists of the following hierarchies:

Design Attributes (DC)
Design Elements (DG)
Colors (DL)

Design Attributes Hierarchy

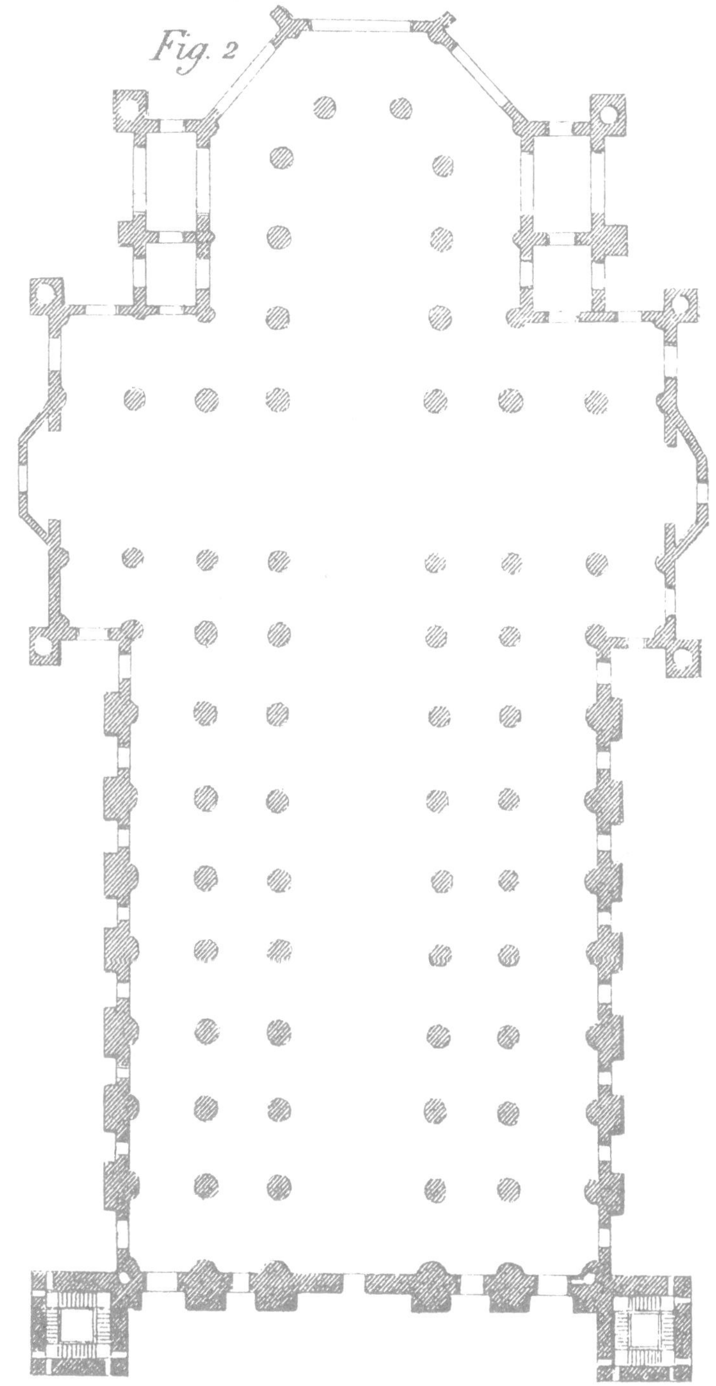

DESIGN ATTRIBUTES

Scope The Design Attributes hierarchy contains descriptors for physical qualities relating to position, shape, size, surface, and other characteristics suggesting frequently occurring aspects of design.

Organization Descriptors are grouped into broad sections, such as <*color-related attributes*> (e.g., **monochrome**), <*positional attributes*> relating to orientation, or relative or directional location (e.g., **diagonal, northeast**), <*shape attributes*> relating to the physical forms of objects or natural elements (e.g., **oxbow, pear-shaped**), <*volume-related attributes*> expressing qualities of mass or capacity (e.g., **hollow**), and <*weight-related attributes*> for relative qualities of weight (e.g., **lightweight**).

Relation to Other Hierarchies Descriptors for geometric figures are found in the Associated Concepts hierarchy (e.g., **hemispheres**), while descriptors for shapes which are not specifically geometric are found here (e.g., **concave**). Descriptors for colors are found in the Colors hierarchy (e.g., **brilliant green**), although descriptors for attributes related to color are found here (e.g., **polychrome**). Descriptors for individual and repeating design elements such as signs and symbols, motifs, patterns, and areas of decoration are in the Design Elements hierarchy (e.g., **crosses, Tudor roses, frets**). Descriptors for styles of art and architecture and names of art movements that are visually distinctive are in the Styles and Periods hierarchy (e.g., **Curvilinear Decorated**).

Descriptor Form and Use Descriptors are in adjectival form, and are meant to be combined with descriptors in other hierarchies (e.g., **broken** + **meander pattern**; **round** + **barns**; **Latin cross-plan** + **churches**).

Number of Descriptors 129

Synopsis

DC.1 *<design attributes>*
DC.2 *<color-related attributes>*
DC.3 **monochrome**
DC.4 **polychrome**
DC.5 *<positional attributes>*
DC.6 *<positional attributes by orientation>*
DC.13 *<positional attributes by portion of a whole>*
DC.25 *<positional attributes by relative position>*
DC.45 *<compass points>*
DC.54 *<shape attributes>*
DC.55 **angular**
|
DC.76 **undulating**
DC.77 *<building plan attributes>*
DC.100 *<furniture shape attributes>*
DC.112 *<naturalistic shape attributes>*
DC.119 *<size attributes>*
DC.120 **large**
|
DC.124 **small**
DC.125 *<photographic plate sizes>*
DC.134 *<surface attributes>*
DC.135 **glossy**
|
DC.141 **smooth**
DC.142 *<volume-related attributes>*
DC.143 **hollow**
DC.144 **solid**
DC.145 *<weight-related attributes>*
DC.146 **heavyweight**
DC.147 **lightweight**

DESIGN ATTRIBUTES (DC)

DC.1	*<design attributes>*
DC.2	*<color-related attributes>*
DC.3	**monochrome**
DC.4	**polychrome**
DC.5	*<positional attributes>*
DC.6	*<positional attributes by orientation>*
DC.7	**diagonal**
DC.8	**frontal**
DC.9	**longitudinal**
DC.10	**perpendicular**
DC.11	**radial**
DC.12	**transverse**
DC.13	*<positional attributes by portion of a whole>*
DC.14	**bottom**
DC.15	**corner**
DC.16	**end**
DC.17	**front**
DC.18	**obverse**
DC.19	**rear**
DC.20	**recto**
DC.21	**reverse**
DC.22	**side**
DC.23	**top**
DC.24	**verso**
DC.25	*<positional attributes by relative position>*
DC.26	**attached**
DC.27	**centered**
DC.28	**central**
DC.29	**concentric**
DC.30	**detached**
DC.31	**elevated**
DC.32	**engaged**
DC.33	**exterior**
DC.34	**freestanding**
DC.35	**interior**
DC.36	**intersecting**
DC.37	**lateral**
DC.38	**left**
DC.39	**lower**
DC.40	**parallel**
DC.41	**projecting**
DC.42	**right**
DC.43	**suspended**
DC.44	**upper**
DC.45	*<compass points>*
DC.46	**east**
DC.47	**north**
DC.48	**northeast**
DC.49	**northwest**

May be used in combination with other descriptors, especially in the Objects facet (e.g., **central-plan** + **churches**; **serpentine-front** + **chests**; **front** + **views**).

DC.50	**south**
DC.51	**southeast**
DC.52	**southwest**
DC.53	**west**
DC.54	*<shape attributes>*
DC.55	**angular**
DC.56	**annular**
DC.57	**arched**
DC.58	**bell-shaped**
DC.59	**broken**
DC.60	**columnar**
DC.61	**curved**
DC.62	**concave**
DC.63	**convex**
DC.64	**curvilinear**
DC.65	**fan-shaped**
DC.66	**flat**
DC.67	**irregular**
DC.68	**pointed**
DC.69	**quadrant**
DC.70	**round**
DC.71	**serpentine**
DC.72	**splayed**
DC.73	**three-dimensional**
DC.74	**two-dimensional**
DC.75	**unbroken**
DC.76	**undulating**
DC.77	*<building plan attributes>*
DC.78	**axial-plan**
DC.79	**central-plan**
DC.80	**Greek cross-plan**
DC.81	**Latin cross-plan**
DC.82	**open-plan**
DC.83	*<building plan attributes: column layouts>*
DC.84	**amphiprostyle**
DC.85	**decastyle**
DC.86	**dipteral**
DC.87	**distyle in antis**
DC.88	**enneastyle**
DC.89	**hexastyle**
DC.90	**octastyle**
DC.91	**peripteral**
DC.92	**prostyle**
DC.93	**pseudodipteral**
DC.94	**pseudoperipteral**
DC.95	**tetrastyle**
DC.96	*<building plan attributes: number of stories>*
DC.97	**single-story**
DC.98	**two-story**

May be used in combination with other descriptors, especially in the Objects facet (e.g., **central-plan** + **churches**; **serpentine-front** + **chests**; **front** + **views**).

DC.99	**three-story**
DC.100	*<furniture shape attributes>*
DC.101	**blockfront**
DC.102	**bombé**
DC.103	**bowfront**
DC.104	**breakfront**
DC.105	**circular-front**
DC.106	**demi-lune**
DC.107	**half-serpentine**
DC.108	**oxbow**
DC.109	**round-front**
DC.110	**serpentine-front**
DC.111	**straight-front**
DC.112	*<naturalistic shape attributes>*
DC.113	**almond-shaped**
DC.114	**anthropomorphic**
DC.115	**egg-shaped**
DC.116	**pear-shaped**
DC.117	**stellate**
DC.118	**zoomorphic**
DC.119	*<size attributes>*
DC.120	**large**
DC.121	**life-size**
DC.122	**miniature**
DC.123	**monumental**
DC.124	**small**
DC.125	*<photographic plate sizes>*
DC.126	**double whole plate**
DC.127	**half plate**
DC.128	**mammoth plate**
DC.129	**ninth plate**
DC.130	**quarter plate**
DC.131	**sixteenth plate**
DC.132	**sixth plate**
DC.133	**whole plate**
DC.134	*<surface attributes>*
DC.135	**glossy**
DC.136	**lustrous**
DC.137	**matte**
DC.138	**raised**
DC.139	**rough**
DC.140	**shiny**
DC.141	**smooth**
DC.142	*<volume-related attributes>*
DC.143	**hollow**
DC.144	**solid**
DC.145	*<weight-related attributes>*
DC.146	**heavyweight**
DC.147	**lightweight**

May be used in combination with other descriptors, especially in the Objects facet (e.g., **central-plan** + **churches**; **serpentine-front** + **chests**; **front** + **views**).

Design Elements Hierarchy

Scope The Design Elements hierarchy contains descriptors for conventionalized and recurring shapes and arrangements of forms used in the design of many types of objects and their ornament. These may be two-dimensional such as painted zigzags, in relief such as carved rosettes, or may refer to the shape of discrete objects, such as Celtic crosses sculpted in stone.

Organization The hierarchy consists of sections for individual **motifs** (e.g., **palmettes**), for repetitive **patterns** (e.g., **interlace**), and for areas of ornamental designs (e.g., **borders**).

Relation to Other Hierarchies Descriptors for geometric figures, which are sometimes used as decorative motifs, are found in the Associated Concepts hierarchy (e.g., **hemispheres**). Other descriptors for certain attributes related to shape or position (e.g., **convex, concentric**) are in the Design Attributes hierarchy. Three-dimensional ornamental elements that derive from architecture but have been adapted to furniture and other decorative arts (e.g., **finials, moldings**), are found in the Built Works Components hierarchy.

Descriptor Form and Use Descriptors appear as plural nouns, except where usage dictates the singular, which includes most pattern types (e.g., **herringbone**). For motifs based on objects or figures, use descriptors from other hierarchies in combination with the descriptor **motif** (e.g., **column** + **motif**; **shell** + **motif**).

Number of Descriptors 144

Synopsis

DG.1	*<design elements>*
DG.2	**motifs**
DG.3	**cabochons**
	|
DG.73	**zodiac symbols**
DG.86	*<ornament areas>*
DG.87	**borders**
	|
DG.92	**panels (ornament areas)**
DG.93	**patterns (design elements)**
DG.94	*<patterns by general type>*
DG.95	**allover patterns**
	|
DG.99	**running patterns**
DG.102	*<patterns by specific type>*
DG.103	**arabesques**
	|
DG.153	**wave pattern**

DESIGN ELEMENTS (DG)

DG.1	*<design elements>*
DG.2	motifs
DG.3	cabochons
DG.4	coquillage
DG.5	crosses
DG.6	ankhs
DG.7	Celtic crosses
DG.8	crosses of Lorraine
DG.9	Greek crosses
DG.10	Latin crosses
DG.11	Calvary crosses
DG.12	Maltese crosses
DG.13	papal crosses
DG.14	patriarchal crosses
DG.15	Saint Andrew's crosses
DG.16	tau crosses
DG.17	wheel crosses
DG.18	drolleries
DG.19	*<figure-derived motifs>*
DG.20	aegicranes
DG.21	bucrania
DG.22	espagnolettes
DG.23	*<geometric motifs>*
DG.24	chevrons
DG.25	cinquefoils
DG.26	dots
DG.27	interlocking circles
DG.28	lozenges
DG.29	multifoils
DG.30	quatrefoils
DG.31	trefoils
DG.32	triquetras
DG.33	grotesques
DG.34	hearts
DG.35	flaming hearts
DG.36	pierced hearts
DG.37	heraldic motifs
DG.38	knots
DG.39	labyrinths
DG.40	linenfold
DG.41	*<natural element motifs>*
DG.42	crescents
DG.43	flames
DG.44	rising suns
DG.45	snowflakes
DG.46	stars
DG.47	Stars of David
DG.48	sunbursts
DG.49	pateras (motifs)

May be used in combination with other descriptors (e.g., **herringbone** + **masonry**; **shell** + **motif**).

DG.50 *<plant-derived motifs>*
DG.51 acanthus
DG.52 anthemions
DG.53 palmettes
DG.54 ballflowers
DG.55 festoons
DG.56 fleurons
DG.57 fleurs-de-lis
DG.58 husks (motifs)
DG.59 lotus
DG.60 rosettes
DG.61 Tudor flowers
DG.62 Tudor roses
DG.63 water leaf
DG.64 scrolls (motifs)
DG.65 C-scrolls
DG.66 leaf scrolls
DG.67 S-scrolls
DG.68 tetraskelions
DG.69 swastikas
DG.70 triskelions
DG.71 trumpet spirals
DG.72 whiplash curves
DG.73 zodiac symbols
DG.74 Aquarius symbols
DG.75 Aries symbols
DG.76 Cancer symbols
DG.77 Capricorn symbols
DG.78 Gemini symbols
DG.79 Leo symbols
DG.80 Libra symbols
DG.81 Pisces symbols
DG.82 Sagittarius symbols
DG.83 Scorpio symbols
DG.84 Taurus symbols
DG.85 Virgo symbols
DG.86 *<ornament areas>*
DG.87 borders
DG.88 cartouches
DG.89 friezes (ornamental bands)
DG.90 zoophori
DG.91 medallions (ornament areas)
DG.92 panels (ornament areas)
DG.93 patterns (design elements)
DG.94 *<patterns by general type>*
DG.95 allover patterns
DG.96 diaper patterns
DG.97 powderwork
DG.98 counterchange

May be used in combination with other descriptors (e.g., **herringbone** + **masonry**; **shell** + **motif**).

DG.99 **running ornament**
DG.100 **undulate bands**
DG.101 **vertebrate bands**
DG.102 *<patterns by specific type>*
DG.103 **arabesques**
DG.104 **moresques**
DG.105 **cloud bands**
DG.106 *<edging and surfacing patterns>*
DG.107 **banding**
DG.108 **cross banding**
DG.109 **feather banding**
DG.110 **straight banding**
DG.111 **beading (edging pattern)**
DG.112 **fluting**
DG.113 **cabled fluting**
DG.114 **strigillation**
DG.115 **gadrooning**
DG.116 **reeding**
DG.117 **rustication**
DG.118 **scalloping**
DG.119 **vermiculation**
DG.120 **floral patterns**
DG.121 **foliation**
DG.122 **geometric patterns**
DG.123 **checker pattern**
DG.124 **frets**
DG.125 **Chinese frets**
DG.126 **key pattern**
DG.127 **fretwork**
DG.128 **Chinese fretwork**
DG.129 **herringbone**
DG.130 **money pattern**
DG.131 **reticular pattern**
DG.132 **step pattern**
DG.133 **stripes**
DG.134 **zigzags**
DG.135 **guilloche**
DG.136 **imbrication**
DG.137 **scale pattern**
DG.138 **interlace**
DG.139 **knotwork**
DG.140 **lacertine ornament**
DG.141 **meanders (patterns)**
DG.142 **stepped frets**
DG.143 **moiré**
DG.144 **scrollwork**
DG.145 **cloud scrolls**
DG.146 **inhabited scrolls**
DG.147 **scrolling foliage**

May be used in combination with other descriptors (e.g., **herringbone** + **masonry**; **shell** + **motif**).

DG.148 rinceaux
DG.149 vine scrolls
DG.150 wave scrolls
DG.151 Vitruvian scrolls
DG.152 strapwork
DG.153 wave pattern

May be used in combination with other descriptors (e.g., **herringbone** + **masonry**; **shell** + **motif**).

Colors
Hierarchy

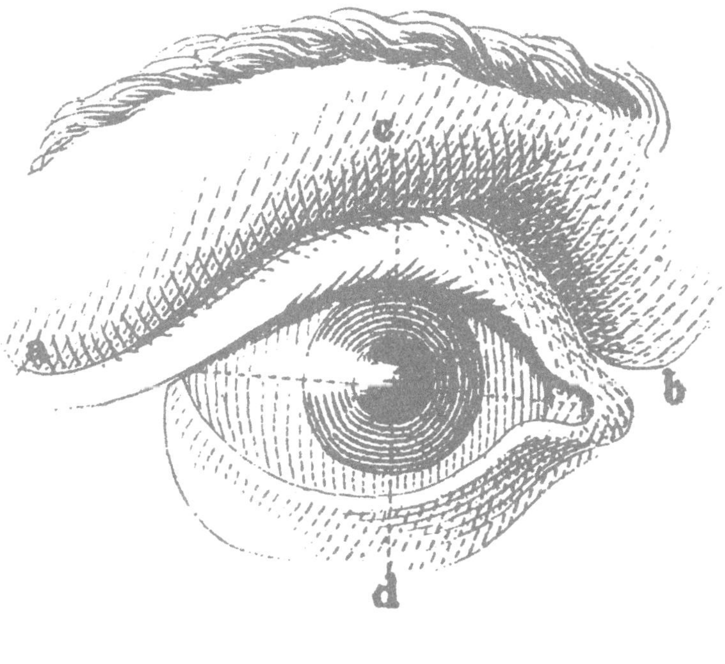

Scope The Colors hierarchy contains descriptors for the names of colors from the Universal Color Language (UCL), as found in Kenneth L. Kelly and Deane B. Judd, *Color: Universal Language and Dictionary of Color Names* (Washington, D.C.: U.S. Department of Commerce, National Bureau of Standards, 1976). Variant color names from other well-known color-order systems and methods of designating color are provided as non-preferred descriptors to their corresponding UCL color names. Centroid color numbers, which refer the user to the appropriate color-blocks on the Inter-Society Color Council and National Bureau of Standards color-name charts given in *Color* are also provided as non-preferred descriptors. The charts supply the range of Munsell notations for each block; however, a user who needs to describe the color of an item in hand very precisely is advised to consult the *Munsell Book of Color*, (Baltimore: Munsell Color Company, 1976) to make comparison with the given samples in order to determine the specific notation.

Organization The descriptors are grouped in two sections: <*chromatic colors*> and **neutrals**. The arrangement given in *Color* is followed, except where a more strictly hierarchical structure is appropriate (e.g., **very pale green** is a narrower descriptor to **pale green**; **dark grayish yellow** is a narrower descriptor to **grayish yellow**).

Relation to Other Hierarchies Color-related attributes (e.g., **monochrome**, **polychrome**) are found in the Design Attributes hierarchy. Descriptors for individual and repeating design elements such as signs and symbols, motifs, patterns, and areas of decoration are in the Design Elements hierarchy (e.g., **crosses**, **Tudor roses**, **frets**). Descriptors for types of color (e.g., **cool colors**, **reflected color**) and color-related concepts (e.g., **color mixture**, **intensity**, **tone**) are found in the Associated Concepts hierarchy.

Descriptor Form and Use Descriptors are in adjectival form, and are intended to modify descriptors from other hierarchies (e.g., **dark gray** + **paving tile**; **deep greenish blue** + **silk**).

Number of Descriptors 296

Synopsis

DL.1	colors
DL.2	<*chromatic colors*>
DL.3	pink
DL.34	red
DL.60	orange
DL.76	brown
DL.111	yellow
DL.144	olive (color)
DL.154	yellow green
DL.163	green
DL.212	blue
DL.266	purple
DL.299	neutrals
DL.300	white
DL.301	gray
DL.305	black

COLORS (DL)

DL.1	colors
DL.2	*<chromatic colors>*
DL.3	pink
DL.4	vivid pink
DL.5	strong pink
DL.6	deep pink
DL.7	light pink
DL.8	moderate pink
DL.9	dark pink
DL.10	pale pink
DL.11	grayish pink
DL.12	pinkish white
DL.13	pinkish gray
DL.14	*<intermediate pinks>*
DL.15	purplish pink
DL.16	brilliant purplish pink
DL.17	strong purplish pink
DL.18	deep purplish pink
DL.19	light purplish pink
DL.20	moderate purplish pink
DL.21	dark purplish pink
DL.22	pale purplish pink
DL.23	grayish purplish pink
DL.24	yellowish pink
DL.25	vivid yellowish pink
DL.26	strong yellowish pink
DL.27	deep yellowish pink
DL.28	light yellowish pink
DL.29	moderate yellowish pink
DL.30	dark yellowish pink
DL.31	pale yellowish pink
DL.32	grayish yellowish pink
DL.33	brownish pink
DL.34	red
DL.35	vivid red
DL.36	strong red
DL.37	deep red
DL.38	very deep red
DL.39	moderate red
DL.40	dark red
DL.41	very dark red
DL.42	grayish red
DL.43	dark grayish red
DL.44	light grayish red
DL.45	blackish red
DL.46	reddish gray
DL.47	dark reddish gray
DL.48	reddish black
DL.49	*<intermediate reds>*

May be used in combination with other descriptors (e.g., **dark gray** + **paving tile**; **deep greenish blue** + **silk**).

DL.50 purplish red
DL.51 vivid purplish red
DL.52 strong purplish red
DL.53 deep purplish red
DL.54 very deep purplish red
DL.55 moderate purplish red
DL.56 dark purplish red
DL.57 very dark purplish red
DL.58 grayish purplish red
DL.59 light grayish purplish red
DL.60 orange
DL.61 vivid orange
DL.62 brilliant orange
DL.63 strong orange
DL.64 deep orange
DL.65 light orange
DL.66 moderate orange
DL.67 *<intermediate oranges>*
DL.68 reddish orange
DL.69 vivid reddish orange
DL.70 strong reddish orange
DL.71 deep reddish orange
DL.72 moderate reddish orange
DL.73 dark reddish orange
DL.74 grayish reddish orange
DL.75 brownish orange
DL.76 brown
DL.77 strong brown
DL.78 deep brown
DL.79 light brown
DL.80 moderate brown
DL.81 dark brown
DL.82 grayish brown
DL.83 light grayish brown
DL.84 dark grayish brown
DL.85 brownish gray
DL.86 light brownish gray
DL.87 brownish black
DL.88 *<intermediate browns>*
DL.89 reddish brown
DL.90 strong reddish brown
DL.91 deep reddish brown
DL.92 light reddish brown
DL.93 moderate reddish brown
DL.94 dark reddish brown
DL.95 grayish reddish brown
DL.96 light grayish reddish brown
DL.97 dark grayish reddish brown
DL.98 yellowish brown

May be used in combination with other descriptors (e.g., **dark gray** + **paving tile**; **deep greenish blue** + **silk**).

<chromatic colors>
brown
<intermediate browns>
yellowish brown

DL.99	strong yellowish brown
DL.100	deep yellowish brown
DL.101	light yellowish brown
DL.102	moderate yellowish brown
DL.103	dark yellowish brown
DL.104	grayish yellowish brown
DL.105	light grayish yellowish brown
DL.106	dark grayish yellowish brown
DL.107	olive brown
DL.108	light olive brown
DL.109	moderate olive brown
DL.110	dark olive brown
DL.111	yellow
DL.112	vivid yellow
DL.113	brilliant yellow
DL.114	strong yellow
DL.115	deep yellow
DL.116	light yellow
DL.117	moderate yellow
DL.118	dark yellow
DL.119	pale yellow
DL.120	grayish yellow
DL.121	dark grayish yellow
DL.122	yellowish white
DL.123	yellowish gray
DL.124	*<intermediate yellows>*
DL.125	orange yellow
DL.126	vivid orange yellow
DL.127	brilliant orange yellow
DL.128	strong orange yellow
DL.129	deep orange yellow
DL.130	light orange yellow
DL.131	moderate orange yellow
DL.132	dark orange yellow
DL.133	pale orange yellow
DL.134	greenish yellow
DL.135	vivid greenish yellow
DL.136	brilliant greenish yellow
DL.137	strong greenish yellow
DL.138	deep greenish yellow
DL.139	light greenish yellow
DL.140	moderate greenish yellow
DL.141	dark greenish yellow
DL.142	pale greenish yellow
DL.143	grayish greenish yellow
DL.144	olive (color)
DL.145	light olive
DL.146	moderate olive
DL.147	dark olive

May be used in combination with other descriptors (e.g., **dark gray** + **paving tile**; **deep greenish blue** + **silk**).

DL.148 grayish olive
DL.149 light grayish olive
DL.150 dark grayish olive
DL.151 olive gray
DL.152 light olive gray
DL.153 olive black
DL.154 yellow green
DL.155 vivid yellow green
DL.156 brilliant yellow green
DL.157 strong yellow green
DL.158 deep yellow green
DL.159 light yellow green
DL.160 moderate yellow green
DL.161 pale yellow green
DL.162 grayish yellow green
DL.163 green
DL.164 vivid green
DL.165 brilliant green
DL.166 strong green
DL.167 deep green
DL.168 light green
DL.169 very light green
DL.170 moderate green
DL.171 dark green
DL.172 very dark green
DL.173 pale green
DL.174 very pale green
DL.175 grayish green
DL.176 dark grayish green
DL.177 blackish green
DL.178 greenish white
DL.179 greenish gray
DL.180 light greenish gray
DL.181 dark greenish gray
DL.182 greenish black
DL.183 *<intermediate greens>*
DL.184 yellowish green
DL.185 vivid yellowish green
DL.186 brilliant yellowish green
DL.187 strong yellowish green
DL.188 deep yellowish green
DL.189 very deep yellowish green
DL.190 light yellowish green
DL.191 very light yellowish green
DL.192 moderate yellowish green
DL.193 dark yellowish green
DL.194 very dark yellowish green
DL.195 bluish green
DL.196 vivid bluish green

May be used in combination with other descriptors (e.g., **dark gray** + **paving tile**; **deep greenish blue** + **silk**).

DL.197	**brilliant bluish green**
DL.198	**strong bluish green**
DL.199	**deep bluish green**
DL.200	**light bluish green**
DL.201	**very light bluish green**
DL.202	**moderate bluish green**
DL.203	**dark bluish green**
DL.204	**very dark bluish green**
DL.205	**olive green**
DL.206	**strong olive green**
DL.207	**deep olive green**
DL.208	**moderate olive green**
DL.209	**dark olive green**
DL.210	**grayish olive green**
DL.211	**dark grayish olive green**
DL.212	**blue**
DL.213	**vivid blue**
DL.214	**brilliant blue**
DL.215	**strong blue**
DL.216	**deep blue**
DL.217	**light blue**
DL.218	**very light blue**
DL.219	**moderate blue**
DL.220	**dark blue**
DL.221	**pale blue**
DL.222	**very pale blue**
DL.223	**grayish blue**
DL.224	**dark grayish blue**
DL.225	**blackish blue**
DL.226	**bluish white**
DL.227	**bluish gray**
DL.228	**light bluish gray**
DL.229	**dark bluish gray**
DL.230	**bluish black**
DL.231	*<intermediate blues>*
DL.232	**greenish blue**
DL.233	**vivid greenish blue**
DL.234	**brilliant greenish blue**
DL.235	**strong greenish blue**
DL.236	**deep greenish blue**
DL.237	**light greenish blue**
DL.238	**very light greenish blue**
DL.239	**moderate greenish blue**
DL.240	**dark greenish blue**
DL.241	**very dark greenish blue**
DL.242	**purplish blue**
DL.243	**vivid purplish blue**
DL.244	**brilliant purplish blue**
DL.245	**strong purplish blue**

May be used in combination with other descriptors (e.g., **dark gray** + **paving tile**; **deep greenish blue** + **silk**).

DL.246 deep purplish blue
DL.247 light purplish blue
DL.248 very light purplish blue
DL.249 moderate purplish blue
DL.250 dark purplish blue
DL.251 pale purplish blue
DL.252 very pale purplish blue
DL.253 grayish purplish blue
DL.254 violet
DL.255 vivid violet
DL.256 brilliant violet
DL.257 strong violet
DL.258 deep violet
DL.259 light violet
DL.260 very light violet
DL.261 moderate violet
DL.262 dark violet
DL.263 pale violet
DL.264 very pale violet
DL.265 grayish violet
DL.266 purple
DL.267 vivid purple
DL.268 brilliant purple
DL.269 strong purple
DL.270 deep purple
DL.271 very deep purple
DL.272 light purple
DL.273 very light purple
DL.274 moderate purple
DL.275 dark purple
DL.276 very dark purple
DL.277 pale purple
DL.278 very pale purple
DL.279 grayish purple
DL.280 dark grayish purple
DL.281 blackish purple
DL.282 purplish white
DL.283 purplish gray
DL.284 light purplish gray
DL.285 dark purplish gray
DL.286 purplish black
DL.287 *<intermediate purples>*
DL.288 reddish purple
DL.289 vivid reddish purple
DL.290 strong reddish purple
DL.291 deep reddish purple
DL.292 very deep reddish purple
DL.293 light reddish purple
DL.294 moderate reddish purple

May be used in combination with other descriptors (e.g., **dark gray** + **paving tile**; **deep greenish blue** + **silk**).

DL.295 dark reddish purple
DL.296 very dark reddish purple
DL.297 pale reddish purple
DL.298 grayish reddish purple
DL.299 neutrals
DL.300 white
DL.301 gray
DL.302 light gray
DL.303 medium gray
DL.304 dark gray
DL.305 black

May be used in combination with other descriptors (e.g., **dark gray** + **paving tile**; **deep greenish blue** + **silk**).

Styles and Periods facet

The Styles and Periods facet provides commonly accepted names for stylistic groupings and distinct chronological periods that are relevant to art and architecture.

The Styles and Periods facet consists of the following hierarchy:

Styles and Periods (FL)

Styles and Periods Hierarchy

STYLES AND PERIODS

Scope The Styles and Periods hierarchy contains the names of art and architecture styles, historical periods, and art movements. Names of peoples, cultures, individuals, and sites are included only if they designate distinct styles or periods (e.g., **Yoruba**, **Louis XIV**). Geographic descriptors are included only for broad cultural regions. Emphasis is on the Western world, though less detailed sections for African, Asian, Islamic, and Pacific art and architecture are included. Subsections related to the decorative arts are under develpment.

Organization The hierarchy is divided into two broad sections. The first, *<styles and periods by general era>*, contains descriptors that apply generally to several regions and cultures (e.g., **prehistoric**). The second, *<styles and periods by region>*, contains descriptors that are specific to certain regions or cultures and is divided into the following: **African**, *<The Americas>*, **Asian**, *<Early Western World>*, **European**, *<The Islamic World>*, **Pacific**, *<international post-1945 styles and movements>*. Under these broad divisions, descriptors may be represented chronologically, where a clear chronological order exists, alphabetically by geographical region, or alphabetically by other relevant divisions, such as architecture, fine arts, or decorative arts styles.

A descriptor for a style or period appears only once in the hierarchy and is placed either with respect to its earliest chronological occurrence, or where the descriptor has its broadest meaning. In general, descriptors should be considered as clarified by their hierarchical location but not limited in meaning by it. For example, although descriptors for styles brought to colonized regions (e.g., **Georgian**) are listed only under the colonizing country, such as Great Britain, they may be relevant to any area where the styles are found.

Relation to Other Hierarchies Descriptors for broad types of art and architecture that are not specific to a given people or period (e.g., **amateur art**) are found in the Associated Concepts hierarchy, as are descriptors for general approaches to art (e.g., **realism**), while specific movements named after such terms are found here (e.g., **Realist**). Descriptors for styles and movements which are primarily associated with fields other than art (e.g., **concrete poetry**) are also located in the Associated Concepts hierarchy, although descriptors applicable to both the visual and nonvisual arts (e.g., **Decadent Movement**) are here.

Descriptor Form and Use Descriptors from the Styles and Periods hierarchy are intended to be used as modifiers and therefore are in adjectival form, where one exists (e.g., **Greek**). Otherwise they are in noun form to be used as noun modifiers (e.g., **Shawnee**). In the modern and post-1945 sections, where a descriptor is an adjective derived from the name of an artistic movement, the name of that movement appears as an alternate form (e.g., **Cubist**, alternate: **Cubism**).

Some style names must be combined from two or more descriptors in this hierarchy (e.g., **French** + **Empire**). For styles brought to colonized regions, use the style name plus the appropriate geographic place name (e.g., **Tudor** + **United States**).

Number of Descriptors 3284

Synopsis

FL.1	*<styles and periods by general era>*
FL.2	**ancient**
FL.3	**Dark Ages**
FL.4	**prehistoric**
FL.5	**protohistoric**
FL.6	*<three-age system>*
FL.7	**Stone Age**
FL.18	*<transitional periods Stone Age to Bronze Age>*
FL.26	**Bronze Age**
FL.30	**Iron Age**
FL.34	*<styles and periods by region>*
FL.35	**African**
FL.36	*<prehistoric African periods>*
FL.75	*<ancient African styles and periods>*
FL.171	*<Colonial African styles>*
FL.175	*<African styles by region>*
FL.699	*<African sculpture styles>*
FL.702	*<The Americas>*
FL.703	*<American regions>*
FL.726	**Pre-Columbian**
FL.1194	**Native American**
FL.1701	*<Colonial American styles>*
FL.1719	*<modern American styles and movements>*
FL.1761	**Asian**
FL.1762	**Central Asian**
FL.1831	**East Asian**
FL.2119	**Siberian**
FL.2151	**South Asian**
FL.2307	**Southeast Asian**
FL.2447	*<Early Western World>*
FL.2448	*<ancient European styles and periods>*
FL.2528	**Mediterranean**
FL.2846	**Near Eastern**

FL.3034 **European**
FL.3035 *<European regions>*
FL.3065 *<European styles and periods>*
FL.3424 *<The Islamic World>*
FL.3425 *<Islamic World dynastic styles and periods>*
FL.3604 **Moorish**
FL.3605 **Saracenic**
FL.3606 **Tartar**
FL.3608 **Pacific**
FL.3609 **Australian**
FL.3618 **Melanesian**
FL.3676 **Micronesian**
FL.3687 **Polynesian**
FL.3703 *<international post-1945 styles and movements>*
FL.3705 *<post-1945 architecture and design styles and movements>*
FL.3712 *<post-1945 fine arts styles and movements>*

STYLES AND PERIODS (FL)

FL.1	*<styles and periods by general era>*
FL.2	ancient
FL.3	Dark Ages
FL.4	prehistoric
FL.5	protohistoric
FL.6	*<three-age system>*
FL.7	Stone Age
FL.8	Paleolithic
FL.9	Lower Paleolithic
FL.10	Middle Paleolithic
FL.11	Upper Paleolithic
FL.12	Epipaleolithic
FL.13	Mesolithic
FL.14	Neolithic
FL.15	Early Neolithic
FL.16	Middle Neolithic
FL.17	Late Neolithic
FL.18	*<transitional periods Stone Age to Bronze Age>*
FL.19	Basal Neolithic
FL.20	Chalcolithic
FL.21	Early Chalcolithic
FL.22	Middle Chalcolithic
FL.23	Late Chalcolithic
FL.24	Eneolithic
FL.25	Final Neolithic
FL.26	Bronze Age
FL.27	Early Bronze Age
FL.28	Middle Bronze Age
FL.29	Late Bronze Age
FL.30	Iron Age
FL.31	Early Iron Age
FL.32	Middle Iron Age
FL.33	Late Iron Age
FL.34	*<styles and periods by region>*
FL.35	African
FL.36	*<prehistoric African periods>*
FL.37	*<prehistoric North African periods>*
FL.38	*<African Paleolithic periods>*
FL.39	Aterian
FL.40	Dabban
FL.41	*<African Epipaleolithic periods>*
FL.42	Capsian
FL.43	Keremian
FL.44	Libyco-Capsian
FL.45	Oranian
FL.46	*<prehistoric Sub-Saharan African periods>*
FL.47	*<Earlier Stone Age>*
FL.48	Pre-Chellean
FL.49	Kafuan

May be used in combination with other descriptors, especially in the Objects facet (e.g., **Baroque** + **churches**; **Japanese** + **enameling**; **Abstract Expressionist** + **drawings**).

FL.50 **Oldowen**
FL.51 **Chelles-Acheul**
FL.52 *<First Intermediate Stone Age>*
FL.53 **Fauresmith**
FL.54 **Sangoan**
FL.55 *<Middle Stone Age>*
FL.56 **Stillbay**
FL.57 **Pietersburg**
FL.58 **Lupemban**
FL.59 *<Second Intermediate Stone age>*
FL.60 **Mangosian**
FL.61 **Lupembo-Tshitolian**
FL.62 *<Later Stone age>*
FL.63 **Smithfield**
FL.64 **Wilton**
FL.65 **Nachikufan**
FL.66 **Tshitolian**
FL.67 *<prehistoric African rock art periods>*
FL.68 **Bubalus phase**
FL.69 **Round Head phase**
FL.70 **Bovidean Pastoral phase**
FL.71 **Horse phase**
FL.72 **Chariot sub-period**
FL.73 **Horseman sub-period**
FL.74 **Horse and Camel sub-period**
FL.75 *<ancient African styles and periods>*
FL.76 *<ancient West African styles and periods>*
FL.77 **Dawu**
FL.78 **Ghana Kingdom**
FL.79 **Koumbi Saleh**
FL.80 **Gonja**
FL.81 **Kanem-Bornu**
FL.82 **Kintampo**
FL.83 **Kong**
FL.84 **Mali Kingdom**
FL.85 *<ancient Inland Niger Delta styles>*
FL.86 **Jenne**
FL.87 **Mopti**
FL.88 **Niani**
FL.89 **Sankore**
FL.90 **Tellem**
FL.91 **Timbuktu**
FL.92 **Nigerian**
FL.93 **Benin**
FL.94 **Early Benin**
FL.95 **Middle Benin**
FL.96 **Late Benin**
FL.97 **Daima**
FL.98 **Eshure**

May be used in combination with other descriptors, especially in the Objects facet (e.g., **Baroque** + **churches**; **Japanese** + **enameling**; **Abstract Expressionist** + **drawings**).

FL.99	Esie
FL.100	Ife
FL.101	Classical Ife
FL.102	Postclassical Ife
FL.103	Igbo-Ukwu
FL.104	Igbo Isaiah
FL.105	Igbo Jonah
FL.106	Igbo Richard
FL.107	Kanuri
FL.108	Birnin Gazargamo
FL.109	Niger Delta
FL.110	Nok
FL.111	Taruga
FL.112	Old Oyo
FL.113	Owo
FL.114	Igbo Laja
FL.115	Tsoede
FL.116	Jebba
FL.117	Tada
FL.118	Yelwa
FL.119	Sao Empire
FL.120	Songhai
FL.121	Gaô
FL.122	*<ancient Central African styles and periods>*
FL.123	Kongo Kingdom
FL.124	Kuba Kingdom
FL.125	Luba-Lunda Kingdoms
FL.126	Luba Empire
FL.127	Lunda Empire
FL.128	*<ancient Southern African styles and periods>*
FL.129	Karanga
FL.130	*<Karanga periods>*
FL.131	Pre-Monomotapa
FL.132	Monomotapa
FL.133	Mambo
FL.134	Lydenburg
FL.135	Mapungubwe
FL.136	Mtoko
FL.137	Rozwi
FL.138	Dhlo Dhlo
FL.139	Khami
FL.140	Naletali
FL.141	Regina
FL.142	Thabas-zi-ka-Mambo
FL.143	Van Niekirk Ruins
FL.144	*<ancient Southern African pottery styles>*
FL.145	channeled ware
FL.146	dimple based ware
FL.147	stamped ware

May be used in combination with other descriptors, especially in the Objects facet (e.g., **Baroque** + **churches**; **Japanese** + **enameling**; **Abstract Expressionist** + **drawings**).

FL.148 *<ancient East African styles and periods>*
FL.149 **Axum**
FL.150 **Azanian**
FL.151 **Kilwa**
FL.152 **Lamu**
FL.153 **Mombasa**
FL.154 **Ingombe Ilede**
FL.155 **Nubian**
FL.156 **Kerma**
FL.157 *<Kerma periods>*
FL.158 **Early Kerma**
FL.159 **Middle Kerma**
FL.160 **Classic Kerma**
FL.161 **Kushite**
FL.162 *<Kushite periods>*
FL.163 **Napatan**
FL.164 **Meroitic**
FL.165 **Songa Mnara**
FL.166 **Zanj**
FL.167 *<ancient North African styles and periods>*
FL.168 **Darfur**
FL.169 **Jebel Uri**
FL.170 **Numidian**
FL.171 *<Colonial African styles>*
FL.172 **Afro-Portuguese**
FL.173 **Bini-Portuguese**
FL.174 **Sapi-Portuguese**
FL.175 *<African styles by region>*
FL.176 *<West African styles>*
FL.177 *<Northeastern Nigerian styles>*
FL.178 *<Cameroon grasslands>*
FL.179 **Bamileke**
FL.180 **Bagam**
FL.181 **Bamenjo**
FL.182 **Batie**
FL.183 **Cham (Bamileke)**
FL.184 **Ngwa**
FL.185 *<Cameroonian groups below the escarpment>*
FL.186 **Bafo**
FL.187 **Bassa**
FL.188 **Fia**
FL.189 **Kossi**
FL.190 **Kpe**
FL.191 **Kundu**
FL.192 **Lundu**
FL.193 **Seke**
FL.194 **Tikar**
FL.195 **Bamum**
FL.196 **Banki**

May be used in combination with other descriptors, especially in the Objects facet (e.g., **Baroque** + **churches**; **Japanese** + **enameling**; **Abstract Expressionist** + **drawings**).

FL.197	**Fum**
FL.198	**Kom**
FL.199	**Li**
FL.200	**Wum**
FL.201	*<Niger-Congo language groups>*
FL.202	*<Adamawa-Eastern branch>*
FL.203	**Chamba (Nigerian)**
FL.204	**Mumuye**
FL.205	**Waja**
FL.206	*<Benue-Congo branch>*
FL.207	**Afo**
FL.208	**Gwari**
FL.209	**Jaba**
FL.210	**Jarawa**
FL.211	**Barawa**
FL.212	**Jibu**
FL.213	**Jukun**
FL.214	**Kaleri**
FL.215	**Koro**
FL.216	**Mama**
FL.217	**Mambila**
FL.218	**Nupe**
FL.219	**Rinderi**
FL.220	**Rukuba**
FL.221	**Tigong**
FL.222	**Tiv**
FL.223	**Zumper**
FL.224	*<Chad subfamily Afroasiatic language groups>*
FL.225	**Angas**
FL.226	**Bachama**
FL.227	**Bura**
FL.228	**Ga'anda**
FL.229	**Goemai**
FL.230	**Gwandara**
FL.231	**Montol**
FL.232	**Wurkun**
FL.233	*<Southern Nigerian styles>*
FL.234	*<Cross River region>*
FL.235	**Abua**
FL.236	**Anyang (Nigerian)**
FL.237	**Boki**
FL.238	**Ejagham**
FL.239	**Keaka**
FL.240	**Ibibio**
FL.241	**Anang**
FL.242	**Efik**
FL.243	**Eket**
FL.244	**Mbembe**
FL.245	**Ogoni**

May be used in combination with other descriptors, especially in the Objects facet (e.g., **Baroque** + **churches**; **Japanese** + **enameling**; **Abstract Expressionist** + **drawings**).

FL.246 **Oron**
FL.247 *<Edo-speaking cultures>*
FL.248 **Bini**
FL.249 **Edo (African)**
FL.250 **Etsako**
FL.251 **Ishan**
FL.252 **Isoko**
FL.253 **Itsekiri**
FL.254 **Okpella**
FL.255 **Urhobo**
FL.256 *<Igbo region>*
FL.257 **Ebira**
FL.258 **Idoma**
FL.259 **Igala**
FL.260 **Igbo**
FL.261 **Achi**
FL.262 **Afikpo**
FL.263 **Bende (Igbo)**
FL.264 **Udi**
FL.265 *<Niger Delta>*
FL.266 **Ijo**
FL.267 **Brass (Ijo)**
FL.268 **Kalabari**
FL.269 **Yoruba**
FL.270 *<Yoruba architectural styles>*
FL.271 **Brazilian Style**
FL.272 *<Yoruba fine arts styles>*
FL.273 **Egba**
FL.274 **Ekiti**
FL.275 **Igbomina**
FL.276 **Ijebu**
FL.277 **Ketu**
FL.278 **Oyo**
FL.279 *<Western Guinea coast styles>*
FL.280 *<Akan cultures>*
FL.281 **Akan**
FL.282 **Akyem**
FL.283 **Akwamu**
FL.284 **Akwapim**
FL.285 **Anyi**
FL.286 **Aowin**
FL.287 **Ashanti**
FL.288 **Baulé**
FL.289 **Yaure**
FL.290 **Fanti**
FL.291 **Coastal Akan**
FL.292 **Ajukru**
FL.293 **Alagya**
FL.294 **Attie**

May be used in combination with other descriptors, especially in the Objects facet (e.g., **Baroque** + **churches**; **Japanese** + **enameling**; **Abstract Expressionist** + **drawings**).

FL.295	Ebrie
FL.296	Eotile
FL.297	Guang
FL.298	Brong
FL.299	*<Ewe cultures>*
FL.300	Adangme
FL.301	Krobo
FL.302	Ewe
FL.303	Fon
FL.304	Adja
FL.305	Aizo
FL.306	Gä
FL.307	Gun
FL.308	Tofinu
FL.309	Namba
FL.310	Shai
FL.311	*<Kru-speaking peoples>*
FL.312	Bété
FL.313	Kru
FL.314	Wee
FL.315	Sapo
FL.316	Tien
FL.317	*<Kwa-speaking peoples>*
FL.318	De
FL.319	Grebo
FL.320	*<Mande region peoples>*
FL.321	Dan
FL.322	Tura
FL.323	Gbande
FL.324	Gbundi
FL.325	Guro
FL.326	Kissi
FL.327	Kono
FL.328	Kpelle
FL.329	Loma
FL.330	Mano
FL.331	Mende
FL.332	Sherbro
FL.333	Temne
FL.334	Vai
FL.335	*<West Atlantic peoples>*
FL.336	Banyun
FL.337	Bijogo
FL.338	Diola
FL.339	Felup
FL.340	Gola
FL.341	Koniagui
FL.342	Serer
FL.343	*<Simo society cultures>*

May be used in combination with other descriptors, especially in the Objects facet (e.g., **Baroque** + **churches**; **Japanese** + **enameling**; **Abstract Expressionist** + **drawings**).

FL.344 Baga
FL.345 Landuma
FL.346 Nalu
FL.347 Wolof
FL.348 *<Western Sudanese styles>*
FL.349 *<Gur-speaking peoples>*
FL.350 Bargu
FL.351 Basari
FL.352 Dogon
FL.353 Grunshi
FL.354 Kurumba
FL.355 Lobi
FL.356 Minianka
FL.357 Mossi
FL.358 Nafana
FL.359 Nioniosse
FL.360 Nunuma
FL.361 Senufo
FL.362 Kulango
FL.363 Ligbi
FL.364 Sisala
FL.365 Tallensi
FL.366 *<Lake Chad region peoples>*
FL.367 Bagirmi
FL.368 Fali
FL.369 Kotoko
FL.370 Mandara
FL.371 Masa
FL.372 Saô
FL.373 Manding
FL.374 Bamana
FL.375 Bozo
FL.376 Malinke
FL.377 Marka
FL.378 Soninke
FL.379 *<Voltaic peoples>*
FL.380 Bobo
FL.381 Bobo-Fing
FL.382 Bwa
FL.383 Gurunsi
FL.384 Kabre
FL.385 Konkomba
FL.386 Moba
FL.387 Tamberma
FL.388 Tem
FL.389 *<Western Sudanese fringe-dwelling peoples>*
FL.390 Adarawa
FL.391 Fulani
FL.392 Bororo (African)

May be used in combination with other descriptors, especially in the Objects facet (e.g., **Baroque** + **churches**; **Japanese** + **enameling**; **Abstract Expressionist** + **drawings**).

<West African styles>
  <Western Sudanese styles>
    <Western Sudanese fringe-dwelling peoples>
      Fulani

FL.393 **Fula**
FL.394 **Wodaabe**
FL.395 **Hausa**
FL.396 *<Central and Equatorial African styles>*
FL.397   *<Gabon region styles>*
FL.398   **Kuyu**
FL.399   *<Ogowe River area>*
FL.400   **Galwa**
FL.401   **Lali**
FL.402   **Lumbu**
FL.403   **Mpongwe**
FL.404   **Nzebi**
FL.405   **Punu**
FL.406   **Sangu**
FL.407   **Shira**
FL.408   **Pahouin**
FL.409   **Beti**
FL.410   **Bulu**
FL.411   **Fang (Pahouin)**
FL.412   *<Reliquary figure area>*
FL.413   **Duma**
FL.414   **Hongwe**
FL.415   **Kande**
FL.416   **Kota**
FL.417   **Mbete**
FL.418   **Ndumbo**
FL.419   **Ngom**
FL.420   **Ngumba**
FL.421   **Shake**
FL.422   **Wumu**
FL.423   **Tsogo**
FL.424   *<Upper Sangha River area>*
FL.425   **Duala**
FL.426   **Kwele**
FL.427   *<Western Zaire styles>*
FL.428   *<Central Zaire>*
FL.429   **Kuba**
FL.430   **Biombo**
FL.431   **Kete**
FL.432   **Kuba Court Style**
FL.433   **Kuba Revived Court Style**
FL.434   **Kuba Folk Style**
FL.435   **Kele**
FL.436   **Mbala (Kuba Folk Style)**
FL.437   **Ngendi**
FL.438   **Ngongo**
FL.439   **Pianga**
FL.440   **Shobwa**
FL.441   **Lele**

May be used in combination with other descriptors, especially in the Objects facet (e.g., **Baroque** + **churches**; **Japanese** + **enameling**; **Abstract Expressionist** + **drawings**).

FL.442	Luntu
FL.443	Lwalwa
FL.444	Mbagani
FL.445	Ndengese
FL.446	Nkutshu
FL.447	Salampasu
FL.448	Wongo
FL.449	Yaelima
FL.450	Lulua
FL.451	<*Chokwe-Lunda*>
FL.452	Chokwe
FL.453	Lozi
FL.454	Luchazi
FL.455	Lunda
FL.456	Lwena
FL.457	Mbundu
FL.458	Ndembu
FL.459	Songo
FL.460	<*Kwango-Kwilu*>
FL.461	Boma
FL.462	Fumu
FL.463	Holo
FL.464	Huana
FL.465	Hum
FL.466	Kwese
FL.467	Mbala (Western Zaire)
FL.468	Mbun
FL.469	Pende
FL.470	Suku
FL.471	Teke
FL.472	Tsaya
FL.473	Yaka
FL.474	Yanzi
FL.475	<*Lower Zaire*>
FL.476	Bembe (Lower Zaire)
FL.477	Bwende
FL.478	Dondo
FL.479	Kongo
FL.480	Mbamba
FL.481	Mbata
FL.482	Mpangu
FL.483	Mpemba
FL.484	Sonyo
FL.485	Sorongo
FL.486	Sundi
FL.487	Vili
FL.488	Yombe
FL.489	Woyo
FL.490	<*Luba region*>

May be used in combination with other descriptors, especially in the Objects facet (e.g., **Baroque** + **churches**; **Japanese** + **enameling**; **Abstract Expressionist** + **drawings**).

FL.491 **Holoholo**
FL.492 **Jiji**
FL.493 **Kanioka**
FL.494 **Kusu**
FL.495 **Luba**
FL.496 **Buli**
FL.497 **Hemba**
FL.498 **Shankadi**
FL.499 **Mwanza**
FL.500 **Songye**
FL.501 **Nsapo-Nsapo**
FL.502 **Tabwa**
FL.503 **Tetela**
FL.504 *<Northern Zaire>*
FL.505 *<Northeastern Zaire>*
FL.506 *<Lega region>*
FL.507 **Amba**
FL.508 **Bembe (Northeastern Zaire)**
FL.509 **Boyo**
FL.510 **Kasingo**
FL.511 **Komo (Northeastern Zaire)**
FL.512 **Lega**
FL.513 **Lengola**
FL.514 **Mbole**
FL.515 **Metoko**
FL.516 **Pere**
FL.517 **Yela**
FL.518 *<Zande-Mangbetu region>*
FL.519 **Babwa**
FL.520 **Babeo**
FL.521 **Budu**
FL.522 **Lese**
FL.523 **Mangbetu**
FL.524 **Zande**
FL.525 *<Northwestern Zaire>*
FL.526 **Bangi**
FL.527 **Bolia**
FL.528 **Gobu**
FL.529 **Loi**
FL.530 **Mbanza**
FL.531 **Ngbaka**
FL.532 **Ngbandi**
FL.533 **Ngombe**
FL.534 **Ntomba**
FL.535 **Sango**
FL.536 **Sengele**
FL.537 **Togbo**
FL.538 **Yangere**
FL.539 **Pygmy**

May be used in combination with other descriptors, especially in the Objects facet (e.g., **Baroque** + **churches**; **Japanese** + **enameling**; **Abstract Expressionist** + **drawings**).

FL.540 **Twa**
FL.541 *<Southern African styles>*
FL.542 *<Eastern Zambian, Zimbabwe, and Western Mozambique styles>*
FL.543 **Bemba**
FL.544 **Chewa**
FL.545 **Lungu**
FL.546 **Maravi**
FL.547 **Shanga**
FL.548 **Shona**
FL.549 **Thonga**
FL.550 *<Khoisan-speaking peoples styles>*
FL.551 **Bergdama**
FL.552 **KhoiKhoi**
FL.553 **San**
FL.554 *<Malagasi styles>*
FL.555 **Antandroy**
FL.556 **Antanosy**
FL.557 **Bara**
FL.558 **Mahafaly**
FL.559 **Merina**
FL.560 **Sakalava**
FL.561 *<Ngoni styles>*
FL.562 **Ndebele**
FL.563 **Pondo**
FL.564 **Swazi**
FL.565 **Tembu**
FL.566 **Xhosa**
FL.567 **Zulu**
FL.568 **Bhaca**
FL.569 *<Sotho styles>*
FL.570 **Lovedu**
FL.571 **Pedi**
FL.572 **Sotho**
FL.573 **Tswana**
FL.574 **Venda**
FL.575 *<Southern Angolan and Northern Namibian styles>*
FL.576 **Ambo**
FL.577 **Herero**
FL.578 *<Zambezi River region styles>*
FL.579 **Chopi**
FL.580 **Tonga**
FL.581 *<East African styles>*
FL.582 *<Central Tanzanian styles>*
FL.583 **Bena**
FL.584 **Fipa**
FL.585 **Gogo**
FL.586 **Ha**
FL.587 **Hehe**
FL.588 **Mbunga**

African

<African styles by region>

<East African styles>

<Central Tanzanian styles>

FL.589	Nyamwanga
FL.590	Nyamwezi
FL.591	Sandawe
FL.592	Turu
FL.593	Vinza
FL.594	*<Coastal East African styles>*
FL.595	Bondei
FL.596	Doe
FL.597	Jibana
FL.598	Kambe
FL.599	Kami
FL.600	Luguru
FL.601	Mijikenda
FL.602	Chonyi
FL.603	Digo
FL.604	Duruma
FL.605	Giriama
FL.606	Rabai
FL.607	Ribe
FL.608	Swahili
FL.609	Bajun
FL.610	Pemba
FL.611	Rufijic
FL.612	Zaramo
FL.613	Zigula
FL.614	Eastern Hamitic
FL.615	Afar
FL.616	Arusi
FL.617	Bari
FL.618	Bimal
FL.619	Bongo
FL.620	Borana
FL.621	Dinka
FL.622	Eile
FL.623	Gabbra
FL.624	*<Konso cluster>*
FL.625	Gato
FL.626	Konso
FL.627	Nuba
FL.628	Ometo
FL.629	Pokot
FL.630	Rendile
FL.631	Samburu
FL.632	Shilluk
FL.633	Somali
FL.634	Topotha
FL.635	Turkana
FL.636	*<Ethiopian styles>*
FL.637	Amhara

May be used in combination with other descriptors, especially in the Objects facet (e.g., **Baroque** + **churches**; **Japanese** + **enameling**; **Abstract Expressionist** + **drawings**).

FL.638 **Falasha**
FL.639 **Gurage**
FL.640 **Kemant**
FL.641 *<Kenyan and Great Rift Valley styles>*
FL.642 **Arusha**
FL.643 **Bende (Kenya)**
FL.644 **Chagga**
FL.645 **Dorobo**
FL.646 **Kamba**
FL.647 **Kikuyu**
FL.648 **Kipsigis**
FL.649 **Luo**
FL.650 **Masai**
FL.651 **Meru**
FL.652 **Pare**
FL.653 **Shambala**
FL.654 **Sukuma**
FL.655 **Sumbwa**
FL.656 **Teita**
FL.657 *<Makonde region and Lake Nyasa area styles>*
FL.658 **Lomwe**
FL.659 **Makonde**
FL.660 **Makua**
FL.661 **Matambwe**
FL.662 **Matengo**
FL.663 **Mawia**
FL.664 **Mwera**
FL.665 **Ngindo**
FL.666 **Ngoni**
FL.667 **Nyakyusa**
FL.668 **Nyanja**
FL.669 **Pangwa**
FL.670 **Pogoro**
FL.671 **Yao**
FL.672 *<Upper Great Lakes African styles>*
FL.673 **Acholi**
FL.674 **Bantu Kavirondo**
FL.675 **Dumbo**
FL.676 **Ganda**
FL.677 **Gisu**
FL.678 **Gusii**
FL.679 **Haya**
FL.680 **Jie**
FL.681 **Karagwe**
FL.682 **Karamojong**
FL.683 **Kerewe**
FL.684 **Lango**
FL.685 **Nkole**
FL.686 **Nyoro**

May be used in combination with other descriptors, especially in the Objects facet (e.g., **Baroque** + **churches**; **Japanese** + **enameling**; **Abstract Expressionist** + **drawings**).

FL.687	**Ruanda**
FL.688	**Soga (African)**
FL.689	**Teso**
FL.690	*<North African styles>*
FL.691	**Baggara**
FL.692	**Bedouin**
FL.693	**Cyrenaican**
FL.694	**Beja**
FL.695	**Amer**
FL.696	**Berber**
FL.697	**Kabyle**
FL.698	**Tuareg**
FL.699	*<African sculpture styles>*
FL.700	**Pole Style**
FL.701	**Round Style**
FL.702	*<The Americas>*
FL.703	*<American regions>*
FL.704	**Central American**
FL.705	**Guatemalan**
FL.706	**Nicaraguan**
FL.707	**Caribbean**
FL.708	**Cuban**
FL.709	**Haitian**
FL.710	**Jamaican**
FL.711	**Puerto Rican**
FL.712	**North American**
FL.713	**American**
FL.714	**Canadian**
FL.715	**Mexican**
FL.716	**South American**
FL.717	**Argentine**
FL.718	**Bolivian**
FL.719	**Brazilian**
FL.720	**Chilean**
FL.721	**Colombian**
FL.722	**Paraguayan**
FL.723	**Peruvian**
FL.724	**Uruguayan**
FL.725	**Venezuelan**
FL.726	**Pre-Columbian**
FL.727	*<Pre-Columbian North American styles and periods>*
FL.728	*<Pre-Columbian North American periods>*
FL.729	**Pre-projectile Point**
FL.730	**Archaic (North American)**
FL.731	**Eastern Archaic**
FL.732	**Western Archaic**
FL.733	**Desert Tradition**
FL.734	**Old Cordilleran**
FL.735	**Paleo-Indian**

May be used in combination with other descriptors, especially in the Objects facet (e.g., **Baroque** + **churches**; **Japanese** + **enameling**; **Abstract Expressionist** + **drawings**).

FL.736 <*Eastern North American Paleo-Indian periods*>
FL.737 **Quad**
FL.738 **Cumberland Fluted**
FL.739 **Dalton**
FL.740 **Hardaway**
FL.741 **Reagen**
FL.742 **Suwannee**
FL.743 <*Western North American Paleo-Indian periods*>
FL.744 **Llano**
FL.745 **Clovis**
FL.746 **Sandia**
FL.747 **Folsom**
FL.748 **Plano**
FL.749 **Plainview**
FL.750 **Meserve**
FL.751 **Midland**
FL.752 **Milnesand**
FL.753 **Parallel-flaked**
FL.754 **Agate Basin**
FL.755 **Angostura**
FL.756 **Cody**
FL.757 **Eden**
FL.758 **Scottsbluff**
FL.759 <*Pre-Columbian Eastern North American periods*>
FL.760 <*Pre-Columbian Midwestern Woodland periods*>
FL.761 **Woodland Tradition**
FL.762 <*Pre-Columbian Southeastern Woodland periods*>
FL.763 **Burial Mound period**
FL.764 **Burial Mound I**
FL.765 **Burial Mound II**
FL.766 **Temple Mound period**
FL.767 **Temple Mound I**
FL.768 **Temple Mound II**
FL.769 <*Pre-Columbian Western North American periods*>
FL.770 <*Pre-Columbian Californian periods*>
FL.771 **Early period Californian**
FL.772 **Middle period Californian**
FL.773 **Late period Californian**
FL.774 <*Pre-Columbian Plains North American periods*>
FL.775 **Plains Village**
FL.776 <*Pre-Columbian Plateau North American periods*>
FL.777 **Early period Plateau**
FL.778 **Transitional period Plateau**
FL.779 **Middle period Plateau**
FL.780 **Late period Plateau**
FL.781 <*Pre-Columbian North American styles*>
FL.782 <*Pre-Columbian Arctic and Subarctic styles*>
FL.783 <*Pre-Columbian Aleutian styles*>
FL.784 **Aleut**

FL

May be used in combination with other descriptors, especially in the Objects facet (e.g., **Baroque** + **churches**; **Japanese** + **enameling**; **Abstract Expressionist** + **drawings**).

FL.785	**Anangula**
FL.786	**Kodiak**
FL.787	**Kachemak**
FL.788	**Takli**
FL.789	**Ocean Bay**
FL.790	**Eskimo**
FL.791	*<Pre-Columbian Eastern Eskimo styles>*
FL.792	**Dorset**
FL.793	**Pre-Dorset**
FL.794	**Sarqaq**
FL.795	**Thule**
FL.796	*<Pre-Columbian Western Eskimo styles>*
FL.797	*<Pre-Columbian Choris area styles>*
FL.798	**Choris**
FL.799	**Ipiutak**
FL.800	**Norton**
FL.801	**Palisades (Eskimo style)**
FL.802	**Western Thule**
FL.803	*<Pre-Columbian Maritime area styles>*
FL.804	**Akmak**
FL.805	**Birnick**
FL.806	**Denbigh**
FL.807	**Nukleet**
FL.808	**Kobuk**
FL.809	**Northern Archaic**
FL.810	**Old Bering Sea**
FL.811	**Punuk**
FL.812	*<Pre-Columbian Eastern North American styles>*
FL.813	*<Pre-Columbian Great Lakes styles>*
FL.814	**Aztalan**
FL.815	**Dustin**
FL.816	**Effigy Mound**
FL.817	**Glacial Kame**
FL.818	**Goodall**
FL.819	**Moccasin Bluff**
FL.820	**Norton-Hopewell**
FL.821	**Old Copper Culture**
FL.822	**Osceola**
FL.823	**Riverton**
FL.824	**Trempealeau**
FL.825	*<Pre-Columbian Middle Atlantic North American styles>*
FL.826	**Badin**
FL.827	**Caraway**
FL.828	**Savannah River**
FL.829	**Uwharrie**
FL.830	**Yadkin**
FL.831	*<Pre-Columbian Mississippi Valley styles>*
FL.832	*<Pre-Columbian Upper Mississippi Valley styles>*
FL.833	**Baehr Hopewell**

May be used in combination with other descriptors, especially in the Objects facet (e.g., **Baroque** + **churches**; **Japanese** + **enameling**; **Abstract Expressionist** + **drawings**).

FL.834 **Faulkner**
FL.835 **Fisher**
FL.836 **Havana Hopewellian**
FL.837 **Hidden Valley**
FL.838 **Jersey Bluff**
FL.839 **Kincaid**
FL.840 **Maples Mills**
FL.841 **Morton**
FL.842 **Oneota**
FL.843 **Red Ocher (style)**
FL.844 *<Pre-Columbian Central Mississippi Valley styles>*
FL.845 **Baumer**
FL.846 **Baytown**
FL.847 **Cahokia**
FL.848 **Obion**
FL.849 **Old Village**
FL.850 **Tchula**
FL.851 *<Pre-Columbian Lower Mississippi Valley styles>*
FL.852 **Caddo**
FL.853 **Fulton Caddo**
FL.854 **Gibson Caddo**
FL.855 **Coles Creek**
FL.856 **Issaquena**
FL.857 **Marksville**
FL.858 **Mississippian**
FL.859 **Middle Mississippian**
FL.860 **Natchez**
FL.861 **Plaquemine**
FL.862 **Poverty Point**
FL.863 **Tchefuncte**
FL.864 **Troyville**
FL.865 *<Pre-Columbian Northeastern North American styles>*
FL.866 **Bare Island**
FL.867 **Boreal Archaic**
FL.868 **Boylston**
FL.869 **Huron-Iroquois**
FL.870 **Lamoka**
FL.871 **Laurel (style)**
FL.872 **Laurentian**
FL.873 **Meadowood**
FL.874 **Monongahela**
FL.875 **Owasco**
FL.876 **Point Peninsula**
FL.877 *<Pre-Columbian Ohio Valley styles>*
FL.878 **Adena**
FL.879 **Fort Ancient**
FL.880 **Hopewell**
FL.881 **Indian Knoll**
FL.882 **Intrusive Mound**

May be used in combination with other descriptors, especially in the Objects facet (e.g., **Baroque** + **churches**; **Japanese** + **enameling**; **Abstract Expressionist** + **drawings**).

FL

FL.883 *<Pre-Columbian Ozark Plateau styles>*
FL.884 **Bluff-dweller**
FL.885 **Grove**
FL.886 *<Pre-Columbian Southeastern North American styles>*
FL.887 **Appalachee**
FL.888 **Candy Creek**
FL.889 **Copena**
FL.890 **Deptford**
FL.891 **Etowah**
FL.892 **Fort Walton**
FL.893 **Hamilton**
FL.894 **Lauderdale**
FL.895 **Macon Plateau**
FL.896 **Santa Rosa-Swift Creek**
FL.897 **Weeden Island**
FL.898 *<Pre-Columbian Western North American styles>*
FL.899 *<Pre-Columbian Californian styles>*
FL.900 **Amargosa**
FL.901 **Canaliño**
FL.902 **La Jolla**
FL.903 **Malaga Cove**
FL.904 **Topanga**
FL.905 *<Pre-Columbian Great Basin styles>*
FL.906 **Catlow**
FL.907 **Danger Cave**
FL.908 **Lake Mojave**
FL.909 **Lovelock**
FL.910 **Pinto Basin**
FL.911 *<Pre-Columbian Northwest Coast North American styles>*
FL.912 **Coast Salish**
FL.913 **Cold Springs**
FL.914 **Locarno Beach**
FL.915 **Marpole**
FL.916 **Stselax**
FL.917 *<Pre-Columbian Plains North American styles>*
FL.918 **Dismal River**
FL.919 **Edwards Plateau**
FL.920 **Lower Loup**
FL.921 **McKean**
FL.922 **Nebraska**
FL.923 **Upper Republican**
FL.924 *<Pre-Columbian Plateau North American styles>*
FL.925 **Congdon**
FL.926 **Late Cremation**
FL.927 *<Pre-Columbian Southwestern North American styles>*
FL.928 **Casas Grandes**
FL.929 **Cochise**
FL.930 **Chiricahua Cochise**
FL.931 **San Pedro Cochise**

FL.932 **Sulphur Spring Cochise**
FL.933 **Fremont**
FL.934 **Hohokam**
FL.935 **Mogollon**
FL.936 **Chiricahua stage Mogollon**
FL.937 **Georgetown Mogollon**
FL.938 **Mimbres**
FL.939 *<Mimbres pottery styles>*
FL.940 **Mimbres black-on-white**
FL.941 **Mimbres corrugated**
FL.942 **Pine Lawn Mogollon**
FL.943 *<Pine Lawn Mogollon pottery styles>*
FL.944 **Alma**
FL.945 **Alma plain**
FL.946 **Alma rough**
FL.947 **San Francisco red**
FL.948 **Reserve Mogollon**
FL.949 **San Francisco Mogollon**
FL.950 **Three Circle Mogollon**
FL.951 **Patayan**
FL.952 **Cerbat**
FL.953 **Cohonina**
FL.954 **Sinagua**
FL.955 *<Pre-Columbian Pueblo styles>*
FL.956 **Anasazi**
FL.957 **Basketmaker**
FL.958 *<Pre-Columbian Middle American styles and periods>*
FL.959 **Mesoamerican**
FL.960 *<Mesoamerican periods>*
FL.961 **Paleo-Indian (Mesoamerican)**
FL.962 **Preclassic**
FL.963 **Early Preclassic**
FL.964 **Middle Preclassic**
FL.965 **Late Preclassic**
FL.966 **Protoclassic**
FL.967 **Classic**
FL.968 **Early Classic**
FL.969 **Middle Classic**
FL.970 **Late Classic**
FL.971 **Postclassic**
FL.972 **Early Postclassic**
FL.973 **Late Postclassic**
FL.974 *<Mesoamerican regional styles and periods>*
FL.975 *<Central Plateau Mesoamerican styles and periods>*
FL.976 *<Central Plateau Mesoamerican periods>*
FL.977 **Tlalpan**
FL.978 **Tlatilco**
FL.979 **Zacatenco**
FL.980 **El Arbolillo**

FL

May be used in combination with other descriptors, especially in the Objects facet (e.g., **Baroque** + **churches**; **Japanese** + **enameling**; **Abstract Expressionist** + **drawings**).

FL.981 **La Pastora**
FL.982 **Cuautepec**
FL.983 **Ticomán**
FL.984 **Tezoyuca**
FL.985 **Patlichique**
FL.986 **Chimalhuacán**
FL.987 **Tzacualli**
FL.988 **Miccaotli**
FL.989 **Tlamimilolpa**
FL.990 **Xolalpan**
FL.991 **Metepec**
FL.992 **Oxtotícpac**
FL.993 **Coyotlatelco**
FL.994 **Aztec I**
FL.995 **Aztec II**
FL.996 **Aztec III**
FL.997 **Aztec IV**
FL.998 *<Central Plateau Mesoamerican styles>*
FL.999 **Aztec**
FL.1000 **Mixteca-Puebla**
FL.1001 **Teotihuacán**
FL.1002 **Toltec**
FL.1003 *<Gulf Coast Mesoamerican styles>*
FL.1004 **Classic Veracruz**
FL.1005 **Tajin**
FL.1006 **Olmec**
FL.1007 *<Maya area styles and periods>*
FL.1008 *<Maya area periods>*
FL.1009 *<Lowland Maya area periods>*
FL.1010 **Xe**
FL.1011 **Mamon**
FL.1012 **Chicanel**
FL.1013 **Matzanel**
FL.1014 **Tzakol**
FL.1015 **Tepeu**
FL.1016 *<Highland Maya area periods>*
FL.1017 **Arévalo**
FL.1018 **Esperanza**
FL.1019 **Las Charcas**
FL.1020 **Providencia**
FL.1021 **Arenal**
FL.1022 **Miraflores**
FL.1023 **Aurora**
FL.1024 **Amatle**
FL.1025 **Tohil**
FL.1026 **Chinautla**
FL.1027 *<Pacific Coast Maya area periods>*
FL.1028 **Ocós**
FL.1029 **Cuadros**

May be used in combination with other descriptors, especially in the Objects facet (e.g., **Baroque** + **churches**; **Japanese** + **enameling**; **Abstract Expressionist** + **drawings**).

FL.1030	**Jocotal**
FL.1031	**Conchas**
FL.1032	**Crucero**
FL.1033	**Izapa**
FL.1034	**Ilusiones**
FL.1035	**Laguneta**
FL.1036	**Cotzumalhuapa**
FL.1037	*<Maya area styles>*
FL.1038	*<Maya area architecture styles>*
FL.1039	**Chenes**
FL.1040	**Puuc**
FL.1041	**Rio Bec**
FL.1042	*<Maya area pottery styles>*
FL.1043	**Fine Orange**
FL.1044	**Plumbate**
FL.1045	**Robles**
FL.1046	**San Juan (pottery style)**
FL.1047	**Tohil Plumbate**
FL.1048	**Thin Orange**
FL.1049	**Usulután**
FL.1050	**Oaxacan**
FL.1051	*<Oaxacan periods>*
FL.1052	**San José Mogote**
FL.1053	**Guadalupe**
FL.1054	**Monte Albán**
FL.1055	**Monte Albán I**
FL.1056	**Monte Albán II**
FL.1057	**Monte Albán III**
FL.1058	**Monte Albán IV**
FL.1059	**Monte Albán V**
FL.1060	*<Oaxacan styles>*
FL.1061	**Mixtec**
FL.1062	**Ñuiñe**
FL.1063	**Zapotec**
FL.1064	*<West Coast Mesoamerican styles>*
FL.1065	**Aztatlán**
FL.1066	**Colima**
FL.1067	**Los Ortices**
FL.1068	**Jalisco**
FL.1069	**Ameca-Zacoalco**
FL.1070	**Mezcala**
FL.1071	**Nayarit**
FL.1072	**Ixtlán**
FL.1073	*<Pre-Columbian Central American styles and periods>*
FL.1074	*<Pre-Columbian Northern Central American styles>*
FL.1075	**Chontales**
FL.1076	**Chorotegan**
FL.1077	*<Chorotegan pottery styles>*
FL.1078	**Luna ware**

FL

FL.1079	**Nicoya polychrome**
FL.1080	**Copador**
FL.1081	**Naco**
FL.1082	**Tazumal**
FL.1083	**Ulúa**
FL.1084	*<Pre-Columbian Panamanian styles and periods>*
FL.1085	*<Pre-Columbian Panamanian periods>*
FL.1086	**Cerro Mangote**
FL.1087	**Monagrillo**
FL.1088	**Scarified-Guacamayo**
FL.1089	**Santa Maria**
FL.1090	**Conte Polychrome**
FL.1091	**Macaracas**
FL.1092	**Herrera**
FL.1093	**Chiriqui**
FL.1094	**Veraguas**
FL.1095	*<Pre-Columbian Panamanian styles>*
FL.1096	**Coclé**
FL.1097	**Darién**
FL.1098	**Diquis**
FL.1099	*<Pre-Columbian Panamanian pottery styles>*
FL.1100	**Guacamayo**
FL.1101	**lost color ware**
FL.1102	**scarified ware**
FL.1103	*<Pre-Columbian Caribbean styles>*
FL.1104	**Couri**
FL.1105	**Los Barrancos**
FL.1106	**Taino**
FL.1107	*<Pre-Columbian South American styles and periods>*
FL.1108	*<Pre-Columbian Colombian styles>*
FL.1109	**Calima**
FL.1110	**Sinú**
FL.1111	**Tolima**
FL.1112	*<Pre-Columbian Ecuadorian periods>*
FL.1113	**Valdivia**
FL.1114	**Machalilla**
FL.1115	**Chorrera**
FL.1116	**Jambeli**
FL.1117	**Bahía**
FL.1118	**Guangala**
FL.1119	**Manteño**
FL.1120	**Milagro**
FL.1121	*<Pre-Columbian Amazonian styles and periods>*
FL.1122	*<Pre-Columbian Amazonian periods>*
FL.1123	**Zoned Hachure horizon**
FL.1124	**Incised Rim horizon**
FL.1125	**Polychrome horizon**
FL.1126	**Incised and Punctate horizon**
FL.1127	*<Pre-Columbian Amazonian styles>*

FL.1128 Marajoara
FL.1129 Santarém
FL.1130 *<Pre-Columbian Andean styles and periods>*
FL.1131 *<Pre-Columbian Andean periods>*
FL.1132 Preceramic
FL.1133 Junín
FL.1134 Lauricocha
FL.1135 Siches
FL.1136 Initial period
FL.1137 Early Chiripa
FL.1138 Kotosh
FL.1139 Early horizon
FL.1140 Cerro Sechín
FL.1141 Chavín
FL.1142 Moxeke
FL.1143 Cupisnique
FL.1144 Kotosh Chavín
FL.1145 Chanapata
FL.1146 Late Chiripa
FL.1147 Paracas
FL.1148 Paracas Cavernas
FL.1149 Paracas Necropolis
FL.1150 Early Intermediate period
FL.1151 Salinar
FL.1152 Pucará
FL.1153 Gallinazo
FL.1154 Recuay
FL.1155 Mochica
FL.1156 Nazca
FL.1157 Huari
FL.1158 Middle horizon
FL.1159 Atarco
FL.1160 Pacheco
FL.1161 Tiahuanaco
FL.1162 Pachacamac
FL.1163 Late Intermediate period
FL.1164 Lambayeque
FL.1165 Ica
FL.1166 Chancay
FL.1167 Chimú
FL.1168 Chincha
FL.1169 Huamachuco
FL.1170 Inca
FL.1171 Late horizon
FL.1172 *<Pre-Columbian Andean styles>*
FL.1173 Chavín horizon
FL.1174 *<Pre-Columbian Andean pottery styles>*
FL.1175 black-white-red
FL.1176 cursive

May be used in combination with other descriptors, especially in the Objects facet (e.g., **Baroque** + **churches**; **Japanese** + **enameling**; **Abstract Expressionist** + **drawings**).

FL.1177 **Inca horizon**
FL.1178 **interlocking**
FL.1179 **negative**
FL.1180 **Viñaque**
FL.1181 **white-on-red**
FL.1182 *<Pre-Columbian Chilean styles>*
FL.1183 **Atacameño**
FL.1184 **Diaguita**
FL.1185 *<Diaguita pottery styles>*
FL.1186 **Belén**
FL.1187 **Chilean Diaguite**
FL.1188 **Draconian**
FL.1189 **Santa Maria (pottery style)**
FL.1190 *<Pre-Columbian Argentine periods>*
FL.1191 **Aguada**
FL.1192 **Barreales**
FL.1193 **Candelaria**
FL.1194 **Native American**
FL.1195 *<Native North American styles>*
FL.1196 *<Arctic and Subarctic Native American styles>*
FL.1197 *<Arctic Native American styles>*
FL.1198 *<Alaskan Native styles>*
FL.1199 **Chugach**
FL.1200 **Inupiaq**
FL.1201 **Koniag**
FL.1202 **Saint Lawrence Island Eskimo**
FL.1203 **Yuit**
FL.1204 **Yupik**
FL.1205 *<Canadian Arctic Native styles>*
FL.1206 **Inuit**
FL.1207 **Baffin Island Inuit**
FL.1208 **Caribou Inuit**
FL.1209 **Copper Inuit**
FL.1210 **Iglulik**
FL.1211 **Labrador Inuit**
FL.1212 **Netsilik**
FL.1213 **Ungava**
FL.1214 **Western Arctic Inuit**
FL.1215 *<Greenlandic Native styles>*
FL.1216 **Katladlit**
FL.1217 *<Eastern Subarctic Native American>*
FL.1218 **Algonkin**
FL.1219 **Beothuk**
FL.1220 **Cree**
FL.1221 **Montagnais**
FL.1222 **Ottawa**
FL.1223 **Saulteaux**
FL.1224 *<Western Subarctic Native American styles>*
FL.1225 **Ahtena**

May be used in combination with other descriptors, especially in the Objects facet (e.g., **Baroque** + **churches**; **Japanese** + **enameling**; **Abstract Expressionist** + **drawings**).

FL.1226 Athabaskan
FL.1227 Beaver
FL.1228 Carrier
FL.1229 Chilcotin
FL.1230 Chipewyan
FL.1231 Dogrib
FL.1232 Han (Native American)
FL.1233 Hare
FL.1234 Ingalik
FL.1235 Kaska
FL.1236 Koyukon
FL.1237 Kutchin
FL.1238 Sarsi
FL.1239 Sekani
FL.1240 Slave
FL.1241 Tahltan
FL.1242 Tanaina
FL.1243 Tanana
FL.1244 Tsetsaut
FL.1245 Tutchone
FL.1246 *<Californian Native American styles>*
FL.1247 Achomawi
FL.1248 Atsugewi
FL.1249 Cahuilla
FL.1250 Chumash
FL.1251 Costanoan
FL.1252 Cupeño
FL.1253 Gabrieliño
FL.1254 Halchidhoma
FL.1255 Hupa
FL.1256 Karok
FL.1257 Luiseño
FL.1258 Miwok
FL.1259 Mono
FL.1260 Patwin
FL.1261 Pomo
FL.1262 Salinan
FL.1263 Serrano
FL.1264 Shasta
FL.1265 Tübatulabal
FL.1266 Tulare
FL.1267 Wintun
FL.1268 Wiyot
FL.1269 Yana
FL.1270 Yokuts
FL.1271 Yuki
FL.1272 Yurok
FL.1273 *<Baja Californian Native American>*
FL.1274 California Yuman

May be used in combination with other descriptors, especially in the Objects facet (e.g., **Baroque** + **churches**; **Japanese** + **enameling**; **Abstract Expressionist** + **drawings**).

FL.1275	**Diegueño**
FL.1276	**Kamia**
FL.1277	**Kiliwa**
FL.1278	**Nakipa**
FL.1279	**Paipai**
FL.1280	**Guaicurian**
FL.1281	**Guaicura**
FL.1282	**Huchiti**
FL.1283	**Pericú**
FL.1284	**Peninsula Yuman**
FL.1285	**Borjeño**
FL.1286	**Ignacieño**
FL.1287	*<Eastern Woodland and Eastern Great Lake Native American styles>*
FL.1288	**Abnaki**
FL.1289	**Conestoga**
FL.1290	**Delaware**
FL.1291	**Erie**
FL.1292	**Iroquois**
FL.1293	**Cayuga**
FL.1294	**Mohawk**
FL.1295	**Oneida**
FL.1296	**Onondaga**
FL.1297	**Seneca**
FL.1298	**Tuscarora (Iroquois)**
FL.1299	**Mahican**
FL.1300	**Malecite**
FL.1301	**Massachusett**
FL.1302	**Micmac**
FL.1303	**Pennacook**
FL.1304	**Penobscot**
FL.1305	**Susquehanna**
FL.1306	**Wappinger**
FL.1307	*<Great Basin Native American styles>*
FL.1308	**Bannock**
FL.1309	**Chemehuevi**
FL.1310	**Eastern Mono**
FL.1311	**Gosiute**
FL.1312	**Kawaiisu**
FL.1313	**Lemhi**
FL.1314	**Northern Paiute**
FL.1315	**Panamint**
FL.1316	**Shoshone**
FL.1317	**Western Shoshone**
FL.1318	**Wind River Shoshone**
FL.1319	**Southern Paiute**
FL.1320	**Ute**
FL.1321	**Washo**
FL.1322	*<Great Lake and Central Woodland Native American styles>*
FL.1323	**Fox**

May be used in combination with other descriptors, especially in the Objects facet (e.g., **Baroque** + **churches**; **Japanese** + **enameling**; **Abstract Expressionist** + **drawings**).

- FL.1324 Huron
- FL.1325 Illinois
- FL.1326 Kickapoo
- FL.1327 Menomini
- FL.1328 Miami
- FL.1329 Ojibwa
- FL.1330 Potawatomi
- FL.1331 Sauk
- FL.1332 Winnebago

FL.1333 *<Northwest Coast Native American styles>*

- FL.1334 Alsea
- FL.1335 Bella Bella
- FL.1336 Bella Coola
- FL.1337 Chehalis
- FL.1338 Chinook
- FL.1339 Coos
- FL.1340 Cowlitz
- FL.1341 Eyak
- FL.1342 Gitksan
- FL.1343 Haida
- FL.1344 Haisla
- FL.1345 Heiltsuk
- FL.1346 Kalapuya
- FL.1347 Klallam
- FL.1348 Kwakiutl
- FL.1349 Lummi
- FL.1350 Makah
- FL.1351 Niska
- FL.1352 Nootka
- FL.1353 Puyallup
- FL.1354 Quileute
- FL.1355 Quinault
- FL.1356 Salish
  - FL.1357 Comox
  - FL.1358 Cowichan
- FL.1359 Sitka
- FL.1360 Siuslaw
- FL.1361 Skagit
- FL.1362 Snuqualmi
- FL.1363 Tillamook
- FL.1364 Tlingit
- FL.1365 Tolowa
- FL.1366 Tsimshian
- FL.1367 Twana

FL.1368 *<Plains Native American styles>*

- FL.1369 Arapaho
- FL.1370 Arikara
- FL.1371 Assiniboin
- FL.1372 Atsina

May be used in combination with other descriptors, especially in the Objects facet (e.g., **Baroque** + **churches**; **Japanese** + **enameling**; **Abstract Expressionist** + **drawings**).

FL.1373	**Blackfoot**
FL.1374	**Blood (Native American)**
FL.1375	**Piegan**
FL.1376	**Cheyenne**
FL.1377	**Northern Cheyenne**
FL.1378	**Southern Cheyenne**
FL.1379	**Sutaio**
FL.1380	**Comanche**
FL.1381	**Crow**
FL.1382	**Hidatsa**
FL.1383	**Iowa**
FL.1384	**Kansa**
FL.1385	**Kiowa**
FL.1386	**Kiowa Apache**
FL.1387	**Mandan**
FL.1388	**Missouri**
FL.1389	**Omaha**
FL.1390	**Osage**
FL.1391	**Oto**
FL.1392	**Pawnee**
FL.1393	**Ponca**
FL.1394	**Plains Cree**
FL.1395	**Plains Ojibwa**
FL.1396	**Sioux**
FL.1397	**Dakota**
FL.1398	**Santee Dakota**
FL.1399	**Teton**
FL.1400	**Yankton**
FL.1401	**Wichita**
FL.1402	**Tawakoni**
FL.1403	**Waco**
FL.1404	*<Plateau Native American styles>*
FL.1405	**Cayuse**
FL.1406	**Coeur d'Alène**
FL.1407	**Flathead**
FL.1408	**Kalispel**
FL.1409	**Klamath**
FL.1410	**Klikitat**
FL.1411	**Kutenai**
FL.1412	**Lake**
FL.1413	**Lillooet**
FL.1414	**Modoc**
FL.1415	**Molala**
FL.1416	**Nespelem**
FL.1417	**Nez Percé**
FL.1418	**Okanagan**
FL.1419	**Sanpoil**
FL.1420	**Shuswap**
FL.1421	**Sinkiuse**

May be used in combination with other descriptors, especially in the Objects facet (e.g., **Baroque** + **churches**; **Japanese** + **enameling**; **Abstract Expressionist** + **drawings**).

FL.1422 Spokan
FL.1423 Tenino
FL.1424 Thompson
FL.1425 Umatilla
FL.1426 Wenatchi
FL.1427 Wishram
FL.1428 Yakima
FL.1429 *<Southeastern Native American styles>*
FL.1430 Atakapa
FL.1431 Cherokee
FL.1432 Chickasaw
FL.1433 Chitimacha
FL.1434 Choctaw
FL.1435 Creek
FL.1436 Karankawa
FL.1437 Powhatan
FL.1438 Quapaw
FL.1439 Seminole
FL.1440 Shawnee
FL.1441 Timucua
FL.1442 Tonkawa
FL.1443 Tunica
FL.1444 Tuscarora
FL.1445 Tutelo
FL.1446 Yuchi
FL.1447 *<Southwestern Native American styles>*
FL.1448 Apache
FL.1449 Chiricahua Apache
FL.1450 Eastern Apache
FL.1451 Jicarilla Apache
FL.1452 Lipan Apache
FL.1453 Mescalero Apache
FL.1454 Western Apache
FL.1455 Cocopa
FL.1456 Concho
FL.1457 Havasupai
FL.1458 Maricopa
FL.1459 Mojave
FL.1460 Navajo
FL.1461 Opata
FL.1462 Paiute
FL.1463 Papago
FL.1464 Pima
FL.1465 Pueblo
FL.1466 *<Rio Grande Pueblo styles>*
FL.1467 Acoma
FL.1468 Cochiti
FL.1469 Jemez
FL.1470 Laguna

FL.1471 **Picuris**
FL.1472 **San Ildefonso**
FL.1473 **San Juan (Rio Grande Pueblo)**
FL.1474 **Santa Ana**
FL.1475 **Santa Clara**
FL.1476 **Santo Domingo**
FL.1477 **Taos**
FL.1478 **Tesuque**
FL.1479 **Zia**
FL.1480 *<Western Pueblo styles>*
FL.1481 **Hopi**
FL.1482 **Zuñi**
FL.1483 **Seri**
FL.1484 **Walapai**
FL.1485 **Yavapai**
FL.1486 **Yuman**
FL.1487 *<Native Middle American styles>*
FL.1488 *<Native Northwestern Mexican styles>*
FL.1489 **Cora**
FL.1490 **Huichol**
FL.1491 **Mayo**
FL.1492 **Tarahumara**
FL.1493 **Tepecano**
FL.1494 **Tepehuan**
FL.1495 **Yaqui**
FL.1496 *<Native Western Mexican styles>*
FL.1497 **Tarascan**
FL.1498 *<Native Central Mexican styles>*
FL.1499 **Chichimec**
FL.1500 **Huastec**
FL.1501 **Matlatzinca**
FL.1502 **Mazahua**
FL.1503 **Nahua**
FL.1504 **Tlahuica**
FL.1505 **Tlaxcalan**
FL.1506 **Otomi**
FL.1507 **Pame**
FL.1508 **Totonac**
FL.1509 *<Native Southern Mexican styles>*
FL.1510 **Amuzgo**
FL.1511 **Chatino**
FL.1512 **Chinantec**
FL.1513 **Chocho**
FL.1514 **Chontal**
FL.1515 **Cuicatec**
FL.1516 **Huave**
FL.1517 **Izcatec**
FL.1518 **Mazatec**
FL.1519 **Mixe**

May be used in combination with other descriptors, especially in the Objects facet (e.g., **Baroque** + **churches**; **Japanese** + **enameling**; **Abstract Expressionist** + **drawings**).

FL.1520 **Popoloca**
FL.1521 **Popoluca**
FL.1522 **Tequislatec**
FL.1523 **Tlapanec**
FL.1524 **Trique**
FL.1525 **Zoque**
FL.1526 *<Native Yucatan styles>*
FL.1527 **Itzá**
FL.1528 **Mopan**
FL.1529 **Yucatec**
FL.1530 *<Native Highland Mexican and Guatemalan styles>*
FL.1531 **Mayan**
FL.1532 **Cakchiquel**
FL.1533 **Ixil**
FL.1534 **Kekchi**
FL.1535 **Lacandón**
FL.1536 **Mam**
FL.1537 **Pokomam**
FL.1538 **Quiche**
FL.1539 **Rabinal**
FL.1540 **Tojolabal**
FL.1541 **Tzeltal**
FL.1542 **Tzotzil**
FL.1543 **Chamula**
FL.1544 **Zinacantec**
FL.1545 **Tzutujil**
FL.1546 **Uspantec**
FL.1547 *<Native Central American styles>*
FL.1548 **Cuna**
FL.1549 **Cueva-Cuna**
FL.1550 **San Blas**
FL.1551 **Dorasque**
FL.1552 **Guaymí**
FL.1553 **Guetar**
FL.1554 **Jicaque**
FL.1555 **Lenca**
FL.1556 **Mangue**
FL.1557 **Mosquito**
FL.1558 **Nicarao**
FL.1559 **Paya**
FL.1560 **Sumo**
FL.1561 *<Native Caribbean styles>*
FL.1562 **Arawak**
FL.1563 **Carib**
FL.1564 **Ciboney**
FL.1565 **Guanahatabey**
FL.1566 *<Native South American styles>*
FL.1567 *<Native Amazonian styles>*
FL.1568 **Amahuaca**

FL

May be used in combination with other descriptors, especially in the Objects facet (e.g., **Baroque** + **churches**; **Japanese** + **enameling**; **Abstract Expressionist** + **drawings**).

FL.1569	**Apalai**
FL.1570	**Arua**
FL.1571	**Caquetío**
FL.1572	**Caríjona**
FL.1573	**Caripuna**
FL.1574	**Catukina**
FL.1575	**Cayapó**
FL.1576	**Chiriguano**
FL.1577	**Conibo**
FL.1578	**Cubeo**
FL.1579	**Encabellado**
FL.1580	**Galibi**
FL.1581	**Guahibo**
FL.1582	**Ipuriná**
FL.1583	**Jivaro**
FL.1584	**Kuikuru**
FL.1585	**Macú**
FL.1586	**Macuna**
FL.1587	**Macusi**
FL.1588	**Makiritaré**
FL.1589	**Manao**
FL.1590	**Maué**
FL.1591	**Mojo**
FL.1592	**Mundurucú**
FL.1593	**Mura**
FL.1594	**Parintintin**
FL.1595	**Shipaya**
FL.1596	**Shipibo**
FL.1597	**Sinabo**
FL.1598	**Tembé**
FL.1599	**Tucano**
FL.1600	**Waiwai**
FL.1601	**Xingú**
FL.1602	*<Native Andean styles>*
FL.1603	*<Native Central Andean styles>*
FL.1604	**Atsahuaca**
FL.1605	**Campa**
FL.1606	**Cañari**
FL.1607	**Masco**
FL.1608	**Patagón**
FL.1609	**Piro**
FL.1610	**Puná**
FL.1611	**Quechua**
FL.1612	**Tepqui**
FL.1613	**Tumbez**
FL.1614	**Uru**
FL.1615	**Yunca**
FL.1616	*<Native South Andean styles>*
FL.1617	**Araucanian**

May be used in combination with other descriptors, especially in the Objects facet (e.g., **Baroque** + **churches**; **Japanese** + **enameling**; **Abstract Expressionist** + **drawings**).

FL.1618 **Aymará**
FL.1619 **Comechingón**
FL.1620 **Huarpe**
FL.1621 **Huilliche**
FL.1622 **Lipe**
FL.1623 **Lule**
FL.1624 **Picunche**
FL.1625 **Sanaviron**
FL.1626 **Tonocoté**
FL.1627 *<Native South American Caribbean Coast styles>*
FL.1628 **Achagua**
FL.1629 **Carajá**
FL.1630 **Chaima**
FL.1631 **Jirajara**
FL.1632 **Palenque**
FL.1633 **Timote**
FL.1634 **Warrau**
FL.1635 *<Native Chaco styles>*
FL.1636 **Abipón**
FL.1637 **Ashluslay**
FL.1638 **Caduveo**
FL.1639 **Cañar**
FL.1640 **Chamacoco**
FL.1641 **Chané**
FL.1642 **Chorotí**
FL.1643 **Guaná**
FL.1644 **Lengua**
FL.1645 **Matará**
FL.1646 **Mbayá**
FL.1647 **Mocoví**
FL.1648 **Payaguá**
FL.1649 **Pilagá**
FL.1650 **Toba (Chaco)**
FL.1651 **Zamuco**
FL.1652 *<Native Coastal Ecuadorian and Colombian styles>*
FL.1653 **Andaqui**
FL.1654 **Andoke**
FL.1655 **Barbacoa**
FL.1656 **Calamari**
FL.1657 **Cara**
FL.1658 **Chibcha**
FL.1659 **Chocó**
FL.1660 **Esmeralda**
FL.1661 **Huancavilca**
FL.1662 **Manta**
FL.1663 **Páez**
FL.1664 **Pasto**
FL.1665 **Pijao**
FL.1666 **Puruhá**

FL.1667 **Quillacinga**
FL.1668 **Quimbaya**
FL.1669 **Tairona**
FL.1670 **Tolú**
FL.1671 **Urabá**
FL.1672 *<Native Eastern Brazillian styles>*
FL.1673 **Bororo (South American)**
FL.1674 **Botocudo**
FL.1675 **Caingang**
FL.1676 **Camacan**
FL.1677 **Central Ge**
FL.1678 **Guaitacá**
FL.1679 **Guaraní**
FL.1680 **Patashó**
FL.1681 **Potiguara**
FL.1682 **Puri-Coroado**
FL.1683 **Timbira**
FL.1684 **Tupí**
FL.1685 **Tupinamba**
FL.1686 **Tupinikin**
FL.1687 *<Native Pampean and Fuegian styles>*
FL.1688 **Alacaluf**
FL.1689 **Chaná**
FL.1690 **Charrúa**
FL.1691 **Chono**
FL.1692 **Colastiné**
FL.1693 **Corondá**
FL.1694 **Mbeguá**
FL.1695 **Ona**
FL.1696 **Puelche**
FL.1697 **Querandí**
FL.1698 **Tehuelche**
FL.1699 **Timbú**
FL.1700 **Yahgan**
FL.1701 *<Colonial American styles>*
FL.1702 *<Colonial North American styles>*
FL.1703 **American Colonial**
FL.1704 **Pennsylvania Dutch**
FL.1705 **Pilgrim**
FL.1706 **Latin American**
FL.1707 *<Colonial Latin American styles>*
FL.1708 **Altoperuvian**
FL.1709 **Puebla**
FL.1710 *<Colonial Latin American architecture styles>*
FL.1711 **Arequipa**
FL.1712 **Poblano**
FL.1713 **Provincial Highland**
FL.1714 **Tepalcingo**
FL.1715 **Ultrabaroque**

FL.1716 *<Colonial Latin American fine arts styles>*
FL.1717 **Cuzco**
FL.1718 **Quito**
FL.1719 *<modern American styles and movements>*
FL.1720 *<modern North American styles and movements>*
FL.1721 **African American**
FL.1722 **Carpenter's Gothic**
FL.1723 **Colonial Revival**
FL.1724 **Spanish Colonial Revival**
FL.1725 **Mission Style**
FL.1726 **Craftsman**
FL.1727 **Federal**
FL.1728 **Gingerbread**
FL.1729 **Harlem Renaissance**
FL.1730 *<modern North American architecture styles and movements>*
FL.1731 **Château Style**
FL.1732 **City Beautiful Movement**
FL.1733 **Italianate**
FL.1734 **Italian Villa Style**
FL.1735 **Mayan Revival**
FL.1736 **Prairie School**
FL.1737 **Pueblo Revival**
FL.1738 **Richardsonian Romanesque**
FL.1739 **Shingle Style**
FL.1740 **Stick Style**
FL.1741 *<modern North American decorative arts styles and movements>*
FL.1742 **Cottage Style**
FL.1743 **Eastlake**
FL.1744 **Fancy**
FL.1745 **Grand Rapids**
FL.1746 **Mission**
FL.1747 *<modern North American fine arts styles and movements>*
FL.1748 **American Scene**
FL.1749 **Regionalist**
FL.1750 **Ashcan School**
FL.1751 **Luminist**
FL.1752 **Photo-Secession**
FL.1753 **Precisionist**
FL.1754 **Synchromist**
FL.1755 **Tonalist**
FL.1756 *<modern Latin American fine arts styles and movements>*
FL.1757 **Creationist**
FL.1758 **Estridentismo**
FL.1759 **Indigenismo**
FL.1760 **Mexican Muralist**
FL.1761 Asian
FL.1762 Central Asian
FL.1763 *<Central Asian Paleolithic styles and periods>*
FL.1764 **Aman-Kutan**

May be used in combination with other descriptors, especially in the Objects facet (e.g., **Baroque** + **churches**; **Japanese** + **enameling**; **Abstract Expressionist** + **drawings**).

FL.1765 **Karatau**
FL.1766 **Teshik-Tash**
FL.1767 **Zaraut-Say**
FL.1768 *<Central Asian Neolithic styles and periods>*
FL.1769 **Anau**
FL.1770 **Dzhanbas-Kala**
FL.1771 **Dzhebel Cave**
FL.1772 **Dzheytun**
FL.1773 **Geokysur**
FL.1774 **Kara Depe**
FL.1775 **Kelteminar**
FL.1776 **Khorezm**
FL.1777 **Kobadian**
FL.1778 **Namazga-Tepe**
FL.1779 *<Central Asian Bronze Age styles and periods>*
FL.1780 **Anan'ino**
FL.1781 **Chust**
FL.1782 **Hissar**
FL.1783 **Kayrakkum**
FL.1784 **Tazaba-Gyab**
FL.1785 **Zaman-Baba**
FL.1786 *<Central Asian early historic styles and periods>*
FL.1787 **Adzhina-Tepe**
FL.1788 **Ai-Hanum**
FL.1789 **Ak-Beshim**
FL.1790 **Bactrian**
FL.1791 **Greco-Bactrian**
FL.1792 **Balalyk-Tepe**
FL.1793 **Dalverzin-Tepe**
FL.1794 **Key-Kobad-Shakh**
FL.1795 **Khalchayan**
FL.1796 **Khaydarabad-Tepe**
FL.1797 **Kukhn-Kala**
FL.1798 **Kuva**
FL.1799 **Nisa**
FL.1800 **Perm**
FL.1801 **Lomatov**
FL.1802 **Pianobor**
FL.1803 **Sarmatian**
FL.1804 **Alani**
FL.1805 **Shakhrinau**
FL.1806 **Tali-Barzu**
FL.1807 **Toprak-Kala**
FL.1808 **Tup-Khona**
FL.1809 **Uighur**
FL.1810 *<Central Asian early historic painting styles>*
FL.1811 **Balawaste**
FL.1812 **Bäzäklik**
FL.1813 **Dandan Oilik**

May be used in combination with other descriptors, especially in the Objects facet (e.g., **Baroque** + **churches**; **Japanese** + **enameling**; **Abstract Expressionist** + **drawings**).

FL.1814 Khocho
FL.1815 Khotan
FL.1816 Kizil
FL.1817 Kuça
FL.1818 Kumutra
FL.1819 Miran
FL.1820 Shorchuk
FL.1821 Sogdian
FL.1822 Afrasiab
FL.1823 Panjikent
FL.1824 Shahristan
FL.1825 Varakhsha
FL.1826 Toyok
FL.1827 Tumshuk
FL.1828 Tun-huang
FL.1829 Turfan
FL.1830 Yarkhoto
FL.1831 East Asian
FL.1832 Chinese
FL.1833 *<Chinese styles and periods>*
FL.1834 *<Chinese prehistoric periods>*
FL.1835 *<Chinese Paleolithic periods>*
FL.1836 Choukoutien
FL.1837 *<Chinese Mesolithic periods>*
FL.1838 Microlithic
FL.1839 Hoabinhian
FL.1840 Qingliangang
FL.1841 *<Chinese Neolithic periods>*
FL.1842 Sheng-wen
FL.1843 Yangshao
FL.1844 Chungwan
FL.1845 Gansu
FL.1846 Longshan
FL.1847 *<Chinese dynastic styles and periods>*
FL.1848 Han (Chinese)
FL.1849 Eastern Han
FL.1850 Western Han
FL.1851 Jin
FL.1852 Xia
FL.1853 Erlitou
FL.1854 Shang
FL.1855 *<Shang periods>*
FL.1856 Erligang
FL.1857 *<Shang styles>*
FL.1858 Anyang (Shang style)
FL.1859 Xiaotun
FL.1860 Zhengzhou
FL.1861 Zhou
FL.1862 Eastern Zhou

May be used in combination with other descriptors, especially in the Objects facet (e.g., **Baroque** + **churches**; **Japanese** + **enameling**; **Abstract Expressionist** + **drawings**).

FL.1863	Spring and Autumn Annals
FL.1864	Warring States
FL.1865	Western Zhou
FL.1866	Qin
FL.1867	Six Dynasties
FL.1868	Northern and Southern Dynasties
FL.1869	Northern Dynasties
FL.1870	Northern Wei
FL.1871	Eastern Wei
FL.1872	Western Wei
FL.1873	Northern Qi
FL.1874	Northern Zhou
FL.1875	Southern Dynasties
FL.1876	Southern Qi
FL.1877	Liu Song
FL.1878	Liang
FL.1879	Chen
FL.1880	Three Kingdoms (Chinese)
FL.1881	Jin (Six Dynasties)
FL.1882	Eastern Jin
FL.1883	Western Jin
FL.1884	Sui
FL.1885	Tang
FL.1886	Five Dynasties
FL.1887	Later Jin
FL.1888	Later Tang
FL.1889	Later Liang
FL.1890	Later Han
FL.1891	Later Zhou
FL.1892	Liao
FL.1893	Song
FL.1894	Northern Song
FL.1895	Southern Song
FL.1896	Yüan
FL.1897	Ming
FL.1898	Hongwu
FL.1899	Yongle
FL.1900	Xuande
FL.1901	Chenghua
FL.1902	Hongzhi
FL.1903	Zhengde
FL.1904	Jiajing
FL.1905	Longqing
FL.1906	Wanli
FL.1907	Tianqi
FL.1908	Chongzhen
FL.1909	Qing
FL.1910	Shunzhi
FL.1911	Kangxi

May be used in combination with other descriptors, especially in the Objects facet (e.g., **Baroque** + **churches**; **Japanese** + **enameling**; **Abstract Expressionist** + **drawings**).

FL.1912 Yongzheng
FL.1913 Qianlong
FL.1914 Jiaqing
FL.1915 Daoguang
FL.1916 Xianfeng
FL.1917 Tongzhi
FL.1918 Guangxu
FL.1919 Xuantong
FL.1920 *<modern Chinese styles and periods>*
FL.1921 Hongxian
FL.1922 *<Chinese styles>*
FL.1923 *<Chinese architecture styles>*
FL.1924 Karayo
FL.1925 *<Chinese painting styles>*
FL.1926 Bai miao
FL.1927 blue-and-green
FL.1928 Canton
FL.1929 Dong-Ju
FL.1930 Gongan
FL.1931 Individualist
FL.1932 Loudong
FL.1933 Ma-Xia
FL.1934 Northern School
FL.1935 Shanghai
FL.1936 Southern School
FL.1937 Su-Song
FL.1938 Wen ren
FL.1939 Wu
FL.1940 Zhe
FL.1941 *<Chinese pottery styles>*
FL.1942 Chinese export porcelain
FL.1943 Compagnie des Indes ware
FL.1944 Jesuit ware
FL.1945 Ding ware
FL.1946 Jun ware
FL.1947 Kraak porcelain
FL.1948 Qingbai ware
FL.1949 Ru ware
FL.1950 Sancai
FL.1951 Shufu
FL.1952 Swatow ware
FL.1953 Wucai
FL.1954 Xing ware
FL.1955 Japanese
FL.1956 *<Japanese periods>*
FL.1957 *<Japanese prehistoric periods>*
FL.1958 Pre-pottery
FL.1959 Jomon
FL.1960 Proto-Jomon

May be used in combination with other descriptors, especially in the Objects facet (e.g., **Baroque** + **churches**; **Japanese** + **enameling**; **Abstract Expressionist** + **drawings**).

FL.1961 **Early Jomon**
FL.1962 **Middle Jomon**
FL.1963 **Late Jomon**
FL.1964 **Final Jomon**
FL.1965 *<Medieval Japanese periods>*
FL.1966 **Kamakura**
FL.1967 **Nambokucho**
FL.1968 **Muromachi**
FL.1969 **Sengoku**
FL.1970 *<Japanese protohistoric periods>*
FL.1971 **Yayoi**
FL.1972 **Kofun**
FL.1973 *<early historical Japanese periods>*
FL.1974 **Asuka**
FL.1975 **Nara**
FL.1976 **Early Nara**
FL.1977 **Late Nara**
FL.1978 **Heian**
FL.1979 **Early Heian**
FL.1980 **Late Heian**
FL.1981 *<early modern Japanese periods>*
FL.1982 **Edo (Japanese period)**
FL.1983 **Early Edo**
FL.1984 **Middle Edo**
FL.1985 **Late Edo**
FL.1986 **Momoyama**
FL.1987 *<modern Japanese periods>*
FL.1988 **Meiji**
FL.1989 **Taisho**
FL.1990 **Showa**
FL.1991 *<Japanese styles>*
FL.1992 *<Japanese architecture styles>*
FL.1993 **Daibutsuyo**
FL.1994 **Gongen**
FL.1995 **Hachiman**
FL.1996 **Hie**
FL.1997 **Izumo Taisha**
FL.1998 **Kasuga**
FL.1999 **Minka**
FL.2000 **Nagare**
FL.2001 **Settchuyo**
FL.2002 **Shimmei**
FL.2003 **Shinden**
FL.2004 **Shoin**
FL.2005 **Sukiya**
FL.2006 **Sumiyoshi (architecture style)**
FL.2007 **Wayo**
FL.2008 **Zenshuyo**
FL.2009 *<Japanese decorative arts styles>*

May be used in combination with other descriptors, especially in the Objects facet (e.g., **Baroque** + **churches**; **Japanese** + **enameling**; **Abstract Expressionist** + **drawings**).

FL.2010 *<Japanese lacquer styles>*
FL.2011 Negoro
FL.2012 *<Japanese pottery styles>*
FL.2013 Agano
FL.2014 Arita
FL.2015 Imari
FL.2016 Kakiemon
FL.2017 Nabeshima
FL.2018 Banko
FL.2019 Bizen
FL.2020 Hagi
FL.2021 Hirado
FL.2022 Iga
FL.2023 Karatsu
FL.2024 Kuniyaki
FL.2025 Kutani
FL.2026 Ao Kutani
FL.2027 Ko Kutani
FL.2028 Saiko Kutani
FL.2029 Kyoto
FL.2030 Nisai
FL.2031 Oribe
FL.2032 Ryokuyo
FL.2033 Sanage
FL.2034 Yamachawan
FL.2035 Satsuma
FL.2036 Seto ware
FL.2037 Ki Seto
FL.2038 Ko Seto
FL.2039 Seto-guro
FL.2040 Shigaraki
FL.2041 Shiki
FL.2042 Shino
FL.2043 Sue ware
FL.2044 Takatori ware
FL.2045 Tamba
FL.2046 Tokoname
FL.2047 Yakishime
FL.2048 *<Japanese painting styles>*
FL.2049 Ami School
FL.2050 Akita Ranga School
FL.2051 Haboku
FL.2052 Hasegawa School
FL.2053 Kaiho School
FL.2054 Kano School
FL.2055 Kara-e
FL.2056 Kasuga School
FL.2057 Kose School
FL.2058 Maruyama School

FL

May be used in combination with other descriptors, especially in the Objects facet (e.g., **Baroque** + **churches**; **Japanese** + **enameling**; **Abstract Expressionist** + **drawings**).

FL.2059 Nagasaki
FL.2060 Namban
FL.2061 Nanga
FL.2062 Nara-e
FL.2063 Nihonga
FL.2064 Otsu-e
FL.2065 Shijo
FL.2066 Soga (Japanese painting style)
FL.2067 Sotatsu-Korin School
FL.2068 Takuma
FL.2069 Suibokuga
FL.2070 Sumiyoshi (painting style)
FL.2071 Tosa School
FL.2072 Unkoku School
FL.2073 Yamato-e
FL.2074 Yoga
FL.2075 *<Japanese printmaking styles>*
FL.2076 Benizuri-e
FL.2077 Ishizuri-e
FL.2078 Kamigata-e
FL.2079 Mizui-e
FL.2080 Nagasaki-e
FL.2081 Osaka Print School
FL.2082 Torii School
FL.2083 Uki-e
FL.2084 Ukiyo-e
FL.2085 Edo-e
FL.2086 Hanabusa School
FL.2087 Hiroshige School
FL.2088 Hishigawa School
FL.2089 Hokusai School
FL.2090 Kaigetsudo School
FL.2091 Katsukawa School
FL.2092 Kitagawa School
FL.2093 Kitao School
FL.2094 Nishimura School
FL.2095 Suzuki School
FL.2096 Utagawa School
FL.2097 Yokohama-e
FL.2098 *<Japanese sculpture styles>*
FL.2099 Chuguji
FL.2100 Jocho
FL.2101 Kudara Kannon
FL.2102 Sanjo Street School
FL.2103 Shichijo Street School
FL.2104 Tori
FL.2105 Unkei
FL.2106 Korean
FL.2107 *<Korean periods>*

May be used in combination with other descriptors, especially in the Objects facet (e.g., **Baroque** + **churches**; **Japanese** + **enameling**; **Abstract Expressionist** + **drawings**).

FL.2108 Koryo
FL.2109 Three Kingdoms (Korean)
FL.2110 Old Silla
FL.2111 Koguryo
FL.2112 Paekche
FL.2113 Unified Silla Kingdom
FL.2114 Yi
FL.2115 Chosen
FL.2116 *<Korean styles>*
FL.2117 *<Korean pottery styles>*
FL.2118 Punch'ong ware
FL.2119 Siberian
FL.2120 *<Siberian periods>*
FL.2121 Afanasievo
FL.2122 Okunev
FL.2123 Andronovo
FL.2124 Karasuk
FL.2125 Kamenny Log phase
FL.2126 Early Nomads Age
FL.2127 Bol'shaia Rechka
FL.2128 Biysk phase
FL.2129 Berëzovsk phase
FL.2130 Maiemir
FL.2131 Pazyryk
FL.2132 Shibe
FL.2133 Tagar
FL.2134 Bainov phase
FL.2135 Podgornoe phase
FL.2136 Saragash phase
FL.2137 Tes phase
FL.2138 Tashtyk
FL.2139 *<Siberian styles>*
FL.2140 Altai
FL.2141 Bashadar
FL.2142 Goldi
FL.2143 Saka
FL.2144 Tuva
FL.2145 Kuznetsk Basin
FL.2146 Minusinsk Basin
FL.2147 Ordos
FL.2148 *<Siberian Arctic Native styles>*
FL.2149 Chukchi
FL.2150 Koryak
FL.2151 South Asian
FL.2152 Himalayan
FL.2153 Bhutanese
FL.2154 Kashmiri
FL.2155 Ladakhi
FL.2156 Nepalese

FL.2157 <*Nepalese dynastic periods*>
FL.2158 Pre-Licchavi
FL.2159 Licchavi
FL.2160 Utpala
FL.2161 Thakuri
FL.2162 Malla
FL.2163 Early Malla
FL.2164 Late Malla
FL.2165 Gurkha
FL.2166 <*Nepalese regional styles*>
FL.2167 Bhatgaon
FL.2168 Kathmandu
FL.2169 Kusinagara
FL.2170 Patan
FL.2171 Vaisali (Nepalese)
FL.2172 Sikkimese
FL.2173 Swat
FL.2174 Swat Valley
FL.2175 Tibetan
FL.2176 <*Tibetan painting styles*>
FL.2177 Bal-bris
FL.2178 Guge
FL.2179 Kadam School
FL.2180 Karma Gardri School
FL.2181 Menri School
FL.2182 New Menri School
FL.2183 Pala-Tibetan
FL.2184 Sakya School
FL.2185 Indian
FL.2186 <*Indian styles and periods*>
FL.2187 Indus Valley
FL.2188 Harappan
FL.2189 Mohenjo-daro
FL.2190 Vedic
FL.2191 <*Indian dynastic styles and periods*>
FL.2192 Saisunaga-Nanda
FL.2193 Maurya
FL.2194 Asóka
FL.2195 Sunga
FL.2196 Andhra
FL.2197 Early Andra
FL.2198 Later Andhra
FL.2199 Kushan
FL.2200 Gandharan
FL.2201 Gupta
FL.2202 Sarnath
FL.2203 Mathura
FL.2204 Post-Gupta
FL.2205 Pallava

May be used in combination with other descriptors, especially in the Objects facet (e.g., **Baroque** + **churches**; **Japanese** + **enameling**; **Abstract Expressionist** + **drawings**).

FL.2206 Mamalla
FL.2207 Rajasimha
FL.2208 Chalukyan
FL.2209 Ganga
FL.2210 Pala
FL.2211 Sena
FL.2212 Rashtrakuta
FL.2213 Solanki
FL.2214 Paramara
FL.2215 Candella
FL.2216 Gurjara-Partihara
FL.2217 Chola
FL.2218 Hoysala
FL.2219 Yadava
FL.2220 Pandya
FL.2221 *<Late Indian styles and periods>*
FL.2222 Nayak
FL.2223 Vijayanagar
FL.2224 *<Islamic Indian styles and periods>*
FL.2225 Delhi Sultanate
FL.2226 Mughal
FL.2227 *<Mughal periods>*
FL.2228 Shah Alam
FL.2229 Babur
FL.2230 Humayun
FL.2231 Akbar
FL.2232 Jahangir
FL.2233 Shah Jahan
FL.2234 Aurangzeb
FL.2235 Muhammad Shah
FL.2236 *<Mughal styles>*
FL.2237 Popular Mughal
FL.2238 Provincial Mughal
FL.2239 Sub-Imperial Mughal
FL.2240 Tughluq
FL.2241 *<Colonial Indian styles>*
FL.2242 *<British Colonial Indian styles>*
FL.2243 Company
FL.2244 *<Portuguese Colonial Indian styles>*
FL.2245 Goan
FL.2246 *<Indian architecture styles>*
FL.2247 Dravidian
FL.2248 Nagara
FL.2249 Vesara
FL.2250 *<Indian painting styles>*
FL.2251 Deccani
FL.2252 Ahmadnagar
FL.2253 Aurangabad
FL.2254 Bijapur

FL.2255 **Daulatabad**
FL.2256 **Golconda**
FL.2257 **Hyderabad**
FL.2258 **Eastern Indian**
FL.2259 **Kalighat**
FL.2260 **Orissa**
FL.2261 **Oudh**
FL.2262 **Fyzabad**
FL.2263 **Jaunpur**
FL.2264 **Paithan**
FL.2265 **Rajput**
FL.2266 **Central Indian**
FL.2267 **Bundelkhand**
FL.2268 **Datia**
FL.2269 **Malwa**
FL.2270 **Pahari**
FL.2271 **Basohli**
FL.2272 **Bhoti**
FL.2273 **Bilaspur**
FL.2274 **Chamba (Pahari)**
FL.2275 **Garwhal**
FL.2276 **Guler**
FL.2277 **Hindur**
FL.2278 **Jammu**
FL.2279 **Kangra**
FL.2280 **Kulu**
FL.2281 **Mandi**
FL.2282 **Mankot**
FL.2283 **Nurpur**
FL.2284 **Raghogarh**
FL.2285 **Rajasthani**
FL.2286 **Ajmer**
FL.2287 **Amber (painting style)**
FL.2288 **Bikaner**
FL.2289 **Bundi**
FL.2290 **Deogarh**
FL.2291 **Jodhpur**
FL.2292 **Kishangarh**
FL.2293 **Kotah**
FL.2294 **Marwar**
FL.2295 **Mewar**
FL.2296 **Sirohi**
FL.2297 **South Indian**
FL.2298 **Kerala**
FL.2299 **Mysore**
FL.2300 **Sirmur**
FL.2301 **Sittanavasal**
FL.2302 **Sultanate**
FL.2303 **Western Indian**

May be used in combination with other descriptors, especially in the Objects facet (e.g., **Baroque** + **churches**; **Japanese** + **enameling**; **Abstract Expressionist** + **drawings**).

FL.2304 Sri Lankan
FL.2305 Anuradhapura
FL.2306 Polonnaruwa
FL.2307 Southeast Asian
FL.2308 Burmese
FL.2309 Mandalay
FL.2310 Mon
FL.2311 Thatôn
FL.2312 Pagán
FL.2313 Pyu
FL.2314 Talaing
FL.2315 Pegu
FL.2316 Cambodian
FL.2317 Pre-Angkorean
FL.2318 Funan
FL.2319 Phnom Da
FL.2320 Chen-la
FL.2321 Kompong Preah
FL.2322 Prasat Andet
FL.2323 Prei Kmeng
FL.2324 Sambor Prei Kuk
FL.2325 *<Pre-Angkorean periods by reign>*
FL.2326 Mahendravarman
FL.2327 Jayavarman I
FL.2328 Transitional
FL.2329 Jayavarman II
FL.2330 Jayavarman III
FL.2331 Angkorean
FL.2332 *<Angkorean periods by reign>*
FL.2333 Indravarman I
FL.2334 Suryavarman I
FL.2335 Yasovarman I
FL.2336 Jayavarman IV
FL.2337 Rajendravarman
FL.2338 Jayavarman V
FL.2339 Udayadityavarman I
FL.2340 Harshavarman III
FL.2341 Jayavarman VI
FL.2342 Dharanindravarman I
FL.2343 Suryavarman II
FL.2344 Dharanindravarman II
FL.2345 Yasovarman II
FL.2346 Tribhuvanadityavarman
FL.2347 Jayavarman VII
FL.2348 Indravarman II
FL.2349 Jayavarman VIII
FL.2350 Srindravarman
FL.2351 Srindrajayavarman
FL.2352 Jayavarmadiparamesvara

FL.2353	*<Angkorean styles>*
FL.2354	Angkor Thom
FL.2355	Baphuon
FL.2356	Bayon
FL.2357	Angkor Vat
FL.2358	Bakheng
FL.2359	Banteay Chmar
FL.2360	Banteay Srei
FL.2361	Kulên
FL.2362	Koh Ker
FL.2363	Phi Mai
FL.2364	Pré Rup
FL.2365	Preah Khan
FL.2366	Preah Vihear
FL.2367	Post-Angkorean
FL.2368	Indonesian
FL.2369	*<Indonesian periods>*
FL.2370	Dông-Son
FL.2371	Late Zhou
FL.2372	*<Indonesian regional styles and periods>*
FL.2373	Balinese
FL.2374	Javanese period (Balinese)
FL.2375	Bornean
FL.2376	Flores
FL.2377	Javanese
FL.2378	Central Javanese
FL.2379	Srivijaya
FL.2380	Sailendra
FL.2381	East Javanese
FL.2382	*<East Javanese periods>*
FL.2383	Singhasari
FL.2384	Majapahit
FL.2385	Mataram
FL.2386	Wayang
FL.2387	Sulawesi
FL.2388	Sumatran
FL.2389	Malayu
FL.2390	Sumba
FL.2391	Sumbawa
FL.2392	Timor
FL.2393	Laotian
FL.2394	Lan Xang
FL.2395	Luang Prabang
FL.2396	Vientiane
FL.2397	Malaysian
FL.2398	Malayan
FL.2399	Sarawak
FL.2400	Philippine
FL.2401	Thai

May be used in combination with other descriptors, especially in the Objects facet (e.g., **Baroque** + **churches**; **Japanese** + **enameling**; **Abstract Expressionist** + **drawings**).

FL.2402 <*Thai periods*>
FL.2403 **Ayudhya**
FL.2404 **Ban Chieng**
FL.2405 **Dvaravati**
FL.2406 **Nakhon Pathom**
FL.2407 **Pra Patom**
FL.2408 **Khmer**
FL.2409 **Lopburi-Khmer**
FL.2410 **Haripunjaya**
FL.2411 **Nakhon Si Thammarat**
FL.2412 **Peninsular**
FL.2413 **Northern Thai**
FL.2414 **Sri Deb**
FL.2415 **Sukhothai**
FL.2416 **Thonburi**
FL.2417 **Wat Kukut**
FL.2418 **Srivijaya (Thai)**
FL.2419 **Lopburî**
FL.2420 **Chiang Mai**
FL.2421 **U Tong**
FL.2422 **Bangkok**
FL.2423 <*Thai pottery styles*>
FL.2424 **Bencharong**
FL.2425 **Sawankhalok**
FL.2426 **Vietnamese**
FL.2427 <*Vietnamese periods*>
FL.2428 **Dai-La**
FL.2429 **Dông-Son (Vietnamese)**
FL.2430 **Ly**
FL.2431 **Trân**
FL.2432 **Lê**
FL.2433 **Nguyên**
FL.2434 <*Vietnamese regional styles and periods*>
FL.2435 **Annamese**
FL.2436 **Cham (Vietnamese)**
FL.2437 <*Cham periods*>
FL.2438 **Binh Dinh**
FL.2439 **Mi-son**
FL.2440 **Mi-son A 1**
FL.2441 **Mi-son E 1**
FL.2442 **Tra-kieu**
FL.2443 **Dong-duong**
FL.2444 **Hoa Lai**
FL.2445 **Cochin Chinese**
FL.2446 **Tonkin**
FL.2447 <*Early Western World*>
FL.2448 <*Ancient European styles and periods*>
FL.2449 <*European Lower Paleolithic styles and periods*>
FL.2450 **Abbevillian**

May be used in combination with other descriptors, especially in the Objects facet (e.g., **Baroque** + **churches**; **Japanese** + **enameling**; **Abstract Expressionist** + **drawings**).

FL.2451	**Acheulian**
FL.2452	**Clactonian**
FL.2453	**Levalloisian**
FL.2454	**Tayacian**
FL.2455	*<European Middle Paleolithic styles and periods>*
FL.2456	**Levalloiso-Mousterian**
FL.2457	**Micoquian**
FL.2458	**Mousterian**
FL.2459	*<European Upper Paleolithic styles and periods>*
FL.2460	*<Eastern European Upper Paleolithic styles and periods>*
FL.2461	**East Gravettian**
FL.2462	**Pavlovian**
FL.2463	**Szeletian**
FL.2464	*<Western European Upper Paleolithic styles and periods>*
FL.2465	**Aurignacian**
FL.2466	**Châtelperronian**
FL.2467	**Gravettian**
FL.2468	**Magdalenian**
FL.2469	**Perigordian**
FL.2470	**Lower Perigordian**
FL.2471	**Upper Perigordian**
FL.2472	**Solutrian**
FL.2473	**Uluzzian**
FL.2474	*<European Mesolithic styles and periods>*
FL.2475	**Asturian**
FL.2476	**Azilian**
FL.2477	**Campignian**
FL.2478	**Epi-gravettian**
FL.2479	**Ertebølle**
FL.2480	**Hamburgian**
FL.2481	**Maglemosian**
FL.2482	**Romanellian**
FL.2483	**Sauveterrian**
FL.2484	**Tardenoisian**
FL.2485	*<European Neolithic styles and periods>*
FL.2486	**Almerian**
FL.2487	**Chasseen**
FL.2488	**Corded ware**
FL.2489	**Cris**
FL.2490	**Danubian**
FL.2491	**Koros**
FL.2492	**Kurgan**
FL.2493	**Lagozza**
FL.2494	**Rossen**
FL.2495	**Starcevo**
FL.2496	**Tripolye**
FL.2497	**Vinca**
FL.2498	**Vinca-Plocnik**
FL.2499	**Vinca-Tordos**

May be used in combination with other descriptors, especially in the Objects facet (e.g., **Baroque** + **churches**; **Japanese** + **enameling**; **Abstract Expressionist** + **drawings**).

FL.2500	**Windmill Hill**
FL.2501	*<European Neolithic pottery styles>*
FL.2502	**Bandkeramik**
FL.2503	**Linienbandkeramik**
FL.2504	**Stichbandkeramik**
FL.2505	**Bell Beaker**
FL.2506	**Funnel Beaker**
FL.2507	*<European Bronze Age styles and periods>*
FL.2508	*<European Bronze Age periods>*
FL.2509	**Dagger period**
FL.2510	**Hallstatt**
FL.2511	**Tumulus period**
FL.2512	**Unetician**
FL.2513	**Urnfield**
FL.2514	**Wessex**
FL.2515	*<European Bronze Age styles>*
FL.2516	**Boss Style**
FL.2517	*<European Iron Age styles and periods>*
FL.2518	*<European Iron Age periods>*
FL.2519	**Jastorf**
FL.2520	**La Tène**
FL.2521	*<European Iron Age styles>*
FL.2522	**Celtic**
FL.2523	*<LaTene styles>*
FL.2524	**Early Style**
FL.2525	**Plastic Style**
FL.2526	**Sword Style**
FL.2527	**Waldalgesheim Style**
FL.2528	**Mediterranean**
FL.2529	**Aegean**
FL.2530	*<Aegean periods>*
FL.2531	*<Aegean Neolithic periods>*
FL.2532	**Proto-Sesklo**
FL.2533	**Sesklo**
FL.2534	**Dimini**
FL.2535	*<Aegean Bronze Age periods>*
FL.2536	**Cycladic**
FL.2537	**Early Cycladic**
FL.2538	**Pelos phase**
FL.2539	**Grotta-Pelos**
FL.2540	**Keros-Syros**
FL.2541	**Syros phase**
FL.2542	**Kastri group**
FL.2543	**Amorgos group**
FL.2544	**Lefkandi I**
FL.2545	**Phylakopi I phase**
FL.2546	**Middle Cycladic**
FL.2547	**Late Cycladic**
FL.2548	**Helladic**

FL

May be used in combination with other descriptors, especially in the Objects facet (e.g., **Baroque** + **churches**; **Japanese** + **enameling**; **Abstract Expressionist** + **drawings**).

FL.2549	Early Helladic
FL.2550	Middle Helladic
FL.2551	Shaft Grave period
FL.2552	Late Helladic
FL.2553	Mycenaean
FL.2554	Sub-Mycenaean
FL.2555	Minoan
FL.2556	Early Minoan
FL.2557	Middle Minoan
FL.2558	Subminoan
FL.2559	Late Minoan
FL.2560	Old Palace period
FL.2561	New Palace period
FL.2562	Greek
FL.2563	Protogeometric
FL.2564	Geometric
FL.2565	Early Geometric
FL.2566	Middle Geometric
FL.2567	Late Geometric
FL.2568	Sub-geometric
FL.2569	Orientalizing
FL.2570	Early Orientalizing
FL.2571	Developed Orientalizing
FL.2572	Late Orientalizing
FL.2573	Archaic
FL.2574	Early Archaic
FL.2575	Middle Archaic
FL.2576	Late Archaic
FL.2577	Classical
FL.2578	Early Classical
FL.2579	High Classical
FL.2580	Late Classical
FL.2581	Hellenistic
FL.2582	Late Hellenistic
FL.2583	*<Aegean styles>*
FL.2584	Cretan
FL.2585	Creto-Mycenaean
FL.2586	*<Aegean architecture styles>*
FL.2587	Aeolic
FL.2588	Corinthian (architectural style)
FL.2589	Doric
FL.2590	Ionic
FL.2591	*<Aegean pottery styles>*
FL.2592	*<Cycladic pottery styles>*
FL.2593	Curvilinear Style
FL.2594	Cycladic white ware
FL.2595	dark-burnished ware
FL.2596	dark-faced incised ware
FL.2597	yellow-slipped ware

May be used in combination with other descriptors, especially in the Objects facet (e.g., **Baroque** + **churches**; **Japanese** + **enameling**; **Abstract Expressionist** + **drawings**).

FL.2598 *<Greek pottery styles>*
FL.2599 *<Central Italian Greek pottery styles>*
FL.2600 **Caeretan**
FL.2601 **East Greek**
FL.2602 **Clazomenian**
FL.2603 **Ionian**
FL.2604 **Wild Goat Style**
FL.2605 *<Island Greek pottery styles>*
FL.2606 **Chian**
FL.2607 **Chalice Style**
FL.2608 **Daphne ware**
FL.2609 **Linear Island Style**
FL.2610 **Rhodian**
FL.2611 **Fikellura**
FL.2612 **Theran**
FL.2613 *<Mainland Greek pottery styles>*
FL.2614 **Attic**
FL.2615 **Free Style (pottery)**
FL.2616 **Early Free Style**
FL.2617 **Proto-Attic**
FL.2618 **Boeotian**
FL.2619 **Chalcidian**
FL.2620 **Eretrian**
FL.2621 **Euboean**
FL.2622 **Megarian**
FL.2623 **West Slope ware**
FL.2624 *<Peloponnesian pottery styles>*
FL.2625 **Corinthian (pottery style)**
FL.2626 **Proto-Corinthian**
FL.2627 **Early Corinthian**
FL.2628 **Middle Corinthian**
FL.2629 **Late Corinthian**
FL.2630 **Laconian**
FL.2631 **South Italian**
FL.2632 **Apulian**
FL.2633 **Gnathian**
FL.2634 **Calene ware**
FL.2635 **Campanian**
FL.2636 **Canosa**
FL.2637 **Centuripe**
FL.2638 **Lucanian**
FL.2639 **Paestan**
FL.2640 **Sicilian**
FL.2641 *<Greek vase painting styles>*
FL.2642 **Black and White Style (pottery)**
FL.2643 **Black-figure**
FL.2644 **Outline Style**
FL.2645 **Red-figure**
FL.2646 **Florid Style**

FL.2647 Kerch Style
FL.2648 Ornate Style
FL.2649 Simple Style
FL.2650 White-ground
FL.2651 *<Helladic pottery styles>*
FL.2652 black burnished ware (Helladic pottery)
FL.2653 Close Style
FL.2654 crusted ware
FL.2655 dark-on-light painted ware
FL.2656 Ephyraean ware
FL.2657 matt-painted ware
FL.2658 Minyan ware
FL.2659 Argive Minyan ware
FL.2660 Gray Minyan ware
FL.2661 Yellow Minyan ware
FL.2662 Palace style (Mycenaean pottery)
FL.2663 Urfirnis ware
FL.2664 *<Minoan pottery styles>*
FL.2665 Ayios Onouphrios ware
FL.2666 eggshell ware
FL.2667 Floral Style
FL.2668 Kamares ware
FL.2669 light-on-dark ware
FL.2670 Marine Style
FL.2671 Octopus Style
FL.2672 Plant Style
FL.2673 Pyrgos ware
FL.2674 Vasiliki ware
FL.2675 *<Aegean sculpture styles>*
FL.2676 *<Cycladic sculpture styles>*
FL.2677 Dokathismata type
FL.2678 folded-arm type
FL.2679 Plastiras type
FL.2680 Spedos type
FL.2681 *<Greek sculpture styles>*
FL.2682 Archaistic
FL.2683 Argive School
FL.2684 Polykleitan
FL.2685 Daedalic
FL.2686 Ionian Island Style
FL.2687 Lysippic
FL.2688 Melian
FL.2689 Naxian
FL.2690 Parian
FL.2691 Pergamene
FL.2692 Phidian
FL.2693 Praxitelean
FL.2694 Samian
FL.2695 Severe Style

May be used in combination with other descriptors, especially in the Objects facet (e.g., **Baroque** + **churches**; **Japanese** + **enameling**; **Abstract Expressionist** + **drawings**).

FL.2696 **Skopasian**
FL.2697 *<Ancient Italian styles and periods>*
FL.2698 *<Ancient Italian periods>*
FL.2699 *<Italian Bronze Age periods>*
FL.2700 **Apennine**
FL.2701 **Ausonian**
FL.2702 **Morgetian**
FL.2703 **Proto-Villanovan**
FL.2704 **Sub-Apennine**
FL.2705 **Terramare**
FL.2706 **Villanovan**
FL.2707 **Etruscan**
FL.2708 **Early Etruscan**
FL.2709 **Late Etruscan**
FL.2710 **Tarquinian**
FL.2711 **Roman**
FL.2712 **Republican**
FL.2713 **Late Republican**
FL.2714 **Caesarian**
FL.2715 **Sullan**
FL.2716 **Imperial**
FL.2717 **Early Imperial**
FL.2718 **Augustan**
FL.2719 **Julio-Claudian**
FL.2720 **Flavian**
FL.2721 **Trajanic**
FL.2722 **Hadrianic**
FL.2723 **Antonine**
FL.2724 **Severan**
FL.2725 **Late Antique**
FL.2726 **Tetrarchic**
FL.2727 **Constantinian**
FL.2728 *<Ancient Italian styles>*
FL.2729 **Etrusco-Italic**
FL.2730 **Etrusco-Roman**
FL.2731 **Greco-Etruscan**
FL.2732 **Italic**
FL.2733 *<Roman provincial styles>*
FL.2734 **Gallo-Roman**
FL.2735 **Romano-British**
FL.2736 *<Villanovan styles>*
FL.2737 **Arnoaldi**
FL.2738 **Benacci**
FL.2739 *<Ancient Italian architecture styles>*
FL.2740 **Composite**
FL.2741 **Tuscan**
FL.2742 *<Ancient Italian pottery styles>*
FL.2743 *<Etruscan pottery styles>*
FL.2744 **Bucchero ware**

FL

May be used in combination with other descriptors, especially in the Objects facet (e.g., **Baroque** + **churches**; **Japanese** + **enameling**; **Abstract Expressionist** + **drawings**).

FL.2745	Civitavecchia
FL.2746	Faliscan ware
FL.2747	*<Roman pottery styles>*
FL.2748	brittle ware
FL.2749	gray ware
FL.2750	micaceous ware
FL.2751	Pergamene ware
FL.2752	red-gloss pottery
FL.2753	Terra sigillata
FL.2754	Samian ware
FL.2755	Western sigillata ware
FL.2756	Arretine ware
FL.2757	thorn ware
FL.2758	*<Ancient Italian sculpture styles>*
FL.2759	*<Roman sculpture styles>*
FL.2760	Aphrodisian
FL.2761	Greco-Roman
FL.2762	Hard Style
FL.2763	Neo-Attic
FL.2764	*<Ancient Italian wall painting styles>*
FL.2765	*<Pompeian wall painting styles>*
FL.2766	First Style
FL.2767	Second Style
FL.2768	Third Style
FL.2769	Fourth Style
FL.2770	Egyptian
FL.2771	*<Egyptian periods>*
FL.2772	Predynastic (Egyptian)
FL.2773	*<Lower Egyptian Predynastic periods>*
FL.2774	Fayum A
FL.2775	Merimde
FL.2776	El-Omari
FL.2777	Ma'adi
FL.2778	*<Upper Egyptian Predynastic periods>*
FL.2779	Badarian
FL.2780	Amratian
FL.2781	Gerzean
FL.2782	Early Gerzean
FL.2783	Late Gerzean
FL.2784	*<Egyptian Paleolithic periods>*
FL.2785	Qadan
FL.2786	Sebilian
FL.2787	Old Kingdom
FL.2788	Third Dynasty
FL.2789	Fourth Dynasty
FL.2790	Fifth Dynasty
FL.2791	Sixth Dynasty
FL.2792	Early Dynastic (Egyptian)
FL.2793	First Dynasty

May be used in combination with other descriptors, especially in the Objects facet (e.g., **Baroque** + **churches**; **Japanese** + **enameling**; **Abstract Expressionist** + **drawings**).

FL.2794 Second Dynasty
FL.2795 Thinite
FL.2796 First Intermediate period
FL.2797 Seventh Dynasty
FL.2798 Eighth Dynasty
FL.2799 Ninth Dynasty
FL.2800 Tenth Dynasty
FL.2801 Heracleopolitan period
FL.2802 Memphite
FL.2803 Middle Kingdom
FL.2804 Eleventh Dynasty
FL.2805 Twelfth Dynasty
FL.2806 Second Intermediate period
FL.2807 Thirteenth Dynasty
FL.2808 Fourteenth Dynasty
FL.2809 Fifteenth Dynasty
FL.2810 Sixteenth Dynasty
FL.2811 Seventeenth Dynasty
FL.2812 Hyksos
FL.2813 Theban
FL.2814 New Kingdom
FL.2815 Eighteenth Dynasty
FL.2816 Nineteenth Dynasty
FL.2817 Ramesside period
FL.2818 Twentieth Dynasty
FL.2819 Amarna period
FL.2820 Third Intermediate period
FL.2821 Twenty-first Dynasty
FL.2822 Twenty-second Dynasty
FL.2823 Twenty-third Dynasty
FL.2824 Twenty-fourth Dynasty
FL.2825 Twenty-fifth Dynasty
FL.2826 Late period (Egyptian)
FL.2827 Twenty-sixth Dynasty
FL.2828 Twenty-seventh Dynasty
FL.2829 Twenty-eighth Dynasty
FL.2830 Twenty-ninth Dynasty
FL.2831 Thirtieth Dynasty
FL.2832 Thirty-first Dynasty
FL.2833 Ptolemaic
FL.2834 Coptic (period)
FL.2835 *<Egyptian styles>*
FL.2836 *<Egyptian pottery styles>*
FL.2837 black-mouthed ware
FL.2838 black-topped pottery
FL.2839 black-topped red ware
FL.2840 Hadra
FL.2841 orange-burnished ware
FL.2842 red-polished ware

FL

May be used in combination with other descriptors, especially in the Objects facet (e.g., **Baroque** + **churches**; **Japanese** + **enameling**; **Abstract Expressionist** + **drawings**).

FL.2843 ripple-burnished ware
FL.2844 white-lined pottery
FL.2845 white cross-lined pottery
FL.2846 Near Eastern
FL.2847 Anatolian
FL.2848 *<Anatolian periods>*
FL.2849 *<Anatolian Paleolithic periods>*
FL.2850 Belbasi
FL.2851 Beldibi
FL.2852 Kemerian
FL.2853 Assyrian Colony period
FL.2854 Hittite
FL.2855 Old Hittite Kingdom
FL.2856 Middle Hittite Kingdom
FL.2857 Hittite Empire
FL.2858 Neo-Hittite
FL.2859 Urartian
FL.2860 Phrygian
FL.2861 Lydian
FL.2862 *<Anatolian styles>*
FL.2863 Lycian
FL.2864 Syro-Hittite
FL.2865 *<Anatolian pottery styles>*
FL.2866 black-on-red ware
FL.2867 brown-on-cream ware
FL.2868 brown-slipped ware
FL.2869 Cappadocian ware
FL.2870 Çatal West ware
FL.2871 gritty buff ware
FL.2872 intermediate ware
FL.2873 knobbed ware
FL.2874 metallic ware (Anatolian pottery)
FL.2875 multiple-brush painted ware
FL.2876 red-on-cream ware
FL.2877 red-slipped ware
FL.2878 white-on-red pottery
FL.2879 white-slipped red ware
FL.2880 Arabian
FL.2881 *<Arabian periods>*
FL.2882 Dilmun
FL.2883 Early Dilmun
FL.2884 Middle Dilmun
FL.2885 Late Dilmun
FL.2886 Nabatean
FL.2887 Qatabian
FL.2888 Sabaean
FL.2889 Umm an-Nar
FL.2890 Cypriote
FL.2891 *<Cypriote periods>*

May be used in combination with other descriptors, especially in the Objects facet (e.g., **Baroque** + **churches**; **Japanese** + **enameling**; **Abstract Expressionist** + **drawings**).

FL.2892 Early Cypriote
FL.2893 Philia stage
FL.2894 Vounous stage
FL.2895 Middle Cypriote
FL.2896 Late Cypriote
FL.2897 *<Cypriote styles>*
FL.2898 Cypro-Phoenician
FL.2899 *<Cypriote pottery styles>*
FL.2900 base ring ware
FL.2901 black lustrous ware
FL.2902 black-slip-and-combed ware
FL.2903 red lustrous ware
FL.2904 red polished ware
FL.2905 red-on-black ware
FL.2906 red-on-white ware
FL.2907 white painted ware
FL.2908 white slip ware
FL.2909 Levantine
FL.2910 *<Levantine periods>*
FL.2911 *<Levantine Paleolithic periods>*
FL.2912 Jabrudian
FL.2913 Levanto-Aurignacian
FL.2914 Kebaran
FL.2915 Natufian
FL.2916 *<Levantine Neolithic periods>*
FL.2917 Pre-pottery Neolithic A
FL.2918 Yarmukian
FL.2919 Pre-pottery Neolithic B
FL.2920 Munhatta phase
FL.2921 Jericho Pottery Neolithic B
FL.2922 Proto-Ghassulian
FL.2923 Ghassulian
FL.2924 Mitannian
FL.2925 *<Levantine styles>*
FL.2926 Canaanite
FL.2927 Palestinian
FL.2928 Philistine
FL.2929 Phoenician
FL.2930 Syro-Phoenician
FL.2931 Syrian
FL.2932 *<Levantine pottery styles>*
FL.2933 Amuq B ware
FL.2934 Atchana ware
FL.2935 basket ware
FL.2936 brittle-painted ware
FL.2937 dark-faced burnished ware
FL.2938 Khabur ware
FL.2939 Khirbet Kerak ware
FL.2940 metallic ware (Levantine pottery)

May be used in combination with other descriptors, especially in the Objects facet (e.g., **Baroque** + **churches**; **Japanese** + **enameling**; **Abstract Expressionist** + **drawings**).

FL.2941	pattern-burnished ware
FL.2942	red wash ware
FL.2943	red-pattern burnished ware
FL.2944	red-washed buff ware
FL.2945	Syrian gray-black ware
FL.2946	Wadi Rabah pottery
FL.2947	white ware
FL.2948	Mesopotamian
FL.2949	*<Mesopotamian periods>*
FL.2950	*<Prehistoric Mesopotamian periods>*
FL.2951	*<Prehistoric Northern Mesopotamian periods>*
FL.2952	Jarmo
FL.2953	Hassuna
FL.2954	Samarra
FL.2955	Halaf
FL.2956	*<Prehistoric Southern Mesopotamian periods>*
FL.2957	Eridu
FL.2958	Hajji Muhammed
FL.2959	Ubaid
FL.2960	Protoliterate
FL.2961	Gawra period
FL.2962	Uruk
FL.2963	Jamdat Nasr
FL.2964	Sumerian
FL.2965	Early Dynastic
FL.2966	Protoimperial
FL.2967	Akkadian
FL.2968	Post-Akkadian
FL.2969	Sargonid
FL.2970	Neo-Sumerian
FL.2971	Third Dynasty of Ur
FL.2972	Old Babylonian
FL.2973	First Dynasty of Babylon
FL.2974	Isin-Larsa
FL.2975	Mari Age
FL.2976	Kassite
FL.2977	Assyrian
FL.2978	Old Assyrian
FL.2979	Middle Assyrian
FL.2980	Late Assyrian
FL.2981	Neo-Babylonian
FL.2982	Chaldean
FL.2983	*<Mesopotamian styles>*
FL.2984	Assyro-Babylonian
FL.2985	Babylonian
FL.2986	Sumero-Akkadian
FL.2987	*<Mesopotamian glyptic styles>*
FL.2988	Brocade Style
FL.2989	*<Mesopotamian pottery styles>*

FL.2990 black-burnished ware
FL.2991 black-on-buff ware
FL.2992 gray burnished ware
FL.2993 Hassuna Archaic ware
FL.2994 Hassuna standard ware
FL.2995 Ninevite
FL.2996 scarlet ware
FL.2997 Persian
FL.2998 *<Persian periods>*
FL.2999 *<Zagros Mountain prehistoric periods>*
FL.3000 Baradostian
FL.3001 Zarzian
FL.3002 Zawi Chemi Shanidar
FL.3003 Karim Shaharian
FL.3004 Bus Mordeh
FL.3005 Ali Kosh
FL.3006 Muhammed Jafar
FL.3007 Khazineh
FL.3008 Memeh
FL.3009 Bayat
FL.3010 Elamite
FL.3011 Old Elamite
FL.3012 Proto-Elamite
FL.3013 Middle Elamite
FL.3014 Achaemenid
FL.3015 Seleucid
FL.3016 Parthian
FL.3017 Sassanian
FL.3018 *<Persian styles>*
FL.3019 Animal Style
FL.3020 Median (Persian style)
FL.3021 Scythian
FL.3022 *<Persian pottery styles>*
FL.3023 Archaic ware
FL.3024 buff ware
FL.3025 Choga Mami Transitional
FL.3026 early red ware
FL.3027 Ismailabad ware
FL.3028 red burnished ware
FL.3029 red-on-red ware
FL.3030 Sarab ware
FL.3031 Sialk pottery
FL.3032 soft ware
FL.3033 standard painted ware
FL.3034 European
FL.3035 *<European regions>*
FL.3036 Albanian
FL.3037 Austrian
FL.3038 Belgian

May be used in combination with other descriptors, especially in the Objects facet (e.g., **Baroque** + **churches**; **Japanese** + **enameling**; **Abstract Expressionist** + **drawings**).

FL.3039	**British**
FL.3040	**English**
FL.3041	**Scottish**
FL.3042	**Welsh**
FL.3043	**Bulgarian**
FL.3044	**Czech**
FL.3045	**French**
FL.3046	**German**
FL.3047	**Hungarian**
FL.3048	**Irish**
FL.3049	**Italian**
FL.3050	**Netherlandish**
FL.3051	**Dutch**
FL.3052	**Flemish**
FL.3053	**Polish**
FL.3054	**Portuguese**
FL.3055	**Romanian**
FL.3056	**Russian**
FL.3057	**Scandinavian**
FL.3058	**Danish**
FL.3059	**Finnish**
FL.3060	**Norwegian**
FL.3061	**Swedish**
FL.3062	**Spanish**
FL.3063	**Swiss**
FL.3064	**Yugoslav**
FL.3065	*<European styles and periods>*
FL.3066	*<Early Christian-Byzantine styles and periods>*
FL.3067	**Early Christian**
FL.3068	**Byzantine**
FL.3069	**Early Byzantine**
FL.3070	**Theodosian**
FL.3071	**Justinianic**
FL.3072	**Middle Byzantine**
FL.3073	**Comnenian**
FL.3074	**Macedonian Renaissance**
FL.3075	**Latin Empire**
FL.3076	**Late Byzantine**
FL.3077	**Palaeologan**
FL.3078	**Early Palaeologan**
FL.3079	**High Palaeologan**
FL.3080	*<Byzantine regional styles>*
FL.3081	**Constantinopolitan**
FL.3082	**Italo-Byzantine**
FL.3083	*<Russian Byzantine styles>*
FL.3084	**Muscovite**
FL.3085	**Vladimir-Suzdalian**
FL.3086	*<Medieval styles and periods>*
FL.3087	**Medieval**

May be used in combination with other descriptors, especially in the Objects facet (e.g., **Baroque** + **churches**; **Japanese** + **enameling**; **Abstract Expressionist** + **drawings**).

FL.3088 Early Medieval
FL.3089 Migration period
FL.3090 Carolingian
FL.3091 Ottonian
FL.3092 Romanesque
FL.3093 Gothic
FL.3094 Early Gothic
FL.3095 High Gothic
FL.3096 Late Gothic
FL.3097 Late Medieval
FL.3098 Proto-Renaissance
FL.3099 International Gothic
FL.3100 *<Medieval regional styles>*
FL.3101 Crusader
FL.3102 *<Migration period styles>*
FL.3103 Avar
FL.3104 Germanic
FL.3105 Alamannic
FL.3106 Burgundian
FL.3107 Frankish
FL.3108 Merovingian
FL.3109 Gothic (Migration period)
FL.3110 Ostrogothic
FL.3111 Visigothic
FL.3112 Lombard
FL.3113 Marcomannic
FL.3114 Vandal
FL.3115 Polychrome Style
FL.3116 Slavic
FL.3117 *<Northern European Medieval styles>*
FL.3118 Anglo-Norman
FL.3119 *<British Isles Medieval styles>*
FL.3120 Anglo-Saxon
FL.3121 Hiberno-Saxon
FL.3122 Insular
FL.3123 *<British Isles Medieval architecture styles>*
FL.3124 Decorated Style
FL.3125 Early Decorated
FL.3126 Curvilinear Decorated
FL.3127 Early English
FL.3128 Perpendicular Style
FL.3129 *<British Isles Medieval pottery styles>*
FL.3130 Humber ware
FL.3131 *<Carolingian styles>*
FL.3132 Franco-Saxon
FL.3133 Reims Style
FL.3134 Channel Style
FL.3135 Franco-Flemish
FL.3136 *<French Medieval styles>*

May be used in combination with other descriptors, especially in the Objects facet (e.g., **Baroque** + **churches**; **Japanese** + **enameling**; **Abstract Expressionist** + **drawings**).

FL.3137	Norman
FL.3138	*<French Medieval architecture styles>*
FL.3139	Angevin Gothic
FL.3140	Flamboyant
FL.3141	Rayonnant
FL.3142	*<German Medieval styles>*
FL.3143	*<German Medieval architecture styles>*
FL.3144	Backsteingotik
FL.3145	Sondergotik
FL.3146	*<Scandinavian Medieval styles>*
FL.3147	Jellinge Style
FL.3148	Mammen Style
FL.3149	Ringerike Style
FL.3150	Urnes Style
FL.3151	Viking
FL.3152	*<Southern European Medieval styles>*
FL.3153	First Romanesque
FL.3154	*<Italian Medieval styles>*
FL.3155	*<Italian Medieval pottery styles>*
FL.3156	Forum ware
FL.3157	*<Portuguese Medieval styles>*
FL.3158	Manueline
FL.3159	*<Spanish Medieval styles>*
FL.3160	Hispano-Flemish
FL.3161	Hispano-Moresque
FL.3162	Isabelline
FL.3163	Mozarabic
FL.3164	Mudéjar
FL.3165	*<Renaissance-Baroque styles and periods>*
FL.3166	Renaissance
FL.3167	Early Renaissance
FL.3168	High Renaissance
FL.3169	Late Renaissance
FL.3170	Reformation
FL.3171	Counter-Reformation
FL.3172	Baroque
FL.3173	Early Baroque
FL.3174	High Baroque
FL.3175	Late Baroque
FL.3176	Rococo
FL.3177	*<Renaissance-Baroque styles>*
FL.3178	Mannerist
FL.3179	Proto-Baroque
FL.3180	Romanist
FL.3181	*<Renaissance-Baroque architecture styles>*
FL.3182	Palladian
FL.3183	*<Renaissance-Baroque decorative arts styles>*
FL.3184	Auricular
FL.3185	Chinoiserie

May be used in combination with other descriptors, especially in the Objects facet (e.g., **Baroque** + **churches**; **Japanese** + **enameling**; **Abstract Expressionist** + **drawings**).

FL.3186 **Rocaille**
FL.3187 *<Renaissance-Baroque pottery styles>*
FL.3188 **Tiger ware**
FL.3189 *<Renaissance-Baroque regional styles>*
FL.3190 *<British Renaissance-Baroque styles>*
FL.3191 *<British Renaissance-Baroque styles by reign>*
FL.3192 **Tudor**
FL.3193 **Elizabethan**
FL.3194 **Stuart**
FL.3195 **Jacobean**
FL.3196 **Restoration (period)**
FL.3197 **William and Mary**
FL.3198 **Queen Anne**
FL.3199 **Georgian**
FL.3200 *<British Renaissance-Baroque architecture styles>*
FL.3201 **Artisan Mannerist**
FL.3202 **Black and White Style (architecture)**
FL.3203 *<Eastern European Renaissance-Baroque styles>*
FL.3204 *<Eastern European Renaissance-Baroque pottery styles>*
FL.3205 **Brancovan**
FL.3206 **Habaner ware**
FL.3207 *<French Renaissance-Baroque styles>*
FL.3208 **French Colonial**
FL.3209 *<French Renaissance-Baroque decorative arts styles>*
FL.3210 **Aubusson**
FL.3211 **Gobelins**
FL.3212 *<French Renaissance-Baroque decorative arts styles by reign>*
FL.3213 **François I**
FL.3214 **Henri II**
FL.3215 **Louis XIII**
FL.3216 **Régence**
FL.3217 **Louis XIV**
FL.3218 **Louis XV**
FL.3219 *<French Renaissance-Baroque pottery styles>*
FL.3220 **Haguenau pottery**
FL.3221 **Limoges porcelain**
FL.3222 **Palissy ware**
FL.3223 **Strasbourg faïence**
FL.3224 *<German Renaissance-Baroque styles>*
FL.3225 *<German Renaissance-Baroque pottery styles>*
FL.3226 **Böttger ware**
FL.3227 **Hanau pottery**
FL.3228 **Regensburg porcelain**
FL.3229 **Westerwald stoneware**
FL.3230 *<Italian Renaissance-Baroque styles>*
FL.3231 **Barocchetto**
FL.3232 *<Italian Renaissance-Baroque pottery styles>*
FL.3233 **Castelli maiolica**
FL.3234 **Vezzi porcelain**

FL

May be used in combination with other descriptors, especially in the Objects facet (e.g., **Baroque** + **churches**; **Japanese** + **enameling**; **Abstract Expressionist** + **drawings**).

FL.3235	*<Netherlandish Renaissance-Baroque styles>*
FL.3236	**Dutch Colonial**
FL.3237	*<Netherlandish Renaissance-Baroque pottery styles>*
FL.3238	**Delft**
FL.3239	**Tournai porcelain**
FL.3240	*<Portuguese Renaissance-Baroque styles>*
FL.3241	**Portuguese Colonial**
FL.3242	*<Spanish Renaissance-Baroque styles>*
FL.3243	**Churrigueresque**
FL.3244	**Plateresque**
FL.3245	**First Plateresque**
FL.3246	**Second Plateresque**
FL.3247	**Spanish Colonial**
FL.3248	*<Spanish Renaissance-Baroque architecture styles>*
FL.3249	**Herreran**
FL.3250	*<modern European styles and movements>*
FL.3251	**Art Deco**
FL.3252	**Art Nouveau**
FL.3253	**Biedermeier**
FL.3254	**Expressionist**
FL.3255	**fin de siècle**
FL.3256	**Decadent Movement**
FL.3257	**Modernist**
FL.3258	**Neo-Romantic**
FL.3259	**Neoclassical**
FL.3260	**Romantic**
FL.3261	**Secession Movement**
FL.3262	*<modern European revival styles>*
FL.3263	**Baroque Revival**
FL.3264	**Byzantine Revival**
FL.3265	**Classical Revival**
FL.3266	**Greek Revival**
FL.3267	**Egyptian Revival**
FL.3268	**Etruscan Style**
FL.3269	**Gothic Revival**
FL.3270	**Islamic Revival**
FL.3271	**Mudejar Revival**
FL.3272	**Pompeian Style**
FL.3273	**Renaissance Revival**
FL.3274	**Rococo Revival**
FL.3275	**Romanesque Revival**
FL.3276	**Norman Revival**
FL.3277	*<modern European architecture styles and movements>*
FL.3278	**Beaux-Arts**
FL.3279	**International Style**
FL.3280	**Modern Movement**
FL.3281	**Neues Bauen**
FL.3282	*<modern European decorative arts styles and movements>*
FL.3283	**Abbotsford**

May be used in combination with other descriptors, especially in the Objects facet (e.g., **Baroque** + **churches**; **Japanese** + **enameling**; **Abstract Expressionist** + **drawings**).

FL.3284 **Japonaiserie**
FL.3285 **Rustic**
FL.3286 *<modern European pottery styles>*
FL.3287 **armorial porcelain**
FL.3288 *<modern European fine arts styles and movements>*
FL.3289 **Abstract**
FL.3290 **Nonobjective**
FL.3291 **Concrete art**
FL.3292 **Cubist**
FL.3293 **Analytical Cubist**
FL.3294 **Synthetic Cubist**
FL.3295 **Dada**
FL.3296 **Impressionist**
FL.3297 **Magic Realist**
FL.3298 **Neo-Florentine**
FL.3299 **Pictorialist**
FL.3300 **Post-Impressionist**
FL.3301 **Realist**
FL.3302 **Rosicrucian**
FL.3303 **Straight**
FL.3304 **Surrealist**
FL.3305 **Symbolist**
FL.3306 **Unanimist**
FL.3307 *<modern European regional styles and movements>*
FL.3308 *<modern Austrian styles and movements>*
FL.3309 **Sezessionstil**
FL.3310 *<modern British styles and movements>*
FL.3311 **Adam Style**
FL.3312 **Aesthetic Movement**
FL.3313 **Arts and Crafts**
FL.3314 **Queen Anne Style**
FL.3315 *<modern British styles by reign>*
FL.3316 **Regency**
FL.3317 **Victorian**
FL.3318 **Early Victorian**
FL.3319 **High Victorian**
FL.3320 **Late Victorian**
FL.3321 **Edwardian**
FL.3322 *<modern British revival styles>*
FL.3323 **Elizabethan Revival**
FL.3324 **Georgian Revival**
FL.3325 **Jacobean Revival**
FL.3326 **Jacobethan**
FL.3327 **Regency Revival**
FL.3328 **Stuart Revival**
FL.3329 **Tudor Revival**
FL.3330 **Victorian Revival**
FL.3331 *<modern British architecture styles and movements>*
FL.3332 **Free Style (architecture)**

FL

May be used in combination with other descriptors, especially in the Objects facet (e.g., **Baroque** + **churches**; **Japanese** + **enameling**; **Abstract Expressionist** + **drawings**).

FL.3333 **Old English**
FL.3334 **Scottish Baronial**
FL.3335 *<modern British decorative arts styles and movements>*
FL.3336 **Chippendale**
FL.3337 **Chinese Chippendale**
FL.3338 **Hepplewhite**
FL.3339 **Sheraton**
FL.3340 *<modern British pottery styles>*
FL.3341 **Minton**
FL.3342 **Parian ware**
FL.3343 *<modern British fine arts styles and movements>*
FL.3344 **New Sculpture Movement**
FL.3345 **Pre-Raphaelite**
FL.3346 **Vorticist**
FL.3347 *<modern Danish styles and movements>*
FL.3348 **Hellenerne**
FL.3349 *<modern Dutch styles and movements>*
FL.3350 **De Stijl**
FL.3351 **Elementarist**
FL.3352 **Neo-Plastic**
FL.3353 **Nieuwe Zakelijkheid**
FL.3354 *<modern French styles and movements>*
FL.3355 **Troubadour**
FL.3356 *<modern French styles by reign>*
FL.3357 **Directoire**
FL.3358 **Consulat**
FL.3359 **Empire**
FL.3360 **Louis XVI**
FL.3361 **Restauration**
FL.3362 **Louis Philippe**
FL.3363 **Second Empire**
FL.3364 *<modern French architecture styles and movements>*
FL.3365 **Neo-Grec**
FL.3366 *<modern French decorative arts styles and movements>*
FL.3367 **goût grec**
FL.3368 *<modern French pottery styles>*
FL.3369 **Saint Clément pottery**
FL.3370 **Sarreguemines pottery**
FL.3371 *<modern French fine arts styles and movements>*
FL.3372 **Animalier**
FL.3373 **Cloisonnist**
FL.3374 **Fauve**
FL.3375 **Intimist**
FL.3376 **Neo-Impressionist**
FL.3377 **Orphist**
FL.3378 **Purist**
FL.3379 **Synthetist**
FL.3380 *<modern German styles and movements>*
FL.3381 **Bauhaus**

May be used in combination with other descriptors, especially in the Objects facet (e.g., **Baroque** + **churches**; **Japanese** + **enameling**; **Abstract Expressionist** + **drawings**).

FL.3382 **Jugendstil**
FL.3383 **Zopfstil**
FL.3384 *<modern German architecture styles and movements>*
FL.3385 **Rundbogenstil**
FL.3386 *<modern German pottery styles>*
FL.3387 **Bunzlau pottery**
FL.3388 **Kelsterbach porcelain**
FL.3389 **Thuringian ware**
FL.3390 *<modern German fine arts styles and movements>*
FL.3391 **Entartete Kunst**
FL.3392 **Gedankenmalerei**
FL.3393 **Merz**
FL.3394 **Neue Sachlichkeit**
FL.3395 *<modern Italian styles and movements>*
FL.3396 **Futurist**
FL.3397 **Stile Liberty**
FL.3398 *<modern Italian architecture styles and movements>*
FL.3399 **Stile Boito**
FL.3400 **Stile Umberto**
FL.3401 *<modern Italian decorative arts styles and movements>*
FL.3402 **Dantesque**
FL.3403 *<modern Italian fine arts styles and movements>*
FL.3404 **Aeropittura**
FL.3405 **Metaphysical**
FL.3406 **Scapigliatura**
FL.3407 **Tactilist**
FL.3408 **Verismo**
FL.3409 *<modern Polish fine arts styles and movements>*
FL.3410 **Zonist**
FL.3411 *<modern Russian styles and movements>*
FL.3412 **Constructivist**
FL.3413 *<modern Russian fine arts styles and movements>*
FL.3414 **Cubo-Futurist**
FL.3415 **Mir Iskusstva**
FL.3416 **Primitivist**
FL.3417 **Rayonist**
FL.3418 **Socialist Realist**
FL.3419 **Suprcmatist**
FL.3420 **Unist**
FL.3421 *<modern Spanish fine arts styles and movements>*
FL.3422 **Ultraist**
FL.3423 **Vibrationist**
FL.3424 *<The Islamic World>*
FL.3425 *<Islamic World dynastic styles and periods>*
FL.3426 **Abbasid (Dynasty)**
FL.3427 *<Abbasid pottery styles>*
FL.3428 **Amol ware**
FL.3429 **Samarra ware**
FL.3430 **Aghlabid**

May be used in combination with other descriptors, especially in the Objects facet (e.g., **Baroque** + **churches**; **Japanese** + **enameling**; **Abstract Expressionist** + **drawings**).

FL.3431	**Almohad**
FL.3432	**Almoravid**
FL.3433	**Atabeg**
FL.3434	**Zengid**
FL.3435	**Ayyubid**
FL.3436	*<Ayyubid painting styles>*
FL.3437	**Mesopotamian School**
FL.3438	**Baghdad School**
FL.3439	*<Ayyubid pottery styles>*
FL.3440	**Raqqa ware**
FL.3441	**Buyid**
FL.3442	**Fatimid**
FL.3443	*<Fatimid pottery styles>*
FL.3444	**Fostat ware**
FL.3445	**Ghaznavid**
FL.3446	**Ghurid**
FL.3447	**Hafsid**
FL.3448	**Hamdanid**
FL.3449	**Idrisid**
FL.3450	**Ikhshidid**
FL.3451	**Il-Khanid**
FL.3452	*<Il-Khanid painting styles>*
FL.3453	**Mongol School**
FL.3454	**Inju School**
FL.3455	**Tabriz School (Il-Khanid)**
FL.3456	*<Il-Khanid pottery styles>*
FL.3457	**Kashan ware**
FL.3458	**Rayy ware**
FL.3459	**Sultanabad ware**
FL.3460	**Veramin ware**
FL.3461	**Jalairid**
FL.3462	**Karamanid**
FL.3463	**Karaman b. Nura Sufi**
FL.3464	**Muhammad I**
FL.3465	**Badr-al-Din Mahmud**
FL.3466	**`Ala'-ad-Din Khalil**
FL.3467	**`Ala'-ad-Din b. Khalil**
FL.3468	**Muhammad II**
FL.3469	**`Ala'-ad-Din `Ali**
FL.3470	**Ishaq**
FL.3471	**Pir Ahmad**
FL.3472	**Qasim**
FL.3473	**Khalji**
FL.3474	**Lodi**
FL.3475	**Mamluk**
FL.3476	**Mongol**
FL.3477	**Muzaffarid**
FL.3478	**Nasrid**
FL.3479	**Orthodox Caliphate**

May be used in combination with other descriptors, especially in the Objects facet (e.g., **Baroque** + **churches**; **Japanese** + **enameling**; **Abstract Expressionist** + **drawings**).

FL.3480 **Ottoman**
FL.3481 *<Ottoman styles and periods by reign>*
FL.3482 **Osman I**
FL.3483 **Orhan**
FL.3484 **Murad I**
FL.3485 **Bayazid I**
FL.3486 **Mehmed I**
FL.3487 **Süleyman I**
FL.3488 **Murad II**
FL.3489 **Mehmed II**
FL.3490 **Bayazid II**
FL.3491 **Selim I**
FL.3492 **Süleyman II**
FL.3493 **Selim II**
FL.3494 **Murad III**
FL.3495 **Mehmed III**
FL.3496 **Ahmed I**
FL.3497 **Mustafa I**
FL.3498 **Osman II**
FL.3499 **Murad IV**
FL.3500 **Ibrahim**
FL.3501 **Mehmed IV**
FL.3502 **Ahmed II**
FL.3503 **Mustafa II**
FL.3504 **Ahmed III**
FL.3505 **Mahmud I**
FL.3506 **Osman III**
FL.3507 **Mustafa III**
FL.3508 **Abdülhamid I**
FL.3509 **Selim III**
FL.3510 **Mustafa IV**
FL.3511 **Mahmud II**
FL.3512 **Abdülmecid I**
FL.3513 **Abdülâziz**
FL.3514 **Murad V**
FL.3515 **Abdülhamid II**
FL.3516 **Mehmed V**
FL.3517 **Mehmed VI**
FL.3518 *<Ottoman pottery styles>*
FL.3519 **Chanak Kalé**
FL.3520 **Iznik ware**
FL.3521 **Damascus ware**
FL.3522 **Kütahya ware**
FL.3523 **Rhodian ware**
FL.3524 *<Ottoman rug styles>*
FL.3525 **Holbein**
FL.3526 **Lotto**
FL.3527 **Pahlevi**
FL.3528 **Qajar**

May be used in combination with other descriptors, especially in the Objects facet (e.g., **Baroque** + **churches**; **Japanese** + **enameling**; **Abstract Expressionist** + **drawings**).

FL.3529	**Qarakhanid**
FL.3530	**Rasulid**
FL.3531	**Safavid**
FL.3532	*<Safavid painting styles>*
FL.3533	**Isfahan School**
FL.3534	**Kazvin School**
FL.3535	**Meshhed**
FL.3536	**Tabriz School (Safavid)**
FL.3537	**Bihzad School**
FL.3538	*<Safavid pottery styles>*
FL.3539	**Gombroon ware**
FL.3540	**Kirman ware**
FL.3541	**Kubachi ware**
FL.3542	**Meshhed ware**
FL.3543	**Yezd ware**
FL.3544	**Saffarid**
FL.3545	**Samanid**
FL.3546	*<Samanid pottery styles>*
FL.3547	**Nishapur ware**
FL.3548	**Sari ware**
FL.3549	**Seljuk**
FL.3550	**Great Seljuk**
FL.3551	**Seljuk of Kirman**
FL.3552	**Seljuk of Rum**
FL.3553	**Sulayman b. Qutalmish**
FL.3554	**Qïlïch Arslan I**
FL.3555	**Malikshah**
FL.3556	**Ghiyath-al-Din Kaykhusraw I, first reign**
FL.3557	**Rukn-ad-Din Sulayman II**
FL.3558	**`Izz-ad-Din Qïlïch Arslan III**
FL.3559	**Ghiyath-al-Din Kaykhusraw I, second reign**
FL.3560	**Ghiyath-al-Din Kaykhusraw II**
FL.3561	**Seljuk of Syria**
FL.3562	*<Seljuk pottery styles>*
FL.3563	**Agkhand ware**
FL.3564	**Garrus ware**
FL.3565	**Gurgan ware**
FL.3566	**Lakabi ware**
FL.3567	**Minai ware**
FL.3568	**Rusapha ware**
FL.3569	**Sava**
FL.3570	**Sulayhid**
FL.3571	**Timurid**
FL.3572	*<Timurid painting styles>*
FL.3573	**Herat School**
FL.3574	**Baysunghur Style**
FL.3575	**Samarkand School**
FL.3576	**Tulunid**
FL.3577	**Turkman**

FL.3578 Akkoyunlu
FL.3579 Qara Yawlaq Arslan
FL.3580 Hamza
FL.3581 Baysonqur
FL.3582 Rüstem
FL.3583 Murad
FL.3584 Muhammad Mirza
FL.3585 Ya`qub
FL.3586 Karakoyunlu
FL.3587 *<Turkman rug styles>*
FL.3588 Afghan
FL.3589 Chodor
FL.3590 Ersari
FL.3591 Salor
FL.3592 Saryk
FL.3593 Tekke
FL.3594 Yomud
FL.3595 Umayyad
FL.3596 *<Umayyad pottery styles>*
FL.3597 Gabri ware
FL.3598 Uzbek
FL.3599 *<Uzbek painting styles>*
FL.3600 Bukhara School
FL.3601 Ya` Furid
FL.3602 Zand
FL.3603 Zirid
FL.3604 Moorish
FL.3605 Saracenic
FL.3606 Tartar
FL.3607 Kipchak Khanate
FL.3608 Pacific
FL.3609 Australian
FL.3610 Australian Aboriginal
FL.3611 Arunta
FL.3612 Murngin
FL.3613 Washkuk
FL.3614 *<Australian regional styles>*
FL.3615 Arnhem Land
FL.3616 Kimberly
FL.3617 Tasmanian
FL.3618 Melanesian
FL.3619 Fijian
FL.3620 Manus
FL.3621 New Britain
FL.3622 Baining
FL.3623 Sulka
FL.3624 Tolai
FL.3625 New Caledonian
FL.3626 New Guinea

May be used in combination with other descriptors, especially in the Objects facet (e.g., **Baroque** + **churches**; **Japanese** + **enameling**; **Abstract Expressionist** + **drawings**).

FL.3627 Irian Jaya
FL.3628 *<Irian Jaya native styles>*
FL.3629 Asmat
FL.3630 Dani
FL.3631 *<Irian Jaya regional styles>*
FL.3632 Geelvinck Bay
FL.3633 Humboldt Bay
FL.3634 Lake Sentani
FL.3635 Papua New Guinea
FL.3636 Astrolabe Bay
FL.3637 Huon Gulf
FL.3638 Massim Area
FL.3639 D'Entrecasteaux
FL.3640 Louisiade
FL.3641 Trobriand Island
FL.3642 Papuan Gulf
FL.3643 Elema
FL.3644 Kiwai
FL.3645 Sepik
FL.3646 *<Sepik native styles>*
FL.3647 Abelam
FL.3648 Chambri
FL.3649 Iatmul
FL.3650 Kapriman
FL.3651 Mundugumor
FL.3652 Sawos
FL.3653 *<Sepik regional styles>*
FL.3654 Lower Sepik
FL.3655 Maprik
FL.3656 Middle Sepik
FL.3657 Upper Sepik
FL.3658 Torres Strait
FL.3659 New Ireland
FL.3660 *<New Ireland sculpture styles>*
FL.3661 Málanggan
FL.3662 Solomon Island
FL.3663 Bougainville
FL.3664 Buka
FL.3665 Choiseul
FL.3666 Malaita
FL.3667 New Georgia Island
FL.3668 San Cristoval Island
FL.3669 Santa Cruz Island
FL.3670 Tikopia
FL.3671 Vanuatu
FL.3672 Ambrym
FL.3673 Banks Island
FL.3674 Malekula
FL.3675 Oba

May be used in combination with other descriptors, especially in the Objects facet (e.g., **Baroque** + **churches**; **Japanese** + **enameling**; **Abstract Expressionist** + **drawings**).

- FL.3676 Micronesian
    - FL.3677 Aua
    - FL.3678 Caroline Island
        - FL.3679 Palau
        - FL.3680 Truk
        - FL.3681 Yap
    - FL.3682 Kiribati
    - FL.3683 Marianas Island
    - FL.3684 Marshall Island
    - FL.3685 Tuvalu
    - FL.3686 Wuvulu Island
- FL.3687 Polynesian
    - FL.3688 Austral Island
    - FL.3689 Cook Island
        - FL.3690 Mangaian
    - FL.3691 Easter Island
    - FL.3692 Gambier Island
        - FL.3693 Mangarevan
    - FL.3694 Hawaiian
    - FL.3695 Marquesan
    - FL.3696 New Zealand
        - FL.3697 Maori
            - FL.3698 Classic Maori
    - FL.3699 Samoan
    - FL.3700 Society Island
        - FL.3701 Tahitian
    - FL.3702 Tongan

FL.3703 *<international post-1945 styles and movements>*

- FL.3704 Postmodern
- FL.3705 *<post-1945 architecture and design styles and movements>*
    - FL.3706 Bolidist
    - FL.3707 Brutalist
    - FL.3708 Deconstructivist
    - FL.3709 High-Tech
    - FL.3710 Neo-Rationalist
    - FL.3711 Nuovo Design
- FL.3712 *<post-1945 fine arts styles and movements>*
    - FL.3713 Abstract Expressionist
        - FL.3714 Abstract Imagist
        - FL.3715 Action painting
    - FL.3716 Abstract Impressionist
    - FL.3717 Art Informel
        - FL.3718 Tachiste
    - FL.3719 Arte Povera
    - FL.3720 Chicago Imagist
    - FL.3721 Color-field
    - FL.3722 Conceptual
    - FL.3723 Constructionist
    - FL.3724 Direct art

May be used in combination with other descriptors, especially in the Objects facet (e.g., **Baroque** + **churches**; **Japanese** + **enameling**; **Abstract Expressionist** + **drawings**).

FL

FL.3725 **Fantastic Realist**
FL.3726 **Fluxus**
FL.3727 **Funk**
FL.3728 **Hard-edge**
FL.3729 **Kinetic**
FL.3730 **Lettrism**
FL.3731 **Lyrical Abstraction**
FL.3732 **Matter art**
FL.3733 **Minimal**
FL.3734 **Neo-Constructivist**
FL.3735 **Neo-Dada**
FL.3736 **Neo-Expressionist**
FL.3737 **Neo-Geo**
FL.3738 **Neue Rheinische Sezession**
FL.3739 **New Figuration**
FL.3740 **New Realist**
FL.3741 **Op art**
FL.3742 **Pattern painting**
FL.3743 **Photorealist**
FL.3744 **Pittura Colta**
FL.3745 **Pop**
FL.3746 **Post-Conceptual**
FL.3747 **Post-Minimal**
FL.3748 **Process art**
FL.3749 **Auto-destructive**
FL.3750 **Psychedelic**
FL.3751 **Spatialist**
FL.3752 **Supermannerist**
FL.3753 **Systemic**
FL.3754 **Systems art**
FL.3755 **Trans-avantgarde**
FL.3756 **Wiener Aktionismus**

May be used in combination with other descriptors, especially in the Objects facet (e.g., **Baroque** + **churches**; **Japanese** + **enameling**; **Abstract Expressionist** + **drawings**).

Agents facet

The purpose of the agents facet is to allow the designation of persons, groups of persons, and organizations identified by some role or occupation.

The Agents facet consists of the following hierarchies:

People and Organizations (HG)

People and Organizations Hierarchy

PEOPLE AND ORGANIZATIONS

Scope The People and Organizations hierarchy contains descriptors for occupational titles and role names, and for groups, industries, collections, and institutions.

Organization The hierarchy is divided into two sections: **people** and **organizations. People** is comprised of seven parts: <*people by age group*> (e.g., **adults**), <*people by family relationship*> (e.g., **offspring**), <*people by gender*> (e.g., **women**), <*people by occupation*> (e.g., **auditors**), <*people by activity*>, (e.g., **collectors**), <*people by degree of qualification*>, (e.g., **amateurs**), and <*people by state or condition*> (e.g., **handicapped**). Descriptors in the second section, **organizations**, are arranged, wherever possible, in generic groups such as **collections**, **institutions**, and **societies**.

Relation to Other Hierarchies Descriptors for branches of learning, areas of specialization, and professions are found in the Disciplines hierarchy (e.g., **mathematics**, **zoning law**, **museum administration**).

Descriptor Form and Use Descriptors appear as plural nouns, with the singular added as an alternate form. Descriptors may be combined with those from other hierarchies (e.g., **popes** + **palaces**; **presidents** + **personal papers**; **teacher** + **education**; **slide** + **collections**).

Number of Descriptors 852

HG

Synopsis

HG.1	**people**
HG.2	*<people by age group>*
HG.8	*<people by family relationship>*
HG.18	*<people by gender>*
HG.21	*<people by occupation>*
HG.36	*<people in service occupations>*
HG.56	*<people in the humanities>*
HG.249	*<people in the social sciences and related occupations>*
HG.323	*<people in science and related occupations>*
HG.391	*<people in commerce and business>*
HG.437	*<people in crafts and trades>*
HG.580	*<people in engineering, building trades and planning>*
HG.649	*<people in government and administration>*
HG.705	*<people by activity>*
HG.761	*<people by degree of qualification>*
HG.775	*<people by state or condition>*
HG.799	**organizations**
HG.800	**academies**
	|
HG.906	**workshops**

PEOPLE AND ORGANIZATIONS (HG)

- HG.1 **people**
  - HG.2 *<people by age group>*
    - HG.3 **adults**
    - HG.4 **aged**
    - HG.5 **youth**
      - HG.6 **children**
      - HG.7 **teenagers**
  - HG.8 *<people by family relationship>*
    - HG.9 **offspring**
      - HG.10 **daughters**
      - HG.11 **sons**
    - HG.12 **parents**
      - HG.13 **fathers**
      - HG.14 **mothers**
    - HG.15 **spouses**
      - HG.16 **husbands**
      - HG.17 **wives**
  - HG.18 *<people by gender>*
    - HG.19 **men**
    - HG.20 **women**
  - HG.21 *<people by occupation>*
    - HG.22 **personnel**
    - HG.23 **workers**
      - HG.24 **blue collar workers**
        - HG.25 **laborers**
      - HG.26 **migrant workers**
      - HG.27 **semiskilled workers**
      - HG.28 **skilled workers**
        - HG.29 **technicians**
      - HG.30 **unskilled labor**
      - HG.31 **volunteers**
      - HG.32 **white collar workers**
        - HG.33 **clerical workers**
          - HG.34 **secretaries (clerical workers)**
          - HG.35 **stenographers**
    - HG.36 *<people in service occupations>*
      - HG.37 **bellmen**
      - HG.38 **cleaners (people)**
      - HG.39 **custodians**
        - HG.40 **caretakers**
      - HG.41 **domestics**
      - HG.42 **fire fighters**
      - HG.43 **househusbands**
      - HG.44 **housewives**
      - HG.45 **maintenance men**
        - HG.46 **janitors**
      - HG.47 **messengers**
      - HG.48 **packers**
      - HG.49 **policemen**

May be used in combination with other descriptors, especially in the Objects facet (e.g., **popes** + **palaces**; **slide** + **collections**).

HG.50 **porters**
HG.51 **repairmen**
HG.52 **security guards**
HG.53 **servants**
HG.54 **shippers**
HG.55 **watchmen**
HG.56 *<people in the humanities>*
HG.57 *<people in the arts and related occupations>*
HG.58 *<people in the arts>*
HG.59 *<people in the performing arts>*
HG.60 **cameramen**
HG.61 **choreographers**
HG.62 **costumers (people)**
HG.63 **directors (performing arts)**
HG.64 **filmmakers**
HG.65 **performing artists**
HG.66 **actors**
HG.67 **clowns**
HG.68 **comedians**
HG.69 **dancers**
HG.70 **jesters**
HG.71 **musicians**
HG.72 **arrangers**
HG.73 **bandsmen**
HG.74 **bandmasters**
HG.75 **composers**
HG.76 **conductors (music)**
HG.77 **instrumentalists**
HG.78 **lyricists**
HG.79 **singers**
HG.80 **television personalities**
HG.81 *<people in the visual arts>*
HG.82 **animators**
HG.83 **architects**
HG.84 **associated architects**
HG.85 **government architects**
HG.86 **landscape architects**
HG.87 **naval architects**
HG.88 **project architects**
HG.89 **supervising architects**
HG.90 **art directors**
HG.91 **artists**
HG.92 **artists-in-residence**
HG.93 **caricaturists**
HG.94 **cartoonists**
HG.95 **collagists**
HG.96 **conceptual artists**
HG.97 **dissident artists**
HG.98 **draftsmen**

HG

May be used in combination with other descriptors, especially in the Objects facet (e.g., **popes** + **palaces**; **slide** + **collections**).

HG.99	renderers
HG.100	environmental artists
HG.101	fiber artists
HG.102	folk artists
HG.103	illuminators
HG.104	miniaturists
HG.105	painters
HG.106	*<painters by subject of work>*
HG.107	animal painters
HG.108	limners
HG.109	marine painters
HG.110	*<painters by technique, implement, or material employed>*
HG.111	grainers
HG.112	muralists
HG.113	stencilers
HG.114	watercolorists
HG.115	pastelists
HG.116	performance artists
HG.117	photographers
HG.118	architectural photographers
HG.119	cinematographers
HG.120	photojournalists
HG.121	scientific photographers
HG.122	medical photographers
HG.123	still photographers
HG.124	war photographers
HG.125	printmakers
HG.126	engravers
HG.127	photoengravers
HG.128	stipple engravers
HG.129	etchers
HG.130	lithographers
HG.131	photolithographers
HG.132	mezzotinters
HG.133	serigraphers
HG.134	wood engravers
HG.135	woodcutters
HG.136	sculptors
HG.137	animal sculptors
HG.138	tattoo artists
HG.139	designers
HG.140	commercial artists
HG.141	benday artists
HG.142	graphic designers
HG.143	calligraphers
HG.144	illustrators
HG.145	book illustrators
HG.146	fashion illustrators
HG.147	scientific illustrators

May be used in combination with other descriptors, especially in the Objects facet (e.g., **popes** + **palaces**; **slide** + **collections**).

HG.148 medical illustrators
HG.149 letterers
HG.150 costume designers
HG.151 display designers
HG.152 window dressers
HG.153 exhibition designers
HG.154 fashion designers
HG.155 floral designers
HG.156 industrial designers
HG.157 product engineers
HG.158 interior decorators
HG.159 interior designers
HG.160 drapers
HG.161 theater designers
HG.162 *<people in arts-related occupations>*
HG.163 architectural critics
HG.164 architectural historians
HG.165 art critics
HG.166 art historians
HG.167 musicologists
HG.168 ethnomusicologists
HG.169 *<people in linguistics and related occupations>*
HG.170 *<people in linguistics>*
HG.171 grammarians
HG.172 linguists
HG.173 semanticists
HG.174 *<people in linguistics-related occupations>*
HG.175 cryptographers
HG.176 philologists
HG.177 *<people in literature and related occupations>*
HG.178 *<people in literature>*
HG.179 authors
HG.180 biographers
HG.181 hagiographers
HG.182 chroniclers
HG.183 diarists
HG.184 essayists
HG.185 fabulists
HG.186 humorists
HG.187 librettists
HG.188 playwrights
HG.189 poets
HG.190 satirists
HG.191 screen writers
HG.192 *<people in literature-related occupations>*
HG.193 bibliographers
HG.194 compilers
HG.195 encyclopedists
HG.196 lexicographers

May be used in combination with other descriptors, especially in the Objects facet (e.g., **popes** + **palaces**; **slide** + **collections**).

HG.197 critics
HG.198 literary critics
HG.199 editors
HG.200 literary historians
HG.201 *<people in museology>*
HG.202 curators
HG.203 docents
HG.204 preparators
HG.205 registrars
HG.206 philosophers
HG.207 aestheticians
HG.208 logicians
HG.209 metaphysicians
HG.210 phenomenologists
HG.211 *<people in religion and related occupations>*
HG.212 *<people in religion>*
HG.213 ayatollahs
HG.214 cantors
HG.215 clergy
HG.216 abbots
HG.217 archbishop-electors
HG.218 archbishops
HG.219 bishops
HG.220 canons
HG.221 cardinals
HG.222 chaplains
HG.223 deacons
HG.224 elders
HG.225 evangelists
HG.226 metropolitans
HG.227 missionaries
HG.228 mullahs
HG.229 pastors
HG.230 patriarchs
HG.231 popes
HG.232 priests
HG.233 confessors
HG.234 rabbis
HG.235 rectors
HG.236 dervishes
HG.237 imams
HG.238 laity
HG.239 mystics
HG.240 religious
HG.241 monks
HG.242 nuns
HG.243 theologians
HG.244 *<people in religion-related occupations>*
HG.245 church historians

May be used in combination with other descriptors, especially in the Objects facet (e.g., **popes** + **palaces**; **slide** + **collections**).

HG.246 historians of religion
HG.247 mohel
HG.248 rhetoricians
HG.249 *<people in the social sciences and related occupations>*
HG.250 *<people in the social sciences>*
HG.251 anthropologists
HG.252 ethnologists
HG.253 physical anthropologists
HG.254 social anthropologists
HG.255 archaeologists
HG.256 anthropological archaeologists
HG.257 industrial archaeologists
HG.258 demographers
HG.259 economists
HG.260 geographers
HG.261 cartographers
HG.262 paleogeographers
HG.263 gerontologists
HG.264 *<people in history and related occupations>*
HG.265 historians
HG.266 historiographers
HG.267 urban historians
HG.268 *<people in history-related occupations>*
HG.269 archivists
HG.270 epigraphers
HG.271 genealogists
HG.272 numismatists
HG.273 paleographers
HG.274 philatelists
HG.275 political scientists
HG.276 psychologists
HG.277 therapists
HG.278 sociologists
HG.279 *<people in social science-related occupations>*
HG.280 *<people in communications>*
HG.281 announcers
HG.282 broadcasters
HG.283 newscasters
HG.284 radio broadcasters
HG.285 journalists
HG.286 columnists
HG.287 editorial writers
HG.288 reporters
HG.289 correspondents
HG.290 foreign correspondents
HG.291 law reporters
HG.292 publishers
HG.293 translators
HG.294 interpreters

May be used in combination with other descriptors, especially in the Objects facet (e.g., **popes** + **palaces**; **slide** + **collections**).

people
<people by occupation>
<people in the social sciences and related occupations>
<people in social science-related occupations>

HG.295	**counselors**
HG.296	**educators**
HG.297	**deans**
HG.298	**principals**
HG.299	**teachers**
HG.300	**professors**
HG.301	**tutors**
HG.302	**graphologists**
HG.303	**information scientists**
HG.304	**indexers**
HG.305	**librarians**
HG.306	**audiovisual librarians**
HG.307	**catalogers**
HG.308	**circulation librarians**
HG.309	**reference librarians**
HG.310	**special librarians**
HG.311	**government librarians**
HG.312	*<people in law>*
HG.313	**arbitrators**
HG.314	**industrial arbitrators**
HG.315	**judges**
HG.316	**justices of the peace**
HG.317	**lawyers**
HG.318	**barristers**
HG.319	**public defenders**
HG.320	**public prosecutors**
HG.321	**solicitors**
HG.322	**social workers**
HG.323	*<people in science and related occupations>*
HG.324	*<people in science>*
HG.325	**scientists**
HG.326	**astronomers**
HG.327	**biologists**
HG.328	**botanists**
HG.329	**marine biologists**
HG.330	**ichthyologists**
HG.331	**physiologists**
HG.332	**zoologists**
HG.333	**chemists**
HG.334	**assayers**
HG.335	**conservators**
HG.336	**crystallographers**
HG.337	**cyberneticians**
HG.338	**ecologists**
HG.339	**entomologists**
HG.340	**geologists**
HG.341	**geomorphologists**
HG.342	**mineralogists**
HG.343	**paleontologists**

May be used in combination with other descriptors, especially in the Objects facet (e.g., **popes** + **palaces**; **slide** + **collections**).

HG.344 stratigraphers
HG.345 hydrographers
HG.346 mathematicians
HG.347 statisticians
HG.348 medical scientists
HG.349 metallurgists
HG.350 meteorologists
HG.351 metrologists
HG.352 naturalists
HG.353 oceanographers
HG.354 physicists
HG.355 *<people in science-related occupations>*
HG.356 computer programmers
HG.357 historians of science
HG.358 systems analysts
HG.359 *<people in agriculture, landscape and natural resources>*
HG.360 agriculturists
HG.361 farmers
HG.362 herdsmen
HG.363 shepherds
HG.364 horticulturists
HG.365 nurserymen
HG.366 vintners
HG.367 livestock breeders
HG.368 horse breeders
HG.369 plantation owners
HG.370 ranchers
HG.371 fishermen
HG.372 foresters
HG.373 game wardens
HG.374 gardeners
HG.375 hunters
HG.376 lumbermen
HG.377 loggers
HG.378 miners
HG.379 trappers
HG.380 *<people in health and medicine>*
HG.381 anatomists
HG.382 chiropractors
HG.383 dentists
HG.384 dietitians
HG.385 nurses
HG.386 physical therapists
HG.387 physicians
HG.388 surgeons
HG.389 psychiatrists
HG.390 psychoanalysts
HG.391 *<people in commerce and business>*
HG.392 *<people in accounting>*

May be used in combination with other descriptors, especially in the Objects facet (e.g., **popes** + **palaces**; **slide** + **collections**).

HG.393	accountants
HG.394	actuaries
HG.395	auditors
HG.396	bookkeepers
HG.397	comptrollers
HG.398	appraisers
HG.399	auctioneers
HG.400	bankers
HG.401	bidders
HG.402	subbidders
HG.403	businessmen
HG.404	buyers
HG.405	clients
HG.406	commercial agents
HG.407	brokers
HG.408	stockbrokers
HG.409	insurance agents
HG.410	real estate agents
HG.411	travel agents
HG.412	commission merchants
HG.413	consumers
HG.414	dealers
HG.415	entrepreneurs
HG.416	exporters
HG.417	financiers
HG.418	hotelkeepers
HG.419	importers
HG.420	industrialists
HG.421	manufacturers
HG.422	investment advisors
HG.423	investors
HG.424	partners
HG.425	proprietors
HG.426	sales personnel
HG.427	booksellers
HG.428	merchants
HG.429	retailers
HG.430	shopkeepers
HG.431	wholesalers
HG.432	peddlers
HG.433	suppliers
HG.434	undertakers
HG.435	vendors
HG.436	online vendors
HG.437	*<people in crafts and trades>*
HG.438	craftsmen
HG.439	*<people in crafts and trades by activity>*
HG.440	assemblers
HG.441	bakers

May be used in combination with other descriptors, especially in the Objects facet (e.g., **popes** + **palaces**; **slide** + **collections**).

HG.442 carvers
HG.443 casters (people)
HG.444 foundrymen
HG.445 machinists
HG.446 mechanics (people)
HG.447 millwrights
HG.448 millers
HG.449 molders
HG.450 *<people in the printing industry>*
HG.451 bookbinders
HG.452 colorers
HG.453 bronzers
HG.454 compositors
HG.455 linotype operators
HG.456 makeup arrangers
HG.457 opaquers
HG.458 pressmen
HG.459 printers (people)
HG.460 impression printers
HG.461 job printers
HG.462 rectification printers
HG.463 siderographers
HG.464 stereotypers
HG.465 typesetters
HG.466 typographers
HG.467 restorers
HG.468 scribes
HG.469 copyists
HG.470 setters-out
HG.471 *<people in crafts and trades by material>*
HG.472 ceramists
HG.473 enamelers
HG.474 gilders
HG.475 ciseleurs-doreurs
HG.476 glassworkers
HG.477 glassblowers
HG.478 glassmakers
HG.479 glaziers
HG.480 hornworkers
HG.481 inlayers
HG.482 lacquerers
HG.483 japanners
HG.484 lapidaries
HG.485 leatherworkers
HG.486 curriers
HG.487 dressers (leatherworkers)
HG.488 fellmongers
HG.489 tanners
HG.490 metalworkers

May be used in combination with other descriptors, especially in the Objects facet (e.g., **popes** + **palaces**; **slide** + **collections**).

<people by occupation>
<people in crafts and trades>
<people in crafts and trades by material>
metalworkers

HG.491 *<metalworkers by type of metal>*
HG.492 braziers
HG.493 bronzeworkers
HG.494 coppersmiths
HG.495 goldsmiths
HG.496 ironsmiths
HG.497 blacksmiths
HG.498 farriers
HG.499 pewterers
HG.500 silversmiths
HG.501 tinsmiths
HG.502 *<metalworkers by process or technique>*
HG.503 electroplaters
HG.504 founders (metalworkers)
HG.505 furnacemen
HG.506 grinders (metalworkers)
HG.507 smeltermen
HG.508 welders
HG.509 *<metalworkers by product>*
HG.510 armorers
HG.511 bell-founders
HG.512 boilermakers
HG.513 coremakers
HG.514 gunsmiths
HG.515 locksmiths
HG.516 medalists
HG.517 nail makers
HG.518 sheet metal workers
HG.519 swordsmiths
HG.520 tinkers
HG.521 mosaicists
HG.522 papermakers
HG.523 dominotiers
HG.524 marbreurs
HG.525 textile workers
HG.526 dyers
HG.527 embroiderers
HG.528 furriers
HG.529 knitters
HG.530 sewers (textile workers)
HG.531 spinners
HG.532 stylists
HG.533 tailors
HG.534 weavers
HG.535 *<textile workers by product>*
HG.536 dressmakers
HG.537 hatters
HG.538 milliners
HG.539 lace makers

May be used in combination with other descriptors, especially in the Objects facet (e.g., **popes** + **palaces**; **slide** + **collections**).

HG.540 quiltmakers
HG.541 tapissiers
HG.542 veneerers
HG.543 woodworkers
HG.544 coopers
HG.545 planers (woodworkers)
HG.546 sawyers
HG.547 turners
HG.548 wood-carvers
HG.549 *<people in crafts and trades by product>*
HG.550 artists' colormen
HG.551 basket makers
HG.552 brickmakers
HG.553 broommakers
HG.554 brushmakers
HG.555 clockmakers
HG.556 dollmakers
HG.557 furniture workers
HG.558 cabinetmakers
HG.559 ébénistes
HG.560 chairmakers
HG.561 joiners
HG.562 menuisiers
HG.563 upholsterers
HG.564 glovers
HG.565 jewelers
HG.566 luthiers
HG.567 violin makers
HG.568 modelers
HG.569 patternmakers
HG.570 potters
HG.571 rope-makers
HG.572 saddlers
HG.573 sailmakers
HG.574 sealmakers
HG.575 shoemakers
HG.576 toolmakers
HG.577 watchmakers
HG.578 wheelwrights
HG.579 wigmakers
HG.580 *<people in engineering, building trades and planning>*
HG.581 construction workers
HG.582 asphalters
HG.583 blasters
HG.584 borers
HG.585 builders
HG.586 carpenters
HG.587 clerks of the works
HG.588 concreters

May be used in combination with other descriptors, especially in the Objects facet (e.g., **popes** + **palaces**; **slide** + **collections**).

  - HG.589 cranemen
    - HG.590 slingers
  - HG.591 derrickmen
  - HG.592 drillers
  - HG.593 electricians
  - HG.594 erectors
  - HG.595 hammermen
  - HG.596 industrial painters
  - HG.597 masons
    - HG.598 banker masons
    - HG.599 bricklayers
    - HG.600 fixer masons
    - HG.601 stonemasons
  - HG.602 pipe fitters
  - HG.603 pipelayers
  - HG.604 plasterers
  - HG.605 plumbers
  - HG.606 riveters
  - HG.607 roofers
  - HG.608 scaffolders
  - HG.609 shipbuilders
    - HG.610 constructors
  - HG.611 shorers
  - HG.612 steeplejacks
  - HG.613 stonecutters
    - HG.614 quarriers
  - HG.615 wreckers
- HG.616 contractors
  - HG.617 general contractors
  - HG.618 prime contractors
  - HG.619 subcontractors
- HG.620 developers
- HG.621 draftsmen (technical)
  - HG.622 architectural draftsmen
  - HG.623 delineators
- HG.624 engineers
  - HG.625 acoustical engineers
  - HG.626 aerospace engineers
    - HG.627 aeronautical engineers
  - HG.628 biomedical engineers
  - HG.629 chemical engineers
  - HG.630 civil engineers
    - HG.631 hydraulic engineers
      - HG.632 water-supply engineers
    - HG.633 sanitary engineers
    - HG.634 structural engineers
    - HG.635 traffic engineers
    - HG.636 transportation engineers
  - HG.637 electrical engineers

HG.638 industrial engineers
HG.639 marine engineers
HG.640 mechanical engineers
HG.641 military engineers
HG.642 municipal engineers
HG.643 nuclear engineers
HG.644 safety engineers
HG.645 planners
HG.646 city planners
HG.647 quantity surveyors
HG.648 surveyors
HG.649 *<people in government and administration>*
HG.650 administrators
HG.651 executives
HG.652 directors
HG.653 gallery directors
HG.654 presidents
HG.655 superintendents
HG.656 vice presidents
HG.657 managers
HG.658 supervisors
HG.659 foremen
HG.660 gangers
HG.661 bureaucrats
HG.662 cabinet officers
HG.663 commissioners
HG.664 courtiers
HG.665 government employees
HG.666 public administrators
HG.667 tax collectors
HG.668 military personnel
HG.669 notaries
HG.670 politicians
HG.671 public officers
HG.672 constables
HG.673 consuls
HG.674 diplomats
HG.675 governors
HG.676 legislators
HG.677 Members of Congress
HG.678 Members of the House of Representatives
HG.679 Members of Parliament
HG.680 Senators
HG.681 lieutenant governors
HG.682 magistrates
HG.683 mayors
HG.684 postmasters
HG.685 procurators
HG.686 sheriffs

May be used in combination with other descriptors, especially in the Objects facet (e.g., **popes** + **palaces**; **slide** + **collections**).

HG.687 viceroys
HG.688   governors general
HG.689 registrars (government and administration)
HG.690 rulers (people)
HG.691   chieftains
HG.692   czars
HG.693   doges
HG.694   duchesses (people)
HG.695   dukes
HG.696   emperors
HG.697   empresses
HG.698   kings
HG.699   pharaohs
HG.700   princes
HG.701   princesses
HG.702   queens
HG.703   regents
HG.704 statesmen
HG.705 *<people by activity>*
HG.706 advisors
HG.707 antiquaries
HG.708 checkers (people)
HG.709 coaches
HG.710 collectors
HG.711 consultants
HG.712 criminals
HG.713   counterfeiters
HG.714   forgers
HG.715   thieves
HG.716 detectives
HG.717 donors
HG.718 explorers
HG.719 founders
HG.720 inscribers
HG.721 inventors
HG.722 jurors
HG.723 landlords
HG.724 lecturers
HG.725 models (people)
HG.726 orators
HG.727 patrons
HG.728 pedestrians
HG.729 philanthropists
HG.730 pioneers
HG.731 preservationists
HG.732   historic preservationists
HG.733 researchers
HG.734 revisers
HG.735 seamen

May be used in combination with other descriptors, especially in the Objects facet (e.g., **popes** + **palaces**; **slide** + **collections**).

HG.736   shipmasters
HG.737 signers
HG.738 squatters
HG.739 tenants
HG.740 theorists
HG.741 travelers
HG.742 trustees
HG.743 users
HG.744   end users
HG.745 visitors
HG.746 yachtsmen
HG.747 *<people by ideology or political activity>*
HG.748   activists
HG.749   anarchists
HG.750   conservationists
HG.751   dissenters
HG.752   feminists
HG.753   lobbyists
HG.754   pacifists
HG.755   reformers
HG.756   abolitionists
HG.757   suffragists
HG.758   suffragettes
HG.759   visionaries
HG.760   zionists
HG.761 *<people by degree of qualification>*
HG.762 amateurs
HG.763 assistants
HG.764 experts
HG.765 interns
HG.766 journeymen
HG.767 masters
HG.768 professionals
HG.769 scholars
HG.770   classicists
HG.771 specialists
HG.772 students
HG.773 trainees
HG.774   apprentices
HG.775 *<people by state or condition>*
HG.776 blessed
HG.777 dedicatees
HG.778 ethnic groups
HG.779   African Americans
HG.780   Latinos
HG.781   Mexican Americans
HG.782 exceptional persons
HG.783   gifted
HG.784   handicapped

May be used in combination with other descriptors, especially in the Objects facet (e.g., **popes** + **palaces**; **slide** + **collections**).

HG.785 mentally handicapped
HG.786 physically handicapped
HG.787 blind
HG.788 deaf
HG.789 mutes
HG.790 expatriates
HG.791 homeless persons
HG.792 immigrants
HG.793 minorities
HG.794 prisoners
HG.795 hostages
HG.796 refugees
HG.797 saints
HG.798 terminally ill
HG.799 organizations
HG.800 academies
HG.801 *<administrative bodies>*
HG.802 cantons
HG.803 counties
HG.804 departments
HG.805 empires
HG.806 nations
HG.807 parishes (administrative bodies)
HG.808 provinces
HG.809 shires
HG.810 states
HG.811 territories
HG.812 agencies
HG.813 funding agencies
HG.814 armed forces
HG.815 air forces
HG.816 armies
HG.817 navies
HG.818 associations
HG.819 clubs
HG.820 garden clubs
HG.821 commonwealths
HG.822 consortia
HG.823 credit unions
HG.824 granges
HG.825 guilds
HG.826 professional associations
HG.827 standards organizations
HG.828 trade associations
HG.829 trade unions
HG.830 user groups
HG.831 voluntary associations
HG.832 boards (organizations)
HG.833 art commissions

May be used in combination with other descriptors, especially in the Objects facet (e.g., **popes** + **palaces**; **slide** + **collections**).

HG.834 boards of directors
HG.835 boards of trade
HG.836 boards of trustees
HG.837 health boards
HG.838 park commissions
HG.839 planning commissions
HG.840 zoning boards
HG.841 business enterprises
HG.842 companies
HG.843 corporations
HG.844 partnerships
HG.845 firms
HG.846 architectural firms
HG.847 collections
HG.848 clearinghouses
HG.849 corporate collections
HG.850 private collections
HG.851 visual resource collections
HG.852 committees
HG.853 task forces
HG.854 foundations (organizations)
HG.855 industries
HG.856 cottage industries
HG.857 institutes
HG.858 institutions
HG.859 charities
HG.860 public institutions
HG.861 social institutions
HG.862 public utilities
HG.863 electric utilities
HG.864 *<services>*
HG.865 information services
HG.866 abstracting and indexing services
HG.867 bibliographic utilities
HG.868 information retrieval services
HG.869 reference services
HG.870 online reference services
HG.871 library service agencies
HG.872 public services
HG.873 emergency services
HG.874 public works
HG.875 social services
HG.876 day care
HG.877 welfare services
HG.878 *<social groups>*
HG.879 *<kinship groups>*
HG.880 clans
HG.881 families
HG.882 tribes

May be used in combination with other descriptors, especially in the Objects facet (e.g., **popes** + **palaces**; **slide** + **collections**).

HG.883 social classes
HG.884 middle class
HG.885 bourgeoisie
HG.886 peasantry
HG.887 upper classes
HG.888 aristocracy
HG.889 nobility
HG.890 working class
HG.891 proletariat
HG.892 societies
HG.893 archaeological societies
HG.894 architectural societies
HG.895 brotherhoods
HG.896 charitable societies
HG.897 confraternities
HG.898 educational societies
HG.899 historical societies
HG.900 horticultural societies
HG.901 scientific societies
HG.902 secret societies
HG.903 technical societies
HG.904 studios
HG.905 workshops
HG.906 *<organizations by location or context>*
HG.907 community organizations
HG.908 international organizations
HG.909 national organizations

May be used in combination with other descriptors, especially in the Objects facet (e.g., **popes** + **palaces**; **slide** + **collections**).

Activities facet

The Activities facet encompasses areas of endeavor, physical and mental actions, discrete occurrences, and methods employed toward a certain end. These range from branches of learning and professional fields to specific life events, from mentally executed tasks to processes performed on or with materials and objects. Although descriptors for a wide range of disciplines are included, the focus is activities specific to the scope of the thesaurus.

The Activities facet consists of the following hierarchies:

Disciplines (KD)
Functions (HG)
Events (KM)
Processes and Techniques (KT)

Disciplines
Hierarchy

DISCIPLINES

Scope The Disciplines hierarchy contains descriptors for branches of learning, areas of specialization, and professions and professional specialities.

Organization Most descriptors are collocated under one of the traditional fields of study: **humanities, social sciences**, and **sciences**. Disciplines that incorporate aspects of more than one of the above areas are classed under *<cross-disciplinary studies>* (e.g., **forensic medicine**).

Relation to Other Hierarchies Material-specific or object-specific activities appear primarily in the Processes and Techniques hierarchy (e.g., **metalworking, carpentry**) while more general professional activities appear here (e.g., **architectural engineering**). Theories relating to disciplines appear in the Associated Concepts hierarchy, (e.g., **criticism, structuralism**). Descriptors for activities conducted in order to accomplish specific purposes appear in the Functions hierarchy (e.g., **researching**).

Descriptor Form and Use Descriptors appear as singular nouns, except where common usage dictates the plural (e.g., **sciences**). They may be combined with descriptors from other hierarchies (e.g., **dance** + **photography**; **Gothic** + **architecture**; **Greek** + **art**).

Number of Descriptors 290

KD

Synopsis

KD.1	**disciplines**
KD.2	**humanities**
KD.3	*<art and related disciplines>*
	|
KD.88	**rhetoric**
KD.89	**social sciences**
KD.90	**anthropology**
	|
KD.193	**urban studies**
KK.194	**sciences**
KD.195	**aeronautics**
	|
KD.258	**physical sciences**
KD.291	*<cross-disciplinary studies>*
KD.294	*<Medieval studies>*
KD.300	*<occult sciences>*

DISCIPLINES (KD)

KD.1	disciplines
KD.2	humanities
KD.3	*<arts and related disciplines>*
KD.4	arts
KD.5	performing arts
KD.6	dance
KD.7	ballet
KD.8	tap dance
KD.9	film (performing arts)
KD.10	music
KD.11	opera
KD.12	theater
KD.13	video
KD.14	visual arts
KD.15	architecture
KD.16	landscape architecture
KD.17	naval architecture
KD.18	art
KD.19	decorative arts
KD.20	fine arts
KD.21	*<arts-related disciplines>*
KD.22	architectural criticism
KD.23	architectural history
KD.24	art criticism
KD.25	art history
KD.26	art therapy
KD.27	musicology
KD.28	ethnomusicology
KD.29	classics
KD.30	languages
KD.31	*<linguistics and related disciplines>*
KD.32	linguistics
KD.33	applied linguistics
KD.34	anthropological linguistics
KD.35	computational linguistics
KD.36	graphemics
KD.37	psycholinguistics
KD.38	sociolinguistics
KD.39	theoretical linguistics
KD.40	historical linguistics
KD.41	metalinguistics
KD.42	morphology (linguistics)
KD.43	phonetics
KD.44	phonology
KD.45	pragmatics
KD.46	semantics
KD.47	syntax
KD.48	*<linguistics-related disciplines>*
KD.49	etymology

May be used in combination with other descriptors (e.g., **dance** + **photography**; **Gothic** + **architecture**; **Greek** + **art**).

KD.50 toponymy
KD.51 philology
KD.52 semiotics
KD.53 literature
KD.54 comparative literature
KD.55 drama
KD.56 literary criticism
KD.57 literary history
KD.58 poetics
KD.59 museology
KD.60 museum administration
KD.61 philosophy
KD.62 aesthetics
KD.63 axiology
KD.64 cosmography
KD.65 epistemology
KD.66 ethics (philosophy)
KD.67 logic
KD.68 metaphysics
KD.69 cosmology
KD.70 ontology
KD.71 phenomenology
KD.72 process philosophy
KD.73 *<religion and related disciplines>*
KD.74 religion
KD.75 anthropology of religion
KD.76 comparative religion
KD.77 philosophy of religion
KD.78 psychology of religion
KD.79 sociology of religion
KD.80 *<religion-related disciplines>*
KD.81 Biblical studies
KD.82 church history
KD.83 ecclesiology
KD.84 eschatology
KD.85 history of religion
KD.86 religious ethics
KD.87 theology
KD.88 rhetoric
KD.89 social sciences
KD.90 anthropology
KD.91 demographic anthropology
KD.92 ethnography
KD.93 ethnology
KD.94 material culture
KD.95 philosophical anthropology
KD.96 physical anthropology
KD.97 anthropometry
KD.98 paleoanthropology

May be used in combination with other descriptors (e.g., **dance** + **photography**; **Gothic** + **architecture**; **Greek** + **art**).

KD

KD.99	social anthropology
KD.100	structural anthropology
KD.101	archaeology
KD.102	anthropological archaeology
KD.103	archaeometry
KD.104	classical archaeology
KD.105	ethnoarchaeology
KD.106	industrial archaeology
KD.107	underwater archaeology
KD.108	communications
KD.109	advertising
KD.110	broadcasting
KD.111	radio broadcasting
KD.112	television broadcasting
KD.113	journalism
KD.114	public relations
KD.115	telecommunications
KD.116	criminology
KD.117	demography
KD.118	economics
KD.119	education
KD.120	*<education by grade level>*
KD.121	early childhood education
KD.122	preschool education
KD.123	elementary education
KD.124	primary education
KD.125	secondary education
KD.126	higher education
KD.127	continuing education
KD.128	*<education by subdiscipline>*
KD.129	architectural education
KD.130	art appreciation
KD.131	art education
KD.132	ekistics
KD.133	geography
KD.134	paleogeography
KD.135	physical geography
KD.136	population geography
KD.137	urban geography
KD.138	gerontology
KD.139	*<history and related disciplines>*
KD.140	history
KD.141	industrial history
KD.142	intellectual history
KD.143	local history
KD.144	oral history
KD.145	social history
KD.146	urban history
KD.147	*<history-related disciplines>*

May be used in combination with other descriptors (e.g., **dance** + **photography**; **Gothic** + **architecture**; **Greek** + **art**).

KD.148 epigraphy
KD.149 genealogy
KD.150 heraldry
KD.151 historiography
KD.152 numismatics
KD.153 paleography
KD.154 philately
KD.155 home economics
KD.156 human factors
KD.157 industrial relations
KD.158 information science
KD.159 library science
KD.160 law
KD.161 civil law
KD.162 criminal law
KD.163 environmental law
KD.164 international law
KD.165 land law
KD.166 public law
KD.167 zoning law
KD.168 planning
KD.169 campus planning
KD.170 city planning
KD.171 regional planning
KD.172 rural planning
KD.173 transportation planning
KD.174 highway planning
KD.175 political science
KD.176 comparative government
KD.177 international relations
KD.178 public policy
KD.179 *<psychology and related disciplines>*
KD.180 psychology
KD.181 ethnopsychology
KD.182 psychoanalysis
KD.183 social psychology
KD.184 *<psychology-related disciplines>*
KD.185 phrenology
KD.186 physiognomy
KD.187 psychohistory
KD.188 sociology
KD.189 historical sociology
KD.190 rural sociology
KD.191 sociology of knowledge
KD.192 urban sociology
KD.193 urban studies
KD.194 sciences
KD.195 aeronautics
KD.196 agriculture

May be used in combination with other descriptors (e.g., **dance** + **photography**; **Gothic** + **architecture**; **Greek** + **art**).

KD.197	horticulture
KD.198	floriculture
KD.199	ornamental horticulture
KD.200	biological sciences
KD.201	anatomy
KD.202	biology
KD.203	botany
KD.204	ecology
KD.205	genetics
KD.206	microbiology
KD.207	molecular biology
KD.208	physiology
KD.209	zoology
KD.210	computer science
KD.211	cybernetics
KD.212	engineering
KD.213	acoustical engineering
KD.214	aerospace engineering
KD.215	aeronautical engineering
KD.216	chemical engineering
KD.217	civil engineering
KD.218	architectural engineering
KD.219	environmental engineering
KD.220	sanitary engineering
KD.221	hydraulic engineering
KD.222	structural engineering
KD.223	traffic engineering
KD.224	transportation engineering
KD.225	highway engineering
KD.226	electrical engineering
KD.227	geological engineering
KD.228	industrial engineering
KD.229	marine engineering
KD.230	mechanical engineering
KD.231	military engineering
KD.232	plant engineering
KD.233	systems engineering
KD.234	environmental sciences
KD.235	forestry
KD.236	urban forestry
KD.237	health sciences
KD.238	chiropractic
KD.239	dentistry
KD.240	medicine
KD.241	nursing
KD.242	pharmacology
KD.243	pharmacy
KD.244	psychiatry
KD.245	materials sciences

May be used in combination with other descriptors (e.g., **dance** + **photography**; **Gothic** + **architecture**; **Greek** + **art**).

KD.246 ceramic science
KD.247 metallurgy
KD.248 polymer science
KD.249 textile science
KD.250 mathematics
KD.251 algebra
KD.252 applied mathematics
KD.253 arithmetic
KD.254 biometrics
KD.255 calculus
KD.256 geometry
KD.257 trigonometry
KD.258 physical sciences
KD.259 astronomy
KD.260 astrophysics
KD.261 chemistry
KD.262 biochemistry
KD.263 inorganic chemistry
KD.264 organic chemistry
KD.265 earth sciences
KD.266 geochemistry
KD.267 geodesy
KD.268 geology
KD.269 petrology
KD.270 structural geology
KD.271 tectonics (geology)
KD.272 geomorphology
KD.273 geophysics
KD.274 hydrography
KD.275 meteorology
KD.276 mineralogy
KD.277 oceanography
KD.278 paleontology
KD.279 soil science
KD.280 physics
KD.281 acoustics
KD.282 architectural acoustics
KD.283 applied physics
KD.284 engineering physics
KD.285 high energy physics
KD.286 hydraulics
KD.287 mathematical physics
KD.288 mechanics (physics)
KD.289 nuclear physics
KD.290 optics
KD.291 *<cross-disciplinary studies>*
KD.292 forensic medicine
KD.293 liberal arts
KD.294 *<Medieval studies>*

May be used in combination with other descriptors (e.g., **dance** + **photography**; **Gothic** + **architecture**; **Greek** + **art**).

KD.295	forbidden arts
KD.296	liberal arts (Medieval studies)
KD.297	trivium
KD.298	quadrivium
KD.299	mechanical arts
KD.300	occult sciences
KD.301	alchemy
KD.302	astrology
KD.303	magic
KD.304	voodoo

May be used in combination with other descriptors (e.g., **dance** + **photography**; **Gothic** + **architecture**; **Greek** + **art**).

Functions
Hierarchy

FUNCTIONS

Scope The Functions hierarchy contains descriptors for activities which are conducted in order to accomplish specific purposes, as well as methodologies associated with specific areas of endeavor. It includes descriptors for activities relating to the manipulation of data, the collecting of objects, human communication, economics, business, law, and government, as well as other professional activities.

Organization The Functions hierarchy is divided into two main sections: <*functions by general context*> and <*functions by specific context*>. The first section consists of activities common to a wide range of institutions, professions, and occupations, such as: <*analytical functions*> (e.g., **inspecting**), <*economic and financial functions*> (e.g., **bidding**), <*information handling functions*> (e.g., **accessioning**), and <*organizational functions*> (e.g., **scheduling**). The second section includes activities usually found in a particular context, such as: <*educational functions*> (e.g., **teaching**), <*governmental functions*> (e.g., **taxing**), <*legal functions*> (e.g., **paroling**), and <*religious functions*> (e.g., **baptizing**).

Relation to Other Hierarchies Descriptors for operations and processes performed on or with objects and materials (e.g., **polishing**), are found in the Processes and Techniques hierarchy. Descriptors describing branches of learning, (e.g., **history**) and areas of specialization, (e.g., **law**), are found in the Disciplines hierarchy. Descriptors denoting occasions and happenings of a social, cultural, religious, or personal nature, (e.g., **exhibitions**), are found in the Events hierarchy.

Descriptor Form and Use Descriptors appear in gerund form or in the most commonly used noun form. They may be combined with descriptors from other appropriate hierarchies to identify the functions or activities of organizations (e.g., **inspecting** + **nursing homes**; **coordinating** + **social services**). Alternate adjectival forms may also be used as modifiers (e.g., **protected** + **public land**; **licensed** + **architects**).

Number of Descriptors 204

Synopsis

KG.1	**functions**
KG.2	*<functions by general context>*
KG.3	*<analytical functions>*
KG.32	*<communication functions>*
KG.43	*<economic functions>*
KG.64	*<information handling functions>*
KG.110	**maintaining**
KG.138	*<organizational functions>*
KG.162	*<functions by specific context>*
KG.163	**business**
KG.173	*<educational functions>*
KG.176	*<governmental functions>*
KG.188	*<health care functions>*
KG.191	*<legal functions>*
KG.211	*<religious functions>*
KG.216	*<social functions>*

FUNCTIONS (KG)

- KG.1 **functions**
  - KG.2 *<functions by general context>*
    - KG.3 *<analytical functions>*
      - KG.4 **adjudicating**
      - KG.5 **analyzing**
        - KG.6 **cost benefit analysis**
        - KG.7 **needs assessment**
      - KG.8 **arbitrating**
      - KG.9 **auditing**
      - KG.10 **authenticating**
      - KG.11 **comparing**
      - KG.12 **decision making**
        - KG.13 **selecting**
      - KG.14 **describing**
      - KG.15 **diagnosing**
        - KG.16 **building diagnostics**
          - KG.17 **building pathology**
          - KG.18 **post-occupancy evaluation**
      - KG.19 **evaluating**
        - KG.20 **expertizing**
      - KG.21 **experimenting**
      - KG.22 **identifying**
      - KG.23 **inspecting**
      - KG.24 **investigating**
        - KG.25 **feasibility studies**
      - KG.26 **researching**
        - KG.27 **fieldwork**
      - KG.28 **resolving**
      - KG.29 **reviewing**
        - KG.30 **design review**
      - KG.31 **testing**
    - KG.32 *<communication functions>*
      - KG.33 **advocating**
      - KG.34 **communicating**
      - KG.35 **consulting**
      - KG.36 **counseling**
        - KG.37 **vocational guidance**
      - KG.38 **lobbying**
      - KG.39 **negotiating**
      - KG.40 **protesting**
      - KG.41 **publicizing**
      - KG.42 **reporting**
    - KG.43 *<economic and financial functions>*
      - KG.44 **appraising**
        - KG.45 **land valuation**
      - KG.46 **assisting**
        - KG.47 **funding**
          - KG.48 **subsidizing**
      - KG.49 **bidding**

May be used in combination with other descriptors (e.g., **inspecting** + **nursing homes**; **coordinating** + **social services**; **protected** + **public land**; **licensed** + **architects**).

KG.50 billing
KG.51 bonding (financial)
KG.52 budgeting
KG.53 cost control
KG.54 disbursing
KG.55 distributing
KG.56 estimating
KG.57 fund raising
KG.58 insuring
KG.59 investing
KG.60 marketing
KG.61 mortgaging
KG.62 procuring
KG.63 purchasing
KG.64 *<information handling functions>*
KG.65 abstracting
KG.66 censoring
KG.67 classifying
KG.68 collections management
KG.69 accessioning
KG.70 acquisition
KG.71 archiving
KG.72 cataloging
KG.73 descriptive cataloging
KG.74 subject cataloging
KG.75 circulation
KG.76 collecting
KG.77 collection development
KG.78 curating
KG.79 deaccessioning
KG.80 inventorying
KG.81 lending
KG.82 marking
KG.83 computer programming
KG.84 data processing
KG.85 data conversion
KG.86 retrospective conversion
KG.87 document delivery
KG.88 documenting
KG.89 editing
KG.90 exhibiting
KG.91 indexing
KG.92 information management
KG.93 authority control
KG.94 information retrieval
KG.95 searching
KG.96 online searching
KG.97 subject searching
KG.98 information storage

May be used in combination with other descriptors (e.g., **inspecting** + **nursing homes**; **coordinating** + **social services**; **protected** + **public land**; **licensed** + **architects**).

KG.99   records management
KG.100   thesaurus construction
KG.101   monitoring
KG.102   publishing
KG.103   electronic publishing
KG.104   recording
KG.105   registering (information handling)
KG.106   subject analysis
KG.107   technical writing
KG.108   specification writing
KG.109   translating
KG.110 maintaining
KG.111   crime prevention
KG.112   burglary protection
KG.113   environmental protection
KG.114   avalanche protection
KG.115   fire prevention
KG.116   flood control
KG.117   humidity control
KG.118   landscape protection
KG.119   landslide protection
KG.120   lightning protection
KG.121   noise control
KG.122   pollution control
KG.123   air purification
KG.124   smoke abatement
KG.125   solid waste management
KG.126   waste disposal
KG.127   refuse disposal
KG.128   sewage disposal
KG.129   water quality management
KG.130   preservation
KG.131   historic preservation
KG.132   protecting
KG.133   providing
KG.134   water resources development
KG.135   reclamation
KG.136   rehabilitating
KG.137   relocating
KG.138 <*organizational functions*>
KG.139   administering
KG.140   facility management
KG.141   admitting
KG.142   authorizing
KG.143   accrediting
KG.144   certifying
KG.145   campaigning
KG.146   coordinating
KG.147   enforcing

May be used in combination with other descriptors (e.g., **inspecting** + **nursing homes**; **coordinating** + **social services**; **protected** + **public land**; **licensed** + **architects**).

KG.148 licensing
KG.149 managing
KG.150 appointing
KG.151 employing
KG.152 firing
KG.153 hiring
KG.154 recruiting
KG.155 supervising
KG.156 programming
KG.157 punishing
KG.158 regulating
KG.159 releasing
KG.160 scheduling
KG.161 striking
KG.162 *<functions by specific context>*
KG.163 business
KG.164 accounting
KG.165 cost accounting
KG.166 banking
KG.167 exporting
KG.168 importing
KG.169 manufacturing
KG.170 quality control
KG.171 selling
KG.172 speculating
KG.173 *<educational functions>*
KG.174 matriculating
KG.175 teaching
KG.176 *<governmental functions>*
KG.177 annexing
KG.178 apportioning
KG.179 assessing
KG.180 condemning
KG.181 confiscating
KG.182 legislating
KG.183 nationalization
KG.184 pardoning
KG.185 representing
KG.186 taxing
KG.187 zoning
KG.188 *<health care functions>*
KG.189 surgery
KG.190 treating
KG.191 *<legal functions>*
KG.192 contracting
KG.193 design-build
KG.194 subcontracting
KG.195 evicting
KG.196 extraditing

May be used in combination with other descriptors (e.g., **inspecting** + **nursing homes**; **coordinating** + **social services**; **protected** + **public land**; **licensed** + **architects**).

KG.197 **foreclosing**
KG.198 **impeaching**
KG.199 **issuing**
KG.200 *<judicial functions>*
KG.201 **convicting**
KG.202 **executing**
KG.203 **incarcerating**
KG.204 **indicting**
KG.205 **litigating**
KG.206 **sentencing**
KG.207 **law enforcing**
KG.208 **naturalizing**
KG.209 **paroling**
KG.210 **probating**
KG.211 *<religious functions>*
KG.212 **baptizing**
KG.213 **blessing**
KG.214 **ministering**
KG.215 **tithing**
KG.216 *<social functions>*
KG.217 **celebrating**
KG.218 **entertaining**

May be used in combination with other descriptors (e.g., **inspecting** + **nursing homes**; **coordinating** + **social services**; **protected** + **public land**; **licensed** + **architects**).

Events Hierarchy

EVENTS

Scope The Events hierarchy contains descriptors for occurrences, happenings, and occasions of a social, cultural, religious, or personal nature (e.g., **anniversaries, concerts, birth**).

Organization Decriptors are collocated under broad groupings such as *<religious ceremonies>* (e.g., **communion**), *<entertainment events>* (e.g., **performances**), *<religious holidays>* (e.g., **Passover**), and **meetings** (e.g., **conferences**).

Relation to Other Hierarchies Descriptors for activities and methodologies associated with specific contexts (e.g., **researching, taxing**) are found in the Functions hierarchy. Descriptors relating to actions performed with concrete objects and materials (e.g., **polishing**), are found in the Processes and Techniques hierarchy.

Descriptor Form and Use Descriptors appear as plural nouns, unless common usage dictates the singular. Descriptors may be combined with those from other hierarchies (e.g., **Native American** + **ceremonies**; **Roman** + **festivals**; **presidents** + **inaugurations**).

Number of Descriptors 148

Synopsis

KM.1	**events**
KM.2	**campaigns**
KM.5	**celebrations**
KM.11	**ceremonies**
KM.12	*<academic ceremonies>*
KM.15	*<building ceremonies>*
KM.17	*<cultural ceremonies>*
KM.28	*<religious ceremonies>*
KM.41	**contests**
KM.46	*<educational events>*
KM.52	**elections**
KM.53	*<entertainment events>*
KM.64	**exhibitions**
KM.70	**fasts**
KM.71	**holidays**
KM.91	**journeys**
KM.96	**meetings**
KM.101	*<natural events>*
KM.127	**openings (events)**
KM.129	**parties**
KM.133	*<personal life events>*
KM.140	**previews**
KM.142	*<religious events>*
KM.146	**rituals**
KM.147	*<sales events>*
KM.157	**trials**
KM.158	*<work-related events>*

EVENTS (KM)

KM.1	events
KM.2	campaigns
KM.3	advertising campaigns
KM.4	political campaigns
KM.5	celebrations
KM.6	anniversaries
KM.7	birthdays
KM.8	feasts
KM.9	festivals
KM.10	Carnival
KM.11	ceremonies
KM.12	*<academic ceremonies>*
KM.13	commencements
KM.14	convocations
KM.15	*<building ceremonies>*
KM.16	toppings out
KM.17	*<cultural ceremonies>*
KM.18	christenings
KM.19	coronations
KM.20	dedications (ceremonies)
KM.21	funerals
KM.22	inaugurations
KM.23	initiations
KM.24	potlaches
KM.25	processions
KM.26	wakes
KM.27	weddings
KM.28	*<religious ceremonies>*
KM.29	baptism
KM.30	bar mitzvahs
KM.31	bath mitzvahs
KM.32	circumcision
KM.33	communion
KM.34	confirmation
KM.35	consecration
KM.36	deconsecration
KM.37	extreme unction
KM.38	mass (liturgy)
KM.39	ordinations
KM.40	Seders
KM.41	contests
KM.42	competitions
KM.43	games
KM.44	rodeos
KM.45	tournaments
KM.46	*<educational events>*
KM.47	charettes
KM.48	critiques
KM.49	juries

May be used in combination with other descriptors, especially in the Styles and Periods and Agents facets (e.g., **Native American** + **ceremonies**; **Roman** + **festivals**; **presidents** + **inaugurations**).

KM.50 seminars
KM.51 workshops (seminars)
KM.52 elections
KM.53 *<entertainment events>*
KM.54 carnivals
KM.55 fêtes
KM.56 parades
KM.57 performances
KM.58 circuses
KM.59 concerts
KM.60 naumachias
KM.61 pageants
KM.62 recitals
KM.63 side shows
KM.64 exhibitions
KM.65 fairs
KM.66 world's fairs
KM.67 garden shows
KM.68 industrial expositions
KM.69 traveling exhibitions
KM.70 fasts
KM.71 holidays
KM.72 legal holidays
KM.73 national holidays
KM.74 Independence Day
KM.75 New Year
KM.76 Thanksgiving
KM.77 *<religious holidays>*
KM.78 Ascension Day
KM.79 Ash Wednesday
KM.80 Christmas
KM.81 Easter
KM.82 Good Friday
KM.83 Hanukkah
KM.84 Lent
KM.85 Palm Sunday
KM.86 Passover
KM.87 Ramadan
KM.88 Rosh Hashanah
KM.89 Sukkot
KM.90 Yom Kippur
KM.91 journeys
KM.92 expeditions
KM.93 pilgrimages
KM.94 tours
KM.95 grand tours
KM.96 meetings
KM.97 conferences
KM.98 symposia

May be used in combination with other descriptors, especially in the Styles and Periods and Agents facets (e.g., **Native American** + **ceremonies**; **Roman** + **festivals**; **presidents** + **inaugurations**).

KM.99 hearings
KM.100 town meetings
KM.101 *<natural events>*
KM.102 avalanches
KM.103 earth movements
KM.104 continental drift
KM.105 earthquakes
KM.106 frost heaves
KM.107 mudflows
KM.108 subsidences (earth movements)
KM.109 fires
KM.110 forest fires
KM.111 floods
KM.112 landslides
KM.113 storms
KM.114 blizzards
KM.115 cyclones
KM.116 hurricanes
KM.117 tornadoes
KM.118 typhoons
KM.119 duststorms
KM.120 ice storms
KM.121 monsoons
KM.122 sandstorms
KM.123 snowstorms
KM.124 thunderstorms
KM.125 windstorms
KM.126 tidal waves
KM.127 openings (events)
KM.128 premieres
KM.129 parties
KM.130 balls (parties)
KM.131 galas
KM.132 receptions
KM.133 *<personal life events>*
KM.134 birth
KM.135 death
KM.136 executions
KM.137 murders
KM.138 assassinations
KM.139 suicides
KM.140 retreats
KM.141 previews
KM.142 *<religious events>*
KM.143 beatifications
KM.144 canonizations
KM.145 excommunications
KM.146 rituals
KM.147 *<sales events>*

May be used in combination with other descriptors, especially in the Styles and Periods and Agents facets (e.g., **Native American** + **ceremonies**; **Roman** + **festivals**; **presidents** + **inaugurations**).

KM.148 **auctions**
KM.149 **garage sales**
KM.150 **markets (events)**
KM.151 **farmers' markets**
KM.152 **flea markets**
KM.153 **periodic markets**
KM.154 **promotions**
KM.155 **rummage sales**
KM.156 **trade shows**
KM.157 **trials**
KM.158 *<work-related events>*
KM.159 **lockouts**
KM.160 **strikes (events)**

May be used in combination with other descriptors, especially in the Styles and Periods and Agents facets (e.g., **Native American** + **ceremonies**; **Roman** + **festivals**; **presidents** + **inaugurations**).

Processes and Techniques Hierarchy

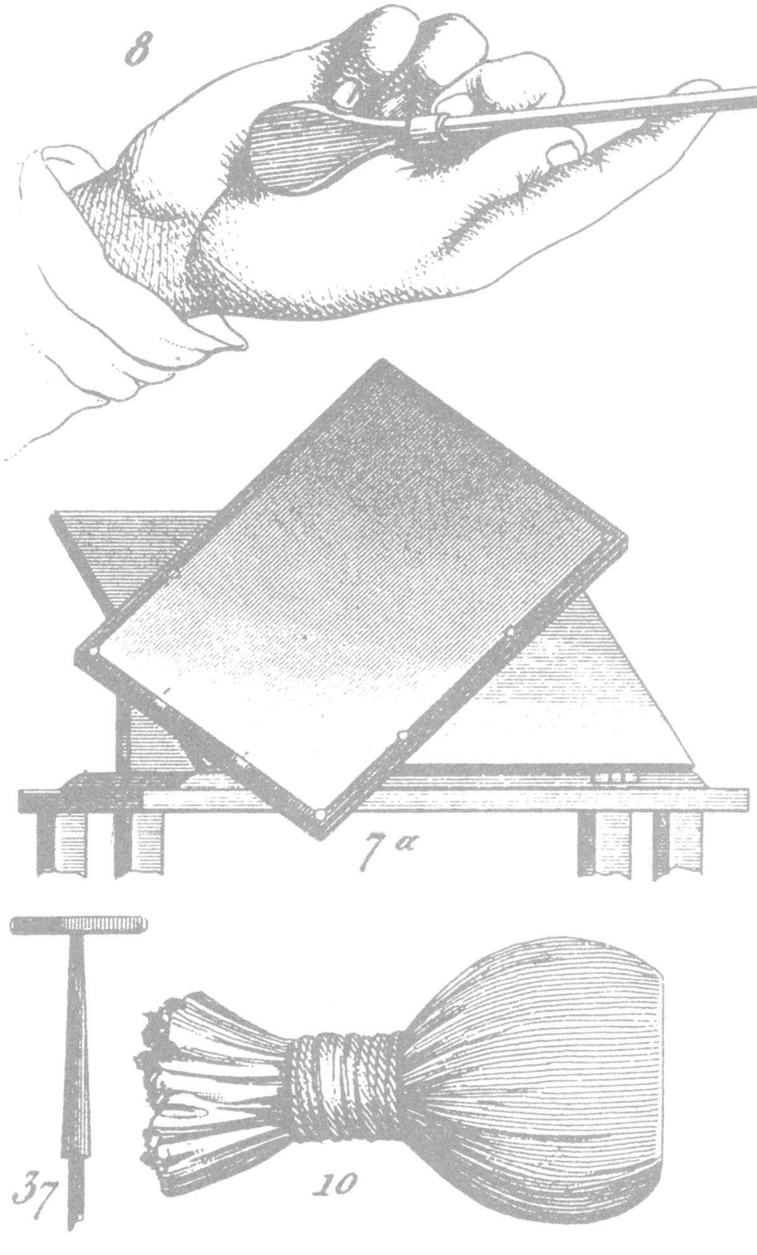

Scope The Processes and Techniques hierarchy contains descriptors for actions and methods performed on or with materials and objects. Included are descriptors for types of processes that occur in more than one context (e.g., **assembling**), as well as descriptors specific to either the production of images and other objects (e.g., **drawing**, **tapestry**) or to the manipulation or processing of certain materials (e.g., **soldering**). Also included are descriptors for conditions and effects, that is, processes that are usually the result of natural forces rather than human direction and usually associated with the degeneration of physical objects (e.g., **deterioration**).

Organization This hierarchy consists of three main sections. The first, *<processes and techniques by general type>*, includes only the descriptors **processes** and **techniques**. The second, *<processes and techniques by specific type>*, is the largest section. Descriptors for processes and techniques used in more than one context (e.g., **carving**) appear directly under this guide term, while those usually associated with a particular material or object type (e.g., **metalworking**, **sculpture techniques**) appear under one of the following guide terms: *<processes and techniques by material>*, *<image-making processes and techniques>*, or *<object-making processes and techniques>*. The last section, *<conditions and effects>*, includes descriptors for phenomena resulting from environmental, chemical, or other processes (e.g., **erosion**).

Relation to Other Hierarchies Descriptors for operations that pertain to abstract or conceptual processes (e.g., **identifying**, **analyzing**), as well as descriptors relating to the manipulation of data, the collecting of objects, and various other professional or organizational activities (e.g., **collections management**, **recruiting**) are found in the Functions hierarchy. Descriptors that designate branches of learning (e.g., **anthropology**) are found in the Disciplines hierarchy, while the processes and techniques associated with these fields are contained here. Certain descriptors that apply to degenerative forces on materials or structures (e.g., **stress**) are found in the Associated Concepts hierarchy.

Descriptor Form and Use Most descriptors appear in the gerund form (e.g., **planishing**, **plastering**). Where common usage dictates, other forms are used (e.g., **abrasion**, **tapestry**). Adjectival forms of many descriptors (e.g., **painted**, **burnished**) are provided as an alternate. Descriptors may be combined with those from other hierarchies (e.g., **painted** + **ceilings**; **conservation** + **techniques**; **Medieval** + **painting**; **half-timber** + **cottages**).

Number of Descriptors 871

Synopsis

KT.1	*<processes and techniques>*
KT.2	*<processes and techniques by general type>*
KT.3	**processes**
KT.4	**techniques**
KT.5	*<processes and techniques by process>*
KT.6	**absorption**
	|
KT.756	**transporting**
KT.760	*<processes and techniques by material>*
KT.761	**caning**
	|
KT.877	**paperworking techniques**
KT.885	*<conditions and effects>*
KT.886	**buckling**
	|
KT.929	**warping**

PROCESSES AND TECHNIQUES (KT)

KT.1	*<processes and techniques>*
KT.2	*<processes and techniques by general type>*
KT.3	processes
KT.4	techniques
KT.5	*<processes and techniques by specific type>*
KT.6	absorption
KT.7	adsorption
KT.8	alteration
KT.9	retouching
KT.10	*<analysis and testing techniques>*
KT.11	chemical analysis
KT.12	trace element analysis
KT.13	neutron activation analysis
KT.14	colorimetry
KT.15	microscopy
KT.16	site analysis
KT.17	fengshui
KT.18	systems analysis
KT.19	terrain analysis
KT.20	x-ray spectroscopy
KT.21	assembling
KT.22	adhesion
KT.23	gluing
KT.24	pasting
KT.25	bonding (joining)
KT.26	construction
KT.27	*<construction by form>*
KT.28	cantilever construction
KT.29	composite construction
KT.30	drywall construction
KT.31	frame construction
KT.32	half-timber construction
KT.33	lightweight construction
KT.34	sandwich construction
KT.35	stressed-skin construction
KT.36	log construction
KT.37	stovewood construction
KT.38	modular construction
KT.39	monocoque construction
KT.40	prefabrication
KT.41	wattle and daub
KT.42	*<construction by function>*
KT.43	bombproof construction
KT.44	earthquake-resistant construction
KT.45	fire-resistive construction
KT.46	reconstruction
KT.47	stormproof construction
KT.48	facing
KT.49	fastening

May be used in combination with other descriptors (e.g., **upholstered** + **chairs**; **half-timber** + **cottages**; **Medieval** + **painting**; **gilded** + **bronze**).

KT.50 bolting
KT.51 nailing
KT.52 pinning
KT.53 riveting
KT.54 screwing
KT.55 stapling
KT.56 joining
KT.57 laminating
KT.58 layering
KT.59 mitering
KT.60 mixing
KT.61 blending
KT.62 splicing
KT.63 tipping in
KT.64 tying
KT.65 cleaning
KT.66 abrasive cleaning
KT.67 sandblasting
KT.68 shotblasting
KT.69 chemical cleaning
KT.70 detoxification
KT.71 disinfecting
KT.72 fumigating
KT.73 poulticing (masonry)
KT.74 washing
KT.75 coloring
KT.76 bleaching
KT.77 dyeing
KT.78 chiné technique
KT.79 resist dyeing
KT.80 batik
KT.81 tie-dyeing
KT.82 hand coloring
KT.83 staining
KT.84 tinting
KT.85 cutting
KT.86 carving
KT.87 direct carving
KT.88 sawing
KT.89 snipping
KT.90 stonecutting
KT.91 trimming
KT.92 cropping
KT.93 decoration
KT.94 design
KT.95 advertising design
KT.96 architectural design
KT.97 participatory design
KT.98 computer-aided design

KT.99 costume design
KT.100 fashion design
KT.101 graphic design
KT.102 industrial design
KT.103 interior decoration
KT.104 interior design
KT.105   space planning
KT.106 theater design
KT.107 destruction
KT.108 blasting
KT.109   mud-capping
KT.110 breaking
KT.111 crushing
KT.112 demolition
KT.113 dismantling
KT.114 *<exploring and investigating techniques>*
KT.115 dowsing
KT.116 remote sensing
KT.117 surveying
KT.118   archaeological surveying
KT.119   photographic surveying
KT.120   topographical surveying
KT.121 filling
KT.122 grouting
KT.123 hydraulic filling
KT.124 pointing
KT.125 spackling
KT.126 fixing
KT.127 forming
KT.128 bending
KT.129 beveling
KT.130 casting
KT.131   continuous casting
KT.132   die casting
KT.133   lost-wax process
KT.134   centrifugal casting
KT.135   sand casting
KT.136 chamfering
KT.137 cold-working
KT.138 compaction
KT.139   puddling
KT.140 crimping
KT.141 extrusion
KT.142 knurling
KT.143 leveling
KT.144 modeling (forming)
KT.145 molding
KT.146   blow molding
KT.147   compression molding

May be used in combination with other descriptors (e.g., **upholstered** + **chairs**; **half-timber** + **cottages**; **Medieval** + **painting**; **gilded** + **bronze**).

KT.148 injection molding
KT.149 reaction injection molding
KT.150 rotational molding
KT.151 transfer molding
KT.152 vacuum forming
KT.153 peening
KT.154 planishing
KT.155 pressing
KT.156 calendering
KT.157 squaring
KT.158 stamping
KT.159 check stamping
KT.160 rocker stamping
KT.161 stereotomy
KT.162 streamlining
KT.163 stretching
KT.164 *<forming by removal of material>*
KT.165 honing
KT.166 machining
KT.167 reaming
KT.168 scoring
KT.169 turning
KT.170 whittling
KT.171 *<image-making processes and techniques>*
KT.172 animation
KT.173 computer animation
KT.174 cartography
KT.175 cartooning
KT.176 cerography
KT.177 collage
KT.178 computer graphics
KT.179 copying
KT.180 photocopying
KT.181 electrostatic printing
KT.182 xerography
KT.183 spirit duplicating
KT.184 stencil duplicating
KT.185 décollage
KT.186 *<drawing and drawing techniques>*
KT.187 drawing
KT.188 architectural drawing
KT.189 drawing techniques
KT.190 à deux crayons
KT.191 à trois crayons
KT.192 blot drawing
KT.193 contour drawing
KT.194 blind contour drawing
KT.195 cross-contour drawing
KT.196 doodling

May be used in combination with other descriptors (e.g., **upholstered** + **chairs**; **half-timber** + **cottages**; **Medieval** + **painting**; **gilded** + **bronze**).

KT.197 drafting
KT.198 freehand drawing
KT.199 gesture drawing
KT.200 rendering
KT.201 fumage
KT.202 illustration
KT.203 archaeological illustration
KT.204 book illustration
KT.205 fashion illustration
KT.206 manuscript illumination
KT.207 newspaper illustration
KT.208 periodical illustration
KT.209 scientific illustration
KT.210 biological illustration
KT.211 anatomical illustration
KT.212 botanical illustration
KT.213 zoological illustration
KT.214 medical illustration
KT.215 technical illustration
KT.216 micrographics
KT.217 *<painting and painting techniques>*
KT.218 painting
KT.219 painting techniques
KT.220 *<painting techniques by application method>*
KT.221 alla prima
KT.222 dragging
KT.223 drip painting
KT.224 dry-brush painting
KT.225 fat over lean technique
KT.226 fresco painting
KT.227 mezzo fresco
KT.228 stucco-lustro technique
KT.229 grattage
KT.230 impasto
KT.231 lifting (painting technique)
KT.232 oiling out
KT.233 pointillism
KT.234 scumbling
KT.235 secco
KT.236 soak-stain technique
KT.237 spray painting
KT.238 airbrushing
KT.239 *<painting techniques by medium>*
KT.240 aquarelle
KT.241 encaustic painting
KT.242 burning in (painting)
KT.243 *<painting techniques by stage>*
KT.244 priming
KT.245 underpainting

May be used in combination with other descriptors (e.g., **upholstered** + **chairs**; **half-timber** + **cottages**; **Medieval** + **painting**; **gilded** + **bronze**).

KT.246 **laying in**
KT.247 **overpainting**
KT.248 *<painting techniques by tool>*
KT.249 **finger painting**
KT.250 **roller painting**
KT.251 **stumping**
KT.252 *<painting techniques for special effects>*
KT.253 **camaieu**
KT.254 **cirage**
KT.255 **grisaille**
KT.256 **faux finishing**
KT.257 **antiquing**
KT.258 **graining**
KT.259 **marbling**
KT.260 **sumie**
KT.261 **toning**
KT.262 *<perspective and shading techniques>*
KT.263 **chiaroscuro**
KT.264 **foreshortening**
KT.265 **hatching**
KT.266 **cross-hatching**
KT.267 **heightening**
KT.268 **modeling (shading)**
KT.269 **perspective**
KT.270 **aerial perspective**
KT.271 **axial perspective**
KT.272 **inverted perspective**
KT.273 **linear perspective**
KT.274 **one-point perspective**
KT.275 **two-point perspective**
KT.276 **three-point perspective**
KT.277 **parallel perspective**
KT.278 **projection**
KT.279 **central projection**
KT.280 **parallel projection**
KT.281 **axonometric projection**
KT.282 **dimetric projection**
KT.283 **isometric projection**
KT.284 **oblique projection**
KT.285 **trimetric projection**
KT.286 **orthographic projection**
KT.287 **multiview projection**
KT.288 **sfumato**
KT.289 **shading**
KT.290 *<photography and photographic processes and techniques>*
KT.291 **photography**
KT.292 **advertising photography**
KT.293 **architectural photography**
KT.294 **astronomical photography**

KT

May be used in combination with other descriptors (e.g., **upholstered** + **chairs**; **half-timber** + **cottages**; **Medieval** + **painting**; **gilded** + **bronze**).

KT.295	cinematography
KT.296	commercial portraiture
KT.297	documentary photography
KT.298	ethnographic photography
KT.299	fashion photography
KT.300	industrial photography
KT.301	medical photography
KT.302	military photography
KT.303	nature photography
KT.304	photojournalism
KT.305	psychic photography
KT.306	scientific photography
KT.307	spirit photography
KT.308	travel photography
KT.309	war photography
KT.310	wedding photography
KT.311	photographic processes
KT.312	additive color processes
KT.313	Autochrome process
KT.314	screen processes
KT.315	Dufaycolor
KT.316	Finlaycolor
KT.317	albumen process
KT.318	aniline process
KT.319	aristotype
KT.320	collodion processes
KT.321	ambrotype
KT.322	dry collodion process
KT.323	tintype
KT.324	wet collodion process
KT.325	diazo process
KT.326	diffusion transfer process
KT.327	dye diffusion transfer process
KT.328	internal dye diffusion transfer process
KT.329	direct positive processes
KT.330	Bayard's process
KT.331	daguerreotype
KT.332	heliochromy
KT.333	heliography
KT.334	Hillotype
KT.335	electrophotography
KT.336	gelatin silver process
KT.337	gelatin dry plate process
KT.338	interference processes
KT.339	holography
KT.340	Lippmann process
KT.341	iron processes
KT.342	blueprint process
KT.343	ferrogallic process

KT.344 kallitype
KT.345 lenticular processes
KT.346 palladium process
KT.347 pigment processes
KT.348 bichromate processes
KT.349 carbon process
KT.350 Artigue process
KT.351 dusting-on process
KT.352 ceramic process
KT.353 Fresson
KT.354 gum bichromate process
KT.355 oil processes
KT.356 bromoil process
KT.357 carbro process
KT.358 three-color carbro process
KT.359 platinum process
KT.360 sepia platinotype
KT.361 salted paper processes
KT.362 calotype
KT.363 photogenic drawing
KT.364 waxed-paper process
KT.365 subtractive color processes
KT.366 chromogenic processes
KT.367 Agfacolor (TM)
KT.368 Ektachrome (TM)
KT.369 Kodachrome (TM)
KT.370 Kodacolor (TM)
KT.371 silver-dye bleach process
KT.372 Cibachrome (TM)
KT.373 Gasparcolor
KT.374 three-color processes
KT.375 two-color processes
KT.376 Wothlytype
KT.377 photographic techniques
KT.378 black-and-white photography
KT.379 color photography
KT.380 *<picture-taking techniques>*
KT.381 chronophotography
KT.382 stroboscopic photography
KT.383 time-lapse photography
KT.384 high-speed photography
KT.385 Kirlian photography
KT.386 multiple exposure
KT.387 photomicrography
KT.388 radiography
KT.389 autoradiography
KT.390 stereoscopic photography
KT.391 telephotography
KT.392 *<picture-taking techniques by location or context>*

KT

KT.393	**aerial photography**
KT.394	**close-up photography**
KT.395	**indoor photography**
KT.396	**night photography**
KT.397	**space photography**
KT.398	**underwater photography**
KT.399	*<picture-taking techniques by lighting>*
KT.400	**available light photography**
KT.401	**infrared photography**
KT.402	**schlieren photography**
KT.403	**ultraviolet photography**
KT.404	*<photographic processing and presentation techniques>*
KT.405	**archival processing**
KT.406	**burning in (photography)**
KT.407	**burnishing (photography)**
KT.408	**combination printing**
KT.409	**contact printing**
KT.410	**developing (photography)**
KT.411	**dodging**
KT.412	**enlarging**
KT.413	**ferrotyping**
KT.414	**glycerine process**
KT.415	**intensification**
KT.416	**macrophotography**
KT.417	**microphotography**
KT.418	**reduction (photography)**
KT.419	**solarization**
KT.420	**toning (photography)**
KT.421	**dye toning**
KT.422	**metallic toning**
KT.423	**photomechanical processes**
KT.424	**dye transfer process**
KT.425	**Eastman Wash-off Relief (TM)**
KT.426	**Pinatype**
KT.427	**Woodburytype**
KT.428	*<photomechanical processes: intaglio>*
KT.429	**etched daguerreotype process**
KT.430	**photogalvanography**
KT.431	**photogravure**
KT.432	**photoaquatint**
KT.433	*<photomechanical processes: planographic>*
KT.434	**photolithography**
KT.435	**collotype**
KT.436	*<photomechanical processes: relief>*
KT.437	**photoengraving**
KT.438	**relief halftone**
KT.439	*<printmaking and printmaking techniques>*
KT.440	**printmaking**
KT.441	**printmaking techniques**

May be used in combination with other descriptors (e.g., **upholstered** + **chairs**; **half-timber** + **cottages**; **Medieval** + **painting**; **gilded** + **bronze**).

KT.442 acid-biting
KT.443 color printing
KT.444 color separation
KT.445 imposition process
KT.446 zincography
KT.447 *<printmaking techniques by transfer method>*
KT.448 intaglio printing
KT.449 collagraph printing
KT.450 die stamping
KT.451 engraving (printmaking)
KT.452 drypoint
KT.453 line engraving
KT.454 mezzotint
KT.455 stipple engraving
KT.456 etching (printmaking)
KT.457 aquatint
KT.458 lift-ground
KT.459 deep etching
KT.460 soft-ground etching
KT.461 planographic printing
KT.462 lithography
KT.463 chromolithography
KT.464 transfer lithography
KT.465 monotype
KT.466 offset printing
KT.467 serigraphy
KT.468 relief printing
KT.469 anastatic printing
KT.470 block printing
KT.471 linocut
KT.472 potato printing
KT.473 tile block printing
KT.474 wood-block printing
KT.475 nature printing
KT.476 white line process
KT.477 wood engraving
KT.478 sgraffito
KT.479 dry sgraffito
KT.480 sketching
KT.481 tattooing
KT.482 thermography
KT.483 writing
KT.484 calligraphy
KT.485 lettering
KT.486 dimensioning
KT.487 skywriting
KT.488 *<landscaping and related processes>*
KT.489 gardening
KT.490 greenhouse gardening

May be used in combination with other descriptors (e.g., **upholstered** + **chairs**; **half-timber** + **cottages**; **Medieval** + **painting**; **gilded** + **bronze**).

KT.491 **indoor gardening**
KT.492 **landscape gardening**
KT.493 **planting**
KT.494 **landscaping**
KT.495 **measuring**
KT.496 **dating**
KT.497 *<bone dating techniques>*
KT.498 **fluorine dating**
KT.499 **nitrogen dating**
KT.500 **dendrochronology**
KT.501 **obsidian hydration dating**
KT.502 **paleomagnetic dating**
KT.503 **radioactive dating**
KT.504 **fission track dating**
KT.505 **potassium-argon dating**
KT.506 **radiocarbon dating**
KT.507 **thermoluminescence dating**
KT.508 **photogrammetry**
KT.509 **aerial photogrammetry**
KT.510 **sensitometry**
KT.511 **photographic sensitometry**
KT.512 *<object-making processes and techniques>*
KT.513 **basketmaking**
KT.514 **beadmaking**
KT.515 **bookbinding**
KT.516 **Japanese binding**
KT.517 **saw-kerf binding**
KT.518 **side sewing**
KT.519 **candlemaking**
KT.520 **clock making**
KT.521 **coopering**
KT.522 **dressmaking**
KT.523 **furniture making**
KT.524 **cabinetmaking**
KT.525 **gunsmithing**
KT.526 **jewelry making**
KT.527 **kitemaking**
KT.528 **maskmaking**
KT.529 **model-making**
KT.530 **rugmaking**
KT.531 *<sculpture and sculpture techniques>*
KT.532 **sculpture**
KT.533 **sculpture techniques**
KT.534 **assemblage**
KT.535 **ganosis**
KT.536 **pointing (sculpture)**
KT.537 **relief**
KT.538 **bas-relief**
KT.539 **high relief**

May be used in combination with other descriptors (e.g., **upholstered** + **chairs**; **half-timber** + **cottages**; **Medieval** + **painting**; **gilded** + **bronze**).

KT.540	**taxidermy**
KT.541	**textile working**
KT.542	*<interworking processes and techniques>*
KT.543	**braiding**
KT.544	**hooking**
KT.545	**knitting**
KT.546	**knotting**
KT.547	**macramé**
KT.548	**netting**
KT.549	**lace making**
KT.550	**tatting**
KT.551	**weaving**
KT.552	**brocade**
KT.553	**brocatelle**
KT.554	**hand weaving**
KT.555	**loom weaving**
KT.556	**tapestry**
KT.557	**needlework**
KT.558	**appliqué**
KT.559	**beadwork**
KT.560	**crochet**
KT.561	**embroidery**
KT.562	**couching**
KT.563	**crewelwork**
KT.564	**overstitching**
KT.565	**needlepoint**
KT.566	**quilting**
KT.567	**sewing**
KT.568	**basting**
KT.569	**stitching**
KT.570	**spinning**
KT.571	**hand spinning**
KT.572	**toy making**
KT.573	**dollmaking**
KT.574	**watch making**
KT.575	*<placing processes and techniques>*
KT.576	**bricklaying**
KT.577	**installing**
KT.578	**cable laying**
KT.579	**glazing (glass)**
KT.580	**pipe-fitting**
KT.581	**gas fitting**
KT.582	**pipelaying**
KT.583	**paperhanging**
KT.584	**paving**
KT.585	**pile driving**
KT.586	**pouring concrete**
KT.587	**shingling**
KT.588	**slating**

May be used in combination with other descriptors (e.g., **upholstered** + **chairs**; **half-timber** + **cottages**; **Medieval** + **painting**; **gilded** + **bronze**).

KT.589 **thatching**
KT.590 **tile laying**
KT.591 **preparing**
KT.592 **processing**
KT.593 **production**
KT.594 *<protective processes>*
KT.595 **fireproofing**
KT.596 **frostproofing**
KT.597 **rustproofing**
KT.598 **soundproofing**
KT.599 **waterproofing**
KT.600 *<removal processes and techniques>*
KT.601 **abrasion**
KT.602 **sanding**
KT.603 **broaching**
KT.604 **dehumidification**
KT.605 **desalination**
KT.606 **dewatering**
KT.607 **dredging**
KT.608 **drilling**
KT.609 **drying**
KT.610 **erasing**
KT.611 **excavation**
KT.612 **grading**
KT.613 **tunneling**
KT.614 **filing**
KT.615 **grinding**
KT.616 **levigation**
KT.617 **mining**
KT.618 **strip mining**
KT.619 **picking**
KT.620 **planing**
KT.621 **quarrying**
KT.622 **scraping**
KT.623 **skinning**
KT.624 **stripping**
KT.625 *<restorative processes and techniques>*
KT.626 **compensation (restoring)**
KT.627 **inpainting**
KT.628 **conservation**
KT.629 **remodeling**
KT.630 **renovation**
KT.631 **repairing**
KT.632 **anastylosis**
KT.633 **restoration**
KT.634 **retrofitting**
KT.635 **separating**
KT.636 **carding**
KT.637 **combing**

KT.638 dispersion
KT.639 diffusion
KT.640 filtration
KT.641 leaching
KT.642 stabilizing
KT.643 strengthening
KT.644 consolidation (masonry)
KT.645 lining
KT.646 strip-lining
KT.647 matting
KT.648 prestressing
KT.649 post tensioning
KT.650 pretensioning
KT.651 shoring
KT.652 supporting
KT.653 mounting
KT.654 dry mounting
KT.655 *<surface coating and decorating processes and techniques>*
KT.656 coating
KT.657 colorwashing
KT.658 enameling
KT.659 basse-taille
KT.660 champlevé
KT.661 cloisonné
KT.662 filigree enameling
KT.663 copper enameling
KT.664 counter-enameling
KT.665 en ronde bosse
KT.666 plique-à-jour
KT.667 flocking
KT.668 lacquering
KT.669 japanning
KT.670 painting (coating)
KT.671 sealing
KT.672 heat-sealing
KT.673 varnishing
KT.674 whitewashing
KT.675 embossing
KT.676 goffering
KT.677 engraving (surface decorating)
KT.678 diamond-point engraving
KT.679 siderography
KT.680 wheel-engraving
KT.681 etching (surface decorating)
KT.682 pyrography
KT.683 finishing
KT.684 barreling
KT.685 floating (surface finishing)
KT.686 polishing

May be used in combination with other descriptors (e.g., **upholstered** + **chairs**; **half-timber** + **cottages**; **Medieval** + **painting**; **gilded** + **bronze**).

KT.687 burnishing
KT.688 ball-burnishing
KT.689 electropolishing
KT.690 incising
KT.691 scarifying
KT.692 infusing
KT.693 *<ink and paint application techniques>*
KT.694 brushwork
KT.695 rolling-up
KT.696 spattering
KT.697 splashing
KT.698 stippling
KT.699 tapping out
KT.700 inlay
KT.701 Cosmati work
KT.702 mosaic
KT.703 pietra dure
KT.704 niello
KT.705 lathing
KT.706 marquetry
KT.707 boulle work
KT.708 intarsia
KT.709 parquetry
KT.710 metallizing
KT.711 bronzing
KT.712 gilding
KT.713 amalgam-gilding
KT.714 garm-mulamma
KT.715 mordant gilding
KT.716 water gilding
KT.717 silvering
KT.718 amalgam-silvering
KT.719 plastering
KT.720 furring
KT.721 sizing
KT.722 stuccoing
KT.723 tooling
KT.724 upholstery
KT.725 veneering
KT.726 *<temperature related processes>*
KT.727 combustion
KT.728 cooling
KT.729 freezing
KT.730 refrigeration
KT.731 heating
KT.732 annealing
KT.733 tempering
KT.734 thawing
KT.735 *<transferring and transferring techniques>*

May be used in combination with other descriptors (e.g., **upholstered** + **chairs**; **half-timber** + **cottages**; **Medieval** + **painting**; **gilded** + **bronze**).

KT.736 **transferring**
KT.737 **stacco**
KT.738 **strappo**
KT.739 *<transferring techniques>*
KT.740 **brass rubbing**
KT.741 **decalcomania**
KT.742 **frottage**
KT.743 **pouncing**
KT.744 **spolvero**
KT.745 **pricking**
KT.746 **printing**
KT.747 **double-printing**
KT.748 **overprinting**
KT.749 **registering**
KT.750 **transfer printing**
KT.751 **squaring (transferring technique)**
KT.752 **stenciling**
KT.753 **film-stencil method**
KT.754 **pochoir**
KT.755 **tracing**
KT.756 **transporting**
KT.757 **lifting**
KT.758 **mailing**
KT.759 **shipping**
KT.760 *<processes and techniques by material>*
KT.761 **caning**
KT.762 **glassworking**
KT.763 **fire polishing**
KT.764 **flashing (glassworking)**
KT.765 **glassblowing**
KT.766 *<glass painting techniques>*
KT.767 **reverse painting on glass**
KT.768 **verre églomisé**
KT.769 **lapidary**
KT.770 **glyptics**
KT.771 **leatherworking**
KT.772 **curing (leather)**
KT.773 **currying**
KT.774 **tanning**
KT.775 **dressing (leather)**
KT.776 *<metalworking and metalworking processes and techniques>*
KT.777 **metalworking**
KT.778 **art metalworking**
KT.779 **brass-smithing**
KT.780 **coppersmithing**
KT.781 **goldsmithing**
KT.782 **ironworking**
KT.783 **blacksmithing**
KT.784 **pewtersmithing**

May be used in combination with other descriptors (e.g., **upholstered** + **chairs**; **half-timber** + **cottages**; **Medieval** + **painting**; **gilded** + **bronze**).

KT.785 silversmithing
KT.786 tinsmithing
KT.787 *<metalworking processes and techniques>*
KT.788 *<metal assembling processes and techniques>*
KT.789 soldering
KT.790 brazing
KT.791 arc brazing
KT.792 dip brazing
KT.793 furnace brazing
KT.794 induction brazing
KT.795 resistance brazing
KT.796 torch brazing
KT.797 vacuum brazing
KT.798 welding
KT.799 braze welding
KT.800 electric welding
KT.801 arc welding
KT.802 projection welding
KT.803 shielded metal arc welding
KT.804 stud welding
KT.805 resistance welding
KT.806 forge welding
KT.807 friction welding
KT.808 fusion welding
KT.809 electron beam welding
KT.810 gas welding
KT.811 laser welding
KT.812 pressure welding
KT.813 cold welding
KT.814 ultrasonic welding
KT.815 *<metal coating processes and techniques>*
KT.816 aluminizing
KT.817 galvanizing
KT.818 electrogalvanizing
KT.819 hot-dip galvanizing
KT.820 plating
KT.821 electroless plating
KT.822 electroplating
KT.823 ion plating
KT.824 sherardizing
KT.825 metal-cutting
KT.826 blanking
KT.827 electric metal-cutting
KT.828 electrochemical cutting
KT.829 laser beam cutting
KT.830 thermal cutting
KT.831 ultrasonic metal-cutting
KT.832 *<metal decorating techniques>*
KT.833 chasing

May be used in combination with other descriptors (e.g., **upholstered** + **chairs**; **half-timber** + **cottages**; **Medieval** + **painting**; **gilded** + **bronze**).

KT.834 ciselure
KT.835 damascening
KT.836 granulation (metal finishing)
KT.837 repoussé
KT.838 *<metal finishing processes and techniques>*
KT.839 anodizing
KT.840 hammering
KT.841 pickling (metal finishing)
KT.842 surface hardening
KT.843 case-hardening
KT.844 *<metal forming processes and techniques>*
KT.845 drawing (metalworking)
KT.846 forging
KT.847 upset forging
KT.848 founding
KT.849 hot-rolling
KT.850 metal-spinning
KT.851 milling (metalworking)
KT.852 smelting
KT.853 swaging
KT.854 paperworking techniques
KT.855 origami
KT.856 papermaking
KT.857 couching (papermaking)
KT.858 deckling
KT.859 *<pottery techniques>*
KT.860 coiling
KT.861 cord marking
KT.862 firing (ceramics)
KT.863 bonfire firing
KT.864 *<pottery decorating techniques>*
KT.865 bat printing
KT.866 encaustic decoration
KT.867 glazing
KT.868 cuenca
KT.869 cuerda seca
KT.870 overglazing
KT.871 underglazing
KT.872 mishima
KT.873 slip trailing
KT.874 slab method
KT.875 slip casting
KT.876 throwing (pottery technique)
KT.877 *<woodworking and woodworking processes and techniques>*
KT.878 woodworking
KT.879 carpentry
KT.880 woodcarving
KT.881 chip carving
KT.882 *<woodworking processes and techniques>*

May be used in combination with other descriptors (e.g., **upholstered** + **chairs**; **half-timber** + **cottages**; **Medieval** + **painting**; **gilded** + **bronze**).

KT.883	kerfing
KT.884	pickling (woodworking)
KT.885	*<conditions and effects>*
KT.886	buckling
KT.887	elastic buckling
KT.888	inelastic buckling
KT.889	lateral buckling
KT.890	curling
KT.891	damage
KT.892	defects
KT.893	deterioration
KT.894	chipping
KT.895	corrosion
KT.896	electrochemical corrosion
KT.897	rusting
KT.898	crumbling
KT.899	decay
KT.900	embrittlement
KT.901	erosion
KT.902	oxidative-reductive deterioration
KT.903	silver mirroring
KT.904	sulfiding
KT.905	weathering
KT.906	discoloration
KT.907	color shift
KT.908	fading
KT.909	foxing
KT.910	*<photographic reversal effects>*
KT.911	Sabattier effect
KT.912	*<size-related conditions and effects>*
KT.913	contraction
KT.914	expansion
KT.915	shrinkage
KT.916	*<surface changing conditions and effects>*
KT.917	bleeding
KT.918	blistering
KT.919	cracking
KT.920	crazing
KT.921	peeling
KT.922	delamination
KT.923	flaking
KT.924	pitting
KT.925	spalling
KT.926	wrinkling
KT.927	thermal bridges
KT.928	vitrification
KT.929	warping

May be used in combination with other descriptors (e.g., **upholstered** + **chairs**; **half-timber** + **cottages**; **Medieval** + **painting**; **gilded** + **bronze**).

Materials facet

The Materials facet deals with physical substances, whether naturally or synthetically derived. These range from specific materials to types of materials designated by their function, such as adhesives, and from raw materials to those that have been formed or processed into products that are used in fabricating structures or objects.

The Materials facet consists of the following hierarchy:

Materials (MT)

Materials Hierarchy

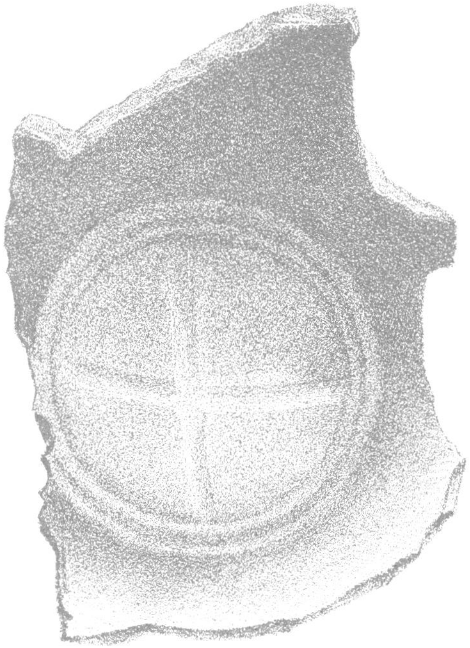

MATERIALS

Scope The Materials hierarchy contains descriptors for a broad range of substances, from natural and synthetic raw materials to material products. Material products are included here rather than in the Objects facet because they can be used in the construction of various objects (e.g., **panel** for doors or walls), and because they are not necessary constituent parts of objects (e.g., **shingles** are not essential to roofs in the same way as **roof ridges** or **eaves**).

Organization The Materials hierarchy consists of six sections. The organization of this hierarchy reflects an emphasis on the substance quality of materials rather than their numerous forms and functions, thus the majority of descriptors appear under the heading <*materials by composition or origin*>. This section is divided into the categories of <*inorganic materials*> (e.g., **cement**), **organic materials** (e.g., **coal**), and <*materials of inorganic and organic origin*> (e.g., **pigments**). Under the heading <*materials by form*> are descriptors for common forms in which materials are produced (e.g., **sheet**). Under <*materials by function*> are descriptors for classes of materials that denote the particular purpose they serve (e.g., **adhesives**, **solvents**) as well as broad headings for materials relating to specific activities (e.g., **building materials**). Other sections are <*materials by technique*> (e.g., **metalwork**, **pargeting**) and <*materials by property*> (e.g., **fire-resistant materials**).

Relation to Other Hierarchies Descriptors denoting activities performed on or with materials are found in the Processes and Techniques hierarchy (e.g., **glassworking**). Tools used in the creation of image types (e.g., **pen**, **brush**) appear in the Tools and Equipment hierarchy.

Descriptor Form and Use Most descriptors appear as singular nouns. Classes of materials (e.g., **flammable materials**) appear as plural nouns. Descriptors may be combined with those from other hierarchies (e.g., **stained glass** + **windows**; **tortoise shell** + **faux finish**).

Number of Descriptors 2626

Synopsis

MT.1 **materials**
MT.2 *<materials by composition or origin>*
MT.3 *<inorganic materials*
MT.4 **argon**
|
MT.578 **stone**
MT.909 **organic materials**
MT.910 **animal materials**
|
MT.1466 **resin**
MT.1510 *<materials of inorganic and organic origin>*
MT.1511 **colorant**
|
MT.2187 **wax**
MT.2208 *<materials by form>*
MT.2209 **aerosol**
|
MT.2285 **wicker**
MT.2286 *<materials by form: state>*
MT.2287 **gases**
|
MT.2290 **solids**
MT.2291 *<materials by function>*
MT.2292 **abrasives**
|
MT.2737 **wrapping materials**
MT.2738 *<materials by technique>*
MT.2739 **canework**
|
MT.2784 **woodwork**
MT.2787 *<materials by property>*
MT.2788 **abrasion-resistant materials**
|
MT.2811 **pyroclastic materials**

MATERIALS (MT)

MT.1	materials
MT.2	*<materials by composition or origin>*
MT.3	*<inorganic materials>*
MT.4	argon
MT.5	*<cement and cement products>*
MT.6	cement
MT.7	*<cement by composition or origin>*
MT.8	aluminous cement
MT.9	asbestos-cement
MT.10	asphalt cement
MT.11	portland cement
MT.12	high-early-strength cement
MT.13	low-heat cement
MT.14	masonry cement
MT.15	modified portland cement
MT.16	portland-pozzolan cement
MT.17	portland slag cement
MT.18	standard portland cement
MT.19	sulfate-resistant cement
MT.20	glass reinforced cement
MT.21	granite-powder cement
MT.22	gypsum cement
MT.23	Keene's cement
MT.24	Mack's cement
MT.25	Martin's cement
MT.26	Parian cement
MT.27	magnesia cement
MT.28	natural cement
MT.29	neat cement
MT.30	oxychloric cement
MT.31	polymer-impregnated cement
MT.32	pozzolan cement
MT.33	slag cement
MT.34	soil cement
MT.35	sulfur cement
MT.36	tabby
MT.37	*<cement by property>*
MT.38	accelerated cement
MT.39	brick cement
MT.40	expanding cement
MT.41	*<cement products>*
MT.42	calcium silicate brick
MT.43	sand-lime brick
MT.44	chalk
MT.45	black chalk
MT.46	fabricated chalk
MT.47	Conté crayon (TM)
MT.48	precipitated chalk
MT.49	red chalk

May be used in combination with other descriptors (e.g., **marble** + **floors**; **granite** + **faux finishing**).

MT.50 <*clay and clay products*>
MT.51   **clay**
MT.52   <*clay by composition or origin*>
MT.53   **ball clay**
MT.54   **banco**
MT.55   **catlinite**
MT.56   **kaolin**
MT.57   **malm**
MT.58   **marl**
MT.59   **slip**
MT.60   **Albany slip clay**
MT.61   **bentonite**
MT.62   <*clay by function*>
MT.63   **fireclay**
MT.64   **potter's clay**
MT.65   **clay products**
MT.66   **brick**
MT.67   <*brick by form*>
MT.68   <*brick by form: shape or size*>
MT.69   **angle brick**
MT.70   **brick slip**
MT.71   **bullnose brick**
MT.72   **compass brick**
MT.73   **cutter**
MT.74   **dogleg brick**
MT.75   **great brick**
MT.76   **tax brick**
MT.77   **jumbo brick**
MT.78   **modular building brick**
MT.79   **SCR brick**
MT.80   **Norman brick**
MT.81   **plinth brick**
MT.82   **Roman brick**
MT.83   **soap (brick)**
MT.84   **splay brick**
MT.85   **squint brick**
MT.86   <*brick by form: solidity*>
MT.87   **cellular brick**
MT.88   **hollow brick**
MT.89   **perforated brick**
MT.90   **solid brick**
MT.91   <*brick by function*>
MT.92   **air brick**
MT.93   **backing brick**
MT.94   **building brick**
MT.95   **capping brick**
MT.96   **saddle-back coping brick**
MT.97   **engineering brick**
MT.98   **blue brick**

May be used in combination with other descriptors (e.g., **marble** + **floors**; **granite** + **faux finishing**).

MT

MT.99 face brick
MT.100 ashlar brick
MT.101 rustic brick
MT.102 fire brick
MT.103 copper brick
MT.104 floor brick
MT.105 furring brick
MT.106 paving brick
MT.107 Flemish brick
MT.108 pamment
MT.109 pilaster brick
MT.110 *<brick by location or context>*
MT.111 closer
MT.112 king closer
MT.113 quarter closer
MT.114 queen closer
MT.115 *<brick by technique>*
MT.116 *<brick by technique: drying process>*
MT.117 fired brick
MT.118 hard-burned brick
MT.119 clinker brick
MT.120 soft brick
MT.121 grizzle
MT.122 place brick
MT.123 sammel brick
MT.124 sun-dried brick
MT.125 adobe
MT.126 bitudobe
MT.127 torchis
MT.128 *<brick by technique: shaping process>*
MT.129 handmade brick
MT.130 axed brick
MT.131 gauged brick
MT.132 stock brick
MT.133 molded brick
MT.134 fletton
MT.135 soft-mud brick
MT.136 sand-struck brick
MT.137 water-struck brick
MT.138 pressed brick
MT.139 stiff-mud brick
MT.140 wire-cut brick
MT.141 end-cut brick
MT.142 side-cut brick
MT.143 *<ceramics and ceramic products>*
MT.144 ceramics
MT.145 porcelain
MT.146 hard paste porcelain
MT.147 soft paste porcelain

May be used in combination with other descriptors (e.g., **marble** + **floors**; **granite** + **faux finishing**).

MT.148	pottery
MT.149	earthenware
MT.150	creamware
MT.151	delftware
MT.152	faience
MT.153	maiolica
MT.154	majolica
MT.155	redware
MT.156	raku
MT.157	stoneware
MT.158	*<ceramic products>*
MT.159	ceramic tile
MT.160	*<ceramic tile by form>*
MT.161	book tile
MT.162	carreau
MT.163	imbrex
MT.164	quarry tile
MT.165	*<ceramic tile by function>*
MT.166	draintile
MT.167	mathematical tile
MT.168	structural clay tile
MT.169	fireproofing tile
MT.170	partition tile
MT.171	weather tile
MT.172	roofing tile
MT.173	*<roofing tile by form>*
MT.174	French tile
MT.175	pan-and-roll roofing tile
MT.176	Roman tile
MT.177	shingle tile
MT.178	Spanish tile
MT.179	*<roofing tile by function>*
MT.180	cover tile
MT.181	pantile
MT.182	*<roofing tile by location or context>*
MT.183	crest tile
MT.184	eaves tile
MT.185	hip tile
MT.186	bonnet hip tile
MT.187	ridge tile
MT.188	valley tile
MT.189	*<ceramic tile by technique>*
MT.190	azulejo
MT.191	faience tile
MT.192	cob
MT.193	terracotta
MT.194	*<concrete and concrete products>*
MT.195	concrete
MT.196	*<concrete by composition or origin>*

MT

May be used in combination with other descriptors (e.g., **marble** + **floors**; **granite** + **faux finishing**).

MT.197	asphalt concrete
MT.198	béton
MT.199	cinder concrete
MT.200	colloidal concrete
MT.201	cyclopean concrete
MT.202	fibro-concrete
MT.203	lime concrete
MT.204	polymer-impregnated concrete
MT.205	rubble concrete
MT.206	slag concrete
MT.207	*<concrete by function>*
MT.208	insulating concrete
MT.209	Zonolite concrete (TM)
MT.210	*<concrete by technique>*
MT.211	air-entrained concrete
MT.212	foamed concrete
MT.213	foamed sand concrete
MT.214	foamed slag concrete
MT.215	gunite
MT.216	precast concrete
MT.217	prestressed concrete
MT.218	post-tensioned prestressed concrete
MT.219	ready-mixed concrete
MT.220	reinforced concrete
MT.221	*<concrete by property>*
MT.222	expansive concrete
MT.223	frost-resistant concrete
MT.224	heat-resistant concrete
MT.225	high-strength concrete
MT.226	lightweight concrete
MT.227	no-fines concrete
MT.228	normal-weight concrete
MT.229	porous concrete
MT.230	sulfate-resistant concrete
MT.231	concrete products
MT.232	concrete block
MT.233	cinder block
MT.234	*<glass and glass products>*
MT.235	glass
MT.236	*<glass by composition or origin>*
MT.237	borosilicate glass
MT.238	Pyrex (TM)
MT.239	flint glass
MT.240	paste (glass)
MT.241	rhinestone
MT.242	fused silica glass
MT.243	lead glass
MT.244	crystal
MT.245	soda lime glass

May be used in combination with other descriptors (e.g., **marble** + **floors**; **granite** + **faux finishing**).

MT.246 *<glass by form>*
MT.247 glass wool
MT.248 leaded glass
MT.249 plate glass
MT.250 sheet glass
MT.251 double strength window glass
MT.252 greenhouse glass
MT.253 single strength window glass
MT.254 *<glass by technique>*
MT.255 blown glass
MT.256 cased glass
MT.257 cellular glass
MT.258 crown glass
MT.259 cylinder glass
MT.260 drawn glass
MT.261 float glass
MT.262 ground glass
MT.263 pot glass
MT.264 rolled glass
MT.265 silvered glass
MT.266 stained glass
MT.267 Venetian glass
MT.268 *<glass by property>*
MT.269 architectural glass
MT.270 Carrara structural glass
MT.271 figured glass
MT.272 spandrel glass
MT.273 Vitrolite (TM)
MT.274 glare-reducing glass
MT.275 heat-absorbing glass
MT.276 heat-resisting glass
MT.277 heat-strengthened glass
MT.278 insulating glass
MT.279 nonreflective glass
MT.280 opal glass
MT.281 optical glass
MT.282 photosensitive glass
MT.283 prismatic glass
MT.284 reflective glass
MT.285 safety glass
MT.286 bullet-resistant glass
MT.287 wired glass
MT.288 x-ray protective glass
MT.289 *<glass products>*
MT.290 glass block
MT.291 glassware
MT.292 *<inorganic compounds>*
MT.293 acid
MT.294 acetic acid

May be used in combination with other descriptors (e.g., **marble** + **floors**; **granite** + **faux finishing**).

MT.295	vinegar
MT.296	carbolic acid
MT.297	fatty acid
MT.298	hydrochloric acid
MT.299	aqua regia
MT.300	hydrofluoric acid
MT.301	nitric acid
MT.302	sulfuric acid
MT.303	alkali
MT.304	potassium hydroxide
MT.305	sodium hydroxide
MT.306	ammonia
MT.307	halide
MT.308	silver halide
MT.309	silver bromide
MT.310	silver chloride
MT.311	silver iodide
MT.312	nitrous oxide
MT.313	sulfur dioxide
MT.314	water
MT.315	*<water by property>*
MT.316	fresh water
MT.317	hard water
MT.318	salt water
MT.319	soft water
MT.320	*<water by quality>*
MT.321	distilled water
MT.322	drinking water
MT.323	*<water by state>*
MT.324	ice
MT.325	water vapor
MT.326	steam
MT.327	lime
MT.328	hydrated lime
MT.329	quicklime
MT.330	fat lime
MT.331	meager lime
MT.332	*<metal and metal products>*
MT.333	metal
MT.334	*<metal by composition or origin>*
MT.335	alloys
MT.336	iron alloys
MT.337	cast iron
MT.338	ductile iron
MT.339	gray iron
MT.340	high-alloy iron
MT.341	white iron
MT.342	steel
MT.343	*<steel by composition or origin>*

May be used in combination with other descriptors (e.g., **marble** + **floors**; **granite** + **faux finishing**).

MT.344 carbon steel
MT.345 low-carbon steel
MT.346 medium-carbon steel
MT.347 high-carbon steel
MT.348 steel alloys
MT.349 chrome steel
MT.350 chrome-vanadium steel
MT.351 stainless steel
MT.352 austenitic stainless steel
MT.353 martensitic stainless steel
MT.354 high-strength low-alloy steel
MT.355 nickel steel
MT.356 steel-aluminum alloys
MT.357 titanium steel
MT.358 *<steel by function>*
MT.359 structural steel
MT.360 structural iron
MT.361 wrought iron
MT.362 nonferrous alloys
MT.363 aluminum alloys
MT.364 aluminum-silicon alloy
MT.365 aluminum-zinc alloy
MT.366 duralumin
MT.367 chromium alloys
MT.368 copper alloys
MT.369 aluminum bronze
MT.370 copper-beryllium alloys
MT.371 copper-nickel alloys
MT.372 copper-silicon alloys
MT.373 copper-tin alloys
MT.374 admiralty metal
MT.375 bronze
MT.376 architectural bronze
MT.377 bell metal
MT.378 manganese bronze
MT.379 nickel bronze
MT.380 statuary bronze
MT.381 gunmetal
MT.382 lead bronze
MT.383 phosphor bronze
MT.384 copper-zinc alloys
MT.385 brass
MT.386 cartridge brass
MT.387 naval brass
MT.388 red brass
MT.389 Muntz metal
MT.390 silicon bronze
MT.391 gold alloys
MT.392 *<gold alloys by composition or origin>*

May be used in combination with other descriptors (e.g., **marble** + **floors**; **granite** + **faux finishing**).

MT.393	electrum
MT.394	green gold
MT.395	rose gold
MT.396	white gold
MT.397	*<gold alloys by quality>*
MT.398	eighteen-carat gold
MT.399	fourteen-carat gold
MT.400	lead alloys
MT.401	nickel alloys
MT.402	German silver
MT.403	monel
MT.404	silver alloys
MT.405	sterling silver
MT.406	tin alloys
MT.407	Babbitt metal
MT.408	pewter
MT.409	Ashberry metal
MT.410	britannia metal
MT.411	English britannia metal
MT.412	minofor
MT.413	queen's metal
MT.414	Dutch white metal
MT.415	English pewter
MT.416	Hanover white metal
MT.417	Koeller's alloy
MT.418	Roman pewter
MT.419	Tutanic metal
MT.420	solder
MT.421	fine solder
MT.422	hard solder
MT.423	medium solder
MT.424	white metal
MT.425	bidri
MT.426	zinc alloys
MT.427	iron
MT.428	nonferrous metals
MT.429	aluminum
MT.430	structural aluminum
MT.431	antimony
MT.432	cadmium
MT.433	chromium
MT.434	copper
MT.435	gold
MT.436	lead
MT.437	magnesium
MT.438	manganese
MT.439	mercury
MT.440	nickel
MT.441	palladium

May be used in combination with other descriptors (e.g., **marble** + **floors**; **granite** + **faux finishing**).

MT.442 platinum
MT.443 <*silver and silver compounds*>
MT.444 silver
MT.445 <*silver compounds*>
MT.446 silver nitrate
MT.447 silver phosphate
MT.448 tin
MT.449 titanium
MT.450 tungsten
MT.451 uranium
MT.452 vanadium
MT.453 zinc
MT.454 <*metal by form*>
MT.455 foil
MT.456 ingots
MT.457 leaf
MT.458 plate
MT.459 <*plate by material*>
MT.460 gold plate
MT.461 vermeil
MT.462 silver plate
MT.463 Sheffield plate
MT.464 <*plate by technique*>
MT.465 electroplate
MT.466 ormolu
MT.467 terneplate
MT.468 <*metal by quality*>
MT.469 precious metal
MT.470 scrap metal
MT.471 metal products
MT.472 bidriware
MT.473 cermets
MT.474 cladding
MT.475 expanded metal
MT.476 forgings
MT.477 metalware
MT.478 tinware
MT.479 scoria
MT.480 steel wool
MT.481 wire
MT.482 barbed wire
MT.483 chicken wire
MT.484 piano wire
MT.485 minerals
MT.486 <*minerals by composition or origin*>
MT.487 apatite
MT.488 asbestos
MT.489 augite
MT.490 beryl

May be used in combination with other descriptors (e.g., **marble** + **floors**; **granite** + **faux finishing**).

MT.491	aquamarine
MT.492	emerald
MT.493	golden beryl
MT.494	morganite
MT.495	borax
MT.496	calcite
MT.497	chlorite
MT.498	corundum
MT.499	emery
MT.500	ruby
MT.501	sapphire
MT.502	diamond
MT.503	enstatite
MT.504	epidote
MT.505	feldspar
MT.506	microcline
MT.507	moonstone
MT.508	orthoclase
MT.509	plagioclase
MT.510	*<ferrous minerals>*
MT.511	hematite
MT.512	limonite
MT.513	magnetite
MT.514	marcasite
MT.515	pyrite
MT.516	siderite
MT.517	fluorite
MT.518	garnet
MT.519	graphite
MT.520	gypsum
MT.521	alabaster
MT.522	calcined gypsum
MT.523	selenite
MT.524	uncalcined gypsum
MT.525	jade
MT.526	nephrite
MT.527	jadeite
MT.528	jet
MT.529	lapis lazuli
MT.530	lepidolite
MT.531	magnesite
MT.532	malachite
MT.533	meerschaum
MT.534	mica
MT.535	muscovite (mica)
MT.536	phlogopite
MT.537	vermiculite
MT.538	olivine
MT.539	opal

May be used in combination with other descriptors (e.g., **marble** + **floors**; **granite** + **faux finishing**).

MT.540 **ore**
MT.541 **silica**
MT.542 **quartz**
MT.543 **amethyst**
MT.544 **bitstone**
MT.545 **chalcedony**
MT.546 **agate**
MT.547 **carnelian**
MT.548 **onyx**
MT.549 **sardonyx**
MT.550 **bloodstone**
MT.551 **chert**
MT.552 **chrysoprase**
MT.553 **jasper**
MT.554 **flint**
MT.555 **gunflint**
MT.556 **potter's flint**
MT.557 **touchstone**
MT.558 **quartz crystal**
MT.559 **aventurine**
MT.560 **rose quartz**
MT.561 **sulfur**
MT.562 **talc**
MT.563 **asbestine**
MT.564 **French chalk**
MT.565 **topaz**
MT.566 **tourmaline**
MT.567 **turquoise**
MT.568 **zircon**
MT.569 **hyacinth**
MT.570 **gems**
MT.571 **birthstones**
MT.572 **industrial jewels**
MT.573 **precious stones**
MT.574 **semiprecious stones**
MT.575 **ocher**
MT.576 **selenium**
MT.577 **silicon**
MT.578 **stone**
MT.579 *<stone by composition or origin>*
MT.580 **igneous rock**
MT.581 *<igneous rock by composition>*
MT.582 *<igneous rock by composition: chemical>*
MT.583 **acid igneous rock**
MT.584 **dacite**
MT.585 **felsite**
MT.586 **granite**
MT.587 *<granite by composition: physical>*
MT.588 **microgranite**

May be used in combination with other descriptors (e.g., **marble** + **floors**; **granite** + **faux finishing**).

MT.589 pegmatite
MT.590 graphic granite
MT.591 petuntze
MT.592 *<granite by color>*
MT.593 gray granite
MT.594 Barre granite
MT.595 Cornish granite
MT.596 Wicklow granite
MT.597 pink granite
MT.598 Milford granite
MT.599 shap granite
MT.600 red granite
MT.601 luxullianite
MT.602 Minnesota granite
MT.603 rapakivi
MT.604 granodiorite
MT.605 rhyolite
MT.606 basic igneous rock
MT.607 basalt
MT.608 pietra di paragone
MT.609 diabase
MT.610 gabbro
MT.611 intermediate igneous rock
MT.612 andesite
MT.613 diorite
MT.614 mica diorite
MT.615 quartz diorite
MT.616 syenite
MT.617 *<igneous rock by composition: physical>*
MT.618 porphyry
MT.619 quartz porphyry
MT.620 elvan
MT.621 red antique porphyry
MT.622 *<igneous rock by origin>*
MT.623 plutonic rock
MT.624 volcanic rock
MT.625 lava
MT.626 pumice
MT.627 pyroclastic rock
MT.628 obsidian
MT.629 marekanite
MT.630 perlite
MT.631 tachylite
MT.632 trass
MT.633 tufa
MT.634 tuff
MT.635 peperino
MT.636 sperone
MT.637 santorin

May be used in combination with other descriptors (e.g., **marble** + **floors**; **granite** + **faux finishing**).

- MT.638 **sedimentary rock**
  - MT.639 *<sedimentary rock by composition>*
    - MT.640 **argillaceous rock**
      - MT.641 **argillite**
      - MT.642 **clay stone**
      - MT.643 **marlstone**
      - MT.644 **mudstone**
      - MT.645 **shale**
        - MT.646 **clay shale**
    - MT.647 **carbonate rock**
      - MT.648 **caliche**
      - MT.649 **limestone**
        - MT.650 *<limestone by composition>*
          - MT.651 *<limestone by composition: aggregate type>*
            - MT.652 *<fossiliferous limestone>*
              - MT.653 **algal limestone**
              - MT.654 **bryozoa limestone**
              - MT.655 **coral limestone**
              - MT.656 **crinoidal limestone**
              - MT.657 **Shelly limestone**
                - MT.658 **beer stone**
                - MT.659 **clipsham stone**
                - MT.660 **coquina rock**
                - MT.661 **purbeck marble**
            - MT.662 **oolitic limestone**
              - MT.663 **Alabama limestone**
              - MT.664 **Bangor limestone**
              - MT.665 **Batesville marble**
              - MT.666 **Bath stone**
              - MT.667 **Caen stone**
              - MT.668 **Indiana limestone**
                - MT.669 **Bedford stone**
              - MT.670 **Ketton stone**
              - MT.671 **Portland stone**
              - MT.672 **Weldon stone**
            - MT.673 **pisolitic limestone**
            - MT.674 **poros**
            - MT.675 **travertine**
              - MT.676 **onyx marble**
              - MT.677 **Tabrez marble**
          - MT.678 *<limestone by composition: binder type>*
            - MT.679 **argillaceous limestone**
              - MT.680 **hydraulic limestone**
              - MT.681 **Queenston limestone**
            - MT.682 **carbonaceous limestone**
            - MT.683 **ferruginous limestone**
            - MT.684 **magnesian limestone**
              - MT.685 **dolomite**
              - MT.686 **solnhofen stone**

May be used in combination with other descriptors (e.g., **marble** + **floors**; **granite** + **faux finishing**).

MT.687 siliceous limestone
MT.688 *<limestone by pattern or texture>*
MT.689 ragstone
MT.690 Barnack stone
MT.691 river marble
MT.692 rottenstone
MT.693 ruin marble
MT.694 variegated limestone
MT.695 *<limestone by quality>*
MT.696 Old Gothic limestone
MT.697 rustic limestone
MT.698 select limestone
MT.699 standard limestone
MT.700 statuary limestone
MT.701 sandstone
MT.702 *<sandstone by composition>*
MT.703 *<sandstone by composition: aggregate type>*
MT.704 gritstone
MT.705 holystone
MT.706 siltstone
MT.707 *<sandstone by composition: binder type>*
MT.708 argillaceous sandstone
MT.709 bluestone
MT.710 Hudson bluestone
MT.711 North River bluestone
MT.712 Wyoming Valley stone
MT.713 graywacke
MT.714 calcareous sandstone
MT.715 reigate stone
MT.716 feldspathic sandstone
MT.717 ferruginous sandstone
MT.718 Arizona flagstone
MT.719 brownstone
MT.720 Portland sandstone
MT.721 Seneca sandstone
MT.722 micaceous sandstone
MT.723 siliceous sandstone
MT.724 Amherst sandstone
MT.725 Aquia Creek sandstone
MT.726 Dunville sandstone
MT.727 Potsdam sandstone
MT.728 Stancliffe sandstone
MT.729 *<sedimentary rock by form>*
MT.730 concretionary stone
MT.731 septaria
MT.732 oolite
MT.733 rudaceous rock
MT.734 breccia
MT.735 Potomac breccia

May be used in combination with other descriptors (e.g., **marble** + **floors**; **granite** + **faux finishing**).

MT.736 conglomerate
MT.737 carstone
MT.738 puddingstone
MT.739 metamorphic rock
MT.740 gneiss
MT.741 hornfels
MT.742 marble
MT.743 *<marble by composition or origin>*
MT.744 calcite marble
MT.745 Minnesota stone
MT.746 *<marble by form or function>*
MT.747 breccia marble
MT.748 breccia a semesanto
MT.749 breccia corallina
MT.750 breccia di Settebasi
MT.751 breccia traccagnina
MT.752 breche violette marble
MT.753 broccatellone
MT.754 Egyptian breccia marble
MT.755 marmor Africano
MT.756 mischio marble
MT.757 rosso brecciato
MT.758 Sarrancolin marble
MT.759 forest marble
MT.760 fortification marble
MT.761 Lyonaise marble
MT.762 madrepore marble
MT.763 pagoda stone
MT.764 shell marble
MT.765 brocatello
MT.766 lepanto marble
MT.767 lumachella
MT.768 occhio di pavone
MT.769 Sussex marble
MT.770 statuary marble
MT.771 *<marble by color or pattern>*
MT.772 black marble
MT.773 Belgian black marble
MT.774 Eleusinian marble
MT.775 Irish black marble
MT.776 lucullite
MT.777 nero antico
MT.778 Rockingham royal black marble
MT.779 Saint Anne marble
MT.780 gray marble
MT.781 bardiglio
MT.782 bardiglio 'scuro
MT.783 bardiglio fiorito
MT.784 bigio antico

May be used in combination with other descriptors (e.g., **marble** + **floors**; **granite** + **faux finishing**).

MT.785 bigio e nero antico
MT.786 bigio e nero di francia
MT.787 bigio morato
MT.788 bougard marble
MT.789 Formosa marble
MT.790 parmazo marble
MT.791 green marble
MT.792 Connemara marble
MT.793 Iona marble
MT.794 verd antique
MT.795 pink marble
MT.796 Tennessee pink marble
MT.797 red marble
MT.798 griotte marble
MT.799 Languedoc marble
MT.800 rance
MT.801 rosso de levanto marble
MT.802 rouge antique marble
MT.803 variegated marble
MT.804 bianco e giallo antico
MT.805 brocatelle marble
MT.806 campan marble
MT.807 cipollino
MT.808 cottanello
MT.809 fiore di Persico
MT.810 fiorto marble
MT.811 giallo tigrato
MT.812 Numidian marble
MT.813 paonazzo marble
MT.814 pavonazzetto
MT.815 Porta Santa marble
MT.816 portor marble
MT.817 rosso di francia
MT.818 white marble
MT.819 Alabama cream marble
MT.820 cream blanc marble
MT.821 madre cream marble
MT.822 Carrara marble
MT.823 Cockeysville marble
MT.824 Colorado yule statuary marble
MT.825 Georgia marble
MT.826 Hymettian marble
MT.827 Istrian marble
MT.828 Lee marble
MT.829 lesbio
MT.830 Luna marble
MT.831 Missouri marble
MT.832 palombino
MT.833 Parian marble

May be used in combination with other descriptors (e.g., **marble** + **floors**; **granite** + **faux finishing**).

MT.834 Pentelic marble
MT.835 porino
MT.836 tasio
MT.837 Tennessee marble
MT.838 Texas marble
MT.839 tirio
MT.840 Vermont white statuary marble
MT.841 white Cherokee marble
MT.842 Winooski marble
MT.843 yellow marble
MT.844 Lisbon yellow marble
MT.845 Siena marble
MT.846 phyllite
MT.847 quartzite
MT.848 ganister
MT.849 schist
MT.850 serpentine (rock)
MT.851 amianto
MT.852 marmolite
MT.853 pietra nefritica
MT.854 serpentina comune
MT.855 verde di genoa
MT.856 verde di levanto
MT.857 verde di pegli
MT.858 verde di ponsevera
MT.859 verde di prato
MT.860 verde di ranocchia
MT.861 slate
MT.862 *<slate by color or quality>*
MT.863 gray slate
MT.864 black slate
MT.865 blue slate
MT.866 green slate
MT.867 red slate
MT.868 purple slate
MT.869 ribbon slate
MT.870 *<slate by form or function>*
MT.871 blackboard slate
MT.872 roofing slate
MT.873 wrestler slate
MT.874 structural slate
MT.875 soapstone
MT.876 Alberene stone
MT.877 steatite
MT.878 potstone
MT.879 Virginia greenstone
MT.880 *<stone by form>*
MT.881 boulder
MT.882 cobblestone

May be used in combination with other descriptors (e.g., **marble** + **floors**; **granite** + **faux finishing**).

MT.883 beach cobble
MT.884 crushed stone
MT.885 fieldstone
MT.886 flagstone
MT.887 freestone
MT.888 gravel
MT.889 pea gravel
MT.890 megaliths
MT.891 pebble
MT.892 rock
MT.893 rubble
MT.894 sarsen
MT.895 stone dust
MT.896 marble dust
MT.897 terrazzo
MT.898 *<stone by function>*
MT.899 building stone
MT.900 dimension stone
MT.901 ashlar
MT.902 dressed stone
MT.903 roofing granules
MT.904 thackstone
MT.905 curbing
MT.906 monumental stone
MT.907 paving stone
MT.908 Belgian block
MT.909 organic materials
MT.910 animal materials
MT.911 albumin
MT.912 albumen
MT.913 antler
MT.914 blood
MT.915 bone
MT.916 casein
MT.917 coral
MT.918 star coral
MT.919 dung
MT.920 cow manure
MT.921 guano
MT.922 egg
MT.923 egg yolk
MT.924 feather
MT.925 down
MT.926 fur
MT.927 gelatin
MT.928 *<hair and hair products>*
MT.929 hair
MT.930 *<hair by composition or origin>*
MT.931 camel hair

May be used in combination with other descriptors (e.g., **marble** + **floors**; **granite** + **faux finishing**).

MT.932	goat hair
MT.933	horsehair
MT.934	human hair
MT.935	*<hair by form>*
MT.936	bristles
MT.937	whiskers
MT.938	*<hair products>*
MT.939	velum
MT.940	horn
MT.941	pearl
MT.942	quill
MT.943	shell
MT.944	abalone
MT.945	cowrie
MT.946	mother of pearl
MT.947	oyster shell
MT.948	scallop shell
MT.949	skin
MT.950	fish scales
MT.951	fishskin
MT.952	sharkskin
MT.953	hide
MT.954	leather
MT.955	buckskin
MT.956	chamois
MT.957	lizard leather
MT.958	pigskin
MT.959	snakeskin
MT.960	parchment
MT.961	vellum
MT.962	sponge
MT.963	tooth
MT.964	tusk
MT.965	ivory
MT.966	tortoise shell
MT.967	bituminous materials
MT.968	asphalt
MT.969	*<asphalt by composition or origin>*
MT.970	artificial asphalt
MT.971	petroleum asphalt
MT.972	natural asphalt
MT.973	bitumen
MT.974	maltha
MT.975	natural bitumen
MT.976	gilsonite
MT.977	lake asphalt
MT.978	rock asphalt
MT.979	*<asphalt by form>*
MT.980	liquid asphalt

May be used in combination with other descriptors (e.g., **marble** + **floors**; **granite** + **faux finishing**).

MT.981	emulsified asphalt
MT.982	*<asphalt by function>*
MT.983	paving asphalt
MT.984	*<asphalt by property>*
MT.985	rapid-curing asphalt
MT.986	slow-curing asphalt
MT.987	tar
MT.988	coal tar
MT.989	wood tar
MT.990	pine tar
MT.991	navy pitch
MT.992	coal
MT.993	anthracite
MT.994	bituminous coal
MT.995	cannel coal
MT.996	organic compounds
MT.997	camphor
MT.998	carbon dioxide
MT.999	carbon monoxide
MT.1000	chlorofluorocarbons
MT.1001	formaldehyde
MT.1002	latex
MT.1003	lipids
MT.1004	fat
MT.1005	lecithin
MT.1006	sulfide
MT.1007	*<petroleum and petroleum products>*
MT.1008	petroleum
MT.1009	petroleum products
MT.1010	gasoline
MT.1011	liquefied petroleum gas
MT.1012	butane
MT.1013	pentane
MT.1014	propane
MT.1015	petrochemicals
MT.1016	petroleum jelly
MT.1017	plant materials
MT.1018	bark
MT.1019	bark strip
MT.1020	cork
MT.1021	cane
MT.1022	rattan
MT.1023	fruit
MT.1024	berry
MT.1025	gourd
MT.1026	grass
MT.1027	bamboo
MT.1028	split bamboo
MT.1029	cutch-grass

May be used in combination with other descriptors (e.g., **marble** + **floors**; **granite** + **faux finishing**).

MT.1030 eelgrass
MT.1031 reed
MT.1032 bulrush
MT.1033 bur reed
MT.1034 pampas grass
MT.1035 sea reed
MT.1036 rush
MT.1037 husk
MT.1038 leaves
MT.1039 palm leaf
MT.1040 tobacco
MT.1041 nut
MT.1042 *<plant derivatives>*
MT.1043 agar-agar
MT.1044 cellulose
MT.1045 charcoal
MT.1046 wood charcoal
MT.1047 fusain
MT.1048 gum
MT.1049 apricot gum
MT.1050 cherry gum
MT.1051 gum arabic
MT.1052 gum karaya
MT.1053 gum thus
MT.1054 gum tragacanth
MT.1055 sarcocolla
MT.1056 pulp
MT.1057 soda pulp
MT.1058 wood-pulp
MT.1059 sap
MT.1060 saponin
MT.1061 starch
MT.1062 arrowroot
MT.1063 cassava
MT.1064 root
MT.1065 *<seed and seed components>*
MT.1066 seed
MT.1067 bean
MT.1068 corn
MT.1069 grain
MT.1070 *<seed components>*
MT.1071 pods
MT.1072 locust bean pod
MT.1073 stalk
MT.1074 cornstalk
MT.1075 guinea corn stalk
MT.1076 leafstalk
MT.1077 straw
MT.1078 barley straw

May be used in combination with other descriptors (e.g., **marble** + **floors**; **granite** + **faux finishing**).

MT.1079 rice straw
MT.1080 wheat straw
MT.1081 thorn
MT.1082 *<wood and wood products>*
MT.1083 wood
MT.1084 *<wood by composition or origin>*
MT.1085 hardwood
MT.1086 *<genus Aesculus>*
MT.1087 buckeye
MT.1088 California buckeye
MT.1089 dwarf buckeye
MT.1090 Ohio buckeye
MT.1091 yellow buckeye
MT.1092 alder
MT.1093 Alnus cremastogyne
MT.1094 Alnus pendula
MT.1095 American green alder
MT.1096 common alder
MT.1097 European green alder
MT.1098 red alder
MT.1099 seaside alder
MT.1100 ash (wood)
MT.1101 European ash
MT.1102 white ash
MT.1103 balaustre
MT.1104 beech
MT.1105 American beech
MT.1106 Chinese beech
MT.1107 European beech
MT.1108 Japanese beech
MT.1109 New Zealand beech
MT.1110 Oriental beech
MT.1111 red beech
MT.1112 Siebold's beech
MT.1113 white beech
MT.1114 birch
MT.1115 downy birch
MT.1116 dwarf birch
MT.1117 European birch
MT.1118 gray birch
MT.1119 Himalayan birch
MT.1120 paper birch
MT.1121 river birch
MT.1122 silver birch
MT.1123 sweet birch
MT.1124 yellow birch
MT.1125 boxwood
MT.1126 Maracaibo boxwood
MT.1127 brazilwood

May be used in combination with other descriptors (e.g., **marble** + **floors**; **granite** + **faux finishing**).

MT.1128 sappanwood
MT.1129 camphorwood
MT.1130 catalpa
MT.1131 chestnut
MT.1132 American chestnut
MT.1133 Chinese chestnut
MT.1134 European chestnut
MT.1135 horse chestnut
MT.1136 Japanese chestnut
MT.1137 dogwood
MT.1138 ebony
MT.1139 black ebony
MT.1140 Diospyros ebenum
MT.1141 Diospyros melanoxylos
MT.1142 kaki
MT.1143 marblewood
MT.1144 elm
MT.1145 American elm
MT.1146 Chinese elm
MT.1147 English elm
MT.1148 rock elm
MT.1149 slippery elm
MT.1150 wych elm
MT.1151 eucalyptus
MT.1152 blackbutt
MT.1153 bloodwood
MT.1154 gray ironbark
MT.1155 gumwood
MT.1156 blue gum
MT.1157 mountain ash
MT.1158 *<genus Nyssa>*
MT.1159 black gum
MT.1160 ogeche tupelo
MT.1161 swamp tupelo
MT.1162 tupelo
MT.1163 red gum
MT.1164 sweet gum
MT.1165 fig
MT.1166 fruitwood
MT.1167 hackberry
MT.1168 Chinese hackberry
MT.1169 European hackberry
MT.1170 Mississippi hackberry
MT.1171 hawthorn
MT.1172 hickory
MT.1173 big shellbark hickory
MT.1174 bitternut hickory
MT.1175 black hickory
MT.1176 mockernut hickory

May be used in combination with other descriptors (e.g., **marble** + **floors**; **granite** + **faux finishing**).

MT.1177 pecan
MT.1178 pignut hickory
MT.1179 shagbark hickory
MT.1180 holly
MT.1181 hornbeam
MT.1182 European hornbeam
MT.1183 hop hornbeam
MT.1184 American hop hornbeam
MT.1185 European hop hornbeam
MT.1186 iroko
MT.1187 ironwood
MT.1188 gangaw
MT.1189 hackia
MT.1190 Persian ironwood
MT.1191 itaùba
MT.1192 lancewood
MT.1193 lauan
MT.1194 laurel
MT.1195 lemon
MT.1196 lignum vitae
MT.1197 limba
MT.1198 locust
MT.1199 Acacia
MT.1200 koa
MT.1201 Australian locust
MT.1202 black locust
MT.1203 honey locust
MT.1204 silver wattle
MT.1205 lumbayo
MT.1206 magnolia
MT.1207 magnolia graniflora
MT.1208 mahogany
MT.1209 African mahogany
MT.1210 Borneo mahogany
MT.1211 Swietenia
MT.1212 South American mahogany
MT.1213 crotch mahogany
MT.1214 West Indies mahogany
MT.1215 white mahogany
MT.1216 mangrove
MT.1217 maple
MT.1218 bigleaf maple
MT.1219 bird's-eye maple
MT.1220 black maple
MT.1221 box elder
MT.1222 Japanese maple
MT.1223 red maple
MT.1224 silver maple
MT.1225 sugar maple

May be used in combination with other descriptors (e.g., **marble** + **floors**; **granite** + **faux finishing**).

MT.1226 tiger maple
MT.1227 merawan
MT.1228 oak
MT.1229 aleppo oak
MT.1230 Austrian oak
MT.1231 black oak
MT.1232 California black oak
MT.1233 bur oak
MT.1234 California white oak
MT.1235 chestnut oak
MT.1236 Quercus montana
MT.1237 Quercus prinus
MT.1238 chinquapin oak
MT.1239 durmast oak
MT.1240 English oak
MT.1241 European turkey oak
MT.1242 laurel oak
MT.1243 live oak
MT.1244 coast live oak
MT.1245 overcup oak
MT.1246 pin oak
MT.1247 post oak
MT.1248 red oak
MT.1249 scarlet oak
MT.1250 sessile oak
MT.1251 shumard oak
MT.1252 southern red oak
MT.1253 swamp white oak
MT.1254 valonia oak
MT.1255 western white oak
MT.1256 white oak
MT.1257 olive
MT.1258 padouk
MT.1259 partridgewood
MT.1260 pear
MT.1261 applewood
MT.1262 common pear
MT.1263 prairie crabapple
MT.1264 persimmon
MT.1265 common persimmon
MT.1266 plane wood
MT.1267 London plane wood
MT.1268 sycamore
MT.1269 poplar
MT.1270 *<poplar: subgenus aegiros>*
MT.1271 black poplar
MT.1272 eastern cottonwood
MT.1273 *<poplar: subgenus populus>*
MT.1274 American aspen

May be used in combination with other descriptors (e.g., **marble** + **floors**; **granite** + **faux finishing**).

MT.1275 **aspen**
MT.1276 **big toothed aspen**
MT.1277 **cottonwood**
MT.1278 **gray poplar**
MT.1279 **white poplar**
MT.1280 *<poplar: subgenus tacamahaca>*
MT.1281 **balm of gilead**
MT.1282 **balsam poplar**
MT.1283 **black cottonwood**
MT.1284 *<genus Prunus>*
MT.1285 **almond**
MT.1286 **apricot**
MT.1287 **cherry**
MT.1288 **black cherry**
MT.1289 **English cherry**
MT.1290 **sour cherry**
MT.1291 **sweet cherry**
MT.1292 **peach**
MT.1293 **plum**
MT.1294 **purpleheart**
MT.1295 **quebracho**
MT.1296 **rosewood**
MT.1297 **Borneo rosewood**
MT.1298 **Brazilian rosewood**
MT.1299 **Ceylon rosewood**
MT.1300 **Dalbergia**
MT.1301 **African blackwood**
MT.1302 **cocobolo**
MT.1303 **granadilla**
MT.1304 **East Indian rosewood**
MT.1305 **satinee**
MT.1306 **sassafras**
MT.1307 **American sassafras**
MT.1308 **oleum sassafras**
MT.1309 **satinwood**
MT.1310 **teak**
MT.1311 *<genus Tilia>*
MT.1312 **common lime**
MT.1313 **linden**
MT.1314 **small-leafed lime**
MT.1315 **tulipwood**
MT.1316 **violet wood**
MT.1317 **walnut**
MT.1318 **burled walnut**
MT.1319 **East India walnut**
MT.1320 **imbuia**
MT.1321 *<genus Juglans>*
MT.1322 **black walnut**
MT.1323 **butternut**

May be used in combination with other descriptors (e.g., **marble** + **floors**; **granite** + **faux finishing**).

MT.1324 English walnut
MT.1325 mahoe
MT.1326 willow
MT.1327 black willow
MT.1328 Japanese willow
MT.1329 western black willow
MT.1330 white willow
MT.1331 softwood
MT.1332 balsa wood
MT.1333 cedar
MT.1334 American arbor vitae
MT.1335 Atlantic cedar
MT.1336 deodar
MT.1337 incense cedar
MT.1338 Lebanon cedar
MT.1339 Paraguayan cedar
MT.1340 Spanish cedar
MT.1341 toon
MT.1342 chinaberry
MT.1343 cypress
MT.1344 classic cypress
MT.1345 Port Orford cedar
MT.1346 white cypress
MT.1347 yellow cypress
MT.1348 filbert
MT.1349 fir
MT.1350 balsam fir
MT.1351 Fraser's balsam fir
MT.1352 Douglas fir
MT.1353 silver fir
MT.1354 hemlock
MT.1355 eastern hemlock
MT.1356 mountain hemlock
MT.1357 western hemlock
MT.1358 juniper
MT.1359 African cedar
MT.1360 mountain juniper
MT.1361 red cedar
MT.1362 larch
MT.1363 European larch
MT.1364 Japanese larch
MT.1365 Siberian larch
MT.1366 western larch
MT.1367 mesquite
MT.1368 myrtle
MT.1369 Osage orange
MT.1370 pine
MT.1371 Austrian pine
MT.1372 Corsican pine

MT.1373 Cuban pine
MT.1374 jack pine
MT.1375 Japanese stone pine
MT.1376 Japanese white pine
MT.1377 Jeffrey pine
MT.1378 loblolly pine
MT.1379 lodgepole pine
MT.1380 longleaf pine
MT.1381 northern white pine
MT.1382 Norway pine
MT.1383 pond pine
MT.1384 ponderosa pine
MT.1385 Scotch pine
MT.1386 scrub pine
MT.1387 shortleaf pine
MT.1388 southern yellow pine
MT.1389 sugar pine
MT.1390 yellow pine
MT.1391 redwood
MT.1392 dawn redwood
MT.1393 giant sequoia
MT.1394 Humboldt redwood
MT.1395 sandalwood
MT.1396 spruce
MT.1397 black spruce
MT.1398 blue spruce
MT.1399 bog spruce
MT.1400 common spruce
MT.1401 Norway spruce
MT.1402 red spruce
MT.1403 sitka spruce
MT.1404 Engelmann spruce
MT.1405 West Himalayan spruce
MT.1406 white spruce
MT.1407 yew
MT.1408 *<wood by form or function>*
MT.1409 bentwood
MT.1410 driftwood
MT.1411 primary wood
MT.1412 secondary wood
MT.1413 wood products
MT.1414 battens
MT.1415 compressed wood
MT.1416 excelsior
MT.1417 furring strips
MT.1418 impregnated wood
MT.1419 log
MT.1420 lumber
MT.1421 *<lumber by form or function>*

May be used in combination with other descriptors (e.g., **marble** + **floors**; **granite** + **faux finishing**).

MT.1422 form lumber
MT.1423 *<lumber by technique>*
MT.1424 *<lumber by technique: processing method>*
MT.1425 dressed lumber
MT.1426 worked lumber
MT.1427 patterned lumber
MT.1428 matched lumber
MT.1429 rough lumber
MT.1430 *<lumber by technique: sawing method>*
MT.1431 plain-sawed lumber
MT.1432 quarter-sawed lumber
MT.1433 *<lumber by technique: seasoning method>*
MT.1434 air-dried lumber
MT.1435 green lumber
MT.1436 kiln-dried lumber
MT.1437 *<lumber by quality>*
MT.1438 clear lumber
MT.1439 boat lumber
MT.1440 dimension lumber
MT.1441 factory lumber
MT.1442 select lumber
MT.1443 structural lumber
MT.1444 plank
MT.1445 timber
MT.1446 yard lumber
MT.1447 finish lumber
MT.1448 scantling
MT.1449 millwork
MT.1450 plywood
MT.1451 poles
MT.1452 pressure-treated wood
MT.1453 pulpwood
MT.1454 sawdust
MT.1455 shakes
MT.1456 treenware
MT.1457 *<wood boards>*
MT.1458 barnboard
MT.1459 blockboard
MT.1460 corkboard
MT.1461 hardboard
MT.1462 Masonite (TM)
MT.1463 particle board
MT.1464 chipboard
MT.1465 woodchips
MT.1466 resin
MT.1467 balsam
MT.1468 Burgundy turpentine
MT.1469 Burgundy pitch
MT.1470 Canada balsam

May be used in combination with other descriptors (e.g., **marble** + **floors**; **granite** + **faux finishing**).

MT.1471	copaiba balsam
MT.1472	Maracaibo balsam
MT.1473	para balsam
MT.1474	Jura turpentine
MT.1475	Peru balsam
MT.1476	Strasbourg turpentine
MT.1477	tolu balsam
MT.1478	Venice turpentine
MT.1479	benzoin
MT.1480	copal
MT.1481	Congo copal
MT.1482	East African copal
MT.1483	Manila copal
MT.1484	Sierra Leone copal
MT.1485	Zanzibar copal
MT.1486	damar
MT.1487	Batavia damar
MT.1488	Singapore damar
MT.1489	Mata Kuching damar
MT.1490	dragon's blood
MT.1491	elemi
MT.1492	Manila elemi
MT.1493	fossil resin
MT.1494	amber
MT.1495	succinite
MT.1496	galipot
MT.1497	gamboge
MT.1498	gum resin
MT.1499	acaroid resin
MT.1500	rubber
MT.1501	juniper resin
MT.1502	kauri
MT.1503	lac
MT.1504	mastic
MT.1505	pitch
MT.1506	rosin
MT.1507	ester gum
MT.1508	sandarac
MT.1509	storax
MT.1510	*<materials of inorganic and organic origin>*
MT.1511	colorant
MT.1512	*<colorant by form>*
MT.1513	dye
MT.1514	*<dye by composition or origin>*
MT.1515	natural dye
MT.1516	kermes
MT.1517	oxgall
MT.1518	Tyrian purple
MT.1519	vegetable dye

May be used in combination with other descriptors (e.g., **marble** + **floors**; **granite** + **faux finishing**).

MT.1520 alkanet
MT.1521 buckthorn berry
MT.1522 chay
MT.1523 indigo
MT.1524 litmus
MT.1525 lokao
MT.1526 madder
MT.1527 morinda
MT.1528 orchil
MT.1529 purpurin
MT.1530 safflower (colorant)
MT.1531 saffron
MT.1532 turmeric
MT.1533 turnsole
MT.1534 ventilago
MT.1535 weld
MT.1536 woad
MT.1537 synthetic dye
MT.1538 alizarin
MT.1539 aniline dye
MT.1540 magenta
MT.1541 mauve
MT.1542 pink mauve
MT.1543 methyl dye
MT.1544 *<dye by property>*
MT.1545 oil soluble dyes
MT.1546 water soluble dyes
MT.1547 pigment
MT.1548 *<pigments by composition or origin>*
MT.1549 inorganic pigment
MT.1550 artificial inorganic pigment
MT.1551 metallic pigment
MT.1552 natural inorganic pigment
MT.1553 inert pigment
MT.1554 organic pigment
MT.1555 natural organic pigment
MT.1556 animal pigment
MT.1557 plant pigment
MT.1558 anthocyanin
MT.1559 carotene
MT.1560 chlorophyll
MT.1561 melanin
MT.1562 synthetic organic pigment
MT.1563 *<pigments by color>*
MT.1564 black pigment
MT.1565 organic black pigment
MT.1566 carbon black
MT.1567 bone black
MT.1568 ivory black

May be used in combination with other descriptors (e.g., **marble** + **floors**; **granite** + **faux finishing**).

MT

MT.1569 Paris black
MT.1570 charcoal black
MT.1571 fruit stone black
MT.1572 peach black
MT.1573 vine black
MT.1574 graphite (black pigment)
MT.1575 lampblack
MT.1576 artificial inorganic black pigment
MT.1577 Mars black
MT.1578 synthetic organic black pigment
MT.1579 aniline black
MT.1580 blue pigment
MT.1581 inorganic blue pigment
MT.1582 azurite
MT.1583 blue ocher
MT.1584 cendre blue
MT.1585 Mayan blue
MT.1586 ultramarine blue
MT.1587 organic blue pigment
MT.1588 blue carmine
MT.1589 blue lake
MT.1590 campeachy lake
MT.1591 cork (blue pigment)
MT.1592 cornflower blue
MT.1593 artificial inorganic blue pigment
MT.1594 artificial ultramarine blue
MT.1595 blue verditer
MT.1596 Bremen blue
MT.1597 lime blue
MT.1598 cerulean blue
MT.1599 cobalt blue
MT.1600 Leithner's blue
MT.1601 Egyptian blue
MT.1602 manganese blue
MT.1603 smalt
MT.1604 tungsten blue
MT.1605 synthetic organic blue pigment
MT.1606 indanthrone blue
MT.1607 irgazin blue
MT.1608 phthalocyanine blue
MT.1609 Prussian blue
MT.1610 Antwerp blue
MT.1611 brown pigment
MT.1612 inorganic brown pigment
MT.1613 transparent brown
MT.1614 organic brown pigment
MT.1615 asphaltum
MT.1616 mummy
MT.1617 bister

May be used in combination with other descriptors (e.g., **marble** + **floors**; **granite** + **faux finishing**).

MT.1618 bone brown
MT.1619 burnt carmine
MT.1620 cutch
MT.1621 gambier
MT.1622 Spanish licorice
MT.1623 Van Dyke brown
MT.1624 artificial inorganic brown pigment
MT.1625 brown ocher
MT.1626 brown iron oxide
MT.1627 burnt ocher
MT.1628 sienna
MT.1629 burnt sienna
MT.1630 raw sienna
MT.1631 umber
MT.1632 burnt umber
MT.1633 raw umber
MT.1634 green pigment
MT.1635 inorganic green pigment
MT.1636 chrysocolla
MT.1637 green earth
MT.1638 Bohemian earth
MT.1639 Cyprian green earth
MT.1640 Tyrolean green
MT.1641 Verona green
MT.1642 malachite green
MT.1643 organic green pigment
MT.1644 lily green
MT.1645 pansy green
MT.1646 sap green
MT.1647 artificial inorganic green pigment
MT.1648 blue-green oxide
MT.1649 cadmium green
MT.1650 chromium oxide green
MT.1651 cobalt green
MT.1652 copper resinate
MT.1653 emerald green
MT.1654 Scheele's green
MT.1655 permanent green
MT.1656 ultramarine green
MT.1657 verdigris
MT.1658 viridian
MT.1659 zinc chrome green
MT.1660 synthetic organic green pigment
MT.1661 phthalocyanine green
MT.1662 composite green pigment
MT.1663 chrome green
MT.1664 Brunswick green
MT.1665 Elsner green
MT.1666 Hooker's green

May be used in combination with other descriptors (e.g., **marble** + **floors**; **granite** + **faux finishing**).

colorant

<colorant by form>

pigment

<pigments by color>

MT.1667	red pigment
MT.1668	inorganic red pigment
MT.1669	chrome red
MT.1670	iron oxide red
MT.1671	gulf red
MT.1672	Pompeian red
MT.1673	Pozzuoli red
MT.1674	red bole
MT.1675	red ocher
MT.1676	sinopia
MT.1677	Spanish red oxide
MT.1678	Tuscan red
MT.1679	Venetian red
MT.1680	realgar
MT.1681	vermilion
MT.1682	antimony vermilion
MT.1683	Chinese vermilion
MT.1684	English vermilion
MT.1685	orange vermilion
MT.1686	scarlet vermilion
MT.1687	organic red pigment
MT.1688	barwood
MT.1689	carmine
MT.1690	cochineal
MT.1691	crimson lake
MT.1692	lac (red pigment)
MT.1693	logwood
MT.1694	safflower (red pigment)
MT.1695	artificial inorganic red pigment
MT.1696	antimony orange
MT.1697	cadmium red
MT.1698	cadmium red lithopone
MT.1699	Indian red
MT.1700	potter's pink
MT.1701	red lead
MT.1702	synthetic organic red pigment
MT.1703	alizarin madder
MT.1704	geranium red
MT.1705	iodine scarlet
MT.1706	lithol red
MT.1707	para red
MT.1708	quinacridone red
MT.1709	toluidine red
MT.1710	violet pigment
MT.1711	inorganic violet pigment
MT.1712	manganese violet
MT.1713	Mars violet
MT.1714	ultramarine violet
MT.1715	organic violet pigment

May be used in combination with other descriptors (e.g., **marble** + **floors**; **granite** + **faux finishing**).

MT.1716 vegetable violet
MT.1717 violet carmine
MT.1718 artificial inorganic violet pigment
MT.1719 cobalt violet
MT.1720 deep cobalt phosphate
MT.1721 pale cobalt arsenate
MT.1722 synthetic organic violet pigment
MT.1723 alizarin violet
MT.1724 quinacridone violet
MT.1725 thioindigo violet
MT.1726 white pigment
MT.1727 opaque white pigment
MT.1728 antimony oxide
MT.1729 antimony white
MT.1730 bismuth white
MT.1731 Caledonian white
MT.1732 composite white
MT.1733 lithopone
MT.1734 tin white
MT.1735 titanium white
MT.1736 titanium barium white
MT.1737 titanium calcium white
MT.1738 white lead
MT.1739 Dutch process white lead
MT.1740 zinc white
MT.1741 zirconium oxide
MT.1742 transparent white pigment
MT.1743 aluminum hydrate white
MT.1744 aluminum stearate white
MT.1745 anhydrite white
MT.1746 barium carbonate
MT.1747 bianco sangiovanni
MT.1748 blanc fixe
MT.1749 bone white
MT.1750 diatomaceous earth
MT.1751 kaolinite
MT.1752 mica (white pigment)
MT.1753 oyster white
MT.1754 pumice (white pigment)
MT.1755 silica (white pigment)
MT.1756 talc (white pigment)
MT.1757 yellow pigment
MT.1758 inorganic yellow pigment
MT.1759 orpiment
MT.1760 organic yellow pigment
MT.1761 annatto
MT.1762 Dutch pink
MT.1763 fustic
MT.1764 young fustic

May be used in combination with other descriptors (e.g., **marble** + **floors**; **granite** + **faux finishing**).

MT.1765 Indian yellow
MT.1766 Persian berries lake
MT.1767 tumeric
MT.1768 yellow carmine
MT.1769 artificial inorganic yellow pigment
MT.1770 barium yellow
MT.1771 cadmium yellow
MT.1772 cadmium orange
MT.1773 cadmium yellow lithopone
MT.1774 deep cadmium yellow
MT.1775 lemon cadmium yellow
MT.1776 middle cadmium yellow
MT.1777 pale cadmium yellow
MT.1778 chrome yellow
MT.1779 cobalt yellow
MT.1780 lead stannate
MT.1781 litharge
MT.1782 massicot
MT.1783 Mars yellow
MT.1784 Naples yellow
MT.1785 nickel-titanium yellow
MT.1786 *<ochers>*
MT.1787 golden ocher
MT.1788 transparent gold ocher
MT.1789 light ocher
MT.1790 Oxford ocher
MT.1791 spruce ocher
MT.1792 yellow ocher
MT.1793 strontium yellow
MT.1794 Turner's yellow
MT.1795 uranium yellow
MT.1796 zinc yellow
MT.1797 synthetic organic yellow pigment
MT.1798 alizarin yellow
MT.1799 Hansa yellow
MT.1800 yellow lake
MT.1801 quercitron lake
MT.1802 *<pigments by production method>*
MT.1803 composite pigment
MT.1804 drop pigment
MT.1805 dry color
MT.1806 lake pigment
MT.1807 Mars pigment
MT.1808 *<colorant by function>*
MT.1809 cement color
MT.1810 mortar color
MT.1811 ceramic color
MT.1812 *<fiber and fiber products>*
MT.1813 fiber

May be used in combination with other descriptors (e.g., **marble** + **floors**; **granite** + **faux finishing**).

MT.1814 natural fiber
MT.1815 animal fiber
MT.1816 alpaca
MT.1817 angora
MT.1818 silk
MT.1819 Chinese silk
MT.1820 wool
MT.1821 tweed
MT.1822 plant fiber
MT.1823 bagasse
MT.1824 bast
MT.1825 coir
MT.1826 esparto
MT.1827 flax
MT.1828 hemp
MT.1829 Manila hemp
MT.1830 henequen
MT.1831 jute
MT.1832 kapok
MT.1833 kenaf
MT.1834 palm fiber
MT.1835 raffia
MT.1836 ramie
MT.1837 sisal
MT.1838 synthetic fiber
MT.1839 polyester fiber
MT.1840 Dacron (TM)
MT.1841 rayon
MT.1842 *<fiber products>*
MT.1843 bark cloth
MT.1844 cloth
MT.1845 *<cloth by composition or origin>*
MT.1846 chintz
MT.1847 cotton
MT.1848 calico
MT.1849 dimity
MT.1850 fustian
MT.1851 tobacco cloth
MT.1852 denim
MT.1853 linen
MT.1854 Roman linen
MT.1855 moreen
MT.1856 *<cloth by form>*
MT.1857 baize
MT.1858 burlap
MT.1859 canvas
MT.1860 sailcloth
MT.1861 corduroy
MT.1862 cut-pile cloth

May be used in combination with other descriptors (e.g., **marble** + **floors**; **granite** + **faux finishing**).

MT.1863 damask
MT.1864 drafting cloth
MT.1865 duck (cloth)
MT.1866 felt
MT.1867 flannel
MT.1868 gauze
MT.1869 kente
MT.1870 lace
MT.1871   bobbin lace
MT.1872   Valenciennes lace
MT.1873   hairpin lace
MT.1874 muslin
MT.1875 satin
MT.1876 textiles
MT.1877 tracing cloth
MT.1878 velvet
MT.1879 *<cloth by surface treatment>*
MT.1880 adinkra
MT.1881 korhogo cloth
MT.1882 mud cloth
MT.1883 oilcloth
MT.1884 resist-dyed cloth
MT.1885   adire
MT.1886   starch-resist cloth
MT.1887   tie and dye cloth
MT.1888 wax resist cloth
MT.1889 fiberboard
MT.1890   jute board
MT.1891   strawboard
MT.1892 paper
MT.1893   *<paper by composition or origin>*
MT.1894   papyrus
MT.1895   rag paper
MT.1896   rag felt
MT.1897   rice paper
MT.1898   wood pulp paper
MT.1899   kraft paper
MT.1900   Manila paper
MT.1901   cartridge paper
MT.1902   newsprint
MT.1903   *<paper by form>*
MT.1904   crepe paper
MT.1905   glassine
MT.1906   India paper
MT.1907   Japanese paper
MT.1908   onionskin paper
MT.1909   pasteboard
MT.1910   cardboard
MT.1911   bristol board

MT.1912 illustration board
MT.1913 coquille board
MT.1914 ivory board
MT.1915 mat board
MT.1916 millboard
MT.1917 academy board
MT.1918 canvas board
MT.1919 museum board
MT.1920 Ross board (TM)
MT.1921 scratchboard
MT.1922 pulpboard
MT.1923 tissue paper
MT.1924 *<paper by function>*
MT.1925 absorbent paper
MT.1926 blotting paper
MT.1927 building paper
MT.1928 felt paper
MT.1929 tar paper
MT.1930 rosin-sized paper
MT.1931 carbon paper
MT.1932 drawing paper
MT.1933 charcoal paper
MT.1934 graph paper
MT.1935 layout paper
MT.1936 prepared paper
MT.1937 tracing paper
MT.1938 tracing vellum
MT.1939 watercolor paper
MT.1940 filter paper
MT.1941 litmus paper
MT.1942 photographic paper
MT.1943 baryta paper
MT.1944 developing-out paper
MT.1945 gaslight paper
MT.1946 printing-out paper
MT.1947 aristo paper
MT.1948 resin-coated paper
MT.1949 reversal paper
MT.1950 salted paper
MT.1951 single-weight paper
MT.1952 solio paper
MT.1953 stripping film
MT.1954 printing paper
MT.1955 book paper
MT.1956 transfer paper
MT.1957 wrapping paper
MT.1958 butcher paper
MT.1959 writing paper
MT.1960 bond paper

MT

May be used in combination with other descriptors (e.g., **marble** + **floors**; **granite** + **faux finishing**).

MT.1961 *<paper by production method>*
MT.1962 handmade paper
MT.1963 gampi
MT.1964 kozo
MT.1965 mitsumata
MT.1966 washi
MT.1967 laid paper
MT.1968 machine-made paper
MT.1969 moldmade paper
MT.1970 wove paper
MT.1971 papier-mâché
MT.1972 *<spun fiber products>*
MT.1973 cord
MT.1974 rope
MT.1975 string
MT.1976 thread
MT.1977 twine
MT.1978 yarn
MT.1979 roving
MT.1980 stretch yarn
MT.1981 oil
MT.1982 *<oil by composition or origin>*
MT.1983 animal oil
MT.1984 mineral oil
MT.1985 vegetable oil
MT.1986 essential oil
MT.1987 clove oil
MT.1988 lavender oil
MT.1989 spike oil
MT.1990 rosemary oil
MT.1991 *<oil by form or function>*
MT.1992 cutting oil
MT.1993 grease
MT.1994 lubricating oil
MT.1995 *<oil by technique>*
MT.1996 blown oil
MT.1997 cold-pressed oil
MT.1998 raw oil
MT.1999 saponified oil
MT.2000 stand oil
MT.2001 middle oil
MT.2002 strong oil
MT.2003 thin oil
MT.2004 sun-thickened oil
MT.2005 *<oil by property>*
MT.2006 drying oil
MT.2007 bodied oil
MT.2008 candlenut oil
MT.2009 fish oil

May be used in combination with other descriptors (e.g., **marble** + **floors**; **granite** + **faux finishing**).

MT.2010 hempseed oil
MT.2011 linseed oil
MT.2012 boiled oil
MT.2013 black oil
MT.2014 raw linseed oil
MT.2015 oiticica oil
MT.2016 perilla oil
MT.2017 poppy-seed oil
MT.2018 safflower oil
MT.2019 soybean oil
MT.2020 sunflower oil
MT.2021 tobacco seed oil
MT.2022 tung oil
MT.2023 Japanese tung oil
MT.2024 walnut oil
MT.2025 semidrying oil
MT.2026 cottonseed oil
MT.2027 croton oil
MT.2028 curcas oil
MT.2029 kapok oil
MT.2030 maize oil
MT.2031 nondrying oil
MT.2032 almond oil
MT.2033 castor oil
MT.2034 jamba oil
MT.2035 kernel oil
MT.2036 mustard oil
MT.2037 olive oil
MT.2038 peanut oil
MT.2039 rape oil
MT.2040 ravison oil
MT.2041 rice oil
MT.2042 *<residue materials>*
MT.2043 ash (residue)
MT.2044 cinder
MT.2045 clinker
MT.2046 slag
MT.2047 soot
MT.2048 smoke
MT.2049 soap
MT.2050 soft soap
MT.2051 soil
MT.2052 *<soil by form or function>*
MT.2053 borrow soil
MT.2054 daga
MT.2055 burnt daga
MT.2056 earth
MT.2057 pisé
MT.2058 rammed earth

May be used in combination with other descriptors (e.g., **marble** + **floors**; **granite** + **faux finishing**).

MT

MT.2059 tapia
MT.2060 sod
MT.2061 *<soil by composition or origin>*
MT.2062 chika
MT.2063 humus
MT.2064 laterite
MT.2065 loam
MT.2066 mud
MT.2067 peat
MT.2068 sand
MT.2069 building sand
MT.2070 flooring sand
MT.2071 paving sand
MT.2072 roofing sand
MT.2073 foundry sand
MT.2074 glass sand
MT.2075 silica sand
MT.2076 greensand
MT.2077 sandblast sand
MT.2078 zaccab
MT.2079 *<synthetic materials>*
MT.2080 elastomers
MT.2081 *<elastomers by composition or origin>*
MT.2082 butyl rubber
MT.2083 epichlorohydrin elastomer
MT.2084 ethylene-propylene elastomer
MT.2085 fluorocarbon elastomer
MT.2086 neoprene
MT.2087 nitrile elastomer
MT.2088 polybutadiene elastomer
MT.2089 polyethylene elastomer
MT.2090 polyisoprene
MT.2091 silicone rubber
MT.2092 polysulfide elastomer
MT.2093 silicone elastomer
MT.2094 fluorosilicone elastomer
MT.2095 styrene-butadiene rubber
MT.2096 urethane elastomer
MT.2097 *<elastomers by form>*
MT.2098 foam rubber
MT.2099 plastics
MT.2100 *<plastics by composition or origin>*
MT.2101 plastic alloys
MT.2102 *<plastics by form>*
MT.2103 filled plastic
MT.2104 plastic foam
MT.2105 structural foam
MT.2106 unfilled plastic
MT.2107 *<plastics by production method>*

May be used in combination with other descriptors (e.g., **marble** + **floors**; **granite** + **faux finishing**).

MT.2108 **extruded plastic**
MT.2109 **extrusion blown plastic**
MT.2110 **plastic laminate**
MT.2111 **Formica (TM)**
MT.2112 **micarta**
MT.2113 **reinforced plastic**
MT.2114 **glass reinforced plastic**
MT.2115 *<plastics by property>*
MT.2116 **thermoplastic**
MT.2117 **acetal**
MT.2118 **acrylic**
MT.2119 **polyacrylate**
MT.2120 **Lucite (TM)**
MT.2121 **perspex**
MT.2122 **Plexiglas (TM)**
MT.2123 **Rhoplex resin (TM)**
MT.2124 **acrylonitrile-butadiene-styrene copolymer**
MT.2125 **butyrate**
MT.2126 **cellulosic**
MT.2127 **cellulose acetate**
MT.2128 **cellulose diacetate**
MT.2129 **cellulose triacetate**
MT.2130 **cellulose ether**
MT.2131 **ethyl cellulose**
MT.2132 **nitrocellulose**
MT.2133 **celluloid**
MT.2134 **collodion**
MT.2135 **pyroxylin**
MT.2136 **fluoroplastic**
MT.2137 **furan**
MT.2138 **ionomer polymer**
MT.2139 **phenylene-based resin**
MT.2140 **polyamide**
MT.2141 **nylon**
MT.2142 **kevlar**
MT.2143 **polybutylene**
MT.2144 **polycarbonate**
MT.2145 **polyetherimide**
MT.2146 **polyethylene**
MT.2147 **polypropylene**
MT.2148 **polystyrene**
MT.2149 **Styrofoam (TM)**
MT.2150 **styrene-acrylonitrile**
MT.2151 **sulfone polymer**
MT.2152 **vinyl**
MT.2153 **polyvinyl acetal**
MT.2154 **polyvinyl acetate**
MT.2155 **polyvinyl alcohol**
MT.2156 **polyvinyl butyral**

May be used in combination with other descriptors (e.g., **marble** + **floors**; **granite** + **faux finishing**).

MT.2157 polyvinyl chloride
MT.2158 thermoset
MT.2159 alkyd resin
MT.2160 oil-modified alkyd
MT.2161 allyl resin
MT.2162 amino resin
MT.2163 melamine
MT.2164 urea-formaldehyde resin
MT.2165 aminoaldehyde resin
MT.2166 casein plastic
MT.2167 epoxy
MT.2168 basic liquid epoxy
MT.2169 multifunctional epoxy
MT.2170 silicone epoxy
MT.2171 phenolic
MT.2172 Bakelite (TM)
MT.2173 catalin
MT.2174 melamine phenolic
MT.2175 polyvinylidene chloride
MT.2176 silicone
MT.2177 silane
MT.2178 *<plastics by property: thermoplastic or thermoset>*
MT.2179 polyester
MT.2180 thermoplastic polyester
MT.2181 Mylar (TM)
MT.2182 thermoset polyester
MT.2183 polyimide
MT.2184 thermoplastic polyimide
MT.2185 thermoset polyimide
MT.2186 polyurethane
MT.2187 wax
MT.2188 animal wax
MT.2189 insect wax
MT.2190 beeswax
MT.2191 bleached beeswax
MT.2192 punic wax
MT.2193 unbleached beeswax
MT.2194 Chinese insect wax
MT.2195 lanolin
MT.2196 spermaceti
MT.2197 mineral wax
MT.2198 montan wax
MT.2199 ozokerite
MT.2200 ceresin
MT.2201 paraffin
MT.2202 microcrystalline wax
MT.2203 synthetic wax
MT.2204 vegetable wax
MT.2205 candelilla wax

May be used in combination with other descriptors (e.g., **marble** + **floors**; **granite** + **faux finishing**).

MT.2206 carnauba wax
MT.2207 Japan wax
MT.2208 *<materials by form>*
MT.2209 aerosol
MT.2210 block
MT.2211 hollow block
MT.2212 board
MT.2213 building board
MT.2214 wallboard
MT.2215 gypsum board
MT.2216 brickbat
MT.2217 cable
MT.2218 armored cable
MT.2219 castings
MT.2220 cellular materials
MT.2221 honeycomb materials
MT.2222 chain
MT.2223 coil
MT.2224 composite materials
MT.2225 dowel
MT.2226 filament
MT.2227 monofilament
MT.2228 film
MT.2229 American film
MT.2230 photographic film
MT.2231 black-and-white film
MT.2232 collodion pellicle
MT.2233 color film
MT.2234 bipacks
MT.2235 integral bipacks
MT.2236 integral tripacks
MT.2237 tripacks
MT.2238 cut film
MT.2239 disk film
MT.2240 panchromatic film
MT.2241 Polaroid (TM) film
MT.2242 reversal film
MT.2243 roll film
MT.2244 safety film
MT.2245 foam
MT.2246 gel
MT.2247 granular materials
MT.2248 fine-grain materials
MT.2249 dust
MT.2250 powder
MT.2251 medium-grain materials
MT.2252 flake
MT.2253 coarse-grain materials
MT.2254 pellet

May be used in combination with other descriptors (e.g., **marble** + **floors**; **granite** + **faux finishing**).

MT.2255 shot
MT.2256 mesh
MT.2257 paillette
MT.2258 panel
MT.2259 paneling
MT.2260 boiserie
MT.2261 paste
MT.2262 pipe
MT.2263 quadrel
MT.2264 ribbon
MT.2265 rods
MT.2266 shavings
MT.2267 sheet
MT.2268 slat
MT.2269 staff
MT.2270 stave
MT.2271 stick
MT.2272 strap
MT.2273 strip
MT.2274 syrup
MT.2275 tape
MT.2276 tesserae
MT.2277 tile
MT.2278 acoustical tile
MT.2279 arris tile
MT.2280 paving tile
MT.2281 wall tile
MT.2282 tubing
MT.2283 veneer
MT.2284 burl veneer
MT.2285 wicker
MT.2286 *<materials by form: state>*
MT.2287 gases
MT.2288 liquids
MT.2289 raw materials
MT.2290 solids
MT.2291 *<materials by function>*
MT.2292 abrasives
MT.2293 additives
MT.2294 accelerators
MT.2295 aggregates
MT.2296 *<aggregates by size>*
MT.2297 ballast
MT.2298 coarse aggregate
MT.2299 fine aggregate
MT.2300 *<aggregates by weight>*
MT.2301 lightweight aggregate
MT.2302 breeze
MT.2303 heavyweight aggregate

May be used in combination with other descriptors (e.g., **marble** + **floors**; **granite** + **faux finishing**).

MT.2304	air-entraining agents
MT.2305	antifoaming agents
MT.2306	antifreeze
MT.2307	antioxidants
MT.2308	curing agents
MT.2309	dispersing agents
MT.2310	driers
MT.2311	emulsifiers
MT.2312	film formers
MT.2313	foaming agents
MT.2314	hardeners
MT.2315	inhibitors
MT.2316	corrosion inhibitors
MT.2317	rust inhibitors
MT.2318	neutralizers
MT.2319	odorants
MT.2320	penetrants
MT.2321	permeability agents
MT.2322	plasticizers
MT.2323	hydromel
MT.2324	pozzolana
MT.2325	resorcinol
MT.2326	restrainers
MT.2327	retardants
MT.2328	stabilizers
MT.2329	heat stabilizers
MT.2330	ultraviolet stabilizers
MT.2331	suspending agents
MT.2332	thickeners
MT.2333	titanates
MT.2334	water reducers
MT.2335	water softeners
MT.2336	adhesives
MT.2337	*<adhesives by composition or origin>*
MT.2338	*<inorganic adhesives>*
MT.2339	water glass
MT.2340	organic adhesives
MT.2341	dextrine
MT.2342	British gum
MT.2343	glue
MT.2344	*<animal adhesive>*
MT.2345	albumin glue
MT.2346	bone glue
MT.2347	casein glue
MT.2348	fish glue
MT.2349	isinglass
MT.2350	hide glue
MT.2351	vegetable glue
MT.2352	cellulose cement

May be used in combination with other descriptors (e.g., **marble** + **floors**; **granite** + **faux finishing**).

MT.2353	library paste
MT.2354	mucilage
MT.2355	soybean glue
MT.2356	*<adhesives by form>*
MT.2357	adhesive tape
MT.2358	friction tape
MT.2359	masking tape
MT.2360	mounting tissue
MT.2361	*<adhesives by function>*
MT.2362	marine glue
MT.2363	subbing layer
MT.2364	antistatic agents
MT.2365	artists' materials
MT.2366	supports (artists' materials)
MT.2367	mounts (artists' materials)
MT.2368	binders
MT.2369	agglutinin
MT.2370	cera colla
MT.2371	synthetic binders
MT.2372	vehicles
MT.2373	*<biological control agents>*
MT.2374	algicides
MT.2375	disinfectants
MT.2376	antiseptics
MT.2377	fungicides
MT.2378	herbicides
MT.2379	insecticides
MT.2380	bleach
MT.2381	superoxol
MT.2382	building materials
MT.2383	air infiltration barriers
MT.2384	bars (building materials)
MT.2385	reinforcing bars
MT.2386	deformed bars
MT.2387	tie rods
MT.2388	daub
MT.2389	finishings
MT.2390	flooring
MT.2391	linoleum
MT.2392	tile flooring
MT.2393	roofing
MT.2394	built-up roofing
MT.2395	matting (roofing material)
MT.2396	shingles
MT.2397	siding
MT.2398	board and batten
MT.2399	clapboard siding
MT.2400	shiplap siding
MT.2401	wallpaper

May be used in combination with other descriptors (e.g., **marble** + **floors**; **granite** + **faux finishing**).

MT.2402 insulation
MT.2403 acoustical insulation
MT.2404 electrical insulation
MT.2405 thermal insulation
MT.2406 flexible insulation
MT.2407 fill insulation
MT.2408 roll insulation
MT.2409 batt insulation
MT.2410 reflective insulation
MT.2411 rigid insulation
MT.2412 lath
MT.2413 diamond mesh lath
MT.2414 rib lath
MT.2415 sheathing
MT.2416 caraboard
MT.2417 vapor barriers
MT.2418 wattle
MT.2419 catalysts
MT.2420 promoters
MT.2421 cleaning compounds
MT.2422 detergents
MT.2423 coatings
MT.2424 *<coatings by composition or origin>*
MT.2425 bituminous coatings
MT.2426 enamel
MT.2427 japan (enamel)
MT.2428 porcelain enamel
MT.2429 lacquer
MT.2430 Oriental lacquer
MT.2431 shellac
MT.2432 orange shellac
MT.2433 white shellac
MT.2434 plaster
MT.2435 *<plaster by composition or origin>*
MT.2436 coarse stuff
MT.2437 fibrous plaster
MT.2438 fine stuff
MT.2439 gypsum plaster
MT.2440 anhydrous gypsum plaster
MT.2441 gauging plaster
MT.2442 plaster of Paris
MT.2443 casting plaster
MT.2444 slaked plaster of Paris
MT.2445 retarded hemihydrate plaster
MT.2446 hydrostone
MT.2447 mud-plaster
MT.2448 slag plaster
MT.2449 timchent
MT.2450 *<plaster by function>*

May be used in combination with other descriptors (e.g., **marble** + **floors**; **granite** + **faux finishing**).

MT

MT.2451 acoustical plaster
MT.2452 molding plaster
MT.2453 hydrocal
MT.2454 *<plaster by technique>*
MT.2455 arriccio
MT.2456 gatch
MT.2457 intonaco
MT.2458 pebble dash
MT.2459 roughcast
MT.2460 scagliola
MT.2461 stucco
MT.2462 kellastone
MT.2463 powder coatings
MT.2464 stain
MT.2465 oil stain
MT.2466 silver stain
MT.2467 spirit stain
MT.2468 varnish stain
MT.2469 water stain
MT.2470 varnish
MT.2471 *<varnish by function>*
MT.2472 gold varnish
MT.2473 intermediate varnish
MT.2474 isolating varnish
MT.2475 retouch varnish
MT.2476 mixing varnish
MT.2477 picture varnish
MT.2478 rubbing varnish
MT.2479 finishing varnish
MT.2480 spar varnish
MT.2481 *<varnish by production method>*
MT.2482 oil varnish
MT.2483 coach varnish
MT.2484 yellow varnish
MT.2485 simple solution varnish
MT.2486 spirit varnish
MT.2487 copal varnishes
MT.2488 *<varnish by property>*
MT.2489 flat varnish
MT.2490 litho varnish
MT.2491 vert antique
MT.2492 *<coatings by form>*
MT.2493 emulsion
MT.2494 oil-in-water emulsion
MT.2495 ink
MT.2496 atramentum
MT.2497 black carbon ink
MT.2498 Chinese ink
MT.2499 colored ink

May be used in combination with other descriptors (e.g., **marble** + **floors**; **granite** + **faux finishing**).

MT.2500 India ink
MT.2501 invisible ink
MT.2502 iron gall ink
MT.2503 Japanese ink
MT.2504 sepia
MT.2505   Roman sepia
MT.2506 tusche
MT.2507 maroger medium
MT.2508 megilp
MT.2509 paint
MT.2510   *<paint by composition or origin>*
MT.2511   aluminum paint
MT.2512   *<aqueous paint>*
MT.2513   distemper paint
MT.2514   calcimine
MT.2515   poster color
MT.2516   whitewash
MT.2517   emulsion paint
MT.2518   tempera
MT.2519   casein paint
MT.2520   egg tempera
MT.2521   gum tempera
MT.2522   oil tempera
MT.2523   watercolor
MT.2524   body color
MT.2525   gouache
MT.2526   enamel paint
MT.2527   oil paint
MT.2528   lead-based paint
MT.2529   silicate paint
MT.2530   *<synthetic resin paint>*
MT.2531   latex paint
MT.2532   polymer paint
MT.2533   acrylic paint
MT.2534   *<paint by function>*
MT.2535   concrete paint
MT.2536   deck paint
MT.2537   housc paint
MT.2538   *<paint by property>*
MT.2539   antifouling paint
MT.2540   chemical-resistant paint
MT.2541   dampproofing paint
MT.2542   fire-retardant paint
MT.2543   flat paint
MT.2544   frost-proof paint
MT.2545   luminous paint
MT.2546   fluorescent paint
MT.2547   magnetic paint
MT.2548   rust-inhibiting paint

May be used in combination with other descriptors (e.g., **marble** + **floors**; **granite** + **faux finishing**).

MT

MT.2549 patina
MT.2550 wash
MT.2551 *<coatings by location or context>*
MT.2552 concrete coatings
MT.2553 finishes
MT.2554 faux finishes
MT.2555 glaze
MT.2556 ceramic glaze
MT.2557 *<ceramic glaze by composition or origin>*
MT.2558 alkaline glaze
MT.2559 ash glaze
MT.2560 peach bloom
MT.2561 Bristol glaze
MT.2562 celadon
MT.2563 *<ceramic glaze by form>*
MT.2564 clear glaze
MT.2565 *<ceramic glaze by technique>*
MT.2566 blister glaze
MT.2567 crystalline glaze
MT.2568 matte glaze
MT.2569 salt glaze
MT.2570 sang de boeuf
MT.2571 slip glaze
MT.2572 engobe
MT.2573 paper coatings
MT.2574 supercoat
MT.2575 polish (coating)
MT.2576 buffing compositions
MT.2577 rouge
MT.2578 green rouge
MT.2579 conductors
MT.2580 electric conductors
MT.2581 semiconductors
MT.2582 superconductors
MT.2583 coolants
MT.2584 explosives
MT.2585 gunpowder
MT.2586 nitroglycerin
MT.2587 dynamite
MT.2588 TNT
MT.2589 fertilizers
MT.2590 fill
MT.2591 fillers
MT.2592 badigeon
MT.2593 extenders
MT.2594 mortar
MT.2595 *<mortar by composition or origin>*
MT.2596 cement mortar
MT.2597 clay mortar

May be used in combination with other descriptors (e.g., **marble** + **floors**; **granite** + **faux finishing**).

MT.2598	clay-and-hair mortar
MT.2599	gypsum mortar
MT.2600	lime mortar
MT.2601	fat mortar
MT.2602	lean mortar
MT.2603	lime-sand mortar
MT.2604	mud mortar
MT.2605	*<mortar by function>*
MT.2606	grout
MT.2607	hydraulic mortar
MT.2608	*<mortar by property>*
MT.2609	dry mortar
MT.2610	polymer-impregnated mortar
MT.2611	plastic wood
MT.2612	Spackle (TM)
MT.2613	filters
MT.2614	fireproofing agents
MT.2615	fixatives
MT.2616	flux
MT.2617	food products
MT.2618	fuel
MT.2619	firewood
MT.2620	fossil fuels
MT.2621	natural gas
MT.2622	lubricants
MT.2623	media
MT.2624	mixed media
MT.2625	molding materials
MT.2626	packaging materials
MT.2627	parting compounds
MT.2628	bond breakers
MT.2629	form oil
MT.2630	mold release agents
MT.2631	perfume
MT.2632	photographic materials
MT.2633	final image material
MT.2634	photographic plates
MT.2635	preservatives
MT.2636	*<preservatives by composition or origin>*
MT.2637	carbolineum
MT.2638	creosote
MT.2639	coal tar creosote
MT.2640	pentachlorophenol
MT.2641	*<preservatives by function>*
MT.2642	wood preservatives
MT.2643	acid copper chromate
MT.2644	ammoniacal copper arsenate
MT.2645	chromated copper arsenate
MT.2646	chromated zinc chloride

May be used in combination with other descriptors (e.g., **marble** + **floors**; **granite** + **faux finishing**).

MT.2647 **propellants**
MT.2648 **reinforcing materials**
MT.2649 **sealing compounds**
MT.2650   **caulking compounds**
MT.2651   **latex caulk**
MT.2652   **lead wool**
MT.2653   **oakum**
MT.2654   **putty**
MT.2655   **glazier's putty**
MT.2656   **lime putty**
MT.2657   **picture putty**
MT.2658   **water putty**
MT.2659 **solvents**
MT.2660   *<solvents by composition or origin>*
MT.2661   **butyl lactate**
MT.2662   **carbitol**
MT.2663   **carbon disulfide**
MT.2664   **coal tar solvents**
MT.2665   **ethylene glycol monoethyl ether**
MT.2666   *<hydrocarbon solvents>*
MT.2667   **aliphatic hydrocarbons**
MT.2668   **kerosene**
MT.2669   **mineral spirits**
MT.2670   **naphtha**
MT.2671   **aromatic hydrocarbons**
MT.2672   **benzene**
MT.2673   **toluene**
MT.2674   **xylene**
MT.2675   **chlorinated hydrocarbons**
MT.2676   **carbon tetrachloride**
MT.2677   **methylene chloride**
MT.2678   **heptane**
MT.2679   **hexane**
MT.2680   *<oxygenated solvents>*
MT.2681   **alcohol**
MT.2682   **amyl alcohol**
MT.2683   **butyl alcohol**
MT.2684   **butanol**
MT.2685   **diacetone alcohol**
MT.2686   **ethyl alcohol**
MT.2687   **absolute alcohol**
MT.2688   **denatured alcohol**
MT.2689   **isopropyl alcohol**
MT.2690   **methyl alcohol**
MT.2691   **esters**
MT.2692   **amyl acetate**
MT.2693   **butyl acetate**
MT.2694   **ethyl acetate**
MT.2695   **isopropyl acetate**

May be used in combination with other descriptors (e.g., **marble** + **floors**; **granite** + **faux finishing**).

MT.2696 ketones
MT.2697 acetone
MT.2698 methyl acetone
MT.2699 methyl ethyl ketone
MT.2700 methyl isobutyl ketone
MT.2701 styrene
MT.2702 terpenes
MT.2703 dipentene
MT.2704 pine oil
MT.2705 turpentine
MT.2706 gum turpentine
MT.2707 wood turpentine
MT.2708 tricloroethane
MT.2709 *<solvents by function>*
MT.2710 paint removers
MT.2711 ammonia water
MT.2712 thinners
MT.2713 *<surface preparation materials>*
MT.2714 gesso
MT.2715 gesso grosso
MT.2716 gesso sottile
MT.2717 ground (material)
MT.2718 emulsion ground
MT.2719 whiting
MT.2720 mordants
MT.2721 aqua fortis
MT.2722 Dutch mordant
MT.2723 Smillie's bath
MT.2724 primer
MT.2725 polymer primer
MT.2726 resist
MT.2727 rust removing agents
MT.2728 size (materials)
MT.2729 animal size
MT.2730 gold size
MT.2731 viscose size
MT.2732 surface-active agents
MT.2733 dispersants
MT.2734 wetting agents
MT.2735 waterproof materials
MT.2736 waterproofing materials
MT.2737 wrapping materials
MT.2738 *<materials by technique>*
MT.2739 canework
MT.2740 fitching
MT.2741 concretework
MT.2742 featherwork
MT.2743 feltwork
MT.2744 fiberwork

MT

MT.2745	bastwork
MT.2746	*<masonry and masonry units>*
MT.2747	masonry
MT.2748	bonds (masonry)
MT.2749	common bond
MT.2750	English bond
MT.2751	Flemish bond
MT.2752	running bond
MT.2753	stack bond
MT.2754	brickwork
MT.2755	stonework
MT.2756	cyclopean masonry
MT.2757	masonry units
MT.2758	bondstones
MT.2759	perpends
MT.2760	headers
MT.2761	bull header
MT.2762	glazed header
MT.2763	splits
MT.2764	stretchers (masonry units)
MT.2765	metalwork
MT.2766	brasswork
MT.2767	copperwork
MT.2768	goldwork
MT.2769	ironwork
MT.2770	leadwork
MT.2771	punchwork
MT.2772	steelwork
MT.2773	wirework
MT.2774	paperwork
MT.2775	paper quillwork
MT.2776	plasterwork
MT.2777	pargeting
MT.2778	raffiawork
MT.2779	ribbonwork
MT.2780	ropework
MT.2781	rushwork
MT.2782	straw work
MT.2783	wickerwork
MT.2784	woodwork
MT.2785	joinery
MT.2786	nailed joinery
MT.2787	*<materials by property>*
MT.2788	abrasion-resistant materials
MT.2789	absorbent materials
MT.2790	chemical-resistant materials
MT.2791	acid-resistant materials
MT.2792	corrosive materials
MT.2793	fire-resistant materials

May be used in combination with other descriptors (e.g., **marble** + **floors**; **granite** + **faux finishing**).

MT.2794 flammable materials
MT.2795 flexible materials
MT.2796 hazardous substances
MT.2797 heat-resistant materials
MT.2798 refractory materials
MT.2799 *<imitative materials>*
MT.2800 artificial ivory
MT.2801 artificial stone
MT.2802 coade stone
MT.2803 marbelite
MT.2804 marezzo marble
MT.2805 impregnated materials
MT.2806 inert materials
MT.2807 lightweight materials
MT.2808 malleable materials
MT.2809 pollutants
MT.2810 porous materials
MT.2811 pyroclastic materials

May be used in combination with other descriptors (e.g., **marble** + **floors**; **granite** + **faux finishing**).

Objects facet

The Objects facet encompasses those discrete tangible or visible things that are inanimate and man-made, that is, that are either fabricated or given form by human activity. These range, in physical form, from built works to images and written documents, and, in purpose, from the utilitarian to the aesthetic.

The Objects facet consists of the following hierarchies:

Built Environment
Settlements, Systems and Landscapes (RD)
Built Complexes and Districts (RG)
Single Built Works and Open Spaces (RK)
Building Divisions and Site Elements (RM)
Built Works Components (RT)

Furnishings and Equipment
Tools and Equipment (TB)
Hardware and Joints (TF)
Furniture (TG)

Visual and Verbal Communication
Image and Object Genres (VB)
Drawings (VD)
Photographs (VJ)
Document Types (VW)

Built Environment

(RD) Settlements, Systems and Landscapes
(RG) Built Complexes and Districts
(RK) Single Built Works and Open Spaces
(RM) Building Divisions and Site Elements
(RT) Built Works Components

The Built Environment section covers features that comprise all levels of constructed works and their components, forming a continuum from the largest settled and natural landscapes to the smallest components of built works. Descriptors are not repeated; therefore, in those instances where a descriptor may logically appear in more than one level of the continuum (e.g., **chapels** may be both single built works or components of a work), it is placed in the hierarchy containing the smaller scale elements unless factors of common usage, design intent, or historical precedence dictate otherwise.

Settlements, Systems and Landscapes Hierarchy

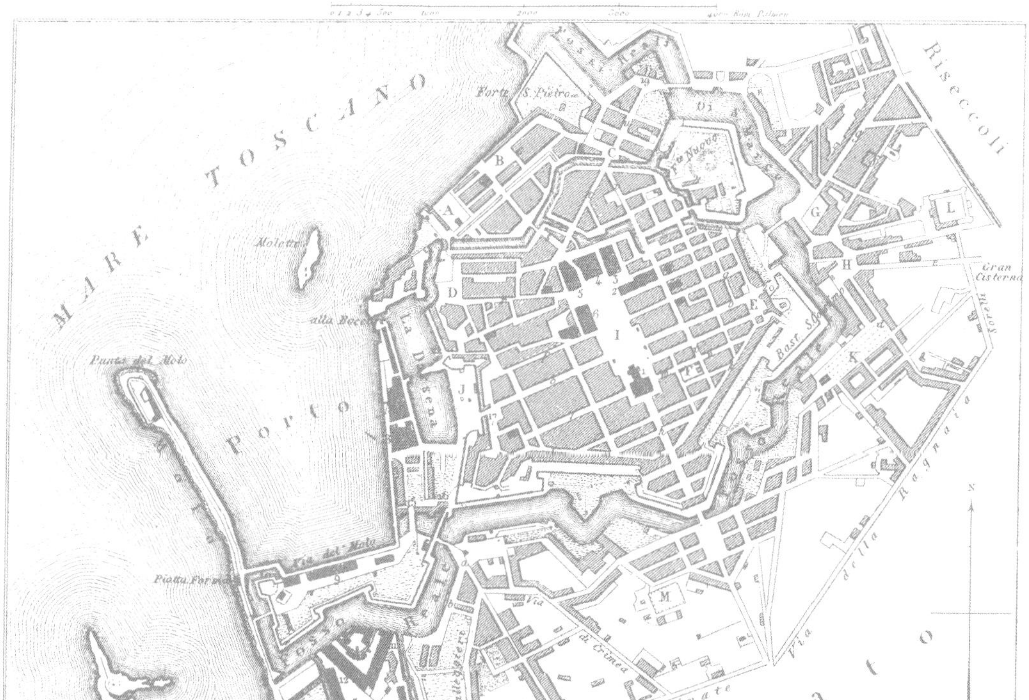

SETTLEMENTS, SYSTEMS AND LANDSCAPES

Scope The Settlements, Systems and Landscapes hierarchy contains descriptors for the largest features of the built environment, whether relatively concentrated (e.g., **cities**) or extensive (e.g., **bus transit systems**). Settlements are defined as all places or areas, however large, occupied or modified by human populations and with enough societal functions to be relatively self-sufficient. The systems covered here are infrastructural systems, which may be defined as networks of buildings, other structures, and equipment that constitute physically ordered entities within settlements and landscapes.

Also included in this hierarchy are descriptors for major types of natural landscapes and cultural landscapes and their components that provide the largest environmental context for built works, By placing natural landscapes in this hierarchy, the *AAT* has chosen not to emphasize a distinction between the natural environment and the built environment. Maintaining such a distinction is often frustrated because (a) there is continuity between the two, (b) much of the natural environment has been subject to human intervention and has the qualities of a cultural artifact, and (c) much of the built environment, at a wide range of scales, functions as an ecological system.

Organization The hierarchy comprises three sections: **settlements**, <*infrastructural systems*>, and **landscapes (environments)**. Descriptors in the **settlements** section are organized according to characteristics such as function (e.g., **capital cities**), economic base (e.g., **fishing villages**), location (e.g., **hill towns**), and planning concept (e.g., **model cities**).

Under <*infrastructural systems*> are such descriptors as **drainage systems**, **transit systems**, and **utilities**.

The landscapes portion of the hierarchy is comprised of two sections: **natural landscapes** and **cultural landscapes**. **Natural landscapes** include **bodies of water** and their components (e.g., **lakes**), **wetlands** (e.g., **bogs**), major **landforms** and their components (e.g., **mountains**, **cliffs**), major categories of **vegetation** (e.g., **herbaceous plants**), and **plant communities** (e.g., **prairies**). **Cultural landscapes** are subdivided into <*cultural landscapes by function*> (e.g., **agricultural land**), <*cultural landscapes by location or context*> (e.g., **urban landscapes**), <*cultural landscapes by development practice*> (e.g., **wasteland**), and <*cultural landscapes by ownership*> (e.g., **demesnes**).

Relation to Other Hierarchies Administrative bodies (e.g., **nations**, **provinces**) are located in the People and Organizations hierarchy. Adjectival attributes of some settlements (e.g., **radial plan**) are found in the Associated Concepts hierarchy. Descriptors referring to individual plants and trees are found in the Materials hierarchy (e.g., **bamboo**, **pine**).

Descriptor Form and Use Descriptors appear as plural nouns, with the singular added as an alternate form where appropriate. Descriptors may be combined with those from other hierarchies (e.g., **city** + **streets**; **protected** + **wetlands**; **Medieval** + **towns**).

Number of Descriptors 268

Synopsis

RD.1	**settlements**
RD.2	*<settlements by form>*
RD.3	*<settlements by form: plan>*
RD.5	*<settlements by form: scale>*
RD.20	*<settlements by function>*
RD.21	*<settlements by function: administrative>*
RD.30	*<settlements by function: military>*
RD.36	*<settlements by condition>*
RD.46	*<settlements by economic base>*
RD.60	*<settlements by location>*
RD.70	*<settlements by occupants>*
RD.76	*<settlements by ownership>*
RD.80	*<settlements by planning concept>*
RD.86	*<infrastructural systems>*
RD.87	**drainage systems**
RD.88	**telecommunications systems**
RD.91	**transit systems**
RD.116	**utilities**
RD.122	**landscapes (environments)**
RD.123	**natural landscapes**
RD.124	*<bodies of water and components of bodies of water>*
RD.166	**deserts**
RD.167	**wetlands**
RD.175	*<landforms and landform components>*
RD.240	*<vegetation and vegetation components>*
RD.280	**cultural landscapes**
RD.281	*<cultural landscapes by function>*
RD.290	*<cultural landscapes by location or context*
RD.302	*<cultural landscapes by development practice>*
RD.308	*<cultural landscapes by ownership>*

RD.1	**settlements**
RD.2	<*settlements by form*>
RD.3	<*settlements by form: plan*>
RD.4	**linear cities**
RD.5	<*settlements by form: scale*>
RD.6	**hamlets**
RD.7	**villages**
RD.8	**kraals**
RD.9	**towns**
RD.10	**oppida**
RD.11	**cities**
RD.12	**medinas**
RD.13	**metropolises**
RD.14	**municipia**
RD.15	**poleis**
RD.16	**metropolitan areas**
RD.17	**agglomerations**
RD.18	**conurbations**
RD.19	**megalopolises**
RD.20	<*settlements by function*>
RD.21	<*settlements by function: administrative*>
RD.22	**capital cities**
RD.23	**cathedral cities**
RD.24	**colonial cities**
RD.25	<*local administrative centers*>
RD.26	**county seats**
RD.27	**parish seats**
RD.28	**missions**
RD.29	**pueblos (settlements)**
RD.30	<*settlements by function: military*>
RD.31	**fortified towns**
RD.32	**bastides**
RD.33	**castelli**
RD.34	**military towns**
RD.35	**presidios**
RD.36	<*settlements by condition*>
RD.37	**ghost towns**
RD.38	**lost cities**
RD.39	**ruined cities**
RD.40	**buried cities**
RD.41	**tells**
RD.42	**hüyüks**
RD.43	**tepes**
RD.44	**deserted villages**
RD.45	**unincorporated areas**
RD.46	<*settlements by economic base*>
RD.47	**agricultural settlements**
RD.48	**boomtowns**
RD.49	**college towns**

May be used in combination with other descriptors (e.g., **grid plan** + **cities**; **Medieval** + **towns**; **protected** + **wetlands**; **city** + **streets**).

RD.50 company towns
RD.51 fishing villages
RD.52 industrial towns
RD.53 factory villages
RD.54 mill towns
RD.55 mining towns
RD.56 market towns
RD.57 ports
RD.58 tourist towns
RD.59 university towns
RD.60 *<settlements by location>*
RD.61 exurbs
RD.62 satellite cities
RD.63 space colonies
RD.64 suburbs
RD.65 garden suburbs
RD.66 *<settlements by location: topographical>*
RD.67 coastal towns
RD.68 hill towns
RD.69 river towns
RD.70 *<settlements by occupants>*
RD.71 artists' colonies
RD.72 Indian reservations
RD.73 retirement communities
RD.74 life care communities
RD.75 squatter settlements
RD.76 *<settlements by ownership>*
RD.77 collective settlements
RD.78 communes
RD.79 kibbutzim
RD.80 *<settlements by planning concept>*
RD.81 future cities
RD.82 ideal cities
RD.83 model cities
RD.84 new towns
RD.85 garden cities
RD.86 *<infrastructural systems>*
RD.87 drainage systems
RD.88 telecommunication systems
RD.89 police communication systems
RD.90 telephone systems
RD.91 transit systems
RD.92 public transit
RD.93 *<public transit by form>*
RD.94 *<free-wheeled transit systems>*
RD.95 bus transit systems
RD.96 trolleybus systems
RD.97 paratransit
RD.98 rail transit systems

May be used in combination with other descriptors (e.g., **grid plan** + **cities**; **Medieval** + **towns**; **protected** + **wetlands**; **city** + **streets**).

RD.99 light rail transit
RD.100 cable railroads
RD.101 funicular railroads
RD.102 rack railroads
RD.103 street-railroads
RD.104 streetcar systems
RD.105 monorails
RD.106 personal rapid transit
RD.107 rapid rail transit systems
RD.108 subways
RD.109 *<public transit by location or context>*
RD.110 commuter railroads
RD.111 elevated railroads
RD.112 local transit
RD.113 urban transit systems
RD.114 urban rail systems
RD.115 railroads
RD.116 utilities
RD.117 municipal lighting
RD.118 street lighting
RD.119 water supply systems
RD.120 irrigation systems
RD.121 water storage systems
RD.122 landscapes (environments)
RD.123 natural landscapes
RD.124 *<bodies of water and components of bodies of water>*
RD.125 bodies of water
RD.126 *<bodies of water by size>*
RD.127 *<marine bodies>*
RD.128 oceans
RD.129 seas
RD.130 *<lacustrine bodies>*
RD.131 lakes
RD.132 oxbow lakes
RD.133 tarns
RD.134 ponds
RD.135 fishponds
RD.136 pools
RD.137 *<riverine bodies>*
RD.138 rivers
RD.139 streams
RD.140 brooks
RD.141 creeks
RD.142 *<bodies of water by location>*
RD.143 aquifers
RD.144 *<coastline bodies of water>*
RD.145 bays
RD.146 coves
RD.147 fiords

May be used in combination with other descriptors (e.g., **grid plan** + **cities**; **Medieval** + **towns**; **protected** + **wetlands**; **city** + **streets**).

RD.148 gulfs
RD.149 harbors
RD.150 lagoons
RD.151 springs
RD.152 *<bodies of water by state>*
RD.153 glaciers
RD.154 icebergs
RD.155 pack ice
RD.156 *<components of bodies of water>*
RD.157 channels
RD.158 estuaries
RD.159 meanders
RD.160 oxbows
RD.161 river beds
RD.162 riverbanks
RD.163 waterfalls
RD.164 cataracts
RD.165 rapids
RD.166 deserts
RD.167 wetlands
RD.168 backwaters
RD.169 bayous
RD.170 bogs
RD.171 peat bogs
RD.172 fens
RD.173 marshes
RD.174 swamps
RD.175 *<landforms and landform components>*
RD.176 landforms
RD.177 *<landforms by formation process>*
RD.178 *<landforms by plate tectonics>*
RD.179 continents
RD.180 faults
RD.181 volcanoes
RD.182 glacial landforms
RD.183 drumlins
RD.184 eskers
RD.185 kames
RD.186 moraines
RD.187 fluvial landforms
RD.188 alluvial fans
RD.189 deltas
RD.190 arroyos
RD.191 beach ridges
RD.192 canyons
RD.193 coulees
RD.194 flood plains
RD.195 gorges
RD.196 ravines

May be used in combination with other descriptors (e.g., **grid plan** + **cities**; **Medieval** + **towns**; **protected** + **wetlands**; **city** + **streets**).

RD.197 aeolian landforms
RD.198 dunes
RD.199 loess
RD.200 *<landforms by shape or position>*
RD.201 *<landforms by shape or position: upward>*
RD.202 mountains
RD.203 hills
RD.204 foothills
RD.205 hillocks
RD.206 plateaus
RD.207 mesas
RD.208 buttes
RD.209 *<landforms by shape or position: downward>*
RD.210 valleys
RD.211 hollows
RD.212 gullies
RD.213 swales
RD.214 *<landforms by shape or position: level>*
RD.215 flats (landforms)
RD.216 salt flats
RD.217 plains
RD.218 *<landforms by position: relation to water>*
RD.219 capes (landforms)
RD.220 islands
RD.221 atolls
RD.222 isthmuses
RD.223 peninsulas
RD.224 promontories
RD.225 reefs
RD.226 sand bars
RD.227 shores
RD.228 beaches
RD.229 coastlines
RD.230 lakeshores
RD.231 seashores
RD.232 *<landform components>*
RD.233 caverns
RD.234 caves
RD.235 cliffs
RD.236 escarpments (landform components)
RD.237 peaks
RD.238 ridges (landform components)
RD.239 slopes
RD.240 *<vegetation and vegetation components>*
RD.241 vegetation
RD.242 *<vegetation components>*
RD.243 plant communities
RD.244 grassland
RD.245 llanos

RD

May be used in combination with other descriptors (e.g., **grid plan** + **cities**; **Medieval** + **towns**; **protected** + **wetlands**; **city** + **streets**).

RD.246 meadows
RD.247 pampas
RD.248 prairies
RD.249 savannas
RD.250 jungles
RD.251 rain forests
RD.252 taigas
RD.253 tundras
RD.254 woodlands
RD.255 woods
RD.256 groves
RD.257 plants
RD.258 nonwoody plants
RD.259 algae
RD.260 ferns
RD.261 fungi
RD.262 herbs
RD.263 woody plants
RD.264 herbaceous plants
RD.265 annuals (plants)
RD.266 biennials
RD.267 bulbs
RD.268 flowers
RD.269 grasses
RD.270 perennials
RD.271 vines
RD.272 shrubs
RD.273 trees
RD.274 *<trees by leaf life>*
RD.275 deciduous trees
RD.276 evergreens
RD.277 *<trees by location or context>*
RD.278 canopy trees
RD.279 understory trees
RD.280 cultural landscapes
RD.281 *<cultural landscapes by function>*
RD.282 agricultural land
RD.283 arable land
RD.284 chinampas
RD.285 cropland
RD.286 farmland
RD.287 smallholdings
RD.288 pastures
RD.289 rangeland
RD.290 *<cultural landscapes by location or context>*
RD.291 oases
RD.292 skylines
RD.293 suburban landscapes
RD.294 townscapes

May be used in combination with other descriptors (e.g., **grid plan** + **cities**; **Medieval** + **towns**; **protected** + **wetlands**; **city** + **streets**).

RD.295 urban landscapes
RD.296 wilderness
RD.297 bush
RD.298 forests
RD.299 forest reserves
RD.300 national forests
RD.301 urban forests
RD.302 *<cultural landscapes by development practice>*
RD.303 improved land
RD.304 polders
RD.305 raw land
RD.306 tracts (land areas)
RD.307 wasteland
RD.308 *<cultural landscapes by ownership>*
RD.309 common land
RD.310 crown land
RD.311 demesnes
RD.312 public land

May be used in combination with other descriptors (e.g., **grid plan** + **cities**; **Medieval** + **towns**; **protected** + **wetlands**; **city** + **streets**).

Built Complexes and Districts Hierarchy

BUILT COMPLEXES AND DISTRICTS

Scope The Built Complexes and Districts hierarchy contains descriptors for coherent groupings of built works and for parts of settlements. Complexes are defined as aggregations of buildings, other structures, and open spaces—often multifunctional and more extensive, and usually shaped over a longer period of time by more participants than single built works. Districts are defined as delineated or perceived components of settlements that are more extensive and less architectonic than built complexes. These areas are likely to be defined by socio-economic characteristics or topographic features, by a sameness of the built works they encompass, or by administratively created boundaries.

Organization The hierarchy is structured under the two broad descriptors **complexes** and **districts**. Descriptors in the **complexes** section of the hierarchy are classified by function (e.g., **plantations**, **power plants**) or by development practice (e.g., **mixed-use developments**). Under the **districts** section, descriptors are found under the headings <*districts by function*> (e.g., **dioceses**, **school districts**), <*districts by location or context*> (e.g., **acropolises**, **inner cities**), or <*districts by condition*> (e.g., **growth centers**).

Relation to Other Hierarchies Types of roads (e.g., **highways**, **streets**) are found in the open spaces portion of the Single Built Works and Open Spaces hierarchy. Public transit systems (e.g., **streetcar systems**) are found in the Settlements, Systems and Landscapes hierarchy. Components of all types of roads (e.g., **bus lanes**, **curbs**) are found in the Building Divisions and Site Elements hierarchy.

Descriptor Form and Use Descriptors appear as plural nouns, with the singular added as an alternate form where appropriate. Descriptors may be combined with those from other hierarchies (e.g, **district** + **zoning**; **prefabricated** + **housing**; **Shaker** + **cemeteries**; **rehabilitated** + **inner cities**).

Number of Descriptors 274

Synopsis

RG.1 **complexes**
RG.2 *<complexes by function>*
RG.3 *<agricultural complexes>*
|
RG.229 **zoos**
RG.235 *<complexes by development practice>*
RG.236 **commercial strips**
RG.237 **mixed-use developments**
RG.238 **subdivisions**
RG.239 **districts**
RG.240 *<districts by function>*
RG.241 *<districts by function: administrative>*
RG.242 **assessment districts**
|
RG.264 **water districts**
RG.265 *<districts by function: land use>*
RG.266 **business districts**
|
RG.285 **zones**
RG.289 *<districts by location or context>*
RG.290 **acropolises**
|
RG.297 **urban fringes**
RG.298 *<districts by condition>*
RG.299 **development areas**
|
RG.300 **growth centers**

BUILT COMPLEXES AND DISTRICTS (RG)

- RG.1 complexes
  - RG.2 *<complexes by function>*
    - RG.3 *<agricultural complexes>*
      - RG.4 farms
        - RG.5 abandoned farms
        - RG.6 historic farms
        - RG.7 *<farms by function>*
          - RG.8 dairy farms
          - RG.9 fish hatcheries
          - RG.10 orchards
          - RG.11 school farms
          - RG.12 sheep farms
          - RG.13 tree farms
          - RG.14 vineyards
        - RG.15 *<farms by ownership>*
          - RG.16 collective farms
            - RG.17 kolkhoz
          - RG.18 granges (farms)
      - RG.19 haciendas
      - RG.20 latifundia
      - RG.21 manors
      - RG.22 plantations
      - RG.23 ranches
        - RG.24 cattle ranches
    - RG.25 cemeteries
      - RG.26 *<cemeteries by form>*
        - RG.27 catacombs
        - RG.28 columbaria
        - RG.29 necropolises
      - RG.30 *<cemeteries by function>*
        - RG.31 churchyards
        - RG.32 cineraria
        - RG.33 national cemeteries
        - RG.34 pet cemeteries
        - RG.35 potter's fields
        - RG.36 war cemeteries
    - RG.37 children's villages
    - RG.38 *<commercial complexes>*
      - RG.39 marketplaces
        - RG.40 bazaars
        - RG.41 festival marketplaces
      - RG.42 shopping centers
        - RG.43 shopping arcades
        - RG.44 shopping malls
        - RG.45 shopping plazas
        - RG.46 underground shopping centers
    - RG.47 *<detention complexes>*
      - RG.48 concentration camps
      - RG.49 penal colonies

May be used in combination with other descriptors (e.g., **wood** + **housing**; **prefabricated** + **temporary housing**; **rehabilitated** + **inner cities**).

RG.50   prison camps
RG.51   educational complexes
RG.52   campuses
RG.53   educational parks
RG.54   housing
RG.55   *<housing by form>*
RG.56   cluster housing
RG.57   homesteads
RG.58   low-rise housing
RG.59   pueblos (housing complexes)
RG.60   *<housing by function>*
RG.61   temporary housing
RG.62   emergency housing
RG.63   labor camps
RG.64   lumber camps
RG.65   *<housing by location or context>*
RG.66   rural housing
RG.67   *<housing by development practice>*
RG.68   affordable housing
RG.69   housing projects
RG.70   low cost housing
RG.71   public housing
RG.72   scattered-site housing
RG.73   low income housing
RG.74   mobile home parks
RG.75   moderate income housing
RG.76   self-help housing
RG.77   housing developments
RG.78   planned unit developments
RG.79   rental housing
RG.80   trade-in housing
RG.81   *<housing by occupants>*
RG.82   housing for the elderly
RG.83   housing for the handicapped
RG.84   military housing
RG.85   olympic villages
RG.86   refugee camps
RG.87   student housing
RG.88   *<housing by ownership>*
RG.89   communal housing
RG.90   phalansteries
RG.91   condominiums
RG.92   cooperative housing
RG.93   industrial housing
RG.94   industrial complexes
RG.95   *<extracting complexes>*
RG.96   gravel pits
RG.97   mines
RG.98   coal mines

May be used in combination with other descriptors (e.g., **wood** + **housing**; **prefabricated** + **temporary housing**; **rehabilitated** + **inner cities**).

RG.99   copper mines
RG.100   diamond mines
RG.101   gold mines
RG.102   iron mines
RG.103   silver mines
RG.104   tin mines
RG.105   oil fields
RG.106   quarries
RG.107 industrial parks
RG.108 power plants
RG.109   gas-turbine power plants
RG.110   hydroelectric power plants
RG.111   pumped storage power plants
RG.112   tidal power plants
RG.113   solar power plants
RG.114   ocean thermal energy conversion plants
RG.115   steam power plants
RG.116   coal-fired power plants
RG.117   geothermal power plants
RG.118   nuclear power plants
RG.119   oil-fired power plants
RG.120   wind power plants
RG.121 tank farms
RG.122 military installations
RG.123 military bases
RG.124   air bases
RG.125   naval air bases
RG.126   army bases
RG.127   guided missile bases
RG.128   naval bases
RG.129   naval shipyards
RG.130   submarine bases
RG.131 military camps
RG.132   army camps
RG.133   cantonments
RG.134   castra
RG.135   ribats
RG.136 military training camps
RG.137   boot camps
RG.138 motion-picture studios
RG.139 museum villages
RG.140 nature centers
RG.141 office complexes
RG.142 office parks
RG.143 proving grounds
RG.144 ranges
RG.145 firing ranges
RG.146 guided missile ranges
RG.147 shooting ranges

May be used in combination with other descriptors (e.g., **wood** + **housing**; **prefabricated** + **temporary housing**; **rehabilitated** + **inner cities**).

RG.148 archery ranges
RG.149 rifle ranges
RG.150 skeet ranges
RG.151 recreation areas
RG.152 amusement parks
RG.153 theme parks
RG.154 bathing beaches
RG.155 campgrounds
RG.156 camps
RG.157 day camps
RG.158 nudist camps
RG.159 religious camps
RG.160 church camps
RG.161 school camps
RG.162 summer camps
RG.163 trailer camps
RG.164 country clubs
RG.165 dude ranches
RG.166 midways
RG.167 preserves
RG.168 resorts
RG.169 health resorts
RG.170 spas
RG.171 seaside resorts
RG.172 summer resorts
RG.173 winter resorts
RG.174 sports complexes
RG.175 obstacle courses
RG.176 racetracks
RG.177 automobile racetracks
RG.178 drag strips
RG.179 dog tracks
RG.180 horse racetracks
RG.181 velodromes
RG.182 skateboarding parks
RG.183 trails
RG.184 heritage trails
RG.185 nature trails
RG.186 ski trails
RG.187 yacht clubs
RG.188 religious communities
RG.189 béguinages
RG.190 convents
RG.191 hermitages
RG.192 lavras
RG.193 mathas
RG.194 monasteries
RG.195 abbeys
RG.196 charterhouses

May be used in combination with other descriptors (e.g., **wood** + **housing**; **prefabricated** + **temporary housing**; **rehabilitated** + **inner cities**).

RG.197 double monasteries
RG.198 friaries
RG.199 priories
RG.200 sanghas
RG.201 tekkes
RG.202 viharas
RG.203 sites
RG.204 archaeological sites
RG.205 dance grounds
RG.206 leys
RG.207 building sites
RG.208 homesites
RG.209 industrial sites
RG.210 endangered places
RG.211 historic sites
RG.212 battlefields
RG.213 pilgrimage centers
RG.214 test sites
RG.215 nuclear test sites
RG.216 *<transportation complexes>*
RG.217 *<air transportation complexes>*
RG.218 airports
RG.219 heliports
RG.220 launch complexes
RG.221 railroad yards
RG.222 marshalling yards
RG.223 *<water transportation complexes>*
RG.224 dockyards
RG.225 hoverports
RG.226 marinas
RG.227 marine terminals
RG.228 shipyards
RG.229 zoos
RG.230 children's zoos
RG.231 menageries
RG.232 open-air zoos
RG.233 safari parks
RG.234 wild animal parks
RG.235 *<complexes by development practice>*
RG.236 commercial strips
RG.237 mixed-use developments
RG.238 subdivisions
RG.239 districts
RG.240 *<districts by function>*
RG.241 *<districts by function: administrative>*
RG.242 assessment districts
RG.243 *<civil divisions>*
RG.244 arrondissements
RG.245 boroughs

May be used in combination with other descriptors (e.g., **wood** + **housing**; **prefabricated** + **temporary housing**; **rehabilitated** + **inner cities**).

RG.246 precincts
RG.247 townships
RG.248 election districts
RG.249 congressional districts
RG.250 legislative districts
RG.251 park districts
RG.252 planning districts
RG.253 *<religious districts>*
RG.254 archdioceses
RG.255 closes
RG.256 dioceses
RG.257 parishes
RG.258 temene
RG.259 school districts
RG.260 seigneuries
RG.261 statistical areas
RG.262 census tracts
RG.263 Standard Metropolitan Statistical Areas
RG.264 water districts
RG.265 *<districts by function: land use>*
RG.266 business districts
RG.267 red-light districts
RG.268 shopping districts
RG.269 civic centers
RG.270 historic districts
RG.271 industrial districts
RG.272 residential districts
RG.273 neighborhoods
RG.274 barrios
RG.275 Chinatowns
RG.276 ghettos
RG.277 skid rows
RG.278 slums
RG.279 shantytowns
RG.280 barriadas
RG.281 bidonvilles
RG.282 favelas
RG.283 vici
RG.284 woonerven
RG.285 zones
RG.286 buffer zones
RG.287 demilitarized zones
RG.288 transition zones
RG.289 *<districts by location or context>*
RG.290 acropolises
RG.291 central business districts
RG.292 central cities
RG.293 inner cities
RG.294 old towns

May be used in combination with other descriptors (e.g., **wood** + **housing**; **prefabricated** + **temporary housing**; **rehabilitated** + **inner cities**).

districts

<districts by location or context>

RG.295	**quarters (districts)**
RG.296	**urban areas**
RG.297	**urban fringes**
RG.298	*<districts by condition>*
RG.299	**development areas**
RG.300	**growth centers**

May be used in combination with other descriptors (e.g., **wood** + **housing**; **prefabricated** + **temporary housing**; **rehabilitated** + **inner cities**).

Single
Built Works
and Open Spaces
Hierarchy

Scope The Single Built Works and Open Spaces hierarchy contains descriptors for two aspects of the built environment. In addition to freestanding buildings and other structures commonly considered individual built works or architectural types (e.g., **museums, towers, banks**), this hierarchy includes certain open spaces (e.g., **gardens, plazas**) because they are relatively coherent areas created and modified by many of the same concepts and processes that shape buildings and other structures.

Descriptors in the <*single built works*> portion of the hierarchy cover a range from complex buildings to minimal accessory structures. Wherever possible, buildings are distinguished from other structures. Buildings are defined as walled or roofed constructions used or intended for shelter or occupancy (e.g, **apartment houses, restaurants**), generally more substantial than other structures that provide only some shelter or enclosure (e.g., **tents, cow sheds**). "Other structures" are considered to be constructions having partial or virtual enclosure or shelter (e.g., **cromlechs, arbors**) or freestanding constructions providing no enclosure or shelter (e.g., **mounds, signal towers**). Some structures may be relatively small and exist as accessories to other built works (e.g., **fountains, tombs**).

The **open spaces** portion of the hierarchy includes exterior spaces that are designed as units or designated as units and may contain buildings and other structures (e.g., **quadrangles, parks**).

Organization The <*single built works*> portion of the hierarchy has two main sections to distinguish between the general types of built works (**buildings** and **structures**) and specific types (e.g., **cottages, post offices**, and **temples**). The <*single built works by specific type*> section is then further subdivided as follows: Under the heading <*single built works by form*> are found general morphological types that do not necessarily denote any specific function (e.g., **apsidal buildings, skyscrapers**). Under <*single built works by function*> are descriptors for classes of built works that are denoted by their use (e.g., **commercial buildings, dwellings**). Under <*single built works by location or context*> are found descriptors defined by their placement in the landscape in relation to other structures or in relation to landscape features (e.g., **garden structures, outbuildings**). A small number of descriptors are found under additional headings classifying single built works <*by design*>, and <*by condition*>.

Descriptors in the open spaces portion of the hierarchy are classified by form (e.g., **gardens, quadrangles**), by function (e.g., **nature preserves, roads**), and by location or context (e.g., **city blocks, yards**).

Relation to Other Hierarchies Some descriptors located in the Single Built Works and Open Spaces hierarchy (e.g., **schools, libraries**) can be used to mean the built works, the organizations, or the institutions.

Descriptors for the structural systems and individual building parts (e.g., **balloon frames, doors**) that make up single built works are found in the Built Works Components hierarchy. Rooms, spaces, and other large building subdivisions (e.g., **kitchens, ells**) are found in the Building Divisions and Site Elements hierarchy, as are descriptors for the component parts of open spaces and landscapes (e.g., **fences, berms**).

Descriptor Form and Use Descriptors appear as plural nouns, with the singular added as an alternate form where appropriate. For single built works by style, physical attributes, technique, material, or other aspect, combine with descriptors from other hierarchies (e.g., **Georgian** + **saltbox houses**; **three-story** + **parking garages**; **modular** + **houses**; **fieldstone** + **cottages**). Alternate forms may be used as modifiers (e.g., **temple** + **porticoes**).

Number of Descriptors 1427

Synopsis

RK.1 *<single built works>*
RK.2 *<single built works by general type>*
RK.3 **structures**
RK.4 **buildings**
RK.5 *<single built works by specific type>*
RK.6 *<single built works by form>*
RK.7 *<single built works by form: height>*
RK.15 *<single built works by form: massing or shape>*
RK.39 *<single built works by function>*
RK.40 *<agricultural structures>*
|
RK.1325 *<workship buildings>*
RK.1327 *<single built works by location or context>*
RK.1328 **garden structures**
|
RK.1371 **underwater buildings**
RK.1372 *<single built works by design>*
RK.1373 **earth sheltered buildings**
|
RK.1388 **windowless buildings**
RK.1389 *<single built works by condition>*
RK.1390 **derelict buildings**
RK.1391 **illegal buildings**
RK.1392 **ruins**
RK.1393 **open spaces**
RK.1394 *<open spaces by form>*
RK.1395 **gardens**
|
RK.1444 **squares**
RK.1449 *<open spaces by function>*
RK.1451 **nature preserves**
|
RK.1568 **walkways**
RK.1579 *<open spaces by location or context>*
RK.1580 **agoras**
|
RK.1600 yards

RK.1 *<single built works>*
RK.2 *<single built works by general type>*
RK.3 **structures**
RK.4 **buildings**
RK.5 *<single built works by specific type>*
RK.6 *<single built works by form>*
RK.7 *<single built works by form: height>*
RK.8 **multistory buildings**
RK.9 **low-rise buildings**
RK.10 **mid-rise buildings**
RK.11 **high-rise buildings**
RK.12 **point blocks**
RK.13 **skyscrapers**
RK.14 **tower buildings**
RK.15 *<single built works by form: massing or shape>*
RK.16 **apsidal buildings**
RK.17 **tetraconchs**
RK.18 **triconchs**
RK.19 **basilicas**
RK.20 **kiosks**
RK.21 **lean-tos**
RK.22 **megastructures**
RK.23 **mimetic buildings**
RK.24 **monoptera**
RK.25 **panopticons**
RK.26 **quonset huts**
RK.27 **rotundas (buildings)**
RK.28 **slab blocks**
RK.29 **sunken huts**
RK.30 **tholoi**
RK.31 **towers**
RK.32 **bell towers**
RK.33 **campaniles**
RK.34 **shoro**
RK.35 **clock towers**
RK.36 **round towers**
RK.37 **watchtowers**
RK.38 **fire towers**
RK.39 *<single built works by function>*
RK.40 *<agricultural structures>*
RK.41 **agricultural buildings**
RK.42 **barns**
RK.43 *<barns by form>*
RK.44 **crib barns**
RK.45 **Dutch barns**
RK.46 **English barns**
RK.47 *<barns by function>*
RK.48 **cattle barns**
RK.49 **dairy barns**

May be used in combination with other descriptors (e.g., **fieldstone** + **cottages**; **prefabricated** + **ranch houses**; **three-story** + **parking garages**; **Georgian** + **saltbox houses**; **temple** + **porticoes**).

RK.50	horse barns
RK.51	sheep barns
RK.52	tithe barns
RK.53	*<barns by location or context>*
RK.54	bank barns
RK.55	Pennsylvania bank barns
RK.56	connected barns
RK.57	dairies
RK.58	farm buildings
RK.59	grain elevators
RK.60	granaries
RK.61	hop barns
RK.62	horticultural buildings
RK.63	greenhouses
RK.64	forcing houses
RK.65	orangeries
RK.66	palm houses
RK.67	solar greenhouses
RK.68	winter gardens
RK.69	lathhouses
RK.70	nurseries (horticulture)
RK.71	ice houses
RK.72	malthouses
RK.73	milk houses
RK.74	springhouses
RK.75	sugar houses
RK.76	woolsheds
RK.77	animal housing
RK.78	apiaries
RK.79	beehives
RK.80	aviaries
RK.81	birdhouses
RK.82	dovecotes
RK.83	corrals
RK.84	cow sheds
RK.85	doghouses
RK.86	kennels
RK.87	pig houses
RK.88	pigsties
RK.89	poultry houses
RK.90	chicken houses
RK.91	chicken hatcheries
RK.92	rabbit hutches
RK.93	sheepfolds
RK.94	stables
RK.95	mews
RK.96	*<food storage structures>*
RK.97	corncribs
RK.98	grain bins

May be used in combination with other descriptors (e.g., **fieldstone** + **cottages**; **prefabricated** + **ranch houses**; **three-story** + **parking garages**; **Georgian** + **saltbox houses**; **temple** + **porticoes**).

<single built works by specific type>
<single built works by function>
<agricultural structures>
<food storage structures>

RK.99 **silos**
RK.100 **tobacco barns**
RK.101 **commercial buildings**
RK.102 *<eating and drinking buildings>*
RK.103 **bars**
RK.104 **milk bars**
RK.105 **pubs**
RK.106 **saloons**
RK.107 **beer halls**
RK.108 **snack bars**
RK.109 **beer gardens**
RK.110 **coffeehouses**
RK.111 **restaurants**
RK.112 **Automats (TM)**
RK.113 **brasseries**
RK.114 **cafés**
RK.115 **coffee shops**
RK.116 **diners**
RK.117 **fast food restaurants**
RK.118 **drive-in restaurants**
RK.119 **ice cream parlors**
RK.120 **outdoor cafés**
RK.121 **popinae**
RK.122 **tea rooms**
RK.123 **roadhouses**
RK.124 **taverns**
RK.125 **ordinaries**
RK.126 **financial institutions**
RK.127 **banks**
RK.128 **branch banks**
RK.129 **drive-in banks**
RK.130 **Federal Reserve banks**
RK.131 **mobile banks**
RK.132 **savings banks**
RK.133 **exchanges**
RK.134 **commodity exchanges**
RK.135 **stock exchanges**
RK.136 **mercantile buildings**
RK.137 **art galleries**
RK.138 **auction houses**
RK.139 **design centers**
RK.140 **markets**
RK.141 **macella**
RK.142 **market halls**
RK.143 **supermarkets**
RK.144 *<stands and stalls>*
RK.145 **bookstalls**
RK.146 **newsstands**
RK.147 **produce stands**

May be used in combination with other descriptors (e.g., **fieldstone** + **cottages**; **prefabricated** + **ranch houses**; **three-story** + **parking garages**; **Georgian** + **saltbox houses**; **temple** + **porticoes**).

RK.148 stores
RK.149 *<stores by commodity sold>*
RK.150 antique stores
RK.151 bakeries
RK.152 bookstores
RK.153 clothing stores
RK.154 shoe stores
RK.155 confectioneries
RK.156 delicatessens
RK.157 drugstores
RK.158 florist shops
RK.159 furniture stores
RK.160 grocery stores
RK.161 hardware stores
RK.162 jewelry stores
RK.163 lumberyards
RK.164 pet shops
RK.165 sporting goods stores
RK.166 tea stores
RK.167 toy stores
RK.168 *<stores by merchandising practice>*
RK.169 chain stores
RK.170 company stores
RK.171 convenience stores
RK.172 cooperative stores
RK.173 department stores
RK.174 magasins de nouveautés
RK.175 discount houses
RK.176 outlet stores
RK.177 general stores
RK.178 pawnshops
RK.179 retail stores
RK.180 self-service stores
RK.181 specialty stores
RK.182 boutiques
RK.183 tabernae
RK.184 thrift shops
RK.185 trading posts
RK.186 variety stores
RK.187 trade marts
RK.188 *<service industry buildings>*
RK.189 barbershops
RK.190 beauty shops
RK.191 betting parlors
RK.192 brothels
RK.193 employment agencies
RK.194 laundries
RK.195 massage parlors
RK.196 travel agencies

May be used in combination with other descriptors (e.g., **fieldstone** + **cottages**; **prefabricated** + **ranch houses**; **three-story** + **parking garages**; **Georgian** + **saltbox houses**; **temple** + **porticoes**).

RK.197 *<communications structures>*
RK.198 communications buildings
RK.199 computer centers
RK.200 publishing offices
RK.201 *<telecommunications buildings>*
RK.202 broadcasting stations
RK.203 radio stations
RK.204 television stations
RK.205 relay stations
RK.206 repeater stations
RK.207 satellite tracking stations
RK.208 telegraph offices
RK.209 telegraph stations
RK.210 telephone exchanges
RK.211 *<telecommunications towers>*
RK.212 radio towers
RK.213 television towers
RK.214 transmission towers
RK.215 telephone booths
RK.216 dwellings
RK.217 *<group dwellings>*
RK.218 barracks
RK.219 bunkhouses
RK.220 dormitories
RK.221 fraternity houses
RK.222 interns' residences
RK.223 longhouses
RK.224 nurses' residences
RK.225 sorority houses
RK.226 houses
RK.227 *<houses by form>*
RK.228 bastel houses
RK.229 bungalows
RK.230 cabins
RK.231 chalets
RK.232 cottages
RK.233 cottages ornés
RK.234 Creole cottages
RK.235 domus
RK.236 huts
RK.237 bothies
RK.238 hovels
RK.239 rondavels
RK.240 mansions
RK.241 shacks
RK.242 *<houses by form: height>*
RK.243 three-deckers
RK.244 *<houses by form: massing or shape>*
RK.245 A-frame houses

May be used in combination with other descriptors (e.g., **fieldstone** + **cottages**; **prefabricated** + **ranch houses**; **three-story** + **parking garages**; **Georgian** + **saltbox houses**; **temple** + **porticoes**).

RK.246 beehive houses
RK.247 clochans
RK.248 trulli
RK.249 garrison houses
RK.250 I-houses
RK.251 ranch houses
RK.252 saltbox houses
RK.253 split-level houses
RK.254 stilt houses
RK.255 *<houses by form: plan>*
RK.256 courtyard houses
RK.257 atrium houses
RK.258 peristyle houses
RK.259 detached houses
RK.260 double-pen houses
RK.261 dogtrot houses
RK.262 saddlebag houses
RK.263 double-pile houses
RK.264 megarons
RK.265 row houses
RK.266 brownstones
RK.267 crescents (row houses)
RK.268 terrace houses
RK.269 shotgun houses
RK.270 single-pen houses
RK.271 *<houses by form: roof orientation>*
RK.272 gable-front houses
RK.273 *<houses by function>*
RK.274 decorators' show houses
RK.275 model houses
RK.276 seasonal dwellings
RK.277 summer houses
RK.278 yalis
RK.279 vacation houses
RK.280 tourist cabins
RK.281 second homes
RK.282 *<houses by designer or builder>*
RK.283 architect-designed houses
RK.284 builder-designed houses
RK.285 owner-built houses
RK.286 *<houses by location or context>*
RK.287 *<houses by location: settlement area>*
RK.288 *<rural houses>*
RK.289 country houses
RK.290 châteaux
RK.291 dachas
RK.292 villas
RK.293 villae rusticae
RK.294 villae suburbanae

May be used in combination with other descriptors (e.g., **fieldstone** + **cottages**; **prefabricated** + **ranch houses**; **three-story** + **parking garages**; **Georgian** + **saltbox houses**; **temple** + **porticoes**).

RK.295 villae urbanae
RK.296 farmhouses
RK.297 manor houses
RK.298 plantation houses
RK.299 suburban houses
RK.300 borjs
RK.301 town houses
RK.302 hôtels
RK.303 palazzi
RK.304 *<houses by location: topographical>*
RK.305 beach houses
RK.306 cave dwellings
RK.307 cliff dwellings
RK.308 lake dwellings
RK.309 crannogs
RK.310 pit dwellings
RK.311 tree houses
RK.312 *<houses by construction technique>*
RK.313 earth lodges
RK.314 hogans
RK.315 igloos
RK.316 log cabins
RK.317 log houses
RK.318 solar houses
RK.319 wigwams
RK.320 *<houses by development practice>*
RK.321 speculative houses
RK.322 tract houses
RK.323 *<houses by occupants>*
RK.324 architects' houses
RK.325 artists' houses
RK.326 *<clergy houses>*
RK.327 deaneries
RK.328 manses
RK.329 parsonages
RK.330 rectories
RK.331 vicarages
RK.332 guesthouses
RK.333 haunted houses
RK.334 lockkeepers' houses
RK.335 official residences
RK.336 legations
RK.337 palaces
RK.338 bishops' palaces
RK.339 bît-hilani
RK.340 mahals
RK.341 royal palaces
RK.342 ducal palaces
RK.343 imperial palaces

May be used in combination with other descriptors (e.g., **fieldstone** + **cottages**; **prefabricated** + **ranch houses**; **three-story** + **parking garages**; **Georgian** + **saltbox houses**; **temple** + **porticoes**).

RK.344 summer palaces
RK.345 zimbabwes
RK.346 praetoriums
RK.347 retirement homes
RK.348 single-family dwellings
RK.349 slave quarters
RK.350 *<movable dwellings>*
RK.351 camping trailers
RK.352 caravans
RK.353 houseboats
RK.354 mobile homes
RK.355 motor homes
RK.356 tents
RK.357 tipis
RK.358 yurts
RK.359 travel trailers
RK.360 multiple dwellings
RK.361 apartment hotels
RK.362 apartment houses
RK.363 cooperative apartment houses
RK.364 garden apartments
RK.365 tenement houses
RK.366 dumbbell tenements
RK.367 double houses
RK.368 duplex houses
RK.369 insulae
RK.370 exhibition buildings
RK.371 *<animal exhibition buildings>*
RK.372 aquariums
RK.373 marine aquariums
RK.374 elephant houses
RK.375 corn palaces
RK.376 halls of fame
RK.377 museums
RK.378 children's museums
RK.379 *<museums by form>*
RK.380 open-air museums
RK.381 *<museums by subject>*
RK.382 art museums
RK.383 architectural museums
RK.384 architectural centers
RK.385 decorative arts museums
RK.386 folk art museums
RK.387 literature museums
RK.388 photography museums
RK.389 textile museums
RK.390 communications museums
RK.391 costume museums
RK.392 history museums

May be used in combination with other descriptors (e.g., **fieldstone** + **cottages**; **prefabricated** + **ranch houses**; **three-story** + **parking garages**; **Georgian** + **saltbox houses**; **temple** + **porticoes**).

RK.393 agriculture museums
RK.394 archaeological museums
RK.395 historic house museums
RK.396 historical society museums
RK.397 industrial museums
RK.398 maritime museums
RK.399 military museums
RK.400 naval museums
RK.401 technology museums
RK.402 transportation museums
RK.403 aeronautical museums
RK.404 astronautical museums
RK.405 automobile museums
RK.406 railroad museums
RK.407 museums of moving images
RK.408 music museums
RK.409 numismatic museums
RK.410 philatelic museums
RK.411 religious museums
RK.412 science museums
RK.413 anthropology museums
RK.414 ethnological museums
RK.415 astronomical museums
RK.416 botanical museums
RK.417 herbaria
RK.418 geology museums
RK.419 mineralogy museums
RK.420 medical museums
RK.421 natural history museums
RK.422 zoological museums
RK.423 sports museums
RK.424 fishery museums
RK.425 hunting museums
RK.426 theater museums
RK.427 wax museums
RK.428 *<museums by administration>*
RK.429 company museums
RK.430 county museums
RK.431 international museums
RK.432 national museums
RK.433 planetaria
RK.434 fortifications
RK.435 bawns
RK.436 castles
RK.437 châtelets
RK.438 moated castles
RK.439 qasrs
RK.440 city walls
RK.441 coastal fortifications

May be used in combination with other descriptors (e.g., **fieldstone** + **cottages**; **prefabricated** + **ranch houses**; **three-story** + **parking garages**; **Georgian** + **saltbox houses**; **temple** + **porticoes**).

RK.442 field fortifications
RK.443 fortresses
RK.444 alcazars
RK.445 citadels
RK.446 migdols
RK.447 forts
RK.448 bastioned forts
RK.449 fortlets
RK.450 hillforts
RK.451 star-forts
RK.452 limites
RK.453 plant fortifications
RK.454 redoubts
RK.455 stockades
RK.456 *<funerary structures>*
RK.457 burial mounds
RK.458 catafalques
RK.459 funerary buildings
RK.460 *<funerary preparatory buildings>*
RK.461 crematories
RK.462 busta
RK.463 ustrina
RK.464 funeral homes
RK.465 morgues
RK.466 mortuaries
RK.467 towers of silence
RK.468 *<sepulchral buildings>*
RK.469 mausoleums
RK.470 gumbads
RK.471 rauzas
RK.472 ossuaries
RK.473 graves
RK.474 lich stones
RK.475 pyres
RK.476 sepulchral monuments
RK.477 cenotaphs
RK.478 lanterns of the dead
RK.479 tombstones
RK.480 tombs
RK.481 *<tombs by form>*
RK.482 altar tombs
RK.483 chamber tombs
RK.484 hypogea
RK.485 megalithic chamber tombs
RK.486 gallery graves
RK.487 passage graves
RK.488 chullpas
RK.489 cist graves
RK.490 mastabas

May be used in combination with other descriptors (e.g., **fieldstone** + **cottages**; **prefabricated** + **ranch houses**; **three-story** + **parking garages**; **Georgian** + **saltbox houses**; **temple** + **porticoes**).

RK.491 **pyramids**
RK.492 **rock-cut tombs**
RK.493 **shaft graves**
RK.494 **tholos tombs**
RK.495 **tower-tombs**
RK.496 *<tombs by function>*
RK.497 **royal tombs**
RK.498 *<gate structures>*
RK.499 **city gates**
RK.500 **gopuras**
RK.501 **p'ai-lous**
RK.502 **pishtaqs**
RK.503 **propylaea**
RK.504 **pylons**
RK.505 **tetrapylons**
RK.506 **toranas**
RK.507 **torii**
RK.508 **water gates**
RK.509 **historic buildings**
RK.510 **historic houses**
RK.511 **landmark buildings**
RK.512 **hydraulic structures**
RK.513 *<hydraulic structures by form>*
RK.514 *<artificial water channels>*
RK.515 **flumes**
RK.516 **millraces**
RK.517 **sluices**
RK.518 **canals**
RK.519 **interoceanic canals**
RK.520 **dams**
RK.521 *<dams by form>*
RK.522 **arch dams**
RK.523 **buttress dams**
RK.524 **gravity dams**
RK.525 *<dams by function>*
RK.526 **barrages**
RK.527 **check dams**
RK.528 **cofferdams**
RK.529 **diversion dams**
RK.530 **flood dams**
RK.531 **hydroelectric dams**
RK.532 **weirs**
RK.533 **wasteweirs**
RK.534 *<dams by construction>*
RK.535 **earth-fill dams**
RK.536 **rolled-fill dams**
RK.537 **zoned earth dams**
RK.538 **rock-fill dams**
RK.539 *<hydraulic structures by function>*

May be used in combination with other descriptors (e.g., **fieldstone** + **cottages**; **prefabricated** + **ranch houses**; **three-story** + **parking garages**; **Georgian** + **saltbox houses**; **temple** + **porticoes**).

RK.540	*<drainage structures>*
RK.541	culverts
RK.542	sewers
RK.543	*<sewers by function>*
RK.544	combined sewers
RK.545	sanitary sewers
RK.546	storm sewers
RK.547	*<sewers by location or context>*
RK.548	branch sewers
RK.549	cloacae
RK.550	intercepting sewers
RK.551	lateral sewers
RK.552	main sewers
RK.553	outfall sewers
RK.554	erosion protection works
RK.555	breakwaters
RK.556	blockwork breakwaters
RK.557	mound breakwaters
RK.558	seawalls
RK.559	gabions
RK.560	groins (erosion protection works)
RK.561	hydraulic gates
RK.562	jetties
RK.563	riprap
RK.564	wing dams
RK.565	flood protection works
RK.566	dikes
RK.567	levees
RK.568	land reclamation works
RK.569	*<water distribution structures>*
RK.570	aqueducts
RK.571	qanats
RK.572	conduits
RK.573	fountain-houses
RK.574	fountains
RK.575	pumping stations
RK.576	reservoirs
RK.577	castelli aquae
RK.578	underground reservoirs
RK.579	settling basins
RK.580	standpipes
RK.581	storm water retention basins
RK.582	water tanks
RK.583	water towers
RK.584	waterworks
RK.585	desalination plants
RK.586	filtration plants
RK.587	sewage treatment plants
RK.588	water treatment plants

May be used in combination with other descriptors (e.g., **fieldstone** + **cottages**; **prefabricated** + **ranch houses**; **three-story** + **parking garages**; **Georgian** + **saltbox houses**; **temple** + **porticoes**).

RK.589 wells
RK.590 *<wells by function>*
RK.591 gas wells
RK.592 oil wells
RK.593 water wells
RK.594 *<wells by construction>*
RK.595 artesian wells
RK.596 baolis
RK.597 driven wells
RK.598 dug wells
RK.599 *<industrial structures>*
RK.600 *<drilling structures>*
RK.601 drilling rigs
RK.602 offshore rigs
RK.603 oil rigs
RK.604 offshore drilling platforms
RK.605 industrial buildings
RK.606 *<accessory industrial buildings>*
RK.607 boiler houses
RK.608 employees' buildings
RK.609 machine shops
RK.610 paint shops
RK.611 repair shops
RK.612 body shops
RK.613 factories
RK.614 *<factories by function>*
RK.615 assembly plants
RK.616 automobile factories
RK.617 furniture factories
RK.618 pilot plants
RK.619 printing plants
RK.620 *<processing plants>*
RK.621 beverage processing plants
RK.622 bottling plants
RK.623 breweries
RK.624 distilleries
RK.625 wineries
RK.626 brickworks
RK.627 cement plants
RK.628 crushing plants
RK.629 food processing plants
RK.630 canneries
RK.631 dairy plants
RK.632 fisheries
RK.633 flour mills
RK.634 *<meat processing plants>*
RK.635 packing plants
RK.636 slaughterhouses
RK.637 saltworks

May be used in combination with other descriptors (e.g., **fieldstone** + **cottages**; **prefabricated** + **ranch houses**; **three-story** + **parking garages**; **Georgian** + **saltbox houses**; **temple** + **porticoes**).

RK.638	smokehouses
RK.639	sugar refineries
RK.640	gasworks
RK.641	glass factories
RK.642	*<metalworking plants>*
RK.643	ironworks
RK.644	shot towers
RK.645	smelters
RK.646	steel mills
RK.647	rolling mills
RK.648	tube mills
RK.649	paper mills
RK.650	planing mills
RK.651	potteries
RK.652	pulp mills
RK.653	refineries
RK.654	petroleum refineries
RK.655	resource recovery facilities
RK.656	roperies
RK.657	sawmills
RK.658	tanneries
RK.659	textile mills
RK.660	cotton mills
RK.661	dyeworks
RK.662	fulling mills
RK.663	woolen mills
RK.664	*<factories by power source>*
RK.665	water mills
RK.666	tide mills
RK.667	windmills
RK.668	smock mills
RK.669	mine buildings
RK.670	*<utilities buildings>*
RK.671	electric substations
RK.672	*<power plant buildings>*
RK.673	powerhouses
RK.674	reactor containment buildings
RK.675	*<metal works structures>*
RK.676	blast furnaces
RK.677	*<mine structures>*
RK.678	mine shafts
RK.679	*<shipyard structures>*
RK.680	slipways
RK.681	*<textile mill structures>*
RK.682	bleacheries
RK.683	weaving sheds
RK.684	*<information handling facilities>*
RK.685	archives
RK.686	chartophylacia

May be used in combination with other descriptors (e.g., **fieldstone** + **cottages**; **prefabricated** + **ranch houses**; **three-story** + **parking garages**; **Georgian** + **saltbox houses**; **temple** + **porticoes**).

RK.687 tabularia
RK.688 documentation centers
RK.689 information centers
RK.690 visitors' centers
RK.691 libraries
RK.692 *<libraries by administration>*
RK.693 national libraries
RK.694 private libraries
RK.695 public libraries
RK.696 branch libraries
RK.697 Carnegie libraries
RK.698 state libraries
RK.699 *<libraries by location or context>*
RK.700 academic libraries
RK.701 school libraries
RK.702 learning resource centers
RK.703 special libraries
RK.704 corporate libraries
RK.705 research libraries
RK.706 *<libraries by subject>*
RK.707 architectural libraries
RK.708 art libraries
RK.709 children's libraries
RK.710 depository libraries
RK.711 medical libraries
RK.712 presidential libraries
RK.713 *<institutional buildings>*
RK.714 correctional institutions
RK.715 ergastula
RK.716 jails
RK.717 gaols
RK.718 lockups
RK.719 prisons
RK.720 *<prisons by form or function>*
RK.721 debtor's prisons
RK.722 maximum-security prisons
RK.723 medium-security prisons
RK.724 minimum-security prisons
RK.725 open prisons
RK.726 *<prisons by administration>*
RK.727 federal prisons
RK.728 military prisons
RK.729 state prisons
RK.730 reformatories
RK.731 detention centers
RK.732 workhouses
RK.733 *<health and welfare facilities>*
RK.734 health facilities
RK.735 *<auxiliary health care facilities>*

May be used in combination with other descriptors (e.g., **fieldstone** + **cottages**; **prefabricated** + **ranch houses**; **three-story** + **parking garages**; **Georgian** + **saltbox houses**; **temple** + **porticoes**).

RK.736 ambulance stations
RK.737 medical laboratories
RK.738 poison control centers
RK.739 vaccination centers
RK.740 clinics
RK.741 birth control clinics
RK.742 dental clinics
RK.743 dispensaries
RK.744 psychiatric clinics
RK.745 surgical clinics
RK.746 comfort stations
RK.747 latrines
RK.748 reredorters
RK.749 extended care facilities
RK.750 nursing homes
RK.751 old age homes
RK.752 rehabilitation centers
RK.753 rest homes
RK.754 labor rest homes
RK.755 sanatoriums
RK.756 terminal care facilities
RK.757 hospitals
RK.758 *<hospitals by form>*
RK.759 cottage hospitals
RK.760 mobile hospitals
RK.761 *<hospitals by function>*
RK.762 aural hospitals
RK.763 children's hospitals
RK.764 convalescent hospitals
RK.765 eye hospitals
RK.766 *<hospitals for contagious diseases>*
RK.767 lazarettos
RK.768 leprosariums
RK.769 pesthouses
RK.770 maternity hospitals
RK.771 military hospitals
RK.772 teaching hospitals
RK.773 veterans' hospitals
RK.774 veterinary hospitals
RK.775 infirmaries
RK.776 medical centers
RK.777 emergency medical centers
RK.778 mental health facilities
RK.779 psychiatric hospitals
RK.780 public baths
RK.781 balnea
RK.782 thermae
RK.783 welfare buildings
RK.784 almshouses

May be used in combination with other descriptors (e.g., **fieldstone** + **cottages**; **prefabricated** + **ranch houses**; **three-story** + **parking garages**; **Georgian** + **saltbox houses**; **temple** + **porticoes**).

RK.785 beadhouses
RK.786 animal shelters
RK.787 asylums
RK.788 group homes
RK.789 halfway houses
RK.790 orphanages
RK.791 sheltered workshops
RK.792 soup kitchens
RK.793 schools
RK.794 *<schools by function>*
RK.795 boarding schools
RK.796 consolidated schools
RK.797 day schools
RK.798 free schools
RK.799 military academies
RK.800 naval schools
RK.801 *<schools by subject>*
RK.802 aeronautical schools
RK.803 architectural schools
RK.804 art schools
RK.805 business schools
RK.806 business colleges
RK.807 dental schools
RK.808 engineering schools
RK.809 Hebrew schools
RK.810 language schools
RK.811 law schools
RK.812 medical schools
RK.813 music schools
RK.814 music conservatories
RK.815 nursing schools
RK.816 riding schools
RK.817 Sunday schools
RK.818 teachers colleges
RK.819 *<theological schools>*
RK.820 madrasas
RK.821 rabbinical seminaries
RK.822 theological seminaries
RK.823 veterinary colleges
RK.824 vocational schools
RK.825 *<schools by ownership>*
RK.826 private schools
RK.827 parochial schools
RK.828 preparatory schools
RK.829 yeshivas
RK.830 public schools
RK.831 *<schools by level of education>*
RK.832 *<pre-primary schools>*
RK.833 day care centers

May be used in combination with other descriptors (e.g., **fieldstone** + **cottages**; **prefabricated** + **ranch houses**; **three-story** + **parking garages**; **Georgian** + **saltbox houses**; **temple** + **porticoes**).

RK

RK.834	kindergartens
RK.835	nursery schools
RK.836	play schools
RK.837	elementary schools
RK.838	middle schools
RK.839	junior high schools
RK.840	high schools
RK.841	*<universities and colleges>*
RK.842	colleges
RK.843	community colleges
RK.844	junior colleges
RK.845	state colleges
RK.846	polytechnics
RK.847	universities
RK.848	state universities
RK.849	urban universities
RK.850	continuing education centers
RK.851	lyceums
RK.852	memorials
RK.853	war memorials
RK.854	military buildings
RK.855	*<military deployment and distribution buildings>*
RK.856	arsenals
RK.857	guided missile silos
RK.858	magazines (military buildings)
RK.859	powder magazines
RK.860	ordnance depots
RK.861	post exchanges
RK.862	*<military security buildings>*
RK.863	blockhouses
RK.864	bunkers
RK.865	guardhouses
RK.866	*<military towers>*
RK.867	*<defensive towers>*
RK.868	brochs
RK.869	nuraghi
RK.870	martello towers
RK.871	sentry boxes
RK.872	*<military social buildings>*
RK.873	officers' clubs
RK.874	*<military training buildings>*
RK.875	armories
RK.876	drill halls
RK.877	monuments
RK.878	*<monuments by form>*
RK.879	effigy mounds
RK.880	markers (monuments)
RK.881	cippi
RK.882	*<cross monuments>*

May be used in combination with other descriptors (e.g., **fieldstone** + **cottages**; **prefabricated** + **ranch houses**; **three-story** + **parking garages**; **Georgian** + **saltbox houses**; **temple** + **porticoes**).

RK.883 market crosses
RK.884 preaching crosses
RK.885 wayside crosses
RK.886 landmarks
RK.887 metae
RK.888 milestones
RK.889 megalithic monuments
RK.890 cromlechs
RK.891 henges
RK.892 standing stones
RK.893 trilithons
RK.894 memorial arches
RK.895 triumphal arches
RK.896 memorial columns
RK.897 rostral columns
RK.898 trinity columns
RK.899 zoophoric columns
RK.900 *<monumental pillars>*
RK.901 lats
RK.902 obelisks
RK.903 stelae
RK.904 *<monuments by function>*
RK.905 choragic monuments
RK.906 historical monuments
RK.907 national monuments
RK.908 soldiers' monuments
RK.909 trophies
RK.910 multipurpose buildings
RK.911 office buildings
RK.912 *<office buildings by form>*
RK.913 office towers
RK.914 *<office buildings by function>*
RK.915 administration buildings
RK.916 architects' offices
RK.917 corporate headquarters
RK.918 dental offices
RK.919 law offices
RK.920 medical offices
RK.921 *<performing arts structures>*
RK.922 band shells
RK.923 bandstands
RK.924 *<performing arts buildings>*
RK.925 cabarets
RK.926 concert halls
RK.927 music halls
RK.928 opera houses
RK.929 nightclubs
RK.930 performing arts centers
RK.931 theaters

May be used in combination with other descriptors (e.g., **fieldstone** + **cottages**; **prefabricated** + **ranch houses**; **three-story** + **parking garages**; **Georgian** + **saltbox houses**; **temple** + **porticoes**).

RK.932 *<theaters by form>*
RK.933 arena theaters
RK.934 miniature theaters
RK.935 open-air theaters
RK.936 amphitheaters
RK.937 *<theaters by function>*
RK.938 movie theaters
RK.939 drive-in theaters
RK.940 nickelodeons
RK.941 odea
RK.942 puppet theaters
RK.943 variety theaters
RK.944 *<public accommodations>*
RK.945 bed-and-breakfasts
RK.946 caravanserais
RK.947 hospices
RK.948 imarets
RK.949 xenodochia
RK.950 hostels
RK.951 youth hostels
RK.952 hotels
RK.953 floating hotels
RK.954 pensions (hotels)
RK.955 railway hotels
RK.956 inns
RK.957 cauponae
RK.958 deversoria
RK.959 lodges
RK.960 fishing lodges
RK.961 hunting lodges
RK.962 ski lodges
RK.963 lodging houses
RK.964 flophouses
RK.965 motels
RK.966 motor courts
RK.967 public buildings
RK.968 *<public buildings by function>*
RK.969 aeraria
RK.970 *<diplomatic buildings>*
RK.971 consulates
RK.972 embassy buildings
RK.973 government office buildings
RK.974 customhouses
RK.975 ministries
RK.976 patent offices
RK.977 *<judicial buildings>*
RK.978 courthouses
RK.979 county courthouses
RK.980 district courts

May be used in combination with other descriptors (e.g., **fieldstone** + **cottages**; **prefabricated** + **ranch houses**; **three-story** + **parking garages**; **Georgian** + **saltbox houses**; **temple** + **porticoes**).

RK.981 legislative buildings
RK.982   bouleuteria
RK.983   capitols
RK.984   curiae
RK.985   parliament buildings
RK.986 mints
RK.987 post offices
RK.988 prytaneia
RK.989 public safety buildings
RK.990   fire stations
RK.991   police stations
RK.992 *<public buildings by location or context>*
RK.993 municipal buildings
RK.994   city halls
RK.995   county halls
RK.996   hôtels de ville
RK.997   palazzi pubblichi
RK.998   rathäuser
RK.999   town halls
RK.1000   broletti
RK.1001 *<recreation structures>*
RK.1002   *<amusement park structures>*
RK.1003   amusement rides
RK.1004   ferris wheels
RK.1005   merry-go-rounds
RK.1006   roller coasters
RK.1007   water slides
RK.1008 courts
RK.1009   badminton courts
RK.1010   ball courts
RK.1011   basketball courts
RK.1012   canchas
RK.1013   croquet courts
RK.1014   handball courts
RK.1015   fives courts
RK.1016   racquetball courts
RK.1017   shuffleboard courts
RK.1018   squash courts
RK.1019   tennis courts
RK.1020   indoor tennis courts
RK.1021   volleyball courts
RK.1022 grandstands
RK.1023 recreation buildings
RK.1024   children's playhouses
RK.1025   clubhouses
RK.1026   athletic clubs
RK.1027   polo clubs
RK.1028   riding clubs
RK.1029   tennis clubs

May be used in combination with other descriptors (e.g., **fieldstone** + **cottages**; **prefabricated** + **ranch houses**; **three-story** + **parking garages**; **Georgian** + **saltbox houses**; **temple** + **porticoes**).

<single built works by function>
<recreation structures>
recreation buildings
clubhouses

RK.1030 beach clubs
RK.1031 boat clubs
RK.1032 entertainment buildings
RK.1033 amusement arcades
RK.1034 penny arcades
RK.1035 video arcades
RK.1036 bingo halls
RK.1037 casinos
RK.1038 gambling casinos
RK.1039 dance halls
RK.1040 discotheques
RK.1041 fun houses
RK.1042 pool halls
RK.1043 recreation centers
RK.1044 shooting galleries
RK.1045 sports buildings
RK.1046 *<sports buildings by form>*
RK.1047 arenas
RK.1048 circuses (Roman arenas)
RK.1049 hippodromes
RK.1050 skating rinks
RK.1051 ice-skating rinks
RK.1052 ice hockey rinks
RK.1053 roller-skating rinks
RK.1054 stadiums
RK.1055 baseball stadiums
RK.1056 football stadiums
RK.1057 *<sports buildings by function>*
RK.1058 bowling alleys
RK.1059 skittle alleys
RK.1060 bullrings
RK.1061 field houses
RK.1062 physical education buildings
RK.1063 gymnasiums
RK.1064 martial arts training centers
RK.1065 palaestrae
RK.1066 riding halls
RK.1067 ski-lift stations
RK.1068 sphaeristeria
RK.1069 *<water recreation structures>*
RK.1070 bathhouses
RK.1071 cabañas
RK.1072 steam baths
RK.1073 sweathouses
RK.1074 Turkish baths
RK.1075 swimming pools
RK.1076 *<winter sports structures>*
RK.1077 artificial ski slopes
RK.1078 bobsled runs

May be used in combination with other descriptors (e.g., **fieldstone** + **cottages**; **prefabricated** + **ranch houses**; **three-story** + **parking garages**; **Georgian** + **saltbox houses**; **temple** + **porticoes**).

RK.1079 ski jumps
RK.1080 ski lifts
RK.1081 toboggan runs
RK.1082 *<religious structures>*
RK.1083 *<freestanding altars>*
RK.1084 arae
RK.1085 bomoi
RK.1086 fire altars
RK.1087 thymeles
RK.1088 holy wells
RK.1089 idgahs
RK.1090 martyria
RK.1091 minarets
RK.1092 religious buildings
RK.1093 baptisteries
RK.1094 churches
RK.1095 *<churches by form>*
RK.1096 double churches
RK.1097 hall churches
RK.1098 rock-cut churches
RK.1099 stave churches
RK.1100 *<churches by function>*
RK.1101 chapels of ease
RK.1102 pilgrimage churches
RK.1103 procathedrals
RK.1104 *<churches by location or context>*
RK.1105 abbey churches
RK.1106 cathedrals
RK.1107 cave churches
RK.1108 collegiate churches
RK.1109 minsters
RK.1110 mission churches
RK.1111 monastic churches
RK.1112 parish churches
RK.1113 domus ecclesiae
RK.1114 kivas
RK.1115 meeting houses
RK.1116 Quaker meeting houses
RK.1117 mosques
RK.1118 *<mosques by form>*
RK.1119 four-iwan mosques
RK.1120 hypostyle mosques
RK.1121 *<mosques by function>*
RK.1122 jamis
RK.1123 masjids
RK.1124 pagodas
RK.1125 synagogues
RK.1126 temples
RK.1127 *<temples by form>*

May be used in combination with other descriptors (e.g., **fieldstone** + **cottages**; **prefabricated** + **ranch houses**; **three-story** + **parking garages**; **Georgian** + **saltbox houses**; **temple** + **porticoes**).

RK.1128 hypaethral temples
RK.1129 rock-cut temples
RK.1130 speoses
RK.1131 wats
RK.1132 *<temples by function>*
RK.1133 aedes
RK.1134 fire temples
RK.1135 chahar taqs
RK.1136 mortuary temples
RK.1137 *<temples by location or context>*
RK.1138 cave temples
RK.1139 shrines
RK.1140 chaityas
RK.1141 heroa
RK.1142 jinjas
RK.1143 mashhads
RK.1144 mithraea
RK.1145 naiskoi
RK.1146 sacella
RK.1147 t'ai miao
RK.1148 stupas
RK.1149 chortens
RK.1150 dagobas
RK.1151 prachedis
RK.1152 sukkahs
RK.1153 ziggurats
RK.1154 *<research structures>*
RK.1155 particle accelerators
RK.1156 cyclotrons
RK.1157 linear accelerators
RK.1158 research buildings
RK.1159 laboratories
RK.1160 aerodynamical laboratories
RK.1161 aeronautical laboratories
RK.1162 agricultural laboratories
RK.1163 biological laboratories
RK.1164 chemical laboratories
RK.1165 conservation laboratories
RK.1166 crime laboratories
RK.1167 electronics laboratories
RK.1168 environmental laboratories
RK.1169 experiment stations
RK.1170 research laboratories
RK.1171 veterinary laboratories
RK.1172 observatories
RK.1173 astronomical observatories
RK.1174 research stations
RK.1175 ice stations
RK.1176 meteorological stations

May be used in combination with other descriptors (e.g., **fieldstone** + **cottages**; **prefabricated** + **ranch houses**; **three-story** + **parking garages**; **Georgian** + **saltbox houses**; **temple** + **porticoes**).

RK.1177 seismological stations
RK.1178 research centers
RK.1179 research institutes
RK.1180 vivariums
RK.1181 shelters
RK.1182 blinds (shelters)
RK.1183 garden houses
RK.1184 rock shelters
RK.1185 *<social and civic buildings>*
RK.1186 assembly halls
RK.1187 chapter houses
RK.1188 comitia
RK.1189 community centers
RK.1190 adult day care centers
RK.1191 senior centers
RK.1192 youth centers
RK.1193 convention centers
RK.1194 cultural centers
RK.1195 art centers
RK.1196 ekklesiasteria
RK.1197 faculty clubs
RK.1198 parish houses
RK.1199 stoas
RK.1200 student unions
RK.1201 societies' buildings
RK.1202 athenaeums
RK.1203 fraternal lodges
RK.1204 masonic buildings
RK.1205 guildhalls
RK.1206 storage facilities
RK.1207 godowns
RK.1208 helms
RK.1209 hoppers
RK.1210 kura
RK.1211 repositories
RK.1212 sheds
RK.1213 belfrys (sheds)
RK.1214 bicycle sheds
RK.1215 drying sheds
RK.1216 lumber sheds
RK.1217 machinery sheds
RK.1218 toolsheds
RK.1219 woodsheds
RK.1220 storage tanks
RK.1221 gasoline tanks
RK.1222 oil storage tanks
RK.1223 *<vehicle storage buildings>*
RK.1224 carriage houses
RK.1225 garages

May be used in combination with other descriptors (e.g., **fieldstone** + **cottages**; **prefabricated** + **ranch houses**; **three-story** + **parking garages**; **Georgian** + **saltbox houses**; **temple** + **porticoes**).

RK

RK.1226	parking garages
RK.1227	roof parking garages
RK.1228	warehouses
RK.1229	bonded warehouses
RK.1230	horrea
RK.1231	*<transportation structures>*
RK.1232	transportation buildings
RK.1233	airport buildings
RK.1234	airport terminals
RK.1235	control towers
RK.1236	hangars
RK.1237	*<rail transportation buildings>*
RK.1238	railway buildings
RK.1239	freight houses
RK.1240	railroad stations
RK.1241	railroad terminals
RK.1242	union stations
RK.1243	roundhouses
RK.1244	wheelhouses
RK.1245	tram depots
RK.1246	subway stations
RK.1247	*<road transportation structures>*
RK.1248	bus shelters
RK.1249	bus stations
RK.1250	bus terminals
RK.1251	mansiones
RK.1252	mutationes
RK.1253	posthouses
RK.1254	service stations
RK.1255	*<toll-collection structures>*
RK.1256	toll plazas
RK.1257	tollbooths
RK.1258	tollgates
RK.1259	tollhouses
RK.1260	truck stops
RK.1261	truck terminals
RK.1262	weigh stations
RK.1263	stations
RK.1264	terminals
RK.1265	freight terminals
RK.1266	passenger terminals
RK.1267	*<water transportation buildings>*
RK.1268	boathouses
RK.1269	coastguard stations
RK.1270	lighthouses
RK.1271	*<transportation structures by form>*
RK.1272	bridges
RK.1273	*<bridges by form>*
RK.1274	arch bridges

May be used in combination with other descriptors (e.g., **fieldstone** + **cottages**; **prefabricated** + **ranch houses**; **three-story** + **parking garages**; **Georgian** + **saltbox houses**; **temple** + **porticoes**).

RK.1275 continuous bridges
RK.1276 covered bridges
RK.1277 movable bridges
RK.1278 bascule bridges
RK.1279 drawbridges
RK.1280 lift bridges
RK.1281 swing bridges
RK.1282 multispan bridges
RK.1283 single span bridges
RK.1284 skew bridges
RK.1285 trestles (bridges)
RK.1286 *<bridges by function>*
RK.1287 footbridges
RK.1288 skybridges
RK.1289 military bridges
RK.1290 viaducts
RK.1291 railroad bridges
RK.1292 road bridges
RK.1293 toll bridges
RK.1294 *<bridges by construction>*
RK.1295 bailey bridges
RK.1296 cable-stayed bridges
RK.1297 cantilever bridges
RK.1298 girder bridges
RK.1299 pile bridges
RK.1300 pontoon bridges
RK.1301 suspension bridges
RK.1302 truss bridges
RK.1303 deck truss bridges
RK.1304 tunnels
RK.1305 highway tunnels
RK.1306 railroad tunnels
RK.1307 toad tunnels
RK.1308 water tunnels
RK.1309 *<transportation structures by function>*
RK.1310 launch towers
RK.1311 *<rail transportation structures>*
RK.1312 signal towers
RK.1313 turntables (rail transportation structures)
RK.1314 *<water transportation structures>*
RK.1315 dolphins
RK.1316 dry docks
RK.1317 floating docks
RK.1318 landings (marine structures)
RK.1319 piers (marine landings)
RK.1320 quays
RK.1321 wharves
RK.1322 launching ramps
RK.1323 moorings

RK

May be used in combination with other descriptors (e.g., **fieldstone** + **cottages**; **prefabricated** + **ranch houses**; **three-story** + **parking garages**; **Georgian** + **saltbox houses**; **temple** + **porticoes**).

RK.1324 wet docks
RK.1325 *<workshop buildings>*
RK.1326 smithies
RK.1327 *<single built works by location or context>*
RK.1328 garden structures
RK.1329 arbors
RK.1330 pergolas
RK.1331 trellises
RK.1332 eye-catchers
RK.1333 follies
RK.1334 artificial ruins
RK.1335 gazebos
RK.1336 grottoes
RK.1337 nymphaea
RK.1338 musaea
RK.1339 pavilions
RK.1340 teahouses
RK.1341 gatehouses
RK.1342 outbuildings
RK.1343 outhouses
RK.1344 washhouses
RK.1345 well houses
RK.1346 *<single built works by location: topographical>*
RK.1347 artificial islands
RK.1348 cave architecture
RK.1349 earthworks
RK.1350 cuts
RK.1351 ditches
RK.1352 fosses
RK.1353 excavations
RK.1354 trenches
RK.1355 embankments
RK.1356 mounds
RK.1357 cairns
RK.1358 pits
RK.1359 extraterrestrial structures
RK.1360 extraterrestrial bases
RK.1361 lunar bases
RK.1362 space stations
RK.1363 hillside architecture
RK.1364 marine structures
RK.1365 offshore structures
RK.1366 submarine structures
RK.1367 rock-cut architecture
RK.1368 underground structures
RK.1369 fogous
RK.1370 underground buildings
RK.1371 underwater buildings
RK.1372 *<single built works by design>*

May be used in combination with other descriptors (e.g., **fieldstone** + **cottages**; **prefabricated** + **ranch houses**; **three-story** + **parking garages**; **Georgian** + **saltbox houses**; **temple** + **porticoes**).

RK.1373	earth sheltered buildings
RK.1374	energy efficient buildings
RK.1375	experimental buildings
RK.1376	floating buildings
RK.1377	intelligent buildings
RK.1378	loft buildings
RK.1379	portable buildings
RK.1380	demountable buildings
RK.1381	revolving buildings
RK.1382	solar buildings
RK.1383	temporary structures
RK.1384	temporary buildings
RK.1385	ice palaces
RK.1386	macchine
RK.1387	walk-ups
RK.1388	windowless buildings
RK.1389	*<single built works by condition>*
RK.1390	derelict buildings
RK.1391	illegal buildings
RK.1392	ruins
RK.1393	open spaces
RK.1394	*<open spaces by form>*
RK.1395	gardens
RK.1396	*<gardens by form>*
RK.1397	boskets
RK.1398	Chinese gardens
RK.1399	formal gardens
RK.1400	bagh
RK.1401	chahar bagh
RK.1402	French gardens
RK.1403	*<geometric gardens>*
RK.1404	knot gardens
RK.1405	maze gardens
RK.1406	hedge mazes
RK.1407	turf mazes
RK.1408	hanging gardens
RK.1409	landscape gardens
RK.1410	miniature gardens
RK.1411	penjing
RK.1412	peat gardens
RK.1413	rock gardens
RK.1414	walled gardens
RK.1415	water gardens
RK.1416	*<gardens by function>*
RK.1417	arboretums
RK.1418	botanical gardens
RK.1419	children's gardens
RK.1420	historic gardens
RK.1421	kitchen gardens

RK

May be used in combination with other descriptors (e.g., **fieldstone** + **cottages**; **prefabricated** + **ranch houses**; **three-story** + **parking garages**; **Georgian** + **saltbox houses**; **temple** + **porticoes**).

RK.1422 market gardens
RK.1423 pleasure gardens
RK.1424 sculpture gardens
RK.1425 tea gardens
RK.1426 xeriscapes
RK.1427 *<gardens by location or context>*
RK.1428 cloister gardens
RK.1429 giardini segreti
RK.1430 roof gardens
RK.1431 *<gardens by product>*
RK.1432 flower gardens
RK.1433 herb gardens
RK.1434 vegetable gardens
RK.1435 victory gardens
RK.1436 *<gardens by ownership>*
RK.1437 community gardens
RK.1438 allotment gardens
RK.1439 private gardens
RK.1440 bustanim
RK.1441 paradise gardens
RK.1442 public gardens
RK.1443 quadrangles
RK.1444 squares
RK.1445 maydans
RK.1446 piazzas
RK.1447 plazas
RK.1448 plazuelas
RK.1449 *<open spaces by function>*
RK.1450 musallas
RK.1451 nature preserves
RK.1452 wilderness areas
RK.1453 wildlife refuges
RK.1454 bird sanctuaries
RK.1455 parks
RK.1456 *<parks by location or context>*
RK.1457 community parks
RK.1458 marine parks
RK.1459 neighborhood parks
RK.1460 regional parks
RK.1461 urban parks
RK.1462 vest-pocket parks
RK.1463 *<parks by ownership or administration>*
RK.1464 national parks
RK.1465 provincial parks
RK.1466 state parks
RK.1467 *<refuse areas>*
RK.1468 dumps
RK.1469 junkyards
RK.1470 automobile graveyards

May be used in combination with other descriptors (e.g., **fieldstone** + **cottages**; **prefabricated** + **ranch houses**; **three-story** + **parking garages**; **Georgian** + **saltbox houses**; **temple** + **porticoes**).

RK.1471 landfills
RK.1472 sanitary landfills
RK.1473 middens
RK.1474 slag heaps
RK.1475 spoil banks
RK.1476 *<sports and recreation spaces>*
RK.1477 athletic fields
RK.1478 baseball fields
RK.1479 cricket fields
RK.1480 football fields
RK.1481 hockey fields
RK.1482 lacrosse fields
RK.1483 polo fields
RK.1484 rugby fields
RK.1485 soccer fields
RK.1486 softball fields
RK.1487 bowling greens
RK.1488 camp sites
RK.1489 driving ranges
RK.1490 fairgrounds
RK.1491 golf courses
RK.1492 miniature golf courses
RK.1493 picnic areas
RK.1494 playgrounds
RK.1495 adventure playgrounds
RK.1496 neighborhood playgrounds
RK.1497 schoolyards
RK.1498 tot lots
RK.1499 riding rings
RK.1500 running tracks
RK.1501 indoor tracks
RK.1502 *<transportation spaces>*
RK.1503 *<air transportation spaces>*
RK.1504 airfields
RK.1505 helipads
RK.1506 overruns
RK.1507 runways
RK.1508 airstrips
RK.1509 taxiways
RK.1510 *<motor vehicle lots>*
RK.1511 parking lots
RK.1512 used car lots
RK.1513 roads
RK.1514 *<roads by form>*
RK.1515 highways
RK.1516 beltways
RK.1517 divided highways
RK.1518 limited access highways
RK.1519 *<limited access highways by degree of grade separation>*

May be used in combination with other descriptors (e.g., **fieldstone** + **cottages**; **prefabricated** + **ranch houses**; **three-story** + **parking garages**; **Georgian** + **saltbox houses**; **temple** + **porticoes**).

RK.1520 expressways
RK.1521 throughways
RK.1522 *<limited access highways by financial base>*
RK.1523 freeways
RK.1524 turnpikes
RK.1525 parkways
RK.1526 streets
RK.1527 *<streets by form>*
RK.1528 alleys
RK.1529 angiportus
RK.1530 blind alleys
RK.1531 avenues
RK.1532 boulevards
RK.1533 dead-end streets
RK.1534 culs-de-sac
RK.1535 lanes
RK.1536 plateias
RK.1537 *<streets by function>*
RK.1538 one way streets
RK.1539 pedestrian streets
RK.1540 processional ways
RK.1541 *<streets by location or context>*
RK.1542 arterial streets
RK.1543 main streets
RK.1544 cardines
RK.1545 decumani
RK.1546 through streets
RK.1547 *<roads by function>*
RK.1548 access roads
RK.1549 arterials
RK.1550 bypasses
RK.1551 driveways
RK.1552 military roads
RK.1553 post roads
RK.1554 primary roads
RK.1555 private roads
RK.1556 secondary roads
RK.1557 service roads
RK.1558 truck routes
RK.1559 *<roads by design>*
RK.1560 elevated roads
RK.1561 multi-level roads
RK.1562 sunken roads
RK.1563 *<roads by location or context>*
RK.1564 causeways
RK.1565 *<roads by material>*
RK.1566 macadamized roads
RK.1567 stockyards
RK.1568 walkways

May be used in combination with other descriptors (e.g., **fieldstone** + **cottages**; **prefabricated** + **ranch houses**; **three-story** + **parking garages**; **Georgian** + **saltbox houses**; **temple** + **porticoes**).

RK.1569	covered walkways
RK.1570	garden walks
RK.1571	malls (walkways)
RK.1572	paths
RK.1573	bridle paths
RK.1574	cycling paths
RK.1575	footpaths
RK.1576	promenades
RK.1577	alamedas
RK.1578	skywalks
RK.1579	*<open spaces by location or context>*
RK.1580	agoras
RK.1581	city blocks
RK.1582	superblocks
RK.1583	commons
RK.1584	forums
RK.1585	greenbelts
RK.1586	greens
RK.1587	grounds
RK.1588	lots
RK.1589	vacant lots
RK.1590	overlooks
RK.1591	parvises
RK.1592	*<waterfronts and waterfront spaces>*
RK.1593	waterfronts
RK.1594	lakefronts
RK.1595	riverfronts
RK.1596	*<waterfront spaces>*
RK.1597	berths
RK.1598	docks
RK.1599	slips
RK.1600	yards
RK.1601	barnyards
RK.1602	dooryards
RK.1603	farmyards

Building Divisions and Site Elements Hierarchy

BUILDING DIVISIONS AND SITE ELEMENTS

Scope The Building Divisions and Site Elements hierarchy contains descriptors for components of infrastructural systems, man-made landscape features, and parts of built works that are distinguishable by their position or location, whether interior or exterior, relative to the main structure of which they are a part.

Organization The hierarchy consists of two main sections: <*building divisions*> and <*site and infrastructural elements*>. The <*building divisions*> section contains descriptors for portions of built works that are identifiable by their relationship to the main structure or building type (e.g., **annexes**) or their function as habitable spaces (e.g., **dining rooms**). Most of the vocabulary in this section occurs under the guide term <*rooms and spaces*>. Descriptors in the <*rooms and spaces*> section are organized according to characteristics such as form (e.g., **balconies**), function (e.g., **assembly rooms**), location or context (e.g., **loggias**), and the building type in which they occur (e.g., **chevets**). The second section contains descriptors for man-made objects that occupy fixed positions in the landscape, particularly landscapes around buildings, but are not sufficiently large or complex to be considered buildings (e.g., **fences**). Also contained in this section are descriptors for the components of infrastructural systems (e.g., **water mains, overpasses**).

Relation to Other Hierarchies Descriptors for the structural systems and individual building parts (e.g., **balloon frames, doors**) that comprise single built works are found in the Built Works Components hierarchy, while rooms, spaces, and other large building subdivisions (e.g., **kitchens**) are found here. Descriptors for the component parts of open spaces and landscapes (e.g., **terrace walls, berms**) are found here, while descriptors for types of open spaces and landscape features (e.g., **gardens, rivers**) are found in the Settlements, Systems and Landscapes hierarchy.

Descriptor Form and Use Descriptors appear as plural nouns, with the singular added as an alternate form where appropriate. For building divisions and site elements by material, technique, physical attribute, or other aspect, combine with descriptors from other appropriate hierarchies (e.g., **glass** + **conservatories; painted** + **burial chambers; oval** + **rooms**). Alternate terms may be used as modifiers of descriptors in other hierarchies (e.g., **dining room** + **furniture**).

Number of Descriptors 453

Synopsis

RM.1 *<building divisions>*
RM.2 **annexes**
|
RM.24 **podiums**
RM.25 *<rooms and spaces>*
RM.26 *<rooms and spaces by form>*
RM.27 **alcoves**
|
RM.39 *<uncovered spaces>*
RM.58 *<rooms and spaces by function>*
RM.59 *<assembly spaces>*
|
RM.220 *<work and instructional spaces>*
RM.241 *<rooms and spaces by location or context>*
RM.242 *<exterior covered spaces>*
|
RM.253 *<interior spaces>*
RM.287 *<rooms and spaces by building type>*
RM.288 *<health facility spaces>*
|
RM.384 *<tomb spaces>*
RM.388 *<rooms and spaces by occupants>*
RM.389 **andra**
|
RM.394 **servant's halls**
RM.395 *<rooms and spaces by property>*
RM.396 **anechoic rooms**
|
RM.398 **darkrooms**
RM.399 *<steeples and steeple components>*
|
RM.426 **wings (building divisions)**
RM.428 *<site and infrastructural elements>*
RM.429 *<site elements>*
RM.430 **birdbaths**
|
RM.458 **windbreaks**
RM.459 *<infrastructural elements>*
RM.460 *<dam elements>*
|
RM.509 *<utilities components>*

RM

BUILDING DIVISIONS AND SITE ELEMENTS (RM)

RM.1	*<building divisions>*
RM.2	annexes
RM.3	appentices
RM.4	bays (building divisions)
RM.5	corps de logis
RM.6	elevations (building divisions)
RM.7	front elevations
RM.8	garden elevations
RM.9	rear elevations
RM.10	side elevations
RM.11	street elevations
RM.12	fire towers (building divisions)
RM.13	*<Greek and Roman temple substructure components>*
RM.14	crepidomas
RM.15	stereobates
RM.16	stylobates
RM.17	hyphens
RM.18	jetties (building divisions)
RM.19	outshuts
RM.20	bed-outshuts
RM.21	overhangs
RM.22	pavilions (building divisions)
RM.23	penthouses
RM.24	podiums
RM.25	*<rooms and spaces>*
RM.26	*<rooms and spaces by form>*
RM.27	alcoves
RM.28	alae
RM.29	inglenooks
RM.30	balconies
RM.31	balconets
RM.32	cages
RM.33	galleries
RM.34	choir lofts
RM.35	dwarf galleries
RM.36	minstrel galleries
RM.37	organ lofts
RM.38	tribunes
RM.39	*<uncovered spaces>*
RM.40	areaways
RM.41	atriums (Roman halls)
RM.42	courtyards
RM.43	base-courts
RM.44	cloister garths
RM.45	forecourts
RM.46	atriums (church courtyards)
RM.47	light courts
RM.48	peristylia
RM.49	quadriportici

May be used in combination with other descriptors (e.g., **glass** + **conservatories**; **painted** + **burial chambers**; **oval** + **rooms**).

RM.50	**decks**
RM.51	**observation decks**
RM.52	**sun decks**
RM.53	**patios**
RM.54	**rooftops**
RM.55	**stoops**
RM.56	**box stoops**
RM.57	**stoups**
RM.58	*<rooms and spaces by function>*
RM.59	*<assembly spaces>*
RM.60	**auditoriums**
RM.61	**conference rooms**
RM.62	**boardrooms**
RM.63	**courtrooms**
RM.64	**lecture halls**
RM.65	*<bath, dressing and sanitary spaces>*
RM.66	**bathrooms**
RM.67	**dressing rooms**
RM.68	**lavatories (rooms)**
RM.69	**locker rooms**
RM.70	**privies**
RM.71	**rest rooms**
RM.72	*<Roman bath spaces>*
RM.73	**apodyteria**
RM.74	**caldaria**
RM.75	**frigidaria**
RM.76	**natatione**
RM.77	**sudatione**
RM.78	**sudatoria**
RM.79	**tepidaria**
RM.80	**saunas**
RM.81	**shower stalls**
RM.82	**steam rooms**
RM.83	**toilet compartments**
RM.84	*<circulation spaces>*
RM.85	**aisles**
RM.86	**concourses**
RM.87	**escalator wells**
RM.88	**passages**
RM.89	**corridors**
RM.90	**cryptoportici**
RM.91	**fauces**
RM.92	**screens passages**
RM.93	**souterrains**
RM.94	**stairwells**
RM.95	**pressurized stairwells**
RM.96	*<display rooms and spaces>*
RM.97	**conservatories**
RM.98	**period rooms**

May be used in combination with other descriptors (e.g., **glass** + **conservatories**; **painted** + **burial chambers**; **oval** + **rooms**).

<building divisions>
<rooms and spaces>
<rooms and spaces by function>
<display rooms and spaces>

RM.99	**showrooms**
RM.100	**automobile showrooms**
RM.101	**furniture showrooms**
RM.102	**sample rooms**
RM.103	**studiolos**
RM.104	*<eating and drinking spaces>*
RM.105	**banquet halls**
RM.106	**breakfast nooks**
RM.107	**breakfast rooms**
RM.108	**cafeterias**
RM.109	**cocktail lounges**
RM.110	**dinettes**
RM.111	**dining alcoves**
RM.112	**dining halls**
RM.113	**mess halls**
RM.114	**refectories**
RM.115	**dining rooms**
RM.116	**triclinia**
RM.117	**lunchrooms**
RM.118	**pump rooms**
RM.119	**rathskellers**
RM.120	**supper rooms**
RM.121	*<entertainment and recreation spaces>*
RM.122	**assembly rooms**
RM.123	**ballrooms**
RM.124	**gaming rooms**
RM.125	**music rooms**
RM.126	**recreation rooms**
RM.127	**game rooms**
RM.128	**billiard rooms**
RM.129	**cardrooms**
RM.130	**playrooms**
RM.131	**screening rooms**
RM.132	*<entrance spaces>*
RM.133	**anterooms**
RM.134	**entrance halls**
RM.135	**loading docks**
RM.136	**lobbies**
RM.137	**mud rooms**
RM.138	**vestibules**
RM.139	*<equipment spaces>*
RM.140	**belfries**
RM.141	**computer rooms**
RM.142	*<protective spaces>*
RM.143	**air raid shelters**
RM.144	**nuclear bomb shelters**
RM.145	**storm cellars**
RM.146	**train sheds**
RM.147	**vaults (strong rooms)**

May be used in combination with other descriptors (e.g., **glass** + **conservatories**; **painted** + **burial chambers**; **oval** + **rooms**).

RM.148 *<reading and writing spaces>*
RM.149 archives rooms
RM.150 carrels
RM.151 libraries (rooms)
RM.152 reading rooms
RM.153 scriptoria
RM.154 studies (rooms)
RM.155 writing rooms
RM.156 *<reception spaces>*
RM.157 presence chambers
RM.158 reception rooms
RM.159 throne rooms
RM.160 *<sleeping spaces>*
RM.161 bedrooms
RM.162 cubicula
RM.163 dormitories (rooms)
RM.164 *<social and sitting spaces>*
RM.165 cabinets (rooms)
RM.166 boudoirs
RM.167 calefactories
RM.168 common rooms
RM.169 dens
RM.170 drawing rooms
RM.171 family rooms
RM.172 keeping rooms
RM.173 living rooms
RM.174 lanais
RM.175 lounges
RM.176 V.I.P. lounges
RM.177 morning rooms
RM.178 parlors
RM.179 salons
RM.180 sitting rooms
RM.181 smoking rooms
RM.182 waiting rooms
RM.183 headhouses
RM.184 *<storage spaces>*
RM.185 apothecae
RM.186 baggage rooms
RM.187 cellars
RM.188 beer cellars
RM.189 root cellars
RM.190 wine cellars
RM.191 chandleries
RM.192 checkrooms
RM.193 cloakrooms
RM.194 closets
RM.195 broom closets
RM.196 clothes closets

RM

May be used in combination with other descriptors (e.g., **glass** + **conservatories**; **painted** + **burial chambers**; **oval** + **rooms**).

RM.197	linen closets
RM.198	cold storage rooms
RM.199	gun rooms
RM.200	larders
RM.201	pantries
RM.202	butler's pantries
RM.203	stillrooms
RM.204	storerooms
RM.205	treasuries
RM.206	cimeliarchs
RM.207	wardrobes (rooms)
RM.208	*<utility and access spaces>*
RM.209	air locks
RM.210	chases
RM.211	chutes
RM.212	coal chutes
RM.213	laundry chutes
RM.214	mail chutes
RM.215	refuse chutes
RM.216	crawl spaces
RM.217	service cores
RM.218	utility rooms
RM.219	boiler rooms
RM.220	*<work and instructional spaces>*
RM.221	audiovisual centers
RM.222	banking rooms
RM.223	broadcasting studios
RM.224	radio studios
RM.225	television studios
RM.226	classrooms
RM.227	control rooms
RM.228	kitchens
RM.229	kitchenettes
RM.230	language laboratories
RM.231	laundry rooms
RM.232	offices
RM.233	sail lofts
RM.234	sculleries
RM.235	sewing rooms
RM.236	sound studios
RM.237	recording studios
RM.238	sound stages
RM.239	studios (work spaces)
RM.240	workshops (work spaces)
RM.241	*<rooms and spaces by location or context>*
RM.242	*<exterior covered spaces>*
RM.243	breezeways
RM.244	carports
RM.245	dogtrots

May be used in combination with other descriptors (e.g., **glass** + **conservatories**; **painted** + **burial chambers**; **oval** + **rooms**).

RM.246	iwans
RM.247	loggias
RM.248	porches
RM.249	sleeping porches
RM.250	porte-cocheres
RM.251	porticoes
RM.252	cyrtostyles
RM.253	*<interior spaces>*
RM.254	apses
RM.255	apsidioles
RM.256	counter apses
RM.257	atriums (interior spaces)
RM.258	attics (interior spaces)
RM.259	booths
RM.260	exhibition booths
RM.261	cells
RM.262	oubliettes
RM.263	*<combinations of rooms>*
RM.264	apartments
RM.265	duplex apartments
RM.266	flats
RM.267	coldwater flats
RM.268	railroad flats
RM.269	model apartments
RM.270	studio apartments
RM.271	suites
RM.272	exedrae
RM.273	halls
RM.274	hypostyle halls
RM.275	hemicycles
RM.276	long galleries
RM.277	naves
RM.278	oeci
RM.279	rooms
RM.280	rotundas
RM.281	shafts (spaces)
RM.282	air shafts
RM.283	lightwells
RM.284	solariums
RM.285	solars
RM.286	tablina
RM.287	*<rooms and spaces by building type>*
RM.288	*<health facility spaces>*
RM.289	blood banks
RM.290	emergency rooms
RM.291	hospital wards
RM.292	intensive care units
RM.293	burn care units
RM.294	coronary care units

May be used in combination with other descriptors (e.g., **glass** + **conservatories**; **painted** + **burial chambers**; **oval** + **rooms**).

RM.295 **maternity wards**
RM.296 **nurses' stations**
RM.297 **operating rooms**
RM.298 **recovery rooms**
RM.299 *<religious building spaces>*
RM.300 *<Christian religious building spaces>*
RM.301 **ambulatories**
RM.302 **antechoirs**
RM.303 **chancels**
RM.304 **chapels**
RM.305 **antiparabemata**
RM.306 **chantries**
RM.307 **funeral chapels**
RM.308 **lady chapels**
RM.309 **oratories**
RM.310 **private chapels**
RM.311 **protheses**
RM.312 **royal chapels**
RM.313 **sepulchral chapels**
RM.314 **chevets**
RM.315 **choirs**
RM.316 **cloisters**
RM.317 **conventicles**
RM.318 **coretti**
RM.319 **crossings**
RM.320 **crypts**
RM.321 **feretories**
RM.322 **misericords**
RM.323 **narthexes**
RM.324 **esonarthexes**
RM.325 **exonarthexes**
RM.326 **parlatories**
RM.327 **presbyteries**
RM.328 **retrochoirs**
RM.329 **sacristies**
RM.330 **diaconica**
RM.331 **transepts**
RM.332 **sacraria**
RM.333 **sanctuaries**
RM.334 **vimanas**
RM.335 *<temple spaces>*
RM.336 **adyta**
RM.337 **naoi**
RM.338 **opisthodomoi**
RM.339 **pronaoi**
RM.340 **pteromata**
RM.341 *<stable and barn spaces>*
RM.342 **feed rooms**
RM.343 **haylofts**

May be used in combination with other descriptors (e.g., **glass** + **conservatories**; **painted** + **burial chambers**; **oval** + **rooms**).

RM.344 **stalls (stable spaces)**
RM.345 **box stalls**
RM.346 **tack rooms**
RM.347 *<theater spaces>*
RM.348 *<audience spaces>*
RM.349 **boxes (audience spaces)**
RM.350 **caveae**
RM.351 **cunei**
RM.352 **diazomata**
RM.353 **orchestras (audience spaces)**
RM.354 **parodoses**
RM.355 **pits (theater spaces)**
RM.356 **praecinctiones**
RM.357 **theater auditoriums**
RM.358 **vomitories**
RM.359 *<performance and backstage spaces>*
RM.360 **fly lofts**
RM.361 **green rooms**
RM.362 **orchestra pits**
RM.363 **orchestras (stage spaces)**
RM.364 **stage houses**
RM.365 *<stages and stage components>*
RM.366 **stages**
RM.367 **proscaenia**
RM.368 **pulpita**
RM.369 **revolving stages**
RM.370 **thrust stages**
RM.371 *<stage components>*
RM.372 **forestages**
RM.373 **stage machinery**
RM.374 *<tiring houses and tiring house components>*
RM.375 **tiring houses**
RM.376 *<tiring house components>*
RM.377 **turrets (theaters)**
RM.378 *<upper stages and upper stage components>*
RM.379 **upper stages**
RM.380 *<upper stage components>*
RM.381 **chambers**
RM.382 **tarrases**
RM.383 **wings (theaters)**
RM.384 *<tomb spaces>*
RM.385 **burial chambers**
RM.386 **dromoi**
RM.387 **vaults (tomb spaces)**
RM.388 *<rooms and spaces by occupants>*
RM.389 **andra**
RM.390 **gynaecea**
RM.391 **harems**
RM.392 **nurseries (rooms)**

May be used in combination with other descriptors (e.g., **glass** + **conservatories**; **painted** + **burial chambers**; **oval** + **rooms**).

RM.393 night nurseries
RM.394 servants' halls
RM.395 *<rooms and spaces by property>*
RM.396 anechoic rooms
RM.397 clean rooms
RM.398 darkrooms
RM.399 *<steeples and steeple components>*
RM.400 steeples
RM.401 crown steeples
RM.402 *<steeple components>*
RM.403 spires
RM.404 broach spires
RM.405 fleches
RM.406 helm roofs
RM.407 needle spires
RM.408 spirelets
RM.409 stories
RM.410 attics (exterior stories)
RM.411 basements
RM.412 clerestories
RM.413 mezzanines
RM.414 piani nobili
RM.415 subbasements
RM.416 triforiums
RM.417 towers (building divisions)
RM.418 church towers
RM.419 crossing towers
RM.420 gate towers
RM.421 sikharas
RM.422 stair towers
RM.423 turrets
RM.424 wall towers
RM.425 westworks
RM.426 wings (building divisions)
RM.427 ells
RM.428 *<site and infrastructural elements>*
RM.429 *<site elements>*
RM.430 birdbaths
RM.431 bollards
RM.432 boundary stones
RM.433 exedrae (site elements)
RM.434 fences
RM.435 chain link fences
RM.436 electric fences
RM.437 hoardings
RM.438 picket fences
RM.439 rail fences
RM.440 snow fences
RM.441 flagpoles

May be used in combination with other descriptors (e.g., **glass** + **conservatories**; **painted** + **burial chambers**; **oval** + **rooms**).

RM.442 *<freestanding walls>*
RM.443 boundary walls
RM.444 periboloi
RM.445 diaphragm walls
RM.446 terrace walls
RM.447 hitching posts
RM.448 lampposts
RM.449 *<landscaped-site elements>*
RM.450 berms
RM.451 cascades
RM.452 ha-has
RM.453 hedges
RM.454 lawns
RM.455 terraces
RM.456 topiary
RM.457 turf seats
RM.458 windbreaks
RM.459 *<infrastructural elements>*
RM.460 *<dam elements>*
RM.461 fishways
RM.462 penstocks
RM.463 spillways
RM.464 stilling basins
RM.465 *<transportation elements>*
RM.466 *<bridge elements>*
RM.467 bridge approaches
RM.468 cutwaters
RM.469 *<road and roadside elements>*
RM.470 bus stops
RM.471 crosswalks
RM.472 curbs
RM.473 grade separations
RM.474 overpasses
RM.475 underpasses
RM.476 guard rails
RM.477 gutters (roadside elements)
RM.478 intersections
RM.479 interchanges
RM.480 cloverleafs
RM.481 traffic circles
RM.482 lanes (road elements)
RM.483 acceleration lanes
RM.484 bus lanes
RM.485 *<manholes and manhole components>*
RM.486 manholes
RM.487 *<manhole components>*
RM.488 manhole covers
RM.489 medians
RM.490 roadside rest areas

May be used in combination with other descriptors (e.g., **glass** + **conservatories**; **painted** + **burial chambers**; **oval** + **rooms**).

RM.491	**roadsides**
RM.492	**roadways**
RM.493	**rumble strips**
RM.494	**shoulders (roads)**
RM.495	**sidewalks**
RM.496	**street furniture**
RM.497	**fire hydrants**
RM.498	**mailboxes**
RM.499	**parking meters**
RM.500	**streetlights**
RM.501	**traffic signals**
RM.502	**taxi stands**
RM.503	**traffic islands**
RM.504	*<transit system elements>*
RM.505	**grade crossings**
RM.506	**roadbeds**
RM.507	**sidings**
RM.508	**signal gantries**
RM.509	*<utilities components>*
RM.510	**gas pipelines**
RM.511	**power lines**
RM.512	**utility poles**
RM.513	**water mains**

May be used in combination with other descriptors (e.g., **glass** + **conservatories**; **painted** + **burial chambers**; **oval** + **rooms**).

Built Works
Components
Hierarchy

BUILT WORKS COMPONENTS

Scope The Built Works Components hierarchy contains descriptors designating parts of buildings and structures, and descriptors for those parts of the building systems that heat, cool and ventilate interiors, provide water, light, and power, carry off waste, communicate voices or signals, and move occupants by mechanical means.

Organization The sections **architectural elements** and <*building systems*> contain descriptors for components of buildings. A descriptor generally appears only once in the hierarchy in the most appropriate location, even if it designates components of different architectural elements. For example, **stiles** and **rails** appear only under <*surface element components*>. Components that are unique to a particular building type are listed in the section <*architectural elements by building type*>. For example, **keeps** are listed as <*fortification elements*>. Architectural elements that are structural in some circumstances and decorative in others (e.g., **columns**, **entablatures**) are classified according to their structural use.

Relation to Other Hierarchies Ornamental motifs (e.g., **S-scrolls**) other than molding types appear in the Design Elements hierarchy. Building finishes (e.g., **siding**) are found in the Materials hierarchy. Movable elements not integrated into the fabric of buildings or permanently affixed to them are in either the Furniture hierarchy (e.g., **counters**), the Hardware and Joints hierarchy (e.g., **locks**), the Tools and Equipment hierarchy (e.g., **air conditioners**), or other appropriate hierarchies in the Objects facet. Some of the more visible systems elements (e.g., **lighting fixtures**) will be in the Furnishings and Equipment section of the Objects facet as it is developed. Rooms, spaces, and larger interior and exterior elements of building massing (e.g., **organ lofts**, **ells**), which constitute the next more complex set of built relationships are located in the Building Divisions and Site Elements hierarchy.

Descriptor Form and Use Terms appear as plural nouns, with the singular added as an alternate form where appropriate. For architectural elements by material, technique, physical attribute, style, location, or other aspect, combine with descriptors from other hierarchies (e.g., **cast iron** + **railings**; **molded** + **cornices**; **semicircular** + **windows**; **Italianate** + **roofs**; **church** + **doors**).

Number of Descriptors 1295

Synopsis

RT.1 **architectural elements**
RT.2 *<structural elements and structural element components>*
RT.3 *<structural elements>*
RT.4 **structures (architectural elements)**
RT.15 *<structural systems>*
RT.45 *<structural assemblies>*
RT.59 *<supporting and resisting elements>*
RT.215 *<spanning and projecting structural elements>*
RT.387 *<enclosing structural elements>*
RT.680 *<structural element components>*
RT.715 *<surface elements and surface element components>*
RT.716 *<surface elements>*
RT.717 **amortizements**
|
RT.819 **soffits**
RT.820 *<surface element components>*
RT.828 *<openings and opening components>*
RT.829 **openings**
RT.830 *<openings by form>*
RT.983 *<openings by function>*
RT.992 *<openings by location or context>*
RT.1000 *<opening components>*
RT.1001 **coaming**
|
RT.1032 **weather strips**
RT.1033 *<barriers and barrier elements>*
RT.1047 *<culminating and edge ornaments>*
RT.1048 **acroteria**
|
RT.1061 **pinnacles**
RT.1062 *<circulation elements>*
RT.1063 **catwalks**
|
RT.1067 *<stairs and stair components>*
RT.1130 *<heating and cooking elements>*
RT.1131 *<chimneys and chimney components>*
|
RT.1164 **ovens**
RT.1165 *<architectural elements by building type>*
RT.1166 *<fortification elements>*
|
RT.1264 *<theater elements>*
RT.1281 **building systems**

BUILT WORKS COMPONENTS

RT.1282	*<communication systems and communication system components>*
RT.1292	*<conveying systems and conveying system components>*
RT.1331	*<electrical systems and electrical system components>*
RT.1352	**lighting**
RT.1380	**mechanical systems**
RT.1381	*<HVAC and HVAC components>*
RT.1444	*<plumbing and storm water systems and their components>*
RT.1502	*<protection systems>*

RT.1 architectural elements
RT.2 *<structural elements and structural element components>*
RT.3 *<structural elements>*
RT.4 structures (structural elements)
RT.5 *<structures by location or context>*
RT.6 substructures
RT.7 superstructures
RT.8 *<structures by property>*
RT.9 large span structures
RT.10 nonrigid structures
RT.11 rigid structures
RT.12 statically determinate structures
RT.13 statically indeterminate structures
RT.14 tensile structures
RT.15 *<structural systems>*
RT.16 cable structures
RT.17 cable net structures
RT.18 cable-stayed structures
RT.19 double-cable structures
RT.20 suspension structures
RT.21 lamella structures
RT.22 plate structures
RT.23 folded plate structures
RT.24 *<slabs and slab components>*
RT.25 slabs
RT.26 one-way structural systems
RT.27 one-way beam and slab systems
RT.28 one-way joist systems
RT.29 one-way solid slab systems
RT.30 two-way structural systems
RT.31 flat plate systems
RT.32 flat slab systems
RT.33 two-way beam and slab systems
RT.34 waffle slabs
RT.35 *<slab components>*
RT.36 drop panels
RT.37 structural frames
RT.38 balloon frames
RT.39 box frames
RT.40 platform frames
RT.41 post-and-beam structures
RT.42 rigid frames
RT.43 braced frames
RT.44 tube structures
RT.45 *<structural assemblies>*
RT.46 aediculae
RT.47 arcades
RT.48 blind arcades
RT.49 interlacing arcades

May be used in combination with other descriptors (e.g., **cast iron** + **railings**; **molded** + **cornices**; **semicircular** + **windows**; **Italianate** + **roofs**; **church** + **doors**).

RT.50 architectural orders
RT.51 Composite order
RT.52 Corinthian order
RT.53 Doric order
RT.54 Ionic order
RT.55 Rustic order
RT.56 Tuscan order
RT.57 colonnades
RT.58 peristyles
RT.59 *<supporting and resisting elements>*
RT.60 abutments
RT.61 *<anthropomorphic supporting elements>*
RT.62 atlantes
RT.63 caryatids
RT.64 canephores
RT.65 *<bases and base components>*
RT.66 bases
RT.67 socles
RT.68 *<base components>*
RT.69 cinctures
RT.70 griffes
RT.71 plinths
RT.72 buttresses
RT.73 *<corner buttresses>*
RT.74 angle buttresses
RT.75 clasping buttresses
RT.76 diagonal buttresses
RT.77 flying buttresses
RT.78 hanging buttresses
RT.79 lateral buttresses
RT.80 setback buttresses
RT.81 cololches
RT.82 *<columns and column components>*
RT.83 columns
RT.84 *<columns by form>*
RT.85 annulated columns
RT.86 baluster columns
RT.87 banded columns
RT.88 blocked columns
RT.89 colonnettes
RT.90 columnae caelatae
RT.91 diminishing columns
RT.92 estipites
RT.93 knotted columns
RT.94 lally columns
RT.95 monolithic columns
RT.96 serpent columns
RT.97 shafts (Medieval columns)
RT.98 jamb shafts

May be used in combination with other descriptors (e.g., **cast iron** + **railings**; **molded** + **cornices**; **semicircular** + **windows**; **Italianate** + **roofs**; **church** + **doors**).

RT.99 spiral columns
RT.100 *<columns by location or context>*
RT.101 angle columns
RT.102 battened columns
RT.103 coupled columns
RT.104 doubled columns
RT.105 engaged columns
RT.106 flanked columns
RT.107 half columns
RT.108 grouped columns
RT.109 median columns
RT.110 mid-wall columns
RT.111 nook shafts
RT.112 *<column components>*
RT.113 Asiatic bases
RT.114 Attic bases
RT.115 *<capitals and capital components>*
RT.116 capitals
RT.117 Aeolic capitals
RT.118 angle capitals
RT.119 basket capitals
RT.120 bell capitals
RT.121 bowl capitals
RT.122 bracket capitals
RT.123 chalice capitals
RT.124 chaptrels
RT.125 crocket capitals
RT.126 cushion capitals
RT.127 lotus capitals
RT.128 palm capitals
RT.129 papyrus capitals
RT.130 protomai capitals
RT.131 scalloped capitals
RT.132 *<capital components>*
RT.133 abaci
RT.134 baltei
RT.135 bolsters
RT.136 caulicoles
RT.137 echini
RT.138 hypotrachelia
RT.139 necking
RT.140 volutes
RT.141 *<shafts and shaft components>*
RT.142 shafts (column components)
RT.143 *<shaft components>*
RT.144 apophyges
RT.145 cabling
RT.146 drums (column components)
RT.147 shaft rings

May be used in combination with other descriptors (e.g., **cast iron** + **railings**; **molded** + **cornices**; **semicircular** + **windows**; **Italianate** + **roofs**; **church** + **doors**).

RT

RT.148 **cribbing**
RT.149 **foundations**
RT.150 *<pier foundations and pier foundation components>*
RT.151 **pier foundations**
RT.152 *<pier foundation components>*
RT.153 **caissons**
RT.154 **piers (foundation components)**
RT.155 *<pile foundations and pile foundation components>*
RT.156 **pile foundations**
RT.157 *<pile foundation components>*
RT.158 **piles**
RT.159 **cast-in-place piles**
RT.160 **caisson piles**
RT.161 **cased piles**
RT.162 **driven piles**
RT.163 **jacked piles**
RT.164 **precast piles**
RT.165 *<spread foundations and spread foundation components>*
RT.166 **spread foundations**
RT.167 **mat foundations**
RT.168 **raft foundations**
RT.169 **slab foundations**
RT.170 *<spread foundation components>*
RT.171 **footings**
RT.172 **cantilevered footings**
RT.173 **combined footings**
RT.174 **continuous footings**
RT.175 **grillages**
RT.176 **masts**
RT.177 *<pedestals and pedestal components>*
RT.178 **pedestals**
RT.179 *<pedestal components>*
RT.180 **caps (pedestal components)**
RT.181 **dadoes**
RT.182 **pendentives**
RT.183 *<piers and pier components>*
RT.184 **piers**
RT.185 *<piers by form>*
RT.186 **bundle piers**
RT.187 **compound piers**
RT.188 *<piers by location or context>*
RT.189 **antae**
RT.190 **buttress piers**
RT.191 **wall piers**
RT.192 *<pier components>*
RT.193 **alettes**
RT.194 **pilotis**
RT.195 **posts**
RT.196 *<posts by form>*

May be used in combination with other descriptors (e.g., **cast iron** + **railings**; **molded** + **cornices**; **semicircular** + **windows**; **Italianate** + **roofs**; **church** + **doors**).

RT.197	cased posts
RT.198	puncheons
RT.199	*<posts by location or context>*
RT.200	jamb posts
RT.201	stilts
RT.202	shores (structural elements)
RT.203	stays
RT.204	braces
RT.205	angle braces
RT.206	dragon ties
RT.207	knee braces
RT.208	spurs
RT.209	wind braces
RT.210	arch braces
RT.211	bridging
RT.212	cross bridging
RT.213	guys
RT.214	trompes
RT.215	*<spanning and projecting structural elements>*
RT.216	*<arches and arch components>*
RT.217	arches
RT.218	*<arches by form>*
RT.219	bell arches
RT.220	blind arches
RT.221	broken arches
RT.222	catenary arches
RT.223	cusped arches
RT.224	drop arches
RT.225	elliptical arches
RT.226	Florentine arches
RT.227	horseshoe arches
RT.228	inverted arches
RT.229	miter arches
RT.230	pointed arches
RT.231	blunt arches
RT.232	equilateral arches
RT.233	Italian pointed arches
RT.234	lancet arches
RT.235	ogee arches
RT.236	pointed segmental arches
RT.237	pseudo-four-centered arches
RT.238	Tudor arches
RT.239	rampant arches
RT.240	segmental arches
RT.241	semiarches
RT.242	semicircular arches
RT.243	shouldered arches
RT.244	stilted arches
RT.245	surmounted arches

May be used in combination with other descriptors (e.g., **cast iron** + **railings**; **molded** + **cornices**; **semicircular** + **windows**; **Italianate** + **roofs**; **church** + **doors**).

RT.246 **surbased arches**
RT.247 *<arches by form: construction>*
RT.248 **concentric arches**
RT.249 **rowlock arches**
RT.250 **corbel arches**
RT.251 **extradosed arches**
RT.252 **flat arches**
RT.253 **camber arches**
RT.254 **Dutch arches**
RT.255 **pseudo-three-centered arches**
RT.256 **gauged arches**
RT.257 **ribbed arches**
RT.258 **rigid arches**
RT.259 **rustic arches**
RT.260 **soldier arches**
RT.261 **stepped arches**
RT.262 *<arches by form: hinging>*
RT.263 **two-hinged arches**
RT.264 **three-hinged arches**
RT.265 *<arches by form: number of centers>*
RT.266 **one-centered arches**
RT.267 **two-centered arches**
RT.268 **three-centered arches**
RT.269 **four-centered arches**
RT.270 *<arches by form: plan>*
RT.271 **oblique arches**
RT.272 **splayed arches**
RT.273 *<arches by function>*
RT.274 **counter arches**
RT.275 **relieving arches**
RT.276 **straining arches**
RT.277 *<arches by location or context>*
RT.278 **back arches**
RT.279 **chancel arches**
RT.280 **diaphragm arches**
RT.281 **pier arches**
RT.282 **squinches**
RT.283 **subarches**
RT.284 **transverse arches**
RT.285 *<arch components>*
RT.286 **archivolts**
RT.287 **haunches**
RT.288 **impost blocks**
RT.289 **imposts**
RT.290 **beams**
RT.291 *<beams by form>*
RT.292 **balks**
RT.293 **box beams**
RT.294 **built-up beams**

May be used in combination with other descriptors (e.g., **cast iron** + **railings**; **molded** + **cornices**; **semicircular** + **windows**; **Italianate** + **roofs**; **church** + **doors**).

RT.295 flitch beams
RT.296 candle beams
RT.297 cased beams
RT.298 girders
RT.299 continuous girders
RT.300 plate girders
RT.301 joists
RT.302 binding joists
RT.303 common joists
RT.304 ceiling joists
RT.305 floor joists
RT.306 open web joists
RT.307 *<beams by location or context>*
RT.308 collar beams
RT.309 crossbeams
RT.310 dragon beams
RT.311 girts
RT.312 hammer beams
RT.313 jesting beams
RT.314 summerbeams
RT.315 *<beams by support condition>*
RT.316 continuous beams
RT.317 simple beams
RT.318 bents
RT.319 brackets
RT.320 angle brackets
RT.321 consoles
RT.322 ancones
RT.323 cantilevers
RT.324 corbels
RT.325 crucks
RT.326 decking
RT.327 *<entablatures and entablature components>*
RT.328 entablatures
RT.329 architrave cornices
RT.330 *<entablature components>*
RT.331 architraves
RT.332 *<cornices and cornice components>*
RT.333 cornices
RT.334 block cornices
RT.335 cavetto cornices
RT.336 raking cornices
RT.337 *<cornice components>*
RT.338 bed moldings
RT.339 coronas
RT.340 cymatia
RT.341 dentils
RT.342 guttae
RT.343 modillions

May be used in combination with other descriptors (e.g., **cast iron** + **railings**; **molded** + **cornices**; **semicircular** + **windows**; **Italianate** + **roofs**; **church** + **doors**).

RT

RT.344 **mutules**
RT.345 *<friezes and frieze components>*
RT.346 **friezes (entablature components)**
RT.347 **hyperthyra**
RT.348 **pulvinated friezes**
RT.349 *<frieze components>*
RT.350 **hemiglyphs**
RT.351 **metopes**
RT.352 **demimetopes**
RT.353 **triglyphs**
RT.354 **lintels**
RT.355 *<trusses and truss components>*
RT.356 **trusses**
RT.357 *<trusses by form>*
RT.358 **planar trusses**
RT.359 **bowstring trusses**
RT.360 **Burr arch trusses**
RT.361 **crescent trusses**
RT.362 **Fink trusses**
RT.363 **fan Fink trusses**
RT.364 **hammer-beam trusses**
RT.365 **Howe trusses**
RT.366 **king-post trusses**
RT.367 **Pratt trusses**
RT.368 **Parker trusses**
RT.369 **Whipple trusses**
RT.370 **queen-post trusses**
RT.371 **scissors trusses**
RT.372 **Town lattice trusses**
RT.373 **Vierendeel trusses**
RT.374 **Warren trusses**
RT.375 **space frames**
RT.376 **tensegrity structures**
RT.377 *<trusses by location or context>*
RT.378 **bridge trusses**
RT.379 **through trusses**
RT.380 **pony trusses**
RT.381 **roof trusses**
RT.382 **jack trusses**
RT.383 **trussed rafters**
RT.384 *<truss components>*
RT.385 **chords**
RT.386 **web members**
RT.387 *<enclosing structural elements>*
RT.388 *<domes and dome components>*
RT.389 **domes**
RT.390 **beehive domes**
RT.391 **calottes**
RT.392 **geodesic domes**

May be used in combination with other descriptors (e.g., **cast iron** + **railings**; **molded** + **cornices**; **semicircular** + **windows**; **Italianate** + **roofs**; **church** + **doors**).

RT.393 onion domes
RT.394 pendentive domes
RT.395 ribbed domes
RT.396 saucer domes
RT.397 Schwedler domes
RT.398 semidomes
RT.399 umbrella domes
RT.400 *<dome components>*
RT.401 gores
RT.402 tension rings
RT.403 membrane structures
RT.404 pneumatic structures
RT.405 air-inflated structures
RT.406 air-supported structures
RT.407 tent structures
RT.408 *<roofs and roof components>*
RT.409 roofs
RT.410 *<roofs by form>*
RT.411 *<roofs by form: exterior shape>*
RT.412 butterfly roofs
RT.413 canopies
RT.414 baldachins
RT.415 flat roofs
RT.416 terrace roofs
RT.417 hoods (roofs)
RT.418 marquees
RT.419 ogee roofs
RT.420 pitched roofs
RT.421 curb roofs
RT.422 gambrel roofs
RT.423 mansard roofs
RT.424 French roofs
RT.425 false thatched roofs
RT.426 gable-on-hip roofs
RT.427 gable roofs
RT.428 double-gable roofs
RT.429 saddleback roofs
RT.430 hip roofs
RT.431 pyramidal roofs
RT.432 jerkinhead roofs
RT.433 platform roofs
RT.434 shed roofs
RT.435 skirt roofs
RT.436 rainbow roofs
RT.437 sawtooth roofs
RT.438 *<roofs by form: interior shape>*
RT.439 barrel roofs
RT.440 compass roofs
RT.441 open-timbered roofs

May be used in combination with other descriptors (e.g., **cast iron** + **railings**; **molded** + **cornices**; **semicircular** + **windows**; **Italianate** + **roofs**; **church** + **doors**).

RT.442 *<roofs by construction>*
RT.443 **suspension roofs**
RT.444 **velaria**
RT.445 *<roofs by construction: rafter structure>*
RT.446 **single-framed roofs**
RT.447 **double-framed roofs**
RT.448 *<roofs by construction: truss and beam structure>*
RT.449 **collar beam roofs**
RT.450 **couple roofs**
RT.451 **hammer-beam roofs**
RT.452 **king-post roofs**
RT.453 **queen-post roofs**
RT.454 **trussed rafter roofs**
RT.455 *<roof components>*
RT.456 *<exterior roof components>*
RT.457 **cowls**
RT.458 *<eaves and eave components>*
RT.459 **eaves**
RT.460 **closed eaves**
RT.461 **flush eaves**
RT.462 **open eaves**
RT.463 *<eave components>*
RT.464 **eaves boards**
RT.465 **eaves fascias**
RT.466 **gargoyles**
RT.467 **hip rolls**
RT.468 **lightning rods**
RT.469 **lookouts (roof components)**
RT.470 **ridges**
RT.471 *<roof appendages>*
RT.472 **bellcotes**
RT.473 **belvederes**
RT.474 **cupolas**
RT.475 **dormers**
RT.476 **chiens-assis**
RT.477 **curved dormers**
RT.478 **eyebrow dormers**
RT.479 **gabled dormers**
RT.480 **pedimented dormers**
RT.481 **hipped dormers**
RT.482 **shaped dormers**
RT.483 **shed dormers**
RT.484 **stair dormers**
RT.485 **lanterns (roof appendages)**
RT.486 **monitors (roof appendages)**
RT.487 **widow's walks**
RT.488 **saddle boards**
RT.489 **show rafters**
RT.490 **snow guards**

May be used in combination with other descriptors (e.g., **cast iron** + **railings**; **molded** + **cornices**; **semicircular** + **windows**; **Italianate** + **roofs**; **church** + **doors**).

RT.491 **valleys (roof components)**
RT.492 *<verges and verge components>*
RT.493 **verges**
RT.494 *<verge components>*
RT.495 **bargeboards**
RT.496 *<roof frame components>*
RT.497 **rafters**
RT.498 **common rafters**
RT.499 **hip rafters**
RT.500 **jack rafters**
RT.501 **valley jacks**
RT.502 **principal rafters**
RT.503 **valley rafters**
RT.504 *<roof beams>*
RT.505 **pole plates**
RT.506 **purlins**
RT.507 **ridgeboards**
RT.508 **straining beams**
RT.509 **tie beams**
RT.510 *<roof posts>*
RT.511 **crown posts**
RT.512 **king posts**
RT.513 **princess posts**
RT.514 **queen posts**
RT.515 **pendant posts**
RT.516 **sprockets**
RT.517 **room dividers**
RT.518 **shell structures**
RT.519 **stressed skin structures**
RT.520 *<vaults and vault components>*
RT.521 **vaults**
RT.522 **compound vaults**
RT.523 *<compound vaults by form>*
RT.524 *<compound vaults by form: number of compartments>*
RT.525 **tripartite vaults**
RT.526 **quadripartite vaults**
RT.527 **sexpartite vaults**
RT.528 **octopartite vaults**
RT.529 *<compound vaults by form: profile>*
RT.530 **cloister vaults**
RT.531 **groined vaults**
RT.532 **domical vaults**
RT.533 **stilted vaults**
RT.534 **plowshare vaults**
RT.535 **underpitch vaults**
RT.536 **simple vaults**
RT.537 **barrel vaults**
RT.538 **annular vaults**
RT.539 **half barrel vaults**

May be used in combination with other descriptors (e.g., **cast iron** + **railings**; **molded** + **cornices**; **semicircular** + **windows**; **Italianate** + **roofs**; **church** + **doors**).

<vaults and vault components>
vaults
simple vaults
barrel vaults

RT.540	**inclined barrel vaults**
RT.541	**spiral vaults**
RT.542	**rampant barrel vaults**
RT.543	**surmounted vaults**
RT.544	**expanding vaults**
RT.545	**conoidal vaults**
RT.546	**convex conoidal vaults**
RT.547	*<vaults by form>*
RT.548	*<vaults by form: construction>*
RT.549	**pitched-brick vaults**
RT.550	**ribbed vaults**
RT.551	**fan vaults**
RT.552	**lierne vaults**
RT.553	**net vaults**
RT.554	**stellar vaults**
RT.555	**solid vaults**
RT.556	**corbel vaults**
RT.557	**timbrel vaults**
RT.558	**Guastavino vaults**
RT.559	*<vaults by form: profile>*
RT.560	**surbased vaults**
RT.561	*<vault components>*
RT.562	**crowns (architectural elements)**
RT.563	**groins**
RT.564	**vault bays**
RT.565	**vaulting capitals**
RT.566	**vaulting cells**
RT.567	**vaulting courses**
RT.568	**tas-de-charges**
RT.569	*<walls and wall components>*
RT.570	**walls**
RT.571	*<walls by form>*
RT.572	**battened walls**
RT.573	**battered walls**
RT.574	**blank walls**
RT.575	**canted walls**
RT.576	**cavity walls**
RT.577	**dry laid walls**
RT.578	**faced walls**
RT.579	**pierced walls**
RT.580	**veneered walls**
RT.581	*<walls by function>*
RT.582	**fire walls**
RT.583	**loadbearing walls**
RT.584	**nonbearing walls**
RT.585	**curtain walls**
RT.586	**wall systems**
RT.587	**retaining walls**
RT.588	**bulkheads**

May be used in combination with other descriptors (e.g., **cast iron** + **railings**; **molded** + **cornices**; **semicircular** + **windows**; **Italianate** + **roofs**; **church** + **doors**).

RT.589 gravity walls
RT.590 shear walls
RT.591 sleeper walls
RT.592 *<walls by location or context>*
RT.593 drums (walls)
RT.594 exterior walls
RT.595 *<facades and facade components>*
RT.596 facades
RT.597 false fronts
RT.598 screen facades
RT.599 storefronts
RT.600 *<facade components>*
RT.601 frontispieces (facade components)
RT.602 gable ends
RT.603 foundation walls
RT.604 interior walls
RT.605 partitions
RT.606 demountable partitions
RT.607 folding partitions
RT.608 party walls
RT.609 *<wall components>*
RT.610 *<wall components by form or function>*
RT.611 corner boards
RT.612 courses
RT.613 bench tables
RT.614 bond courses
RT.615 chain courses
RT.616 corbel tables
RT.617 damp courses
RT.618 lacing courses
RT.619 lintel courses
RT.620 oversailing courses
RT.621 plinth courses
RT.622 stringcourses
RT.623 dogtooth courses
RT.624 king-tables
RT.625 ledgement tables
RT.626 sill courses
RT.627 tumbling courses
RT.628 *<decorative wall components>*
RT.629 bacini
RT.630 chaînes
RT.631 coronets (architectural elements)
RT.632 roundels
RT.633 *<gables and gable components>*
RT.634 gables
RT.635 ailerons
RT.636 cross gables
RT.637 crow-stepped gables

May be used in combination with other descriptors (e.g., **cast iron** + **railings**; **molded** + **cornices**; **semicircular** + **windows**; **Italianate** + **roofs**; **church** + **doors**).

RT.638   **Dutch gables**
RT.639   **gablets**
RT.640   **shaped gables**
RT.641   **side gables**
RT.642   *<gable components>*
RT.643   **barge stones**
RT.644   **crowsteps**
RT.645   **gable posts**
RT.646   **gable shoulders**
RT.647   **kneelers (gable components)**
RT.648   *<interior wall components>*
RT.649   **baseboards**
RT.650   **chair rails**
RT.651   **coving**
RT.652   **overmantels**
RT.653   **picture rails**
RT.654   **plate rails**
RT.655   **wainscoting**
RT.656   **niches**
RT.657   **conchs**
RT.658   **pilasters**
RT.659   **pilaster strips**
RT.660   **pilastrades**
RT.661   **responds**
RT.662   **revetments**
RT.663   **orthostats**
RT.664   **water tables**
RT.665   **wythes**
RT.666   *<wall components by location or context>*
RT.667   **cantons (wall components)**
RT.668   **cornerstones**
RT.669   **padstones**
RT.670   **parapets**
RT.671   **parastades**
RT.672   **pediments**
RT.673   **broken pediments**
RT.674   **ogee pediments**
RT.675   **segmental pediments**
RT.676   **quoins**
RT.677   **scarcements**
RT.678   **spandrels**
RT.679   **tympana**
RT.680 *<structural element components>*
RT.681   *<arch, dome or vault components>*
RT.682   **extradoses**
RT.683   **intradoses**
RT.684   **ribs**
RT.685   **diagonal ribs**
RT.686   **flying ribs**

May be used in combination with other descriptors (e.g., **cast iron** + **railings**; **molded** + **cornices**; **semicircular** + **windows**; **Italianate** + **roofs**; **church** + **doors**).

RT.687 liernes
RT.688 ridge ribs
RT.689 longitudinal ridge ribs
RT.690 transverse ridge ribs
RT.691 tiercerons
RT.692 transverse ribs
RT.693 wall ribs
RT.694 voussoirs
RT.695 keystones
RT.696 key consoles
RT.697 springers
RT.698 *<balloon and platform frame components>*
RT.699 headers (frame components)
RT.700 ledger boards
RT.701 plates (balloon and platform frame components)
RT.702 sill plates
RT.703 wall plates
RT.704 roof plates
RT.705 rough sills
RT.706 studs
RT.707 trimmers (frame components)
RT.708 *<rolled sections>*
RT.709 angles (rolled sections)
RT.710 channel beams
RT.711 H-beams
RT.712 I-beams
RT.713 T-beams
RT.714 wide-flange beams
RT.715 *<surface elements and surface element components>*
RT.716 *<surface elements>*
RT.717 amortizements
RT.718 ceilings
RT.719 acoustical ceilings
RT.720 barrel ceilings
RT.721 beam ceilings
RT.722 camp ceilings
RT.723 cathedral ceilings
RT.724 *<coffered ceilings and coffered ceiling components>*
RT.725 coffered ceilings
RT.726 *<coffered ceiling components>*
RT.727 coffers (ceiling components)
RT.728 compartment ceilings
RT.729 cove ceilings
RT.730 domed ceilings
RT.731 luminous ceilings
RT.732 suspended ceilings
RT.733 coping
RT.734 fascias
RT.735 flashing

May be used in combination with other descriptors (e.g., **cast iron** + **railings**; **molded** + **cornices**; **semicircular** + **windows**; **Italianate** + **roofs**; **church** + **doors**).

RT.736 base flashing
RT.737 counter flashing
RT.738 stepped flashing
RT.739 *<floors and floor components>*
RT.740 floors
RT.741 access floors
RT.742 floating floors
RT.743 platforms
RT.744 bemas
RT.745 loading platforms
RT.746 sprung floors
RT.747 suspended floors
RT.748 *<floor components>*
RT.749 subfloors
RT.750 underlayment
RT.751 *<moldings and molding components>*
RT.752 moldings
RT.753 *<moldings by form>*
RT.754 applied moldings
RT.755 struck moldings
RT.756 revales
RT.757 stop moldings
RT.758 *<moldings by form: motif>*
RT.759 bead and reel moldings
RT.760 beakhead moldings
RT.761 billet moldings
RT.762 roll billet moldings
RT.763 cable moldings
RT.764 chain moldings
RT.765 dogtooth moldings
RT.766 egg and dart moldings
RT.767 paternosters
RT.768 wave moldings
RT.769 *<moldings by form: section>*
RT.770 cant moldings
RT.771 cavetto moldings
RT.772 cymas
RT.773 cyma rectas
RT.774 cyma reversas
RT.775 fillet moldings
RT.776 annulets
RT.777 beak moldings
RT.778 reglet moldings
RT.779 regulae
RT.780 sunk fillets
RT.781 supercilia
RT.782 taeniae
RT.783 half-round moldings
RT.784 astragals

May be used in combination with other descriptors (e.g., **cast iron** + **railings**; **molded** + **cornices**; **semicircular** + **windows**; **Italianate** + **roofs**; **church** + **doors**).

RT.785 bead moldings
RT.786 quirk beads
RT.787 toruses
RT.788 ovolo moldings
RT.789 quarter-round moldings
RT.790 platbands
RT.791 scotias
RT.792 roll moldings
RT.793 roll-and-fillet moldings
RT.794 *<moldings by location or context>*
RT.795 ataduras
RT.796 bolection moldings
RT.797 cap moldings
RT.798 cover moldings
RT.799 crossettes
RT.800 crown moldings
RT.801 drop moldings
RT.802 fusaroles
RT.803 hood moldings
RT.804 accolades
RT.805 label moldings
RT.806 raking moldings
RT.807 *<molding components>*
RT.808 bâtons rompus
RT.809 quirks
RT.810 muqarnas
RT.811 pavements
RT.812 *<pavements by property>*
RT.813 flexible pavements
RT.814 rigid pavements
RT.815 *<pavements by technique>*
RT.816 asarota
RT.817 opus tessellatum
RT.818 shoji
RT.819 soffits
RT.820 *<surface element components>*
RT.821 muntins
RT.822 panels
RT.823 fielded panels
RT.824 rails
RT.825 stiles
RT.826 hinge stiles
RT.827 lock stiles
RT.828 *<openings and opening components>*
RT.829 openings
RT.830 *<openings by form>*
RT.831 *<doorways and doorway components>*
RT.832 doorways
RT.833 *<doorway components>*

May be used in combination with other descriptors (e.g., **cast iron** + **railings**; **molded** + **cornices**; **semicircular** + **windows**; **Italianate** + **roofs**; **church** + **doors**).

RT.834 **air curtains**
RT.835 *<doorframes and doorframe components>*
RT.836 **doorframes**
RT.837 *<door frame components>*
RT.838 **door bucks**
RT.839 **door jambs**
RT.840 **doorheads**
RT.841 **doorstones**
RT.842 **thresholds**
RT.843 *<doors and door components>*
RT.844 **doors**
RT.845 *<doors by form>*
RT.846 **double doors**
RT.847 **Dutch doors**
RT.848 **false doors**
RT.849 **French doors**
RT.850 **jib doors**
RT.851 **trap doors**
RT.852 *<doors by form: construction>*
RT.853 **fire doors**
RT.854 **flush doors**
RT.855 **hollow-core doors**
RT.856 **solid-core doors**
RT.857 **louver doors**
RT.858 **panel doors**
RT.859 **screen doors**
RT.860 *<doors by function>*
RT.861 **access doors**
RT.862 **secret doors**
RT.863 **storm doors**
RT.864 *<doors by mode of operation>*
RT.865 **folding doors**
RT.866 **hinged doors**
RT.867 **mechanically operated doors**
RT.868 **overhead doors**
RT.869 **pivoted doors**
RT.870 **revolving doors**
RT.871 **roll-up doors**
RT.872 **sliding doors**
RT.873 **pocket doors**
RT.874 **swinging doors**
RT.875 *<doors by location or context>*
RT.876 **elevator doors**
RT.877 **garage doors**
RT.878 *<door components>*
RT.879 **door leaves**
RT.880 **door rails**
RT.881 **bottom rails**
RT.882 **lock rails**

May be used in combination with other descriptors (e.g., **cast iron** + **railings**; **molded** + **cornices**; **semicircular** + **windows**; **Italianate** + **roofs**; **church** + **doors**).

RT.883 doorsills
RT.884 overdoors
RT.885 trumeaux
RT.886 embrasures (openings)
RT.887 *<gateways and gateway components>*
RT.888 gateways
RT.889 sally ports
RT.890 *<gateway components>*
RT.891 *<gates and gate components>*
RT.892 gates
RT.893 dog gates
RT.894 lich-gates
RT.895 portcullises
RT.896 sluice gates
RT.897 *<gate components>*
RT.898 hanging posts
RT.899 heel stones
RT.900 shutting posts
RT.901 hatches
RT.902 buttery hatches
RT.903 oculi
RT.904 portals
RT.905 *<windows and window components>*
RT.906 windows
RT.907 *<windows by form>*
RT.908 abat-jours
RT.909 bay windows
RT.910 bow windows
RT.911 meshrebeeyeh
RT.912 rawashin
RT.913 oriel windows
RT.914 square bay windows
RT.915 camber windows
RT.916 Chicago windows
RT.917 classroom windows
RT.918 combination windows
RT.919 coupled windows
RT.920 double windows
RT.921 false windows
RT.922 fenestellas
RT.923 fenestrals
RT.924 floor to ceiling windows
RT.925 lancet windows
RT.926 lattice windows
RT.927 lunettes
RT.928 picture windows
RT.929 psychiatric windows
RT.930 rose windows
RT.931 strip windows

May be used in combination with other descriptors (e.g., **cast iron** + **railings**; **molded** + **cornices**; **semicircular** + **windows**; **Italianate** + **roofs**; **church** + **doors**).

RT.932 **tombstone lights**
RT.933 *<tripartite windows>*
RT.934 **Diocletian windows**
RT.935 **Palladian windows**
RT.936 *<windows by form: mode of operation>*
RT.937 **fixed windows**
RT.938 **hinged windows**
RT.939 **casement windows**
RT.940 **projected windows**
RT.941 **awning windows**
RT.942 **hopper windows**
RT.943 *<hung windows>*
RT.944 **double-hung windows**
RT.945 **jib-headed windows**
RT.946 **single-hung windows**
RT.947 **triple-hung windows**
RT.948 **louver windows**
RT.949 **jalousie windows**
RT.950 **pivoting windows**
RT.951 **sliding windows**
RT.952 *<windows by function>*
RT.953 **peepholes**
RT.954 **show-windows**
RT.955 **cabinet windows**
RT.956 **storm windows**
RT.957 *<windows by location or context>*
RT.958 **basement windows**
RT.959 **fanlights**
RT.960 **frieze band windows**
RT.961 **lowside windows**
RT.962 **side lights**
RT.963 **spire lights**
RT.964 **squints**
RT.965 **transom windows**
RT.966 *<window components>*
RT.967 **brise-soleils**
RT.968 **cames**
RT.969 **lights**
RT.970 **angel lights**
RT.971 **batement lights**
RT.972 **quarrels**
RT.973 **meeting rails**
RT.974 **sashes**
RT.975 **window boxes**
RT.976 *<window frames and window frame components>*
RT.977 **window frames**
RT.978 *<window frame components>*
RT.979 **window heads**
RT.980 **window sills**

May be used in combination with other descriptors (e.g., **cast iron** + **railings**; **molded** + **cornices**; **semicircular** + **windows**; **Italianate** + **roofs**; **church** + **doors**).

RT.981 **lug sills**
RT.982 **slip sills**
RT.983 *<openings by function>*
RT.984 **entrances**
RT.985 **posterns**
RT.986 **exits**
RT.987 **emergency exits**
RT.988 **gunports**
RT.989 **intakes**
RT.990 **vents**
RT.991 **soffit vents**
RT.992 *<openings by location or context>*
RT.993 **archways**
RT.994 **compluvia**
RT.995 *<toplighting openings>*
RT.996 **lantern lights**
RT.997 **laylights**
RT.998 **pavement lights**
RT.999 **skylights**
RT.1000 *<opening components>*
RT.1001 **coaming**
RT.1002 **jambs**
RT.1003 *<louvers and louver components>*
RT.1004 **louvers**
RT.1005 *<louver components>*
RT.1006 **louver boards**
RT.1007 **mullions**
RT.1008 **reveals**
RT.1009 **shutters**
RT.1010 **folding shutters**
RT.1011 **jalousies**
RT.1012 **persiennes**
RT.1013 **sills**
RT.1014 **surrounds**
RT.1015 *<tracery and tracery components>*
RT.1016 **tracery**
RT.1017 **bar tracery**
RT.1018 **flowing tracery**
RT.1019 **perpendicular tracery**
RT.1020 **reticulated tracery**
RT.1021 **wheel tracery**
RT.1022 **Y-tracery**
RT.1023 **blind tracery**
RT.1024 **drop tracery**
RT.1025 **plate tracery**
RT.1026 *<tracery components>*
RT.1027 **daggers (tracery components)**
RT.1028 **foils**
RT.1029 **mouchettes**

May be used in combination with other descriptors (e.g., **cast iron** + **railings**; **molded** + **cornices**; **semicircular** + **windows**; **Italianate** + **roofs**; **church** + **doors**).

RT

RT.1030 **transoms**
RT.1031 **water bars**
RT.1032 **weather strips**
RT.1033 *<barriers and barrier elements>*
RT.1034 **barriers**
RT.1035 *<barrier elements>*
RT.1036 *<balustrades, railings and their components>*
RT.1037 **balustrades**
RT.1038 **railings**
RT.1039 *<balustrade and railing components>*
RT.1040 **balusters**
RT.1041 **handrails**
RT.1042 **grates**
RT.1043 **grilles**
RT.1044 **window guards**
RT.1045 **lattices**
RT.1046 **turnstiles**
RT.1047 *<culminating and edge ornaments>*
RT.1048 **acroteria**
RT.1049 **antefixes**
RT.1050 **cresting**
RT.1051 **brattishing**
RT.1052 **cheneaux**
RT.1053 **crockets**
RT.1054 **cusps**
RT.1055 **drops**
RT.1056 **épis**
RT.1057 **finials**
RT.1058 **hip knobs**
RT.1059 **pommels (finials)**
RT.1060 **pendants (architectural ornaments)**
RT.1061 **pinnacles**
RT.1062 *<circulation elements>*
RT.1063 **catwalks**
RT.1064 **gangways**
RT.1065 **ramps**
RT.1066 **wheelchair ramps**
RT.1067 *<stairs and stair components>*
RT.1068 **stairs**
RT.1069 *<stairs by form>*
RT.1070 **disappearing stairs**
RT.1071 **flying stairs**
RT.1072 **geometrical stairs**
RT.1073 **newel stairs**
RT.1074 **open well stairs**
RT.1075 **spiral stairs**
RT.1076 **double spiral stairs**
RT.1077 **hollow newel stairs**
RT.1078 **open newel stairs**

May be used in combination with other descriptors (e.g., **cast iron** + **railings**; **molded** + **cornices**; **semicircular** + **windows**; **Italianate** + **roofs**; **church** + **doors**).

RT.1079 solid newel stairs
RT.1080 straight stairs
RT.1081 *<stairs by form: landings>*
RT.1082 quarterpace stairs
RT.1083 halfpace stairs
RT.1084 dogleg stairs
RT.1085 *<stairs by form: turns>*
RT.1086 quarter-turn stairs
RT.1087 half-turn stairs
RT.1088 double return stairs
RT.1089 three-quarter turn stairs
RT.1090 one-turn stairs
RT.1091 *<stairs by location or context>*
RT.1092 fire escapes
RT.1093 fire stairs
RT.1094 ghats
RT.1095 pas-de-souris
RT.1096 stiles (stairs)
RT.1097 water stairs
RT.1098 *<stair components>*
RT.1099 apron pieces
RT.1100 carriage pieces
RT.1101 flights
RT.1102 landings
RT.1103 *<newels and newel components>*
RT.1104 newels
RT.1105 landing newels
RT.1106 *<newel components>*
RT.1107 newel caps
RT.1108 newel collars
RT.1109 newel drops
RT.1110 *<steps and step components>*
RT.1111 steps
RT.1112 commode steps
RT.1113 bullnose steps
RT.1114 fliers
RT.1115 hanging steps
RT.1116 spandrel steps
RT.1117 winders (steps)
RT.1118 balanced steps
RT.1119 turret steps
RT.1120 *<step components>*
RT.1121 nosings
RT.1122 risers
RT.1123 treads
RT.1124 strings
RT.1125 face strings
RT.1126 open strings
RT.1127 wall strings

May be used in combination with other descriptors (e.g., **cast iron** + **railings**; **molded** + **cornices**; **semicircular** + **windows**; **Italianate** + **roofs**; **church** + **doors**).

RT.1128 wreaths (stair components)
RT.1129 subrails
RT.1130 *<heating and cooking elements>*
RT.1131 *<chimneys and chimney components>*
RT.1132 chimneys
RT.1133 chimney stacks
RT.1134 smokestacks
RT.1135 *<chimney components>*
RT.1136 chimney bars
RT.1137 chimney breasts
RT.1138 chimney caps
RT.1139 chimney cheeks
RT.1140 chimney crickets
RT.1141 chimney hoods
RT.1142 chimney pots
RT.1143 tallboys (chimney pots)
RT.1144 chimney throats
RT.1145 chimney wings
RT.1146 flue linings
RT.1147 flues
RT.1148 soot doors
RT.1149 *<fireplaces and fireplace components>*
RT.1150 fireplaces
RT.1151 *<fireplace components>*
RT.1152 ashpits
RT.1153 firebacks
RT.1154 fireplace cheeks
RT.1155 hearths
RT.1156 back hearths
RT.1157 front hearths
RT.1158 hearthstones
RT.1159 hobs
RT.1160 mantels
RT.1161 hypocausts
RT.1162 kangs
RT.1163 on-dols
RT.1164 ovens
RT.1165 *<architectural elements by building type>*
RT.1166 *<fortification elements>*
RT.1167 baileys
RT.1168 inner baileys
RT.1169 outer baileys
RT.1170 *<bastions and bastion components>*
RT.1171 bastions
RT.1172 *<bastion components>*
RT.1173 appareilles
RT.1174 casemates
RT.1175 gorges (bastion components)
RT.1176 batteries

May be used in combination with other descriptors (e.g., **cast iron** + **railings**; **molded** + **cornices**; **semicircular** + **windows**; **Italianate** + **roofs**; **church** + **doors**).

RT.1177	cavaliers
RT.1178	<*defensive walls and defensive wall components*>
RT.1179	defensive walls
RT.1180	breastworks
RT.1181	curtain walls (fortification elements)
RT.1182	enceintes
RT.1183	ramparts
RT.1184	valla
RT.1185	<*defensive wall components*>
RT.1186	banquettes (defensive wall components)
RT.1187	bartizans
RT.1188	<*battlements and battlement components*>
RT.1189	battlements
RT.1190	<*battlement components*>
RT.1191	embrasures (battlement components)
RT.1192	merlons
RT.1193	machicolations
RT.1194	terrepleins
RT.1195	<*fortification openings*>
RT.1196	loop windows
RT.1197	loopholes
RT.1198	keeps
RT.1199	mottes
RT.1200	outworks
RT.1201	barbicans
RT.1202	counterscarps
RT.1203	covered ways (fortification elements)
RT.1204	escarpments
RT.1205	glacis
RT.1206	hornworks
RT.1207	moats
RT.1208	palisades (outworks)
RT.1209	ravelins
RT.1210	redans
RT.1211	<*religious building fixtures*>
RT.1212	ablution fountains
RT.1213	<*altars and altar components*>
RT.1214	altars
RT.1215	high altars
RT.1216	side altars
RT.1217	<*altar components*>
RT.1218	altar frontals
RT.1219	mensas
RT.1220	predellas
RT.1221	sepulchers
RT.1222	tabernacles (altar components)
RT.1223	<*Christian religious building fixtures*>
RT.1224	altar rails
RT.1225	communion rails

RT.1226	altarpieces
RT.1227	reredoses
RT.1228	retables
RT.1229	chrismatories
RT.1230	ciboria
RT.1231	confessionals
RT.1232	Easter sepulchers
RT.1233	fonts
RT.1234	kneelers
RT.1235	*<pews and pew components>*
RT.1236	pews
RT.1237	box pews
RT.1238	*<pew components>*
RT.1239	pew chairs
RT.1240	piscinae
RT.1241	*<pulpits and pulpit components>*
RT.1242	pulpits
RT.1243	ambos
RT.1244	three-deckers (pulpits)
RT.1245	*<pulpit components>*
RT.1246	sounding boards
RT.1247	rood lofts
RT.1248	*<screens in Christian religious buildings>*
RT.1249	altar screens
RT.1250	chancel screens
RT.1251	iconostases
RT.1252	rood screens
RT.1253	choir screens
RT.1254	organ screens
RT.1255	parcloses
RT.1256	sedilia
RT.1257	stalls (church fixtures)
RT.1258	choir stalls
RT.1259	*<Islamic religious building fixtures>*
RT.1260	dikka
RT.1261	mihrabs
RT.1262	minbars
RT.1263	qibla walls
RT.1264	*<theater elements>*
RT.1265	gridirons (theater elements)
RT.1266	parascenia
RT.1267	periaktoi
RT.1268	proscenium arches
RT.1269	proscenium walls
RT.1270	*<scaenae and scaenae components>*
RT.1271	scaenae
RT.1272	*<scaenae components>*
RT.1273	episcaenia
RT.1274	scaenae frontes

May be used in combination with other descriptors (e.g., **cast iron** + **railings**; **molded** + **cornices**; **semicircular** + **windows**; **Italianate** + **roofs**; **church** + **doors**).

RT.1275 **stage floors**
RT.1276 *<stage sets and stage set components>*
RT.1277 **stage sets**
RT.1278 *<stage set components>*
RT.1279 **flats (theater elements)**
RT.1280 **traps (theater elements)**
RT.1281 **building systems**
RT.1282 *<communication systems and communication system components>*
RT.1283 **communication systems**
RT.1284 **clock and program systems**
RT.1285 **doorbells**
RT.1286 **intercom systems**
RT.1287 **intermission alarm systems**
RT.1288 **public address systems**
RT.1289 **television antenna systems**
RT.1290 *<communication system components>*
RT.1291 **beacons**
RT.1292 *<conveying systems and conveying system components>*
RT.1293 **conveying systems**
RT.1294 *<diagonal and multi-directional conveying systems>*
RT.1295 **escalators**
RT.1296 **inclined lifts**
RT.1297 **chair lifts**
RT.1298 **moving ramps**
RT.1299 **pneumatic tubes**
RT.1300 *<horizontal conveying systems>*
RT.1301 **moving walkways**
RT.1302 **people-movers**
RT.1303 *<vertical conveying systems>*
RT.1304 **dumbwaiters**
RT.1305 **elevators**
RT.1306 *<elevators by form>*
RT.1307 **double-deck elevators**
RT.1308 **observation car elevators**
RT.1309 **slant elevators**
RT.1310 *<elevators by function>*
RT.1311 **freight elevators**
RT.1312 **grade-level elevators**
RT.1313 **sidewalk elevators**
RT.1314 **passenger elevators**
RT.1315 **service elevators**
RT.1316 *<elevators by mode of operation>*
RT.1317 **automatic elevators**
RT.1318 **electric elevators**
RT.1319 **hydraulic elevators**
RT.1320 **hydroelectric elevators**
RT.1321 **traction elevators**
RT.1322 **manlifts**
RT.1323 *<conveying system components>*

May be used in combination with other descriptors (e.g., **cast iron** + **railings**; **molded** + **cornices**; **semicircular** + **windows**; **Italianate** + **roofs**; **church** + **doors**).

RT.1324 driving machines
RT.1325 *<horizontal and diagonal conveying system components>*
RT.1326 threshold combs
RT.1327 threshold plates
RT.1328 *<vertical conveying systems components>*
RT.1329 counterweights
RT.1330 hoistways
RT.1331 *<electrical systems and electrical system components>*
RT.1332 electrical systems
RT.1333 emergency power supply
RT.1334 grounded systems
RT.1335 *<electrical system components>*
RT.1336 circuit breakers
RT.1337 circuits
RT.1338 electric cables
RT.1339 electric closets
RT.1340 electric conduits
RT.1341 electric switches
RT.1342 electric wiring
RT.1343 electrical supply stations
RT.1344 ground-fault circuit interruptors
RT.1345 panelboards
RT.1346 power outlets
RT.1347 raceways
RT.1348 busways
RT.1349 receptacles
RT.1350 switchboards
RT.1351 transformers
RT.1352 lighting
RT.1353 *<lighting by form>*
RT.1354 direct lighting
RT.1355 directional lighting
RT.1356 festoon lighting
RT.1357 floodlighting
RT.1358 general diffuse lighting
RT.1359 general lighting
RT.1360 indirect lighting
RT.1361 local lighting
RT.1362 spotlighting
RT.1363 supplementary lighting
RT.1364 *<lighting by function>*
RT.1365 architectural lighting
RT.1366 emergency lighting
RT.1367 exit lights
RT.1368 task lighting
RT.1369 *<lighting by light source>*
RT.1370 electric lighting
RT.1371 fluorescent lighting
RT.1372 gas-lighting

May be used in combination with other descriptors (e.g., **cast iron** + **railings**; **molded** + **cornices**; **semicircular** + **windows**; **Italianate** + **roofs**; **church** + **doors**).

RT.1373 *<lighting by location or context>*
RT.1374 exterior lighting
RT.1375 interior lighting
RT.1376 cornice lighting
RT.1377 cove lighting
RT.1378 valance lighting
RT.1379 stage lighting
RT.1380 mechanical systems
RT.1381 *<HVAC and HVAC components>*
RT.1382 HVAC
RT.1383 air conditioning
RT.1384 central air conditioning
RT.1385 incremental air conditioning
RT.1386 unit air conditioning
RT.1387 air cooling
RT.1388 chilled water systems
RT.1389 ice storage systems
RT.1390 refrigerant systems
RT.1391 heating systems
RT.1392 electric resistance heating
RT.1393 hot water heating
RT.1394 radiant heating
RT.1395 panel heating
RT.1396 solar heating
RT.1397 active solar heating
RT.1398 passive solar heating
RT.1399 steam heating
RT.1400 vacuum heating
RT.1401 warm air heating
RT.1402 forced air heating
RT.1403 gravity heating
RT.1404 ventilation
RT.1405 exhaust ventilation
RT.1406 mechanical ventilation
RT.1407 natural ventilation
RT.1408 *<HVAC components>*
RT.1409 *<cooling, heating and humidifying components>*
RT.1410 air washers
RT.1411 boilers
RT.1412 hot water boilers
RT.1413 steam boilers
RT.1414 cooling towers
RT.1415 furnaces
RT.1416 warm air furnaces
RT.1417 electric furnaces
RT.1418 oil furnaces
RT.1419 heat exchangers
RT.1420 coils
RT.1421 cooling coils

May be used in combination with other descriptors (e.g., **cast iron** + **railings**; **molded** + **cornices**; **semicircular** + **windows**; **Italianate** + **roofs**; **church** + **doors**).

RT.1422	dehumidifying coils
RT.1423	heating coils
RT.1424	condensers
RT.1425	heat pumps
RT.1426	solar-assisted heat pumps
RT.1427	heat-distributing units
RT.1428	baseboard units
RT.1429	convectors
RT.1430	radiators
RT.1431	*<ventilation system components>*
RT.1432	air diffusers
RT.1433	air distribution systems
RT.1434	air ducts
RT.1435	air filters
RT.1436	dry filters
RT.1437	viscous impingement filters
RT.1438	air-handling units
RT.1439	blowers
RT.1440	dampers
RT.1441	plenum chambers
RT.1442	registers (HVAC components)
RT.1443	ventilators
RT.1444	*<plumbing and storm water systems and their components>*
RT.1445	plumbing systems
RT.1446	sanitary drainage systems
RT.1447	*<water distribution systems>*
RT.1448	downfeed systems
RT.1449	upfeed systems
RT.1450	storm water systems
RT.1451	*<plumbing and storm water system components>*
RT.1452	catch basins
RT.1453	cesspools
RT.1454	cisterns
RT.1455	drains
RT.1456	area drains
RT.1457	fixture drains
RT.1458	storm drains
RT.1459	gutters (storm water systems)
RT.1460	arris gutters
RT.1461	back gutters
RT.1462	eaves gutters
RT.1463	valley gutters
RT.1464	impluvia
RT.1465	leaching fields
RT.1466	leader heads
RT.1467	piping (plumbing systems)
RT.1468	conductors (piping)
RT.1469	drainage piping
RT.1470	DWV piping

May be used in combination with other descriptors (e.g., **cast iron** + **railings**; **molded** + **cornices**; **semicircular** + **windows**; **Italianate** + **roofs**; **church** + **doors**).

RT.1471 mains
RT.1472 risers (piping)
RT.1473 service pipes
RT.1474 stacks (piping)
RT.1475 soil stacks
RT.1476 vent stacks
RT.1477 waste stacks
RT.1478 plumbing fixtures
RT.1479 bathtubs
RT.1480 bidets
RT.1481 drinking fountains
RT.1482 laundry trays
RT.1483 showers
RT.1484 sinks
RT.1485 dental sinks
RT.1486 lavatories (sinks)
RT.1487 slop sinks
RT.1488 wash sinks
RT.1489 toilets
RT.1490 waterless toilets
RT.1491 urinals
RT.1492 washfountains
RT.1493 seepage pits
RT.1494 septic tanks
RT.1495 sumps
RT.1496 traps (plumbing systems)
RT.1497 fixture traps
RT.1498 house traps
RT.1499 water heaters
RT.1500 solar water heaters
RT.1501 water storage tanks
RT.1502 *<protection systems>*
RT.1503 fire protection systems
RT.1504 *<fire alarm systems and fire alarm system components>*
RT.1505 fire alarm systems
RT.1506 auxiliary fire alarm systems
RT.1507 local fire alarm systems
RT.1508 proprietary fire alarm systems
RT.1509 remote-station fire alarm systems
RT.1510 *<fire alarm system components>*
RT.1511 fire detectors
RT.1512 flame detectors
RT.1513 temperature detectors
RT.1514 manual stations
RT.1515 smoke detectors
RT.1516 ionization detectors
RT.1517 photoelectric detectors
RT.1518 *<fire extinguishing systems and components>*
RT.1519 fire extinguishing systems

RT

May be used in combination with other descriptors (e.g., **cast iron** + **railings**; **molded** + **cornices**; **semicircular** + **windows**; **Italianate** + **roofs**; **church** + **doors**).

RT.1520 *<fire extinguishing system components>*
RT.1521 **fire sprinklers**
RT.1522 **security systems**

May be used in combination with other descriptors (e.g., **cast iron** + **railings**; **molded** + **cornices**; **semicircular** + **windows**; **Italianate** + **roofs**; **church** + **doors**).

Furnishings and Equipment

(TB) Tools and Equipment
(TF) Hardware and Joints
(TG) Furniture

The Furnishings and Equipment section provides descriptors for artifacts whose primary and original function is utilitarian—to outfit an individual or place, or to provide comfort, convenience, or protection. These artifacts are often embellished and, occasionally, regarded as purely ornamental.

Tools and Equipment Hierarchy

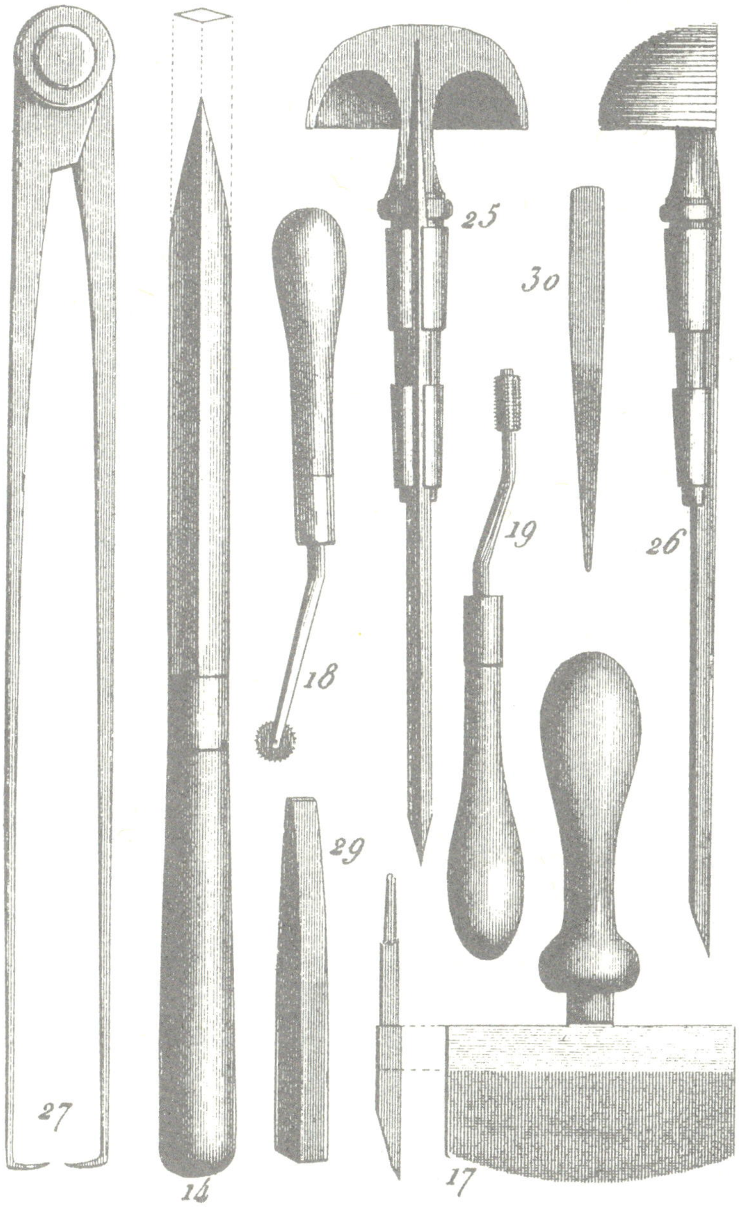

Scope The Tools and Equipment hierarchy contains descriptors for equipment used in processing materials and fabricating objects, as well as descriptors associated with activities and disciplines in the construction industry, design profession, and the arts. Excluded are artifacts, such as measuring devices, which may be considered equipment but which fall within the scope of other hierarchies in the Furnishings and Equipment section. The Tools and Equipment hierarchy consists primarily of descriptors associated with architecture and related disciplines, and will expand in areas relating to the fine and decorative arts as those areas are developed. Place holders, such as <*glassworking equipment*>, have been added in anticipation of this expansion.

Organization The hierarchy is divided into two major categories: **equipment** and <*tool and machinery components*>. The equipment section is further divided into five headings: <*equipment by general type*> (e.g., **machinery**) includes the generic forms of equipment without enumerating their types; <*equipment by mode of operation*> (e.g., **hydraulic equipment**) identifies categories of equipment by their source of power; <*equipment by process*> (e.g., **earthmoving equipment**) organizes equipment according to the basic function it performs; <*equipment by profession or discipline*> (e.g., **scientific instruments**) collocates descriptors for equipment associated with a particular discipline, profession or activity; and <*equipment by material processed*> (e.g., **woodworking tools**) includes descriptors for equipment used exclusively with certain materials. The <*tool and machinery components*> category covers descriptors for the component parts of equipment (e.g., **handles**).

Relation to Other Hierarchies Descriptors for devices used to calculate or measure (e.g., **scales, weights**) will appear in the Measuring Devices hierarchy, still under development. Descriptors for large and small scale items that are necessary to attach, anchor, hold or join materials and objects or their components (e.g., **clips, keys**), appear in the Hardware and Joints hierarchy. HVAC systems can be found in the Built Works Components hierarchy, while the descriptors for HVAC equipment (e.g., **kilns, lehrs**) are found here.

Descriptor Form and Use Descriptors appear as plural nouns, with the singular added as an alternate form where appropriate. Descriptors may be combined with those from other hierarchies (e.g., **pen** + **drawings**; **cast iron** + **anvils**).

Number of Descriptors 994

Synopsis

TB.1	**equipment**
TB.2	*<equipment by general type>*
TB.3	**machinery**
TB.5	**tools**
TB.8	*<equipment by mode of operation>*
TB.9	**hydraulic equipment**
	|
TB.11	*<tools by mode of operation>*
TB.15	*<equipment by process>*
TB.16	**construction equipment**
	|
TB.530	*<upholstering tools>*
TB.535	*<equipment by profession or discipline>*
TB.536	*<equipment for natural resource extraction>*
TB.537	*<equipment for science and technology>*
TB.542	*<equipment by material processed>*
TB.543	*<clayworking tools and equipment>*
	|
TB.791	*<woodworking equipment>*
TB.1093	*<tool and machinery components>*
TB.1094	*<anvil components>*
	|
TB.1132	**wheels**

TB

TOOLS AND EQUIPMENT (TB)

TB.1	equipment
TB.2	*<equipment by general type>*
TB.3	machinery
TB.4	hydraulic machinery
TB.5	tools
TB.6	instruments
TB.7	machine tools
TB.8	*<equipment by mode of operation>*
TB.9	hydraulic equipment
TB.10	mechanical equipment
TB.11	*<tools by mode of operation>*
TB.12	hand tools
TB.13	power tools
TB.14	pneumatic tools
TB.15	*<equipment by process>*
TB.16	construction equipment
TB.17	*<assembling and disassembling construction equipment>*
TB.18	falsework
TB.19	gantries
TB.20	pile drivers
TB.21	stud drivers
TB.22	stud guns
TB.23	wrecking balls
TB.24	compacting equipment
TB.25	compactors
TB.26	tampers
TB.27	rammers
TB.28	rollers (compacting equipment)
TB.29	sheepsfoot rollers
TB.30	steamrollers
TB.31	tandem rollers
TB.32	earthmoving equipment
TB.33	bulldozers
TB.34	angle dozers
TB.35	shovel dozers
TB.36	tilting dozers
TB.37	crawler tractors
TB.38	excavating equipment
TB.39	backhoes
TB.40	dredges
TB.41	post-hole diggers
TB.42	trenching machines
TB.43	graders
TB.44	loaders
TB.45	rippers
TB.46	scarifiers (earthmoving equipment)
TB.47	scrapers (earthmoving equipment)
TB.48	*<shovels: earthmoving>*
TB.49	power shovels

May be used in combination with other descriptors (e.g., **cast iron** + **anvils**; **pen** + **drawings**).

TB.50 steam shovels
TB.51 spreaders
TB.52 *<transferring construction equipment>*
TB.53 bucket loaders
TB.54 chain bucket loaders
TB.55 buckets (construction equipment)
TB.56 clamshell buckets
TB.57 dippers
TB.58 dragline buckets
TB.59 grab buckets
TB.60 cherry pickers
TB.61 cranes
TB.62 bridge cranes
TB.63 climbing cranes
TB.64 crawler cranes
TB.65 davits
TB.66 gantry cranes
TB.67 locomotive cranes
TB.68 tower cranes
TB.69 traveling cranes
TB.70 truck cranes
TB.71 wall cranes
TB.72 wheel-mounted cranes
TB.73 hoisting machinery
TB.74 derricks
TB.75 guy derricks
TB.76 pole derricks
TB.77 gin pole derricks
TB.78 hoists
TB.79 block and tackle
TB.80 come-alongs
TB.81 gins
TB.82 winches
TB.83 windlasses
TB.84 *<cooling, heating and humidifying equipment>*
TB.85 air conditioners
TB.86 dryers
TB.87 *<heating equipment>*
TB.88 kiln forks
TB.89 kilns
TB.90 *<kilns by form>*
TB.91 beehive ovens
TB.92 chamber kilns
TB.93 rotary kilns
TB.94 tunnel kilns
TB.95 *<kilns by function>*
TB.96 brick kilns
TB.97 cement kilns
TB.98 coke ovens

May be used in combination with other descriptors (e.g., **cast iron** + **anvils**; **pen** + **drawings**).

TB.99	dry kilns
TB.100	lime kilns
TB.101	lehrs
TB.102	stoves
TB.103	torches
TB.104	acetylene torches
TB.105	blowtorches
TB.106	kerosene torches
TB.107	oxyacetylene torches
TB.108	oxyhydrogen torches
TB.109	humidifiers
TB.110	*<crushing equipment>*
TB.111	crushing machinery
TB.112	*<cutting equipment>*
TB.113	*<cutting machinery>*
TB.114	lathes
TB.115	*<cutting tools>*
TB.116	adzes
TB.117	augers
TB.118	axes
TB.119	chip axes
TB.120	chisels
TB.121	gouges
TB.122	gravers
TB.123	grozing irons
TB.124	knives
TB.125	pocket knives
TB.126	clasp knives
TB.127	jackknives
TB.128	penknives
TB.129	race knives
TB.130	utility knives
TB.131	rasps
TB.132	razor blades
TB.133	saws
TB.134	band saws
TB.135	crown saws
TB.136	hacksaws
TB.137	scissors
TB.138	shears
TB.139	*<data processing equipment>*
TB.140	calculators
TB.141	pocket calculators
TB.142	computer terminals
TB.143	computers
TB.144	microcomputers
TB.145	laptop computers
TB.146	portable computers
TB.147	minicomputers

May be used in combination with other descriptors (e.g., **cast iron** + **anvils**; **pen** + **drawings**).

TB.148 mainframes
TB.149 peripherals
TB.150 input devices
TB.151 digitizers
TB.152 graphics tablets
TB.153 joysticks
TB.154 keyboards
TB.155 light pens
TB.156 mice
TB.157 modems
TB.158 monitors
TB.159 output devices
TB.160 plotters
TB.161 electrostatic plotters
TB.162 pen plotters
TB.163 printers
TB.164 line printers
TB.165 page printers
TB.166 *<printers by mode of operation>*
TB.167 impact printers
TB.168 daisywheel printers
TB.169 dot matrix printers
TB.170 nonimpact printers
TB.171 ink jet printers
TB.172 laser printers
TB.173 storage devices
TB.174 *<drilling equipment>*
TB.175 drilling machinery
TB.176 boring machinery
TB.177 drill presses
TB.178 *<drilling tools>*
TB.179 drills
TB.180 *<drills by form>*
TB.181 barrel drills
TB.182 bow drills
TB.183 breast drills
TB.184 counterbores
TB.185 pump drills
TB.186 push drills
TB.187 twist drills
TB.188 *<drills by mode of operation>*
TB.189 electric drills
TB.190 hand drills
TB.191 pneumatic drills
TB.192 reamers
TB.193 *<fastening and unfastening equipment>*
TB.194 electronic glue guns
TB.195 screwdrivers
TB.196 offset screwdrivers

May be used in combination with other descriptors (e.g., **cast iron** + **anvils**; **pen** + **drawings**).

TB.197 **Phillips head screwdrivers**
TB.198 **ratchet screwdrivers**
TB.199 **spiral ratchet screwdrivers**
TB.200 **staple guns**
TB.201 **staplers**
TB.202 **wrenches**
TB.203 *<fire-making and controlling equipment>*
TB.204 **firesets**
TB.205 *<grinding and milling equipment>*
TB.206 *<grinding and milling machinery>*
TB.207 **milling machinery**
TB.208 **mower-knife grinders**
TB.209 *<grinding and milling tools>*
TB.210 **grinders**
TB.211 **mortars**
TB.212 **pestles**
TB.213 *<holding and gripping tools>*
TB.214 **clamps**
TB.215 **dovetail clamps**
TB.216 **drill clamps**
TB.217 **hooks**
TB.218 **pincers**
TB.219 **farrier's pincers**
TB.220 **pliers**
TB.221 **needlenose pliers**
TB.222 **tongs**
TB.223 **tweezers**
TB.224 **vises**
TB.225 **bench vises**
TB.226 **hand vises**
TB.227 **wire vises**
TB.228 *<image-making equipment>*
TB.229 *<drafting, drawing and writing equipment>*
TB.230 *<drafting, drawing and writing equipment by general type>*
TB.231 **drafting equipment**
TB.232 **drawing instruments**
TB.233 **writing instruments**
TB.234 *<drafting, drawing and writing equipment by specific type>*
TB.235 **chalk sticks**
TB.236 **charcoal sticks**
TB.237 **compasses**
TB.238 **beam compasses**
TB.239 **drop bow compasses**
TB.240 **proportional compasses**
TB.241 **crayons**
TB.242 **Conté crayons (TM)**
TB.243 **lithographic crayons**
TB.244 **pastels (crayons)**
TB.245 **wax crayons**

May be used in combination with other descriptors (e.g., **cast iron** + **anvils**; **pen** + **drawings**).

TB.246	**drafting machines**
TB.247	**ellipsographs**
TB.248	**erasers**
TB.249	**erasing shields**
TB.250	*<holders: drafting, drawing and writing equipment>*
TB.251	**pencil holders**
TB.252	**portcrayons**
TB.253	**inkstones**
TB.254	**metal points**
TB.255	**copper points**
TB.256	**lead points**
TB.257	**silver points**
TB.258	**micrographs**
TB.259	**pantographs**
TB.260	**pencil sharpeners**
TB.261	**pencils**
TB.262	**charcoal pencils**
TB.263	**colored pencils**
TB.264	**graphite pencils**
TB.265	**grease pencils**
TB.266	**mechanical pencils**
TB.267	**pens**
TB.268	**ball-point pens**
TB.269	**fountain pens**
TB.270	**stylographs**
TB.271	**lettering pens**
TB.272	**markers (drawing instruments)**
TB.273	**felt-tip pens**
TB.274	**quill pens**
TB.275	**reed pens**
TB.276	**ruling pens**
TB.277	**technical pens**
TB.278	**dotting wheels**
TB.279	**perspectographs**
TB.280	**plastic leads**
TB.281	**pointing plates**
TB.282	**stumps**
TB.283	**tortillons**
TB.284	**styluses**
TB.285	*<painting equipment>*
TB.286	**photographic equipment**
TB.287	*<cameras and camera accessories>*
TB.288	**cameras**
TB.289	*<cameras by form or function>*
TB.290	**35mm cameras**
TB.291	**box cameras**
TB.292	**electric eye cameras**
TB.293	**miniature cameras**
TB.294	**subminiature cameras**

May be used in combination with other descriptors (e.g., **cast iron** + **anvils**; **pen** + **drawings**).

TB.295 motion-picture cameras
TB.296 television cameras
TB.297 *<cameras by mode of operation>*
TB.298 panoramic cameras
TB.299 pinhole cameras
TB.300 rangefinder cameras
TB.301 reflex cameras
TB.302 single lens reflex cameras
TB.303 twin-lens cameras
TB.304 stereoscopic cameras
TB.305 view cameras
TB.306 banquet cameras
TB.307 *<camera accessories>*
TB.308 cable releases
TB.309 flash attachments
TB.310 flash cubes
TB.311 lens caps
TB.312 lens hoods
TB.313 light filters
TB.314 light meters
TB.315 photographic lenses
TB.316 convertible lenses
TB.317 fisheye lenses
TB.318 fixed-focus lenses
TB.319 long-focus lenses
TB.320 telephoto lenses
TB.321 standard lenses
TB.322 wide-angle lenses
TB.323 zoom lenses
TB.324 tripods
TB.325 *<photographic processing equipment>*
TB.326 *<brushes: photographic equipment>*
TB.327 background brushes
TB.328 contact printers
TB.329 developing tanks
TB.330 dodgers
TB.331 enlargers
TB.332 film dryers
TB.333 film splicers
TB.334 film washers
TB.335 print dryers
TB.336 safelights
TB.337 stirring rods
TB.338 tacking irons
TB.339 *<photograph viewing equipment>*
TB.340 stereoscopes
TB.341 *<printing and printmaking equipment>*
TB.342 *<maintenance equipment>*
TB.343 *<maintenance machinery>*

May be used in combination with other descriptors (e.g., **cast iron** + **anvils**; **pen** + **drawings**).

TB.344   **incinerators**
TB.345   **washing machines**
TB.346   *<maintenance tools>*
TB.347   **brooms**
TB.348   **whisk brooms**
TB.349   *<brushes: maintenance tools>*
TB.350   **dusting brushes**
TB.351   **file brushes**
TB.352   **scrub brushes**
TB.353   **wire brushes**
TB.354   **mops**
TB.355   **plungers**
TB.356 *<marking tools and accessories>*
TB.357   **brands**
TB.358   **perforating wheels**
TB.359   **pounce bags**
TB.360   **punches**
TB.361   **scorers**
TB.362   **scribers**
TB.363 *<moving and transporting equipment>*
TB.364   *<moving and transporting machinery>*
TB.365   **conveyors**
TB.366   **belt conveyors**
TB.367   **chain conveyors**
TB.368   **roller conveyors**
TB.369   **slat conveyors**
TB.370   **vibrating conveyors**
TB.371   **jacks**
TB.372   **hydraulic jacks**
TB.373   **jackscrews**
TB.374   **trench jacks**
TB.375   **pulley blocks**
TB.376   **pulleys**
TB.377   **pumping machinery**
TB.378   **pumps**
TB.379   *<moving and transporting tools>*
TB.380   **hoses**
TB.381   **shovels**
TB.382 *<piercing tools>*
TB.383   **awls**
TB.384   **needles**
TB.385 **power producing equipment**
TB.386   **compressors**
TB.387   **engines**
TB.388   **animal-powered engines**
TB.389   **steam engines**
TB.390   **generators**
TB.391   **motors**
TB.392   **hydraulic motors**

May be used in combination with other descriptors (e.g., **cast iron** + **anvils**; **pen** + **drawings**).

TB.393 nuclear reactors
TB.394 solar collectors
TB.395 treadmills
TB.396 turbines
TB.397 gas turbines
TB.398 hydraulic turbines
TB.399 impulse turbines
TB.400 steam turbines
TB.401 waterwheels
TB.402 *<protective equipment>*
TB.403 asbestos curtains
TB.404 firefighting equipment
TB.405 fire axes
TB.406 fire extinguishers
TB.407 firehoses
TB.408 respirators
TB.409 dust masks
TB.410 gas masks
TB.411 safety belts
TB.412 safety nets
TB.413 mosquito netting
TB.414 *<prying tools>*
TB.415 chincing irons
TB.416 crowbars
TB.417 claw bars
TB.418 pinch bars
TB.419 flagging irons
TB.420 nail pullers
TB.421 picks
TB.422 flinting picks
TB.423 staple pullers
TB.424 tack pulls
TB.425 *<shaping and guiding equipment>*
TB.426 *<shaping and guiding machinery>*
TB.427 dividing engines
TB.428 goffering machines
TB.429 isographs
TB.430 planing machines
TB.431 *<shaping and guiding tools>*
TB.432 curves
TB.433 Brook's curves
TB.434 flexible curves
TB.435 French curves
TB.436 lathe puppets
TB.437 miter blocks
TB.438 miter boards
TB.439 miter boxes
TB.440 molds
TB.441 patterns (guides)

May be used in combination with other descriptors (e.g., **cast iron** + **anvils**; **pen** + **drawings**).

TB.442 saw sets
TB.443 squares (tools)
TB.444 bevel squares
TB.445 carpenter's squares
TB.446 miter squares
TB.447 set squares
TB.448 T-squares
TB.449 try squares
TB.450 stamps (tools)
TB.451 straightedges
TB.452 parallel rules
TB.453 templates
TB.454 dovetail templates
TB.455 triangles (tools)
TB.456 *<striking tools>*
TB.457 hammers
TB.458 drop hammers
TB.459 peen hammers
TB.460 ball-peen hammers
TB.461 cross-peen hammers
TB.462 straight-peen hammers
TB.463 power hammers
TB.464 jackhammers
TB.465 sledgehammers
TB.466 trip-hammers
TB.467 hammerstones
TB.468 mallets
TB.469 caulking mallets
TB.470 mauls
TB.471 *<supporting equipment>*
TB.472 horses
TB.473 froe horses
TB.474 saw-sharpening horses
TB.475 sawhorses
TB.476 sawing tackles
TB.477 sawyer's props
TB.478 ladders
TB.479 aerial ladders
TB.480 double-cleat ladders
TB.481 extension ladders
TB.482 hook ladders
TB.483 rope ladders
TB.484 sectional ladders
TB.485 single-cleat ladders
TB.486 stepladders
TB.487 trestle ladders
TB.488 scaffolds
TB.489 bracket scaffolding
TB.490 bricklayer's scaffolding

May be used in combination with other descriptors (e.g., **cast iron** + **anvils**; **pen** + **drawings**).

TB.491 **saddle scaffolds**
TB.492 **suspended scaffolding**
TB.493 **trestle scaffolds**
TB.494 **workbenches**
TB.495 *<surface working and finishing equipment>*
TB.496 *<surface working and finishing machinery>*
TB.497 **sandblasting equipment**
TB.498 **sanding machines**
TB.499 *<surface working and finishing tools and accessories>*
TB.500 **abrasive paper**
TB.501 **carborundum paper**
TB.502 **garnet paper**
TB.503 **sandpaper**
TB.504 **brushes**
TB.505 **paintbrushes**
TB.506 **fountain brushes**
TB.507 **wallpaper brushes**
TB.508 **buffs**
TB.509 **burnishers**
TB.510 **carborundum stones**
TB.511 **caulking irons**
TB.512 **countersinks**
TB.513 **crocus cloth**
TB.514 **emery cloth**
TB.515 **files (tools)**
TB.516 **flat files**
TB.517 **rough files**
TB.518 **jeweler's cloth**
TB.519 **paint rollers**
TB.520 **sanders**
TB.521 **belt sanders**
TB.522 **contour sanders**
TB.523 **disk sanders**
TB.524 **power sanders**
TB.525 **spindle sanders**
TB.526 **sanding blocks**
TB.527 **scrapers**
TB.528 **shavehooks**
TB.529 **wall scrapers**
TB.530 *<upholstering tools>*
TB.531 **cabriolet hammers**
TB.532 *<needles: upholstering>*
TB.533 **spring needles**
TB.534 **web strainers**
TB.535 *<equipment by profession or discipline>*
TB.536 *<equipment for natural resource extraction>*
TB.537 *<equipment for science and technology>*
TB.538 **acoustic equipment**
TB.539 **meteorological instruments**

May be used in combination with other descriptors (e.g., **cast iron** + **anvils**; **pen** + **drawings**).

TB.540 optical instruments
TB.541 scientific instruments
TB.542 *<equipment by material processed>*
TB.543 *<clayworking tools and equipment>*
TB.544 *<concrete processing and fabricating equipment>*
TB.545 buggies (equipment)
TB.546 drop chutes
TB.547 *<concrete processing and fabricating machines>*
TB.548 concrete finishing machines
TB.549 concrete mixers
TB.550 concrete pavers
TB.551 concrete pumps
TB.552 concrete spreaders
TB.553 *<concrete processing and fabricating tools>*
TB.554 concrete saws
TB.555 edgers
TB.556 *<glassworking equipment>*
TB.557 *<leatherworking equipment>*
TB.558 *<masonry and plastering equipment>*
TB.559 *<masonry and plastering machinery>*
TB.560 mixers
TB.561 jiffler mixers
TB.562 plastering machines
TB.563 *<masonry and plastering tools>*
TB.564 angle paddles
TB.565 angle planes
TB.566 angle plows
TB.567 *<axes: masonry and plastering tools>*
TB.568 cavils
TB.569 zaxes
TB.570 badgers
TB.571 block scrapers
TB.572 bricklaying profiles
TB.573 *<brushes: masonry and plastering tools>*
TB.574 browning brushes
TB.575 *<chisels: masonry and plastering tools>*
TB.576 blocking chisels
TB.577 brick sets
TB.578 boasters
TB.579 claw chisels
TB.580 pitching chisels
TB.581 splitting chisels
TB.582 tooth chisels
TB.583 cleaving blades
TB.584 *<drills: masonry and plastering tools>*
TB.585 aiguilles
TB.586 hammer drills
TB.587 plugging chisels
TB.588 rock-drills

May be used in combination with other descriptors (e.g., **cast iron** + **anvils**; **pen** + **drawings**).

TB.589	dummies (mallets)
TB.590	featheredge rules
TB.591	feathers (tools)
TB.592	floats
TB.593	angle floats
TB.594	bull floats
TB.595	darbies
TB.596	hand floats
TB.597	texture floats
TB.598	floatstones
TB.599	groovers
TB.600	half hatchets
TB.601	*<hammers: masonry and plastering tools>*
TB.602	axhammers
TB.603	bushhammers
TB.604	crandall hammers
TB.605	face hammers
TB.606	patent hammers
TB.607	scabbling hammers
TB.608	hawks
TB.609	hods
TB.610	jointers
TB.611	*<knives: masonry and plastering tools>*
TB.612	elastic knives
TB.613	plaster knives
TB.614	putty knives
TB.615	lewises
TB.616	*<mauls: masonry and plastering tools>*
TB.617	rakers
TB.618	scotches
TB.619	mud spoons
TB.620	rabs
TB.621	radius tools
TB.622	*<saws: masonry and plastering tools>*
TB.623	grub saws
TB.624	scratch tools
TB.625	cock's combs
TB.626	devil floats
TB.627	drags (scratch tools)
TB.628	scarifiers
TB.629	screeds
TB.630	trowels
TB.631	brick trowels
TB.632	buttering trowels
TB.633	corner trowels
TB.634	inside corner trowels
TB.635	outside corner trowels
TB.636	margin trowels
TB.637	mechanical trowels

May be used in combination with other descriptors (e.g., **cast iron** + **anvils**; **pen** + **drawings**).

TB.638 **pointing trowels**
TB.639 **mixing troughs**
TB.640 *<metalworking equipment>*
TB.641 *<forging and metal-shaping equipment>*
TB.642 *<forging and metal-shaping machinery>*
TB.643 **forges**
TB.644 **punch presses**
TB.645 *<forging and metal-shaping tools>*
TB.646 *<anvils and anvil accessories>*
TB.647 **anvils**
TB.648 **bench anvils**
TB.649 *<anvil accessories>*
TB.650 **hardies**
TB.651 **bench plates**
TB.652 *<blocks: metalworking tools>*
TB.653 **dapping blocks**
TB.654 **filing blocks**
TB.655 **holding blocks**
TB.656 **punch blocks**
TB.657 **striking blocks**
TB.658 **drawplates**
TB.659 **drifts (metalworking tools)**
TB.660 *<hammers: metalworking tools>*
TB.661 **file-cutting hammers**
TB.662 **helve hammers**
TB.663 **planishing hammers**
TB.664 **plow hammers**
TB.665 **set hammers**
TB.666 **mandrels**
TB.667 **nail headers**
TB.668 *<punches: metalworking tools>*
TB.669 **backing-out punches**
TB.670 **counterpunches**
TB.671 **dapping punches**
TB.672 **drift punches**
TB.673 **fore punches**
TB.674 **hand lever punches**
TB.675 **prick punches**
TB.676 **scalloping punches**
TB.677 **rivet sets**
TB.678 **seamers**
TB.679 **double seamers**
TB.680 **snarling irons**
TB.681 **stakes**
TB.682 **beakhorn stakes**
TB.683 **blowhorn stakes**
TB.684 **creasing stakes**
TB.685 **double-creasing stakes**
TB.686 **hatchet stakes**

May be used in combination with other descriptors (e.g., **cast iron** + **anvils**; **pen** + **drawings**).

TB.687	hollow-mandrel stakes
TB.688	needle case stakes
TB.689	planishing stakes
TB.690	swages
TB.691	*<founding tools>*
TB.692	flasks (founding tools)
TB.693	melting ladles
TB.694	riddles (founding tools)
TB.695	shanks
TB.696	skimmers (founding tools)
TB.697	*<metal-cutting and grinding equipment>*
TB.698	*<metal-cutting and grinding machinery>*
TB.699	*<lathes: metalworking equipment>*
TB.700	turret lathes
TB.701	screw-cutting machines
TB.702	*<metal-cutting and grinding tools>*
TB.703	*<chisels: metalworking tools>*
TB.704	cold chisels
TB.705	cape chisels
TB.706	hot chisels
TB.707	*<cutters: metalworking tools>*
TB.708	buffers
TB.709	milling cutters
TB.710	pinion cutters
TB.711	pipe cutters
TB.712	sprue cutters
TB.713	wire cutters
TB.714	*<files: metalworking tools>*
TB.715	clockmaker's files
TB.716	joint files
TB.717	needle files
TB.718	round files
TB.719	flute reamers
TB.720	nippers
TB.721	*<shears: metalworking tools>*
TB.722	bench shears
TB.723	bolt clippers
TB.724	circle shears
TB.725	lever shears
TB.726	sheet shears
TB.727	tin snips
TB.728	strops
TB.729	*<thread-cutters: metalworking tools>*
TB.730	bolt cutters
TB.731	chasers
TB.732	dies (metalwork)
TB.733	screw plates
TB.734	taps
TB.735	plug taps

May be used in combination with other descriptors (e.g., **cast iron** + **anvils**; **pen** + **drawings**).

TB.736	taper taps
TB.737	whetstones
TB.738	gouge slips
TB.739	oil stones
TB.740	*<metal-joining and holding equipment>*
TB.741	*<metal-joining and holding machinery>*
TB.742	arc welding machines
TB.743	drawbenches
TB.744	*<metal-joining and holding tools>*
TB.745	*<pliers: metalworking tools>*
TB.746	combination pliers
TB.747	soldering guns
TB.748	soldering irons
TB.749	*<tongs: metalworking tools>*
TB.750	bolt tongs
TB.751	box tongs
TB.752	clip tongs
TB.753	crook-bit tongs
TB.754	flat tongs
TB.755	hammer tongs
TB.756	box hammer tongs
TB.757	hollow-bit tongs
TB.758	hoop tongs
TB.759	nail tongs
TB.760	pickup tongs
TB.761	pincer tongs
TB.762	round-lip tongs
TB.763	shoe tongs
TB.764	side tongs
TB.765	sliding tongs
TB.766	*<vises: metalworking tools>*
TB.767	chain-pipe vises
TB.768	leg vises
TB.769	*<wrenches: metalworking tools>*
TB.770	adjustable wrenches
TB.771	monkey wrenches
TB.772	spud wrenches
TB.773	Allen wrenches
TB.774	bed wrenches
TB.775	chain tongs
TB.776	impact wrenches
TB.777	open-end wrenches
TB.778	pipe wrenches
TB.779	socket wrenches
TB.780	tap wrenches
TB.781	*<plastics processing equipment>*
TB.782	*<rushworking tools>*
TB.783	fids
TB.784	*<knives: rushworking>*

May be used in combination with other descriptors (e.g., **cast iron** + **anvils**; **pen** + **drawings**).

TB.785	**picking knives**
TB.786	**willow knives**
TB.787	**peg awls**
TB.788	**side cutters**
TB.789	**spline chisels**
TB.790	*<textileworking equipment>*
TB.791	*<woodworking equipment>*
TB.792	**woodworking machinery**
TB.793	*<lathes: woodworking equipment>*
TB.794	**great wheel lathes**
TB.795	**mandrel lathes**
TB.796	**pole lathes**
TB.797	**spoke lathes**
TB.798	**wheel lathes**
TB.799	**bark mills**
TB.800	**barkers**
TB.801	**chippers**
TB.802	*<sawmills: woodworking tools>*
TB.803	**gang sawmills**
TB.804	**gate saws**
TB.805	**muley sawmills**
TB.806	**up-and-down sawmills**
TB.807	**woodworking tools**
TB.808	*<wood-cutting and finishing tools>*
TB.809	*<adzes: woodworking tools>*
TB.810	**bunging adzes**
TB.811	**carpenter's adzes**
TB.812	**cleaving adzes**
TB.813	**cooper's adzes**
TB.814	**hatchet-adzes**
TB.815	**hollowing adzes**
TB.816	**guttering adzes**
TB.817	**lipped adzes**
TB.818	**shipwright's adzes**
TB.819	**trussing adzes**
TB.820	**wheelwright's adzes**
TB.821	*<augers: woodworking tools>*
TB.822	**breast augers**
TB.823	**burn augers**
TB.824	**cylinder augers**
TB.825	**nose augers**
TB.826	**raft augers**
TB.827	**shell augers**
TB.828	**spiral augers**
TB.829	**taper augers**
TB.830	*<awls: woodworking tools>*
TB.831	**bradawls**
TB.832	**burning awls**
TB.833	**scribe awls**

May be used in combination with other descriptors (e.g., **cast iron** + **anvils**; **pen** + **drawings**).

TB.834 *<axes: woodworking tools>*
TB.835 barking axes
TB.836 beginning axes
TB.837 broadaxes
TB.838 goosewing axes
TB.839 felling axes
TB.840 lopping axes
TB.841 marking axes
TB.842 mast axes
TB.843 mortising axes
TB.844 twivels
TB.845 shipwright's axes
TB.846 barking irons
TB.847 braces (woodworking tools)
TB.848 ratchet braces
TB.849 smith's braces
TB.850 breastplates (tools)
TB.851 *<chisels: woodworking tools>*
TB.852 barking chisels
TB.853 bench chisels
TB.854 butt chisels
TB.855 corner chisels
TB.856 forming chisels
TB.857 framing chisels
TB.858 mortise chisels
TB.859 paring chisels
TB.860 slicks
TB.861 fishtail tools
TB.862 floor chisels
TB.863 hinge chisels
TB.864 ripping chisels
TB.865 sash chisels
TB.866 skew chisels
TB.867 socket chisels
TB.868 turning chisels
TB.869 veiners
TB.870 *<cutters: woodworking tools>*
TB.871 dovetail cutters
TB.872 peg cutters
TB.873 *<files: woodworking tools>*
TB.874 cabinet files
TB.875 float files
TB.876 knife files
TB.877 riffler files
TB.878 froes
TB.879 knife froes
TB.880 gimlets
TB.881 *<gouges: woodworking tools>*
TB.882 bent gouges

May be used in combination with other descriptors (e.g., **cast iron** + **anvils**; **pen** + **drawings**).

TB

<woodworking equipment>
woodworking tools
<wood-cutting and finishing tools>
<gouges: woodworking tools>

TB.883	bowl gouges
TB.884	carving gouges
TB.885	firmer gouges
TB.886	fluters
TB.887	paring gouges
TB.888	parting tools
TB.889	turning gouges
TB.890	hatchets
TB.891	adze-hatchets
TB.892	hewing hatchets
TB.893	lathing hatchets
TB.894	shingling hatchets
TB.895	claw hatchets
TB.896	jumpers
TB.897	*<knives: woodworking tools>*
TB.898	bench knives
TB.899	block knives
TB.900	drawknives
TB.901	backing drawknives
TB.902	barking drawknives
TB.903	chamfer knives
TB.904	heading drawknives
TB.905	hollowing drawknives
TB.906	jiggers
TB.907	mast drawknives
TB.908	hoop-notching knives
TB.909	sloyd knives
TB.910	planes
TB.911	combination planes
TB.912	grooving planes
TB.913	badger planes
TB.914	banding planes
TB.915	dado planes
TB.916	edge planes
TB.917	fillisters
TB.918	moving fillister planes
TB.919	sash fillister planes
TB.920	miter planes
TB.921	plow planes
TB.922	rabbet planes
TB.923	bullnose planes
TB.924	horned rabbets
TB.925	skew planes
TB.926	sash planes
TB.927	shoulder planes
TB.928	table round planes
TB.929	tongue planes
TB.930	tongue-and-groove planes
TB.931	leveling planes

May be used in combination with other descriptors (e.g., **cast iron** + **anvils**; **pen** + **drawings**).

TB.932 bench planes
TB.933 block planes
TB.934 jack planes
TB.935 jointer planes
TB.936 cooper's jointer planes
TB.937 long planes
TB.938 short-jointer planes
TB.939 smoothing planes
TB.940 strike blocks
TB.941 trying planes
TB.942 compass planes
TB.943 cooper's stoup planes
TB.944 finger planes
TB.945 floor planes
TB.946 howell planes
TB.947 panel planes
TB.948 sun-planes
TB.949 toothing planes
TB.950 molding planes
TB.951 *<simple molding planes>*
TB.952 bead planes
TB.953 capping planes
TB.954 centerboard planes
TB.955 cove planes
TB.956 guttering planes
TB.957 hollow planes
TB.958 forkstaffs
TB.959 nosing planes
TB.960 round planes
TB.961 *<complex molding planes>*
TB.962 cornice planes
TB.963 handrail planes
TB.964 molding pull planes
TB.965 ogee planes
TB.966 ovolo planes
TB.967 modeling planes
TB.968 roughing planes
TB.969 rounder planes
TB.970 scooper planes
TB.971 splint planes
TB.972 thumb planes
TB.973 *<punches: woodworking tools>*
TB.974 carver's punches
TB.975 handrail punches
TB.976 nail sets
TB.977 shingle punches
TB.978 starting punches
TB.979 veneer punches
TB.980 *<rasps: woodworking tools>*

TB.981	cabinet rasps
TB.982	riffler rasps
TB.983	*<reamers: woodworking tools>*
TB.984	hooked reamers
TB.985	routers
TB.986	*<saws: woodworking tools>*
TB.987	backsaws
TB.988	bead saws
TB.989	blitz-back saws
TB.990	dovetail saws
TB.991	miter-box saws
TB.992	rabbet saws
TB.993	stairbuilder's saws
TB.994	tenon saws
TB.995	carcass saws
TB.996	bench saws
TB.997	chain saws
TB.998	circular saws
TB.999	drunken saws
TB.1000	electric-portable saws
TB.1001	pendulum saws
TB.1002	radial-arm saws
TB.1003	table saws
TB.1004	frame saws
TB.1005	bow saws
TB.1006	web saws
TB.1007	bucksaws
TB.1008	coping saws
TB.1009	felloe saws
TB.1010	fretsaws
TB.1011	buhl saws
TB.1012	pit saws
TB.1013	frame pit saws
TB.1014	scroll saws
TB.1015	hand saws
TB.1016	jigsaws
TB.1017	open saws
TB.1018	cabinet saws
TB.1019	compass saws
TB.1020	keyhole saws
TB.1021	locksaws
TB.1022	square hole saws
TB.1023	crosscut saws
TB.1024	one-man crosscut saws
TB.1025	two-handed crosscut saws
TB.1026	open pit saws
TB.1027	panel saws
TB.1028	ripsaws
TB.1029	half-ripsaws

May be used in combination with other descriptors (e.g., **cast iron** + **anvils**; **pen** + **drawings**).

TB.1030 saber saws
TB.1031 veneer saws
TB.1032 scorpers
TB.1033 closed scorpers
TB.1034 open scorpers
TB.1035 *<scrapers: woodworking tools>*
TB.1036 box scrapers
TB.1037 cabinet scrapers
TB.1038 screw boxes
TB.1039 spokeshaves
TB.1040 chamfer spokeshaves
TB.1041 wedges
TB.1042 splitting wedges
TB.1043 *<wood-holding and assembling tools>*
TB.1044 bench hooks
TB.1045 bench stops
TB.1046 brad pushers
TB.1047 cauls
TB.1048 *<clamps: woodworking tools>*
TB.1049 bench clamps
TB.1050 C-clamps
TB.1051 corner clamps
TB.1052 joiner's clamps
TB.1053 sash clamps
TB.1054 panel clamps
TB.1055 saw clamps
TB.1056 screw clamps
TB.1057 slat-bending clamps
TB.1058 spring clamps
TB.1059 universal clamps
TB.1060 web clamps
TB.1061 dogs (woodworking tools)
TB.1062 bench dogs
TB.1063 spoke dogs
TB.1064 door jacks
TB.1065 holdfasts
TB.1066 *<hooks: woodworking tools>*
TB.1067 cant hooks
TB.1068 ring dogs
TB.1069 peavies
TB.1070 pickaroons
TB.1071 jam pikes
TB.1072 raft shackles
TB.1073 shaving blocks
TB.1074 *<vises: woodworking tools>*
TB.1075 box vises
TB.1076 chair vises
TB.1077 *<wood-striking tools>*
TB.1078 *<hammers: woodworking tools>*

May be used in combination with other descriptors (e.g., **cast iron** + **anvils**; **pen** + **drawings**).

TB.1079 **claw hammers**
TB.1080 **clench hammers**
TB.1081 **framing hammers**
TB.1082 **tack hammers**
TB.1083 **top maul hammers**
TB.1084 **veneer hammers**
TB.1085 **Warrington-pattern hammers**
TB.1086 *<mallets: woodworking tools>*
TB.1087 **beetles (mallets)**
TB.1088 **bungstarts**
TB.1089 **carpenter's mallets**
TB.1090 **carver's mallets**
TB.1091 **dead-blow mallets**
TB.1092 **froe clubs**
TB.1093 *<tool and machinery components>*
TB.1094 *<anvil components>*
TB.1095 **beak irons**
TB.1096 **belts (tool components)**
TB.1097 **bits**
TB.1098 **auger bits**
TB.1099 **ship auger bits**
TB.1100 **brush bits**
TB.1101 **button bits**
TB.1102 **center bits**
TB.1103 **countersink bits**
TB.1104 **expansion bits**
TB.1105 **forstner bits**
TB.1106 **gimlet bits**
TB.1107 **gouge bits**
TB.1108 **nose bits**
TB.1109 **plug cutters**
TB.1110 **pod-bits**
TB.1111 **reamer bits**
TB.1112 **shell bits**
TB.1113 **spiral bits**
TB.1114 **spoon bits**
TB.1115 **tenon-cutting bits**
TB.1116 **blades**
TB.1117 **saw blades**
TB.1118 **bows (tools)**
TB.1119 **chucks**
TB.1120 **cogs**
TB.1121 **collets**
TB.1122 **gears**
TB.1123 **hafts**
TB.1124 **handles (tool components)**
TB.1125 **helves**
TB.1126 **hitches**
TB.1127 *<hoist components>*

May be used in combination with other descriptors (e.g., **cast iron** + **anvils**; **pen** + **drawings**).

TB.1128 **slings**
TB.1129 **nibs**
TB.1130 **sanding disks**
TB.1131 **shafts (tool components)**
TB.1132 **wheels**
TB.1133 **grinding wheels**
TB.1134 **grindstones**
TB.1135 **sanding wheels**

TB

May be used in combination with other descriptors (e.g., **cast iron** + **anvils**; **pen** + **drawings**).

Hardware and Joints Hierarchy

HARDWARE AND JOINTS

Scope The Hardware and Joints hierarchy contains descriptors for the large and small items that are necessary to attach, anchor, hold, or join materials and components of furniture, structures, and other objects (e.g., **catches, tongue-and-groove joints**). Also included are descriptors for items used in the finishing of buildings and objects (e.g., **hinges**, **escutcheons**) and descriptors for decorative and accessory hardware (e.g., **doorplates**).

Organization The hierarchy is composed of two major sections: **hardware** and **joints**. The hardware section is divided into <*hardware by form*> (e.g., **locks**) and <*hardware by location or context*> (e.g., **window hardware**). The majority of descriptors appear under the category <*hardware by form*>, which is subdivided into **rough hardware** (e.g., **nails**) and **finishes hardware** (e.g., **handles**). The second section contains descriptors for **joints**.

Relation to Other Hierarchies Descriptors for HVAC, conveying, electrical, lighting, signal, and water systems are found in the Built Works Components hierarchy (e.g, **heating systems, cisterns**). Descriptors for moldings also appear in Built Works Components (e.g., **crown moldings**). Tools used for construction and fabrication can be found in the Tools and Equipment hierarchy (e.g., **hammers**). Descriptors for weighing and measuring instruments will appear in the Measuring Devices hierarchy, still under development.

Descriptor Form and Use Descriptors appear as plural nouns, with the singular added as an alternate form where appropriate. For hardware by material, technique, or other aspect, combine with descriptors from other appropriate hierarchies (e.g., **brass** + **pulls**; **gilded** + **mounts**; **oval** + **backplates**).

Number of Descriptors 644

Synopsis

TF.1 *<hardware and hardware components>*
TF.2 **hardware**
TF.3 *<hardware by form>*
TF.4 **finish hardware**
TF.286 **rough hardware**
TF.502 *<hardware by location or context>*
TF.503 **awning hardware**
TF.504 **bathroom hardware**
TF.505 **closet hardware**
TF.506 **door hardware**
TF.507 **furniture hardware**
TF.508 **gate hardware**
TF.509 **plumbing hardware**
TF.510 **shelf hardware**
TF.511 **window hardware**
TF.512 *<hardware components>*
TF.513 *<bolts components>*
TF.521 *<hinge components>*
TF.526 *<keys and key components>*
TF.547 *<latch and lock components>*
TF.571 **joints**
TF.572 <joints by form>
TF.573 **angle joints**
|
TF.601 **rubbed joints**
TF.602 *<joints by function>*
TF.603 **contraction joints**
|
TF.608 **thermal breaks**
TF.609 *<joints by material joined>*
TF.610 *<concrete joints>*
TF.615 *<masonry joints>*
TF.641 *<metal joints>*
TF.665 *<wood joints>*

HARDWARE AND JOINTS (TF)

TF.1	*<hardware and hardware components>*
TF.2	hardware
TF.3	*<hardware by form>*
TF.4	finish hardware
TF.5	*<accessory door hardware>*
TF.6	barn-door rollers
TF.7	barn-door stays
TF.8	door bumpers
TF.9	door checks
TF.10	door holders
TF.11	overhead door holders
TF.12	door knockers
TF.13	door rings
TF.14	door silencers
TF.15	doorknobs
TF.16	doorplates
TF.17	armor plates
TF.18	card frames
TF.19	kickplates
TF.20	name plates
TF.21	number plates
TF.22	push plates
TF.23	doorstops
TF.24	letter-box plates
TF.25	pull bars
TF.26	push bars
TF.27	*<accessory window and shutter hardware>*
TF.28	drapery holdbacks
TF.29	sash chains
TF.30	sash cords
TF.31	sash lifts
TF.32	sash pins
TF.33	sash weights
TF.34	shutter bars
TF.35	shutter dogs
TF.36	*<brackets>*
TF.37	handrail brackets
TF.38	shelf brackets
TF.39	campaign trim
TF.40	catches
TF.41	back catches
TF.42	ball catches
TF.43	blind catches
TF.44	bullet catches
TF.45	casement-window fasteners
TF.46	cupboard catches
TF.47	friction catches
TF.48	magnetic catches
TF.49	magnetic push catches

May be used in combination with other descriptors (e.g., **brass** + **faucets**; **metal** + **plated** + **towel bars**; **round** + **backplates**).

TF.50 transom catches
TF.51 castors
TF.52 cupboard turns
TF.53 faucets
TF.54 foot sockets
TF.55 handles
TF.56   bar handles
TF.57   casement stays
TF.58   entrance handles
TF.59   knobs
TF.60   *<knobs by form>*
TF.61   dummy knobs
TF.62   screwless knobs
TF.63   thru-screw knobs
TF.64   *<knobs by location or context>*
TF.65   cabinet knobs
TF.66   closet knobs
TF.67   shutter knobs
TF.68   pulls
TF.69   *<pulls by form>*
TF.70   bail pulls
TF.71   ball and spear pulls
TF.72   bean pulls
TF.73   button pulls
TF.74   drop pulls
TF.75   pear drop handles
TF.76   flush-cup pulls
TF.77   flush rings
TF.78   heart pulls
TF.79   offset pulls
TF.80   onion pulls
TF.81   recessed pulls
TF.82   ring handles
TF.83   lion and ring handles
TF.84   spade pulls
TF.85   *<pulls by location or context>*
TF.86   barn-door pulls
TF.87   bin pulls
TF.88   door pulls
TF.89   door edge pulls
TF.90   sliding-door pulls
TF.91   drawer pulls
TF.92   store-door handles
TF.93 hinges
TF.94   *<hinges by form>*
TF.95   adjustable ball hinges
TF.96   backflap hinges
TF.97   butt hinges
TF.98   ball-bearing hinges

May be used in combination with other descriptors (e.g., **brass** + **faucets**; **metal** + **plated** + **towel bars**; **round** + **backplates**).

TF.99 loose-joint hinges
TF.100 paumelle hinges
TF.101 olive knuckle hinges
TF.102 pocket butt hinges
TF.103 rising hinges
TF.104 butterfly hinges
TF.105 capped butt hinges
TF.106 continuous hinges
TF.107 cotter pin hinges
TF.108 double-acting hinges
TF.109 electric hinges
TF.110 fast-pin hinges
TF.111 friction hinges
TF.112 full-mortise hinges
TF.113 full-surface hinges
TF.114 H hinges
TF.115 H /L hinges
TF.116 half-mortise hinges
TF.117 half-surface hinges
TF.118 harmon hinges
TF.119 hydraulic hinges
TF.120 lift-off hinges
TF.121 rattail hinges
TF.122 loose-pin hinges
TF.123 offset hinges
TF.124 oilite bearing hinges
TF.125 pivot-reinforced hinges
TF.126 spring hinges
TF.127 double-acting spring hinges
TF.128 jamb spring hinges
TF.129 surface hinges
TF.130 strap hinges
TF.131 T hinges
TF.132 *<hinges by location or context>*
TF.133 anchor hinges
TF.134 casement hinges
TF.135 floor hinges
TF.136 checking floor hinges
TF.137 ice box hinges
TF.138 shutter hinges
TF.139 *<hinges by visibility>*
TF.140 concealed hinges
TF.141 exposed hinges
TF.142 invisible hinges
TF.143 *<holders>*
TF.144 hand towel dispensers
TF.145 soap dispensers
TF.146 toilet paper holders
TF.147 toothbrush holders

May be used in combination with other descriptors (e.g., **brass** + **faucets**; **metal** + **plated** + **towel bars**; **round** + **backplates**).

TF.148 towel bars
TF.149 tumbler holders
TF.150 hooks (hardware)
TF.151 bathroom hooks
TF.152 cabin door hooks
TF.153 cabin hooks
TF.154 ceiling hooks
TF.155 chimney hooks
TF.156 ladder hooks
TF.157 utility hooks
TF.158 wardrobe hooks
TF.159 keyhole surrounds
TF.160 *<latches, locks and other securing devices>*
TF.161 chain bolts
TF.162 chain door fasteners
TF.163 door bolts
TF.164 bottom bolts
TF.165 double-door bolts
TF.166 Dutch-door bolts
TF.167 extension flush bolts
TF.168 flush bolts
TF.169 mortise bolts
TF.170 thumb bolts
TF.171 latch bolts
TF.172 latches
TF.173 *<latches by form>*
TF.174 auxiliary dead latches
TF.175 knob latches
TF.176 lift latches
TF.177 night latches
TF.178 roller latches
TF.179 spring latches
TF.180 thumb latches
TF.181 barn-door latches
TF.182 *<latches by location or context>*
TF.183 cabinet latches
TF.184 cottage latches
TF.185 Dutch-door quadrants
TF.186 fire-door latches
TF.187 two-point latches
TF.188 hospital latches
TF.189 ice box latches
TF.190 screen-door latches
TF.191 secret gate latches
TF.192 vestibule latches
TF.193 locks
TF.194 *<locks by form>*
TF.195 bit key locks
TF.196 bored locks

May be used in combination with other descriptors (e.g., **brass** + **faucets**; **metal** + **plated** + **towel bars**; **round** + **backplates**).

TF.197	combination locks
TF.198	cylinder locks
TF.199	deadlocks
TF.200	guarded front locks
TF.201	janus-face locks
TF.202	key changing locks
TF.203	knob locks
TF.204	lever tumbler locks
TF.205	master-keyed locks
TF.206	duplex locks
TF.207	hotel locks
TF.208	mortise locks
TF.209	integral locks
TF.210	rabbeted locks
TF.211	half-rabbeted locks
TF.212	padlocks
TF.213	patio locks
TF.214	preassembled locks
TF.215	reverse bevel locks
TF.216	reversible locks
TF.217	rim locks
TF.218	auxiliary rim locks
TF.219	tubular locks
TF.220	subtreasury locks
TF.221	three-point locks
TF.222	time locks
TF.223	instant locks
TF.224	subsequent locks
TF.225	upright locks
TF.226	warded locks
TF.227	*<locks by location or context>*
TF.228	asylum locks
TF.229	door locks
TF.230	combined store-door locks
TF.231	communicating-door locks
TF.232	French-door locks
TF.233	cremorne bolts
TF.234	espagnolette bolts
TF.235	front-door locks
TF.236	office locks
TF.237	panicproof locks
TF.238	permutation locks
TF.239	prison locks
TF.240	hasp locks
TF.241	jamb locks
TF.242	room-door locks
TF.243	sliding-door locks
TF.244	store-door locks
TF.245	vestibule-door locks

May be used in combination with other descriptors (e.g., **brass** + **faucets**; **metal** + **plated** + **towel bars**; **round** + **backplates**).

TF.246 furniture locks
TF.247 cabinet locks
TF.248 push-pull cabinet locks
TF.249 cupboard locks
TF.250 desk locks
TF.251 drawer locks
TF.252 ship locks
TF.253 window locks
TF.254 air conditioning locks
TF.255 window spring bolts
TF.256 levers
TF.257 toilet tank levers
TF.258 mounts
TF.259 *<plates>*
TF.260 backplates
TF.261 roses (backplates)
TF.262 escutcheons (hardware)
TF.263 combined escutcheon plates
TF.264 cup escutcheons
TF.265 drop escutcheons
TF.266 thread escutcheons
TF.267 wall plates (finish hardware)
TF.268 switch plates
TF.269 racks
TF.270 belt racks
TF.271 shoe racks
TF.272 tie racks
TF.273 safety rails
TF.274 grab bars
TF.275 toilet safety rails
TF.276 stair carpet holders
TF.277 valves
TF.278 ball valves
TF.279 float valves
TF.280 ball cocks
TF.281 flush valves
TF.282 foot pedal valves
TF.283 mixing pressure valves
TF.284 shut-off valves
TF.285 soap valves
TF.286 rough hardware
TF.287 fasteners
TF.288 anchors (fasteners)
TF.289 adhesive anchors
TF.290 anchor plates
TF.291 beam anchors
TF.292 buck anchors
TF.293 dowel anchors
TF.294 drive anchors

May be used in combination with other descriptors (e.g., **brass** + **faucets**; **metal** + **plated** + **towel bars**; **round** + **backplates**).

TF.295   joist anchors
TF.296   lewis bolt anchors
TF.297   rawl plugs
TF.298   rod anchors
TF.299   screw anchors
TF.300   slot anchors
TF.301   double end anchors
TF.302   dovetail wire anchors
TF.303   stone anchors
TF.304   strap anchors
TF.305   Z anchors
TF.306 bolts
TF.307   *<bolts by form>*
TF.308   anchor bolts
TF.309   assembling bolts
TF.310   carriage bolts
TF.311   expansion bolts
TF.312   star expansion bolts
TF.313   eye bolts
TF.314   foot bolts
TF.315   hanger bolts
TF.316   lag bolts
TF.317   machine bolts
TF.318   necked bolts
TF.319   toggle bolts
TF.320   *<bolts by location or context>*
TF.321   bed bolts
TF.322   bookcase bolts
TF.323   gutter bolts
TF.324   handrail bolts
TF.325   sill anchors
TF.326   stove bolts
TF.327 clips
TF.328   angle cleats
TF.329   back clips
TF.330   corner clips
TF.331   nailing clips
TF.332   truss clips
TF.333 grommets
TF.334 gussets
TF.335 hammer fasteners
TF.336 hangers (rough hardware)
TF.337   *<hangers by form>*
TF.338   adjustable pipe hangers
TF.339   straphangers
TF.340   *<hangers by location or context>*
TF.341   barn-door hangers
TF.342   *<ceiling hangers>*
TF.343   clip hangers

May be used in combination with other descriptors (e.g., **brass** + **faucets**; **metal** + **plated** + **towel bars**; **round** + **backplates**).

TF.344 drive type hangers
TF.345 snap-tie hangers
TF.346 standard coil hangers
TF.347 tie hangers
TF.348 *<hangers by material hung>*
TF.349 *<hangers for concrete>*
TF.350 beam hangers
TF.351 bottom and flange bend hangers
TF.352 bottom bend hangers
TF.353 cut and straight hangers
TF.354 nicked hanging wire hangers
TF.355 *<hangers for steel>*
TF.356 steel-to-steel beam hangers
TF.357 channel saddle hangers
TF.358 plate saddle hangers
TF.359 *<hangers for wood>*
TF.360 metal-to-wood wire hangers
TF.361 drop hangers
TF.362 flange hangers
TF.363 wood-to-masonry hangers
TF.364 saddle style hangers
TF.365 variable hangers
TF.366 wood-to-steel joist hangers
TF.367 hook-over hangers
TF.368 pocket style hangers
TF.369 wood-to-wood hangers
TF.370 formed ridge hangers
TF.371 joist hangers
TF.372 double style hangers
TF.373 flush top hangers
TF.374 formed seat hangers
TF.375 nook type hangers
TF.376 hook-and-eye fasteners
TF.377 inserts (hardware)
TF.378 adjustable inserts
TF.379 channel inserts
TF.380 concrete inserts
TF.381 furring inserts
TF.382 nailer inserts
TF.383 nut inserts
TF.384 reglet inserts
TF.385 wedge inserts
TF.386 nails
TF.387 *<nails by form>*
TF.388 box nails
TF.389 cement-coated nails
TF.390 Chinese nails
TF.391 common nails
TF.392 cut nails

May be used in combination with other descriptors (e.g., **brass** + **faucets**; **metal** + **plated** + **towel bars**; **round** + **backplates**).

TF.393 dog nails
TF.394 helical nails
TF.395 hook nails
TF.396 hurdle nails
TF.397 jobent nails
TF.398 ratchet nails
TF.399 ring-shank nails
TF.400 scupper nails
TF.401 *<nails by form: head type>*
TF.402 brads
TF.403 flat-head wire brads
TF.404 casing nails
TF.405 chatônes
TF.406 clout nails
TF.407 cupped nails
TF.408 doornails
TF.409 double-headed nails
TF.410 flat-head nails
TF.411 headless nails
TF.412 hoop fastener nails
TF.413 rose nails
TF.414 rose clench nails
TF.415 rose flat nails
TF.416 rose sharp nails
TF.417 staple nails
TF.418 umbrella nails
TF.419 *<nails by form: point type>*
TF.420 barbed nails
TF.421 blunt nails
TF.422 chisel nails
TF.423 diamond nails
TF.424 drivescrews
TF.425 duck bill nails
TF.426 needle nails
TF.427 side nails
TF.428 *<nails by location or context>*
TF.429 clamp nails
TF.430 concrete nails
TF.431 cut slating nails
TF.432 deck nails
TF.433 fencing nails
TF.434 finishing nails
TF.435 flooring nails
TF.436 gate nails
TF.437 gimp nails
TF.438 gypsum board nails
TF.439 horseshoe nails
TF.440 frost horseshoe nails
TF.441 lath nails

May be used in combination with other descriptors (e.g., **brass** + **faucets**; **metal** + **plated** + **towel bars**; **round** + **backplates**).

TF.442 metal lath nails
TF.443 masonry nails
TF.444 roofing nails
TF.445 lead-capped nails
TF.446 shade roller pin nails
TF.447 sheathing nails
TF.448 shingle nails
TF.449 trunk nails
TF.450 nuts
TF.451 adjusting nuts
TF.452 back nuts
TF.453 locknuts
TF.454 wing nuts
TF.455 pegs
TF.456 pins (hardware)
TF.457 cotter pins
TF.458 dowel pins
TF.459 barbed dowel pins
TF.460 driftpins
TF.461 escutcheon pins
TF.462 line pins
TF.463 push pins
TF.464 veneer pins
TF.465 rivets
TF.466 screws
TF.467 *<screws by form>*
TF.468 Allen screws
TF.469 clamping screws
TF.470 cylinder screws
TF.471 machine screws
TF.472 sems
TF.473 setscrews
TF.474 adjusting screws
TF.475 sheet metal screws
TF.476 stop screws
TF.477 stop bead screws
TF.478 thumbscrews
TF.479 wood screws
TF.480 *<screws by form: head type>*
TF.481 cap screws
TF.482 Phillips head screws
TF.483 *<screws by location or context>*
TF.484 shutter screws
TF.485 skotch fasteners
TF.486 spikes
TF.487 boat spikes
TF.488 gutter spikes
TF.489 staples
TF.490 straps (hardware)

May be used in combination with other descriptors (e.g., **brass** + **faucets**; **metal** + **plated** + **towel bars**; **round** + **backplates**).

TF.491 studs (fasteners)
TF.492 upholstery studs
TF.493 tacks
TF.494 carpet tacks
TF.495 double pointed tacks
TF.496 thumbtacks
TF.497 ties (hardware)
TF.498 anchor ties
TF.499 angle bonds
TF.500 treenails
TF.501 washers (fasteners)
TF.502 *<hardware by location or context>*
TF.503 awning hardware
TF.504 bathroom hardware
TF.505 closet hardware
TF.506 door hardware
TF.507 furniture hardware
TF.508 gate hardware
TF.509 plumbing hardware
TF.510 shelf hardware
TF.511 window hardware
TF.512 *<hardware components>*
TF.513 *<bolt components>*
TF.514 bed bolt covers
TF.515 strikes
TF.516 box strikes
TF.517 dustproof strikes
TF.518 mortise strikes
TF.519 surface strikes
TF.520 universal strikes
TF.521 *<hinge components>*
TF.522 hinge straps
TF.523 knuckles
TF.524 leaves (hinge components)
TF.525 pins (hinge components)
TF.526 *<keys and key components>*
TF.527 keys
TF.528 adjustable keys
TF.529 card keys
TF.530 detachable keys
TF.531 double-bitted keys
TF.532 drop keys
TF.533 master keys
TF.534 night keys
TF.535 push keys
TF.536 round keys
TF.537 pipe keys
TF.538 skeleton keys
TF.539 sliding-door keys

May be used in combination with other descriptors (e.g., **brass** + **faucets**; **metal** + **plated** + **towel bars**; **round** + **backplates**).

TF.540 stop keys
TF.541 submaster keys
TF.542 warded keys
TF.543 wing keys
TF.544 *<key components>*
TF.545 bits (key components)
TF.546 changes (key components)
TF.547 *<latch and lock components>*
TF.548 bolts (latch and lock components)
TF.549 antifriction latch bolts
TF.550 barrel bolts
TF.551 tower bolts
TF.552 box bolts
TF.553 cane bolts
TF.554 dead bolts
TF.555 split dead bolts
TF.556 double throw bolts
TF.557 panic bolts
TF.558 self-latching bolts
TF.559 square bolts
TF.560 swinging latch bolts
TF.561 caps (lock components)
TF.562 cases (lock components)
TF.563 cylinders (lock components)
TF.564 faces (lock components)
TF.565 hasps
TF.566 hubs (lock components)
TF.567 compensating hubs
TF.568 lips (lock components)
TF.569 thumb turns
TF.570 tumblers (lock components)
TF.571 joints
TF.572 *<joints by form>*
TF.573 angle joints
TF.574 abutting joints
TF.575 beaded joints
TF.576 beaking joints
TF.577 bolted joints
TF.578 break joints
TF.579 butt joints
TF.580 hopper joints
TF.581 oblique joints
TF.582 cogged joints
TF.583 coopered joints
TF.584 covered joints
TF.585 dap joints
TF.586 deformed joints
TF.587 flush joints
TF.588 hook-and-butt joints

May be used in combination with other descriptors (e.g., **brass** + **faucets**; **metal** + **plated** + **towel bars**; **round** + **backplates**).

TF.589   **integral joints**
TF.590   **keyed joints**
TF.591   **knuckle joints**
TF.592   **matched joints**
TF.593   **pinned joints**
TF.594   **rabbet joints**
TF.595   **double rabbet joints**
TF.596   **fillistered joints**
TF.597   **rabbeted ledge and miter joints**
TF.598   **random joints**
TF.599   **recessed joints**
TF.600   **roller joints**
TF.601   **rubbed joints**
TF.602 *<joints by function>*
TF.603   **contraction joints**
TF.604   **control joints**
TF.605   **expansion joints**
TF.606   **isolation joints**
TF.607   **seismic joints**
TF.608   **thermal breaks**
TF.609 *<joints by material joined>*
TF.610   *<concrete joints>*
TF.611   **cold joints**
TF.612   **construction joints**
TF.613   **sawed joints**
TF.614   **topping joints**
TF.615   *<masonry joints>*
TF.616   *<masonry joints by form>*
TF.617   **abreuvoirs**
TF.618   **joggle joints**
TF.619   *<mortar joints>*
TF.620   **rough-cut joints**
TF.621   **struck joints**
TF.622   **galletted joints**
TF.623   **shoved joints**
TF.624   **tooled joints**
TF.625   **concave joints**
TF.626   **flush and rodded joints**
TF.627   **raked joints**
TF.628   **stripped joints**
TF.629   **V-shaped joints**
TF.630   **rustic joints**
TF.631   **slip joints**
TF.632   **water joints**
TF.633   **weather-struck joints**
TF.634   *<masonry joints by location or context>*
TF.635   **bed joints**
TF.636   **blind joints**
TF.637   **collar joints**

May be used in combination with other descriptors (e.g., **brass** + **faucets**; **metal** + **plated** + **towel bars**; **round** + **backplates**).

TF.638 exposed joints
TF.639 face joints
TF.640 head joints
TF.641 *<metal joints>*
TF.642 ball joints
TF.643 bell-and-spigot joints
TF.644 blown joints
TF.645 calk joints
TF.646 cup joints
TF.647 dog-eared fold joints
TF.648 interlocking joints
TF.649 *<metal seams>*
TF.650 beaded dovetail seams
TF.651 bottom double seams
TF.652 cap strip seams
TF.653 corner double seams
TF.654 elbow seams
TF.655 flange dovetail seams
TF.656 grooved seams
TF.657 insert bottom seams
TF.658 lap bottom seams
TF.659 Pittsburgh lock seams
TF.660 plain dovetail seams
TF.661 single bottom seams
TF.662 standing seams
TF.663 rigid joints
TF.664 rust joints
TF.665 *<wood joints>*
TF.666 housed joints
TF.667 dado joints
TF.668 dado and rabbet joints
TF.669 dado, tongue and rabbet joints
TF.670 locking joints
TF.671 coped joints
TF.672 dovetail joints
TF.673 blind dovetail joints
TF.674 shouldered dovetail joints
TF.675 feather joints
TF.676 finger joints
TF.677 mortise-and-tenon joints
TF.678 bridle joints
TF.679 round mortise-and-tenon joints
TF.680 simple joints
TF.681 batten joints
TF.682 fished joints
TF.683 heading joints
TF.684 lap joints
TF.685 crosslap joints
TF.686 end lap joints

May be used in combination with other descriptors (e.g., **brass** + **faucets**; **metal** + **plated** + **towel bars**; **round** + **backplates**).

TF.687	**half-lap joints**
TF.688	**miter joints**
TF.689	**rule joints**
TF.690	**scarf joints**
TF.691	**spline joints**
TF.692	**butterfly joints**
TF.693	**squeezed joints**
TF.694	**starved joints**
TF.695	**tongue-and-groove joints**
TF.696	**tongue-and-lip joints**
TF.697	**V-joints**

Furniture Hierarchy

FURNITURE

Scope The Furniture hierarchy contains descriptors for primarily movable articles of convenience used for such functions as seating, sleeping and reclining, storage and display, and support. These articles may be useful or ornamental, may be located in dwellings, places of business, or other public spaces, and may be used in indoor or outdoor spaces. Trade names and proper names for particular forms of furniture which have come to be used generically or near-generically are included in the hierarchy.

Organization The hierarchy is divided into two major categories: **furniture** and *<furniture components>*. The majority of descriptors appear in the **furniture** section under *<furniture by form or function>*. This is further divided into five headings: **screens** (e.g., **fire screens**, **folding screens**), **seating furniture** (e.g., **benches**, **chairs**), *<sleeping and reclining furniture>* (e.g., **beds**, **couches**), *<storage and display furniture>* (e.g., **cabinets**, **cupboards**), and *<support furniture>* (e.g., **easels**, **tables**). Other divisions of the furniture section are *<furniture by location or context>*; and *<furniture by design>*, which includes descriptors which identify furniture by aspects of design without enumerating their types.

Relation to Other Hierarchies Some descriptors for objects traditionally made by cabinetmakers, but that do not fill the functions noted above will be found in other hierarchies in the Furnishings and Equipment section (e.g., **looking glasses**, **mirrors**). Small scale objects such as storage receptacles (e.g., **knife boxes**), will also be found in other hierarchies in this section. Permanent installations integrated into the fabric of buildings (e.g., **altars**, **choir screens**, **pulpits**), appear in the Built Works Components hierarchy. Instruments and other similar objects (e.g., **clocks**, **barometers**) will appear in the Measuring Devices hierarchy. Descriptors for the shape of furniture (e.g., **serpentine**) appear in the Design Attributes hierarchy. Descriptors for architectural elements that often appear on furniture (e.g., **columns**, **finials**) appear in the Built Works Components hierarchy. Abstract or stylized motifs and conventionalized patterns (e.g., **gadrooning**, **trefoils**) which represent a visual vocabulary used throughout the decorative arts, appear in the Design Elements hierarchy. Forms of furniture hardware appear in the Hardware and Joints hierarchy.

Descriptor Form and Use Descriptors appear as plural nouns with the singular supplied as an alternate form. They may be used in combination with descriptors from other appropriate hierarchies (e.g., **blockfront** + **desks**; **Baroque** + **furniture**; **dining room** + **furniture**; **upholstered** + **chairs**).

Number of Descriptors 932

Synopsis

TG.1 **furniture**
TG.2 *<furniture by form or function>*
TG.3 **screens**
TG.18 **seating furniture**
TG.320 *<sleeping and reclining furniture>*
TG.321 **beds**
|
TG.393 **hammocks**
TG.394 *<storage and display furniture>*
TG.395 **bookshelves**
|
TG.604 **étagères**
TG.605 **suites (furniture)**
TG.606 *<support furniture>*
TG.607 **canterburies**
|
TG.665 **tables**
TG.786 *<furniture by location or context>*
TG.787 **outdoor furniture**
TG.788 *<furniture by design>*
TG.789 **adjustable furniture**
TG.790 **architectural furniture**
TG.791 **art furniture**
TG.792 **built-in furniture**
TG.793 **folding furniture**
TG.794 **inflatable furniture**
TG.795 **mechanical furniture**
TG.797 **multipurpose furniture**
TG.798 **portable furniture**
TG.803 **unit furniture**
TG.805 **utility furniture**
TG.806 *<furniture components>*
TG.807 **aprons (furniture components)**
|
TG.989 **supports (furniture components)**

FURNITURE (TG)

- TG.1 furniture
  - TG.2 *<furniture by form or function>*
    - TG.3 screens
      - TG.4 fire screens
        - TG.5 cheval fire screens
        - TG.6 extension fire screens
        - TG.7 folding fire screens
        - TG.8 pole screens
          - TG.9 écrans à pivot
        - TG.10 sliding fire screens
          - TG.11 double sliding fire screens
        - TG.12 writing fire screens
          - TG.13 écrans à secrétaire
          - TG.14 gentleman's writing fire screens
          - TG.15 lady's writing fire screens
      - TG.16 folding screens
        - TG.17 paravents
    - TG.18 seating furniture
      - TG.19 *<single seating furniture>*
        - TG.20 chairs
          - TG.21 *<chairs by form>*
            - TG.22 Adirondack chairs
            - TG.23 armchairs
              - TG.24 bergères
              - TG.25 elbow chairs
                - TG.26 fauteuils
                - TG.27 French elbow chairs
              - TG.28 great chairs
                - TG.29 Brewster chairs
                - TG.30 Carver chairs
            - TG.31 ax chairs
            - TG.32 backstools
              - TG.33 farthingale chairs
            - TG.34 Barcelona chairs
            - TG.35 barrel chairs
            - TG.36 Barwa chairs
            - TG.37 basket chairs
            - TG.38 beanbag chairs
            - TG.39 board chairs
              - TG.40 Brettstuhls
              - TG.41 sgabelles
            - TG.42 Boston chairs
            - TG.43 Brno chairs
            - TG.44 cabriole chairs
            - TG.45 caquetoires
            - TG.46 Cesca chairs
            - TG.47 chair-tables
            - TG.48 chaises longues
              - TG.49 duchesses

May be used in combination with other descriptors (e.g., **mahogany** + **pedestals**; **turned** + **legs**; **serpentine-front** + **chests of drawers**; **Federal** + **pier tables**).

TG.50 duchesses brisées
TG.51 chauffeuses
TG.52 club chairs
TG.53 coiffeuses (chairs)
TG.54 corner chairs
TG.55 crapauds
TG.56 Cromwellian chairs
TG.57 curricles
TG.58 diamond chairs
TG.59 director's chairs
TG.60 easy chairs
TG.61 bergères en confessional
TG.62 fauteuils à orielles
TG.63 circular easy chairs
TG.64 cloath chairs
TG.65 square easy chairs
TG.66 egg chairs
TG.67 elastic chairs
TG.68 Elda 1005 upholstered chairs
TG.69 gondola chairs
TG.70 bergères en gondole
TG.71 hammock chairs
TG.72 Hitchcock chairs
TG.73 hunting chairs
TG.74 India chairs
TG.75 klismoi
TG.76 Kubbestols
TG.77 lolling chairs
TG.78 Morris chairs
TG.79 MR chairs
TG.80 136 armchairs
TG.81 pedestal chairs
TG.82 rout chairs
TG.83 S chairs
TG.84 sedan chairs
TG.85 side chairs
TG.86 Sleepy Hollow chairs
TG.87 sling chairs
TG.88 Hardoy chairs
TG.89 slipper chairs
TG.90 swan chairs
TG.91 tall chairs
TG.92 Trafalgar chairs
TG.93 Turkish chairs
TG.94 Wassily chairs
TG.95 Westport chairs
TG.96 Windsor chairs
TG.97 balloon-back Windsor chairs
TG.98 bow-back Windsor chairs

May be used in combination with other descriptors (e.g., **mahogany** + **pedestals**; **turned** + **legs**; **serpentine-front** + **chests of drawers**; **Federal** + **pier tables**).

TG.99 continuous-bow Windsor armchairs
TG.100 fan-back Windsor chairs
TG.101 gunstock Windsor chairs
TG.102 high-back Windsor chairs
TG.103 low-back Windsor chairs
TG.104 sack-back Windsor chairs
TG.105 splat-back Windsor chairs
TG.106 square-back Windsor chairs
TG.107 double rod-back Windsor chairs
TG.108 lath-back Windsor chairs
TG.109 Mendlesham chairs
TG.110 roll-top Windsor chairs
TG.111 single rod-back Windsor chairs
TG.112 slat-back Windsor chairs
TG.113 tablet-top Windsor chairs
TG.114 writing-arm Windsor chairs
TG.115 womb chairs
TG.116 X-chairs
TG.117 Dante chairs
TG.118 Savonarola chairs
TG.119 sillónes de cadera
TG.120 Y chairs
TG.121 *<chairs by form: back form>*
TG.122 balloon-back chairs
TG.123 banister-back chairs
TG.124 hearts and crown chairs
TG.125 bended-back chairs
TG.126 *<concave-back chairs>*
TG.127 bergères en cabriolet
TG.128 chaises en cabriolet
TG.129 fauteuils en cabriolet
TG.130 fan-back chairs
TG.131 fiddle-back chairs
TG.132 *<flat-back chairs>*
TG.133 bergères à la reine
TG.134 chaises à la reine
TG.135 fauteuils à la reine
TG.136 fret-back chairs
TG.137 Chinese chairs
TG.138 grotto chairs
TG.139 heart-back chairs
TG.140 lunette-back chairs
TG.141 oval-back chairs
TG.142 chaises à la d'artois
TG.143 chaises à médaillon
TG.144 *<pierced splat-back chairs>*
TG.145 cypher-back chairs
TG.146 lyre-back chairs
TG.147 sheaf-back chairs

May be used in combination with other descriptors (e.g., **mahogany** + **pedestals**; **turned** + **legs**; **serpentine-front** + **chests of drawers**; **Federal** + **pier tables**).

TG.148 press-back chairs
TG.149 ribbon-back chairs
TG.150 shield-back chairs
TG.151 bar-back chairs
TG.152 slat-back chairs
TG.153 Chiavari chairs
TG.154 pretzel-back chairs
TG.155 spindle-back chairs
TG.156 spoon-back chairs
TG.157 square-back chairs
TG.158 lattice-back chairs
TG.159 wainscot chairs
TG.160 wheel-back chairs
TG.161 *<chairs by function>*
TG.162 barber's chairs
TG.163 bed chairs
TG.164 *<ceremonial chairs>*
TG.165 cathedrae
TG.166 state chairs
TG.167 thrones
TG.168 thronoi
TG.169 chamber horses
TG.170 child's chairs
TG.171 highchairs
TG.172 carriage chairs
TG.173 commode chairs
TG.174 cabinet chairs
TG.175 dentist's chairs
TG.176 desk chairs
TG.177 fauteuils de bureau
TG.178 office chairs
TG.179 dressing chairs
TG.180 fraileros
TG.181 invalid's chairs
TG.182 garden machines
TG.183 gouty chairs
TG.184 wheelchairs
TG.185 bath chairs
TG.186 lady's chairs
TG.187 music chairs
TG.188 nursing chairs
TG.189 pattern chairs
TG.190 porter's chairs
TG.191 preaching chairs
TG.192 prie-dieus
TG.193 reading chairs
TG.194 student chairs
TG.195 reception chairs
TG.196 sleeping chairs

May be used in combination with other descriptors (e.g., **mahogany** + **pedestals**; **turned** + **legs**; **serpentine-front** + **chests of drawers**; **Federal** + **pier tables**).

TG.197 smoking chairs
TG.198 step chairs
TG.199 tablet-arm chairs
TG.200 touring chairs
TG.201 typewriter chairs
TG.202 voyeuses
TG.203 voyeuses à genoux
TG.204 *<chairs by location or context>*
TG.205 beach chairs
TG.206 deck chairs
TG.207 *<chairs by location or context: position>*
TG.208 sièges courants
TG.209 sièges meublants
TG.210 *<chairs by location or context: rooms or spaces>*
TG.211 dining chairs
TG.212 hall chairs
TG.213 ice-cream parlor chairs
TG.214 kitchen chairs
TG.215 parlor chairs
TG.216 window chairs
TG.217 *<chairs by design>*
TG.218 folding chairs
TG.219 camp chairs
TG.220 Glastonbury chairs
TG.221 Plia folding chairs
TG.222 Plona folding armchairs
TG.223 reclining chairs
TG.224 centripetal spring chairs
TG.225 rocking chairs
TG.226 Boston rockers
TG.227 Lincoln rockers
TG.228 platform rockers
TG.229 Windsor rocking chairs
TG.230 stacking chairs
TG.231 swivel chairs
TG.232 stools
TG.233 *<stools by form>*
TG.234 box stools
TG.235 bidets (box stools)
TG.236 portable bidets
TG.237 traveling bidets
TG.238 close stools
TG.239 buffet stools
TG.240 cricket stools
TG.241 cutty stools
TG.242 diphroi
TG.243 footstools
TG.244 gout stools
TG.245 hassocks

May be used in combination with other descriptors (e.g., **mahogany** + **pedestals**; **turned** + **legs**; **serpentine-front** + **chests of drawers**; **Federal** + **pier tables**).

TG.246 ottoman footstools
TG.247 joint stools
TG.248 music stools
TG.249 placets
TG.250 tabourets
TG.251 tabourets en chancelière
TG.252 Thebes stools
TG.253 three-legged stools
TG.254 Windsor stools
TG.255 *<stools by function>*
TG.256 dressing stools
TG.257 milking stools
TG.258 prayer stools
TG.259 step stools
TG.260 *<stools by location or context>*
TG.261 barstools
TG.262 counter stools
TG.263 fender stools
TG.264 *<stools by design>*
TG.265 folding stools
TG.266 campstools
TG.267 diphroi okladias
TG.268 faldstools
TG.269 fishing stools
TG.270 pliants
TG.271 perroquets
TG.272 sellae curulis
TG.273 revolving stools
TG.274 stacking stools
TG.275 *<multiple-seating furniture>*
TG.276 benches
TG.277 *<benches by form or function>*
TG.278 banquettes
TG.279 cassapanche
TG.280 cradle benches
TG.281 deacon's benches
TG.282 forms (benches)
TG.283 settles
TG.284 box settles
TG.285 hooded settles
TG.286 settle-tables
TG.287 *<benches by location or context>*
TG.288 garden seats
TG.289 hall seats
TG.290 piano benches
TG.291 picnic benches
TG.292 window seats
TG.293 banquettes de croisée
TG.294 bisellia

May be used in combination with other descriptors (e.g., **mahogany** + **pedestals**; **turned** + **legs**; **serpentine-front** + **chests of drawers**; **Federal** + **pier tables**).

TG.295 divans
TG.296 gliders
TG.297 méridiennes
TG.298 ottomans
TG.299 pouffes
TG.300 settees
TG.301 chair-back settees
TG.302 indiscrets
TG.303 Knole settees
TG.304 love seats
TG.305 marquises
TG.306 Windsor settees
TG.307 sofas
TG.308 bornes
TG.309 boudeusses
TG.310 cabriole sofas
TG.311 canapés
TG.312 canapés à confident
TG.313 canapés à corbeille
TG.314 chesterfields
TG.315 confidantes
TG.316 sofa beds
TG.317 davenports
TG.318 veilleuses
TG.319 wagon seats
TG.320 *<sleeping and reclining furniture>*
TG.321 beds
TG.322 *<beds by form or function>*
TG.323 box beds
TG.324 bunk beds
TG.325 canopy beds
TG.326 dome beds
TG.327 lits à la duchesse
TG.328 sparver beds
TG.329 *<children's beds>*
TG.330 bassinets
TG.331 cradles
TG.332 carriage cradles
TG.333 swinging cradles
TG.334 cribs
TG.335 folding cribs
TG.336 swinging cribs
TG.337 cots
TG.338 folding beds
TG.339 deception beds
TG.340 bookcase beds
TG.341 bureau beds
TG.342 cabinet beds
TG.343 chiffonier beds

May be used in combination with other descriptors (e.g., **mahogany** + **pedestals**; **turned** + **legs**; **serpentine-front** + **chests of drawers**; **Federal** + **pier tables**).

TG.344	piano beds
TG.345	press beds
TG.346	library press beds
TG.347	table beds
TG.348	toilet table beds
TG.349	hideaway beds
TG.350	Murphy beds
TG.351	trundle beds
TG.352	French beds
TG.353	half-tester beds
TG.354	high-post beds
TG.355	pencil-post beds
TG.356	tester beds
TG.357	camas de bilros
TG.358	field beds
TG.359	Herrera beds
TG.360	lits à la polonaise
TG.361	summer beds
TG.362	hospital beds
TG.363	lits à l'antique
TG.364	lits à la romaine
TG.365	lits à la turque
TG.366	lits d'ange
TG.367	livery beds
TG.368	low-post beds
TG.369	platform beds
TG.370	settle beds
TG.371	sleigh beds
TG.372	lits en bateau
TG.373	spool beds
TG.374	state beds
TG.375	lits de parade
TG.376	stump beds
TG.377	suitcase beds
TG.378	water beds
TG.379	*<beds by size>*
TG.380	twin beds
TC.381	hollywood beds
TG.382	double beds
TG.383	three-quarter size beds
TG.384	queen-size beds
TG.385	king-size beds
TG.386	couches
TG.387	biclinia
TG.388	couch beds
TG.389	Grecian couches
TG.390	lecti
TG.391	triclinia (couches)
TG.392	daybeds

May be used in combination with other descriptors (e.g., **mahogany** + **pedestals**; **turned** + **legs**; **serpentine-front** + **chests of drawers**; **Federal** + **pier tables**).

TG.393	hammocks
TG.394	*<storage and display furniture>*
TG.395	bookshelves
TG.396	case furniture
TG.397	arks
TG.398	bookcases
TG.399	bibliothèques
TG.400	book cupboards
TG.401	counting-house bookcases
TG.402	dwarf bookcases
TG.403	gentleman's repositories
TG.404	library bookcases
TG.405	moving libraries
TG.406	revolving bookcases
TG.407	secretary-bookcases
TG.408	sectional bookcases
TG.409	cabinets
TG.410	*<cabinets by form>*
TG.411	cabinets of drawers
TG.412	cabinets on stands
TG.413	contadores
TG.414	corner cabinets
TG.415	hanging cabinets
TG.416	lyre-shaped cabinets
TG.417	meubles à hauteur d'appui
TG.418	meubles d'entre deux
TG.419	*<cabinets by function>*
TG.420	bonnetières
TG.421	cartonniers
TG.422	china cabinets
TG.423	*<collector's cabinets>*
TG.424	medal cabinets
TG.425	print cabinets
TG.426	shell cabinets
TG.427	coquilliers
TG.428	vitrines
TG.429	dental cabinets
TG.430	filing cabinets
TG.431	gun cabinets
TG.432	jewel cabinets
TG.433	kitchen cabinets
TG.434	Hoosier cabinets
TG.435	kitchen safes
TG.436	map cabinets
TG.437	music cabinets
TG.438	pianola roll cabinets
TG.439	papeleras
TG.440	record cabinets
TG.441	serre papiers

May be used in combination with other descriptors (e.g., **mahogany** + **pedestals**; **turned** + **legs**; **serpentine-front** + **chests of drawers**; **Federal** + **pier tables**).

TG.442 spice cabinets
TG.443 thread cabinets
TG.444 utility cabinets
TG.445 chests
TG.446 arcae
TG.447 blanket chests
TG.448 board chests
TG.449 bottle cases
TG.450 campaign chests
TG.451 caskets (chests)
TG.452 cassoni
TG.453 cellerets
TG.454 chests with drawers
TG.455 clothes chests
TG.456 coffers (furniture)
TG.457 armada chests
TG.458 bahuts
TG.459 trussing coffers
TG.460 dower chests
TG.461 hembras
TG.462 machos
TG.463 dug-out chests
TG.464 lobby chests
TG.465 medicine chests
TG.466 mule chests
TG.467 Nonsuch chests
TG.468 sea chests
TG.469 spice chests
TG.470 sugar chests
TG.471 taquillónes
TG.472 tea chests
TG.473 tea caddies
TG.474 tilting chests
TG.475 chests of drawers
TG.476 bachelor's chests
TG.477 butler's desks
TG.478 chests-on-chests
TG.479 chests-on-frames
TG.480 cheval dressers
TG.481 chiffoniers
TG.482 chiffonnières
TG.483 chifforobes
TG.484 commodes
TG.485 commodes à encoignures
TG.486 commodes à la régence
TG.487 commodes à vantaux
TG.488 commodes en console
TG.489 corner commodes
TG.490 demi-commodes

May be used in combination with other descriptors (e.g., **mahogany** + **pedestals**; **turned** + **legs**; **serpentine-front** + **chests of drawers**; **Federal** + **pier tables**).

TG.491	petites commodes
TG.492	high chests of drawers
TG.493	tallboys
TG.494	Rudd dressing chests
TG.495	semainiers
TG.496	corner shelves
TG.497	counters
TG.498	cupboards
TG.499	armadios
TG.500	armaria
TG.501	armarios
TG.502	aumbries
TG.503	corner cupboards
TG.504	encoignures
TG.505	court cupboards
TG.506	dole cupboards
TG.507	dressers
TG.508	dry sinks
TG.509	hanging cupboards
TG.510	hasters
TG.511	livery cupboards
TG.512	fresqueras
TG.513	presses
TG.514	clothes presses
TG.515	low clothes presses
TG.516	wing clothes presses
TG.517	linen presses
TG.518	press cupboards
TG.519	tridarns
TG.520	spice cupboards
TG.521	water benches
TG.522	desks
TG.523	bureau tables
TG.524	counting-house desks
TG.525	double counting-house desks
TG.526	cylinder fall desks
TG.527	bureaux à cylindre
TG.528	davenports (desks)
TG.529	desks and bookcases
TG.530	bureau-bookcases
TG.531	cylinder desks and bookcases
TG.532	desks-on-frames
TG.533	desks-over-bookcases
TG.534	fall-front desks
TG.535	secrétaires à abattant
TG.536	slant-front desks
TG.537	bureaus
TG.538	bureaux en pente
TG.539	Governor Winthrop desks

May be used in combination with other descriptors (e.g., **mahogany** + **pedestals**; **turned** + **legs**; **serpentine-front** + **chests of drawers**; **Federal** + **pier tables**).

TG.540 vargueños
TG.541 kneehole desks
TG.542 bureaux Mazarins
TG.543 lady's desks
TG.544 lady's cabinet dressing tables
TG.545 partner's desks
TG.546 pedestal desks
TG.547 portable desks
TG.548 reading desks
TG.549 rolltop desks
TG.550 secrétaires à la Bourgogne
TG.551 secretaries
TG.552 gentleman's secretaries
TG.553 lady's secretaries
TG.554 spinet desks
TG.555 standing desks
TG.556 bureaux debout
TG.557 tambour desks
TG.558 tambour writing tables
TG.559 traveling desks
TG.560 wall desks
TG.561 Wooton desks
TG.562 rotary desks
TG.563 Wooton cabinet office secretaries
TG.564 writing desks
TG.565 escritoires
TG.566 writing tables
TG.567 bufetillos
TG.568 bureaux en pupitre
TG.569 bureaux plats
TG.570 bureaux à gradin
TG.571 Carlton House tables
TG.572 cheverets
TG.573 crofts
TG.574 gentleman's writing tables
TG.575 lady's writing tables
TG.576 bonheurs-du-jour
TG.577 bureaux de dame
TG.578 lady's screen writing tables
TG.579 library tables
TG.580 rising-top writing tables
TG.581 sofa writing tables
TG.582 tables à écrire
TG.583 dispensaries (furniture)
TG.584 exhibit cases
TG.585 showcases
TG.586 sideboards
TG.587 abaci (sideboards)
TG.588 buffets (sideboards)

May be used in combination with other descriptors (e.g., **mahogany** + **pedestals**; **turned** + **legs**; **serpentine-front** + **chests of drawers**; **Federal** + **pier tables**).

TG.589	celleret sideboards
TG.590	chiffoniers (sideboards)
TG.591	console dessertes
TG.592	credenzas
TG.593	huntboards
TG.594	pedestal end sideboards
TG.595	servers
TG.596	slab sideboards
TG.597	wardrobes
TG.598	armoires
TG.599	armoires à deux corps
TG.600	kassen
TG.601	schranks
TG.602	wine coolers
TG.603	china shelves
TG.604	étagères
TG.605	suites (furniture)
TG.606	*<support furniture>*
TG.607	canterburies
TG.608	easels
TG.609	pedestals (furniture)
TG.610	plate warmers (furniture)
TG.611	racks
TG.612	clotheshorses
TG.613	hat racks
TG.614	magazine racks
TG.615	towel racks
TG.616	stands
TG.617	*<stands by form>*
TG.618	cabinet stands
TG.619	canterburies (stands)
TG.620	tiered stands
TG.621	dumbwaiters (stands)
TG.622	Windsor stands
TG.623	*<stands by form: base form>*
TG.624	pies de puente
TG.625	tripods (stands)
TG.626	athéniennes
TG.627	*<stands by function>*
TG.628	bookstands
TG.629	Koran stands
TG.630	candlestands
TG.631	guéridons
TG.632	ratchet candlestands
TG.633	card stands
TG.634	costumers
TG.635	dressing stands
TG.636	gentleman's dressing stands
TG.637	lady's dressing stands

May be used in combination with other descriptors (e.g., **mahogany** + **pedestals**; **turned** + **legs**; **serpentine-front** + **chests of drawers**; **Federal** + **pier tables**).

TG.638 drinking stands
TG.639 globe stands
TG.640 hall stands
TG.641 hat stands
TG.642 kettle stands
TG.643 lecterns
TG.644 map stands
TG.645 muffin stands
TG.646 music stands
TG.647 plant stands
TG.648   ferneries
TG.649   jardinières
TG.650 portfolio stands
TG.651 shaving stands
TG.652 smokers
TG.653 smoking stands
TG.654 torchères
TG.655 tray stands
TG.656 umbrella stands
TG.657 washstands
TG.658   basin stands
TG.659   corner basin stands
TG.660   corner enclosed basin stands
TG.661   enclosed basin stands
TG.662 *<steps: furniture>*
TG.663   bed steps
TG.664   library steps
TG.665 tables
TG.666   *<tables by form>*
TG.667   capstan tables
TG.668   cricket tables
TG.669   draw tables
TG.670   dropleaf tables
TG.671   butterfly tables
TG.672   fly tables
TG.673   gate-leg tables
TG.674   handkerchief tables
TG.675   Pembroke tables
TG.676   harlequin tables
TG.677   pillar and claw Pembroke tables
TG.678   Sutherland tables
TG.679   end tables
TG.680   grotto tables
TG.681   horseshoe tables
TG.682   kidney tables
TG.683   occasional tables
TG.684   tables ambulantes
TG.685   tables de salon
TG.686   ratonas

May be used in combination with other descriptors (e.g., **mahogany** + **pedestals**; **turned** + **legs**; **serpentine-front** + **chests of drawers**; **Federal** + **pier tables**).

TG.687 refectory tables
TG.688 slab tables
TG.689 tables à la tronchin
TG.690 tables volantes
TG.691 tavern tables
TG.692 Windsor tables
TG.693 *<tables by form: base form>*
TG.694 console tables
TG.695 eagle console tables
TG.696 pedestal tables
TG.697 pillar and claw tables
TG.698 sawbuck tables
TG.699 spider-leg tables
TG.700 trestle tables
TG.701 tripod tables
TG.702 *<tables by form: top form>*
TG.703 flip-top tables
TG.704 piecrust tables
TG.705 tables en crachoir
TG.706 tilt-top tables
TG.707 *<tables by function>*
TG.708 bed tables
TG.709 billiard tables
TG.710 bagatelle tables
TG.711 breakfast tables
TG.712 déjeuner tables
TG.713 card tables
TG.714 basset tables
TG.715 loo tables
TG.716 ombre tables
TG.717 tables de brelan
TG.718 tripod card tables
TG.719 cocktail tables
TG.720 coffee tables
TG.721 communion tables
TG.722 credences
TG.723 dining tables
TG.724 extension dining tables
TG.725 telescope tables
TG.726 horseshoe dining tables
TG.727 pillar and claw dining tables
TG.728 three-part dining tables
TG.729 drawing tables
TG.730 dressing tables
TG.731 chamber tables
TG.732 commode dressing tables
TG.733 gentleman's dressing tables
TG.734 Beau-Brummel dressing tables
TG.735 lady's dressing tables

May be used in combination with other descriptors (e.g., **mahogany** + **pedestals**; **turned** + **legs**; **serpentine-front** + **chests of drawers**; **Federal** + **pier tables**).

TG.736 bufetes
TG.737 Rudd tables
TG.738 toilettes
TG.739 coiffeuses
TG.740 toilettes en papillon
TG.741 low chests
TG.742 gaming tables
TG.743 backgammon tables
TG.744 chess tables
TG.745 tables de tric-trac
TG.746 ironing boards
TG.747 mixing tables
TG.748 drinking tables
TG.749 night tables
TG.750 somnoes
TG.751 oyster tables
TG.752 pastry tables
TG.753 picnic tables
TG.754 pool tables
TG.755 radio tables
TG.756 rent tables
TG.757 sideboard tables
TG.758 snack tables
TG.759 tailor's tables
TG.760 tea tables
TG.761 china tables
TG.762 tea wagons
TG.763 telephone tables
TG.764 tocineras
TG.765 trespoli
TG.766 vide-poches
TG.767 work tables
TG.768 serviteurs-fidèle
TG.769 tables en chiffonnière
TG.770 tricoteuses
TG.771 *<tables by location or context>*
TG.772 *<tables by location or context: position>*
TG.773 center tables
TG.774 side tables
TG.775 pier tables
TG.776 enclosed pier tables
TG.777 sofa tables
TG.778 *<tables by location or context: rooms or spaces>*
TG.779 ice-cream tables
TG.780 kitchen tables
TG.781 parlor tables
TG.782 saloon tables
TG.783 *<tables by design>*
TG.784 nesting tables

May be used in combination with other descriptors (e.g., **mahogany** + **pedestals**; **turned** + **legs**; **serpentine-front** + **chests of drawers**; **Federal** + **pier tables**).

TG.785	quartetto tables
TG.786	*<furniture by location or context>*
TG.787	outdoor furniture
TG.788	*<furniture by design>*
TG.789	adjustable furniture
TG.790	architectural furniture
TG.791	art furniture
TG.792	built-in furniture
TG.793	folding furniture
TG.794	inflatable furniture
TG.795	mechanical furniture
TG.796	patent furniture
TG.797	multipurpose furniture
TG.798	portable furniture
TG.799	camp furniture
TG.800	campaign furniture
TG.801	knock-down furniture
TG.802	crate furniture
TG.803	unit furniture
TG.804	sectional furniture
TG.805	utility furniture
TG.806	*<furniture components>*
TG.807	aprons (furniture components)
TG.808	*<arms and arm components>*
TG.809	arms (furniture components)
TG.810	*<arms by form>*
TG.811	hollowed arms
TG.812	knuckled arms
TG.813	open arms
TG.814	rolled arms
TG.815	scrolled arms
TG.816	swan arms
TG.817	*<arms by function>*
TG.818	writing arms
TG.819	*<arm components>*
TG.820	arm pads
TG.821	arm rails
TG.822	arm supports
TG.823	handholds
TG.824	backboards
TG.825	splashboards
TG.826	*<backs and back components>*
TG.827	backs
TG.828	mirrored backs
TG.829	scrolled backs
TG.830	*<back components>*
TG.831	back rails
TG.832	crest rails
TG.833	ears (furniture components)

May be used in combination with other descriptors (e.g., **mahogany** + **pedestals**; **turned** + **legs**; **serpentine-front** + **chests of drawers**; **Federal** + **pier tables**).

TG.834 **shoes (furniture components)**
TG.835 **shoulders (furniture components)**
TG.836 **slats**
TG.837 **splats**
TG.838 **wings (furniture components)**
TG.839 **yokes**
TG.840 **bases (furniture components)**
TG.841 **trestles**
TG.842 **A trestles**
TG.843 *<bed components>*
TG.844 **bed slats**
TG.845 **bedboards**
TG.846 **bedframes**
TG.847 **bedposts**
TG.848 **footposts**
TG.849 **headposts**
TG.850 **bedsprings**
TG.851 **blanket rails**
TG.852 **box springs**
TG.853 **canopies (bed components)**
TG.854 **footboards**
TG.855 **headboards**
TG.856 **mattresses**
TG.857 **French mattresses**
TG.858 **testers**
TG.859 **drop testers**
TG.860 **flying testers**
TG.861 **half-testers**
TG.862 **bends**
TG.863 **birdcages (furniture components)**
TG.864 **carcases**
TG.865 **cleats**
TG.866 **corner blocks**
TG.867 *<corners: furniture components>*
TG.868 **canted corners**
TG.869 **hollow corners**
TG.870 **ovolo corners**
TG.871 *<doors: furniture components>*
TG.872 **prospect doors**
TG.873 *<drawers and drawer components>*
TG.874 **drawers**
TG.875 *<drawers by form>*
TG.876 **blind drawers**
TG.877 **lipped drawers**
TG.878 **nests of drawers**
TG.879 *<drawers by function>*
TG.880 **celleret drawers**
TG.881 **document drawers**
TG.882 **dressing drawers**

May be used in combination with other descriptors (e.g., **mahogany** + **pedestals**; **turned** + **legs**; **serpentine-front** + **chests of drawers**; **Federal** + **pier tables**).

<furniture components>
<drawers and drawer components>
drawers
<drawers by function>

TG.883	secret drawers
TG.884	secretary drawers
TG.885	tills
TG.886	*<drawers by location or context>*
TG.887	quadrant drawers
TG.888	*<drawer components>*
TG.889	runners
TG.890	dustboards
TG.891	end boards
TG.892	*<ends: furniture components>*
TG.893	astragal ends
TG.894	hollow ends
TG.895	*<feet and foot components>*
TG.896	feet
TG.897	ball feet
TG.898	turnip feet
TG.899	block feet
TG.900	bootjack feet
TG.901	bracket feet
TG.902	French feet
TG.903	ogee bracket feet
TG.904	bun feet
TG.905	melon feet
TG.906	club feet
TG.907	pad feet
TG.908	toupie feet
TG.909	pointed shod feet
TG.910	runner feet
TG.911	scroll feet
TG.912	slipper feet
TG.913	Spanish feet
TG.914	therm feet
TG.915	trifid feet
TG.916	*<feet by motif: animal-derived>*
TG.917	claw feet
TG.918	claw-and-ball feet
TG.919	rat claw feet
TG.920	retracted claw feet
TG.921	winged claw feet
TG.922	colt feet
TG.923	dolphin feet
TG.924	dragon feet
TG.925	hoof feet
TG.926	paw feet
TG.927	dog's paw feet
TG.928	hairy paw feet
TG.929	lion's paw feet
TG.930	snake feet
TG.931	*<foot components>*

May be used in combination with other descriptors (e.g., **mahogany** + **pedestals**; **turned** + **legs**; **serpentine-front** + **chests of drawers**; **Federal** + **pier tables**).

TG.932 **balls (foot components)**
TG.933 **bracelets (foot components)**
TG.934 **discs (foot components)**
TG.935 **talons**
TG.936 **footrests**
TG.937 **fronts (furniture components)**
TG.938 **galleries (furniture components)**
TG.939 **hoods (furniture components)**
TG.940 **bonnet tops**
TG.941 **leaves (furniture components)**
TG.942 *<legs and leg components>*
TG.943 **legs**
TG.944 *<legs by form>*
TG.945 **baluster legs**
TG.946 **cabriole legs**
TG.947 **cluster legs**
TG.948 **curule legs**
TG.949 **Marlborough legs**
TG.950 **sabre legs**
TG.951 **stump legs**
TG.952 **therm legs**
TG.953 **trumpet legs**
TG.954 *<legs by design>*
TG.955 **detachable legs**
TG.956 **swing legs**
TG.957 **gate legs**
TG.958 *<leg components>*
TG.959 **cuffs (leg components)**
TG.960 *<knees and knee components>*
TG.961 **knees**
TG.962 **hipped knees**
TG.963 *<knee components>*
TG.964 **knee brackets**
TG.965 **lopers**
TG.966 **noix**
TG.967 **pigeonholes**
TG.968 **pupitres**
TG.969 *<seats and seat components>*
TG.970 **seats**
TG.971 **compass seats**
TG.972 **hollowed seats**
TG.973 **saddle seats**
TG.974 *<upholstered seats>*
TG.975 **coil-spring seats**
TG.976 **slip seats**
TG.977 *<seat components>*
TG.978 **seat frames**
TG.979 **seat rails**
TG.980 **medial braces**

May be used in combination with other descriptors (e.g., **mahogany** + **pedestals**; **turned** + **legs**; **serpentine-front** + **chests of drawers**; **Federal** + **pier tables**).

TG.981 **squabs**
TG.982 **shelves**
TG.983 **sliding shelves**
TG.984 **slides (furniture components)**
TG.985 **candle slides**
TG.986 **spindles**
TG.987 **arrow spindles**
TG.988 **split spindles**
TG.989 **supports (furniture components)**
TG.990 *<supports by form>*
TG.991 **dolphin supports**
TG.992 **melon bulb supports**
TG.993 **monopodia**
TG.994 *<supports by location or context>*
TG.995 **drawer supports**
TG.996 **stretchers**
TG.997 **block and spindle stretchers**
TG.998 **box stretchers**
TG.999 **crescent stretchers**
TG.1000 **cross stretchers**
TG.1001 **saltire stretchers**
TG.1002 **shaped stretchers**

May be used in combination with other descriptors (e.g., **mahogany** + **pedestals**; **turned** + **legs**; **serpentine-front** + **chests of drawers**; **Federal** + **pier tables**).

Visual and Verbal Communication

(VB) Image and Object Genres
(VD) Drawings
(VJ) Photographs
(VW) Document Types

The Visual and Verbal Communication section includes terms for artifacts, as well as genres of images and texts, whose primary and original function is to communicate ideas, concepts, and aesthetic experience through visual or verbal media. Though almost any artifact may be considered to communicate visually something about its maker, its origin, or its use, terms in this section of the thesaurus are those originally produced with the purpose of transmitting an informational, symbolic, or aesthetic message.

Image and Object Genres Hierarchy

IMAGE AND OBJECT GENRES

Scope The Image and Object Genres hierarchy includes descriptors relevant to art and architecture that identify an image or object that can exist in a variety of media (e.g., **portraits, fragments**).

Organization Under <*image genres*> are descriptors for types of images, whether representational, abstract, or symbolic, that are not specific to one artistic medium. Under <*image genres by form*> appear descriptors that suggest the way the image is composed or executed (e.g., **silhouettes**), and <*image genres by function*> brings together descriptors that indicate how an image is employed (e.g., **illustrations**). Included as <*subject genres*> are descriptors for those conventional genres of subject matter that exist in a variety of media (e.g., **landscapes**).

In the <*object genres*> section are descriptors for types of objects that may or may not support an image, may be relevant to a variety of media, and are not specific to one of the other object hierarchies, such as Tools and Equipment or Personal Artifacts (e.g., **antiques**). Descriptors that identify a general object type by aspects of its physical form (e.g., **foldouts**) appear under <*object genres by form*>, and those that emphasize how the object is used are under <*object genres by function*> (e.g., **models**). Under <*derivative objects*> are descriptors for types of objects or images derived from an original work (e.g., **forgeries**).

Relation to Other Hierarchies Descriptors for works of art that are primarily in one medium, such as types of paintings or sculpture, will appear in the hierarchies for those media which are under development. Some related descriptors for object types and record types that are mainly informational (e.g., **maps**), are found in the Document Types hierarchy.

Descriptor Form and Use Descriptors appear as plural nouns, with the singular supplied as an alternate form, where appropriate. For image genres by style, physical attributes, material, instrument, or other aspect, combine with descriptors from other appropriate hierarchies (e.g., **Victorian + reproductions; side + views; ink + sketches; pencil + sketches**). The alternate form may be used as a modifier of other descriptors (e.g., **portrait + drawings**).

Number of Descriptors 113

Synopsis

VB.1	<*image genres*>
VB.2	<*image genres by form*>
VB.3	**anamorphoses**
VB.32	**vignettes**
VB.33	<*image genres by function*>
VB.34	**cartoons (humorous images)**
VB.65	**symbols**
VB.66	<*image genres by location or context*>
VB.67	**graffiti**
VB.68	**tattoos**
VB.69	<*subject genres*>
VB.71	**city views**
VB.78	**still lifes**
VB.82	<*object genres*>
VB.83	**antiques**
VB.88	**works of art**
VB.89	<*object genres by form*>
VB.90	**additions**
VB.99	**sets**
VB.100	<*object genres by function*>
VB.101	**exercises**
VB.112	**spolia**
VB.113	<*derivative objects*>
VB.114	**copies**
VB.126	**proofs**

IMAGE AND OBJECT GENRES (VB)

VB.1	*<image genres>*
VB.2	*<image genres by form>*
VB.3	anamorphoses
VB.4	caricatures
VB.5	panoramas
VB.6	silhouettes
VB.7	sketches
VB.8	composition sketches
VB.9	esquisses
VB.10	pochades
VB.11	preliminary sketches
VB.12	bozzetti
VB.13	travel sketches
VB.14	stencils (images)
VB.15	views
VB.16	*<views by scope>*
VB.17	general views
VB.18	partial views
VB.19	*<views by vantage point or orientation>*
VB.20	aerial views
VB.21	bird's-eye views
VB.22	close-up views
VB.23	distant views
VB.24	exterior views
VB.25	eye-level views
VB.26	interior views
VB.27	oblique views
VB.28	three-quarter views
VB.29	plan views
VB.30	profiles (figures)
VB.31	worm's-eye views
VB.32	vignettes
VB.33	*<image genres by function>*
VB.34	cartoons (humorous images)
VB.35	comics
VB.36	editorial cartoons
VB.37	political cartoons
VB.38	emblems (allegorical pictures)
VB.39	illuminations
VB.40	miniatures (illuminations)
VB.41	illustrations
VB.42	*<illustrations by location or context>*
VB.43	book illustrations
VB.44	newspaper illustrations
VB.45	periodical illustrations
VB.46	*<illustrations by subject type>*
VB.47	courtroom illustrations
VB.48	fashion illustrations
VB.49	scientific illustrations

May be used in combination with other descriptors (e.g., **Victorian** + **reproductions**; **side** + **views**; **ink** + **sketches**; **pencil** + **sketches**; **portrait** + **drawings**).

VB.50 biological illustrations
VB.51 anatomical illustrations
VB.52 botanical illustrations
VB.53 zoological illustrations
VB.54 medical illustrations
VB.55 technical illustrations
VB.56 modelli
VB.57 pictographs
VB.58 studies
VB.59 anatomical studies
VB.60 drapery studies
VB.61 figure studies
VB.62 preparatory studies
VB.63 composition studies
VB.64 detail studies
VB.65 symbols
VB.66 *<image genres by location or context>*
VB.67 graffiti
VB.68 tattoos
VB.69 *<subject genres>*
VB.70 capricci
VB.71 city views
VB.72 genre
VB.73 landscapes
VB.74 portraits
VB.75 group portraits
VB.76 self-portraits
VB.77 seascapes
VB.78 still lifes
VB.79 topographical views
VB.80 vedute
VB.81 vedute ideate
VB.82 *<object genres>*
VB.83 antiques
VB.84 art objects
VB.85 artifacts
VB.86 collectibles
VB.87 originals
VB.88 works of art
VB.89 *<object genres by form>*
VB.90 additions
VB.91 alterations
VB.92 details
VB.93 flaps
VB.94 foldouts
VB.95 fragments
VB.96 sherds
VB.97 inserts
VB.98 overlays

May be used in combination with other descriptors (e.g., **Victorian** + **reproductions**; **side** + **views**; **ink** + **sketches**; **pencil** + **sketches**; **portrait** + **drawings**).

VB.99	**sets**
VB.100	*<object genres by function>*
VB.101	**exercises**
VB.102	**memorabilia**
VB.103	**models**
VB.104	**anatomical models**
VB.105	**écorchés**
VB.106	**architectural models**
VB.107	**ornament**
VB.108	**prototypes**
VB.109	**reconstructions**
VB.110	**samples**
VB.111	**souvenirs**
VB.112	**spolia**
VB.113	*<derivative objects>*
VB.114	**copies**
VB.115	**duplicates**
VB.116	**forgeries**
VB.117	**counterfeits**
VB.118	**reductions**
VB.119	**reproductions**
VB.120	**facsimiles**
VB.121	**replicas**
VB.122	**versions**
VB.123	**editions**
VB.124	**limited editions**
VB.125	**pastiches**
VB.126	**proofs**

May be used in combination with other descriptors (e.g., **Victorian** + **reproductions**; **side** + **views**; **ink** + **sketches**; **pencil** + **sketches**; **portrait** + **drawings**).

Drawings
Hierarchy

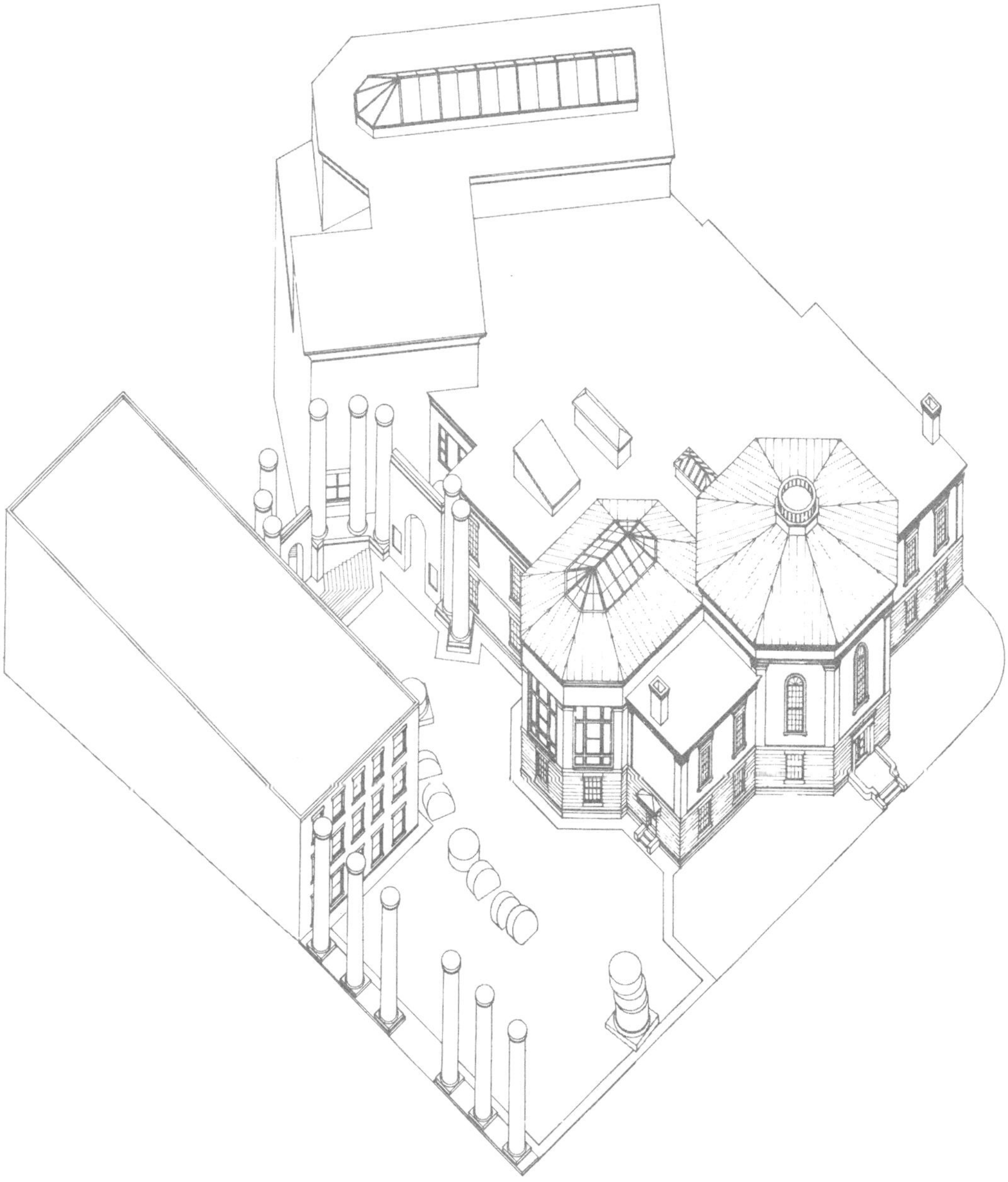

DRAWINGS

Scope The Drawings hierarchy includes terminology for images produced primarily by delineation, usually by the direct application of material or instrument by the draftsman to the surface of the support. The descriptor **drawings** is also applicable to the discrete physical objects that contain such images. The hierarchy reflects vocabulary used for drawings that are considered fine art works in themselves as well as those that constitute part of the design and execution processes of works of art and architecture. Also included here are pastels and watercolors, though they are not always primarily linear, because they, like the majority of drawings, are unique originals that are usually on paper.

Organization The three broadest descriptors in the hierarchy are **drawings**, **pastels**, and **watercolors**; most of the other descriptors in the hierarchy appear under **drawings**. Those for <*drawings by method of representation*> (e.g., **cutaway drawings**) refer to the way in which the representation is formed; under this is a subcategory of <*drawings by method of projection*> (eg., **orthographic drawings**). <*Drawings by function*> includes such items as **working drawings** used both for art and for architecture. Other categories are <*drawings by location or context*> (e.g., **cave drawings**), <*drawings by technique*> (e.g., **doodles**), and <*drawings by maker*> (e.g., **master drawings**). Under <*drawings by subject type*> are general types, such as **architectural drawings**.

Relation to Other Hierarchies Descriptors for the media, supports, and techniques of drawings may be found in the Materials hierarchy (e.g., **ink**, **paper**), in the Tools and Equipment hierarchy (e.g., **crayons**), and in Processes and Techniques (e.g., **rendering**). Descriptors for works done in paint other than watercolor will appear in the Paintings hierarchy, which is under development. Image types that are not exclusively in the drawing medium (e.g., **illustrations**, **sketches**, **studies**, **views**), are in the Image and Object Genres hierarchy. Some other related descriptors (e.g., **sketchbooks**, **maps**) are in the Document Types hierarchy.

Descriptor Form and Use Descriptors appear as plural nouns, with the singular added as an alternate form where appropriate. For drawings by style, material, instrument, subject, or other aspect, combine with descriptors from other appropriate hierarchies (e.g., **Japanese** + **watercolors**; **ink** + **drawings**; **brush** + **drawings**). descriptors from other hierarchies may also be used to specify subject type (e.g., **landscape** + **drawings**; **basement** + **plans**).

Number of Descriptors 151

Synopsis

VD.1	**drawings**
VD.2	*<drawings by method of representation>*
VD.3	**composite drawings**
	|
VD.7	**scale drawings**
VD.9	*<drawings by method of projection>*
VD.10	**axonometric drawings**
	|
VD.79	**perspective drawings**
VD.90	*<drawings by function>*
VD.91	**as-built drawings**
	|
VD.111	**working drawings**
VD.120	*<drawings by location or context>*
VD.121	**cave drawings**
VD.122	*<drawings by technique>*
VD.123	**blot drawings**
	|
VD.139	**tracings**
VD.140	*<drawings by maker>*
VD.141	**master drawings**
VD.142	**student drawings**
VD.144	*<drawings by subject type>*
VD.145	**architectural drawings**
	|
VD.159	**structural drawings**
VD.160	**pastels**
VD.161	**watercolors**

DRAWINGS (VD)

- VD.1 drawings
  - VD.2 *<drawings by method of representation>*
    - VD.3 composite drawings
    - VD.4 cutaway drawings
    - VD.5 exploded drawings
    - VD.6 pictorial drawings
    - VD.7 scale drawings
      - VD.8 full-scale drawings
    - VD.9 *<drawings by method of projection>*
      - VD.10 axonometric drawings
        - VD.11 dimetric drawings
        - VD.12 isometric drawings
        - VD.13 oblique drawings
          - VD.14 elevation oblique drawings
            - VD.15 cabinet oblique drawings
            - VD.16 cavalier oblique drawings
            - VD.17 general oblique drawings
          - VD.18 plan oblique drawings
        - VD.19 trimetric drawings
      - VD.20 orthographic drawings
        - VD.21 auxiliary views
        - VD.22 elevations
          - VD.23 exterior elevations
          - VD.24 interior elevations
          - VD.25 laid-out elevations
          - VD.26 partial elevations
            - VD.27 half elevations
          - VD.28 sectional elevations
          - VD.29 *<ship elevations>*
            - VD.30 body plans
            - VD.31 outboard profiles
            - VD.32 rigging plans
            - VD.33 sail plans
            - VD.34 sheer plans
        - VD.35 multiview drawings
        - VD.36 plans
          - VD.37 *<area plans>*
            - VD.38 city plans
            - VD.39 site plans
              - VD.40 block plans
              - VD.41 grading plans
              - VD.42 landscaping plans
                - VD.43 planting plans
            - VD.44 traces (area plans)
          - VD.45 *<building plans>*
            - VD.46 floor plans
              - VD.47 ground plans
              - VD.48 typical floor plans
            - VD.49 foundation plans

May be used in combination with other descriptors (e.g., **Japanese** + **watercolors**; **ink** + **drawings; brush** + **drawings**; **landscape** + **drawings**).

VD.50 framing plans
VD.51 piling plans
VD.52 reflected ceiling plans
VD.53 utility plans
VD.54 electrical plans
VD.55 HVAC plans
VD.56 heating plans
VD.57 plumbing plans
VD.58 deck plans
VD.59 ichnographic plans
VD.60 key plans
VD.61 master plans
VD.62 partial plans
VD.63 half plans
VD.64 half-breadth plans
VD.65 profiles
VD.66 soil profiles
VD.67 sections
VD.68 broken-out sections
VD.69 cross sections
VD.70 half sections
VD.71 longitudinal sections
VD.72 inboard profiles
VD.73 oblique sections
VD.74 auxiliary sections
VD.75 offset sections
VD.76 partial sections
VD.77 removed sections
VD.78 revolved sections
VD.79 perspective drawings
VD.80 exterior perspectives
VD.81 interior perspectives
VD.82 partial perspectives
VD.83 sectional perspectives
VD.84 *<perspective drawings by point of view>*
VD.85 bird's-eye perspectives
VD.86 one-point perspectives
VD.87 three-point perspectives
VD.88 two-point perspectives
VD.89 worm's-eye perspectives
VD.90 *<drawings by function>*
VD.91 as-built drawings
VD.92 competition drawings
VD.93 contract drawings
VD.94 change order drawings
VD.95 clarification drawings
VD.96 design drawings
VD.97 conceptual drawings
VD.98 design development drawings

May be used in combination with other descriptors (e.g., **Japanese** + **watercolors**; **ink** + **drawings; brush** + **drawings**; **landscape** + **drawings**).

VD.99 schematic drawings
VD.100 measured drawings
VD.101 pattern drawings
VD.102 preliminary drawings
VD.103 underdrawings
VD.104 sinopie
VD.105 preparatory drawings
VD.106 presentation drawings
VD.107 presentation drawings (gifts)
VD.108 record drawings
VD.109 technical drawings
VD.110 theoretical drawings
VD.111 working drawings
VD.112 assembly drawings
VD.113 minor assembly drawings
VD.114 subassembly drawings
VD.115 cartoons (working drawings)
VD.116 auxiliary cartoons
VD.117 construction drawings
VD.118 shop drawings
VD.119 erection drawings
VD.120 *<drawings by location or context>*
VD.121 cave drawings
VD.122 *<drawings by technique>*
VD.123 blot drawings
VD.124 computer drawings
VD.125 plots (computer drawings)
VD.126 doodles
VD.127 freehand drawings
VD.128 gesture drawings
VD.129 line drawings
VD.130 contour drawings
VD.131 blind contour drawings
VD.132 cross-contour drawings
VD.133 outline drawings
VD.134 mechanical drawings
VD.135 renderings
VD.136 three-tone drawings
VD.137 thumbnail sketches
VD.138 tone drawings
VD.139 tracings
VD.140 *<drawings by maker>*
VD.141 master drawings
VD.142 student drawings
VD.143 envois
VD.144 *<drawings by subject type>*
VD.145 architectural drawings
VD.146 mechanical drawings (building systems drawings)
VD.147 HVAC drawings

May be used in combination with other descriptors (e.g., **Japanese** + **watercolors**; **ink** + **drawings; brush** + **drawings**; **landscape** + **drawings**).

VD.148 plumbing drawings
VD.149 composition drawings
VD.150 detail drawings
VD.151 standard detail drawings
VD.152 electrical drawings
VD.153 figure drawings
VD.154 life drawings
VD.155 ornament drawings
VD.156 ships plans
VD.157 docking plans
VD.158 lines drawings
VD.159 structural drawings
VD.160 pastels
VD.161 watercolors
VD.162 gouaches

May be used in combination with other descriptors (e.g., **Japanese** + **watercolors**; **ink** + **drawings; brush** + **drawings**; **landscape** + **drawings**).

Photographs
Hierarchy

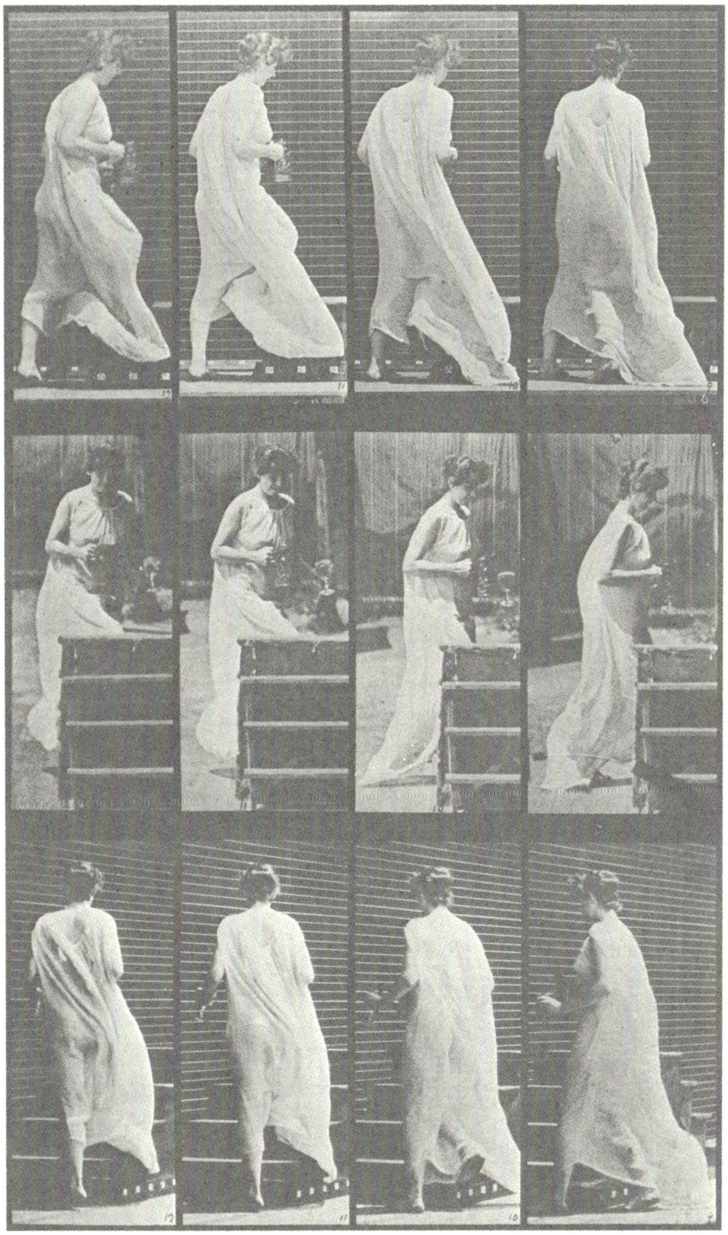

PHOTOGRAPHS

Scope The Photographs hierarchy contains descriptors for still images produced by the action of radiant energy on sensitized materials, as well as the discrete physical objects that contain such images. The energy used is most often light but may also be electron beams or nuclear radiation. The images may be positive or negative, opaque or transparent. Also included here are names of photomechanical prints and a few other descriptors for images that are produced from photographs but were not at any point radiation-sensitive themselves. Not included are types of prints used mainly to reproduce documents and technical drawings, (e.g., **blueprints**), which, though produced by light-sensitive processes, are not in common usage considered photographs.

Organization The hierarchy is organized into sections concerning the form, function, technique, and subject type of photographs. <*Photographs by form*> includes those descriptors used to identify the basic physical characteristics of a photograph (e.g., **negatives**), as well as more specific descriptors that indicate the physical and chemical make-up of the photograph, usually as a result of the photographic process used (e.g., **albumen prints**). <*Photographs by technique*> begins with descriptors for <*photographs by picture-taking technique*>, indicating the manner in which, or location from which, a photograph was captured (e.g., **aerial photographs**). Also under <*photographs by technique*> are descriptors for <*photographs by processing or presentation technique*>, indicating special methods, other than the basic chemical processes, used to produce or mount a photograph (e.g., **contact prints**).

Relation to Other Hierarchies Descriptors for the materials used to make photographs as well as for their constituent parts (e.g., **roll film**, **binders**) are found in the Materials hierarchy. Descriptors for approaches to photography and applications of photography (e.g., **documentary photography**, **medical photography**) and for photographic and photomechanical processes (e.g., **gum bichromate process**, **photolithography**) are found in the Processes and Techniques hierarchy. Descriptors for the equipment used in photography are in the Tools and Equipment hierarchy (e.g., **pinhole cameras**). Descriptors for reproductive prints of technical drawings and documents (e.g., **electrostatic copies**, **blueprints**) are in the Document Types hierarchy under <*reprographic documents*>.

Descriptor Form and Use Descriptors appear as plural nouns, with the singular added as an alternate form where appropriate. For photographs by style, physical attributes, or other aspects, combine with descriptors from other appropriate hierarchies (e.g., **Pictorialist** + **photographs**; **quarter plate** + **photographs**). Descriptors from other hierarchies may be used to specify subject matter (e.g., **fashion** + **photographs**; **still life** + **photographs**).

Number of Descriptors 116

Synopsis

VJ.1 photographs
VJ.2 *<photographs by form>*
VJ.3 negatives
VJ.4 color separation negatives
|
VJ.10 *<negatives by process>*
VJ.16 photomechanical prints
VJ.17 dye transfer prints
|
VJ.26 Woodburytypes
VJ.27 positives
VJ.28 direct positives
VJ.35 holograms
VJ.38 photographic prints
VJ.59 transparencies
VJ.69 *<photographs by form: color>*
VJ.70 black-and-white photographs
VJ.71 color photographs
VJ.72 *<photographs by form: format>*
VJ.73 card photographs
|
VJ.85 slides
VJ.88 *<photographs by function>*
VJ.89 identification photographs
VJ.91 news photographs
VJ.92 *<photographs by technique>*
VJ.93 *<photographs by picture-taking technique>*
VJ.94 aerial photographs
|
VJ.101 stereoscopic photographs
VJ.106 *<photographs by processing or presentation technique>*
VJ.107 cameotypes
|
VJ.124 wire photographs
VJ.125 *<photographs by subject type>*
VJ.126 astrophotographs
|
VJ.130 spirit photographs

PHOTOGRAPHS (VJ)

VJ.1	**photographs**
VJ.2	*<photographs by form>*
VJ.3	**negatives**
VJ.4	**color separation negatives**
VJ.5	**halftone negatives**
VJ.6	**internegatives**
VJ.7	*<negatives by color>*
VJ.8	**black-and-white negatives**
VJ.9	**color negatives**
VJ.10	*<negatives by process>*
VJ.11	**calotypes**
VJ.12	**gelatin silver negatives**
VJ.13	**gelatin dry plate negatives**
VJ.14	**photogenic drawings**
VJ.15	**wet collodion negatives**
VJ.16	**photomechanical prints**
VJ.17	**dye transfer prints**
VJ.18	**etched daguerreotype prints**
VJ.19	**photoengravings**
VJ.20	**line photoengravings**
VJ.21	**relief halftones**
VJ.22	**photogalvanographs**
VJ.23	**photogravures**
VJ.24	**photolithographs**
VJ.25	**collotypes**
VJ.26	**Woodburytypes**
VJ.27	**positives**
VJ.28	**direct positives**
VJ.29	**ambrotypes**
VJ.30	**daguerreotypes**
VJ.31	**Hillotypes**
VJ.32	**instant camera photographs**
VJ.33	**dye diffusion transfer prints**
VJ.34	**tintypes**
VJ.35	**holograms**
VJ.36	**reflection holograms**
VJ.37	**transmission holograms**
VJ.38	**photographic prints**
VJ.39	**negative prints**
VJ.40	**vintage prints**
VJ.41	*<photographic prints by color>*
VJ.42	**black-and-white prints (photographs)**
VJ.43	**color prints (photographs)**
VJ.44	*<photographic prints by process>*
VJ.45	**albumen prints**
VJ.46	**aristotypes**
VJ.47	**collodion prints**
VJ.48	**collodion transfers**
VJ.49	**cyanotypes**

May be used in combination with other descriptors (e.g., **quarter plate** + **photographs**; **Pictorialist** + **photographs**; **fashion** + **photographs**; **still life** + **photographs**).

VJ.50 gelatin silver prints
VJ.51 palladium prints
VJ.52 pigment prints
VJ.53 carbon prints
VJ.54 gum bichromate prints
VJ.55 oil prints
VJ.56 bromoil prints
VJ.57 platinum prints
VJ.58 salted paper prints
VJ.59 transparencies
VJ.60 color separation positives
VJ.61 interpositives
VJ.62 masks (transparencies)
VJ.63 *<transparencies by color>*
VJ.64 black-and-white transparencies
VJ.65 color transparencies
VJ.66 *<transparencies by process>*
VJ.67 Autochromes
VJ.68 gelatin silver transparencies
VJ.69 *<photographs by form: color>*
VJ.70 black-and-white photographs
VJ.71 color photographs
VJ.72 *<photographs by form: format>*
VJ.73 card photographs
VJ.74 boudoir prints
VJ.75 boudoir midget mounts
VJ.76 cabinet photographs
VJ.77 cartes-de-visite
VJ.78 cameo prints
VJ.79 imperial prints
VJ.80 panel prints
VJ.81 promenade prints
VJ.82 victoria prints
VJ.83 gem photographs
VJ.84 lantern slides
VJ.85 slides
VJ.86 black-and-white slides
VJ.87 color slides
VJ.88 *<photographs by function>*
VJ.89 identification photographs
VJ.90 passport photographs
VJ.91 news photographs
VJ.92 *<photographs by technique>*
VJ.93 *<photographs by picture-taking technique>*
VJ.94 aerial photographs
VJ.95 chronophotographs
VJ.96 motion photographs
VJ.97 instantaneous photographs
VJ.98 photomicrographs

May be used in combination with other descriptors (e.g., **quarter plate** + **photographs**; **Pictorialist** + **photographs**; **fashion** + **photographs**; **still life** + **photographs**).

VJ.99 radiographs
VJ.100 snapshots
VJ.101 stereoscopic photographs
VJ.102 anaglyphs
VJ.103 parallax stereographs
VJ.104 stereographs
VJ.105 tissue stereographs
VJ.106 *<photographs by processing or presentation technique>*
VJ.107 cameotypes
VJ.108 cased photographs
VJ.109 clichés-verre
VJ.110 contact prints
VJ.111 contact sheets
VJ.112 enlargements
VJ.113 crayon enlargements
VJ.114 ivorytypes
VJ.115 macrophotographs
VJ.116 manipulated photographs
VJ.117 composite photographs
VJ.118 photomontages
VJ.119 microphotographs
VJ.120 stanhopes
VJ.121 photograms
VJ.122 photomosaics
VJ.123 photomurals
VJ.124 wire photographs
VJ.125 *<photographs by subject type>*
VJ.126 astrophotographs
VJ.127 film stills
VJ.128 frame enlargements
VJ.129 psychic photographs
VJ.130 spirit photographs

May be used in combination with other descriptors (e.g., **quarter plate + photographs**; **Pictorialist + photographs**; **fashion + photographs**; **still life + photographs**).

Document Types Hierarchy

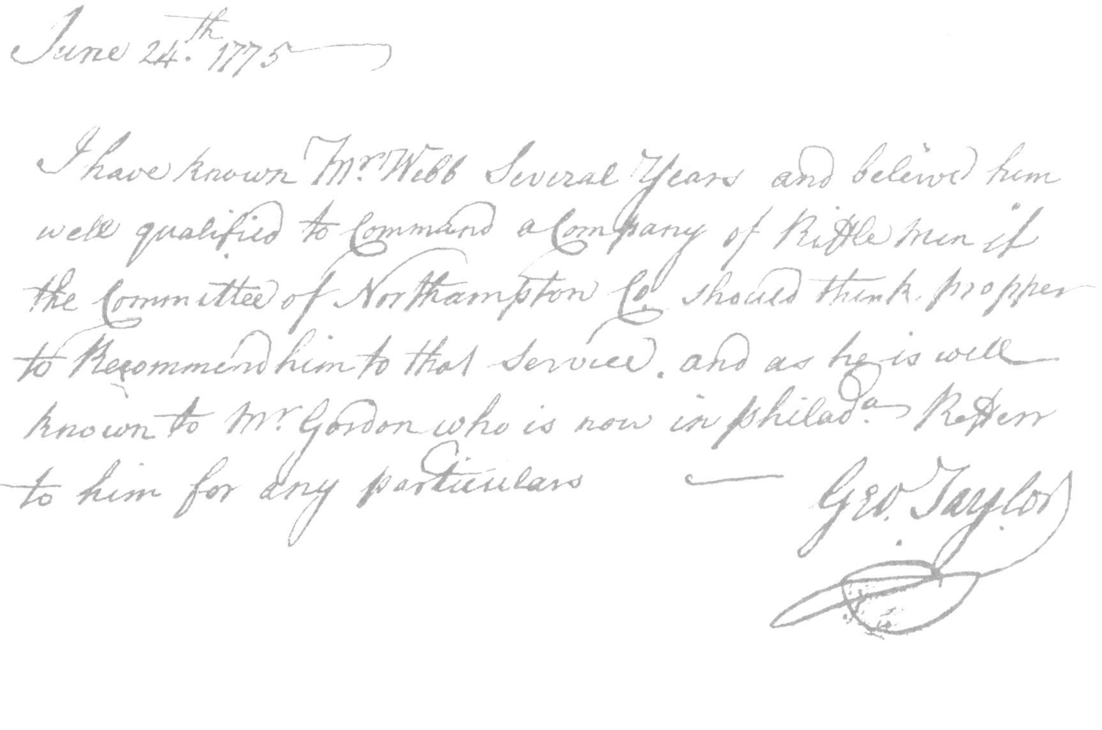

June 24th. 1775

I have known Mr. Webb Several Years and believe him well qualified to Command a Company of Riffle Men if the Committee of Northampton Co. should think propper to Recommend him to that Service. and as he is well known to Mr. Gordon who is now in Philada. Refer to him for any particulars — Geo. Taylor

Scope The Document Types hierarchy contains descriptors for forms of material pertinent to archival description as well as for documents associated with the production, collection, and exhibition of works of art and architecture. Documents are broadly defined as objects that contain recorded information, regardless of their medium.

Organization Descriptors for documents are organized into three main sections: <*document genres*>, <*documentary artifacts*>, and <*record types*>. *Document genres*> includes document types that must be analyzed for their intellectual content, subject coverage, or for the manner in which the information or data they contain is presented before they can be identified (e.g., **essays, eulogies, lists**) <*Documentary artifacts*> collocates descriptors for documents distinguishable by their overall physical form (e.g., **broadsides, cards**). The section <*record types*> includes descriptors for broad classes of documents that denote their purpose or the type of entity which produced them. Under <*record types by function*> are descriptors for functional classes of record types, regardless of their specific provenance (e.g., **administrative records, legal documents**). Under <*record types by provenance*> are descriptors for records whose original context can be specified (e.g., **government records**). Descriptors that denote document types uniquely associated with a type of function or instutution are listed as narrower terms under these generic headings (e.g., **marriage certificates** appears as a narrower descriptor to **marriage records** rather than to **certificates**).

Relation to Other Hierarchies Descriptors for the major classes of two- and three-dimensional works in the visual arts, (e.g., **drawings** and **photographs**), that might be considered documents in some contexts, will be found in other hierarchies within the Visual and Verbal Communication section. Descriptors for books by textual type (e.g., **cookbooks**) appear here, while descriptors for book components and other descriptors necessary for the physical description of rare and other books fall within the scope of the Book Arts hierarchy scheduled for future development. Descriptors for forms of writing (e.g., **hieroglyphics**) also fall within the scope of the Book Arts hierarchy, while descriptors for marks and symbols (e.g., **inscriptions**, **hallmarks**) are found here. Names of prints used primarily to reproduce documents and technical drawings (e.g., **blueprints**) which, though produced by light-sensitive processes, are not considered photographs, appear here, while photographs and photomechanical prints (e.g., **photogravures**) are found in the Photographs hierarchy.

Descriptor Form and Usage Descriptors appear as plural nouns, with the singular added as an alternate form where appropriate. For document types by material or other aspect, combine with descriptors from other appropriate hierarchies (e.g., **plastic** + **relief maps**). Descriptors from other hierarchies may also be used to specify the subject or provenance of a particular document type (e.g., **furniture** + **pattern books**; **artists** + **diaries**).

Number of Descriptors 994

Synopsis

VW.1	**documents**
VW.2	*<document genres>*
VW.3	*<document genres by form>*
VW.4	**addenda**
	|
VW.85	**treatises**
VW.86	*<document genres by form: arrangement of data>*
VW.87	**calendars**
	|
VW.290	**schedules**
VW.293	*<document genres by function>*
VW.294	**acknowledgements**
	|
VW.479	**travelogues**
VW.480	*<documentary artifacts>*
VW.481	*<documentary artifacts by form>*
VW.482	**books**
	|
VW.627	**tickets**
VW.629	*<documentary artifacts by form: medium>*
VW.630	**audiovisual materials**
	|
VW.695	**visual materials**
VW.696	*<documentary artifacts by function>*
VW.697	*<identifying symbols>*
	|
VW.763	**seals**
VW.764	*<record types>*
VW.765	*<record types by function>*
VW.766	**accession records**
	|
VW.946	**vital statistics records**
VW.960	*<record types by provenance>*
VW.961	**business records**
	|
VW.1073	**ship's papers**

VW.1 documents
VW.2   *<document genres>*
VW.3   *<document genres by form>*
VW.4   addenda
VW.5   articles
VW.6   newspaper columns
VW.7   autographs
VW.8   holographs
VW.9   collected works
VW.10   anthologies
VW.11   compendiums
VW.12   correspondence
VW.13   *<correspondence by form>*
VW.14   dispatches
VW.15   electronic mail
VW.16   letters
VW.17   business letters
VW.18   circular letters
VW.19   encyclicals
VW.20   papal encyclicals
VW.21   form letters
VW.22   letters of advice
VW.23   letters of intent
VW.24   letters of introduction
VW.25   letters of recommendation
VW.26   love letters
VW.27   sales letters
VW.28   memorandums
VW.29   telegrams
VW.30   *<correspondence by function>*
VW.31   commercial correspondence
VW.32   legal correspondence
VW.33   personal correspondence
VW.34   dialogues
VW.35   drafts (documents)
VW.36   first drafts
VW.37   essays
VW.38   excerpts
VW.39   quotations
VW.40   excursuses
VW.41   inscriptions
VW.42   colophons
VW.43   epigraphs
VW.44   epitaphs
VW.45   signatures
VW.46   initials
VW.47   interviews
VW.48   journals
VW.49   commonplace books

May be used in combination with other descriptors (e.g., **plastic** + **relief maps**; **furniture** + **pattern books**; **artists** + **diaries**).

VW.50 diaries
VW.51 housebooks
VW.52 ships' logs
VW.53 weather diaries
VW.54 monographs
VW.55 *<music documents>*
VW.56 scores
VW.57 sheet music
VW.58 songs
VW.59 hymns
VW.60 news bulletins
VW.61 press releases
VW.62 notes
VW.63 field notes
VW.64 laboratory notes
VW.65 lecture notes
VW.66 poems
VW.67 elegies
VW.68 programs
VW.69 building programs
VW.70 theater programs
VW.71 scripts
VW.72 prompt books
VW.73 radio scripts
VW.74 screenplays
VW.75 television scripts
VW.76 series
VW.77 monographic series
VW.78 summaries
VW.79 abstracts
VW.80 outlines
VW.81 prospectuses
VW.82 synopses
VW.83 transcripts
VW.84 translations
VW.85 treatises
VW.86 *<document genres by form: arrangement of data>*
VW.87 calendars
VW.88 computus manuscripts
VW.89 perpetual calendars
VW.90 religious calendars
VW.91 devotional calendars
VW.92 catalogs
VW.93 *<catalogs by form>*
VW.94 book catalogs
VW.95 card catalogs
VW.96 classified catalogs
VW.97 dictionary catalogs
VW.98 author catalogs

May be used in combination with other descriptors (e.g., **plastic** + **relief maps**; **furniture** + **pattern books**; **artists** + **diaries**).

VW.99 subject catalogs
VW.100 loose-leaf catalogs
VW.101 online catalogs
VW.102 union catalogs
VW.103 *<catalogs by function or subject>*
VW.104 accession catalogs
VW.105 catalogues raisonnés
VW.106 commercial catalogs
VW.107 *<commercial catalogs by function>*
VW.108 auction catalogs
VW.109 mail order catalogs
VW.110 sale catalogs
VW.111 *<commercial catalogs by source>*
VW.112 booksellers' catalogs
VW.113 manufacturers' catalogs
VW.114 publishers' catalogs
VW.115 exhibition catalogs
VW.116 forms
VW.117 application forms
VW.118 billheads
VW.119 order forms
VW.120 worksheets
VW.121 *<graphic document types>*
VW.122 cartographic materials
VW.123 atlases
VW.124 *<atlases by subject>*
VW.125 historical atlases
VW.126 portolanos
VW.127 statistical atlases
VW.128 *<atlases by subject: location>*
VW.129 city atlases
VW.130 county atlases
VW.131 state atlases
VW.132 regional atlases
VW.133 national atlases
VW.134 world atlases
VW.135 globes
VW.136 celestial globes
VW.137 terrestrial globes
VW.138 maps
VW.139 *<maps by form>*
VW.140 braille maps
VW.141 cartograms
VW.142 chorochromatic maps
VW.143 chorographic maps
VW.144 choroschematic maps
VW.145 dot maps
VW.146 flow-line maps
VW.147 location maps

May be used in combination with other descriptors (e.g., **plastic** + **relief maps**; **furniture** + **pattern books**; **artists** + **diaries**).

<graphic document types>
cartographic materials
maps
<maps by form>

VW.148 isoline maps
VW.149 outline maps
VW.150 base maps
VW.151 pictorial maps
VW.152 planimetric maps
VW.153 cadastral maps
VW.154 index maps
VW.155 line-route maps
VW.156 strip maps
VW.157 quadrangle maps
VW.158 relief maps
VW.159 contour maps
VW.160 raised-relief maps
VW.161 shaded-relief maps
VW.162 topographic maps
VW.163 engineering maps
VW.164 *<maps by function>*
VW.165 fire insurance maps
VW.166 tactical maps
VW.167 thematic maps
VW.168 tourist maps
VW.169 zoning maps
VW.170 *<maps by production method>*
VW.171 computer-assisted maps
VW.172 digital maps
VW.173 manuscript maps
VW.174 photomaps
VW.175 orthophotomaps
VW.176 photomosaic maps
VW.177 sketch maps
VW.178 *<maps by subject>*
VW.179 astronautical charts
VW.180 astronomical charts
VW.181 climatic maps
VW.182 forestry maps
VW.183 geological maps
VW.184 coastal zone maps
VW.185 mine maps
VW.186 flood-prone-area maps
VW.187 hydrologic maps
VW.188 watershed maps
VW.189 isogonic charts
VW.190 mineral resource maps
VW.191 seismicity maps
VW.192 soil maps
VW.193 historical maps
VW.194 land use maps
VW.195 military maps
VW.196 battlefield maps

May be used in combination with other descriptors (e.g., **plastic** + **relief maps**; **furniture** + **pattern books**; **artists** + **diaries**).

VW.197 polar charts
VW.198 population maps
VW.199 census maps
VW.200 postal code maps
VW.201 zip code maps
VW.202 *<public utility maps>*
VW.203 buried cable maps
VW.204 natural-gas-pipelines maps
VW.205 watermain maps
VW.206 telephone area code maps
VW.207 time zone maps
VW.208 transportation maps
VW.209 bus route maps
VW.210 navigation charts
VW.211 aeronautical charts
VW.212 airline maps
VW.213 nautical charts
VW.214 coastal charts
VW.215 marine charts
VW.216 bathymetric maps
VW.217 river charts
VW.218 plotting charts
VW.219 railroad maps
VW.220 road maps
VW.221 street maps
VW.222 weather maps
VW.223 *<maps by subject: location>*
VW.224 village maps
VW.225 township maps
VW.226 city maps
VW.227 parish maps
VW.228 county maps
VW.229 regional maps
VW.230 state maps
VW.231 national maps
VW.232 world maps
VW.233 plats
VW.234 charts
VW.235 astrological charts
VW.236 climatic charts
VW.237 color charts
VW.238 color wheels
VW.239 flowcharts
VW.240 organizational charts
VW.241 solar charts
VW.242 diagrams
VW.243 block diagrams
VW.244 Venn diagrams
VW.245 graphs

May be used in combination with other descriptors (e.g., **plastic** + **relief maps**; **furniture** + **pattern books**; **artists** + **diaries**).

VW.246	bar graphs
VW.247	circular graphs
VW.248	line graphs
VW.249	tables (documents)
VW.250	conversion tables
VW.251	lists
VW.252	*<lists by form or function>*
VW.253	attendance lists
VW.254	bibliographies
VW.255	annotated bibliographies
VW.256	national bibliographies
VW.257	selective bibliographies
VW.258	subject bibliographies
VW.259	bibliographies of bibliographies
VW.260	local bibliographies
VW.261	systematic enumerative bibliographies
VW.262	trade bibliographies
VW.263	checklists
VW.264	mailing lists
VW.265	subscription lists
VW.266	menus
VW.267	registers (lists)
VW.268	cartularies
VW.269	rosters
VW.270	rolls
VW.271	shelf lists
VW.272	union lists
VW.273	want lists
VW.274	*<lists by subject>*
VW.275	discographies
VW.276	donor lists
VW.277	guest registers
VW.278	hotel registers
VW.279	visitors' books
VW.280	job lists
VW.281	membership lists
VW.282	passenger lists
VW.283	ships' passenger lists
VW.284	price lists
VW.285	tariff schedules
VW.286	reading lists
VW.287	voters' lists
VW.288	wine lists
VW.289	questionnaires
VW.290	schedules
VW.291	records schedules
VW.292	general records schedules
VW.293	*<document genres by function>*
VW.294	acknowledgments

May be used in combination with other descriptors (e.g., **plastic** + **relief maps**; **furniture** + **pattern books**; **artists** + **diaries**).

VW.295	awards
VW.296	biographies
VW.297	autobiographies
VW.298	collective biographies
VW.299	certificates
VW.300	certificates of occupancy
VW.301	certificates of origin
VW.302	copyright certificates
VW.303	commentaries
VW.304	annotations
VW.305	marginalia
VW.306	editorials
VW.307	reviews
VW.308	book reviews
VW.309	exhibition reviews
VW.310	film reviews
VW.311	credentials
VW.312	citizenship papers
VW.313	*<declaratory documents>*
VW.314	announcements
VW.315	business announcements
VW.316	legal notices
VW.317	playbills
VW.318	declarations
VW.319	decrees
VW.320	decretals
VW.321	manifestoes
VW.322	proclamations
VW.323	testimonials
VW.324	dedications
VW.325	eulogies
VW.326	examinations
VW.327	Festschriften
VW.328	histories
VW.329	case histories
VW.330	chronicles
VW.331	family histories
VW.332	genealogies
VW.333	genealogical tables
VW.334	pedigrees
VW.335	instructional materials
VW.336	examination study guides
VW.337	finding aids
VW.338	archival calendars
VW.339	archival catalogs
VW.340	archival guides
VW.341	archival inventories
VW.342	archival registers
VW.343	guidelines

May be used in combination with other descriptors (e.g., **plastic** + **relief maps**; **furniture** + **pattern books**; **artists** + **diaries**).

VW.344 design guidelines
VW.345 instructions
VW.346 recipes
VW.347 learning modules
VW.348 manuals
VW.349 buyers' guides
VW.350 collectors' guides
VW.351 employees' manuals
VW.352 style manuals
VW.353 technical manuals
VW.354 data dictionaries
VW.355 operating manuals
VW.356 training manuals
VW.357 primers
VW.358 hornbooks
VW.359 procedures
VW.360 self-instructional materials
VW.361 do-it-yourself manuals
VW.362 workbooks
VW.363 inventories
VW.364 building surveys
VW.365 architectural surveys
VW.366 structural surveys
VW.367 merchandise inventories
VW.368 records surveys
VW.369 invitations
VW.370 wedding invitations
VW.371 obituaries
VW.372 *<permissions>*
VW.373 commissions
VW.374 consents
VW.375 licenses
VW.376 registrations
VW.377 permits
VW.378 building permits
VW.379 demolition permits
VW.380 prescriptions
VW.381 releases
VW.382 warrants
VW.383 petitions
VW.384 prayers
VW.385 proposals
VW.386 grant proposals
VW.387 records
VW.388 *<reference sources>*
VW.389 almanacs
VW.390 concordances
VW.391 dictionaries
VW.392 *<dictionaries by form>*

May be used in combination with other descriptors (e.g., **plastic** + **relief maps**; **furniture** + **pattern books**; **artists** + **diaries**).

VW.393	etymological dictionaries
VW.394	lexicons
VW.395	picture dictionaries
VW.396	*<dictionaries by subject>*
VW.397	biographical dictionaries
VW.398	dictionaries of synonyms
VW.399	foreign-language dictionaries
VW.400	polyglot dictionaries
VW.401	gazetteers
VW.402	heraldic dictionaries
VW.403	sign and symbol handbooks
VW.404	technical dictionaries
VW.405	directories
VW.406	*<directories by subject>*
VW.407	alumni directories
VW.408	commercial directories
VW.409	manufacturers' registers
VW.410	post office directories
VW.411	professional directories
VW.412	social registers
VW.413	telephone directories
VW.414	*<directories by subject: location>*
VW.415	street directories
VW.416	city directories
VW.417	county directories
VW.418	state directories
VW.419	regional directories
VW.420	national directories
VW.421	international directories
VW.422	encyclopedias
VW.423	glossaries
VW.424	indexes
VW.425	*<indexes by form>*
VW.426	card indexes
VW.427	glossarial indexes
VW.428	rotated indexes
VW.429	key-word-and-context indexes
VW.430	key-word-in-context indexes
VW.431	key-word-out-of-context indexes
VW.432	key-word-out-of-title indexes
VW.433	*<indexes by function>*
VW.434	annual indexes
VW.435	citation indexes
VW.436	cumulative indexes
VW.437	periodical indexes
VW.438	newspaper indexes
VW.439	*<indexes by subject>*
VW.440	author indexes
VW.441	subject indexes

May be used in combination with other descriptors (e.g., **plastic** + **relief maps**; **furniture** + **pattern books**; **artists** + **diaries**).

VW.442 title indexes
VW.443 thesauri
VW.444 monolingual thesauri
VW.445 multilingual thesauri
VW.446 reminiscences
VW.447 reports
VW.448 *<administrative reports>*
VW.449 *<administrative reports by function>*
VW.450 accident reports
VW.451 corporation reports
VW.452 damage reports
VW.453 *<administrative reports by frequency>*
VW.454 daily reports
VW.455 monthly reports
VW.456 quarterly reports
VW.457 annual reports
VW.458 official reports
VW.459 communiques
VW.460 plans (reports)
VW.461 *<plans by function>*
VW.462 comprehensive plans
VW.463 *<plans by location or context>*
VW.464 municipal plans
VW.465 regional plans
VW.466 proceedings
VW.467 technical reports
VW.468 environmental impact statements
VW.469 test reports
VW.470 speeches
VW.471 lectures
VW.472 orations
VW.473 sermons
VW.474 supplements
VW.475 testimonies
VW.476 depositions
VW.477 oaths
VW.478 transliterations
VW.479 travelogs
VW.480 *<documentary artifacts>*
VW.481 *<documentary artifacts by form>*
VW.482 books
VW.483 *<books by form or function>*
VW.484 address books
VW.485 albums
VW.486 autograph albums
VW.487 letter books
VW.488 photograph albums
VW.489 view albums
VW.490 postcard albums

May be used in combination with other descriptors (e.g., **plastic** + **relief maps**; **furniture** + **pattern books**; **artists** + **diaries**).

VW.491 presentation albums
VW.492 souvenir albums
VW.493 stamp albums
VW.494 appointment books
VW.495 baby books
VW.496 bridal books
VW.497 chapbooks
VW.498 copybooks
VW.499 emblem books
VW.500 guidebooks
VW.501 *<guidebooks by function>*
VW.502 pilgrimage guidebooks
VW.503 shippers' guides
VW.504 travel guidebooks
VW.505 *<guidebooks by location or context>*
VW.506 city guidebooks
VW.507 state guidebooks
VW.508 national guidebooks
VW.509 *<guidebooks by subject>*
VW.510 architectural guidebooks
VW.511 field guides
VW.512 letterpress copybooks
VW.513 notebooks
VW.514 laboratory notebooks
VW.515 picture books
VW.516 coloring books
VW.517 scrapbooks
VW.518 sketchbooks
VW.519 artists' sketchbooks
VW.520 textbooks
VW.521 programmed textbooks
VW.522 *<books by subject>*
VW.523 casebooks
VW.524 choirbooks
VW.525 cookbooks
VW.526 deed books
VW.527 design books
VW.528 builders' guides
VW.529 drawing books
VW.530 painting books
VW.531 pattern books
VW.532 stylebooks
VW.533 domestic stylebooks
VW.534 librettos
VW.535 price books
VW.536 religious books
VW.537 Bibles
VW.538 Biblia pauperum
VW.539 books of hours

May be used in combination with other descriptors (e.g., **plastic** + **relief maps**; **furniture** + **pattern books**; **artists** + **diaries**).

VW.540	breviaries
VW.541	catechisms
VW.542	christening books
VW.543	graduals
VW.544	hymnals
VW.545	lectionaries
VW.546	epistolaries
VW.547	evangeliaries
VW.548	litanies
VW.549	martyrologies
VW.550	missals
VW.551	passionals
VW.552	prayer books
VW.553	psalters
VW.554	sample books
VW.555	song books
VW.556	carol books
VW.557	studbooks
VW.558	broadsides
VW.559	cards
VW.560	baseball cards
VW.561	business cards
VW.562	catalog cards
VW.563	cigarette cards
VW.564	credit cards
VW.565	dance cards
VW.566	greeting cards
VW.567	birthday cards
VW.568	Christmas cards
VW.569	Easter cards
VW.570	Hanukkah cards
VW.571	valentines
VW.572	identity cards
VW.573	library cards
VW.574	mass cards
VW.575	memorial cards
VW.576	playing cards
VW.577	postcards
VW.578	picture postcards
VW.579	postal cards
VW.580	visiting cards
VW.581	clippings
VW.582	ephemera
VW.583	files
VW.584	*<files by form>*
VW.585	card files
VW.586	clippings files
VW.587	vertical files
VW.588	*<files by function>*

May be used in combination with other descriptors (e.g., **plastic** + **relief maps**; **furniture** + **pattern books**; **artists** + **diaries**).

VW.589	authority files
VW.590	name authority files
VW.591	subject authority files
VW.592	office files
VW.593	*<files by subject>*
VW.594	biography files
VW.595	case files
VW.596	legal files
VW.597	dockets
VW.598	project files
VW.599	map files
VW.600	order files
VW.601	organization files
VW.602	galley proofs
VW.603	handbills
VW.604	advertising fliers
VW.605	leaves (sheets)
VW.606	pamphlets
VW.607	tracts (pamphlets)
VW.608	plaques
VW.609	printouts
VW.610	publications
VW.611	serials
VW.612	annuals
VW.613	yearbooks
VW.614	school yearbooks
VW.615	gazettes
VW.616	newsletters
VW.617	market letters
VW.618	newspapers
VW.619	periodicals
VW.620	digests (periodicals)
VW.621	house organs
VW.622	illustrated periodicals
VW.623	racing forms
VW.624	scrolls
VW.625	tablets
VW.626	tear sheets
VW.627	tickets
VW.628	admission tickets
VW.629	*<documentary artifacts by form: medium>*
VW.630	audiovisual materials
VW.631	sound recordings
VW.632	audio tapes
VW.633	audio cassettes
VW.634	phonograph cylinders
VW.635	phonograph records
VW.636	graphophone records
VW.637	wire recordings

May be used in combination with other descriptors (e.g., **plastic** + **relief maps**; **furniture** + **pattern books**; **artists** + **diaries**).

VW.638	video recordings
VW.639	filmstrips
VW.640	videodiscs
VW.641	videotapes
VW.642	videocassettes
VW.643	machine-readable records
VW.644	compact disks
VW.645	databases
VW.646	bibliographic databases
VW.647	magnetic disks
VW.648	floppy disks
VW.649	magnetic tapes
VW.650	optical disks
VW.651	paper tapes
VW.652	punched cards
VW.653	software
VW.654	manuscripts
VW.655	*<manuscripts by form or function>*
VW.656	codices
VW.657	illuminated manuscripts
VW.658	manuscripts for publication
VW.659	palimpsests
VW.660	typescripts
VW.661	*<manuscripts by subject>*
VW.662	legal manuscripts
VW.663	liturgical manuscripts
VW.664	microforms
VW.665	computer-output microforms
VW.666	computer-output microfiche
VW.667	computer-output microfilms
VW.668	microfiche
VW.669	aperture cards
VW.670	ultrafiche
VW.671	microfilms
VW.672	microfilm strips
VW.673	microopaques
VW.674	motion pictures
VW.675	children's films
VW.676	*<reprographic documents>*
VW.677	blueprints
VW.678	brownprints
VW.679	carbon copies
VW.680	diazotypes
VW.681	letterpress copies
VW.682	master copies
VW.683	mimeograph copies
VW.684	multigraphs
VW.685	photocopies
VW.686	electrostatic copies

May be used in combination with other descriptors (e.g., **plastic** + **relief maps**; **furniture** + **pattern books**; **artists** + **diaries**).

VW.687 xerographic copies
VW.688 reprints
VW.689 stats
VW.690 whiteprints
VW.691 blackline prints
VW.692 blueline prints
VW.693 brownline prints
VW.694 sepia prints
VW.695 visual materials
VW.696 *<documentary artifacts by function>*
VW.697 *<identifying symbols>*
VW.698 devices
VW.699 *<coats of arms and coat of arms components>*
VW.700 coats of arms
VW.701 *<coat of arms components>*
VW.702 escutcheons (coats of arms)
VW.703 impresas
VW.704 insignias
VW.705 emblems
VW.706 logos
VW.707 marks
VW.708 *<marks by form>*
VW.709 punch marks
VW.710 watermarks
VW.711 impressed watermarks
VW.712 *<marks by function>*
VW.713 bench marks
VW.714 cancellation marks
VW.715 collectors' marks
VW.716 date marks
VW.717 dealers' marks
VW.718 excise marks
VW.719 factory marks
VW.720 hallmarks
VW.721 marks of origin
VW.722 country of origin marks
VW.723 ownership marks
VW.724 registry marks
VW.725 trademarks
VW.726 *<marks by location or context>*
VW.727 back stamps
VW.728 bookbinding marks
VW.729 brick stamps
VW.730 furniture marks
VW.731 glass marks
VW.732 house marks
VW.733 pewter marks
VW.734 porcelain marks
VW.735 poster stamps

May be used in combination with other descriptors (e.g., **plastic** + **relief maps**; **furniture** + **pattern books**; **artists** + **diaries**).

VW.736 **pottery marks**
VW.737 **silver marks**
VW.738 **tapestry marks**
VW.739 *<marks by maker>*
VW.740 **architects' marks**
VW.741 **armorers' marks**
VW.742 **artisans' marks**
VW.743 **artists' marks**
VW.744 **painters' marks**
VW.745 **bottle makers' marks**
VW.746 **cabinetmakers' marks**
VW.747 **calligraphers' marks**
VW.748 **engravers' marks**
VW.749 **gilders' marks**
VW.750 **goldsmiths' marks**
VW.751 **masons' marks**
VW.752 **modellers' marks**
VW.753 **potters' marks**
VW.754 **printers' marks**
VW.755 **printers' ornaments**
VW.756 **silversmiths' marks**
VW.757 **swordsmiths' marks**
VW.758 **monograms**
VW.759 **labels**
VW.760 **bookplates**
VW.761 **union labels**
VW.762 **wine labels**
VW.763 **seals**
VW.764 *<record types>*
VW.765 *<record types by function>*
VW.766 **accession records**
VW.767 **accession registers**
VW.768 **administrative records**
VW.769 **agendas**
VW.770 **amendments**
VW.771 **ballots**
VW.772 **bylaws**
VW.773 **constitutions**
VW.774 **election returns**
VW.775 **minute books**
VW.776 **minutes**
VW.777 **personnel records**
VW.778 **attendance records**
VW.779 **job applications**
VW.780 **personnel evaluations**
VW.781 **resumes**
VW.782 **resolutions**
VW.783 **rules**
VW.784 **rules of procedure**

May be used in combination with other descriptors (e.g., **plastic** + **relief maps**; **furniture** + **pattern books**; **artists** + **diaries**).

VW.785 <*work-flow documents*>
VW.786 progress reports
VW.787 progress schedules
VW.788 project calendars
VW.789 architectural records
VW.790 contract documents
VW.791 change orders
VW.792 owner-contractor agreements
VW.793 specifications
VW.794 base bid specifications
VW.795 closed specifications
VW.796 commercial specifications
VW.797 master specifications
VW.798 or-equal specifications
VW.799 outline specifications
VW.800 performance specifications
VW.801 preliminary specifications
VW.802 product specifications
VW.803 proprietary specifications
VW.804 project manuals
VW.805 schedules (contract documents)
VW.806 bidding documents
VW.807 bid forms
VW.808 bidding announcements
VW.809 bids
VW.810 instructions to bidders
VW.811 quantity surveys
VW.812 census records
VW.813 financial records
VW.814 appraisals
VW.815 audits
VW.816 bankbooks
VW.817 budgets
VW.818 check stubs
VW.819 checkbooks
VW.820 estimates
VW.821 financial statements
VW.822 bank statements
VW.823 profit and loss statements
VW.824 mortgages
VW.825 hypothecation certificates
VW.826 negotiable instruments
VW.827 bank drafts
VW.828 bonds (financial records)
VW.829 checks
VW.830 certified checks
VW.831 travelers' checks
VW.832 letters of credit
VW.833 money orders

May be used in combination with other descriptors (e.g., **plastic** + **relief maps**; **furniture** + **pattern books**; **artists** + **diaries**).

VW.834 promissory notes
VW.835 stock certificates
VW.836 portfolios (financial records)
VW.837 trust receipts
VW.838 *<financial records by function>*
VW.839 bookkeeping records
VW.840 account books
VW.841 accounts
VW.842 balance sheets
VW.843 blotters
VW.844 bookkeeping registers
VW.845 cashbooks
VW.846 journals (bookkeeping records)
VW.847 daybooks
VW.848 ledgers
VW.849 payroll records
VW.850 paybooks
VW.851 payrolls
VW.852 time books
VW.853 time cards
VW.854 time sheets
VW.855 credit records
VW.856 insurance records
VW.857 insurance claims
VW.858 insurance policies
VW.859 insurance surveys
VW.860 sales records
VW.861 bills of sale
VW.862 invoices
VW.863 purchase orders
VW.864 requisitions
VW.865 receipts
VW.866 vouchers
VW.867 legal documents
VW.868 bankruptcy proceedings
VW.869 petitions for bankruptcy
VW.870 briefs
VW.871 claims
VW.872 contract awards
VW.873 digests (legal documents)
VW.874 discharges
VW.875 discharges of contracts
VW.876 legal instruments
VW.877 affidavits
VW.878 agreements
VW.879 collective labor agreements
VW.880 contracts
VW.881 *<contracts by form or function>*
VW.882 divided contracts

May be used in combination with other descriptors (e.g., **plastic** + **relief maps**; **furniture** + **pattern books**; **artists** + **diaries**).

VW.883 leases
VW.884 separate contracts
VW.885 single contracts
VW.886 subcontracts
VW.887 syngraphai
VW.888 turnkey contracts
VW.889 *<contracts by manner of payment>*
VW.890 cost plus fee agreements
VW.891 cost reimbursement contracts
VW.892 fixed-price contracts
VW.893 *<contracts by party>*
VW.894 architect-consultant contracts
VW.895 artists' contracts
VW.896 government contracts
VW.897 guarantees
VW.898 warranties
VW.899 international agreements
VW.900 treaties
VW.901 partnership agreements
VW.902 articles of incorporation
VW.903 bonds (legal records)
VW.904 bail bonds
VW.905 bid bonds
VW.906 labor and material bonds
VW.907 payment bonds
VW.908 performance bonds
VW.909 subcontractor bonds
VW.910 surety bonds
VW.911 certificates of incorporation
VW.912 charters
VW.913 escrows
VW.914 franchises
VW.915 indentures
VW.916 articles of apprenticeship
VW.917 indictments
VW.918 powers of attorney
VW.919 submittals
VW.920 traffic tickets
VW.921 wills
VW.922 medical records
VW.923 *<property records>*
VW.924 conveyances
VW.925 deed registers
VW.926 land registers
VW.927 deeds
VW.928 mortgage deeds
VW.929 land grants
VW.930 land surveys
VW.931 topographic surveys

May be used in combination with other descriptors (e.g., **plastic** + **relief maps**; **furniture** + **pattern books**; **artists** + **diaries**).

VW.932 plat books
VW.933 shipping records
VW.934 bills of lading
VW.935 manifests
VW.936 ships' manifests
VW.937 tax records
VW.938 tax bills
VW.939 tax returns
VW.940 warrant books
VW.941 *<travel documents>*
VW.942 itineraries
VW.943 passports
VW.944 visas
VW.945 vital records
VW.946 vital statistics records
VW.947 birth records
VW.948 birth certificates
VW.949 birth registers
VW.950 death records
VW.951 burial records
VW.952 death certificates
VW.953 death registers
VW.954 marriage records
VW.955 divorce records
VW.956 marriage applications
VW.957 marriage certificates
VW.958 marriage licenses
VW.959 marriage registers
VW.960 *<record types by provenance>*
VW.961 business records
VW.962 church records
VW.963 *<church records by form or function>*
VW.964 baptismal certificates
VW.965 briefs (papal)
VW.966 bulls
VW.967 church bulletins
VW.968 church registers
VW.969 baptismal registers
VW.970 burial registers
VW.971 funeral registers
VW.972 communion records
VW.973 *<church records by provenance>*
VW.974 churchwardens' accounts
VW.975 diocesan records
VW.976 parochial records
VW.977 parish inventories
VW.978 parish registers
VW.979 corporation records
VW.980 estate records

May be used in combination with other descriptors (e.g., **plastic** + **relief maps**; **furniture** + **pattern books**; **artists** + **diaries**).

VW.981 government records
VW.982 *<government records by function>*
VW.983 executive records
VW.984 *<executive records by function>*
VW.985 customs records
VW.986 executive orders
VW.987 immigration records
VW.988 letters of marque
VW.989 letters patent
VW.990 lettres de cachet
VW.991 military records
VW.992 military commissions
VW.993 military passes
VW.994 muster rolls
VW.995 naturalization records
VW.996 pardons
VW.997 patents
VW.998 design patents
VW.999 regulations
VW.1000 administrative regulations
VW.1001 codes
VW.1002 building codes
VW.1003 *<executive records by provenance>*
VW.1004 chancery documents
VW.1005 charter rolls
VW.1006 liberate rolls
VW.1007 presidential papers
VW.1008 judicial records
VW.1009 *<judicial records by form or function>*
VW.1010 decisions
VW.1011 subpoenas
VW.1012 summonses
VW.1013 writs
VW.1014 *<judicial records by location or context>*
VW.1015 civil court records
VW.1016 probate records
VW.1017 estate administration records
VW.1018 estate inventories
VW.1019 room-by-room inventories
VW.1020 letters of administration
VW.1021 letters testamentary
VW.1022 criminal court records
VW.1023 legislative records
VW.1024 *<legislative records by form or function>*
VW.1025 bills (legislative records)
VW.1026 legislative acts
VW.1027 statutes
VW.1028 laws
VW.1029 poor laws

May be used in combination with other descriptors (e.g., **plastic** + **relief maps**; **furniture** + **pattern books**; **artists** + **diaries**).

VW.1030	ordinances
VW.1031	zoning ordinances
VW.1032	*<legislative records by location or context>*
VW.1033	congressional records
VW.1034	congressional committee records
VW.1035	congressional committee reports
VW.1036	House of Representatives records
VW.1037	Senate records
VW.1038	parliamentary papers
VW.1039	House of Commons papers
VW.1040	House of Commons bills
VW.1041	House of Lords papers
VW.1042	House of Lords bills
VW.1043	*<government records by provenance>*
VW.1044	local government records
VW.1045	county government records
VW.1046	municipal government records
VW.1047	state government records
VW.1048	national government records
VW.1049	federal government records
VW.1050	intergovernmental records
VW.1051	territorial records
VW.1052	hospital records
VW.1053	manorial records
VW.1054	museum records
VW.1055	exhibition records
VW.1056	exhibit scripts
VW.1057	official documents
VW.1058	notarial documents
VW.1059	personal papers
VW.1060	family papers
VW.1061	Bible records
VW.1062	professional papers
VW.1063	school records
VW.1064	curricula
VW.1065	diplomas
VW.1066	faculty papers
VW.1067	grade books
VW.1068	report cards
VW.1069	syllabi
VW.1070	theses
VW.1071	dissertations
VW.1072	masters theses
VW.1073	ships' papers

May be used in combination with other descriptors (e.g., **plastic** + **relief maps**; **furniture** + **pattern books**; **artists** + **diaries**).